Rediscovering the Golden State
California Geography

William A. Selby
Santa Monica College

John Wiley & Sons, Inc.
New York Chichester Weinheim Brisbane Singapore Toronto

Acquisitions Editor   Diane McDaniel
Full Service Manager   Jeanine Furino
Text Design and Project Management   Elm Street Publishing Services, Inc.

This book was set in ITC Garamond Light by UG / GGS Information Services, Inc. and printed and bound by Victor Graphics. The cover was printed by Victor Graphics.

This book is printed on acid-free paper. ∞

To order books or for customer service please, call 1(800)-CALL-WILEY (225-5945).

ISBN 0-471-31589-3 (pbk)

Printed in the United States of America

10 9 8 7 6 5 4

Preface

In writing *Rediscovering the Golden State: California Geography,* my objective was to reach out to a wide audience of people who want to better understand and appreciate California's diverse natural and human systems and landscapes. A primary component of this audience is made up of students and teachers studying the geography of California.

Increasingly, Californians are searching for new ways to improve their state and plan for the future. As their discipline has become more relevant and applicable to our modern world, modern geographers are responding by reaching out to these concerned citizens. Following that spirit, *Rediscovering the Golden State: California Geography* is written for those who want to better understand issues, solve problems, and help direct the path California will take in the twenty-first century. Accordingly, *Rediscovering the Golden State: California Geography* demonstrates how modern geography has evolved into a discipline that cuts across traditional boundaries, linking seemingly disparate real-world issues in a practical and useful fashion.

◆ SOME UNIFYING THEMES

Three very general themes shape my examination of California geography in this text. The *diversity* of California's physical and cultural landscapes is exceptional. The array of geologic processes and landforms, climates, plant and animal communities, and waterscapes in California continues to challenge our best natural scientists. And, though California's diverse human geography is more than a reflection of the state's natural history, its myriad human landscapes and cultures are sometimes products of the natural settings on which they are founded.

A good understanding of California's geography must include the *connections and relationships* in time and space among so many aspects of the state's natural and human environments. The first step is to appreciate how humans have depended on California's natural settings and resources, and then to see how and why humans have impacted, modified, and exploited these natural landscapes. We can then begin to focus on more specific connections and issues within this larger framework. One example is how the distribution of natural resources and primary industries has influenced the nature and location of California's modern economies and urban landscapes. The scales or scopes of interconnected problems and issues are often more specific, but they must always be considered under that larger, more general umbrella of connections and relationships.

Finally, the rate of *change* in California's natural and human landscapes is remarkable when compared to any other state and to most other locations on our planet. These changes range from active geologic processes to unpredictable and anomalous patterns in weather and climate, from the expansion or destruction of certain species and entire communities of plants and animals to the enormous water diversion and flood control projects that have radically changed California's waterscapes. Change helped define California's natural environments even before the great human settlements and developments.

The changes wrought by California's people are even more dynamic. Great migrations, which have contributed to exploding populations, occur not only into the state, but within the state. Migrations have brought a diversity of cultures into California, and the geographic and economic movement of these cultures has a significant impact on the state. There are few places in the world where people have such mobile and versatile lifestyles and careers. The ability to change continues to be an essential survival strategy in the state.

◆ ACKNOWLEDGMENTS

Hundreds of California geography students read my original manuscript and made helpful suggestions. Colleagues, who included professional geographers and professors from throughout the state, helped revise and refine this work and offered moral support. I am grateful to the following reviewers whose suggestions, criticisms, comments, and different perspectives were used to modify and improve the book: Joan Clemons, University of California, Los Angeles; C. Michael Costanzo, University of California, Santa Barbara; Matt Ebiner, El Camino College; Myron Gershenson, Chabot College; Carolyn Haiman, California State University, Chico; Richard Haiman, California State University, Chico; Mark Purcell, University of California, Los Angeles; Tim Smith, California State University, Northridge; Steven G. Spear, Palomar College; and Charles Thomsen, American River College.

A special note of appreciation goes to the following students who helped with my source research: Margaret Ford, Deborah and René Francois, Kelly Taylor, Bruce Piscitello, Alexandra Malaspinas, and Kathy Nichols. Among the numerous professionals at John Wiley and Sons who made this book possible, Diane McDaniel was a patient and steady editor. Suzi Kuromiya of Magellan Geographix created exceptional maps. Martha Beyerlein of Elm Street Publishing Services used her extraordinary organizational skills to coordinate the efforts of editors, cartographers, and artists. Thanks to all of you.

Thanks to my family and all my friends and colleagues who were patient and supportive while I completed this monumental task. Karen Ayoub (who took time to make suggestions) and Edward Nino (an exceptional friend) helped with their encouragement. Without years of moral support from Jim, the world's number one brother, and his partner, Julie Clayton, I would not have made this goal. Sorry, Dad, that you didn't make it to see the final product. At every turn in this rewarding experience, I am challenged to learn more.

◆ ABOUT THE AUTHOR

William Selby is a native Californian who has explored every corner of the Golden State. He earned his undergraduate degree in southern California (California State University, Fullerton) and his graduate degree in northern California (San Francisco State University). He has lived and worked in many diverse California landscapes and neighborhoods, from rural to urban, in both southern and northern areas of the state.

Professor Selby had extensive experience in private industry before beginning his teaching career in 1981. He then taught geography and science to a variety of grade levels and age groups before taking up his current position at Santa Monica College in 1985. In addition to teaching a wide range of earth science and geography courses, Professor Selby organizes and leads many field trips throughout the state with his colleagues and students. He is recognized as an accomplished speaker on a wide range of subjects in geography and earth science.

His diverse research interests and professional and personal activities reflect Professor Selby's devotion to geography, his love for the Golden State, and his concern for its future. This book combines his academic expertise and his practical experiences within California's myriad landscapes to present an invaluable guide to the issues California brings into the twenty-first century.

Contents

Chapter 1

Getting to Know the Golden State

California has always been a land of legendary extremes. Stories of its incredible natural beauty, its enormous wealth and diversity of natural resources and landscapes, and its violent and destructive natural disasters make world news headlines each year. These stories have been repeated since the first Spanish explorers and then settlers arrived here centuries ago. And, California's people, both real and imagined, have always successfully competed with nature for the spotlight. Even its name originated from a mythical location.

Exploiting imaginations after the European "discovery" of America, the Spanish writer Garcí Ordóñez de Montalvo first named a place called California in his *Las Sergas de Esplandián* (*The Exploits of Esplandián*). Even in this first use of California in 1510, he fabricated an island paradise near the Indies where beautiful black Amazons were surrounded with riches such as gold and pearls.

The name California first appeared on Spanish maps labelling the Gulf of California and the Baja Peninsula in the 1560s. After the Spanish "discovered" California in 1542 and began moving and settling north in 1769, what is today's California was often given the name Nueva (New) or Alta (Upper) California.

As the first real Spanish explorers and settlers sent their actual impressions back to their homeland, they described a landscape hauntingly similar to today's. They painted pictures of wildly different landscapes that ranged between a comfortable paradise and a harsh land where agonizingly hard work and plenty of luck were required for survival. Similar expressions were recorded throughout the Spanish and Mexican Eras; such reports continued even after California became the thirty-first state in the United States in 1850.

More recent writings continue to conflict as they portray a land of remarkable contrasts and contradictions.

Today, California's unsettled population is always evolving, always moving on, creating repeated social upheavals that leave its past in the dust like a forgotten stranger. It is as if California's people are trying to emulate the turbulent forces that shape its natural landscapes as the world looks on. The result is the most diverse population and economy on our planet. California is and will continue to be a celebrated culture hearth in the twenty-first century. Critics beyond its borders have tried to minimize the importance of this nucleus for our civilization, and although some Californians fear the responsibilities that accompany such esteem, California has taken center stage. As the reality of the state's stature, with all its positive and negative features, sets in, every Californian will play a role in molding this great experiment, this model we call California.

KEY ISSUES AND CONCEPTS

◆ This book is a systematic, topical survey of the modern geography of California. It is designed to provide useful information that can help us understand the state, examine modern issues, and solve problems.

◆ California's diverse natural and human landscapes represent ideal laboratories; they provide a wealth of opportunities to make scientific/geographic discoveries and to research a variety of processes, cycles, and systems that are shaping landscapes on many scales.

◆ The five fundamental geographic themes and six essential elements of geography are common threads that tie together topics covered in this and other chapters of this book.

◆ Diversity, connections, and change are evident in all California landscapes and in the processes responsible for shaping them; consequently, they are common themes used in this chapter and this book.

◆ Critical to our understanding of California is recognition of some important geographic factors. They include its large area and elongated shape, its situation in relation to the rest of the world, and the human/environment interaction that has shaped its landscapes.

◆ Early California remained relatively isolated even after the Spanish, Russians, and other invaders discovered and began settling it. Strong ties to Latin America developed, continued during the Mexican Era, and have been recently renewed. Since the mid-1800s and the Gold Rush, growing populations and advanced technologies have strengthened connections with other cultures and nations, particularly on the Pacific Rim.

◆ The state can be divided into diverse physiographic regions which are connected in profound ways and are experiencing different types and rates of change.

◆ The survey of the regional geography of California in this chapter introduces the state's general landscapes and some of the processes that change them. In the survey, we sweep clockwise around the state from region to region. This information will serve as a foundation on which the more dynamic and scientific, systematic, and topical study of the state is constructed in later chapters.

◆ Though each physiographic region demonstrates unique and recognizable qualities, each also shares processes and landscapes with its neighbors. These differences and divisions and relationships and connections combine to shape modern California.

◆ GEOGRAPHERS STUDY CALIFORNIA

Some observers use a microscopic viewpoint to pick apart the very details that eventually come together to build California's landscapes. Some of their precise observations and studies may pinpoint particular locations or focus on specific issues or problems, but investigators of detail must never forget the big picture. How are surrounding locations connected, and how are seemingly disparate events related? At the other end of the spectrum are those who would use a telescope to view California. They see the major trends and paint the state and its people with sweeping generalizations. Though this may be an easy method, it can provide an unrealistic picture that denies the specific exceptions and the uniqueness within California's landscapes and its people.

Therefore, it is necessary to zigzag between these two approaches, going from the smallest to the largest scales and back again. A balance must be found between them in any meaningful study of California. This is a great challenge in a state that is so big and that has so many diverse landscapes with so many powerful stories to tell. It is also a challenge because most of California's landscapes and its people fit somewhere between the extreme stereotypes that constantly bombard us from popular sources of information. The reality is that most Californians share the same basic values and dreams of most Americans and of people in other countries.

The big difference is that California landscapes and their people always seem a little closer to the edge. Although Californians' dreams are lofty and spectacular, they *are* possible to realize. However, Californians' fears of impending failure and disaster may also be deeper than other Americans. Like California's landscapes, its people seem a little more willing to participate in the next experiment. They are always evolving, but they are also waiting for that next surprise, that next unexpected drama which must lie ahead in such a dynamic state.

Consequently, this state is now ripe for research and planning by modern geographers, whether they are formally trained professionals or amateurs and volunteers just testing the waters. Like California, geography has evolved and is experiencing a renaissance. Modern geography has become a more practical, more useful discipline. It is being used by all of us to assess the **sites** or the environments of places where we live, work, and visit. And it is being used to understand the **situations** (or surrounding environments) of those specific locations and the relationships and connections between them.

◆ MODERN GEOGRAPHY IN CALIFORNIA

Just as California continued to experience extraordinary change on the brink of the twenty-first century, geographers around the nation and the world organized to define and direct profound changes caused by the renaissance in their own discipline. They identified and agreed on eighteen National Geography Standards and organized them under six essential elements of geography. All of these were built on the five original and fundamental geographic themes which focus on location, place, human/environment interaction, movement and regions. These themes and standards are also among the common threads that stitch together this work on the geography of California.

What are those essential elements and standards and how are they addressed in this book? We will see California in spatial terms as we organize and analyze natural and human processes, systems, and landscapes. This requires the use of maps (both physical and mental) and other geographic tools and modern techniques. We will learn about the many places and regions that make up California. We will examine California's physical (natural) landscapes and the processes that change them. We will also learn about the people and cultures of California, their human landscapes, and the processes that are changing them. Additionally, we will look at the connections and relationships between California's natural environment and its people. Specifically, how has the physical environment affected human populations and landscapes? Then, how and why have humans modified California's physical landscapes and used its natural resources? Finally, after interpreting California's past, we will use geography to understand present landscapes and to plan for California in the twenty-first century.

Another way of looking at modern geography is to break it down into its basic subdisciplines. *Physical geography* focuses on natural landscapes and the processes responsible for them. Geomorphologists, climatologists, biogeographers, and hydrologists are among the many physical geographers. *Human geographers* study human landscapes and the people who shape them. They may have more specific interests, such as population, migration, cultures, economies, and rural or urban landscapes. Finally, *modern geographic techniques* are being used by all geographers. Computer cartography, air photo interpretation and other remote sensing methods, and widespread applications of geographic information systems (GIS) are tools of the twenty-first century geographer. *Regional geographers* who study specific geographic regions must incorporate each of these subdisciplines and methods into their research.

Regardless of the specific method of study, it is obvious that California's natural history and landscapes and its human history, its people and their landscapes are more than dynamic and diverse; they are connected and related in profound ways. They offer hidden secrets yet to be discovered, and they offer astounding surprises yet to be experienced. This is why modern geographers—and all Californians—must play key roles in the understanding of California's natural and human landscapes and the people who inhabit them. They must also help drive California in a direction that will improve the living environments of all its people. If geography and geographers are left out of the critical decision making that will shape the future of our state, it will be unfortunate for geographers and a lost opportunity for all Californians.

A knowledge of geography will enable us to better understand our state and direct it toward a more promising future.

◆ HERE'S CALIFORNIA

Finding the Golden State and Its Boundaries

Study your state map for this section. California's northern border with Oregon is at 42 degrees N. The southern border with Mexico does not follow a line of latitude. It starts on California's southwest corner just north of 32 degrees, 30′ N on the coast, and follows a line running slightly north of east, until it ends at the Arizona border (the most southeast corner of California).

The eastern border with Nevada follows the 120 degree line of longitude south—from the state's northeast corner on the Oregon border—to Lake Tahoe. From here, another straight line then trends southeast, still marking the California/Nevada border, and slices across lines of latitude and longitude until it ends at a point shared with the Nevada and Arizona borders in the Colorado River. From here, the border with Arizona follows the Colorado River south until it reaches Mexico at the far southeast corner of California. This eastern border and the Colorado River meander near, but never make it to, 114 degrees W just east of the Whipple Mountains.

California's coast veers from just past 117 degrees W at the Mexican border, toward the northwest, far west of the 124 degree longitude at Cape Mendocino (the westernmost extension of California's coastline). The coastline's enormous range of longitude might surprise those who consider this a north–south trending state. San Diego's longitude is the same as parts of Death Valley and central Nevada, up to 650 km (400 miles) of longitude east of Cape Mendocino!

Consequently, this northwest–southeast tending, elongated state covers about 9-1/2 degrees of latitude and more than 10 degrees of longitude on our earth.

Depending on the method and map projection used (use a good map in this section), the geographic center of California is somewhere in the area between these two example measurements:

Latitude 37°, 9′ 58.23″ N
Longitude 119°, 26′ 59.3″ W

Latitude 36°, 51′ 21.60″ N
Longitude 119°, 32′ 59.3″ W

The first location was often accepted after the 1970s, but some geographers have since noted that the term "center" is somewhat subjective in such a strangely shaped state. The second location is one of the latest examples. It was presented by Alon Yaar, a student at USC, at the 1996 Annual Meeting of the California Geographical Society. The average of these and other measurements puts the center somewhere in the Sierra Nevada foothills about 35 km (just more than 20 miles) northeast of Fresno.

Therefore, if you find yourself around 37 degrees N and 119 degrees, 30′ W, you are near California's geographic center, although our review of California's odd shape and borders may seem to diminish the importance of finding this center (see Map 1.1).

Size and Shape Help Define California

So much of California is about being big. With approximately 411,013 sq km (158,693 square miles), or 101,563,520 acres, it is the third largest state, ranking behind Alaska and Texas. It is larger than Japan, Great Britain, Italy, or Norway. It is much longer than it is wide. A straight line from northwest to southeast along its coast runs about 1,220 km (nearly 760 miles), but there are at least 2,027 km (1,260 miles) of entire jagged coastline. (California's entire tidal shorelines—including inlets into bays and rivers and the outer coast and offshore islands—total far more than 5,000 km (more than 3,000 miles) long.) In contrast, California is barely more than 240 km (150 miles) wide from San Francisco to Lake Tahoe. At its widest, it is barely more than 400 km (250 miles) from Point Arguello to the Nevada border.

Diverse Natural Landscapes

This large area and long shape have contributed to the state's number one ranking in so many categories within its natural and human landscapes. Its Death Valley has the lowest point in North America at 86 m (282 feet) below sea level. There are other desert valleys all the way to the Mexican border that drop below sea level. California has the highest mountain peak in the United States

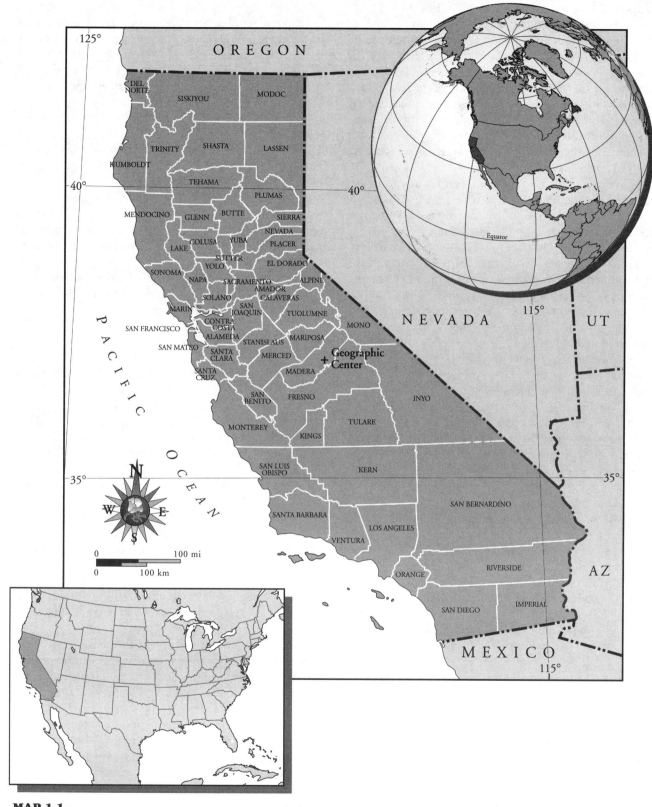

MAP 1.1

Its location and situation and its size and shape help define the state of California. The boundaries and names of counties reflect a rich history.

outside Alaska: Mount Whitney, at 4,421 m (14,495 feet). There are numerous other peaks higher than 14,000 feet, and they are all in the Sierra Nevada except White Mountain Peak (14,246 feet) and majestic Mount Shasta (14,162 feet). The variety of high mountains and deep valleys are a result of the many different geologic processes and landscapes contained in such a large state situated along active tectonic plate boundaries. California also has some of the most varied and abundant earth resources on our planet. These geologic processes and landscapes are reviewed in Chapters 2 and 3.

Across such diverse topography and nearly 9-1/2 degrees of latitude, there must also be a wide variation of climates. From near Death Valley to the northwest coast, mean annual precipitation ranges from less than 5 cm (2 inches) to about 250 cm (100 inches). Each year, temperatures in the state will range above 49°C (120°F) in the southern deserts to well below −18°C (0°F) on numerous occasions in the northern mountains. (The hottest temperature ever recorded in North America was 57°C (134°F) in Death Valley.) These climates are explored in Chapter 4.

A splendid assortment of plants and animals have adapted to these variations in climate and other physical conditions. The tallest living things in the world— Coast Redwoods (*Sequoia sempervirens*)—grow on California's northwest coast. The largest living trees in the world—Sequoia Redwoods (*Sequoiadendron giganteum*)—grow in the western Sierra Nevada. The oldest living trees in the world—Bristlecone Pines (*Pinus longaeva*)—grow in eastern California's White Mountains. The oldest living plants in the world—Creosote Bushes (*Larrea tridentata*)—grow as rings of clones in the southeast deserts. As this list of records grows, these "firsts" serve only as examples of the fascinating variety of plants and animals surveyed in Chapter 5.

All of these natural factors have combined with humans to produce diverse waterscapes scattered throughout California. Humans have now exploited these water resources by building some of the largest water projects in the world. This hydrology is the subject of Chapter 6.

Diverse Human Landscapes

The assorted human invaders and settlers were just as diverse as the landscapes into which they moved (topics of Chapter 7). Their human landscapes have evolved to reflect California's impressive size. By the end of the 1990s, California's population (according to the U.S. Census Bureau and the California Department of Finance) soared past 34 million. It has not only the largest population of any state, it is also the most diverse. California contains the greatest populations in the world of several ethnic groups living outside their countries of origin. These are topics of Chapters 7 and 8.

California also has, by far, the largest and most pow-

erful economy in the United States, and it ranks well into the top ten list of economies worldwide. Southern California alone would be thirteenth in a worldwide list. Our state is the standout leader in agriculture, where it leads in the production of several crops. (It even surpassed Wisconsin to lead the nation in cheese production.) These are topics for Chapter 9.

The state's powerful primary industries are only surpassed by its modern, advanced industrial powerhouses. The trade, high-tech, finance, entertainment, and service industries in California are not only exploding past traditional industries, but they are overshadowing developments in other states and nations. Perhaps this helps explain why Los Angeles has the number one port in the country. These are topics for Chapter 10. Chapter 11 highlights some of the greatest urban landscapes in the world.

Supported by countless ways of making a living, Californians have built an assortment of fascinating and unrivaled rural and urban landscapes.

Is Bigger Really Better?

There are disadvantages to having such a large, elongate territory contained in one state. Divisions between the resource-rich, rural north and the economic and political urban powerhouses of the south have always fueled talk of breaking up. The California legislature nearly split the state into north and south in 1965 and 1967. The idea became popular again during the 1990s, when every rural northern county voted to break away into its own state of "Northern California." These water-rich Californians saw their rural values and lifestyles (supported by primary industries such as timber, mining, agriculture, and ecotourism) as no match for the perceived water-grabbing, cutting-edge urban giants to the south. But, statistics show that instead of benefiting from the creation of a new state of Northern California, these rural counties would have isolated themselves and become one of the poorest states in the United States.

Still, whether perceived or real, the divisions are there. Northern Californians often share typical stereotypes and sweeping generalizations about the south, including images of high crime rates, air and water pollution, traffic jams, higher taxes, fast-paced, unrestrained lifestyles, and unmanageable cities. In response, some southern urbanites may try to paint northerners as backward isolationists lacking culture and living where there are fewer conveniences, little social life or excitement, and little opportunity to change and grow.

Meanwhile, the populations of the San Francisco Bay Area and parts of the central coast and Central Valley are often caught in the middle of this philosophical tug-of-war. They may despise southern California attitudes and lifestyles, but they also see themselves as more cosmopolitan and more on the cultural and economic cutting-edge than their rural neighbors to the north. Some claim this calls for a third state—a Central or Middle California.

Such divisions are enhanced by geographic distance. How does a resident of San Diego relate to events in San Francisco or the state capital of Sacramento, more than 800 km (500 miles) to the north, much less to someone in Crescent City, or Alturas, more than 1,300 km (800 miles) north? And how can an effective and efficient state government operate across such disparate landscapes? It becomes apparent that California's very strengths—its size, the diversity of natural and human landscapes, and the various forces shaping them—can be construed as liabilities by those who would divide the state.

Proponents of division do not realize how California's seemingly separate regions and people depend on one another and are connected in profound ways. Just watch as the north's abundant natural resources flow south and the political and economic clout of the southern cities may help balance and stabilize an otherwise isolated north. On the occasions when this enormous state recognizes its diverse economies and cultures as assets, the usual result is long-term stability, balance, and prosperity.

California's Situation

California's **situation** (its regional position in relation to other locations) has also had a profound impact on its evolution, history, and settlement patterns.

Situation and Physical Geography

The state is situated along tectonic plate boundaries, where dynamic geologic processes continue to shape a variety of landforms such as its giant mountain ranges bordered by deep valleys. You will find more details on geologic processes in Chapter 2. California's middle latitude climates are influenced by the Hawaiian (East Pacific) Subtropical High Pressure System, which causes summer drought. Then, the Aleutian Low slips south during winter, ushering in storms to provide much-needed precipitation to the state. California is not far enough south to experience tropical climates; its location on the west coast and east side of the Hawaiian High ensures a cool ocean current (known as the California current) that moderates any tropical air masses moving toward the state. You will find specific definitions and details on weather and climate in Chapter 4.

California's plants and animals have adapted to the middle latitude Mediterranean climates that dominate west of the major mountain ridges. Meanwhile, desert life forms must endure prolonged drought and temperature extremes common on the leeward sides of the very mountain ranges which were shaped by the geologic processes previously mentioned. For more on the state's biogeography and hydrology, refer to Chapters 5 and 6.

Situation and Human History

Isolation   Most modern anthropologists agree that California's first people were descendants of those who crossed over the "land bridge" into North America from Asia. Previously, the greatest ocean in the world had separated these otherwise mobile people from California. (Some California Indians have very different traditional stories and explanations of their origins.) Their populations eventually swelled to more than 300,000 by the time the Spanish arrived. Many Native Americans in California were often *isolated* by deserts and major topographic barriers, not only from other North American Indians but also from groups prospering in other California regions. Later, these same barriers would help keep California *isolated* from the westward expansions of Anglo-Americans through the early 1800s. The Rocky Mountains, great southwestern deserts, and the Sierra Nevada combined to represent formidable barriers to overland parties that may have otherwise considered California.

Consequently, the first European explorers and settlers of California almost always arrived by boat. The Spanish sea expedition from the south headed by Juan Rodríguez Cabrillo was apparently the first to "discover" California for the Europeans in 1542. A number of Spanish and other European powers explored the California coast after him, including Sir Francis Drake, who claimed parts of California for England as early as 1579. The still isolated and distant regions of California would wait until 1769 before Europeans made any serious attempt at settlement. This is when Father Junípero Serra and Captain Gaspar de Portolá established the first settlement at San Diego. They continued north as Spain took formal possession of "Alta California."

Even after 1769, California's continued isolation contributed to slow growth and expansion of the early Spanish settlements. This left the door open to other invaders from the sea. These were the Russians from the north, who hunted sea otters down the northwest coast of California into the mid-1800s, until the otters were nearly extinct. They met little resistance in this wild land and established and settled Fort Ross between 1812–1841. The Russians named California's Russian River and other geographic features after their distant homeland.

The Latin American Connection   By the early 1800s, the Spanish had already gained control of much of California. After the 1769 start, they spread their presidio-mission-pueblo plan across California's coastal valleys. They finally established solid land routes from New Spain north to "Alta California." This introduced another major locational factor in California's history and development: its strong ties to the people and cultures of the south—first Spanish, then Mexican—have had enormous influence on California's human landscapes. This involves much more than the Spanish names of California's streets, towns, and cities. It involves a Latino population and culture that has always played and will continue to play a major role in California. It is a Latino population with roots that often extend far to the south of Mexico, into Central and South America. It is a Latino population that makes up the majority in many California schools, and it is expected to become the statewide majority in the twenty-first century. **Connections to Latin America** were rejuvenated by the late 1900s and they will continue to strengthen in modern California.

Isolation Ends, New Connections Emerge During the mid-1800s, some of these connections to the south temporarily waned after the discovery of gold brought masses of people into California. This trend especially started with the '49ers. The Mexican government had already lost its grip on California as Anglo-Americans and people from all over the globe rushed in to find their fortunes. California's isolation was broken forever, but the gold rush was just the first of many major developments that would gain the world's attention. By 1850, California was already a U.S. state. California's growth was accelerated by major developments in transportation and communication that strengthened its links to the rest of the world.

With these new technologies, the isolation that once thwarted California's growth and development became an asset. As the population and economies of California cities such as San Francisco and Los Angeles soared into the twentieth century, there were few other competitors in nearby states. California was certainly the focus of activity for a radius of more than 2,000 km (1250 miles). San Francisco became the financial center of the west from the mid-1800s through the early 1900s, and Los Angeles has held a commanding lead ever since. Throughout those decades to today, California's situation has increasingly encouraged growth of historical proportions.

By the mid-1900s, the state's population and economy were number one in the nation, and Los Angeles' only rival city in the United States was New York, more than 4,000 km (2,500 miles) away. Today, this state is perfectly positioned to reap the greatest economic benefit from the advanced technologies on the horizon. This brings the third major situational factor into focus.

Advantages of California's Modern Situation

Today's **Pacific Rim** (referring to trading nations facing the Pacific Ocean) has become such an economic and cultural catchword, it is almost cliché. This is because many Pacific Rim locations have become modern economic, political, and cultural powerhouses. They include such giants as Japan, Korea, and China. California looks directly west to many of these economies and cultures, just as they look directly across the Pacific to California, both literally and figuratively. Additionally, the developing economies of growing Latin American countries ring the Pacific to the south. As highly sophisticated technologies, trade, finance, entertainment, and services are fueling California's economic renaissance, the state is in a perfect geographic position to gain from the new world economies.

The connections are dramatic. There are not only more Asians in California than any other state, but Asian populations are growing faster than any other major ethnic group in California except for Latinos. Such changes are evident from the Little Saigons in Westminster and San Jose to Los Angeles' Little Tokyo and Koreatown. From Monterey Park east of Los Angeles to San Francisco's Chinatown and Japanese Cultural Center, the economic and cultural ripples are profound. These ripples are now extending into every California community. Examples include the growing Asian communities along Irving Street in San Francisco, in Millbrae, and throughout the Bay Area especially from San Francisco to San Jose.

California's situation on this planet has certainly shaped its history and influenced its modern landscapes. And thanks to modern communication, transportation, and other advanced technologies, the state is poised to exploit its advantageous situation in even more profound ways. These connections to the rest of the world—particularly to the Pacific Rim—will certainly have significant impacts on California's future landscapes.

Human/Environment Interaction

Obvious connections between California's natural and human landscapes are evident throughout the state. Natural processes and cycles have done more than create California's physical landscapes; they have impacted and often controlled how humans settle and live on the land. And humans have often done their best to modify and exploit these same natural landscapes.

People Controlled by Nature

An overlay showing the state's topography and densest human populations reveals quite a match. With a few exceptions, the most populous regions of the state have always been in flatter valleys and basins. These were, at first, usually locations with more abundant water (especially groundwater) that had drained down from surrounding watersheds and into the most fertile farmland. These lowlands were also easier to build on than surrounding steeper slopes, and they presented fewer topographic obstacles. Obvious exceptions include parts of San Francisco and the early gold rush towns established in the foothills of the Sierra Nevada during the mid- to late-1800s. San Francisco had exceptional advantages, including its convenient location where ships must enter the bay. The miners had to live near the gold, so the towns grew up around foothill and mountain mines.

As California's soaring populations filled most of its

coastal valleys and flatlands during the 1900s, people first began to settle at the foot of adjacent slopes. Those who could afford the extra costs of construction and access crept into the very mountainous terrain that had once confined them. Examples are scattered throughout the state, from San Diego County to the rim of the Los Angeles Basin, from the hills surrounding the San Francisco Bay Area, to recent invasions of former flatlanders into Sierra Nevada foothills.

The price of a better view and distance from the urban basins is often higher than expected. Summer and fall wildfires and the winter mudflows that usually follow have devastated growing hill and mountain settlements from the Laguna Hills to Malibu, from the Oakland Hills to the Sierra Nevada and beyond. Great battles have erupted between the powerful forces of nature, which have always ruled on the slopes and in the canyons, and the pressures from encroaching urban settlers who try to control nature. Though these settlers risk paying the ultimate price by losing their dreams, other California residents are often forced to help protect them and then subsidize their losses when disaster strikes.

A host of other natural factors caused the concentration of early urban growth in the state's coastal valleys and basins (the lowlands of **cismontane** California). Mild coastal climates—compared to nearly every region that was a source of great migrations to California—made for ideal living and working environments. From Hollywood films to aerospace to silicon chips, climate was and is a major drawing card for industry and people in the state's coastal valleys. The coastline itself has more to offer than just a mild climate. Fishing, trade, and recreation draw even more people to the coast.

It is, therefore, no surprise that California's largest metropolitan areas are, in order, housed within the Los Angeles Basin, the San Francisco Bay Area, and western San Diego County. The top five California cities in population at the end of the twentieth century all had ocean-front property, except San Jose, which is on the southern end of San Francisco Bay. (The top five cities are Los Angeles (3,775,000), San Diego (1,250,000), San Jose (900,000), San Francisco (800,000), and Long Beach (450,000). These are estimates based on U.S. Census and state sources near the end of the twentieth century; each city's population continues to grow at the start of the twenty-first century.)

Technology versus Environmental Constraints: Nature Controlled by People

Numerous other natural factors that were once critical no longer play major roles in concentrating human populations in California. The Native Americans once established their densest settlements where there were abundant water resources and native plants and animals. (The water-wise Spanish did the same, but focused on farmable lands.)

Later, the location of certain minerals and other earth resources first broke California from its isolation and led to huge mining camps and towns in the Mother Lode. Especially within northern California forests, from the 1800s and well into the 1900s, towns grew to support the timber industry. And where the richest soils were deposited, agricultural service towns erupted to support productive farms. Today, less than 20 percent of California's modern population is even indirectly involved in these original primary industries or living in what we now consider rural landscapes. Timber, mining, and agricultural activities and populations, although important to the state, are not even in the same league with California's great urban population centers and modern economies.

Recently, as the prime coastal locations filled, the great urban areas quickly spread east away from traditional coastal conveniences and into the inland valleys with hotter, smoggier summers. In southern California, the urban growth more recently spilled farther inland

These teetering structures sliding down to Pacific Coast Highway and the beach from Pacific Palisades cliffs may symbolize crumbling investments and dreams of Californians who have challenged the laws of nature. Or, perhaps they remind us—even with our modern technologies—of limitations to western migration.

into even harsher environments, through mountain passes and into the high desert (including Antelope Valley) and into the lower desert (including Coachella and Imperial Valleys).

In central and northern California, the people have recently poured into rapidly expanding urban areas of the Central Valley, and they are even creeping up many Sierra Nevada slopes. The perception is that many of the prime coastal locations are still attractive, but they have already been discovered and filled (and, some would argue, ruined). Californians are now forced to move farther and farther inland to find their dreams. Fresno (415,000) and Sacramento (397,000) were the sixth and eighth most populated cities in California at the end of the twentieth century. Riverside, Stockton, and Bakersfield (all well over 200,000), were eleventh, twelfth and thirteenth, respectively.

Most modern Californians in these urban fringe areas are rarely forced to consider to confront their natural environments, except for the occasional wildfire or flood, a mountain lion or bear, or the endangered species that may interrupt their perceptions of order and tranquility.

The trend away from our dependence on the natural environment is especially noticeable when it comes to water. Just as the Indians settled along water courses, so the Spanish were careful to locate almost every mission, presidio, or pueblo near a reliable source of water. California's early settlements were also near water courses. However, by the 1900s, Californians were proving that they could live and farm almost anywhere if they could import enough water. The irrigated farmlands of the San Joaquin Valley grew almost as fast as the urban populations of California. This was made possible by building the greatest water projects on the planet to divert water away from the water-rich, but population-poor, north and toward the demanding populations, economies, and political powerhouses of the south.

Examples of how we are controlled by nature and how we are now controlling nature are throughout this book. Although the occasional earthquake, landslide, flood, or drought are reminders of nature's power, Californians are increasingly learning how to control and exploit nature as they make more obvious human imprints on the landscape. Some knowledge of these issues is necessary to understand how the state's natural and human landscapes have evolved and to predict how they will continue to change.

◆ GETTING TO KNOW CALIFORNIA: A BRIEF SURVEY OF ITS DIVERSE REGIONS

This book was *not* designed to take the reader from region to region, simply describing each section of California. Instead, it is designed as a systematic approach to examining some of the more important and interesting topics, issues, and problems facing California today. Such a dynamic state—with so many related and connected forces and landscapes—deserves a modern, dynamic approach. A review of particular regions and more specific locations will be incorporated as those places relate to or offer examples of topics covered in each chapter.

Nevertheless, the remainder of this chapter is designed to introduce the reader to the state and its diverse regions. Remember that these regions, and many of the more specific locations within them, will be referred to in the chapters which follow (see Map 1.2).

California's major topographic features stand out. More than two-thirds of the state is considered mountainous by the most conservative estimates. These topographic features are often the major players in controlling temperature, precipitation, and prevailing wind patterns. The distribution of plants and animals, soils, and drainage patterns are also frequently controlled by topography. We've already considered the powerful controls these topographic features have placed on people and their settlements.

Consequently, geographers and other scientists have tried to divide California into landform divisions sometimes called natural provinces or **physiographic regions**. Regardless of the names or more specific divisions, each region is considered somewhat different from the others. Each region's natural landscapes have often supported people and human landscapes that are also somehow different from other parts of California. Now, we will sweep clockwise around California from region to region, starting with the northwest and ending back at the central coast. We'll look at that middle part of the clock—the Central Valley—last.

Get out your maps and prepare for this brief journey through each of California's diverse regions. Counties and the largest incorporated cities are listed for individual regions. City populations are estimates based on data from the U.S. Census and the State of California at the end of the twentieth century.

Northwestern California and the Klamath Mountains

Counties: Del Norte, western Siskiyou, Humboldt, Trinity, northern Mendocino, southwest corner of Shasta, western edge of Tehama

Largest Cities: Eureka (28,000), Arcata (16,600), Fortuna (10,300), Crescent City (9,000)

Among the obvious features that dominate northwestern California landscapes from the northern end of the Coast Ranges through the Klamath Mountains Physiographic Region are the exceptionally steep, moist, heavily forested mountain slopes. The Klamaths extend nearly

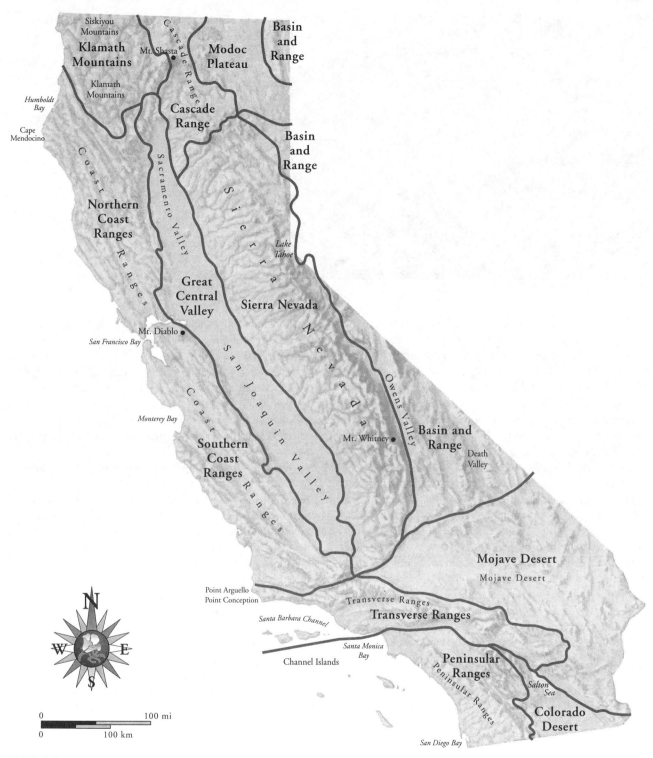

Siskiyou
Mountains

**Klamath
Mountains**

Mt. Shasta

Cascade Range

**Modoc
Plateau**

**Basin
and
Range**

Klamath
Mountains

*Humboldt
Bay*

**Cascade
Range**

**Basin
and
Range**

*Cape
Mendocino*

Sacramento Valley

Sierra

**Northern
Coast
Ranges**

Coast Ranges

**Great
Central
Valley**

*Lake
Tahoe*

Sierra Nevada

Nevada

Mt. Diablo

San Francisco Bay

San Joaquin Valley

Owens Valley

Coast Ranges

Monterey Bay

**Southern
Coast
Ranges**

Mt. Whitney

**Basin and
Range**

Death
Valley

Mojave Desert

Mojave Desert

*Point Arguello
Point Conception*

Transverse Ranges

Transverse Ranges

Santa Barbara Channel

*Santa Monica
Bay*

Channel Islands

**Peninsular
Ranges**

Peninsular Ranges

*Salton
Sea*

**Colorado
Desert**

San Diego Bay

N
W · E
S

0   100 mi

0   100 km

MAP 1.2
California's landform divisions are often considered natural provinces or physiographic
regions.

250 km (150 miles) north–south and are about 160 km (100 miles) wide. This entire region is bordered by the Pacific Ocean on the west, Oregon to the north, Shasta Valley and the Cascades (with Interstate 5 [I-5]) to the east, and the Sacramento Valley to the southeast.

Rocks of the Klamaths have been caught and lifted above the subduction zone where the continental plate rides up over the ocean tectonic plate (as defined in the next chapter). Like most California mountain ranges, granitic rocks are common (such as at Castle Crags State

On California's rugged northwest coast, mighty streams and rivers carry runoff from heavy seasonal rains back to the Pacific Ocean. Summer fog forms in the chilly air over the cold California current and drifts inland with the sea breeze against moist coastal slopes supporting forests down to the shoreline.

Park). However, California's most rugged mountain range also exhibits more old metamorphic rocks than are found in most other provinces. Glacial features also remain as remnants of the Ice Age above about 1,675 m (5,500 feet) in this cool, damp range.

Within a high-density dendritic (branching, treelike) pattern, most major stream canyons of the Klamaths are eroded more than 300–600 m (1,000–2,000 feet) deep. Above these steep, narrow canyons, the Klamath ridges tower higher than 2,100–2,700 m (7,000–9,000 feet). The Scott Valley and Smith River's coastal lowland are considered large valleys for this region. Scott Valley, the largest, is only about .8–8 km (.5–5 miles) wide and 32 km (20 miles) long.

Similar heavily forested terrain south of the Klamaths—in the northern Coast Ranges—is cut by more regularly northwest–southeast trending streams. Throughout this north coast region, from the Oregon Border into the northern Coast Ranges, are some of the state's greatest rivers. Impressive discharges from the Smith, Klamath and Trinity, Mad and Eel, and other rivers and streams (reviewed in detail in Chapter 6) are common especially during winter and spring. As the Coast Ranges trend farther south and away from this region, they generally become drier and less rugged.

Throughout this book there are more details about the natural history of this region that has the heaviest rainfall (up to 200 cm [80 inches] per year) and greatest runoff in California. Deep canyons and rugged terrain have contributed to the region's cultural and economic isolation; residents of southern California may be as unfamiliar with the people of northwestern California as they are with its natural environments.

Historically, primary industries ruled the economies here, but the region saw the peak of the timber industry

come and go in the 1950s. As the timber industry worked overtime to cut the tallest stands of trees in the world, Redwood National Park and other reserves were created to protect some of the less than 10 percent of old-growth forest remaining in California. While the industry waited for its second- and third-growth forests to mature, it was also changing its methods of operation.

Timber jobs were lost as the industry began loading raw, unprocessed timber directly onto boats for processing overseas. Automation replaced many of the remaining jobs, and companies were finding timber at lower prices abroad. Jobs and towns in the region began to wither while environmentalists and industry management engaged in an ongoing controversy. Now, with less than 10 percent of California's old-growth forests remaining, and much of that protected, these economies must rely on sustained-yield timber production as they search for other sources of income.

By the 1970s and 1980s, illegal crops of marijuana had become so valuable to the region's economy that marijuana wars broke out. To the embarrassment of some Californians living in the number one agriculture state, marijuana was reported as the top cash crop in California; much of it was being grown in the northwestern region. The area's still slumping economies are left to depend on small manufacturing, retail trade, tourism, fishing, and a swelling retired population. Some communities have investigated bringing in government prisons or offshore oil drilling to create jobs. With few exceptions, such as the developments around Arcata Bay (including Eureka and Humboldt State) and the connections made by Highway (Hwy.) 101, this land and its people (less than 1 percent of the state's population) remain relatively isolated in some of the world's most beautiful mountain and coastal scenery.

North/Central California with its Southern Cascades

Counties: Siskiyou, Shasta

Largest Cities: Redding (80,000), Shasta Lake (9,500), Yreka (7,150), Mt. Shasta (3,550), Weed (3,050)

If not for its majestic composite volcanoes, this region would serve as a smoother transition from the Klamaths on the west to the Modoc Plateau on the east. However, standing on top of 3,189 m (10,457 feet) Lassen Peak (the most southerly of the major Cascade volcanoes), you can look south out of the Cascades and into the northern Sierra Nevada. Looking north from Lassen, you can see the ominous Mount Shasta in the distance. At 4,319 m (14,162 feet), it is the second largest volcano in the north–south trending Cascade Range. (Only Washington's Mount Rainier is higher.) It rises directly up from Shasta Valley for nearly 3,355 m (11,000 feet). A few active glaciers still creep down its slopes. There are several smaller volcanoes lined up within California's southern Cascades. Some are still active with fumaroles and vents. Lassen erupted from 1914–1917.

This relatively long, slender physiographic region is cut into north and far south sections by the Pit River, which flows west out of the Modoc Plateau and into Shasta Lake. The region is bounded by the edge of Shasta Valley and the Klamaths to the west, Modoc Plateau to the east, and the Central Valley and northern Sierra Nevada to the south. Tucked behind the Klamaths, California's Cascade valleys are drier than valleys draining the slopes facing the Pacific Ocean, but precipitation, vegetation, and forest densities increase toward the higher, cooler, wetter slopes. Winters are colder and summers warmer than on Pacific-facing slopes; continental air masses are more common here.

Mount Shasta is the spectacular landmark in California's Cascades. It is part of the string of volcanoes which extend south from Washington and Oregon into northern California. Ranching and other primary industries are evident throughout these rural landscapes.

Since I-5 follows the western edge of this region, travellers are rewarded with views of impressive mountains on both sides of the interstate—the Klamaths to the west, the Cascades to the east. This major transportation corridor links Pacific coast cities in California with Oregon and Washington; it also breaks the isolation of regions to its west and east. Without it, California north of Sacramento would be even less recognized, with even a smaller population and economy. All of the major towns of California's Cascades, which also serve the ranching and timber industry so important to the region, are located along I-5. It even slices through Shasta Valley, where cattle pastures are interrupted by some farming on the richer soils formed on sediments carried from the surrounding mountains. The farther you wander away from this northern California corridor, the more things have remained unchanged; there has been little population or economic growth beyond it. I-5 extends a similar influential ribbon well to the south, into the Sacramento Valley.

For those travelling north, just up from the Sacramento Valley, Redding welcomes visitors to the southern edge of the Cascades. This is the largest city in the north end of the state, and it represents the antithesis of the state's three northern regions. (It could also be considered a part of the northern edge of the Sacramento Valley.) The city's past aggressive development strategies have resulted in a series of generic malls and businesses, neighborhoods, and urban scenes reminiscent of larger population centers to the south.

While moving to Redding to escape the city, many people brought it with them. This is especially evident on the east side of the Sacramento River, which slices through the city. Today's condominium and apartment complexes rest on bluffs overlooking the Sacramento River, and they overshadow an older town center with a rich history. Redding's influential fingers stretch out for several miles into more extensively populated neighborhoods on the suburban/rural fringe and into nearby small, but growing, towns.

The string of towns along I-5 north to the Oregon border is more characteristic of the region. Many serve as economic and population centers, although occasionally residents may have to travel north into Oregon or south back to Redding for goods or services.

The Northeast and Modoc Plateau

Counties: Modoc, Lassen, north tip of Plumas

Largest Cities: Susanville (17,200), Alturas (3,150)

Moving east from the majestic Cascades, the volcanic peaks are smaller and the broad, flat basaltic lava flows of the Modoc Plateau dominate the landscape. Surfaces of these thick lava flows average more than 1,350 m (about 4,500 feet) above sea level and may represent the southwestern extension of the Columbia Plateau. There are occasional interruptions by volcanic cones rising between 300–1,050 m (1,000–3,500 feet) above the plateau.

Even farther east, the Modoc Plateau breaks up into a series of dramatic fault-block valleys and mountains more characteristic (and actually a part of) the Basin and Range Physiographic Province. Examples include the lofty Warner Mountains in California's northeast corner, which even support impressive stands of cool, damp aspen forest. The inland Alkali Lakes (in Surprise Valley east of the Warners) and Goose Lake to the west are examples of water accumulating in down-faulted basins. Another finger of the Basin and Range Province extends in from Nevada farther south, around Honey Lake. This region is bordered by the Sierra Nevada on the south.

The Pit River represents the only major water course in this region; it drains from northeast to southwest, bisecting it. To the north, some of the best examples of volcanic features such as basaltic flows, lava tubes, and cinder cones are displayed at Lava Beds National Monument. North of that are Tule Lake and the Lower Klamath Lake wildlife refuges up to the Oregon border. Volcanic hillslopes are common south of the Pit.

Since this high plateau is in the rainshadow of the Klamaths and Cascades, it receives little precipitation (about 50 cm [(20 inches] per year), and it experiences long, harsh winters while in the grip of dry continental air masses. Sagebrush steppe and juniper shrub savanna dominate the vegetation of the plateau, where surface water usually drains freely and is lost through the lava flows. Yellow pine and other forests appear on higher slopes, where orographic precipitation enhances water supplies.

Like people in the northwest, residents of northeast California are isolated. Due to drier climates, timber is less important and ranching rules most of the economies. Grazing cattle and farmland stretch across almost every Modoc valley during summer, while events like the rodeo in Surprise Valley's Cedarville evoke the culture of a land unfamiliar to many Californians. There is also some hunting, fishing, and tourism in this mostly culturally conservative region. Local unemployment can rise to 20 percent during the long, cold winters. In 1996, the Pit River Indians started a casino to attract revenue. The region does not tend to attract industry, business, or people because of its isolation and lack of economic development.

Susanville, near Honey Lake, is an exception. First, it is the largest town in the northeast. Second, it lies on the edge of the Basin and Range landforms more common to the east. Finally, it has stronger economic and cultural ties to the east in Reno and Nevada than to California because of easy access along Hwy. 395. Farther north, where Hwy. 395 crosses the Pit River, is the second-largest town, Alturas. This is mostly an agricultural service town and is more typical of the northeast.

How will the high-tech communication and computer revolution affect these northern California towns and their economies? It is too early to tell. However, as more people in higher income groups utilize technology to do more work at home, they are also able to move farther out from the urban fringe. There may be interesting long-term consequences for all California regions that have remained relatively isolated and undeveloped until now.

Basin and Range

Counties: Mono, Inyo

Largest Cities: Bishop (3,550), Mammoth Lakes (5,500, within the eastern Sierra Nevada but services northern heart of Basin and Range)

The heart of the Basin and Range Physiographic Province extends east of the Sierra Nevada and throughout Nevada. It is sometimes referred to as the "Trans-Sierra" to help separate it from the local fault blocks of valleys and mountains that encroach into northeastern California and are actually a part of this province. It is bordered by the Sierra Nevada on the west, and it ends at the Garlock Fault and Mojave Desert to the south. Unlike the Mojave, its ranges are lofty and they trend north–south—parallel to its deep, long valleys—in such regular patterns that the ranges have been likened to caterpillars crawling north.

These uplifted blocks called horsts are highest just east of the Sierra Nevada. They include the White, Inyo, Coso, and Argus Mountains, which form a north–south spine more than 250 km (160 miles) long and culminate at 4,345 m (14,246 feet) White Mountain Peak. To the southeast, the Panamint Mountains are capped by 3,370 m (11,049 feet) Telescope Peak, which looks directly down into the lowest basin in North America (Death Valley at 86 m [282 feet] below sea level). Death Valley is an exaggerated version of the many elongated, down-dropped basins sometimes called grabens (actually, it is a pull-apart basin) that separate the ranges. These basins represent base level for the interior drainage they catch. When underground and surface water evaporates, it leaves the characteristic white salty playas with their borax, potash, soda ash, and other salts.

Volcanic activity, often found along many of these faults and fissures in the thin crust, is reviewed in Chapter 3. Left behind, mostly in and north of the Owens Valley, are hot springs, craters, cones, lava flows, and other volcanic landscapes.

In the rainshadow of the Sierra Nevada, these ranges are relatively dry with much sparser vegetation than their big brother to the west. Their unusual plant communities include bristlecone pines, the oldest living trees in the world, and their more protected valleys rank among some of the hottest and driest places on earth. The climates of some nearby valleys are almost as severe as

Death Valley, where the mean annual precipitation is only 5 cm (2 inches) per year and the hottest temperature in North America was recorded at nearly 57°C (134°F). Even the common desert scrub vegetation struggles to survive in these conditions.

Streams flowing out of the eastern Sierra Nevada toward the Owens Valley once represented the only major source of water for the Basin and Range. Then, starting in the early 1900s, even this water was diverted to Los Angeles, drying first the Owens River and Valley and then Mono Lake and Basin to the north.

Consequently, recreation (including fishing), tourism, and service industries have long since replaced many of the formerly important primary industries, even in the Owens Valley. In contrast to northwestern and northeastern California, the Basin and Range is home to very popular destinations, and it is closer and more accessible to the southern California masses. Visitors crowd Hwy. 395 to Mammoth (one of the greatest ski resorts in the world) during the ski season, and they meander on the roads to those eastern Sierra Nevada fishing holes and retreats or to visit Death Valley, Mono Lake, and other natural attractions in these open landscapes. Familiar small settlements in the Owens Valley along Hwy. 395—such as Little Lake, Lone Pine, Independence and Big Pine—are dwarfed by Bishop, which is becoming more than just a tourist stop.

Sierra Nevada

Counties: Plumas, Sierra, eastern edges of Butte and Yuba, Nevada, eastern Placer, El Dorado, Amador, Alpine, Calaveras, Tuolumne, Mariposa, eastern portions of Madera, Fresno, and Tulare, northeastern Kern, western fringes of Mono and Inyo

Largest Cities: Paradise (27,000), South Lake Tahoe (23,000), Truckee (12,500), Auburn (11,650), Grass Valley (9,600)

Whether it is considered a physiographic province, region, or major landform, the Sierra Nevada competes with the Central Valley as the largest in California. It is nearly 650 km (about 400 miles) long and approximately 110 km (70 miles) wide. Its ridges trend northwest–southeast and several peaks rise well above 4,270 m (14,000 feet). The tallest peak in the United States outside Alaska is Mount Whitney at 4,421 m (14,495 feet), and there are others not far behind. Sierra Nevada's sawtooth ridgelines split in two to couch the Tahoe Basin in the north, and they are also split by the Kern River to the south. Most of the vertical faulting responsible for lifting the range is evident on the magnificently steep eastern wall, where the view from Lone Pine on Hwy. 395 (1,130 m [3,700 feet]) is directly up to Mount Whitney, which is only several miles away.

Yosemite's granitic rock and high country (from near the top of Yosemite Falls) has been carved by glaciers. Since John Muir, so many millions of visitors and naturalists have been inspired by Yosemite's valley and meadows that there is concern the crowds are loving it to death.

In contrast, the western slopes of this mighty range gradually rise above the Central Valley until they reach the top as far as 80 km (50 miles) to the east. This elongate region is bound by the Central Valley on the west, the Cascades on the north, the Basin and Range on the east, and the Mojave Desert to the south. This orientation makes the Sierra Nevada an almost perfect barrier to catch orographic precipitation from the winter storms that sweep from west to east across California from the Pacific. Tremendous winter snowfalls are common at higher elevations. When the snow melts, water pours into streams, rivers, and reservoirs toward the Central Valley, where it is used for farming or diverted to thirsty cities. Even greater snow packs accumulated during the Ice Ages to build glaciers that carved spectacular scenery in the high country and in major canyons. Yosemite and Kings Canyon serve as outstanding examples of these landscapes.

The varied climates—from drier foothills up to towering peaks—have also produced life zones or belts of vegetation containing a fascinating assemblage of plants and animals that have been studied by biologists and biogeographers. They include the only stands of the largest (in bulk) living trees in the world, the Giant Sierra Redwood, or Giant Sequoia, (*Sequoiadendron giganteum*).

The granitic rocks so common in the Sierra Nevada are similar to those forming the cores of almost every other major California mountain range. Gold was discovered along the contact zones between these great granitic batholiths and older mostly metamorphic rocks as some of the gold weathered out and into the streams. The discovery of gold in 1848 in the western Sierra Nevada foothills changed California forever. Thousands flocked from all over the world to the Mother Lode, and many of the gold rush towns they built are still there. Today, powerful human forces are molding new landscapes.

Explorer and naturalist John Muir properly named the Sierra Nevada "The Range of Light." Many Californians still think of the Sierra Nevada as a place where spectacular scenery and rich natural history is protected by the expansive national forests and parks that make it world famous. It has been a barrier to air masses, water, plant and animal species, and people (such as the Donner Party). It contains one of the largest areas without roads in the United States outside Alaska. South of Tioga Pass, only two highways and one railroad cut through the range. During winter through at least early spring, the region becomes more inaccessible; snow typically closes the roads from Walker Pass in the south to the central Sierra Nevada north of Yosemite.

Today, the old mining towns that became agricultural and timber service towns are bulging with tourists, retirees, and even commuters! From Grass Valley and Nevada City to Sonora and beyond, housing developments and suburbs are spreading uphill from the Central Valley. In many cases, the escaping urbanites have brought their freeways, generic shopping malls, and other service-oriented landscapes. And though the higher elevations (such as in Alpine County) are more distant and have escaped this encroachment, there are local exceptions. Residents of Lake Tahoe (with bustling casinos across the state line) and Mammoth Lakes are fighting over how to control the growth of their crowded ski resorts and housing developments.

Public lands and parks are also feeling the pinch as Yosemite receives more than 3.5 million visitors each year. Daytime visitors from the Central Valley and weekend visitors escaping California's great urban centers crowd resorts such as Lake Isabella and the lower Kern River at the Sierra Nevada's southern end.

As many Sierra Nevada towns compete for more growth, jobs, and industry, the regional debate rages: will tomorrow's Sierra Nevada be set aside in parks and wild lands for recreation or will it serve as just another California suburb? As we debated this question, the region's population increased by 400 percent from 1960 to 2000. There is extensive discussion about the Sierra Nevada's natural and human landscapes in this book.

Southern California Deserts (Transmontane Southern California): About 20 Percent of the State

Mojave Desert

Counties: southeastern corner of Kern, northeastern corner of Los Angeles, nearly all of San Bernardino leeward of coastal mountains, much of Riverside leeward of coastal mountains

Largest Cities: Lancaster (130,000), Palmdale (120,000), Victorville (62,000), Hesperia (61,000), Apple Valley (55,000)

The Mojave Desert begins just south of the Garlock Fault at the southern end of the Basin and Range and Sierra Nevada regions. Mountain ranges of the Mojave are not as commonplace or impressive as in the Basin and Range. Many of the Mojave ranges are older and weathered; they have crumbled into and filled the surrounding pediplains with much debris, especially in the western Mojave. Higher ranges of the eastern Mojave soar above 2,150 m (7,050 feet), including the Kingston, Clark, New York, and Providence Mountains. Throughout the Mojave, at the base of the steeper mountains, are the gently sloping alluvial fans and bajadas common to California's desert terrain.

Although the Mojave generally makes up what is often known as the northern deserts, or the "**high desert**," it is punctuated by deep valleys and desert playas (salty lake beds). Just as in the Basin and Range, mineral-laden water may accumulate in these basins and evaporate to leave white, crusty salts on the surface. These lower basins are also home to some of the driest climates and hottest summers in North America. Soda Dry Lake and Silver Dry Lake basins near Baker and I-15 are examples. Like the Basin and Range, there are only a few locations where sand has been blown into dunes. The Devil's Playground and Kelso Dunes are stellar examples southeast of Baker between I-15 and I-40.

The western corner of the Mojave begins east of Frazier Mountain and Tejon Pass within a narrow wedge where the Sierra Nevada has tapered off into the Tehachapis and where these ranges intersect the Transverse Ranges at an acute angle. On the rainshadow side of these intersecting ranges, the wedge opens up into the desert basin toward the east, known as the Antelope Valley. The Mojave continues to widen toward the east until it represents an enormous expanse of diverse desert topography all the way into Nevada and northwestern Arizona. Just as the Garlock Fault separates the Mojave from the Basin and Range, Sierra Nevada, and Tehachapis to the north, so do the San Andreas Fault and other structures separate the Mojave from the Transverse Ranges on its southwestern border. The generally lower Colorado Desert Physiographic Province lies to the south of the Mojave.

Since so much of the Mojave Desert is higher terrain than its neighbor to the south, it is generally cooler and wetter than California's hottest deserts. A few winter storms commonly produce snowfall each year. The thicker desert scrub and Joshua trees of the high desert may even give way to pinyon, juniper, and sparse forest at the highest elevations. These life forms and their surrounding landscapes are spotlighted in Joshua Tree National Park and the Mojave National Preserve.

Substantial military and mining operations and limited grazing fueled the economies of the tiny settlements in the Mojave during the 1900s, but the military presence was most noticeable. The Marine Corps Training Center north of Twentynine Palms, Antelope Valley's Edwards Air Force Base, Fort Irwin north of Barstow, and China Lake Naval Weapons Center are good examples. Military activities required plenty of open space and the Mojave had it. Expansive San Bernardino County—the largest U.S. county and most of it U.S. government land—offered ideal settings for many of these military operations.

Transportation has always been vital to survival in this harsh, wide-open country. This is why most of the few people and economies of the Mojave Desert once clung to the services provided along its major transportation corridors. One example is Barstow, where train tracks and Hwy. 58 meet I-15 and I-40 and where the celebrated Route 66 once made the town famous. The traffic between Barstow and Las Vegas along I-15 and the trickle of sightseers to Death Valley kept little Baker's pulse going. Trains, truckers, and travellers also converged on the little town of Mojave. Later, a huge storage facility for mothballed jet airliners was built in Mojave. Tehachapis' wind farms decorate desert slopes above Mojave. Way out on I-40 near the Colorado River, the little town of Needles has gained fame as the largest settlement near the latest proposed nuclear waste site in Ward Valley.

Recent mass migrations of people from the coastal side of the mountains has transformed the economies and landscapes especially of the western Mojave and Antelope Valley. Some newcomers are retired, and some have found work in the high desert. Many moved their families to this harsher climate for more space and cheap housing, but the price they pay is a commute to and from the L.A. Basin that may total several hours each day. A heavy toll has been placed not only on the breadwinners and their families, but on the very desert environments that once represented an escape from urban life.

Giant malls, congestion, pollution, violence, and other urban problems are now commonplace in Palmdale, Lancaster, and Victorville. Even that charming little Apple Valley of the 1960s—once just a wide spot on Hwy. 18 where a trailer park and hamburger stand were major landmarks—has a population soaring past 55,000. The Joshua trees have come down and the housing projects have gone up. Far to the southeast of Antelope Valley's city lights are the strip of blossoming towns along the north edge of Joshua Tree National Park; landscapes from Twentynine Palms to Joshua Tree to Yucca Valley and Morongo Valley are gaining new populations. Some of this chaotic growth is spreading far into the Mojave, where you can find major malls and occasional traffic jams outside of Barstow.

Population growth in southern California desert counties has averaged nearly 40 percent per decade since the 1960s.

The Colorado Desert

Counties: Imperial, southern and eastern portions of Riverside, far eastern edge of San Diego

Largest Cities: Indio (45,000), Palm Springs (43,000), El Centro (38,000), Cathedral City (36,500), Palm Desert (36,000)

South of the Mojave, extending into the Salton Trough and Mexico and then along a strip of the Colorado River Valley, is the Colorado Desert. Often called the southern deserts, or the "**low desert**," it includes the farmlands and developments of the Coachella and Imperial Valleys. This region is tucked away on the rainshadow side of the Peninsular Ranges to its west and the Transverse Ranges to its northwest. It is generally hotter and drier than the higher Mojave, and it probably has more in common with the deserts of southern Arizona and northern Mexico than it does with the deserts of California.

In contrast to the higher Mojave, the Colorado Desert's annual precipitation is below 13 cm (5 inches) per year, daytime highs frequently break 43°C (110°F), and overnight lows may not drop below 27°C (80°F) during mid-summer. Desert scrub dominated by the ubiquitous creosote bush is common in both regions, but the Colorado Desert lacks Joshua trees, which grow to the north in the Mojave. Also lacking are saguaro cacti, which only grow naturally in California along a thin strip of the Colorado River but are imported into human landscapes of the Imperial and Coachella Valleys. However, several other species of cactus are common in the cactus scrub of the Colorado Desert's lower desert terrain, and in some desert canyons you will find the state's only native palms. They are beautifully displayed in Anza Borrego, California's largest state park.

The Salton Trough is being stretched and dropped in relation to the surrounding mountains, especially the Peninsular Ranges, which are being pulled away from it by tectonic forces reviewed in Chapters 2 and 3. The Palm Springs Tramway lifts travelers over some of these faults on the trip from this desert floor up to the cool forests of the Peninsulars' San Jacinto Mountains. Farther south, the Salton Sea was a mistake created and filled by overflow from the rampaging Colorado River in the early 1900s. It has since served as a sump for agricultural run-off from the Coachella and Imperial Valleys.

People and Their Landscapes Pour into Low Desert Valleys As the inland valleys west of the mountains fill with people, growth spills through Banning (San Gorgonio) Pass, into the Coachella and Imperial Valleys, and even up parts of the Colorado River Valley. Even Blythe, once just a small agricultural service community and pit

Palm Springs and the Coachella Valley (looking toward the west) are tucked behind the San Jacinto Mountains, a wall that blocks moist Pacific air from penetrating east into the desert. Settlements first huddled around natural springs, but resorts and other developments are now spreading across desert scrub and sand dunes.

stop where I-10 crosses the Colorado River, has blossomed to substantial town status. Such population and economic growth has brought division to the Coachella and Imperial Valleys.

Parts of cities like Palm Springs, Rancho Mirage, and Palm Desert still offer the resort atmosphere that once attracted Hollywood stars, the rich, and the famous. In contrast to these traditionally wealthy visitors, there are now a large number of lower-income workers in the service industries that support the resort economy. As we move south, through Indio and into the farming communities where the farm workers live, poverty and unemployment become more visible. Imperial County, with a majority Latino population, is now the poorest county in southern California. Because agribusiness is the only major industry in the area and because there is a large pool of potential farm workers in Mexicali, just across the Mexican border, the future looks bleak for the Imperial Valley's working masses.

The long growing season and irrigation water from the Colorado River made the fertile farms of the Salton Trough possible. The region produces as great a variety and quantity of valuable crops as any area its size. Just a glance across this valley with its lettuce fields, grape vines, citrus groves, and towering date trees will serve as testimony to its productivity. Unfortunately, these advantages are barely translating into a subsistence-level income for much of the Coachella and Imperial Valley working class. A visit to some of the Imperial Valley's little towns provides testimony to this disparity.

While economic disparity is the rule in this region, many Coachella Valley cities, such as Cathedral City, are somewhere in the middle, struggling to find their roles. They often find some answers when the snow birds arrive to escape northern winters and crowd the Coachella Valley from November through April. This clean revenue source evaporates in summer's sizzling sun when the

streets, stores, and restaurants turn quiet again. Some residents look toward the new Shadowrock Golf Course or Palm Springs Air Museum to pump more energy into their economies.

Southern California's Coast and Mountains (Cismontane Southern California)

The dividing line between the Peninsular Ranges and Transverse Ranges Physiographic Provinces is clear near Banning in San Gorgonio Pass along the San Andreas Fault Zone. The San Bernardino Mountains of the Transverse Ranges tower above on the northern side, while to the south, the spectacular San Jacinto Mountains loom as the northern edge of the Peninsular Ranges. However, west of the pass, the coastal and inland valleys of Riverside, San Bernardino, Orange, and Los Angeles Counties begin to blend together both physically and culturally. Elsewhere, it is often difficult to tell where the natural and human landscapes of the Peninsular Ranges to the south yield to those of the Transverse Ranges to the north. We will consider these two landform provinces separately, but under the same Southern California Coast and Mountains heading.

South of Los Angeles: The Peninsular Ranges and South Coast

Counties: San Diego, Orange, western Riverside
Largest Cities: San Diego (1,250,000), Santa Ana (313,000), Anaheim (305,000), Riverside (256,000), Huntington Beach (195,000)

The Peninsular Ranges have much in common with the Sierra Nevada. First, the core is primarily granitic rock

San Diego's natural harbor and ideal climate encouraged earlier settlements with military and then tourist roots. A more diverse population and economy with powerful connections to Mexico and the Pacific Rim are fueling rapid growth throughout modern San Diego County.

that cooled to form a huge batholith after it contacted older, mostly metamorphic rock. Second, active faulting has lifted the block at steep angles above the desert floor on the east side; slopes drop down more gradually toward the coastal plains on the west side. Finally, because of this orientation, the Peninsular Ranges catch considerable orographic precipitation which accumulates and flows along major streams toward the west, mostly down the gentle western slopes toward the very ocean it came from.

However, there remain major differences between the Peninsular Ranges and the Sierra Nevada. First, they are not as tall or as massive as the Sierra Nevada. The highest peak is San Jacinto at 3,295 m (10,804 feet) at the northern tip of the Peninsular Ranges. They trend lower toward the south; the next range south of the San Jacintos is the 1,830 m (6,000 feet) average crest of the Santa Rosas. Second, they are farther south. Not only are they farther away from winter's major storm tracks, which makes them much drier, but they trend for nearly 1,300 km (about 800 miles) out of California and all the way down to southern Baja California.

Finally, the Peninsular Ranges are really a series of ranges interrupted by valleys (some substantial and deep) and parallel faults, many which are still active. One example is the San Jacinto Plain, which sits between the San Jacinto Fault and Mountains to its east and the Elsinore Fault and Santa Ana Mountains to its west. More noticeable, however, is how the entire Peninsular Ranges are pulling away from the Salton Trough and the Gulf of California. They also include the Laguna Mountains, Palomar Mountain, and the islands trending parallel to them just offshore. They are bordered by the Salton Trough on the east, while the Transverse Ranges cut them off on the north.

Starting at the coast, a patchwork of coastal sage scrub yields to grasslands in the inland valleys and to chaparral on inland mountain slopes. In higher elevations of the Peninsular Ranges, oak woodlands and then yellow pine forests become dominant. Isolated patches of cooler, wetter forests grow even higher in the San Jacintos and near a few of the highest peaks to the south. Among the few mountain resorts within these cooler forests are Idyllwild, between Hemet and Palm Springs, and Julian, in the mountains east of San Diego. The Palomar Mountain Observatory, east of Oceanside, ranks as one of the world's premier astronomical observation sites. It also looks down on some of the many inland valleys which interrupt these ranges.

Interesting coastal landforms include the mesas which gradually drop down from the range to marine terraces along the San Diego County coast. As these terraces overlook the ocean, they are occasionally sliced through by the westward flowing streams. The result can be seen in a drive along I-5, mostly on the flat, raised terraces, until there is the occasional drop into a deep stream canyon or valley and a view of the characteristic lagoon or estuary which has formed near the shoreline.

Into the Los Angeles Basin and Orange County: Northern Fringes of the Peninsular Ranges or Southern Fringes of the Transverse Ranges?

Inland Valleys This brings us to some of those eastern inland valley extensions of the Los Angeles Basin (known as the Inland Empire) and to the south part of the basin itself. From the retirement communities that flooded the valley around Hemet, to the gradual growth and more diverse economy of historic Riverside, these inland valleys experienced soaring growth rates after Orange County had filled up. Corona, west of Riverside, caught the population overflow that spilled around the Santa Ana Mountains and through Santa Ana Canyon.

Few communities will ever match the explosive

PEOPLE COME TO THE SOUTH COAST

During the middle part of the 1900s, San Diego County built an economy based on such staples as the military, retirement, tourism, and construction. However, this county with one of the mildest climates in the world became the fastest growing county in the state by the 1980s. It grew so fast that nervous residents began rallying around groups with names such as "Not yet L.A." Regardless of this activity, San Diego's growth—at the expense of its fields of flowers and its citrus and avocado groves—was undeniable, and growth often occurred without plans or controls. The region's history and quaint Spanish atmosphere and architecture were being swept away by a host of developments including generic housing tracts, new urban developments, development along Hotel Circle and the rest of Mission Valley, tourist attractions such as Sea World, a redeveloped downtown, and an enlarged freeway system.

A good place to view the results of these changes is at Cabrillo National Monument, which looks down on San Diego from atop Point Loma. (The monument was named after the Portuguese soldier of fortune who discovered California for Spain in 1542. San Diego was finally claimed and settled for Spain by Portolá and Serra in 1769.)

From Coronado to Mission Bay and Beach, from Old Town to the new Horton Plaza, from the even newer Gaslamp Quarter and the convention center nearby, heroic efforts were made during the 1980s and 1990s to change San Diego for the better and sometimes to even preserve its charm. However, the city had become the second largest in California, and it was still growing. San Diego's population sprawled up the coast through Del Mar and Encinitas and out toward San Diego Zoo's Wild Animal Park. Even Oceanside experienced a burst in population and in construction to house all the newcomers. The masses are now

filling in the gap between San Diego and Tijuana (Chula Vista is the county's second-largest city), and they have spread east into and around communities like La Mesa and El Cajon and along I-15 to cities like Escondido.

Like residents of San Francisco and its Bay Area, many who live in these extended communities often consider themselves a part of that larger domain known as San Diego. At the same time, they have also created their own more independent urban centers as San Diego County's economy is forced to diversify along with its cultures. The county's historic economic dependence on the military and the "zoners" who come to escape southern Arizona's searing summer heat is dwindling. High-tech manufacturing, retail, and services have become new economic staples. Meanwhile, the Latino population has swelled to nearly 25 percent while Asians and Pacific Islanders (especially Filipino-Americans) also play key roles in breaking the old stereotype of a traditionally white San Diego.

Today, residents can no longer blame traffic congestion, air pollution, crime, and economic bumps on Los Angeles. San Diego is in the big city league now, and in the twenty-first century it will be linked with its close neighbor to the south, a bulging and bustling Tijuana.

Predictions of what will become of this great experiment range from exciting to frightening. Already, San Diego is beginning to meet head on the urban sprawl spilling south from southern Orange County, itself an outpost of the urban sprawl from Los Angeles to the north. Only the open space of the United States Marine Corps' Camp Pendleton prevents the merger of San Diego and Los Angeles. Will anything stop these cities from growing together into one coastal megalopolis that will eventually stretch from the San Fernando Valley or even the Ventura/Oxnard Plain well into Mexico?

growth once seen in Moreno Valley, east of Riverside. During the 1980s, this little community grew from less than 10,000 to a city of over 100,000. The influx of commuters eager for inexpensive housing often resulted in a loss of the area's citrus groves and dairy farms. The irony is that residents brought the city they sought to escape with them. Many still must commute through torturous hours of traffic into the cities deep within the Los Angeles Basin to make a living. Whether the valley smog and long commutes are worth the bigger houses and yards is a question pondered in Moreno Valley neighborhoods every day.

The story is similar in San Bernardino and other inland valleys farther to the north, technically on the edge of the Transverse Range Province. The difference is that more urban poor of all ethnicities have flocked to these

suburbs, assembling in neighborhoods troubled by gang activity and higher crime rates.

Orange County If it is now difficult to believe that Riverside is where the first navel orange trees grew, a glance at the modern landscape makes it almost impossible to understand how the county and city or Orange got their names. The city of Orange was founded in 1873; the county was born in 1889. Even into the mid-1900s, fruit trees and strawberry fields were commonplace in Orange County. Orange County began growing as Los Angeles' little sister just after the San Fernando Valley began to fill and long before those valleys to the east began to experience population growth. Newer communities to the east can learn some valuable lessons from the county of Orange.

It first grew as a Los Angeles suburb. As agriculture gave way to land development and construction, an economic strip grew along the Santa Ana Freeway (I-5), the main link to Los Angeles. I-5 slices through inland Orange County, so it is not surprising that Disneyland grew up next to it and Knott's Berry Farm was not far away. Backed by history and the county seat, Santa Ana became and still is the most populated city. Anaheim competed, building its convention center across from Disneyland and not far from Anaheim Stadium ("The Big A"), where major league baseball had arrived in the 1960s in the form of the California Angels. (By the late 1990s, it was known as Edison Field.) Just as economic development increased where I-5 intersected with other new Orange County freeways, the focus of activity and growth shifted south.

By the 1970s, Orange County beaches had solid reputations; surfing, swimming, sunbathing, and the beach culture that supposedly personified Southern California were firmly established in the minds of visitors as typical of the Orange County coast. Laguna, Newport, and Huntington Beaches evolved to represent coastal playgrounds that were more convenient and less crowded than the long-established retreats on Santa Monica Bay to the north. This delighted city officials and developers because people, industry, and jobs flocked to southern Orange County. As this economic activity moved south, it affected communities near the beach and along the San Diego Freeway (I-405), such as Fountain Valley, Costa Mesa, and Irvine. Within about a decade, sprawling farms were converted to housing tracts and industrial sites, the inevitable result of rapid population growth.

Today's economy continues to evolve, pushing high-tech and service industries into the limelight. Some observers make powerful arguments when they claim that the center of Orange County's economy and culture is now somewhere around South Coast Plaza or even farther south. Farther inland, northern Orange County neighborhoods (in parts of Fullerton, Anaheim, and surrounding cities) and Santa Ana have become more ethnically diverse and similar to greater Los Angeles rather than the predominantly middle-class, white, conservative enclaves they once were. Boasting the third-largest county population in California, Orange County is now more than 25 percent Latino and more than 10 percent Asian.

Orange County's wealthiest residents are concentrated along a huge check mark that extends from Huntington Harbor and Beach down through Newport and the Laguna coast. A leg of this area extends north and inland along the hills from the southern edge of Orange County and the San Juan Capistrano area, spilling around the Laguna and Irvine Hills. Evidence of a high-income population is occasionally seen along the western foothills of the Santa Ana Mountains and again in the Anaheim Hills and Santa Ana Canyon. We are now presented with an opportunity to identify trends and patterns of settlement and income distribution common to much of California. To better view and discuss this general pattern, we finally move north and work our way into the heart of Los Angeles and even farther into the Transverse Ranges.

Los Angeles and the Transverse Ranges

Counties: southwestern San Bernardino, Los Angeles, Ventura, Santa Barbara

Largest Cities: Los Angeles (3,775,000), Long Beach (450,000), Glendale (200,000), San Bernardino (183,000), Oxnard (158,000)

In this section, we will continue our review of human landscapes as they blend into Los Angeles (L.A.). We will later review the natural landscapes of the Transverse Ranges. This is the reverse of our approach for previous regions.

Exaggerated Human Landscapes Population, economic, and cultural trends in L.A. are similar to those of its southern neighbors, with three major differences: L.A. is the largest city; L.A. has been the traditional leader in trends; and, if California is a land of extremes, L.A. is a singular place where both ends of social, economic, political, and environmental extremes coexist.

Where else can you find towering skyscrapers dwarfed by the backdrop of spectacular snowcapped mountains one day but obscured in a thick smog the next? The longest parade of Rolls Royce automobiles ever assembled in the world followed by three days of riots and civil unrest attributed to racial strife and charges of police brutality? People living in thirty-room mansions on enormous estates that overlook a city where illegal immigrants making less than minimum wage are forced to work *and* live in sweatshops? The busiest and richest port, but the worst traffic jams in the country? Two thousand violent murders per year in the early 1990s? (Fortunately, murder and violent crime rates were down sharply by the late 1990s.) Many residents, city officials, and astonished onlookers may have stopped trying to make sense of L.A. and assume it to be an unmanageable chameleon. However, there are orderly patterns that repeat themselves around the City of Angels.

Looking for Patterns in L.A.'s Chaos One pattern is true for almost all of California: Where the hills meet the water, wealth is present. From La Jolla and Del Mar to Santa Barbara, there are numerous examples in Southern California. Like so many other trends, this pattern is exaggerated in L.A. Wealthy neighborhoods of the Palos Verdes Peninsula look down toward those of racially diverse working classes (including the largest number of Pacific Islanders on the mainland) in Long Beach, Compton, Carson, and the South Bay. Even farther west in the Palos Verdes hills, expensive properties offer a view away from this city of contradictions and toward the ocean.

From the Hollywood Hills to Beverly Hills, you can look down on the poverty embedded in L.A.'s city lights. But, as you move toward the "West Side," the poverty of the lowlands yields to wealth; generally, real estate prices escalate for land close to the ocean. Residents farther west in the Pacific Palisades or Malibu may find it difficult to believe that there is a poverty-stricken, 57-square-mile segment of the L.A. area (mostly south and east of downtown) where the majority of residents are not even citizens. That is an area larger than the entire city of San Francisco!

Income disparity and racial segregation were not in the original plan when the Spanish founded a little pueblo along the Los Angeles River in 1781. By the early 1900s, newspaper and railroad tycoons and land barons teamed up with William Mulholland to bring water to the swelling population of L.A. The quest for resources grew with the annexations of surrounding lands, the population increase, and the booming economy. The path was paved for the movie industry. By 1915, Hollywood (within the official city limits of L.A.) was already the movie capital of the world. The discovery of oil pulled great industries, such as transportation and defense, to the L.A. area. This growing industrial base and the mild climate attracted increasing numbers of people. As a result, the service economy boomed, thus providing more jobs.

As we have seen in other regions of California, housing developments, construction, aircraft plants, and an impressive tourist industry replaced agriculture and oil wells. Freeways stretched the settlements even farther until they filled the San Fernando, San Gabriel, and more distant inland valleys. The settlements filled Orange County and the pressure finally squeezed them into the canyons. Like chain-reaction explosions, outlying cities erupted almost overnight, mostly along freeways and highways. More recently, they have spilled north toward Magic Mountain and into Canyon Country, creating the city of Santa Clarita, and even farther out along Hwy. 14 to the high desert and Palmdale and Lancaster. (Each of those cities has well over 100,000 people.) To the northwest, cities such as Simi Valley and Thousand Oaks (both also more than 100,000) are demolishing the former gap between L.A. and the Ventura/Oxnard Plain.

Like the developments in southern Orange County, the spread northwest is mostly an extension of the flight of white residents, money, and jobs from the inner city that was common in previous decades. Currently, the spread represents a migration from closer to outlying suburbs. However, in the Antelope Valley and many of the outlying inland valleys, these patterns are changing. This leads us to reassess some of the sweeping generalizations that are so often made about L.A. by those who see it as too complex to understand.

First, although many proclaim that L.A. never had a plan, much of the booming growth through most of the 1900s was not only planned, but welcomed by the city and surrounding communities. Unlike San Francisco, most of L.A.'s growth was ushered in with the automobile. Also, L.A. had a light rail system that was one of the best and most celebrated urban transportation systems in the world. Since people were able to live away from the urban center, along or at the end of red car lines, communities sprang up all around L.A.'s periphery during the early 1900s. When this most efficient transportation system was dismantled, the freeways and their cars took its place during the mid-1900s.

The population spread was further encouraged by land developers who convinced so many families to buy the American dream—a California-style bungalow on a big lot in a new, clean neighborhood away from the city. The San Fernando Valley and other L.A. suburbs were products of those developers' and homeowners' dreams. The plan was to disperse the population and make L.A. an assemblage of individual, loosely connected communities. With more modest population density gradients, Angelenos would be spared the cramped conditions typical of the huddled masses in great European and eastern U.S. cities. Instead, they would have a piece of their own space to enjoy the year-round sunshine delivered by the mild, Mediterranean climate.

Second, it is true that, as in most American cities, institutional racial segregation forced African-Americans and other ethnic groups into specific neighborhoods. It is also true that white flight and the subsequent drain of wealth out of the inner city began to transform L.A. after WWII and accelerated into the 1960s and 1970s. Downtown began to resemble a ghost town at night and on weekends as workers took their paychecks home to spend in suburban shopping malls. Minorities and the poor were generally left behind in the inner city. Meanwhile, the primarily white suburbs thrived as people and money poured in. However, things began to change in the 1980s.

A booming economy brought redevelopment and gentrification to parts of L.A. as YUPPIES, tiring of their long commutes, trickled back toward the city's core. They evicted the poor, fixed up some of the old Victorians and bungalows, and reclaimed several neighborhoods. This trend mixed the population pot again and contributed to a more complex and fascinating human landscape. (Similar trends were affecting the San Francisco area and, to a smaller extent, San Diego and a few of California's smaller cities.) Some of the displaced working class found homes in nearby neighborhoods, and some were left homeless. Many of them moved out to the hinterland. Cities like Palmdale, Lancaster, and San Bernardino have received an influx of these low-income families. Consequently, many distant suburbs have now also become complicated human landscapes with diverse assemblages of families who represent many ethnic groups, cultures, and income levels. They, too, have "escaped" the urban core.

Finally, too often, L.A.'s many rich and diverse communities have been improperly lumped together. It is tempting, especially while travelling through the basin by freeway, to discredit L.A. as a bunch of generic housing projects that eventually grew into one another, emerging as a bland, expansive megalopolis. Such superficial observations are not only incorrect, they are unfair to the many dedicated residents who identify with and are active in their specific communities and neighborhoods. After all, we are talking about more than 3 million people within the city limits and a population nearing 15 million in the basin and its connected settlements.

Divided L.A. Los Angeles still has an economic center that stretches from the central business district, west along the Wilshire Corridor's concrete canyon, into Century City and Westwood. Otherwise, economies and jobs in the basin are so spread out, freeways are often jammed with commuters going in both directions (to and from downtown) during morning and evening rush hours. Perhaps understanding these economies is just as difficult as understanding the complex cultures and neighborhoods that make up L.A. and California. Today, there is a new, powerful economic force that is putting pressure on Californians in general and Angelenos in particular: the global marketplace.

Current economic trends in L.A., as in most other California cities, are toward an economy with two distinct and very distant levels. Middle class manufacturing jobs are being replaced by two very different employment extremes. One extreme is represented by the high-paying, high-tech, research and development jobs and their associated high-level services (finance, trade, professional, and information technologies). On the other end are the growing low-paying, low-tech manufacturing jobs, such as garment sweatshops, and low-level services jobs, such as the fast-food industry.

The growing disparity in incomes and in levels of education and skills is tightening the social vise, increasing tensions between and within these classes, and challenging officials who are trying to figure out how to cope with the situation. To witness the impact these trends

WHERE IS L.A.?

Part of the difficulty in discussing L.A.'s issues and problems is that few can figure out, much less agree on, where this great city begins and ends. Because we've already considered Orange County, the eastern inland valleys, and some high desert suburbs, we are focusing here on Los Angeles County until we later sweep northwest and follow the Transverse Ranges.

There are many individual and unique neighborhoods within the city limits such as Echo Park, Boyle Heights, Hollywood, Van Nuys, Woodland Hills, Westwood, Century City, and Venice, whose residents often identify more with their particular communities than with the city of Los Angeles. Earlier in the 1900s, L.A. annexed many of these locations—especially in the San Fernando Valley—to expand its water rights. By the 1990s, efforts to preserve identity and uniqueness reached a feverish pitch; some residents of the San Fernando Valley saw their communities as so distinct that they launched a movement to secede from L.A.

In contrast, there is the long list of cities that are frequently considered part of the city of L.A. but are actually separate, official cities. A few examples are Santa Monica, Culver City, Beverly Hills, West Hollywood, and Inglewood. Finally, there are the unincorporated communities within Los Angeles County. They don't belong to any city, and they aren't official cities at all! East L.A. and Marina del Rey are examples.

Each of these communities proudly displays its own specific cultures, lifestyles, and human landscapes, but all of them are a part of that sprawling abstract painting, that great experiment we often call Los Angeles.

Decades of growth and redevelopment have transformed the skyline of downtown Los Angeles. Change is particularly evident on and near Bunker Hill. This view is from Los Angeles' oldest park, a redeveloped Pershing Square, looking over the landmark Biltmore Hotel (with its restored Spanish-Italian renaissance architecture) toward a modern landmark (the state's tallest office tower).

have on L.A.'s and California's human landscapes, you need only walk through the streets of Pico-Union or South-Central and then walk through the streets of Brentwood or Beverly Hills.

The increased economic competition is also raising tensions between lower-income groups. These tensions are evident in places like South-Central L.A., where Latinos have recently displaced African Americans to become the majority ethnic group. Intricately entwined economic and cultural trends are producing some fast-changing human landscapes throughout L.A. and California; such trends earn more attention here since they are common to most of California's major cities.

Moving Northwest, into Other Urban Centers in the Transverse Ranges Farther northwest is Ventura County, where the Ventura/Oxnard Plain's rich agricultural fields are being consumed by the same kinds of industrial parks, shopping malls, and housing projects that took the San Fernando Valley and other L.A. suburbs by storm so many years ago. Similar activities blossoming along the strip of Ventura Freeway (such as in Thousand Oaks) and in places like the spreading Simi Valley are strengthening the connections with L.A. Experiencing so many of the same economic trends as L.A., this was one of the fastest growing regions in California during the late 1900s. Oxnard outgrew its older neighbor, Ventura, many years ago.

Still farther to the northwest is the beautiful and still somewhat isolated strip of Santa Barbara coast. Past development has been mostly limited to that thin coastal plain with the ocean on one side and the steep Santa Ynez Mountains on the other. Limited water supplies should play less important roles in the future since many of these communities connected to the California Water Project after 1996.

In spite of tourists, the crowded downtown shops, a growing University of California, and development encroaching from surrounding communities, Santa Barbara retains much of its magic and charm and an atmosphere that is more reminiscent of old California. Perhaps this is because it was just far enough from the explosive growth of L.A. and, more recently, Ventura and Oxnard. Perhaps it is because land values and rents are very high, and there are not many high-paying jobs, and it is too far to commute into L.A. Whatever the reason, when that dry sundowner wind blows through the imported palm trees, over the historic mission and toward its scenic beaches, Santa Barbara can still shine like no other California city.

The Transverse Ranges Now we will review the natural landscapes and processes that combine to form the Transverse Ranges.

They rise above and protect so many southern California cities from winter's cold snaps. This protection is evident when north winds must sink and be heated by

Santa Barbara and its neighbors are confined to a narrow, sheltered lowland strip between the ocean and the rugged Santa Ynez Mountains.

compression to get to the coastal valleys below. What would be cool winds are modified to warm and dry, causing autumn and winter heat waves. When these Santa Anas blow during mid-winter, the mild southern Californian climate is the envy of snow shovelers in more wintery parts of the country.

However, these winds also bring the occasional wildfires that scorch the chaparral and coastal sage and even communities on the lower slopes of the Transverse Ranges. The winter mudflows that follow these fires race out of the mountain canyons and add to the destruction. They also add a little bit more material to the alluvial fans radiating out of the canyons and the more than 9,150 m (30,000 feet) of sediment already accumulated below the Los Angeles Basin.

The Transverse Ranges' name comes from their cutting east-west, across the more common trend of landforms, through California. They represent rocks and slices of crust caught, crumbled, and lifted up throughout a wide region near the big bend in the San Andreas Fault Zone. The Transverse Ranges trend all the way from Points Arguello and Conception and the Channel Islands National Park on the west into the little San Bernardino Mountains and Joshua Tree National Park on the east. They are bordered by the Coast Ranges and Central Valley to the northwest and the Sierra Nevada and Mojave

Physiographic Provinces to the northeast. The Peninsular Ranges make up their southern boundary, and the Coachella Valley is at their southeastern boundary.

The Transverse Ranges are typically quite rugged and especially lofty toward the east. The San Bernardino Mountains include the resorts of Lake Arrowhead and Big Bear and its popular ski slopes. San Gorgonio Mountain is the highest in southern California at 3,507 m (11,499 feet). Across Cajon Pass and trending west are the San Gabriel Mountains, with 3,070 m (10,064 feet) Mount San Antonio (Old Baldy) Peak towering above Wrightwood and its popular ski resort. The rugged topography trends farther west to 1,742 m (5,710 feet) Mount Wilson and its renowned observatory. After becoming one of the world's premier astronomical observatories earlier in the 1900s, its importance faded in later decades. Thanks to new technologies, it enjoyed a rebirth in the 1990s.

Nature and Open Spaces Accessible to Millions The Transverse Ranges have gained much of their fame because of their proximity to the Los Angeles Basin. On clear days, they seem to erupt from the eastern edge of the San Fernando Valley and especially the northern edge of the San Gabriel and northeastern San Bernardino Valleys. The contrast between the basin (with its warm winter sunshine, citrus groves, and palm trees) and the brilliant snowcapped peaks in the background was displayed on magazine covers and promotional brochures for years. Today's Los Angeles skyscrapers have replaced the orange groves in a modern version of these breathtaking views. Residents of the Los Angeles Basin from the valleys to Orange County and Santa Monica Bay beaches will recognize these familiar landmarks looming toward the north and northeast.

The chaparral on these slopes yields to woodland and yellow pine and even cooler forests at higher elevations that receive more than 75 cm (30 inches) of precipitation per year. This serves as important watershed, since much of the water flows down into the basin after accumulating in channels flowing through deep canyons. When the water out of the San Gabriel River and other channels is ponded into spreading basins at the bottom of the mountain front, it recharges future groundwater supplies. However, during heavy winter storms, it can produce dangerous and destructive flooding.

The cool forests and winter snows of the San Gabriels and San Bernardinos have also been magnets for millions of visitors willing to brave winding roads and the short drive to escape the city. Weekend traffic jams bring the crowds who fill every picnic table, campground and trail, or winter ski resort. Here, especially along Angeles Crest Highway, is another example of how so many Californians strain to find a little piece of that remaining wilderness and open space that once helped make Southern California famous.

The same problems plague the smaller Santa Monica Mountains, which are also peppered with developments. Within them are Griffith Park and the Hollywood Hills to the east and the community of Topanga and the city of Malibu toward the west. The Santa Monicas are the most southerly of these Transverse Ranges and they are the only major mountain range to bisect a major U.S. city. Meanwhile, all of these diverse landscapes continue to star as scenery in countless Hollywood movies, TV programs and commercials. Trending farther west, the northern Channel Islands are a structural extension of the Santa Monicas.

From the San Gabriels, the Santa Susana, Topatopa, and Santa Ynez Mountains finally trend out to Points Conception and Arguello. Gradually, the remaining ranches and agricultural service towns like those near the Santa Clara River will probably yield to the same developments that are surrounding them and have already been reviewed previously. North of here, Coast Ranges landforms rule and trend in a more northerly direction. Landforms, coastal features, and coastal waters become decisively central Californian to the north.

A Geographic Pivot Point

There is an outstanding geographic pivot point in California. It stands out because the bending San Andreas Fault meets the Garlock and other faults there. It stands out where the corners of five different physiographic regions intersect (the Coast Ranges, Central Valley, Sierra Nevada's Tehachapi extension, the Mojave, and the Transverse Ranges). It stands near where three different mountain ranges and three different basins (including the Los Angeles Basin) are wedged together with many different rock types. It marks the center for a major mountain barrier between air masses to the north and south. It displays an amazing mix of plants and animals that have crept in from cismontane and transmontane, central and southern California, from lower to higher elevations.

It sits on a definitive natural and cultural boundary between southern California and the rest of the state. Three counties (Ventura, Kern, and Los Angeles) intersect at this geographic pivot point near Frazier Peak and Tejon Pass. Even the cars, buses and trucks on I-5 must strain to get over this barrier, as if some unknown force was trying to make them turn back before it was too late, to discourage them from entering that different world on the other side. All of these factors come together on the map and on the ground to create a unique landscape at this most unusual geographic pivot point.

We are getting closer to the end of our clockwise sweep around the various regions of the Golden State. It's time to head northwest from here, into the Coast Ranges. As usual, we will first look at the physical geography of the entire region, then its human geography, saving the human landscapes of the San Francisco Bay Area for last. We will finally complete our journey with a brief view of the Central Valley.

The Central Coast and Coast Ranges

Counties: far northern tip of Santa Barbara, San Luis Obispo, Monterey, San Benito, Santa Cruz, Santa Clara, San Mateo, Alameda, San Francisco, Contra Costa, western edges of several San Joaquin Valley counties, Marin, southwestern Solano, Sonoma, Napa, southern Mendocino, Lake, western edges of Glenn and Colusa

Largest Cities Beyond the Bay Area: Salinas (130,000), Santa Maria (72,000), Santa Cruz (56,000), San Luis Obispo (43,500)

Here, we consider the Central Coast and Ranges west of the Central Valley. They trend northwest along the coast and the San Andreas Fault Zone from north of the Transverse Ranges, and finally blend in with the northern Coast Ranges and the northwest coast somewhere in Mendocino County. There is no clear northern boundary, but the northern Coast Ranges and Klamath Mountains tend to be higher, more rugged, and wetter.

Major mountain ridges and valleys of the Coast Ranges trend strikingly parallel to the northwest–southeast trending San Andreas and other splinter faults. They present formidable barriers to east–west travel throughout the range. San Francisco Bay is often used as the break between the north and south Coast Ranges, and with good reason. First, the path from the Golden Gate into the Bay and Carquinez Strait and on into the Delta *is* the only major natural break slicing across the Coast Ranges. This gash not only serves as a conduit so that ocean air can flow into the Central Valley, but also as a channel for deep-water vessels into the valley. It is the path followed by both saltwater, when it encroaches in-

land during high tide, and freshwater from the Delta that flushes the system during heavy runoff and low tide.

Ridges of the Coast Ranges tend to be lower in the south, ranging above 600–1200 m (about 2,000–4,000 feet). Major ranges include the Santa Cruz Mountains down to Monterey Bay and the Santa Lucia Range down to Morro Bay. On the inland side are the Diablo Range east and south of the Bay Area and the Temblor Range farther to the southeast. Deep and sometimes broad valleys often parallel these ranges. The greatest is the Salinas. The Salinas River headwaters drain toward the northwest all the way from San Luis Obispo County. The river continues to flow northwest through the productive farmlands of a widening Salinas Valley, past King City and Soledad and toward Salinas. Finally, the valley and its river spill out into the Monterey Bay and its submarine canyon, bounded by Santa Cruz on the north and Monterey on the south. Farther north is the Santa Clara Valley; it trends southeast out of San Jose and the Bay Area and into Hollister.

North of San Francisco Bay, the Coast Range ridges eventually reach higher. The northern ranges also receive considerably more rainfall. This generally results in more lush forests, especially on western slopes, compared to the southern ranges. "The Redwood Empire" was named with these forests in mind. In Lake County, Clear Lake is the largest freshwater lake totally contained within California's boundaries. Even in the northern Coast Ranges, the inland valleys are hot and dry during the summer. Good examples include the Sonoma and Napa Valleys, which receive abundant rainfall in the winter but turn warm and dry during summer, providing perfect grape-growing climates. Even farther north of the Bay Area, the valleys and the coast tend to be more narrow strips.

These coasts north and south of the Bay Area are also some of the most picturesque, photographed, and famous landscapes in the world. From Morro Rock to the

Scenic Morro Bay, with its sand spit, mudflat, and ancient volcanic rock, interrupts the terraces and serenity of the central coast, midway between Los Angeles and San Francisco. Retirees and others escaping California's urban centers are flooding the hills and lowlands from San Luis Obispo to central coast beach communities.

cliffs that erupt out of the sea at Big Sur, from Carmel and Monterey Bays, to Ano Nuevo, Pescadero, and Half Moon Bay, spectacular rock formations combine with a patchwork of plant communities and misty fog for some unparalleled coastal scenery. North of San Francisco, equally accessible and splendid coastal landscapes are on display from Stinson Beach to Point Reyes National Seashore and from Bodega Bay all the way up the Sonoma and Mendocino coastlines. Several of nature's attractions more inland and close to Bay Area populations include Big Basin Redwoods in the Santa Cruz Mountains, Muir Woods in Marin County, and, farther north, the Russian River summer resorts near Santa Rosa. (The Russian River also follows an inland valley, flowing southeast until it turns west just before Santa Rosa and slices through the Coast Ranges to Jenner and the Pacific.)

Human Landscapes of the Central Coast

Monterey Bay and the Salinas Valley probably have the richest history along this coast outside the Bay Area. There were once nearly one-hundred sardine packing plants during the great fishing boom along Cannery Row in Monterey. The fishing boats can still be seen in Monterey, Morro Bay, and other central coast spots. However, none of these coastal communities rely on fishing to fuel their economies as they did many decades ago.

Today, from Monterey Bay Aquarium and Carmel-by-the-Sea to Big Sur, San Simeon, and Morro Bay, tourism is king, and it is enhanced by some impressive art communities. The Monterey Peninsula entertains more than 2 million tourists each year; the shops and other tourist attractions in Monterey and Carmel are testimony to this. To the north, Santa Cruz is an historical tourist destination, especially for working folks escaping the Central Valley's summer heat or the Bay Area's crowds. This tradition continues, but a more diverse economy now includes modern industries and the University of California, Santa Cruz.

Between Monterey and Santa Cruz, once booming communities grew in the shadow of Fort Ord which helped fuel their economies. Since the military announced that the base would close, Seaside, Marina, and many other surrounding communities search for an economic jump-start to replace it. Perhaps the new Cal State University, Monterey Bay, will lead the way.

Meanwhile, nearby Salinas Valley communities have no identity crises. They continue to thrive in some of the most productive farmlands in the world, the same places John Steinbeck wrote about. Here also is that same disparity in income we have noted previously between those who plant and harvest the crops and those who run the farms; it would look very familiar to someone from the Imperial Valley. Today, about 40 percent of the Salinas population is Latino. (That percentage is even higher for nearby San Benito County.) To the south, Cal

Poly, retirees, and transplants from southern California help fuel the economy and increase land values in the San Luis Obispo area. Gone are the days when you could sell your modest home in L.A. and buy a small ranch in these rolling scenic hills.

Finally, way down on the southern tip of the Coast Ranges (or northern Transverse Ranges) along the Santa Maria River is little Santa Maria, which at 68,900 is no longer so little. Santa Maria is not a tourist town, though attempts are being made to diversify its economy. Unfortunately, during the late 1900s, it began to experience some of the problems connected to rapid growth although it is not a suburb attached to any city. It stands in real contrast to the picturesque, gently rolling hills with grasslands and oak woodlands so common to other stretches of Hwy. 101. If there is a nostalgic landscape typical of California's mission days, you may find it along or near central California's Hwy. 101, but not in Santa Maria.

Human Landscapes of the San Francisco Bay Area

Largest Cities: San Jose (900,000), San Francisco (800,000), Oakland (400,000), Fremont (200,000), Santa Rosa (140,000)

Although Bay Area residents may resist the idea, their human landscapes have much in common with Los Angeles. We can make a brief list of those common events that have had similar results in the Bay Area. First, as San Francisco, Oakland, and other traditional centers bulged during the middle to late 1900s, populations broke away to establish enormous outlying suburbs. Many went to the South Bay, others to the East Bay, and today they are even filling North Bay spaces. Second, like Los Angeles, portions of central San Francisco and Oakland experienced urban decay during and after the mid-1900s. Mainly white populations moved to the suburbs along with money and jobs while lower income families and minorities were left behind. This trend eventually impacted even San Jose's downtown. Third, these problems were further exacerbated by redlining and the unwillingness of businesses to invest in some of these blighted communities.

Just as in Los Angeles, in the 1980s and 1990s, urban redevelopment and gentrification attracted YUPPIES back to the city (especially San Francisco), and the poor were squeezed further, many to the outlying suburbs. The result is that some lower-income and minority families have populated a few of the suburbs far out on the urban fringe. As Bay Area suburbs continue to grow, traffic jams, pollution, gangs, and crime may also grow. Today, public officials are straining to create efficient infrastructures that will serve the edges of what has evolved into a complicated megalopolis.

Finally, the economies of the Bay Area, like Los Angeles, are also evolving away from the traditional military and manufacturing emphasis to high-tech, trade, entertainment, and services industries. There is also a growing gap between the rich and poor, though it is less extreme than in Los Angeles. All of these factors are playing important roles in shaping the Bay Area's human landscapes.

The Bay Area is Unique   Perhaps to the delight of northern Californians, there are also some major differences between their Bay Area and the Los Angeles Basin.

First, especially San Francisco experienced most of its growth and development before the automobile. Its narrow, pedestrian-friendly streets and diverse neighborhoods are packed close together. In this respect, San Francisco more resembles Boston rather than a typical California city. Second, unlike L.A. or San Diego, San Francisco is a tiny city in area; once it filled its little end of the peninsula, it could not expand outward. It had to become denser and grow upward, while the overflow populations were sent to neighboring cities. This is why "The City" has often been called the city without a suburb, in contrast to Los Angeles, which has sometimes been considered a group of suburbs without a city.

Second, there are no great lowlands to support the continuous interlocking developments common in Los Angeles. Instead, spreading populations have always been detoured around the huge bays and then often confined between steep hills. When all these factors are considered, it is easy to understand why so much unlikely development has occurred on such steep slopes that would otherwise seem to prohibit settlement. However, the real barriers are the great bays.

San Francisco has one of the world's largest natural harbors. San Francisco Bay spreads out south of San Francisco and Oakland. Some great cities are built on the flatlands surrounding it. They include Alameda, Hayward, San Mateo, Redwood City, Palo Alto, Fremont,

Santa Clara, and San Jose to the south. North of the San Francisco–Oakland Bay Bridge are Berkeley, Richmond, and the Marin County settlements. The sprawling communities north of San Pablo Bay include Petaluma, Rohnert Park, huge Santa Rosa, and the growing communities up along the Napa and Sonoma Valleys. From Vallejo, cities have even grown near the shores of the Carquinez Strait and Suisun Bay and into the Delta. The Bay Bridge and the Richmond–San Rafael, San Mateo, and Dumbarton Bridges represent bold attempts to link these cities. But, that giant bay which separates the city lights continues to be the most conspicuous part of Bay Area landscapes.

Finally, the Bay Area population, at more than six million, is still less than half that of the Los Angeles area. This and the dividing effects of the bay have made this region a little more manageable and user-friendly. As proof of this, in the 1990s the region was temporarily taken off a federal list of urban areas with dangerously polluted air. Another example is how the Bay Area Rapid Transit (BART) system has combined with other transportation services to deliver relatively convenient, reliable, and popular public transportation. The compact city of San Francisco has the finest transportation system with the most options for its riders in California. This convenience also encourages tourism. "The City" is the number two urban tourist destination in the world.

San Francisco erupted as a wild west city almost overnight during the Gold Rush. The City's strategic position had and still has everything to do with the bay and the city's perch atop the entrance to it (the Golden Gate). It quickly became the financial capital of the west and held that distinction from the mid-1800s to the mid-1900s, until Los Angeles took over. Its ability to attract people from so many ethnic groups, cultures, and lifestyles, often shunned by their homelands, has prevailed since its early and wild gold rush days. The African-American popula-

Many of San Francisco's narrow streets and densely populated neighborhoods with Victorian homes were built before the automobile ruled California's urban landscapes. Though today's cable car tracks are used for fun and tourism, this compressed city has remained more committed to successful public transportation than any other California urban center.

tion in the Fillmore, Latinos in the Mission, traditional Italian-Americans at North Beach, the renowned gay community in the Castro, and some of the greatest concentrations of Asians and Pacific Islanders in the country make it difficult to find another city of its size with such cultural diversity.

San Francisco quickly grew from the mid-1800s as a real city with a real skyline and a definite central core. Slicing through today's towering downtown concrete canyons is Market Street; for a short distance it easily triumphs over its southern counterpart—Los Angeles' Wilshire Boulevard—as the city's central strip. San Francisco's central business district is still well defined as are most of its other districts and neighborhoods. It continues to evolve as a walkable, exciting, and entertaining urban center, but a serious housing crunch has been created by those who compete to live in The City. The growing populations were forced to other Bay Area cities. After WWII, Oakland was also developed and the masses spilled away from urban centers and settled south, east, and north around the bay. Just as in the L.A. area, each community has a unique story to tell.

Moving Away from San Francisco and Oakland Just to the south there is Daly City, a bedroom community suburb identified with a 1960s song about "ticky-tacky" little boxes on the hillsides. Across the bay lies Berkeley, famous for its experimental politics and as the location for the state's first University of California. There's quaint Point Richmond, with beautiful views across the bay on one side and Richmond on the other with its refinery, working class, and notable African-American community. From here, across the Richmond-San Rafael Bridge and connected to San Francisco by the Golden Gate Bridge is Marin, one of the wealthiest counties in the United States. Marin County residents have staged some monumental and successful battles to keep out the developers who have filled surrounding lowlands. However, the string of swelling suburbs in counties to the north of San Francisco along Hwy. 101 goes all the way up to Santa Rosa.

Almost as a mirror image with the north, the communities of the South Bay have experienced impressive, but earlier, growth as they culminate in California's third-largest city, San Jose. When communities northwest of San Jose bathed in the industrial and technological riches brought by Stanford researchers and the computer industry during the 1970s, their lowland area took the name "Silicon Valley." San Jose housed many of the workers in these new industries until it earned the reputation of a little L.A. without the culture. As its bedroom communities grew together, they drained San Jose's downtown and created an enormous suburb, complete with malls, traffic jams, and smog.

Unlike San Francisco, San Jose had plenty of room to grow, so it surged ahead of The City in population later

in the 1900s. Currently, the fingers of development are creeping even farther southeast and into the Santa Clara Valley communities of Morgan Hill and Gilroy. However, after the industry slump of the 1980s dragged into the early 1990s recession, the area's cities are considering methods to diversify their economies. If San Jose continues to claim the title, "California's City of the Future," its residents and officials will have to work harder to define what that future city should be.

All of this is similar to the massive developments in the East Bay's inland valleys. Mount Diablo now looks down on the daily traffic jams and congestion created as Concord and Walnut Creek grow together. These inland valleys are shielded from direct sea breezes, so they are hotter and drier during the summer. The valleys with their new developments extend even farther east to Pleasanton and Livermore with its renowned research laboratories. The story is all too familiar as many of these East Bay communities are also competing for high-tech and service industries to fuel their economies.

The developments are now spreading even farther east, into the Delta and Central Valley. Commuters are finding less expensive homes out there, but they are also spending long hours commuting toward Bay Area jobs. Although most residents claim they don't want to create another Los Angeles, it is not difficult to visualize another megalopolis stretching from San Francisco north through Santa Rosa, south past San Jose, east through the East Bay, into the Central Valley, and all the way to Sacramento. Developments are already spilling into and filling these valleys with views of Mount Diablo.

We have reached the Central Valley. This is the center of our clock and the end of our journey.

Central Valley

> *Counties*: southern tip of Shasta, Tehama, eastern Glenn, western Butte, eastern Colusa, Sutter, western Yuba and Placer, Yolo, Sacramento, northeastern Solano, San Joaquin, Stanislaus, Merced, southwestern Madera and Fresno and Tulare, Kings, western Kern
>
> *Largest Cities*: Fresno (415,000), Sacramento (397,000), Stockton (245,000), Bakersfield (228,000), Modesto (185,000)

Natural Setting

The Central Valley (or Great Valley) competes with the Sierra Nevada as the largest province or landform in California. It stretches more than 640 km (400 miles) from southern Shasta County south to the Tehachapis and more than 80 km (50 miles) at its widest from the Coast Ranges to the Sierra Nevada. It is also bordered by the Klamaths and Southern Cascades to the north, while its southern end is near that geographic pivot point with four other physiographic provinces.

This extensive, mostly flat valley near sea level exhibits remarkable uniformity, especially for a California region. It is divided into two sections at the Delta. The Sacramento River and its tributaries drain the northern part of the valley (the Sacramento Valley) into the Delta. The San Joaquin River and its tributaries drain most of the San Joaquin Valley into the Delta, except for far southern portions, which exhibit inland drainage.

This elongate valley has been downwarped for millions of years between the Sierra Nevada and Coast Ranges. It has also been filling with thousands of feet of sediment during that time. Oil is extracted from some of the relatively older sediments in and around the San Joaquin Valley, but the younger surface sediments are even more productive. The soils formed on them are some of the richest in the world.

The Central Valley receives scant precipitation compared to its surrounding mountains. However, for millions of years, rivers and streams flowing out of these mountains (especially off the west slopes of the Sierra Nevada) have delivered rich sediment and abundant water to this basin. Native grasslands once dominated the valley and wide paths of riparian forests grew along its waterways. During heavy runoff, water frequently ponded to form huge lakes in the southern San Joaquin Valley, while the Sacramento and San Joaquin Rivers often flooded much of their valleys and their Delta.

People Bring Changes to the Central Valley

The greatest water projects in the world have controlled these annual floods and distributed the water more evenly throughout the year. These projects have also allowed ocean vessels to navigate along waterways to places like the Port of Stockton and past Sacramento up the Sacramento River. They have also stored tremendous amounts of water for irrigation in what is the greatest and most productive agricultural valley in the world. The result was the early demise of those native grasslands. These topics are addressed in more detail later in this book.

Evidence of agricultural productivity can be witnessed while travelling along Hwy. 99 or I-5 during any summer when caravans of trucks are so full of tomatoes, onions, cotton, and other crops. Great cattle yards, such as those along I-5, harbor thousands of cattle just before they become hamburgers for the fast-food restaurants that originated in California and now line those monotonous strips of Central Valley highways. (The billion-dollar beef and dairy industry produces the number one agricultural commodity in California.) Californians can thank the Central Valley for making the state number one in agriculture in the United States.

The state's remodelled Capitol Building symbolizes a rich history and is the center of California's government activity. Sacramento originally gained fame in a pivotal location on the Sacramento River between the gold fields and San Francisco Bay. Though government jobs are still vital to this urban center in the middle of the Central Valley, the city is growing and spreading with a more diverse population and economy.

Even the weather contributes to this productivity. Sun rules during spring, summer and fall and growing seasons are long, especially in the southern valley. However, stagnant weather conditions that trap summer smog also allow winter's dreaded cold tule fog to settle and thicken out in all directions within this lowland protected by barriers on all sides.

Human populations are now also settling into these massive lowlands, consuming some of the most productive farmlands in the valley, and bringing the same issues and problems we have seen elsewhere: traffic congestion, pollution, inadequate infrastructure, crime, urban sprawl, the loss of open space, and how to diversify and modernize the economy. These are dramas that have already been played out by so many California cities in milder climates closer to the coast.

They are being repeated in the Central Valley as its cities begin to grow and merge together into what could be California's new and most surprising megalopolis of the twenty-first century. The difference in this region is the powerful grip agriculture has had even on many urban economies and cultures since people settled in the valley. Evidence includes the myriad dealers displaying their latest tractors, other farm equipment, and repair services along the highways.

A Journey from South to North in the Central Valley

Bakersfield is king of the southern San Joaquin Valley. This area has taken the nickname "Nashville West" because of country music's traditional popularity. The honky-tonk sound was refined here in the cowboy beer joints and nightclubs as more than one country western performer and native son gained national fame. This city was built on the Kern River where wealth from rich agricultural land and nearby oil fields was enhanced by major transportation corridors which cut through the area.

Fresno combines with its smaller neighbors to the south (including Visalia, Tulare, and Porterville) to represent the focal point of the central San Joaquin Valley. It also straddles Hwy. 99, but it is near the entrance to celebrated Kings Canyon and Sequoia National Parks to the east. It once earned the title "Raisin Capital of the World," a label that could only be attached to such an agricultural giant. (Nearby Selma has claimed that title more recently.)

The agribusiness that dominates throughout the valley also rules here where the valley's ethnic diversity (including an especially large Latino population) stands out. Its economy has been diversified by such additions as a large Cal State University campus. On the western side of the valley opposite Fresno, farms give way to more extensive cattle grazing on drier lands.

North of Fresno, smaller communities are strung out along Hwy. 99 and the major railroad lines that parallel it. They culminate with the larger Modesto and even larger Stockton, with its deep-water port. Here is where the waters of the San Joaquin and Sacramento Rivers converge to flood their delta. The miles of Delta channels meander around below-sea-level islands that are protected by a complicated system of connected and aging levees, zigzagging across the landscape like so many exposed earth worms. Here is also where the East Bay's urban sprawl is spilling farther east to meet valley developments. Mount Diablo seems to punctuate the southwestern horizon of all of these Delta landscapes.

Moving north into the Sacramento Valley, there is Davis, a bicycler's haven made famous by its UC campus with a traditional emphasis on agriculture. Finally, there is Sacramento, the modern state capitol and California's fastest growing urban area where the meandering Sacramento and American Rivers meet. This was another wild west product of the gold rush; it also erupted almost overnight in the mid-1800s. Until sediment from hydraulic mining clogged the Sacramento River and its tributaries, boats hauled people and cargo past Sacramento to the gold fields and towns and back to San Francisco. Ships returned decades later after the sediment had finally been flushed.

Sacramento and Beyond Meanwhile, Sacramento's location at the end of the transcontinental railroad kept the attention of business people, shipping industries, and land barons across the state. Agriculture ruled for decades, but its importance continues to wane within a more diversified economic environment. This includes a reduced military presence, the official state business

for thirty-four million Californians, industrial parks, commercial districts, and a Cal State campus.

It is appropriate to complete our clockwise sweep of California here in Sacramento. It is the center of some of California's most magnificent history. It is in the center of this enormous physiographic region spread along the state's midsection. It is the center of the state's political structure, and it is now experiencing the same profound changes and confronting the same problems and issues common to nearly every California city.

How can we deal with the rapid growth that so often destroys the identities of our cities and communities? What will happen to the open space and productive farmlands consumed by our seemingly insatiable appetites for continued growth? How will we attack the modern urban problems such as congestion, pollution, crime, and quality of life while we build the economies and infrastructures required to serve California's people?

These and other questions continue to haunt Californians, partly because we fail to put aside our partisanships and self-serving agendas long enough to come to some productive compromises. Once again, this time as the Sacramento urban area expands and even begins to meet with developments expanding from the East Bay, we are becoming the victims of change instead of making change work for us. Will we manage to come together and create better living environments that will improve our quality of life? Some answers may be found in landscapes within Sacramento and throughout California.

Perhaps there are clues in the beautiful Victorian homes that have been preserved (some now housing small businesses) along the tree-lined streets and near the old Governor's mansion east of downtown Sacramento. Perhaps there are answers in the displays assembled by each California county in the hallways of the State Capitol building, which may represent attempts by residents and officials to define who they are and show where they are going. A walk down Capitol Avenue and on to the bridge over the Sacramento River, then back into refurbished Old Town reveals a mix of our past and current landscapes and leaves hints of possibilities for the future. Even the simple contrasts between the enclosed Downtown Plaza and the adjacent open K Street Mall suggest that we cannot decide which basic urban environment is best; perhaps it is actually a combination of diverse landscapes and choices which make us most comfortable.

These kinds of observations once again take on a grander scale as we move out of the downtown and into surrounding neighborhoods and outlying communities. How do we deal with the growing gap between rich and poor, the interaction between diverse cultures, and the human landscapes these trends inevitably produce? Look around for the changes and trends that leave their marks on every California town and city.

What is to become of the smaller agricultural service

towns and the sweeping farmlands north of Sacramento? How are the larger settlements strung up through the valley (such as Yuba City and Marysville, and Chico with its CSU campus) dealing with the quiet that returned after busy I-5 bypassed them far to the west years ago? How far will the Central Valley's perfectly square roads and developments encroach up Sierra Nevada slopes after they are forced into the twisted patterns that match the more rugged topography above the valley? Perhaps we can try to imagine what it will be like to climb to the top of the conspicuous Sutter Buttes volcanoes for a view of Sacramento Valley landscapes fifty or one hundred years from now.

As Californians debate so many of these issues, we see once again that California's diverse natural and human landscapes and people are related in profound ways. And they are always changing.

◆ MOVING ON TO A MODERN, SYSTEMATIC GEOGRAPHY OF CALIFORNIA

Layered beneath the Central Valley are thousands of feet of sediments washed down from the surrounding mountains during millions of years of geologic history. These and other California rock formations reveal fascinating clues about some of California's most distant past.

In the next chapters, we will begin with these ancient California landscapes and work our way to modern natural landscapes. In later chapters, we will review the various human patterns and landscapes scattered about the state. This begins our systematic study of the related topics that combine to make modern California geography so captivating and useful.

SOME KEY TERMS AND TOPICS

Basin and Range	Latin American Connection	Sierra Nevada
Central Valley (Great Valley)	low desert	site and situation
Coast Ranges (north and south)	Modoc Plateau	size and shape
Colorado Desert	Mojave Desert	Southern Cascades
high desert	Pacific Rim	Transverse Ranges
human/environment interaction	Peninsular Ranges	
Klamath Mountains	physiographic regions	

Additional Key Terms and Topics

California	geographic isolation	scales of study
cismontane	geographic pivot point	six essential elements of geography
culture hearth	history	South Coast
cycles	human landscapes	systematic
Delta	mission, presidio, and pueblo	systems
diversity, connections, change	processes	topical
five fundamental geographic themes	regional geography	transmontane
geographic center	renaissance in geography	

Chapter 2

Geologic History and Processes

MODERN EARTH RESOURCES ARE CLUES TO CALIFORNIA'S PAST

We are reminded every time a California earthquake adds elevation to another mountain or a landslide rips apart another hillside slope that dynamic and sometimes violent geologic processes are shaping California. Each individual geologic event seems dramatic, but each event is a fleeting moment in California's geologic history. However, the cumulative effects of millions of these events over millions of years are responsible for leaving us a landscape puzzle without rival. The puzzle would be solved if we could fast-forward a film showing crashing tectonic plates, mountains being lifted out of the ocean, and other geologic events that have so gradually distributed various rocks and ores to produce today's California landscapes. Armed with modern tools and techniques and the explosion of new discoveries in earth science, geologists are gradually solving the puzzles of California's past. They are learning that, in terms of geologic time, California's landscapes continue to experience quick and dramatic changes.

In this chapter, we explore the basic geologic concepts that help us understand the constructive and destructive processes responsible for California's past, present, and future physical landscapes. We will use the rock cycle to better understand the geographic distribution of minerals, rocks, and earth resources that have such historic and economic significance. We will step back millions of years into a very different California; this will help us place current and future events and landscapes in proper perspective.

KEY ISSUES AND CONCEPTS

◆ Knowledge of basic concepts in geology, such as geologic time, plate tectonics, and the rock cycle, helps us understand the constructive and destructive processes that have shaped and continue to transform California's physical landscapes.

◆ The geographic distribution of rocks, minerals, and various earth resources are clues left by a tumultuous geologic past in which California remained on or near plate boundaries.

◆ Though the state's rock record dates back nearly 2 billion years, there is far more evidence of more recent geologic events. Although most of the state was submerged below the sea through the Paleozoic and into the Mesozoic Eras, sporadic mountain building gradually lifted landscapes—generally from east to west—above sea level, particularly into and during the Cenozoic Era.

◆ Most Paleozoic Era rocks formed below the sea. Roof pendants of the Sierra Nevada and rock formations particularly in the Basin and Range and Mojave are examples, including extensive Paleozoic Era rocks in Death Valley.

◆ Dominant Mesozoic Era rocks include the *Sierra Nevada batholith* and related granitic plutons (which contain much of the state's gold and other valuable ores). They were formed behind a broad subduction zone and are now found at the cores of most major California mountain ranges. Jumbled masses of Mesozoic Era rocks known as the Franciscan Complex were crushed and squeezed in the subduction zone boundary.

◆ Mountain building pushed the shoreline farther west during the Cenozoic Era. Common Cenozoic Era rock formations (mostly sedimentary with patches of volcanics) are found in sedimentary basins or have been tectonically uplifted in mountains. They sometimes yield fossils, and may provide spectacular scenery.

◆ Later in the Cenozoic Era, toward the end of the Tertiary Period, only sporadic marine encroachments left scattered accumulations of marine sediments. The San Andreas system had already evolved, and California's shoreline and landscapes increasingly resembled those of today.

◆ A variety of valuable *earth resources*, such as gold, silver, other rare earth minerals, and fossil fuels, are scattered about the state, left behind by past geologic events. Some of the most important earth resources are associated with the intrusion of granitic plutons that now make up the cores of most of the state's major mountain ranges. Resulting mining operations helped shape California's history, economy, and cultures.

◆ AN OVERVIEW OF PLATE TECTONICS IN CALIFORNIA

Since there is ample evidence that California has been positioned on or near tectonic plate boundaries for more than one billion years, some knowledge of **plate tectonics** is required to understand the state's geologic history. The relatively thin, brittle lithosphere of Earth, which includes the even thinner crust, is divided into several large and numerous smaller plates. These plates are riding on top of the softer, plastic-like asthenosphere of the earth's upper mantle. As the asthenosphere gradually flows, the brittle tectonic plates riding above are dragged along.

There is tectonic activity (the breaking and bending of the lithosphere and its surface crust) because portions of this upper mantle and its overlying plates are moving. Different types of boundaries and geologic processes are common between these shifting tectonic plates. Three major types of active plate boundaries continue to shape California's landscapes: diverging plates, converging plates, and sliding plate boundaries.

Diverging Plates

A diverging or spreading boundary is currently located far off the Pacific Northwest coast in the eastern Pacific,

GEOLOGIC TIME

Except for rare and dramatic catastrophic events, many of the processes that shape natural landscapes of our planet and our state are excruciatingly slow in human terms. Because we only live to be about 1/60-millionth of the earth's age, we must leave our egos behind to understand geologic time, earth history, and the evolution of California's physical landscapes. With so much geologic activity in California, studies of the state have played major roles in unscrambling earth's complicated history. These studies have also allowed planners to realistically anticipate and prepare for the geologic events and natural hazards that are likely to affect California in the future.

One result of this research is the **Geologic Time Scale**, or Chart, compiled, studied, modified, and used by thousands of scientists from many different fields of study around the world. The scale chronologically organizes earth's and California's natural history into great Eras, which are divided into shorter and more specific Periods or Systems, which are further subdivided into shorter and more specific Epochs or Series as shown in Figure 2.1.

Each time category is recognized for unique events and organisms that are found in the rock record. We will refer to these time categories throughout this chapter.

For example, the Paleozoic Era began at the end of the Precambrian Era; scientists estimate that the Paleozoic Era began nearly 570 million years ago and ended nearly 250 million years ago. From oldest to youngest Periods, the Precambrian Era is followed by the Paleozoic Era, which is divided into the Cambrian, Ordovician, Silurian, Devonian, Mississippian, Pennsylvanian, and Permian Periods. The Mesozoic Era started nearly 250 million years ago with the Triassic Period, then Jurassic Period, and finally ended more than 65 million years ago at the end of the Cretaceous Period. The current Cenozoic Era began more than 65 million years ago with the Tertiary Period, which is divided into Epochs beginning with the Paleocene, then Eocene, Oligocene, Miocene, and ending with the Pliocene Epoch. The Tertiary Period gave way to our current Quaternary Period nearly 2 million years ago. This Period

Continued

Years Ago	Era	Period	Epoch	Some Events in California
10,000	Cenozoic	Quaternary	Holocene	Geographers study California.
Millions			Pleistocene	First people settle California.
				Glaciers erode Sierra Nevada and Northern Mountains.
2		Tertiary	Pliocene	Thick sedimentary basin deposits.
			Miocene	San Andreas Fault System evolves.
			Oligocene	Sporadic mountain building, volcanism, erosion
			Eocene	push shoreline farther west.
			Paleocene	
65	Mesozoic	Cretaceous		Mountain building continues, shoreline pushes
		Jurassic		west: subduction, Nevadan Orogeny, granitic
		Triassic		plutons, Franciscan Complex.
240	Paleozoic	Permian		Violent upheavals, continent encroaches west.
		Pennsylvanian		Deposits in broad marine shelf, subduction,
		Mississippian		metamorphism, metasedimentary "roof
		Devonian		pendants."
		Silurian		"California" is below the sea.
		Ordovician		
		Cambrian		
570	Precambrian			Shallow ocean/continental margin deposits.
				Complex metamorphism/igneous intrusions.

FIGURE 2.1
Geologic Time Scale. Geologic time is divided into Eras, Periods, and Epochs.

GEOLOGIC TIME *continued*

began with the Pleistocene Epoch and its Ice Ages, which gave way to the current Holocene Epoch around 10,000 years ago, at the end of the last Ice Age. We are currently in the Holocene Epoch of the Quaternary Period of the Cenozoic Era.

The many modern rock-dating techniques provide clues to the ages of rock formations and events in California. Absolute dating techniques are used to analyze the decay of radioactive isotopes and indicate the age of a rock within a small percentage of error. Radiocarbon dating is used to date organic matter in very young deposits. Older

rocks are dated using the radioactive decay of unstable elements; each isotope has a known "half life" as it constantly decays into a different product. Potassium-argon, uranium-lead, lead-thorium, and rubidium-strontium are examples of methods used to date older rocks.

Relative dating techniques, such as the use of fossils, layering of sediments, and adjacent geologic structures, are used to determine the sequence of geologic events in a region. Today, there are dozens of modern dating techniques; different methods may be used on the same rocks to verify dates and decrease the range of error.

---

including off the California coast north of Cape Mendocino. As two ocean plates separate, new ocean crust forms to fill the gap, causing older rocks on the two plates to be shoved farther apart. The discovery of this sea-floor spreading zone in the 1960s helped scientists solidify the plate tectonics theory.

Today, ocean floor between Baja California and mainland Mexico is expanding as Baja slides farther away. As the Gulf of California opens wider, this rifting extends into California where the Salton Trough crust is stretching, thinning, and dropping and the Peninsular Ranges are also sliding west, away from the North American Plate. The dynamics of these forces and structures are far more complicated, and extensive volumes on the topic have been published by dedicated geologists.

Converging Plates

A type of converging plate boundary (which once impacted almost all of California and now only occurs off the far north coast) is subduction. In this process, thin dense ocean plate crashes into thicker but less dense continental plate. The continental plate rides up over the sinking ocean crust, sometimes in a series of jerky events causing major earthquakes, compression, folding, and mountain building. Subducted below all of this is the ocean plate, which begins to melt. Major pockets of molten material (magma) form under pressure and frequently erupt to the surface, forming chains of major volcanoes. Today, the Cascades represent such a series of volcanoes, trending north from Lassen, Shasta, and the smaller volcanoes on the northern edge of California into Oregon, Washington, and Canada. Figure 2.2 shows diverging and converging plates.

Historical subduction has influenced at least some part of California's geology since the Precambrian Era. The Sierra Nevada, Coast Ranges, and Klamath Mountains all

contain some rocks dragged from distant regions, then plastered and molded together by these collisions. The complex geology of today's Klamath Mountains is mostly the result of subduction. An ancient sea-floor spreading center was itself jammed into California starting about thirty million years ago, giving birth to another type of plate boundary—a transform fault known as the San Andreas.

Sliding Plate Boundaries

The boundary between two plates which slide past one another is known as a transform fault. The San Andreas is arguably the most famous transform fault in the world. It marks the main boundary where the giant Pacific Plate slides to the northwest at about 5 cm (2 inches) per year against the North American Plate. As we will learn, this is a very complicated fault system. There are places where the two plates seem to jam together, creating a boundary almost resembling converging continental plates, where great mountains are built. There are places where the fault creeps and other places where it is locked until it unleashes tremendous energy in catastrophic shifts. There are hundreds of smaller faults and slivers of crust which are related to this activity. Even the extension that has been pulling the Basin and Range apart may be blamed on stretching along this plate boundary, although other hypotheses might also explain this activity. Figures 2.3a and 2.3b show sliding plate boundaries.

It is clear that California's landscapes have been shaped on an evolving and active **continental margin**, a dynamic boundary between tectonic plates. Geologists have considerable knowledge of the most recent interactions, but the details become fuzzier as the rock records fade away into the hundreds of millions of years past. The accumulating knowledge about recent dynamics will help geologists anticipate future geologic events.

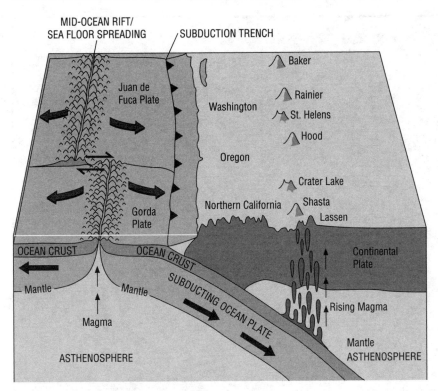

FIGURE 2.2
Diverging and Converging Plates. An oblique view looking north and slicing through a model of earth's crust in northern California. Ocean crust is subducted below the Pacific Northwest's continental crust. Millions of years ago, before the San Andreas Fault system evolved (such as during the Mesozoic Era), subduction dominated most of what is now California.

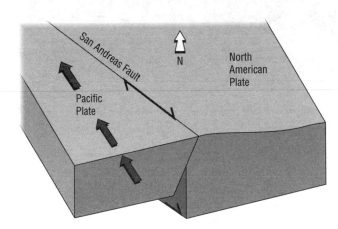

FIGURE 2.3a
Sliding Plate Boundaries. An oblique view (looking north) of right-lateral movement along the San Andreas Fault—one of the world's most famous sliding plate boundaries.

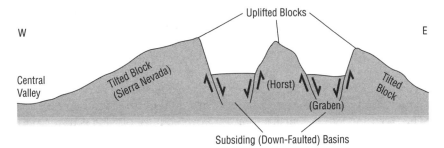

FIGURE 2.3b
Vertical Block Faulting. A side view (looking north) of crustal rupturing and faults common to today's Basin and Range east of the Sierra Nevada. Throughout California's geologic history, such faults have created a series of mountains and valleys.

THE ROCK CYCLE

Before we trace California's geologic history, we must review the **rock cycle**—a basic concept that helps explain the formation, classification, and names of specific rocks (see Figure 2.4). There are three major rock categories: igneous, sedimentary, and metamorphic.

We begin with the igneous rocks, which were completely melted, then cooled and crystallized. Two main criteria are used to classify igneous rocks: the environment where (and how quickly) they cooled, and their chemical composition. Intrusive igneous (plutonic) rocks cooled slowly in an environment deep below the earth's surface; they have large crystals or grains. Extrusive igneous (volcanic) rocks cooled and crystallized quickly near or at the earth's surface; they have much smaller crystals.

The chemical composition criteria show that igneous rocks with the most quartz and feldspar minerals are high in silica (silicon and oxygen). They are usually lighter in color and weight, and they are known as felsic rocks. Igneous rocks with minerals higher in iron and magnesium are usually heavier and darker. They are considered mafic rocks. We are now ready to combine these two criteria to identify some of the more common igneous rocks.

Granitic rocks are intrusive igneous rocks with large crystals that contain abundant quartz and feldspar. These lighter colored rocks with their large grains make up the cores of nearly every major mountain range in California. Anyone who has explored the Klamath, Transverse, or Peninsular Ranges and especially the Sierra Nevada has

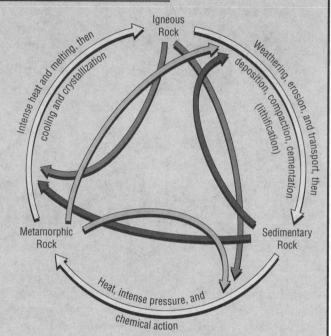

FIGURE 2.4
The Rock Cycle. The rock cycle continues to shape California landscapes.

seen these felsic rocks that cooled deep below the earth's crust from enormous magma chambers. The famous boulders of Joshua Tree National Monument and the Alabama

Continued

◆ CALIFORNIA THROUGH THE AGES: A GEOLOGIC HISTORY

Precambrian Era (Pre-Phanerozoic)

Scientific evidence places earth's age at about 4.6 billion years, but the oldest rocks found in California are dated at just more than 1.8 billion years. A tumultuous geologic past has destroyed older evidence or has greatly altered the oldest survivors, so we know the least about California's most ancient landscapes. However, isolated patches of metamorphic gneisses and schists from 1.7 to more than 1.8 billion years old are scattered particularly about the Basin and Range, Transverse Ranges, and the deserts of California. The Basin and Range contains some of the best remnants, where older rocks are often covered by unaltered and slightly younger sedimentary rocks.

The oldest Proterozoic Eon (later-Precambrian Era) gneisses and schists represent metamorphic basement rock of a continental crust ranging between 1.72 to 1.82

billion years old that contains numerous, slightly younger, granitic intrusions. Whether these rocks are encountered at the base of the San Gabriel, San Bernardino, Chocolate, or Orocopia Mountains or in the northwest Mojave or in such Basin and Range locations as the Black Mountains of Death Valley, they indicate that California's dynamic geology is an ongoing process. Samples from the San Gabriel Mountains suggest deep crustal levels of continental metamorphism and the intrusion of a variety of igneous material—more evidence of California's complex geologic past.

In the Basin and Range, slightly younger sedimentary marine deposits common to continental margins suggest that a Proterozoic (late Precambrian Era) sea must have covered most of what is now California; in other parts of the state, these deposits have been altered or eroded away. Significant exposures of sedimentary rocks from nearly every subdivision of geologic time from the Proterozoic to the Tertiary Period are found in ranges surrounding Death Valley. Shallow ocean deposits and primitive fossils in this area are typical of those along a

---

THE ROCK CYCLE *continued*

Hills are just two examples of how these various grades of granitic-type rocks have been lifted up and are now exposed throughout California.

Exposures of basalt in California are in direct contrast to granitic rocks because they are extrusive igneous lava flows that cooled quickly at the surface. Therefore, they have very small grains. They also have more iron and magnesium, and are, consequently, darker. Since these mafic rocks must get very hot to melt, they often produce runny and less violent eruptions. The flows and lava tubes at Lava Beds National Monument and the flows around the northern Owens Valley serve as just two examples of obvious exposures of this common California extrusive igneous rock. But, the Cascade volcanoes' eruptions often consist of more felsic material that melts at lower temperatures, producing viscous, gooey eruptions that can be very violent. These rocks trend more toward the andesites and sometimes the much more felsic rhyolites. Mount Shasta and Lassen Peak are examples of these majestic composite volcanoes that produce more violent eruptions with slightly lighter materials.

There are excellent examples of almost every other type of intrusive igneous rock (such as the diorites and gabbros) and extrusive igneous rock (such as obsidian, scoria, pumice and tuff) somewhere in California. Most extrusive igneous rocks are remnants of past volcanic activity that has long since ceased.

Completely different criteria are used to classify the second major category of rocks—sedimentary rocks. These rocks are formed when older rocks are exposed to weathering and erosion. The materials are then transported, deposited, and lithified into a different solid rock. Sedimentary rocks are very common because the processes that produce them are constantly at work on the earth's surface. When pieces of the original material are lithified, clastic sedimentary rocks form. They are classified according to grain size: conglomerate, sandstone, siltstone, claystone, shales, etc. When chemicals that were dissolved in water are precipitated out or organic sediments accumulate, nonclastic sedimentary rocks result. These chemical sedimentary rocks are classified by their composition, such as limestone (made of calcite), dolomite, gypsum, chert, and rock salt.

Metamorphic rocks represent the third major category of rock. They are changed by heat and/or pressure that does not totally melt the original rock. In this process, sandstone or chert can be changed to quartzite, limestone to marble, and shale to slate. Schist and gneiss are greatly deformed rocks at higher levels of metamorphism.

In the rock cycle, geologic processes are constantly transforming one major rock type to another. Since every phase of this rock cycle is and has been evident in California, we see every major rock type exposed somewhere in the state. Hiding in each of these rocks is a story, a page in the geologic history of California.

---

passive continental margin and suggest a quieter period during the latest Proterozoic into the early Paleozoic Era in California.

Paleozoic Era

As expected, the younger Paleozoic Era rocks are more widespread in California than their older Precambrian counterparts. Therefore, it follows that we know much more about California's geologic history from the Paleozoic Era of nearly 570 million to nearly 250 million years ago. Rocks from the Paleozoic Era are found throughout eastern and southern California and in portions of west-central California and the Klamath Mountains. These rocks indicate that the shoreline ran north–south from what is now southern Idaho, through central Nevada to southeastern California; coastal waters ranged from very deep in the north (where more than 10,000 m [32,800 feet] of deposits are found) to shallow in the south (where deposits thin to about 1,000 m [3,280 feet]). Great thicknesses of limestone were deposited on the broad, shallow marine shelf that represented most of Paleozoic California. Almost all of California remained below the sea during the Paleozoic Era.

Paleozoic Era Northern California

However, Paleozoic rocks also suggest periods of very complex tectonic activity, especially in the north during the early part of the Era. While most of California was a broad marine shelf, deeper water deposits in the eastern Klamaths and northern Sierra Nevada where volcanic debris from islands to the west was mixed with oceanic crust are typical of a subduction zone. Imbedded fossils common to east Asia indicate the material was dragged on the ocean floor from the western Pacific to the subduction zone in California where it was pinched with island arcs and basins into the continent. As the continent rode over these subducted rocks, material was welded onto its edge where great periods of mountain building occurred (such as the Sonoma orogeny), and the continent grew westward into the Mesozoic Era.

For example, today's Sierra Nevada was a continental shelf and slope environment during the Paleozoic Era. Sediments accumulated up to 9–10 km (5–6 miles) and were compressed and folded with increasing volcanic material to the north. Farther south in the Sierra Nevada, the Paleozoic basement metasedimentary rocks are often called "**roof pendants**." From Tioga Pass in Yosemite to west of Big Pine, these strata represent a nearly complete assemblage of Paleozoic Era history, but the pieces are scattered about. These rocks can often be seen as distinct layers on top of the younger granitic rocks in high Sierra Nevada landscapes. They are a westward extension of the same rocks found in the White and Inyo Mountains, but they are more metamorphosed. These hornfels, cherts, marbles, slates, and quartzites have been dated using radiometric techniques and fossils, and they reach thicknesses near Mount Morrison of about 9,700 m (32,000 feet).

The Shoo Fly complex (in the northwestern Sierra Nevada) and the Duzel and Gazzelle Formations (Klamaths) are typical of Paleozoic Era rock formations to the north and west. They contain more volcanic material mixed with the sediments from the sea floor and continent that were crushed together and metamorphosed in a subduction zone. In the Klamaths, the older Trinity Ophiolite (Ordovician Period) lies below the Silurian Duzel and Gazzelle Formations and represents the largest outcrop of ocean crust and mantle in North America. These conditions are evidence that the area we now call the Klamaths and the entire area northwest of today's central Sierra Nevada must have experienced many violent geologic upheavals during the Paleozoic Era.

Southeastern California During the Paleozoic Era

In the Basin and Range, especially in Death Valley, Cambrian Period strata of up to 5,200 m (17,000 feet) thick lie on top of older Proterozoic (late Precambrian Era) rocks. Above these are younger limestones and dolomites deposited in a warm, shallow sea which represent (in the Inyo Mountains) the thickest Paleozoic Era carbonate deposits in North America. Total thickness of Basin and Range Paleozoic deposits are up to 11,000 m (36,000 feet)! How can exposed rock formation sequences be that thick when surrounding mountains and slopes do not even approach those heights? These formations have been lifted, contorted, and tilted up from their original horizontal positions. Thick deposits and hundreds of millions of years of geologic history are revealed as the edges of these now exposed and steeply dipping layers are eroded.

In the Mojave Desert, Paleozoic Era rocks are not as common and deposits are not as thick as the Basin and Range, and there is evidence of a more stable continental platform. Deposits are especially found in Mojave's eastern ranges. The thickest (in the Providence Mountains)

is up to 3,000 m (10,000 feet); some late Paleozoic rocks are found in the Ord Mountains near Victorville.

Paleozoic Era rocks in the eastern Transverse Range were also deposited on a broad shelf. In the Peninsular Range, outcrops of Paleozoic metasedimentary and metavolcanic rocks appear on some slopes; most of these rocks were later highly metamorphosed into the current schists and gneisses. A Paleozoic Era limestone has been processed for cement near Riverside.

Mesozoic Era

The shoreline and continental margin of North America continued to migrate westward during the Mesozoic Era (starting nearly 250 million years ago). As the ocean plate was subducted below it, additional material was scraped and plastered onto the continent's edge. Most of the widespread igneous, metamorphic, and sedimentary rocks from the Mesozoic Era are a result of continental accretion along this very active plate convergence boundary.

The most common and familiar Mesozoic rocks are the **granitic plutons** that make the core of most of the major mountain ranges in California. These rocks formed after material was subducted with the ocean plate below the continental plate, then melted to form enormous magma bodies. The deep melt eventually cooled and crystallized over millions of years. Perhaps the second most familiar Mesozoic rocks are in the **Franciscan Complex (melange)** of the Coast Ranges. This melange accumulated when exotic igneous and sedimentary material was brought to and crushed against the continental plate by the subducting ocean plate.

An obvious example of the extent of this Mesozoic Era activity is evident even in the Klamaths. Here, both pre-Cretaceous Period plutons (formed from subduction, melting, and recrystallization) and blueschist (scraped onto and squeezed against the continental crust) can be found. A more complete review of these Mesozoic events, and the rocks left behind, follows.

Most of California remained below the sea during the start of the Mesozoic Era, but an exceptionally prolonged and active period of subduction began by the late Triassic Period and continued with only a few interruptions through the Jurassic and Cretaceous Periods. By the end of the Triassic Period, mountains had already been lifted in eastern California and the shoreline was pushed west. By the end of the Jurassic Period, volcanic and sedimentary material subducted below California had melted into enormous granitic magma chambers. By the Cretaceous Period, this melting had intensified, eventually producing the great intrusive igneous rock bodies that are now found throughout California.

Farther west, collision of these plates was also plastering large volumes of exotic materials from the western Pacific and the ocean plate onto the edge of the continental plate. Ocean crust, sea-floor sediments, and volcanic rocks were crushed together and squeezed up to form the Franciscan melanges of the California Coast Ranges. The Franciscan melange includes many different types of rocks contorted together. It has many names, and it is often called the Franciscan Basement in the coast ranges. It is dominated by graywacke and averages many thousands of feet thick. It is found in spots from the northern to southern California coast, but it is especially common in central California. For years, geologists debated the origin of these complex rocks until the extent and importance of Mesozoic Era subduction was understood.

These collisions resulted in one of the greatest mountain-building episodes in California's geologic history—the **Nevadan orogeny** (during the Jurassic and Cretaceous Periods). As the mountains were built higher, the sea was pushed even farther to the west. By the end of the Jurassic Period, the Nevadan Mountains rose abruptly above the ocean along what is now the eastern Great Central Valley; ocean waters would never again encroach east of that line. Toward the end of the Mesozoic Era, those great Nevadan Mountains blocked the sea from eastern California; therefore, the sediments found with other rocks from that time in the Basin and Range and most of the Mojave are terrestrial.

As the Nevadan Mountains were lifted higher during the Jurassic and Cretaceous Periods, near what is today's Sierra Nevada, their weathering and erosion also accelerated. The enormous volumes of sediment were carried west, filling deep ocean basins and then shallower seas; the resulting rock formations are found scattered throughout California west of today's Sierra Nevada. Such Cretaceous Period deposits are more than 7,600 m (25,000 feet) thick below the western Sacramento Valley; total accumulation of the various rock formations is even thicker in other parts of the valley. These Great Valley shales, sandstones, and conglomerates are very orderly compared to their complexly contorted Franciscan melange neighbors to the west.

Mesozoic Era Rocks

Rocks left behind by the geologic processes of the Mesozoic Era are important in many modern California landscapes. These processes and their remnant rocks deserve a more detailed review here, starting at the beginning of the Mesozoic.

Pre-Nevadan rock formations, even in today's Sierra Nevada, indicate that marine sediments were still being deposited at the start of the Mesozoic Era. Examples of these roof pendants, similar to their Paleozoic Era ancestors and up to 3,000–4,000 m (10,000–15,000 feet) thick can be found in Plumas County. They include such rock formations as the Hosselkus limestones and Swearinger slate near Taylorsville and other formations with Triassic Period marine fossils. As expected, no roof pendants (deposits) are found in the record after the Nevadan orogeny of the middle Jurassic Period. Such intense mountain building must have created an erosional environment.

During much of the Triassic Period, a shallow sea deposited mud as it advanced and retreated across the Mojave, but the shoreline usually meandered through it, leaving the eastern Mojave above water. Mesozoic Era wood deposits in the McCoy and Palen Mountains near the Colorado Desert date to this time. Volcanic activity also left rocks behind; examples can be found near Barstow. By the Jurassic Period, terrestrial deposits (such as the red windblown desert Aztec sandstones) were the rule in today's southeastern deserts.

Almost all Mesozoic Era rocks after the Triassic Period in the Coast Ranges, Sierra Nevada, and Klamaths formed as a result of subduction and/or mountain building. This includes the Sierra Nevada batholith rocks dated at 88–206 million years old.

In the Basin and Range, older sedimentary rocks deposited in marine conditions of the Triassic Period yield to volcanic rocks and then to the widespread granitic rocks formed later during subduction from the middle to late Mesozoic Era. Such granitic plutons in the White Mountains are dated at 70–225 million years. It is not surprising that few Mesozoic Era sedimentary rocks have been observed in the Basin and Range because it was dominated by extensive mountain building during that period. Similar plutonic rocks of similar ages are found farther south, underneath the Mojave and at the base of its desert mountain ranges and at the core of the Transverse and Peninsular Ranges. One specific example of the extent of these Mesozoic subduction zone rocks is found at the base of the Fish Creek Mountains (west of the Imperial Valley), where metamorphic gneisses and marbles are mixed with the same granitic rocks found just to the west, in the Peninsular Range.

More Evidence of Mesozoic Era Landscapes

Many geologists recognize that the processes and landscapes shaping today's Andes Mountains resemble those of California during the Mesozoic Era. They also know that the "Klamath-Sierra Nevada volcanic-plutonic arc" system extended far to the south and is responsible for most Mesozoic rocks in the Mojave, Transverse, and Peninsular Ranges and even in a small section of the Salinian block of the Coastal Range. Geologists have used many of these rocks to study the hundreds of miles of displacement that has broken some of them apart along the San Andreas Fault. They have studied (and Californians have exploited) the rare earth minerals found in and near many of the Mesozoic plutons. Great Valley formations and/or Franciscan melange are found even along and off the south coast in such places as the Palos Verdes Peninsula and on Santa Catalina Island; they display evidence of the dominant nature of this subduction activity during the Mesozoic.

Subduction had migrated farther west toward the end of the Mesozoic Era, creating later Cretaceous Period (69–110 million years) granitic plutons and metamorphic rocks found today in the Salinian block in the southern Coast Ranges, west of the San Andreas. By the end of the Mesozoic Era, about 65 million years ago, the Nevadan orogeny had ceased and denudation of the new Sierra and Mojave landscapes was underway.

Paleontologists make use of other evidence to piece together a picture of California's Mesozoic Era landscapes. For example, the fact that California lacks the more abundant dinosaur fossils found in Utah and Arizona is to be expected because much of the state was below the sea during the Mesozoic. Steep, mountainous terrain dominated its more limited land areas, leaving few ideal environments for dinosaurs. There were some exceptions, such as in the Diablo Range west of the San Joaquin Valley, where a scum-scooping duck-billed dinosaur (a kind of "Hadrosaurus") roamed across a small region of swampy coastline.

Cenozoic Era

We have covered about 98.6 percent of California's geologic history, leaving only about 65 million years to go! Since our focus now progresses to more recent and some future processes and landscapes, it is fortunate that nature has left far more evidence of California's recent past. In this section we turn our attention to the Cenozoic Era processes that have left ancient rocks and landscapes behind, especially the processes and landscapes of the Tertiary Period. These rock remains have had less time and opportunity to be altered, so they tell a much more detailed story compared to their older counterparts. As we approach the most recent Quaternary Period, our discussion of California's geologic history will yield to the next chapter and the topic of more recent and current processes that are causing modern landscapes to evolve.

Recall that by the end of the Mesozoic Era, the great Nevadan orogeny had ceased, and the emplacement of Sierran plutonic rocks (including the great granitic plutons in the Klamaths and in ranges to the south) was complete. Degradation destroyed much of the ancient Sierra and Mojave mountains by the end of the Mesozoic and into the Cenozoic Era, though uplifting forces would return to these regions later in the Cenozoic. Just as the ancient shoreline had shifted west early in this era, so had tectonic action shifted west to the Coastal Ranges. That is where we pick up the story.

Sedimentary Deposits Tell the Cenozoic Era Story in Western California

Western Cenozoic Valleys and Basins Fill With Clues to the Past   The Great Valley continued to form as a structurally downwarped basin during the Cenozoic Era. It was also filling with sediment, mostly from the eroding mountains to the east. By the end of the Pliocene Epoch, the sea had retreated west for the last time; except in a few coastal depressions, it would never again visit either the Central Valley or the Coast Ranges. The retreating sea left enormous volumes of marine Cenozoic rocks in almost all California depressions and valleys west of the Sierra slopes. These **Cenozoic basins** include the Eel, San Joaquin and Sacramento, Santa Rosa, Livermore-Santa Clara, Salinas, Santa Maria, Carrizo Plain, Ventura, Los Angeles, San Diego, and Imperial-Coachella Valleys. The Ventura basin's 15,000 m (50,000 feet) of sediments are the most complete middle and late Cenozoic rock records on earth. Similar but much thinner deposits were left in the Colorado Desert and at the base of the Peninsular Ranges.

Where to Find Western California's Cenozoic Record   Record of the entire Cenozoic Era can be found scattered about in the sediments of the Coast Ranges, sediments mostly washed down from adjacent terrestrial environments. One problem is that these sedimentary rocks have been broken apart and displaced (in some cases, hundreds of kms [miles]) by tectonic activity, especially along the San Andreas Fault Zone. Nevertheless, it is clear that the ocean encroached only as far as the Coastal Ranges and into the Central Valley a few times during the Tertiary Period, only to be forced out, time and again, by tectonic activity. The rocks suggest varied landscapes of steep uplands built by rigorous tectonic uplift adjacent to deep, structurally downwarped depressions which filled with the sediments from the uplands. It follows that some Cenozoic sedimentary rocks are terrestrial, but they alternate with thicker and more common accumulations of marine sediments, especially in western California.

To the north, the plant fossils in sedimentary rocks and tuffs of the Weaverville Formation northeast of Weaverville in Trinity County were deposited in a swampy flood plain covered with numerous lakes.

In the Santa Cruz Mountains, more than 6,700 m (22,000 feet) of Tertiary Period mainly marine strata accumulated on top of late Cretaceous Period marine sediments. The deposits formed in deep to shallow sea environments and even alternate with thinner terrestrial deposits. These alternating beds make up the conspicuous ridges and valleys of the Santa Cruz Mountains; they have been quarried and even produced some oil and gas.

Other Tertiary Period formations of the Coast Ranges include Paleocene Epoch submarine fan deposits scattered from Point Reyes south to the Santa Lucias, and Eocene Epoch coal beds and clays that were apparently deposited in tropical conditions. When the sea encroached again in the Miocene Epoch, it deposited diatomaceous material in long, deep basins. The very common Monterey Formation is the result, and it is found from Santa Rosa south into the Transverse and Peninsular ranges. The high organic phosphates and diatoms help make up this thin-bedded, light-colored, deep ocean basin deposit. Beautiful exposures can be observed south and east of Monterey, in the Santa Lucia Range above the Salinas Valley, at Montana de Oro State Beach south of Morro Bay, at Shell Beach, and in other locations along the central coast. Spotty related exposures are seen far to the south, such as at Point Dume, west of Malibu. In the Santa Monica Mountains, this related unit is known as the Modelo Shale.

In the Peninsular Ranges, the Silverado Formation in the northern Santa Ana Mountains is made of Paleocene Epoch nonmarine sands, clays, and coal. Farther south, the source of the rounded pebbles representing stream and submarine deposits of the Eocene Poway Formation in San Diego is probably from northwestern Sonora, Mexico! Some of these deposits were later dragged farther away from their sources, as far northwest as the Channel Islands. Dramatic changes in geography must have occurred since they were deposited. Though thick deposits of Pliocene Epoch rocks in the Peninsular Ranges are nonmarine, the Pliocene San Diego Formation contains abundant and outstanding marine fossils. However, these are limited to the immediate coast in the San Diego area and they are not thick compared to their Pliocene Epoch counterparts in the Los Angeles and Ventura Basins. The location of the Pliocene Epoch San Diego shoreline was probably close to today's.

It is clear that thick nonmarine sections from the Miocene, Pliocene, and Pleistocene Epochs continued to accumulate in local basins up to today. Even since the Pleistocene Epoch, impressive accumulations (thousands of meters) of terrestrial alluvial deposits have filled almost every California coastal and inland valley; many of these lowlands continue to subside at the mercy of sustained tectonic activity.

Sediments Reveal the Cenozoic Era History of Transmontane California

Pre-Miocene Epoch deposits from the Cenozoic Era are probably so rare in the Mojave because a new mountain-building period in the early Cenozoic Era may have lifted the Mojave block up to 4,500 m (15,000 feet) by the start of the Miocene Epoch. This also explains why so much early Tertiary Period sediment accumulated especially in coastal basins to the south and west; one source was this eroding upland. However, there is some record of pre-Miocene Epoch conditions in the Mojave.

Fossil pollen and animals found in the Miocene Barstow Formation of colorful Rainbow Basin suggest deposition in a climate similar to northern Mexico today, with semipermanent inland lakes. The few Oligocene Epoch deposits in the Mojave and Basin and Range (such as in Titus Canyon in Death Valley) indicate a wetter, savanna climate with abundant plant and animal life. Pet-

These sedimentary rock formations at scenic Red Rock Canyon north of Mojave and California City are more than ten million years old. Fossils from many of these red rocks suggest a wetter climate, before the Sierra Nevada to the west was raised high enough to block Pacific air masses.

rified wood and vertebrate fossils found in the Miocene Ricardo Group at Red Rock Canyon north of Mojave were also deposited in savanna grasslands with moderate rainfall.

It is believed that the Sierra Nevada was dominated by lower hills into the Miocene Epoch, having been severely eroded since the Nevadan orogeny. This allowed moist air masses to invade inland more frequently during the Tertiary Period. However, the geology abruptly changed again, and by the early Miocene Epoch, the Mojave block was warped into a structural depression. Inland drainage and deposition would rule thereafter, creating thick accumulations of nonmarine deposits up to today.

Sediments deposited below dry desert lake beds from the Basin and Range south reveal a rich floral and faunal history in the late Cenozoic Era. All Cenozoic deposits in the Mojave are nonmarine, except for a segment in the western Antelope Valley. Layers of volcanic debris alternate with ancient lake sediments, with up to 3,000 m (10,000 feet) locally deposited mostly since the Miocene Epoch. Mojave's Cenozoic volcanic activity began in the Oligocene Epoch, peaked in the Miocene Epoch, and has decreased to today.

Most sedimentary rocks in the Colorado Desert were deposited in the Cenozoic Era, and most of these are nonmarine. The oyster beds that were deposited between the end of the Miocene and early Pliocene Epochs in the Salton Basin are exceptions. These sediments, known as the Split Mountain and Imperial Formations, were deposited when a shallow sea invaded the Salton Basin from the south. By the end of the Pliocene Epoch, the sea was blocked out by the building delta of the Colorado River. Deposits of the nonmarine Palm Springs Formation followed in the Salton Basin.

Volcanic and Tectonic Activity and Landscapes in Cenozoic Era California

Cenozoic Era Events and Landscapes in the Coastal Ranges   Except for the area around Clear Lake (north of San Francisco Bay), the sporadic Cenozoic Era volcanic activity in the Coast Ranges has ceased, leaving behind some spectacular landscapes. About 29 million years ago (mya) the East Pacific Rise was overridden and consumed by the North American Plate. This event produced a series of Miocene Epoch volcanics that have weathered into fascinating landscapes in the Coast Range. A line of fourteen early Miocene Epoch volcanoes that run along the West Huasna fault from San Luis Obispo to Morro Bay (including Morro Rock) have been stripped and eroded down to their more resistant plugs or necks.

In Pinnacles National Monument above Soledad in the Salinas Valley, a variety of volcanic rocks erupted during the Miocene Epoch; they have since been dragged hundreds of kms (miles) to the northwest along the west side of the San Andreas Fault, perhaps from the western Antelope Valley. Some of these rocks (especially the pyroclastics) have weathered into spectacular cliffs, caves, and boulders. Pliocene Epoch volcanic activity has left a variety of volcanic rocks and landscapes above the Napa Valley, including Mount Saint Helena. This activity shifted from the Sonoma area in the Pliocene Epoch to the Clear Lake area today.

To the south, some of the most extensive Miocene Epoch lava flows in California are found in and around the Santa Monica Mountains. These Conejo volcanics were frequently extruded below the sea before the mountains were built; they have weathered into impressive buff- and rust-colored slopes and cliffs.

Volcanics and Tectonics in Transmontane Cenozoic California   Cenozoic Era volcanic activity was far more widespread in much of eastern California, especially on the **Modoc Plateau**. Successive basaltic flows built the plateau during the Tertiary Period. Today's volcanic surface on the Modoc represents the modern southern edge of the Cascade Mountain Range. More recent volcanoes and cones have erupted on top of the older lava plateau. Shasta Valley Cenozoic Era volcanic rocks were first formed from the Eocene through the Miocene Epochs in today's western Cascades. Volcanic activity shifted east after the Miocene Epoch (5 mya), forming the more recent High Cascade volcanic group, including such great volcanoes as Mount Shasta.

Farther south, in the Basin and Range and Mojave, scattered volcanics of the early Tertiary Period were also formed near converging boundaries. Later, the development of right-lateral transform motion and the San Andreas system ended that convergence by the mid-Tertiary Period. Since the Miocene Epoch, east–west crustal extension and crust thinning were mainly responsible for volcanic activity in the region. This stretching has also resulted in the block faulting that has shaped Basin and Range landscapes extending east from eastern California.

Evolution of the San Andreas Fault System   After skipping around California to visit the various Cenozoic Era geologic processes and their landscapes, we have painted a simplified picture of how California's environments evolved to the near present. We will close our Cenozoic Era journey by examining one of the most im-

A series of volcanic plugs (seen on the right) about 22 million years old line the landscapes south of Hwy. 1 between San Luis Obispo and Morro Bay. They represent a geologic history very different from today's geologic processes and plate boundaries. Only the insides of these long extinct volcanoes (mostly made of the rocks andesite and dacite) remain.

portant developments in the geologic history of California—the formation of the San Andreas Fault system (see Map 2.1).

About 29 million years ago, the North American Plate finally began to override and devour the **East Pacific Rise**. As this source of enormous volumes of new ocean crust was itself subducted, tiny portions and then larger segments of the edges of the Pacific and North American Plates began sliding past one another instead of converging. (Many modern geologists consider that explanation too simplistic. They now refer to obduction or underplating to describe these dynamics.) Regardless, the right-lateral movement along the newly born San Andreas strike-slip fault caused forces on California rocks and landscapes to become less compressional and, in some places, more extensional.

In eastern California, the crust was stretched and thinned; block-faulted ranges were elevated as adjacent basins dropped. The eastern Sierra Nevada was faulted upward as its neighbor below (the Owens Valley) dropped. Death Valley and Panamint Valley and so many others like them fell below their adjacent ranges. From the Basin and Range south into California deserts, resulting inland drainage salt basins were already formed and filling by the Pliocene Epoch.

Since the Miocene Epoch in western California, the San Andreas had lengthened and gradually migrated eastward. It represented the boundary where the Pacific Plate (earth's largest crustal plate) was grinding past the North American Plate. Rocks, blocks, and tiny pieces of plates caught near the strike-slip fault zone were rotated, crumbled, and crushed. These independent segments and landscapes were the victims as great mountains (such as the Transverse and Coast Ranges) were folded and faulted, and landscapes contorted near these plate boundaries. Total displacement of some rocks that were first broken along the fault zone is as much as 560 km (350 miles). There are hundreds of smaller, but still significant, branch faults that are at least indirectly related to the same forces.

Regardless of all of the very active geologic processes across the state, a primary focus of our attention remains the San Andreas Fault Zone, the movement between these two plates, and the direct and indirect impact it has had and will have in shaping so many California landscapes. These topics earn more attention in Chapter 3.

◆ MINERALS, ORES, AND OTHER EARTH RESOURCES

In this chapter, we have examined some of the dynamic geologic processes and the remarkable diversity of rocks they have left behind during the last 1.8 billion years. It should not be surprising to find within California some of the most impressive varieties and quantities of valu-able minerals, ores, and other earth resources compared to anywhere on our planet. These valuable earth resources have helped shape human history, and they continue to play a vital role in the state's economy. California's earth resources have attracted so many people and so much industry during the last few centuries. A knowledge of the distribution of those resources will lead to a better understanding of the geography of California. In the following section, we will look at the distribution of some of the more interesting and precious earth resources in California. Previous information covered in this chapter will serve as a foundation for our discussion.

Nearly all of the gold, silver, and many other metallic ores found in California rocks were originally formed by similar processes in or around the Mesozoic Era. In and near subduction zones, ocean and continental crust materials incorporated into magmas would become granitic plutons. As these magmas pushed toward the surface, they came near or contacted older, mostly sedimentary and metamorphic rocks. As the magmas cooled, the most felsic magmas with various minerals in water were often the last to squeeze into cracks and joints we now call veins. These high quartz and feldspar veins then cooled and crystallized with the precious mineral deposits. Since the 1800s, miners followed these veins and contact zones in search of gold and other ores. Today, a map showing these contact zones is inevitably a map showing the location of most of the metallic mineral deposits and mines in the state of California.

There are some important exceptions to this rule. At some locations, after being uplifted and exposed, the minerals were eroded away from their slopes and deposited into the sediments of ancient rivers and lakes; they became **placer deposits**. These processes continue in some areas today. Other rare earth minerals were formed by unusual processes in rocks with unique chemistries.

Gold from the Mother Lode

Since the more than one-hundred million ounces of gold mined in California have had such a dramatic impact on the history and economy of the state, we start with the most famous gold discovery in California. John Sutter commissioned James Marshall to build a sawmill to supply wood for new settlers on the American River. (Sutter's Mill is in modern-day Coloma.) It was Marshall who, on January 24, 1848, first stumbled upon the flakes of gold that would almost instantaneously bring hundreds of thousands of gold seekers to the **Mother Lode**. Most of the gold of the Mother Lode is found along Cretaceous Period white quartz veins dated between 108-127 million years near the Melones Fault. At the Kennedy and Argonaut mines near Jackson, miners dug shafts in the bedrock up to one mile long, following the steeply dipping veins.

This collection of gold was found in Sierra Nevada's gold country and is now displayed at the museum in Sonora. Although we are not likely to stumble across such finds today, we can imagine the excitement felt by miners who hit paydirt after following seemingly endless veins in the granitic rocks or sifting through river sediments carried from such weathered veins.

Much of the originally exposed gold was weathered, eroded, and washed from the veins and deposited downstream millions of years ago during the Eocene Epoch. Miners took these placer deposits and even used **hydraulic placer mining** (with high-powered water hoses) to blast the ancient gold-bearing sediments from hillsides. The tremendous destruction caused by the cutting of slopes and the choking of downstream rivers and streams with sediments is documented at such places as Malakoff Diggins State Park northeast of Grass Valley. Here, steep cliffs remain where monitors blasted hillside gravels in California's largest hydraulic mining operation. Hydraulic mining was banned by the California State Legislature in 1884 to stop this destruction and the disastrous flooding it caused downstream.

In other locations, gold deposits were covered with volcanic ash about 20–25 million years ago. Miners dug through this pink tuff to get to the gold, then used the cinder blocks for building materials. In some areas, dredging of water-deposited sediments has been a successful gold recovery method. Though it has always been an important ore in the state's economy, gold production had already peaked in California by 1852. Today, numerous historical and modern gold mines dot the landscapes of the Mother Lode and represent a variety of gold mining processes. The largest gold nugget ever mined in California weighed 88 kg (195 pounds) and was found at the Carson Hill mine. Near Grass Valley, the Empire Mine produced gold worth up to $1 billion. More recently, the Jamestown and Carson Hill mines have extracted more than 200,000 ounces of gold per year from open pit mines.

Gold in the Klamaths

In the Klamath Mountains, Major Pierson B. Reading first discovered gold in 1848 along the Trinity River near Douglas City south of Weaverville. The French Gulch District became the most productive in the Klamaths; here, granitic and dioritic dikes squeezed out from the Shasta Bally batholith during the Nevadan orogeny were injected into the siltstones, shales, and slates of the Paleozoic Era Bragdon formation. Gold was found along these veins and contact zones. The processes that formed gold and other precious minerals in the Klamaths are similar to the Sierra Nevada and the rest of California.

Again, much of the gold was eroded away from the original veins and deposited along ancient streams, rivers, and shorelines. Such placer deposits are common close to the Oregon border. Extensive dredging has been quite destructive along the south fork of the Scott River in Scott Valley. Near Hornbrook, where I-5 meets the Oregon border, the late Cretaceous Period Hornbrook conglomerate and the mid-Tertiary Period Weaverville Formations contain placer deposits. Farther south, the nonmarine conglomerate, sandstone, shale, and tuff of the Weaverville Formation are exposed around Weaverville and Hayfork. Its lignite and gold were deposited on a wet tropical flood plain dotted with lakes millions of years ago.

In the northwest Klamaths, gold and platinum have been found in the sedimentary deposits of the late Miocene Epoch Wimer Formation. One of the latest gold producers is the Grey Eagle Mine started in the 1980s near Happy Camp. About 20 percent of California's gold comes from the Klamaths, making the region second only to the Sierra Nevada in gold production in California.

A Mix of Valuable Earth Resources in the North

Some deposits and deeply weathered rocks scattered around the Klamaths contain chromium, nickel, and cobalt near the surface. The soils at Gasquet Mountain northeast of Jedediah Smith Redwoods and beach placers near Crescent City are examples. Zinc and copper are found in metamorphic rocks dating back to the Paleozoic Era.

In the West and East Shasta Mining Districts, sulfide minerals carried in solution from nearby plutons have produced iron and more than 400,000 tons of copper and zinc. Specific minerals include the most common: pyrite (with iron), chalcopyrite (with copper), and sphalerite (with zinc). Magnetite (with iron) occurs with an intrusion into the McCloud Limestone near the Shasta Iron Mine. The Altoona mine (west of Castella on the east fork of the Trinity River) takes mercury that was deposited in ancient hot springs. Gravels, clays, and limestone (such as the McCloud Limestone) are also mined in the Klamaths, mostly for construction materials.

Earth Resources and Mines in Transmontane California

Basin and Range

The famous metallic mines of the Basin and Range are now only part of California's history. Like many of the metal mining districts in California, most of the ores were found along the contact zones in older rocks intruded by granites. Of the many mines that dot the landscape, the earliest was Cerro Gordo near the top of the southern Inyo Mountains. It began producing lead and silver, but it became a zinc mine in the 1900s. Silver was mined in the 1870s from mines around Panamint City, which once grew to 1,500 people, near Panamint Pass in the southern part of that range.

There is an exhaustive list of famous, but abandoned gold, silver, lead, and zinc mines scattered about the landscapes of the Basin and Range. The famous Bodie gold mines were producing in the 1870s and 1880s; Bodie is only a ghost town today, preserved as Bodie State Historic Park, but there are plans for renewed mining to the southeast. Most other mines, such as those at Skidoo, Chloride Cliff, and Ballarat had come and gone by the early twentieth century.

Today's mining in the Basin and Range focuses on talc and saline minerals. Talc is also concentrated where igneous plutons have intruded into older metamorphic rocks in the ranges. However, health hazards caused by exposure to dangerous asbestos fibers have taken their tolls on California talc mines. Saline minerals are concentrated as evaporates on and near the dry lake beds in the basins. One of the best examples is Searles Dry Lake, where chemical industries have dominated the economy in little Trona for decades.

Mining from the Mojave to the Southern Deserts

Moving toward the Mojave, along Hwy. 395 (south of Ridgecrest and southeast of the El Paso Mountains), is the Randsburg Mining District, which has mainly produced gold, silver, and tungsten. Once again, where Proterozoic Eon (late Precambrian Era) rocks were intruded by younger plutons, veins with ores were left behind. In the on-and-off-again Yellow Aster deep mine, gold was found along boundaries where granitic ore-rich fluids invaded the Rand schists. Caverns dug at the Kelly Rand silver mine, closed in 1928, followed ore-rich rhyolitic intrusive veins. Sporadic mining activity at the Atolia tungsten mine followed the veins of a Nevadan granitic intrusion, although placer mining has left spoil mounds behind.

Silver was worked during the late 1800s on the south side of the Calico Mountains northeast of Barstow. Here, Pliocene Epoch igneous bodies and their solutions intruded into the sedimentary rocks of the Miocene Barstow Formation. Calico, first a mining town and then a ghost town, is now rebuilt as a tourist spot north of I-15. Colemanite was also mined in the early 1900s from shales of the Barstow Formation in the northeast Calico Mountains.

Many of the volcanic cones from Barstow to Amboy have been mined. Cinder and clay have been taken from Pisgah Crater. Dish Hill is famous for its volcanic bombs with their olivine and granitic cores.

Mines with catchy names such as Antimony Gulch, Copper World Mine, and Birthday Mine near the Mountain Pass Mining District indicate something special. Located north off I-15 between Baker and the Nevada Border south of Clark Mountain, the high desert's Mountain Pass Rare Earth Deposit has the largest known deposits of **rare earth minerals**. Gold was first discovered here; today, 25 percent of the world's rare earth minerals (mainly carbonates) are found at Mountain Pass in a unique high carbonate intrusion and sill that squeezed through older gneiss.

North of Desert Center, the famous Eagle Mountain Mining District contains the largest deposits of iron ore in California. In Mojave's Providence Mountains, where granites intruded into the Cambrian Bonanza King Limestone, scores of minerals formed, including magnetite and hematite, which were processed at the Vulcan mine during the 1940s.

Gold mines in and around the Chocolate Mountains include the Picacho and Mesquite mines, where the ore is found in Jurassic Period metamorphic rocks. The Mesquite began work in 1987, and it may mine more than two million ounces of gold. The Cargo Muchacho Mountains have produced gold since 1781. United Mining Company (Tumco) operations built a town of two thousand in the searing heat at the turn of the twentieth century as they dug into the Jurassic Period Tumco metamorphic rocks. Today's high-tech operations have been dominated by such modern companies as the American Girl Mine. Here, heavy machinery carries the blasted rock out of deep veins. It is then crushed and chemically processed to extract the relatively small quantities of ore. Since worker safety and the environment will always be concerns in the United States, global gold prices and efficiency standards will determine whether such mines can continue to operate.

Salts and other Minerals from Desert Playas

From sodium chloride to carbonates to borates, many salts and mineral deposits have been taken from the mostly dry playas in the Basin and Range and south through California's deserts. Most accumulated as a basin's floodwater, lake water, or groundwater evaporated. Some of the most visible results can be found at Searles Valley and Dry Lake, with their strange tufa formations (the Pinnacles) and the nearby chemical processing plants at Trona.

Borate minerals such as colemanite were taken from the Pleistocene Epoch mud of Death Valley beginning in 1882; this remained California's only commercial source of borax until 1926. The borates were taken all the way to Mojave on wagons pulled by the famous twenty-mule teams. Then, in 1913, the Kramer borates were discovered just one mile north of Boron, including the higher quality kernite which is easier to process into borax. Borax production has been centered at this location since 1928, where the kernite is taken from an open pit mine in the Miocene Kramer deposits.

The salty surface at Bristol Lake near Amboy is packed with evaporite minerals. Trenches are dug up to 6 m (20 feet) and allowed to fill with the high-mineral water. Table salt and calcium chloride are among the salts extracted after the water evaporates.

In the sands of Kelso Dunes in Devil's Playground, previous attempts at mining heavy metals have failed.

Valuable Earth Resources in the Coastal Mountains and Valleys

Peninsular Ranges

In the Peninsular Ranges, gold and nickel were carried into veins when magmas intruded into older Julian Schist near today's Julian Mining District. This geological process should now sound very familiar because we have touched upon it many times in this chapter. This made Julian the historical center for gold and nickel mining in the Peninsular Range.

The famous Mesa Grande, Pala, Rincon, and Ramona gem sites near the headwaters of San Luis Rey River in the Peninsular Ranges formed in conditions typical for California gems. Within these Cretaceous Period pegmatite dike intrusions high in boron and lithium are cavities the size of rooms with giant crystals of tourmaline, beryl, garnet, and topaz. Mining of the tourmaline peaked in the early 1900s. Similar gem sites are scattered throughout the Peninsular Ranges.

New rare earth minerals are being discovered at one of the world's most famous contact metamorphic mineral sites, the Crestmore limestone/marble quarries near Riverside. When Nevadan granitics intruded into these Paleozoic Era limestones, rare trace elements formed more than 140 minerals.

In the northern Santa Ana Mountains, the nonmarine deposits of the Paleocene Epoch Silverado Formation contain some coal, clays with high aluminum content,

and plenty of glass sand. These have been mined for nearly a century.

Coast Ranges Mines

The Coast Ranges did not play a significant role in gold production compared to the Klamaths, Sierra Nevada, and the California deserts until the 1980s. In the northern Coast Ranges' Mayacmas Mountains, north of Lake Berryessa near Knoxville, the McLaughlin Mine quickly became California's number one gold producer into the 1990s. Mercury, arsenic, antimony, tungsten, and thallium are also found in the ores there.

California's Coast Ranges have produced up to 85 percent of all U.S. mercury. Though mercury was discovered first in Santa Barbara County in the 1700s, the New Almaden mine near San Jose was the first to produce mercury in 1824. It later became the deepest mercury mine in the world.

New Idria mine between King City and the Central Valley was established in 1859 and was the largest producer of mercury in the United States until 1965. In the 1800s, it was notorious for the low pay and dangerous working conditions it offered its mostly immigrant workers.

California's state gem (Benitoite) is found only near the San Andreas Rift Zone in southern San Benito County. Appropriately, the large, attractive, six-sided blue-to-white crystals of this mineral are found with serpentine, California's state rock.

This section has covered only some of the more important mineral and ore localities in California. There are many more sites in the state.

Fossil Fuels

History

Fossil fuels, especially oil and gas deposits, have impacted the history and economy of California. In this state, oil and gas have always been far more abundant than coal; they supplied California industries and residents with most of their energy needs during the 1900s. For a few decades during the mid-1900s, California led all other states in petroleum production. Availability of abundant petroleum since the early 1900s has played a major role in the development of California's automobile society.

Fossil fuels usually form in thick layers of sedimentary rocks containing high organic content trapped over millions of years. They accumulate in porous rock along linear folds and faults where the oil and gas is "trapped." (See Figure 2.5.) It should be no surprise to find that most of the fossil fuel discovered in California rocks has been toward the west, below the Central Valley and Coast

Lines of oil platforms are seen off the Ventura/Santa Barbara County coast, anchored above linear geologic structures which naturally trap migrating petroleum. Oil is pumped from these deep reservoirs, while pipelines, oil islands, and storage facilities are evidence of petroleum industry activities along the coast.

Ranges and especially in the deeply folded and faulted structures that make up the coastal and offshore basins toward the south. This is also why you will often notice oil platforms in clusters and lines.

By now, many of these great petroleum reserves, especially the most accessible, are exhausted. The shoulder-to-shoulder oil wells that once covered southern California landscapes such as Signal Hill and Huntington Beach are gone and so is most of the inexpensive, high-quality petroleum. Some of the old oil fields are still productive, such as the cluster of oil rigs near Hwy. 14 along the San Gabriel Fault in the San Gabriel Mountains.

Costly Offshore Reserves

However, many of the operations have been moved out to more expensive and dangerous offshore platforms to tap reserves deep below the sea. These costly offshore rigs can be seen lined up off Huntington Beach and from Ventura to Santa Barbara in the Santa Barbara Channel. Since an offshore platform blew out in January, 1969, consideration of environmental hazards has played a major role in the industry. That 1969 accident produced a devastating oil spill that spoiled twenty miles of Santa Barbara beaches and killed thousands of birds and other wildlife. It and other historical oil disasters have created public relations nightmares for some oil companies. Many potential fields off the northern and central California coast are in, or adjacent to, pristine and delicate wildlife habitats that most Californians are not willing to risk for the sake of oil.

Fossil Fuels in and near the San Joaquin Valley

A series of folds in Tertiary Period sedimentary rocks south of Coalinga along the boundary of the Central Valley and the Coast Ranges down to the southern end of the San Joaquin Valley have produced tremendous amounts of oil and gas. One example, the Kettleman Hills, represents Cenozoic Era rocks with marine fossils that were folded together in a long anticlinal dome and now conspicuously pop above the valley floor. They have produced gas and nearly 500 million barrels (71 million metric tons) of oil. Other domes with oil and gas fields mostly to the south include Elk Hills, Lost Hills, Buena Vista Hills, McKittrick, and Wheeler Ridge. Gas was first discovered in this region in the early 1900s;

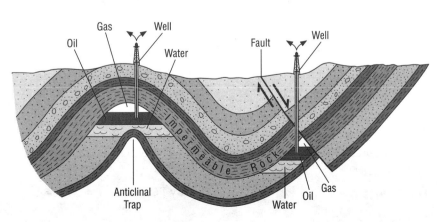

FIGURE 2.5
Drilling for Oil. Oil and gas may pool within various structural traps deep below California. Geologists map these structures before they drill for fossil fuels.

fields at Elk Hills (1919) and Buttonwillow (1927) became major gas producers.

Gas in the Sacramento Valley

Interestingly, gas was first used in Stockton in the 1850s; Cretaceous Period rocks below the Sacramento Valley have since produced most of the gas in California. A few of the major gas fields (usually with high quality gas at high pressure found with little oil) are at Sutter Buttes (discovered in 1933), Willows, Dunnigan, McDonald Island, and Rio Vista. The one field at Rio Vista has produced nearly 100 trillion cubic meters (3,500 trillion cubic feet) of gas.

Few Fossil Fuels in the Coast Ranges

In the Coast Ranges, mostly marine Tertiary Period rocks in the Santa Cruz Mountains produced small amounts of asphalt, oil, and gas into the mid-1900s. Northeast of Mount Diablo, the coal beds and clays of the middle Eocene Epoch nonmarine Comengine Formation were probably deposited in tropical conditions. From 1860–1920, the six mines of the Mount Diablo coal field west of Antioch were California's major coal producers. However, this low-grade lignite was no match for the energy sources provided by the great oil and gas fields discovered later in California. Consequently, these quartz sandstones were finally mined for glass.

◆ SOME FINAL WORDS

In this chapter, we have summarized the geologic history of California. We know more about the many similarities and differences between the processes and landscapes that dominated California millions of years ago and the California we see today. We have also located some of the more common and important rocks and resources that were left behind by those dramatic historical events and landscapes.

The major themes of this book are evident within this chapter. An unrivaled diversity of rocks, landscapes, and earth resources remains from California's tumultuous geologic past. The connections between past and current geologic processes and the landscapes they have created are clear. Connections between the distribution of these landscapes and earth resources and California's diverse human geography (from migration and settlement patterns to economic trends) are also evident. Just as geologic processes and landscapes continue to change, so do the local and global economic forces that determine the value of earth resources such as gold. Which earth resources will be valuable and which mining operations will thrive in the twenty-first century? A host of factors, from environmental quality concerns to the global marketplace, will help determine the answers to such questions and the subsequent impacts on California landscapes.

Chapter 3 will examine current California landscapes and the modern geologic processes that are shaping them.

SOME KEY TERMS AND TOPICS

Cenozoic basins	geologic time scale	plate tectonics
contact metamorphism	granitic pluton	rare earth minerals
continental margin	hydraulic placer mining	rock cycle
earth resources	Modoc Plateau	roof pendants
East Pacific Rise	Mother Lode	Sierra Nevada batholith
fossil fuels	Nevadan orogeny	
Franciscan Complex (melange)	placer deposits	

Additional Key Terms and Topics

Cenozoic Era	lava	ores
diverging plate boundaries	magma	Paleozoic Era
fossils	mercury	Precambrian
granitic intrusion	Mesozoic Era	salt deposits
Great Valley formations	metamorphic rocks	sedimentary rocks
gold	mining districts	serpentine
igneous rocks	oil platforms	Tertiary Period

California Rocks and Minerals: A Brief Field Guide for Rock Hounds and Natural History Detectives

This appendix presents an opportunity to explore in more detail how California's geologic history is revealed by the distribution of so many kinds of rocks in the state. It is provided for those with an appetite for more details about the evidence California's geologic history has left behind.

It would be impossible to find one storage room or laboratory with the variety and quality of mineral and rock samples found in California. Figure 2.4 on page 38 illustrates the rock cycle that yields this variety.

The importance of the distribution of these minerals and rocks ranges far beyond geologic curiosity. We have already followed the clues they provide us about California's tumultuous geologic history. In addition, these rock types and structures often control local and regional geomorphology—the California landscapes which evolve from them. The specific chemistry of soils produced when different rocks are weathered plays a significant role in the distribution of plants and animals in California. Certain types of rocks are associated with specific geologic hazards, especially when we build on them. Ores and gems are also found in and extracted from particular rock bodies, and some are quarried for building materials. Even if you are not a rock hound, you must appreciate the significant roles rock distributions play not only in the landscapes we view, but in California's history and economy.

Most of the minerals and rocks scattered around the state are left behind by past geologic processes. That is why this appendix follows the chapter on geologic history, which described the geologic events that produced California's rocks. This discussion focuses on a search for some of the most common, interesting, and important rocks, minerals, and earth resources in California.

Near the top of Mount Whitney are examples of the Sierra Nevada granitic batholith that slowly cooled and crystallized deep below the surface, mostly during the Mesozoic Era. Millions of years of dramatic tectonic uplift and subsequent weathering and erosion have exposed these intrusive rocks with their large crystals so common to this and other major California ranges.

Plutonic Rocks in California: Lifted and Exposed

Intrusive igneous rocks are found throughout California; they dominate the basement rocks, and they are frequently exposed in the Klamath, Sierra Nevada, Transverse, and Peninsular Ranges and in the mountains of the Basin and Range and Mojave. They make up a large portion of the basement of the Coast Ranges, and they are even buried by more recent volcanic material in northeast California and by recent alluvial deposits in many California valleys. This "Sierra Nevada batholith" is composed of more than one hundred different types of plutons, most referred to as granitic rock. Light-colored speckles that usually dominate this more felsic (high in silica) granitic rock are quartz and feldspar; darker speckles are usually less common and include flat flakes of biotite mica or other more mafic (higher in iron, magnesium, etc.) minerals such as amphibole or pyroxene. Specific names for these salt-and-pepper rocks (granite, quartz-monzonite, granodiorite, quartz diorite, etc.) refer to the specific chemistries of each.

Recall that these rocks formed when an eastward dipping ocean plate was being subducted below the continent, mostly during the Mesozoic Era and the Nevadan orogeny. Though some of this activity began even before the Mesozoic Era and some of it continued into the Cenozoic Era, 100 million years will serve as a convenient, average age for these rocks. Millions of years passed as enormous magma chambers formed below California and gradually cooled and crystallized to produce these rocks with large crystals. Darker plutons are composed of more ocean plate and mantle material from below; lighter granites formed more frequently when large volumes of higher silica continental crust were incorporated into the melt. Many of the once buried batholiths have since been pushed and faulted upward and exposed after overlying rocks were eroded away. About 60 percent of the surface rocks in the central and southern Sierra Nevada are made of these mostly granitic plutons.

Lighter colored dikes, sills, and veins in the batholith represent more felsic (higher silica) magmas that were the last to crystallize. The joints and fractures in the earlier-crystallized plutons served as conduits through which these hot magmas, which were still melted and often mixed with water, were squeezed and finally cooled and crystallized. Rare and valuable earth minerals (such as gold and silver) were sometimes incorporated into the melt and emplaced within the vein. Some of these intrusions are responsible for changing the human history and economy of California.

Today's vertical and horizontal joints and fractures in these plutonic rocks are sometimes a result of compressional and/or extensional tectonic forces that have stressed the buried rocks over millions of years. Other joints and fractures were formed more recently as overlying rocks were eroded away (unloaded), releasing pressure and allowing expansion of the rock masses.

Where to Find Plutonic Rocks and Their Landscapes

Klamath Mountains	Granitic plutons, mostly Jurassic Period, similar to Sierra Nevada batholith
Castle Crags State Park	More resistant granitic rocks form ridges above older, less resistant rocks they once intruded. More rapid weathering along joints isolates the pinnacles.
Coast Ranges West of San Andreas Fault in Salinian Block	Mesozoic Era granitic plutons, similar to Sierra Nevada and Peninsular Ranges. Faulting has moved them up next to the Franciscan melange (the other Coast Ranges basement).
Montara Mountain (Santa Cruz Mountains)	Quartz diorites are strikingly similar to Farallon Islands.
Transverse Ranges	Granitic plutons similar to other California mountains especially near and above San Gabriel and San Bernardino Mountain resorts
Peninsular Range—San Jacinto Mountains from Palm Springs Tram and Above Idyllwild; Laguna Mountains	Southern California batholith dated at 70–120 mya. Slightly less felsic than northern California batholiths, but weather to produce landscapes similar to Sierra Nevada. Numerous pegmatite dikes noticeably cut through to produce gem sites. Upper San Luis Rey River sites have magnificent tourmaline crystals in rock cavities.
Riverside	Common Nevadan plutonic quartz diorites and monzonites intruded into older limestones, creating world-famous assemblage of 140 contact metamorphic minerals at Crestmore limestone quarries. Such minerals are distributed throughout California along edges of Mesozoic Era plutons, where older existing rocks have been heated and metamorphosed.
White-Inyo Mountains East of Big Pine	Papoose Flat pluton (75–81 mya) squeezed through, thinned, and metamorphosed Cambrian Period sedimentary rock formations.
Central and East Mojave	Roots of the Ivanpah Upland are composed of granitic quartz monzonite from the Mesozoic Era, but the rock and its erosional surface have been extensively buried by lava flows and cones since the Miocene Epoch.
Granite Mountains	Named after outcrops of course-grained White Fang quartz monzonite.
Colorado Desert	Plutonic rocks have wide range of ages, from pre- to post-Mesozoic Era. They include the youngest plutons in the state, found in the Chocolate Mountains and dated at just 23–31 mya. Many of these youngest plutons were intruded into some of the oldest rocks in the state.

This exfoliation breaks the rocks at the surface into on-ion-like sheets and sometimes produces great outstanding domes. You might observe some or all of these features in any exposed granitic plutonic body in California. Weathering processes are accelerated in the surface cracks between these rock masses, a topic covered in detail within Chapter 3.

Volcanic Rocks: California's Geologic History Flares Up

It may surprise some Californians that active and potential volcanic hot spots are scattered about in at least four different areas of the state today. They include the majestic volcanoes and lava plateaus of the Cascades and northeastern California, the area above the Napa Valley near Clear Lake (including the geysers), the Basin and Range east of the Sierra Nevada, and south of the Salton Sea in the Imperial Valley. Each of these areas has also experienced some modern volcanic activity, but in this section, we will examine only the distribution of the volcanic rocks that have been left behind by past volcanic activity. Volcanic activity in human history will be examined in Chapter 3.

A few of these ancient hot spots are near areas where volcanic activity happens to have continued to today. Where there is not a clear line, we will yield to Chapter 3's section on modern volcanic processes and landforms. To manage this organizational problem, we ask the question: Where are some of the more common and important volcanic rocks that reflect California's geologic history?

We will discuss the four California volcanic landscapes that contain current volcanic activity in Chapter 3.

Water not only pours over the edge of these lava flows at Burney Falls in northeastern California, but it also pours out of the cliff side. The water has seeped down through a permeable, porous layer only to meet an impermeable layer, where it is forced to seep out the cliff side. A series of lava flows are found below most of northeastern California, particularly the Modoc Plateau.

Metamorphic Rocks Reveal Geologic History

As their name implies, metamorphic rocks are older rocks changed by geologic processes that usually require millions of years. Since most metamorphic rocks form in high pressure and/or heat environments deep below the surface, it takes millions of years of uplift and erosion of overlying rocks to expose them. Therefore, a discussion of the current distribution of metamorphic rocks in California is also a discussion of the geologic history of California.

Most of the metamorphic rocks in California were formed from the late Paleozoic through the Mesozoic Eras and into the early Tertiary Period by two different processes. First, rocks caught between the two plate boundaries of a subduction zone were squeezed and metamorphosed by intense pressure. Second, other rocks were changed, but not totally melted, by intense heat during **contact metamorphism**. These contact zones and their metamorphic rocks formed when deep magmas generated by subduction rose toward the surface. Exceptions to these generalities include some of the oldest rocks in California, which were formed by similar processes much earlier in the Precambrian Era.

Where to Find California's Metamorphic Rocks

The Oldest Rocks The oldest rocks include gneisses and schists dated at 1.72–1.82 billion years old and are basement rocks of a continental crust with slightly younger granitic intrusions. They are scattered about the Transverse Ranges, northwest Mojave, and the Basin and Range. (See the Precambrian Era geologic history section in Chapter 2.)

The Klamaths Metamorphic rocks of the Klamaths were also crushed and molded onto the North American continent. They are related to the Franciscan melange, but numerous plate collisions must have been responsible for their formation because their ages range from mid-Paleozoic Era through the Mesozoic Era, especially during the Nevadan orogeny. The South Fork Mountain Schists (blueschists formed about 120 mya) are examples. They indicate that the Coast Ranges were even attached to the Klamaths during part of the Mesozoic Era.

Coast Ranges The many rocks of the Franciscan Complex (or melange) can be found throughout the Coast Ranges. These sedimentary and metamorphic rocks formed when sea floor materials were dragged east from the western Pacific, then caught and crushed against the continental plate during the Jurassic and Cretaceous Periods. The rocks were carried deep into the subduction zone, but they were pressed and squeezed up toward the surface, like toothpaste. The blue-green schists ex-

Where to Find Ancient Volcanic Rocks and Their Landscapes

Sutter (Marysville) Buttes	With a 25 sq km (10 sq miles) area and at more than 600 m (2000 feet) high, these buttes are the only volcanic outcrops in Central Valley. Pasty eruptions with breccias and tuffs formed these plug domes of andesite and rhyolite. Probably an extension of the southern Cascades, they are very young. (The surrounding late Pliocene Epoch Tehama Formation was warped by these eruptions.) They are included here because they are isolated and detached geographically from the Cascades.
Sierra Nevada Foothills East of Sacramento; Sonora	After erosion denuded the ancient Sierra Nevada to low hills about 20–25 mya, great deposits of volcanic ash invaded from the east to bury gold-rich streams. These are the rhyolitic pink tuffs of the Spring Valley Formation used as building stone during the gold rush. Miners were required to dig through it to reach gold deposits. After some erosion of that surface, extensive volcanic mudflows (including large volcanic cobbles) and basalts covered it. This is known as the Mehrten Formation (4–20 mya). Latite (intermediate between rhyolite and andesite) is found on Table Mountain west of Sonora (9 mya). Basaltic flows were left by the third and youngest volcanic period in this area less than 3.5 mya.
San Luis Obispo; Morro Bay	Along Hwy. 1 from San Luis Obispo to Morro Bay is the chain of fourteen resistant throats of volcanic plugs. Weaker rocks were stripped away from these "insides of volcanoes," which are about 22 million years old, mostly made of andesite. Smaller 160 m (500 feet) Morro Rock is dacite (intermediate between rhyolite and andesite) and was once extensively quarried to make breakwater and fill. Refer to Chapter 2's section on Cenozoic Era geologic history for the origins of these volcanoes.
Pinnacles National Monument East of Salinas	On the Monument's west side, overlooking Soledad and the Salinas Valley, are Miocene Epoch rhyolitic pyroclastic volcanic breccias. They have weathered and eroded into the spectacular caves and landscapes that have made the area famous. Rhyolite and some andesite and basalt are found on the east side of Pinnacles. Again, the origins of these rocks are examined in Chapter 2's Cenozoic Era geologic history section.
Transverse Ranges; Santa Monica Mountains	The Conejo volcanics of the Transverse Ranges (especially in the Santa Monica Mountains and points north) make up many buff- and rust-colored slopes and cliffs. These Miocene Epoch volcanic rocks are sometimes mistaken for sandstone from a distance. They were extruded before the mountains were lifted out of the sea, and they represent one of the most widespread Tertiary Period volcanic formations in California. They stand out along Mulholland Hwy. a few miles north of the ocean; they were so severely fractured, they became a reservoir rock for oil at the Conejo Field east of Camarillo.
Mojave Desert; Eastern Mojave	Outstanding volcanic features are preserved in the Mojave Desert. Cima Volcanic Field on the Ivanpah Upland is south of I-15 in the eastern Mojave. Here, at least forty cinder cones and lava flows up to 90 m (300 feet) formed from the early Miocene to the Holocene Epochs (7.6 million–13,000 years old). Since they formed protective caps on top of the older deeply weathered granitic surface below, they stand out quite nicely. In several locations, entire flows or their remnants have held their ground while surrounding terrain was stripped away. Cima Dome itself is an upwarped granitic mass; scattered volcanic features formed on top of it. Road materials and cinder block are mined from many of the cones.
Barstow to Amboy; Ludlow	A chain of volcanic cones and their lava flows from Barstow east to Amboy exhibit classic examples of pahoehoe (ropy lavas), tubes, tunnels, blisters, collapsed domes, and volcanic bombs—a variety of features difficult to find south of the Cascades. Pisgah Crater, about halfway between Barstow and Amboy, is an extremely young cinder cone formed on top of very fluid and extensive basaltic lava flows. Dish Hill (also known as Siberia Crater) is also large, lies between Ludlow and Amboy, and is famous among rock hounds for granitic and olivine-cored volcanic bombs. Amboy Crater, on the eastern end of the chain, is only about 2,000 years old and may have the greatest variety of impressive features. From the trail up the cone and to Amboy's crater, even the nongeologist can appreciate definitive volcanic features, including dark lava flows that spread from it across Bristol Playa.

"Tombstone rocks" in oak woodlands of the Sierra Nevada foothills, near gold country. These metamorphic rock outcrops were originally volcanic rocks much older than their Sierra Nevada granitic neighbors, but they were later changed by the heat and pressure of mountain-building forces. Sometimes called gravestone slates or gravestone schists, they reminded early miners of tombstones scattered across extensive cemeteries.

posed in the north and south Coast Ranges contain glaucophane, a mineral which forms when mafic marine rocks are exposed to high pressures, not extreme temperatures. Such minerals as jadeite are common in the green pebbles that have weathered off these melanges and washed up on central California beaches.

Many other rocks (such as the common graywacke and chert) in the Franciscan Complex, or melange, show how it got the name melange, which means a mixture of different rocks. Some sedimentary sections of the melange are many thousands of feet thick. Conspicuous red cherts in the slopes of Marin County overlooking San Francisco are examples. California's famous waxy/greasy, greenish serpentines also formed in the Franciscan when deep magma from the upper mantle with high magnesium content flowed into faults and cracks and crystallized. These intrusives can be found on the San Francisco Peninsula because all of the hills of San Francisco are made of Franciscan rock. Mount Diablo east of Walnut Creek (between the Bay Area and Central Valley) is also made of Franciscan rocks and is surrounded by serpentinite, California's official state rock.

Western Sierra Nevada   Various metamorphic rocks are found in the Foothill Metamorphic Belt in the western Sierra Nevada east of Sacramento and west of the Melones thrust fault. They likely formed when colliding plates crushed island arc material against the continent during the Jurassic Period, at the beginning of the Nevadan orogeny.

Sheared Metamorphic Rocks from the Transverse Ranges, South   The Pelona-Orocopia schists are found scattered from the Transverse Ranges down to the Chocolate Mountains east of the Imperial Valley. They formed when a variety of rocks from a deep ocean basin or trench were

thrust together during the late Mesozoic Era. The related Garlock and Rand schists may have been broken off and dragged away from the other side of strike-slip faults to their present locations in the northwest Mojave; these rocks have been the focus of recent studies of the tremendous displacement that has occurred along the San Andreas Fault Zone during the past several million years.

Contact Metamorphism   Examples of rocks metamorphosed millions of years ago by intruding igneous plutons are throughout California. The Crestmore limestone quarries in western Riverside County, where there are more than 140 contact metamorphic minerals, is just one example. You will also find them scattered in road cuts along Hwy. 243 from Banning up to Idyllwild. These are just a few examples of the extensive metamorphic outcrops in the Peninsular Ranges. These events and their rocks are reviewed in other sections within this appendix and Chapter 2 focusing on plutonic intrusions and earth resources.

Sedimentary Rocks and Their Fossils Reveal Geologic History

Sediments and sedimentary rocks make up the majority of the surface of the earth's crust and that is also true for California. Sedimentary rock formations provide some of the most dramatic and beautiful landscapes in California. In addition, they and the materials that were deposited and lithified with them also provide the most detailed accounts of ancient California environments and the processes that must have changed them. They often provide us with energy and mineral resources. Also, because new sediments continue to accumulate on top of their older kin in nearly every California basin and valley, the most productive farmland and almost all of the towns and cities of California are located on sediment and sedimentary rock.

In the following section, we will examine some of the more interesting and important sedimentary rock formations in California. This is an opportunity to differentiate between two very different landscapes in California. There are the relatively flat, sedimentary basins where deposition of sediments continues and where most of the farms and people are located. Standing in contrast are the higher relief, mountainous areas where older sedimentary rocks have been tectonically uplifted and are exposed to differential weathering and erosion.

◆ FOCUS ON THE DISTRIBUTION OF SEDIMENTARY ROCKS: AN IN-DEPTH SECTION

By now, you should have a general working knowledge of California's geologic history and rocks. The following very detailed sections on California's sedimentary rocks are designed for more serious earth scientists—rock hounds who have set a goal to learn more details about the distribution of rocks in California. Human geographers and others who have had enough of rocks and geologic history may want to skip this final appendix section.

First, we will locate some of the oldest sedimentary rocks. Then, we will skip around California to find the most interesting and important sedimentary rock formations. We will investigate landforms these rocks have helped shape and the clues they have left about California's geologic history. This section also serves as an excellent source for planning field trips.

California's Oldest Sedimentary Rocks: Showing Connections

Some of the oldest sedimentary rocks in California are the 800 million–1.2 billion year old Pahrump Group rocks of the Basin and Range. These conglomerates, sandstones, siltstones, shales, limestones, and dolomites of the Crystal Spring, Beck Spring, and Kingston Peak Formations (from oldest to youngest, they are known as the Pahrump Group) are thousands of meters thick. They contain some very primitive single-celled algae fossils and stromatolites deposited in shoreline waters. Deposited on those rocks are the Noonday Dolomite, Johnnie Formation, and Stirling Quartzite that mark the end of the Precambrian Era. Thousands of meters of Cambrian Period rocks were deposited on top of them. These rocks and their fossils (especially found in the White-Inyo Range) were deposited when the first multicellular animals, followed by the invertebrates (hard-shelled ani-

mals), appeared. Cambrian Period limestones and dolomites are also found in the mountains east of Death Valley (such as in Titus Canyon) and are scattered in other Basin and Range and Mojave Desert locations.

The roof pendants of the Sierra Nevada (examined in a previous section of Chapter 2) probably include the same sequence of rocks as found in the Basin and Range, but they were more extensively metamorphosed by the Nevadan orogeny. Additionally, the marine depositional environments that dominated in those locations by the start of the Paleozoic Era were somewhat similar to environments of the Peninsular Range. Evidence that rocks were extensively metamorphosed is found within the limestones near Riverside and in other Paleozoic Era deposits of the region.

In the Mojave, multicolored mudstones were deposited during the Cambrian Period to form the Latham shale with marine fossils. Deposits of iron ore are found in the middle Cambrian Period Bonanza King limestone in the southern Providence Mountains.

Following the Cambrian Period, which begins the Paleozoic Era, the abundance and variety of sedimentary rocks increases with each younger geologic period. Returning to our standard method of reviewing rock formations, we will now discuss some of the most interesting sedimentary rocks from many different ages. We start a sweep around the state with the Great Central Valley region.

Sedimentary Rocks Found Throughout Northern and Central California

Central Valley

Thousands of feet of sediments have been accumulating since the Cretaceous Period in the downwarped basin we call the Central Valley. The layers generally dip down away from the Sierra Nevada and Coast Ranges toward the valley floor, so we see the older rocks only on the edges of the valley and in well samples. Starting with the marine Cretaceous sediments, overlying rocks become more frequently nonmarine into the Quaternary Period. Some produce oil and gas; other rocks are tapped for groundwater. The sedimentary rock layers are more than 7,600 m (25,000 feet) thick in the Sacramento Valley. These rock layers dip toward the valley on its western edge where the Coast Ranges rise above it and have produced long, parallel "hogback" ridges.

It is clear that sediments have washed down from the surrounding steep mountain ranges (especially from the east) into the Central Valley since the Mesozoic Era. The most recent unconsolidated Holocene Epoch sediments cover today's valley floor.

The Kettleman Hills (south of Coalinga) represent a stretched anticlinal dome of Central Valley sedimentary rock folded up above the San Joaquin Valley floor. Rocks of this young structural feature produce not only oil and gas, but many different kinds of Tertiary Period fossils. Here, fossils from a shallow marine environment are found in the younger Pliocene Epoch Etchegoin and San Joaquin Formations. Below, in the late Miocene Epoch Santa Margarita Formation, Ostrea titan giant oyster fossils up to 15 cm (6 inches) long are found. The still deeper and older Miocene Epoch Temblor Formation, which is also exposed in the nearby Coast Ranges, yields Desmostylus sea cow and Merychippus horse fossils.

Northwest California   In the Trinity Forest, limestones between Red Bluff and Humboldt Redwoods State Park on State Hwy. 36 and near Hall City caves contain some of the youngest Permian Period animal fossils in North America; they must have been dragged east to this location on an ocean plate because they match fossils in the western Pacific.

In the Klamaths, Cretaceous Period marine deposits were accumulated when the area was slightly below sea level just after the Nevadan orogeny. Marine fossils include ammonites and pelecypods in the Great Valley Sequence that were deposited before the Klamaths were uplifted. Conglomerates of these formations are exposed south of Weaverville and in the eastern Klamaths. Shallow-water marine fossils are found in the late Cretaceous Period Hornbrook conglomerates, seen near I-5 from Hornbrook to the Oregon border. In contrast, plant fossils in the conglomerates, sandstones, and shales of the Weaverville Formation (found near Weaverville) show it to be nonmarine, deposited on a swampy flood plain during the Oligocene Epoch. A variety of Miocene Epoch Wimer Formation loose clastic rocks are seen in the extreme northwest Klamaths.

Structurally downwarped basins may be smaller on the northwest coast compared to the expansive coastal valleys farther south, but some have accumulated similar rock formations of the same ages. The Eel River Basin is one of the largest. It extends from Cape Mendocino to Eureka and is filled with sedimentary rocks deposited during the last few million years. Pliocene Epoch marine sedimentary mudstones and other rocks of the Wildcat Group include formations with names such as the Eel River, Rio Dell, and St. George. One excellent exposure of the Eel River Formation has been uplifted and is seen at Scotia Bluff along the Eel River.

Cascades and Modoc Plateau   Since the Cascades and Modoc Plateau are dominated by volcanic activity and rocks, they provide relatively few opportunities to study sedimentary rocks. However, there are some basins that have been filling with sediment that includes lake deposits and weathered and eroded volcanic material. At Lava Beds National Monument, fossils of a mastodon and prehistoric camel were found in the lava tubes. Will the recent sedimentary deposits be buried by future ash and cinder deposits or lava flows as some of their ancestors were?

Sierra Nevada   Earlier in Chapter 2, we examined the metamorphosed mostly Paleozoic Era roof pendants of the Sierra Nevada, which lie on top of the granitic rocks, especially in higher terrain. They represent the sedimentary rocks that formed when a depositional environment ruled in the Sierra, but they were later squeezed and faulted on a plate boundary. Most of them have been eroded away. In the northern Sierra Nevada, rock formations of the Silurian Shoo Fly complex include the cherts and limestones of an old ocean crust with accumulated material along a plate boundary.

As expected, there are few deposits left in the Sierra Nevada from the mountain-building episode called the Nevadan orogeny. Today, scattered remnants of sediments accumulated after the Nevadan orogeny and its erosion are more common. Marine sediments and sandstones with fossils from the late Cretaceous Period are found on top of basement rocks along the current boundary between the Central Valley and the Sierra Nevada. In some northern Sierra Nevada foothills, the younger Eocene Epoch Ione Formation consists of sand, clay, and coal beds that have been mined to produce glass, bricks, wax, and fuel.

Sedimentary Rocks in the Coast Ranges

Our search for sedimentary rocks continues in the Coast Ranges. Here, the geology is so complex and the rock formations (dating from the Mesozoic Era to the Pleistocene Epoch) are so diverse, we can only pick out a few examples. For more detail, refer back to the section in Chapter 2 on California geologic history, read articles in other publications, or take field trips to the Coast Ranges region.

The Coast Ranges are dominated by mostly Cenozoic Era sedimentary rocks deposited on two types of basement, one of which is the previously examined Franciscan melange. Mixed with the metamorphic rocks of the melange are graywackes. They were deposited in chaotic currents and mudflows within deep marine basins below steep volcanic highlands, all near the subduction zone which existed during the Mesozoic Era. Thick deposits are exposed in numerous Coast Range locations along with the red cherts which contain single-celled deep sea fossils (radiolarian) and deep sea limestones.

Along the margin between the Coast Ranges and the Great Central Valley are exposures of late Jurassic to late Cretaceous Periods marine conglomerate, sandstone, and shale of the Great Valley Sequence. These several thousand meters of sediments were washed from the east off the continent and lithified. They have been extensively folded and faulted and are now found on the eastern Mendocino and Diablo Ranges and the west edge of the Sacramento Valley.

Extensive thick outcrops of nearly every age of Cenozoic Era sedimentary rocks have been severely faulted and displaced up to 300 km (200 miles) from one another since the Miocene Epoch in the Coast Ranges. They include the Paleocene marine sediments in the Santa Lucia and Diablo Ranges, in San Francisco, and at Point Lobos and Point Reyes. Eocene Epoch coal beds and clays indicate that California experienced tropical conditions; this includes the coal fields northeast of Mount Diablo, which were commercially mined until 1920.

The Emerging Coastline Deep ocean deposits of the Miocene Epoch Monterey Formation have abundant microfossils. This light-colored shale is found from Santa Rosa to near Monterey and from south of Morro Bay to Shell Beach. It is found as far south as the Peninsular Ranges; it is known as the Modelo Shale at Point Dume on the Malibu Coast and in the Santa Monica Mountains. The mostly marine Pliocene Epoch rocks give way to alluvial and lake deposits because the sea retreated for the last time toward the beginning of the Pleistocene Epoch. More recent deposits continue to accumulate to great thicknesses in subsided coastal basins of the Coast Ranges.

Meanwhile, numerous marine fossils are found in rocks along the coast, such as in Pliocene Epoch siltstones at Drakes Beach (Point Reyes) and sandstones at Moss Beach. Additional fossils at other locations, such as near Ano Nuevo State Beach, also confirm that the coastline is being lifted, exposing rocks once deposited below the sea.

Sedimentary Formations in Southern California Coastal Mountains and Valleys

In the Peninsular Ranges You will notice late Cretaceous Period mainly marine sedimentary rocks in the Peninsular Ranges from the Santa Ana Mountains and scattered south into Baja. Among these, the mostly nonmarine Trabuco Conglomerate is common in the western Santa Ana Mountains. In contrast, marine sandstones and shales of the Rosario Formation contain huge ammonites (flat, coiled mollusk fossils from the Mesozoic Era). Exposures of the Rosario sandstones can be found along the coast at La Jolla Cove, Point Loma, and points south into Mexico.

Sedimentary rocks deposited after the Cretaceous Period in the Peninsular Ranges are widespread. Early Tertiary Period rocks include the Paleocene Epoch nonmarine Silverado Formation in the northern Santa Ana Mountains, where coal, clay, and mixed silicates used in glass making have been mined. Eocene Epoch deposits of rounded pebbles at the mouth of the ancient Poway

Vasquez Rocks Park near Hwy. 14 in the San Gabriel Mountains, between Santa Clarita and Palmdale. These sedimentary rocks include sandstones and some conglomerates that were deposited and lithified nearly 25 million years ago. They have been lifted and tilted by mountain-building forces and are now caught near several faults, including the San Gabriel Fault to the southwest and the San Andreas Fault to the northeast. The differentially weathered rock layers have appeared as backdrops in movies, commercials, and TV programs.

River became the Poway Formation in San Diego (examined in the Cenozoic Era discussion in Chapter 2). The Miocene San Onofre breccia, with its chunks of broken schist, is found in spots along the southern coast.

More extensive are the rocks formed since the later Tertiary Period in the Peninsular Ranges. They include the nonmarine conglomerate, sandstone, and siltstone of the Pliocene Epoch Mount Eden and San Timoteo Canyon Formations. Abundant and impressive marine fossils are easily recognized in the Pliocene Epoch San Diego Formation north of Mission Bay. Some of the thickest sedimentary deposits are found in the Imperial and Coachella Valleys, Elsinore trough, Perris Plain, Los Angeles Basin, and offshore basins, as well as in the coastal basins to the north in the Transverse and Coast Ranges. The rocks in these basins were weathered, eroded, and transported from mountain ranges and deposited and lithified in basins that exist to this day.

Sedimentary Formations in the Transverse Ranges In the Transverse Ranges, the Ventura Basin has more than 17,700 m (58,000 feet) of deposits from the Cretaceous Period to today. These include what may be the thickest Pliocene Epoch deposits on earth. This is all part of a structural syncline that also includes the Soledad Basin, which has filled with nonmarine sediments.

Some of the most interesting sedimentary rock formations in the Transverse Ranges have been radically lifted up and exposed by recent tectonic activity along and near the San Andreas Fault Zone. For instance, it might appear that the spectacularly dipping sandstones and conglomerates at three locations in and adjacent to the San Gabriel Mountains are similar: Vasquez Rocks along Hwy. 14 in the San Gabriels, Devil's Punchbowl above Pearblossom, and Mormon Rocks in Cajon Pass. It turns out that the Devil's Punchbowl and Mormon Rocks are both composed of Miocene Epoch deposits of the Punchbowl Formation. Embedded land vertebrate fossils are found at both sites; these two strikingly similar landforms may have been separated by action along the San Andreas Fault Zone. The Vasquez Formation is also nonmarine, but dates back to the Oligocene Epoch. Interestingly, rock outcrops of the Diligencia Formation in the Orocopia Mountains of the Colorado Desert on the other side (east) of the San Andreas Fault match the Vasquez in type and age.

There are so many other beautiful exposures of sedimentary rocks in the Transverse Ranges; this variety of complexly folded and faulted formations makes examination of even the most important ones an impossible task in this book. One example is the drive inland through the Malibu Canyon gorge from Hwy. 1 (PCH) in the Santa Monica Mountains. You will see (in order) more than fifteen million years of earth history from the Oligocene to the Miocene Epochs in exposures of nonmarine pink and purple Sespe, marine Vaqueros, Topanga, Conejo volcanics, and Modelo Shale (related to the Monterey) Formations within fifteen minutes as you drive inland. The folded and faulted rock layers are now dipping at steep angles. Another example is in the Santa Ynez Mountains north of Santa Barbara. Numerous rock formations, from the Jurassic and Cretaceous Periods Franciscan melange to the late Pleistocene Epoch Santa Barbara Formation, have been contorted and lifted upward.

Sedimentary Rocks in Exposed Landscapes of Transmontane California

Basin and Range In the Basin and Range, there are many other interesting sedimentary rock formations in addition to the oldest ones, which we have previously examined. Besides the folded and faulted marine Cambrian Period limestones and dolomites exposed in Titus Canyon in Death Valley and surrounding areas, you will find the Oligocene Epoch Titus Canyon beds, which are also related to the Artist's Drive Formation. Fossils of the great, horse-like herbivore Titanothere, rhinoceros, and camel suggest that a lush savanna existed here during the Oligocene Epoch. Fossils found in Pliocene Epoch rocks at Furnace Creek include leaves, diatoms, and animal footprints, while in the Coso Mountains, late Pliocene Epoch mammal fossils include dogs, peccaries, camel, horses and mastodons. The area apparently became drier (except for occasional wet periods during the Pleistocene Epoch Ice Ages) as the Sierra Nevada was lifted to the west, blocking moisture from the Pacific, as it does today.

Students search for abundant trilobite fossils in Mojave's Marble Mountains just east of Amboy, between Barstow and Needles. Because trilobites are marine index fossils from the Paleozoic Era, they reveal clues about the ages and origins of these lifted and exposed rock layers. This rock formation, the Latham shale, was deposited more than 500 million years ago and contains some trilobites up to 20 cm (8 inches) long.

Of course, the sedimentary rock record in the Basin and Range is far more extensive. (Some of these exposures were reviewed in the section on geologic history in Chapter 2.) You will find more details in specific geology publications.

More recently, in the Basin and Range and into the Mojave Desert since the Pleistocene Epoch, numerous inland basins have been filling with silt and clay during wetter glacial periods and filling with salts during drier periods such as today's. Some of these relatively young sediments, such as the Funeral Formation in Death Valley, have already been folded and faulted.

Early Pleistocene Epoch fossils of horses, camel, deer, pronghorns, hog-like tapirs, and rabbits have been recovered along the shores of ancient Lake Manix in the Mojave. Many different kinds of salts (including chlorides, carbonates, potassium, and borates) are being mined from the saline deposits in these mostly dry lake beds in today's Basin and Range and Mojave.

Mojave Desert Sedimentary Formations Moving toward the Mojave, in Red Rock Canyon, the lighter sandstone layers and the darker lava flows often found above them are commonly oxidized red. The nonmarine sedimentary rocks of this Miocene Epoch Ricardo Group contain fossils of petrified wood, rodents, primitive horses, camel, antelope, mastodons, rhinocerous, and saber-toothed cats that lived in a higher-rainfall savanna when lower hills to the west allowed moist ocean air masses to penetrate farther inland.

Farther east, in Rainbow Basin north of Barstow, are the colorful Miocene Epoch sedimentary rocks of the Barstow Formation. The fossil pollen, rodent, tortoise, dog, cat, rabbit, pronghorn, horse, camel, rhinocerous, and saber-toothed cat suggest that the Miocene was wetter with summer rains.

Continuing east, across the Mojave, in the Providence Mountains, are the limestones of the Permian Bird Spring Formation. Mitchell Caverns were still active during wetter periods as late as the Pleistocene Epoch, when water combined with limestone to produce carbonic acid that dissolved the rock and formed the caverns. Today, Mitchell Caverns are dry, but are open to tour. Geologists recognize the rock record near Mountain Pass to the north to be far more extensive than at popular Mitchell Caverns.

Nearby, brachiopods and trilobites are found in the much older Cambrian Period Latham shale. This formation is made of red, green, and gray mudstones. For many years, fossil collectors have converged on the Marble Mountains east of Amboy, where the relatively accessible and remarkable crustacean trilobite, *Fremontia fremonti*, index fossils of the Paleozoic Era, are up to 20 cm (8 inches) long.

Sedimentary Formations in the Southern Deserts Farther southeast, toward the Colorado Desert, fossil wood has been found in Cretaceous Period sediments of the McCoy and Palen mountains.

The Colorado Desert contains thick accumulations of mostly younger Cenozoic Era rocks. The oldest include Eocene Epoch marine deposits in the Orocopia Mountains (east of the Coachella Valley) and nonmarine rocks in the Palo Verde Mountains (southwest of Blythe). Slightly younger Oligocene Epoch continental deposits of the Diligencia Formation are also found in the Orocopias.

Post-Oligocene Epoch sedimentary rocks are common and are many thousands of meters thick. They are exposed in the western Imperial Valley (including those in Anza Borrego State Park). They also lie below the surface of the valley into Mexico as well as below the Coachella Valley. The majority of these sedimentary rocks are nonmarine, except when the sea encroached in the Miocene Epoch, depositing the brown oyster beds of the Split Mountain Formation and the Pliocene Imperial Formation. After the sea retreated (probably blocked by the building Colorado River delta), the Pliocene Epoch Canebrake Conglomerate and the finer-grained Palm Springs Formation were deposited. The Palm Springs Formation (with some petrified wood) can be seen west of the Salton Sea, where it is folded and being eroded. Still younger Lake Cahuilla deposits since the Pleistocene Epoch were laid flat on the surface of the older rocks and contain marine mollusks. These oyster beds were probably deposited in the high salinity of the late Pleistocene Epoch lake, rather than in ocean water.

Basement rocks of the Valecito and Fish Creek Mountains on the western edge of the Imperial Valley resemble those of the Peninsular Range to the west. However, overlying sedimentary rocks resemble those of the Colorado Desert to the east. Consequently, following deposition of the Anza Formation during a dry period in the Miocene Epoch , many of the younger deposits are somewhat similar to those in the Imperial Valley.

Modern Geology and Geomorphology: California's Recent, Current, and Future Physical Landscapes

In this chapter, we will explore the modern topographic features (geomorphology) of California and some of the more recent and current geologic processes that continue to shape them. This is the nebulous area where the geologic history that left ancient rocks and landscapes behind gradually yields to the current processes that are shaping modern landscapes. The processes are similar, but the magnitude and location of geologic events continues to change. At times, the line separating the past from the present is very blurry, while the connections between past and present geologic events become more clear. Today, we have the privilege of witnessing not only the recently born landscapes that have had little time to be altered, but also the current events which continue to change California landscapes.

Some Californians may consider this privilege a curse. However, the earthquakes, landslides, mudflows, and other events we refer to as natural disasters are simply nature's more dramatic examples of how our landscapes continue to evolve and to change. Without these events, California landscapes would not be as diverse and spectacular. They would become like many quieter places on our planet that are more distant from plate boundaries and therefore more homogeneous—places where connections between natural processes and the landscapes they have created are less evident.

We have learned that California has experienced a tumultuous geologic past. Today, Californians are forced to recognize that the state continues to be a focus of geologic activity. California is still located along plate boundaries where the internal tectonic forces that build mountain ranges (some might call them constructional) are dominant. In turn, the newly emerging landscapes that are so common throughout the state are perfect targets for aggressive attack by agents of weathering, erosion, and mass wasting. The cycles of change continue, seemingly at accelerated rates, in California.

In the first half of this chapter, we will locate and describe some of the more important mountain-building forces at work in California today. These forces have created some of

Mammoths and other large animals roamed the Los Angeles Basin more than ten thousand years ago, when California was cooler and wetter. The proof is preserved in the sediments and tar at the La Brea Tar Pits/George C. Page Museum.

You will find fascinating basaltic lava flows and tubes at Pisgah Crater, east of Barstow. Mojave's climate keeps them looking younger than they are. Related volcanic landscapes throughout the area represent a bridge between California's geologic past and present.

the most spectacular mountainous scenery in the world. In the second half of the chapter, we will examine the denudational (some might call them destructional) forces that are tearing away at California's landscapes and creating new ones at the surface. We will also consider the geologic hazards associated with all of these processes, hazards that Californians must so frequently endure.

KEY ISSUES AND CONCEPTS

◆ **Powerful tectonic forces continue to build spectacular landscapes in California. These emerging landscapes become vulnerable to aggressive denudational (destructional) agents, including weathering, mass wasting, and erosion.**

◆ **Modern volcanic activity is evident in at least four separate regions within the state: the Cascades and Modoc Plateau, the eastern Sierra Nevada into the Basin and Range, the Imperial Valley south of the Salton Sea, and in the mountains north of the Napa and Sonoma Valleys. Generally, such volcanic activity poses no threat to California's major population centers.**

◆ **Because California is located along plate boundaries, a variety of active faults and other geologic structures exist. The most important and famous structural feature is the San Andreas Fault; however, faults are found in almost every region and are responsible for building diverse landscapes.**

◆ **It is likely that major earthquakes will continue to impact the majority of Californians and**

could potentially cause the nation's greatest natural disasters.

◆ **Weathering processes aggressively attack exposed rocks, breaking them into smaller particles which may form soil or be vulnerable to mass wasting and erosion. Differential weathering frequently results in distinct and scenic landscapes throughout the state.**

◆ **A variety of mass wasting processes continue to shape landscapes and threaten Californians in many regions. They range from slow movements that are barely noticeable to sudden, massive, and catastrophic landslides or debris flows and mudflows.**

◆ **Agents that erode, transport, and deposit material in California leave a multitude of landforms. Glaciers modified landscapes in northern California mountains and the Sierra Nevada. The effects of wind are evident in some desert and immediate coast locations. Waves and currents shape our coastline. However, fluvial processes and their landforms (made by running water) are far more important and common.**

◆ INTERNAL MOUNTAIN BUILDING

Modern Volcanic Processes and Landforms

In Chapter 2, we examined some of the widespread ancient volcanic activity and landscapes that have shaped California's past. Today, there are only four general areas in the state where "active" volcanism continues to build and impact modern landscapes. Fortunately, the most populated regions of California (including the south and central coastal regions) are not currently threatened by volcanic activity or eruptions. Areas of modern activity can include areas where ancient volcanic activity has continued to today; it is more difficult to separate the past from the present when similar processes continue to produce similar landscapes in one region. We will now explore the four different **modern volcanic regions** of California: the Cascades and Modoc Plateau, the Basin and Range just east of the Sierra Nevada, the Imperial Valley south of the Salton Sea, and the region above the Sonoma and Napa Valleys north to Clear Lake.

The Cascades and Modoc Plateau

The chain of magnificent volcanoes of the Cascade Range stretches from southern British Colombia through Washington and Oregon and into northern California. The major volcanoes are surrounded by dozens of smaller ones, all lying on the western edge of successive lava flows of the Columbia Plateau. In California, Mount Shasta and Lassen Peak are the most remarkable of the southern Cascades; they merge with the Modoc Plateau lava beds, which extend into California's northeastern corner. These majestic composite volcanoes are formed from a combination of successive and often violent eruptions of ash and cinder and lava flows that occur inland and parallel to a subduction zone. Moving east, less violent eruptions have poured less viscous (more runny)

lava flows over the Modoc Plateau. (The nature and classification of various volcanic rocks is reviewed at the beginning of Chapter 2.) Farther southeast, north-south trending parallel faults are creating valleys and mountains somewhat similar to landscapes of the Basin and Range to the southeast.

Our survey of active volcanism begins on the northern end of California, north of the Mendocino Triple Junction (where the Juan de Fuca, Pacific, and North American Plates meet). Refer to Figure 2.2 on page 37. This is also where the sliding between the Pacific and North American Plates that dominates central and southern California gives way to subduction. North of this point, the Gorda oceanic plate (a southern cousin of the Juan de Fuca oceanic plate) is forced beneath the North American continental plate; this is the only place in California where subduction continues to play a significant role in shaping geologic events and landscapes.

As basaltic crust of the oceanic plate is shoved below the less dense material of northern California's continental crust, sediments and pieces of both crusts are scraped together and carried down with the oceanic plate in a process often termed underplating, rather than subduction. Deeper and now east of the original subduction, these materials are heated and then melted under pressure. Occasionally, portions of these huge magma chambers move toward the surface. They incorporate materials from the less dense continental crust into the melt and finally erupt to form the Cascade chain.

Cascade Volcanoes   Mount Shasta is the most glorious of all California volcanoes and one of the largest and most recently active of all the Cascades. At 4,319 m (14,162 feet) above sea level, this isolated structure rises more than 3,100 m (10,000 feet) above the surrounding countryside. This composite volcano is made of cinder and ash deposits and andesitic lava flows, some more than 17 m (50 feet) thick. It is steepest near the top with a 35 degree slope and grades to only a 5 degree slope

This photo of Lassen Peak erupting (displayed at the historical museum in Weed) is a reminder that Cascade volcanoes are capable of producing catastrophic events. Lassen Volcanic National Park's landscapes are recovering from the devastation left from the 1914-1917 eruption, but this and other Cascade volcanoes are likely to become active again.

at the seventeen-mile diameter base. At the top, the main Hotlum cone is so youthful (last erupted in 1786), there has been very little erosion. A conspicuous satellite cone—Shastina—emerges from the side of the larger structure and is older. The youngest lava flow on Shasta is more than 9,200 years old. Smaller basaltic shield volcanoes and their flows are noticeable north of Shasta.

Lassen Peak (on the southern end of the Cascades east of Redding) began to form more than 11,000 years ago on the remnants of the devastated ancient Mount Tehama. It is now one of the largest plug domes in the world. An explosive eruption began in mid-May, 1915. It included mudflows and a cloud of steam, cinder, and ash up to 7,500 m (25,000 feet) that was seen from Sacramento. Thick, pasty dacite flows were also squeezed up like toothpaste. Less significant steam eruptions ended in 1921, but the volcano exhibits some of the best examples of fresh volcanic features, such as fumaroles, mud pots, boiling lakes, and foul-smelling vents, in the United States.

At 3,187 m (10,457 feet) above sea level, Lassen Peak now looms above the devastating avalanches and mudflows of its latest eruption. A succession of plant communities invading this newborn landscape wait for the next inevitable eruption. A hike through the impressive hot springs and steam vents of Bumpass Hell or to the summit of Lassen Peak could accentuate your experience at today's Lassen Volcanic National Park.

Numerous smaller volcanoes dot the landscapes of the Cascades and Modoc Plateau. Volcanoes surround the Medicine Lake Highland on the eastern edge of Siskiyou County, and lava flows have dammed Medicine Lake. Here, about five million years ago, the Mount Hoffman volcano collapsed, leaving a 65 sq km (25 square mile) caldera. Younger lava flows have filled the caldera. More recent eruptions of at least one hundred cinder and lava cones distributed pumice and tuff across this landscape as recently as 1910. The older basalts grade to more recent rhyolitic eruptions. Some of the best examples of glassy obsidian flows in California cover more than 4,200 acres at nearby Glass Mountain.

The California Cascades have experienced at least seventeen eruptions at Mount Shasta, Lassen Peak, and the Medicine Lake Highland in the last 2,000 years. Future eruptions, including massive landslides, ash and cinder, glowing gas clouds, lava flows, and mud flows typical of felsic composite volcanoes, are probable. Long-term predictions of the exact timing of these eruptions are unlikely, but days of earthquakes and swelling often precede them. Such eruptions since the Pliocene Epoch have produced these landscapes strewn with cinder (weathered from red to black), scoria, pumice, and obsidian.

Modoc's Volcanic Landscapes   The north–south trending faults along which most recent Cascade eruptions have taken place become more pronounced as we move farther east through the Modoc Plateau. The Modoc is actually on the southwestern edge of the Columbia Plateau and has been built up to 1,500 m (5,000 feet) by successive, extensive, runny, basaltic lava flows from the Miocene to today.

At Lava Beds National Monument, some flows are less than 1,000 years old. More than three hundred lava tubes formed here as lava floods cooled and crusted on the surface, allowing magma to drain away below, opening these now cold ice caverns. Prehistoric mastodon, camel, and human remains have been found in these tubes; numerous cinder cones dot the surface above the lava flows.

To the south, Burney Creek plunges over the edge of a resistant basaltic lava flow just before flowing into Lake Britton at McArthur-Burney Falls Memorial State Park. The falls spill over a lava flow that covers porous tuffs and formerly weathered surfaces. All of these rock layers are being cut and exposed by the cascading water, but the lower porous rocks carry groundwater which erupts as impressive natural springs flowing out at up to 4.6 million liters (1.2 million gallons) per day, adding to the spectacle.

In summary, cones, domes, plugs, glass flows, and pumice are common across the Modoc Plateau's basaltic surface. All but the youngest volcanic features have been cut by a series of parallel faults. These north–south trending faults become so dominant toward the east that the Warner Mountains and Surprise Valley are often considered part of the Basin and Range.

Eastern Sierra Nevada/Basin and Range

Extensive and recent (Pleistocene Epoch to today) volcanic activity is common from the eastern Sierra Nevada into and north of the Owens Valley and at points east in the Basin and Range. From Mono Lake to the Mammoth Lakes area and Long Valley, you will find some active or recent volcanic features. They include the impressive Mono and Inyo Craters, Devils Postpile, and pumice covering much of the surface between. Cones and volcanic fields are scattered in, around, and east of the Owens Valley; the valley rises abruptly on the north end, up to the Bishop volcanic tableland.

Mammoth and Beyond   About 730,000 years ago, after nearly three million years of less significant eruptions and lava flows in the area, a spectacular volcanic explosion suddenly blew apart a giant volcano, leaving the Long Valley Caldera. Fiery clouds of ash and pumice rained down and viscous lavas flowed away from the eruption. Deposits of the pinkish Bishop welded tuff (up to 1,500 m [5,000 feet] thick) that make up the tableland are found many kms (miles) away on surrounding landscapes. Traces of airborne material from this eruption have been found as far away as the Great Plains states.

Hundreds of thousands of years ago, there was a magnificent volcano in this area below Mammoth. It was obliterated by a tremendous explosion that left the Long Valley Caldera, a wide region of devastation, and thick accumulations of ash. More recent and smaller volcanic events have impacted these dry landscapes east of the Sierra Nevada, from across the Owens Valley into the Mono Lake area.

The caldera collapsed after the eruption and Long Valley was left behind.

Just to the west is Mammoth Mountain, a volcanic cone built from about ten glassy eruptions between 180,000–40,000 years ago; it is much younger than originally thought. Farther west is Devil's Postpile, where a thin andesitic lava flow cooled about 600,000 years ago. While cooling, it contracted and cracked into nearly perfect six-sided columns. Many of these individual vertical columns have been shaved flat at their tops by glaciers; others are now weathering into piles of rubble.

Volcanic activity in the Mammoth/Long Valley area continues. A series of strong earthquakes (a few at more than 6 magnitude) rocked the area on Memorial Day weekend, 1980. Strong shaking caused visible ground motion east into the Nevada desert, swayed chandeliers in distant Nevada casinos, and caused dangerous rock slides in the Sierra Nevada. By 1982, more than three thousand earthquakes were recorded as a magma chamber moved up to about 5 km (3 miles) from the surface. These earthquakes, increased activity at Hot Creek, and significant ground swelling in Long Valley caused geologists to warn residents and officials that an eruption could occur.

Unlike the Mount Saint Helens disaster, which was unfolding to the north in southern Washington State, there was no eruption. Instead, the activity calmed considerably, only to become active again in significant spasmodic events that continue to keep geologists' and residents' attention. This activity, especially at first, impacted businesses and real estate interests in and around Mammoth Lakes.

To the north, the line of Mono and Inyo Craters have erupted from a few thousand years ago to the last few centuries along a fault zone. Mono Craters are just south of Mono Lake and are composed of viscous rhyolitic materials that squeezed to the surface, forming conspicuous pumice cones and rings and steep-sided flows. They have formed during the last 40,000 years. At the northern end of Mono Craters is Panum crater. It has a pumice and ash ring, a central obsidian plug, and ash deposits that are slightly more than six hundred years old. Five-hundred-year-old Paoha and Negit Islands in Mono Lake experienced minor eruptions in the 1890s. Flows of obsidian and pumice at the steep and deep Inyo Craters are as young as 550 years. There are many other recent volcanic features in the area, such as Wilson Butte and Obsidian Dome near Deadman Summit and Hwy. 395.

To this point, we have examined three very different kinds of volcanic activities and landforms. Runny basaltic flows are characteristic of the Modoc Plateau, viscous rhyolitic eruptions and flows are common north of the Owens Valley, and the composite giants of the Cascades are mostly intermediate in chemical composition. Different volcanic landscapes are evident as we explore south and east into and beyond the Owens Valley.

Exploring Volcanic Activity and Landscapes Into the Owens Valley Heading south, the Owens Valley and surroundings are littered with fresh and often conspicuous ash and cinder cones and dark lava flows. From Crater Mountain and the other outstanding peaks and lava flows south of Big Pine to the 60,000–90,000 year-old basaltic flow at Sawmill Canyon northwest of Independence, it is clear that magma sits just below the surface of the faulted blocks and stretched crust of the Basin and Range.

Farther south, in the less than 25 km (15 miles) area from Little Lake across Rose Valley and northeast to Coso Hot Springs, there are at least fifteen basaltic cinder cones and thirty rhyolitic tuff cones, including pumice, obsidian, and dark lava flows. Some of the youngest landscapes are Red Hill and the prominent, related 10,000-year-old lava flow cut by the Owens River at Fossil Falls north of Little Lake. This is a memorable stop along Hwy. 395 for a view of recent volcanic features. Lava flows that have poured through canyons out of the southern Coso Range to the east are so fresh, one might experience the illusion that they continue to advance. Similarly recent volcanic features stand out along State Hwy. 190 from Olancha to the Panamint Valley in the northern Coso and Argus Ranges.

More Evidence of Volcanic Activity   Other indicators of recent and continued volcanic activity scattered about the Basin and Range include numerous hot springs. Excellent examples are found surrounding the Owens River from the Mammoth/Crowley Lake area south into the Owens Valley to Coso Hot Springs. The subterranean pressurized hot water associated with some of these areas (particularly near Mammoth and Coso) should continue to represent potential sources of hydrothermal energy.

One more example of a recent short-lived eruption is at Ubehebe Crater at the northern edge of Death Valley. This maar volcano erupted when groundwater was superheated by a heat source that neared the surface. The resulting pressurized steam exploded through the older sedimentary rock layers, raining layers of dark ash and cinder down on the surrounding desert surface. There were no lava flows, but the deep, dramatic crater left behind is best described by its name—Ubehebe is an Indian word for "big basket." Smaller craters are prominent on the surrounding desert surface.

The recent volcanics of this region are usually but not always confined to the eastern Sierra Nevada/Basin and Range. Just to the west are remnants of the last Sierra Nevada volcanic episodes (some younger than 3.5 mya), all in the high Sierra Nevada. These are in the headwaters of the San Joaquin River and along Golden Trout Creek before it dumps into the upper Kern River south of Kern Hot Spring. They also include cones along the headwaters of the South Fork of the Kern River.

Imperial Valley South of Salton Sea

Just north of Bombay Beach on the east side of the Salton Sea, the sliding plate boundary defined by the San Andreas Fault gives way to diverging plate boundaries to the south. A series of spreading centers are not only pushing the Peninsular Ranges away from the mainland, but they are stretching and pulling the Imperial Valley apart. These series of transform faults and pull-apart basins in the thinned crust eventually yield to the activity along the East Pacific Rise in the Gulf of California that is pushing the Baja Peninsula away from the Mexican mainland. Modern volcanic features, geothermal fields, and seismic activity south of the Salton Sea are evidence of the active thinning and pull-apart basins.

Southwest of Niland, along the southeastern edge of the Salton Sea, are five young pumice and obsidian domes with names such as Mullet Island, Red Island, and Obsidian Butte. They only rise to about 45 m (150 feet) above the basin surface, but they and the mud volcanoes and hot springs around them are proof that volcanic activity continues to impact the area. Six different geother-

A youthful-looking, but inactive, volcanic landscape is displayed around Ubehebe Crater in Death Valley. A steam explosion such as the one that blew this crater is not expected in the near future in this area, though such an event is possible farther northwest, near Mammoth Mountain. Rare rainstorms produce running water which continues to erode rills and gullies on the sides, filling the crater with sediment.

Boiling mud pots are just a few of the peculiar signs of volcanic activity south of the Salton Sea as the crust stretches, thins, and cracks.

mal fields have been identified in the region, and about a dozen geothermal plants are producing electricity, with great potential for increased production. However, corrosion from the high dissolved mineral content (10–39 percent) of the water continues to hamper the efficiency of these operations. This volcanic activity continues south into Mexico.

Sonoma to Clear Lake

Volcanic activity dominated landscapes starting in the Sonoma area at the end of the Pliocene Epoch and continued migrating north to reach the area around Clear Lake at the present time. Basaltic flows and rhyolites are found, but the dominant rock is andesite. Pyroclastics and lava flows extruded from various volcanoes are common in the mountains above the Sonoma and Napa Valleys. They cover hundreds of square miles in the Coast Ranges's Sonoma, Howell, and Mayacmas Mountains. They include the broken rhyolites of Mount Saint Helena looming above Healdsburg and the Russian River (not to be confused with Mount Saint Helens in Washington). From Lake Berryessa to south of Clear Lake, the cinder cones, pumice, basalt, and obsidian flows are even younger, dated to the last several thousand years. An example is Mount Konocti, which rises above the golf courses and country clubs on the western shores of Clear Lake, with its layers of intermediate lava flows and ash and cinder deposits.

There is still enough activity to boil residual heat water that has seeped through underground fissures, especially in the Mayacmas Mountains. Most of the resulting hot springs are located near the headwaters of Big Sulphur Creek, which eventually pours into the Russian River near Cloverdale. The Geysers Resort and geothermal power plants are also located in this area east of Cloverdale. These wells are some of the largest geothermal energy producers in the world, producing enough energy for a city of more than 500,000. Though the area is small, there are few corrosive chemicals in the dry steam; this contributes to a more efficient energy source. California's popular and dependable Old Faithful Geyser is southeast of this area, near Calistoga.

Summary of Modern Volcanic Activity and Landscapes

There are other hot springs and isolated pockets of related activity that branch away from the four volcanic areas discussed in this section. Perhaps most notable are the springs along the San Jacinto and Elsinore Fault Zones, where underground water has seeped deep into faults and contacted hot rocks. Examples include the historical Elsinore sulfur springs and spa, Warner Springs, and Murrieta Hot Springs. Additional hot springs along the San Jacinto Fault are San Jacinto, Soboba, Eden, and Gilman Springs. Palm Springs and Borrego Springs are other examples of the many hot springs that have attracted visitors and helped shape the history and economy of California.

This concludes our examination of the four major volcanic regions that are currently active in the state. The first two (the Cascades/Modoc Plateau and the east Sierra Nevada/Basin and Range) are the major and extensive regions; the last two (Clear Lake/Sonoma and Imperial Valley) are smaller and less significant in modern California. Each of these landscapes has been built and/or directly impacted by recent and current volcanic activity.

If your favorite volcano or volcanic rock was not mentioned in this section, it may be in an ancient volcanic field that is no longer active. If so, refer to Chapter 2, where the rocks and landscapes left behind by past geologic events are described. When you review some of the ancient Mojave volcanic landscapes covered in Chapter 2, you will better appreciate the thin, fuzzy line separating the past from the present. Once again, you will see how each chapter in this book is connected to the next, just as different events and landscapes are related in California.

Modern Tectonic Processes and Landforms: An Introduction

When you look over a California landscape on a clear day, you are looking across faults or folds in California's crust. You are viewing the structures and surface features that result from the bending and breaking of rocks under stress along or near the boundary between the Pacific and North American Plates. These same **tectonic processes** that move the ground beneath your feet during an earthquake also create diverse and often spectacular landscapes. Because California's unique geologic situation offers the potential of great human disaster, we must continue to learn about tectonic processes and how to live with them.

Unlike the more scattered distribution of volcanic activity, active tectonic landforms dominate or impact every California landscape. In this section, we will focus on more general and widespread tectonic processes and the more interesting and important specific landscapes they have created. We will begin with a very general introduction to these landscapes as we make a clockwise sweep around the state, starting in the northwest.

In the Klamaths, river terraces represent elevated valley floors that have been recently raised up and incised by rejuvenated streams. Numerous volcanoes in the Cascades are lined up along fractures in the crust. To the east, these faults dominate the landscapes into Nevada and south into the Basin and Range, where along them, adjacent blocks of crust are lifted up and dropped down.

Lake Tahoe has filled such a basin. The eastern Sierra Nevada is being lifted above the Owens Valley, and Death Valley is sinking along such faults. Though ancient but similar tectonic activity is often responsible for the older eroding mountains of the eastern Mojave, active faults become more dominant toward the west, closer to the San Andreas Fault Zone.

Farther south, the Coachella and Imperial Valleys continue to stretch and drop as the Peninsular Ranges are lifted and pulled away from them by a series of active faults. Finally, we sweep back north into the Transverse and Coast Ranges, where the tormented crust along the San Andreas Fault Zone and its branches is being folded and faulted, creating dominant landscapes trending mostly parallel to the plate boundary. Fresh **marine terraces** (wave-cut platforms lifted above sea level) so common along the California coast are also indicators of recent mountain building. Caught between much of this activity is the Great Central Valley and some smaller California valleys that have been structurally squeezed and downwarped, only to fill with sediment.

What do we know about specific tectonic processes shaping individual California landscapes, and what future threats do they pose to Californians? To answer these questions, we must always begin with California's situation in relation to global tectonics.

Worldwide, **mountain building** often occurs at much faster rates than **denudation** (landscape destruction) even though the weathering and erosion that causes denudation occurs everywhere, unless an area is being buried beneath sediment. Tectonic activity that causes mountain building only occurs in particular regions and in specific locations, usually along crustal plate boundaries. With few exceptions, active tectonic activity builds young mountain ranges along those plate boundaries faster than they are destroyed; older mountain ranges are now isolated farther away from plate boundaries as they gradually erode to a more subdued or even flat landscape.

Most California landscapes are being built as a result of movement along or near the boundary between the largest tectonic plate on the earth's crust (the **Pacific Plate**) and the continental **North American Plate**. Even in northwestern California north of the San Andreas Fault, a piece of ocean plate spreading away from the Pacific Plate causes folding and faulting as it jams into and is subducted below California's continental crust. Like objects floating on a river of thick mud, the brittle surface plates of California's lithosphere are carried by slow-moving currents within the plastic-like asthenosphere below. At the surface, the brittle Pacific Plate is grinding into and sliding past the North American Plate at about 5 cm (2 inches) per year toward the northwest. (This is roughly the same rate your fingernails grow.)

Specific Tectonic Processes and Landscapes

Though much of this movement occurs along the San Andreas Fault Zone, numerous individual segments of crust caught near plate boundaries are being bent, broken, contorted, and rotated. These forces are so powerful that most of California's mountain ranges and other landscapes are quite youthful. Many are currently being built faster than they are denuded, though the fresh, steep slopes are perfect environments for accelerated weathering and erosion. We will focus on these external processes and the resulting hazards and landscapes in the next section.

Now, we will examine some specific internal tectonic processes common in California, the resultant landscapes, and the hazards they represent. We will begin with the most important structural feature in California, the San Andreas Fault, and then sweep around the state.

The San Andreas Fault System

Two of the greatest earthquakes in California history occurred on the San Andreas Fault. The 1857 Fort Tejon earthquake (magnitude about 8) ripped a segment of the fault more than 300 km (200 miles) long from central California to Cajon Pass. The infamous 1906 San Francisco earthquake was just as powerful, causing more than 5 m (16 feet) of slippage. The quake and subsequent fire nearly destroyed the entire city and heavily damaged other towns and cities in the region. It was this earthquake that brought so many geologists from around the world to focus their attention on California and the **San Andreas Fault Zone**.

Geologists now understand earthquakes along faults to be caused by the stress that builds up in rocks which are locked together along these sliding plate boundaries. As the plates gradually grind past one another, stress builds until the rocks along this boundary must break. Like a rock thrown in a pond of water, energy waves emanate away from where the rocks break and move; these are the seismic waves felt during an earthquake. Geologists have also learned that the San Andreas Fault is more than 1,200 km (740 miles) long, that it has generated such earthquakes for many thousands of years, and that there are branches of hundreds of smaller faults running roughly parallel to it.

The fault began to form at least thirty million years ago when a portion of the East Pacific Rise spreading center was itself subducted and consumed below the North American Plate. The era of subduction that had dominated California's geology for millions of years slowly gave way to sliding along the lengthening San Andreas Fault system. This process continues today as geologists trace the fault south from the Mendocino Tri-

For decades, pilots and geologists have photographed this striking segment of the San Andreas Fault Zone. This boundary between the Pacific and North American plates is most noticeable along the inland edge of San Luis Obispo County, through the Carrizo Plain, and into the Temblor Range.

ple Junction west of Cape Mendocino; subduction is dominant north of this point while sliding rules to the south. Because the San Andreas Fault and its related structures are responsible for so many landscapes and geologic hazards in California, it is prudent to examine it more carefully.

Tracing the San Andreas Fault   From its northern end, the San Andreas Fault roughly parallels the northwest–southeast trending coastline to Point Arena and farther southeast to where the Garcia and Gualala Rivers follow its path. It is sometimes easy to follow along the landscapes it has helped to shape from Bodega Bay to the elongated Tomales Bay and back offshore near Stinson Beach. (The Earthquake Trail near the Nature Center at Point Reyes National Seashore offers a rewarding experience for anyone interested in geology and the San Andreas Fault.)

Trending just a few kms (miles) west of San Francisco, it comes ashore again on the San Francisco Peninsula between Daly City and Pacifica. Outstanding linear ridges, valleys, sag ponds, and offset streams mark its course through the Santa Cruz Mountains. It trends beneath San Andreas Lake and Crystal Springs Reservoir and on southeast through other Coast Ranges. Some of the most remarkable faulted surface features in the world (especially seen from the air) with dramatically offset streams are observed along the San Andreas Fault in the Carrizo Plain (west of the Temblor Range, in the southern Coast Ranges).

Just to the south, near the intersection with the Big Pine and Garlock Faults and other structural features, the San Andreas Fault takes a more easterly turn into Tejon Pass. Just as the fault trends more west–east at the "**Big Bend**," the Transverse Ranges are also aligned in a more west–east trend. Many folds, thrust faults, and other

structural features have built these mountains along the plate boundary that we are following. Once again, the fault is easy to follow by air from the Palmdale area on the inland side of the San Gabriel Mountains into Cajon Pass. As it trends into San Gorgonio (Banning) Pass toward the Coachella Valley, it breaks into several branches; the pass has been dropped along these faults as the San Bernardino and San Jacinto Mountains are being lifted on each side.

The fault zone continues along the east side of the Coachella Valley to just east of Bombay Beach and the Salton Sea. Groves of California fan palms and other green vegetation line the path and identify where crushed and weakened rocks along the fault zone allow ground water to seep toward the desert surface. South of the Salton Sea, the San Andreas Fault yields to the stretching and pulling-apart more typical of the Gulf of California.

Movement Along the Fault   The San Andreas is a right-lateral transform fault, or a right-slip fault. This means that if you stand on a block looking across the San Andreas Fault, the block on the other side of the fault will be moving to your right. This horizontal movement causes streams that flow across the fault to be offset to their right. Rocks on opposite sides of the fault zone have been displaced up to 300 km (185 miles) since the Miocene Epoch. Rocks on the east side of the San Andreas Fault in the Little San Bernardino, Chocolate, and Orocopia Mountains are matched with rocks on the west side of the fault in the San Gabriel Mountains and farther north in the Transverse Ranges. Map 3.1 shows relative movement along the San Andreas Fault.

Likewise, other rocks east of the fault in the San Gabriels and other Transverse Ranges are matched with rocks on the west side of the fault as far as Pinnacles

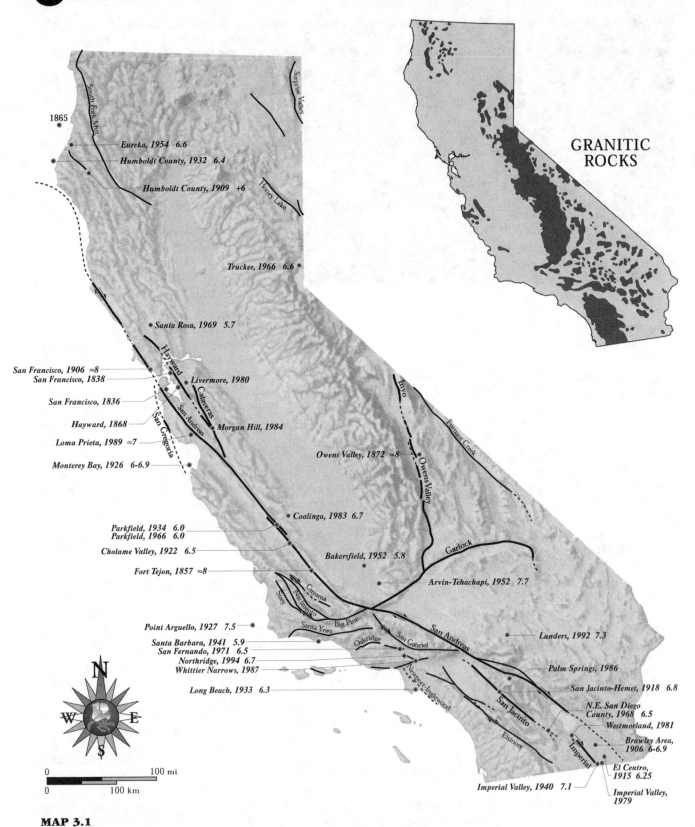

GRANITIC
ROCKS

1865

Eureka, 1954 6.6
Humboldt County, 1932 6.4
Humboldt County, 1909 +6

Truckee, 1966 6.6

Santa Rosa, 1969 5.7

San Francisco, 1906 ≈8
San Francisco, 1838
Livermore, 1980
San Francisco, 1836
Hayward, 1868
Morgan Hill, 1984
Loma Prieta, 1989 ≈7
Monterey Bay, 1926 6-6.9

Owens Valley, 1872 ≈8

Coalinga, 1983 6.7

Parkfield, 1934 6.0
Parkfield, 1966 6.0
Cholame Valley, 1922 6.5
Bakersfield, 1952 5.8
Fort Tejon, 1857 ≈8

Garlock

Arvin-Tehachapi, 1952 7.7

Point Arguello, 1927 7.5
Landers, 1992 7.3
Santa Barbara, 1941 5.9
San Fernando, 1971 6.5
Northridge, 1994 6.7
Whittier Narrows, 1987
Long Beach, 1933 6.3
Palm Springs, 1986
San Jacinto-Hemet, 1918 6.8
N.E. San Diego
County, 1968 6.5
Westmorland, 1981
Brawley Area,
1906 6-6.9
El Centro,
1915 6.25
Imperial Valley, 1940 7.1
Imperial Valley,
1979

0   100 mi
0   100 km

MAP 3.1

The San Andreas Fault and other major faults. As this right-lateral fault slices through
California, edges of the Pacific Plate slide northwest against the North American Plate.
Locations of some major earthquakes are also noted.

(east of the Salinas Valley) and the Santa Cruz Mountains. These rocks were broken apart and dragged away from their original area of formation along opposite sides of the fault. As geologists learn that the San Andreas Fault has been actively sliding for millions of years, they are also gathering much more detailed information about recent movements and the possibility of future activity.

The fault is divided into northern and southern sections, where rocks are locked until there is a major earthquake. However, in portions of central California, where the fault is straighter, it appears to move more frequently in smaller events. Walls and curbs in Hollister are bent along a creeping section of the San Andreas Fault called the Calaveras Fault. Near Parkfield, moderate earthquakes greater than five magnitude have occurred on the average of every twenty-two years. (Many geologists were puzzled when the Parkfield earthquake was several years overdue going into the late-1990s.) Meanwhile, historical earthquakes and recent research have shed light on the frequency of the big events along the more jagged, temporarily locked southern and northern sections.

Numerous geologists have added to our knowledge of California earthquakes and the landscapes they create, but it was Kerry Sieh who, by the late 1970s, had a trench dug across the San Andreas Fault at Pallet Creek south of Pearblossom. There he studied the frequency of earthquakes that break alternating beds of deposited sediments. Using the results of his and others' work, seismologists have shown that major earthquakes of about eight magnitude have broken the rocks along this section of the San Andreas Fault and moved them up to 8–12 m (26–40 feet). Such events have occurred at intervals averaging between 130 and 185 years for the last two thousand years. Since the last great event on this southern section of the fault occurred in 1857, and we know that rocks along the plates are accumulating stress at about 5 cm (2 inches) per year, it is likely that the "Big One," with a magnitude near 8, will occur soon.

What Are the Risks? During the early 1990s, research led seismologists to estimate that there was about a 60 percent chance of a major earthquake along this southern section of the San Andreas Fault within about thirty years. Because the fault southeast of Cajon Pass and east of the Coachella Valley has been locked much longer, the chances for a major earthquake there may even be greater. Conversely, geologists estimate the chance for a major event on the northern section of the San Andreas Fault north of Hollister to be a bit less. However, the fault zone is far more complicated than these estimates might suggest.

Though movement between the plates is mainly relieved by infrequent strong earthquakes along the San Andreas Fault, considerable stress is relieved by smaller earthquakes along nearby branch faults. Some of this movement is vertical, not horizontal. The reason goes back to those tiny slivers and other plate pieces that are caught, crumbled, mangled, and rotated along the plate boundaries. These hundreds of related faults are usually parallel to the San Andreas Fault, but they can be very complex and even difficult to locate. They have also helped build and impact landscapes within many kms (miles) of the San Andreas Fault.

With the inclusion of these smaller faults, geologists put the chance of another disastrous earthquake somewhere in the Los Angeles area at about 80 percent in the next thirty years. Similar conditions caused by different faults led seismologists to estimate about a 67 percent chance of an earthquake of at least 7 magnitude in the San Francisco Bay area within thirty years. These figures reflect studies done by the United States Geological Survey (USGS) near the end of the twentieth century.

It is important to note that seismologists have changed to a more precise method of measuring earthquakes. The older Richter scale used a seismograph to measure the intensity of seismic wave energy released during an earthquake. A one-point increase on the scale represented roughly ten times more wave amplitude, but more than thirty times the amount of released energy. The modern moment-magnitude scale is similar, but measures more precisely the total energy released by quakes, emphasizing the area of rock rupture and the distance the rocks move along a fault during an earthquake.

When rocks break, the primary energy waves move fastest away from the focus, causing the ground to first shake from the compression and rarefaction (expansion) of the ground below. The secondary waves move more slowly away from the focus and represent shearing or undulations that cause the ground to sway and rock during an earthquake. Surface or longitudinal waves are often known as L waves. Many Californians have experienced enough earthquakes to roughly estimate their distance. A hard jolt with no discernable difference in motion could mean the earthquake epicenter was very close. Lengthy shaking from fast-moving primary waves, followed by extended rolling and swaying motions could indicate a very distant quake.

The amount of damage caused by an earthquake depends on two basic factors—distance from the epicenter and makeup of the substrate. In other words, the closer you are, the greater the shaking. Additionally, substrate of solid bedrock moves much less than substrate composed of the unstable loose sediment and fill usually found in California valleys and coastal areas. Especially dangerous is the loose material used to fill wetlands and bays, which may also have high water content, causing liquefaction when shaking begins.

The same two factors which combine to produce the greatest risk from earthquakes in California have also caused the most damaging earthquakes in California history. They occurred on faults along or near the San Andreas Fault system, and they occurred in or near population centers. The greatest damage was often on unstable substrate. The great 1906 San Francisco earthquake ripped more than 400 km (250 miles) of the San Andreas Fault up to 7 m (21 feet) apart in spots from Cape Mendocino to north of Hollister. More than three thousand people were killed, and much of The City was burned to the ground. Cities as far away as Santa Rosa were heavily damaged or nearly destroyed.

During a World Series baseball game between the San Francisco Giants and the Oakland Athletics in October, 1989, the 7.0 magnitude Loma Prieta quake struck along the San Andreas Fault system near Santa Cruz. Geologists believe that compression along a bend in the San Andreas Fault caused the horizontal and vertical thrust movement. The World Series was postponed, and more than 40 percent of downtown Santa Cruz was destroyed.

Though San Francisco was seventy miles north of the epicenter, liquefaction destroyed buildings built on the Marina District fill. A section of the Bay Bridge fell, and across the bay, the double-decker Nimitz Freeway collapsed on helpless commuters. The quake killed sixty-two people and caused $6 billion in damages. Residents and businesses have rebuilt, but retrofitting of older structures continues. The next disaster could be produced by one of several branch faults in the San Francisco Bay Area, where seismic activity has increased in recent years.

Smaller Faults in the Bay Area   From the Calavaras Fault to the south, to the San Gregorio Fault offshore, to the Rodgers Creek Fault to the north, the most dangerous branch fault in the Bay Area is probably the Hayward Fault. It is capable of unleashing an earthquake as powerful as the Loma Prieta quake, but with destruction similar to the January, 1995, earthquake in Kobe, Japan, which killed more than five thousand people. This is because the Hayward Fault runs along a line nearly connecting the major East Bay cities of Richmond, Berkeley, Oakland, and Hayward.

Engineers and scientists at the 1995 meeting of the Earthquake Engineering Research Institute estimated that such a quake, which is overdue, could move rocks along the fault up to 3 m (10 feet) in twenty-two seconds, kill thousands, and cause ten times the damage of the Loma Prieta quake. Perhaps it is geographic irony that many California cities were built along linear lowlands aligned with the dangerous faults which have shaped them. The picture is even more complicated in the Los Angeles area and throughout southern California.

Smaller Faults Cause Big Disasters in Southern California   The Newport-Inglewood Fault Zone trends roughly from Century City through the Baldwin Hills and Inglewood through the South Bay and south to Newport Beach. The geography of this fault is hauntingly similar to that of the Hayward Fault in the Bay Area; it is capable of producing magnitude 7 earthquakes directly below a line of densely populated cities. The 1933 6.4 magnitude Long Beach quake on this fault caused southern Californians to recognize their vulnerability and led to some of California's first stringent building codes to make structures more earthquake resistant.

A relatively quiet period followed, but at 6 A.M. on February 9, 1971, the 6.7 magnitude San Fernando (Sylmar) quake began a new period of activity. This quake killed sixty-four people and caused half a billion dollars damage. Damage to the Van Norman Reservoir left a few feet of dam between a wall of water and residents of the San Fernando Valley. Building codes were further strengthened after this event, due to the additional knowledge gained by engineers. These new building standards would save scores of lives in the years ahead.

The San Fernando quake also focused more attention on the numerous thrust faults that slice their way through

Two meters (more than six feet) of vertical displacement and far more horizontal displacement occurred in less than thirty seconds during the 7.3 magnitude Landers quake of 1992 in the Johnson Valley area northwest of Landers. Imagine the devastation that would result if such an event occurred below one of our urban centers. This photo was taken with the author more than one year after that earthquake.

the Transverse Ranges and the entire "Big Bend" region along the San Andreas Fault. Geologists began to confirm that many other thrust faults like the San Fernando and Santa Susana were capable of causing equally powerful quakes. Many of these faults are called blind thrusts because they are buried beneath sediment, and they do not always leave surface fractures when they move. They are part of the complicated faults and folds of the Transverse Ranges Compressional Zone; the Pacific Plate jams into the North American Plate at this bend, squeezing and folding smaller pieces of crust. The result is formation of the Transverse Ranges and the usually parallel faults that have helped build them.

A remarkable increase in the frequency of earthquakes, mainly along thrust faults, began in the 1980s. To the north, the devastating 1983 Coalinga quake measured 6.7 magnitude, followed by the 1985 5.9 magnitude Kettleman Hills quake. Then, six strong earthquakes hit parts of southern California between 1987 and 1994. Within the Los Angeles area, the 1987 Whittier narrows quake measured 5.9 magnitude, the 1988 Pasadena quake measured 5.0 magnitude and the 1991 Sierra Madre quake measured 5.8 magnitude. These seismic events pale in comparison to the two earthquakes that followed.

The most powerful of these events hit east of the San Andreas Fault near the Mojave desert town of Landers, on the southern edge of the Eastern California shear zone. Occurring in June, 1992, the Landers quake measured 7.3 magnitude. It caused slippage of nearly 7 m (20 feet) along the Landers-Johnson Valley and Homestead Valley Faults. Left behind were fresh scarps more than 2 m (6 feet) high with several meters of noticeable right lateral slippage at the surface. It was followed by another powerful earthquake in the nearby mountains near Big Bear, which was felt in Arizona and Nevada, and it triggered days of numerous earthquakes on faults throughout California and even into Montana.

The Landers quake was significant because it validated the arguments of geologists who believed that major movement between the two plates was migrating east of the San Andreas Fault. Damage was heavy, but the major jolt and aftershocks were centered far from areas with high population densities, sparing many hundreds of lives and billions of dollars of damage. The Landers quake proved once again how earthquakes continue to shape California landscapes and build mountains.

The most destructive earthquake in U.S. history hit Northridge at 4:31 A.M. on January 17, 1994. This 6.7 magnitude earthquake destroyed three thousand homes, entire shopping centers, schools, parking structures, freeway bridges and overpasses; it killed sixty people, including fourteen residents of the collapsed Northridge Meadows apartments who were crushed to death. Extensive damage throughout and north of the San Fernando

Valley and surrounding the base of the Santa Monica Mountains totalled more than $20 billion. The focus of this quake was 18 km (11 miles) below the San Fernando Valley on a blind thrust fault dipping at an angle of 35–45 degrees.

No surface ruptures were found, but parts of the Santa Susana Mountains (including Oat Mountain) moved nearly 21 cm (8 inches) northwest and were pushed up nearly 38 cm (15 inches) during the seconds of the initial quake and its thousands of aftershocks.

There are dozens of similar thrust faults in and near the Transverse Ranges, particularly beneath the Los Angeles Basin. While geologists watched as these processes gradually changed landscapes, they became concerned that this exceptionally active period was a result of increased stress built up in this section of the San Andreas system—stress that may soon be released by a more powerful earthquake. Interestingly, a short period of quiet occurred in the late 1990s. The San Francisco Bay Area also seemed to be in an active period into the last years of the twentieth century, but it too experienced a brief lull in the late 1990s.

Other Signs of Stress, Faults, and Mountain Building
We cannot examine all of the faults and other structural landscapes that surround the complicated San Andreas system, especially as it trends through the parallel Coast Ranges. The Sur-Nacimiento Fault, the anticlinal folds that have pushed up the Diablo Range, and the marine terraces lifted above the sea all result from dynamic mountain-building forces along this system. Various marine terraces have been recently (in geologic time) uplifted to 275 m (900 feet) above sea level; there are five separate terraces near Santa Cruz. The most inexperienced earth scientist can appreciate road cuts similar to those located where Hwy. 14 spills out of the north base of the San Gabriel Mountains into Palmdale. Here, once horizontal rocks are now twisted and contorted into grotesque features on the San Andreas Fault. However, California earthquakes, faults, folds, and their landscapes are not at all confined to the San Andreas Fault Zone.

The area north of Cape Mendocino near the Triple Junction between the Pacific, North American, and Gorda Plates (related to the Juan de Fuca Plate north of California) also experiences earthquakes. This happens as the Gorda Plate is subducted below the northern California continental crust. The 7.2 magnitude Petrolia earthquake hit near this Triple Junction on April 25, 1992. This quake lifted coastal tide pools more than 1 m (3 feet) higher. It also caused extensive damage, especially from Petrolia to Ferndale and even along the coast to Eureka.

This is more evidence of how the mountains of northwestern California are being crunched and folded upward above the subduction zone as the coastline is lifted above sea level. Reverse and thrust faults caused by this compression are common in the Klamaths and in the Transverse Ranges (the other major compressional zone in the state). Numerous coastal and river terraces have also been recently raised.

More recent research suggests that very powerful subduction earthquakes strike this northwestern region every three hundred to six hundred years; it has been about three hundred years since the last one. Many of the tight and complicated folded structures and faults in the Klamaths indicate that mountain building along similar plate boundaries has been repeated on and off for tens of millions of years. Geologists suspect that the Coast Ranges were jammed into the Klamaths more than 100 mya along what is still considered today's boundary, the South Fork Mountain Thrust.

South of the Big Bend   South of the Big Bend in the San Andreas Fault Zone, numerous mostly northwest–southeast trending faults are causing earthquakes and building landscapes. Included are such Peninsular Ranges as the San Jacintos and Santa Rosas and less dramatic features to the west and south all the way offshore.

The San Jacinto Fault veers south away from the San Andreas Fault in the Transverse Range. Geologists have measured more than 28 km (18 miles) of right-slip displacement that has occurred in the last few million years. The San Jacinto Mountains are being squeezed and raised between this fault on the west and branches of the San Andreas to the north and east. Perris Valley and Borrego Valley have been dropped down on the western side, while the impressive San Jacintos and Santa Rosas are lifted on the eastern side of this fault. These mountains are even more abruptly lifted on their eastern slopes by the Banning and other frontal faults. (The resulting scarps make for spectacular scenery, particularly from the Palm Springs desert floor up more than 3,000 m [10,000 feet] to 3,296 m [10,804 foot] Mount San Jacinto.) Back at the San Jacinto Fault, about seven earthquakes near magnitude 6 since 1890 are evidence of recent increased activity.

Farther west, the Elsinore Fault Zone is very similar to the San Jacinto Fault in age and horizontal displacement. Around the Lake Elsinore area, basins drop on this fault's eastern side, and the Santa Ana and other mountains are being lifted on its western side. Parts of the Elsinore Basin are being pulled apart between faults, causing it to drop and fill with thick deposits of sediment. The Elsinore Fault trends southeast from there, through Temecula, Mesa Grande, and Julian. Like the San Jacinto Fault, the Elsinore Fault exhibits many classic fault features, including hot springs. Numerous lesser faults are mapped mostly parallel between and west of these two major faults, to many kms (miles) offshore.

It is interesting that the greatest vertical lifting is found in the higher eastern Peninsular Ranges; this relief tapers off in the gentler slopes toward the west, much like in the Sierra Nevada. Most major rivers also flow to the west and southwest, slicing into these uplifted terrains.

Many of the faults of the Peninsular Range that trend farther southeast toward the Imperial Valley branch off and disappear below the sediment, but interesting structural features, mostly northwest–southeast trending, abound. The San Jacinto Fault Zone branches through Borrego Valley and past Ocotillo Wells, where surface breakage was measured in the 1968 Borrego earthquake. Dramatic surface displacement was measured along the Superstition Hills Fault (a possible branch of the San Jacinto Fault) during a 1987 earthquake. The San Felipe Hills west of Anza Borrego and the Superstition Hills south of the Salton Sea contain so many tight folds that were recently bent up along major faults, they resemble the Indio and Mecca Hills along the San Andreas Fault Zone north of the Salton Sea. Similar forces have created recent folds in the young Palm Springs Formation sediments that stand out on the desert floor west of the Salton Sea.

The numerous northwest–southeast trending faults that are pulling apart the Imperial Valley produced more than twelve major earthquakes during the 1900s, including the 1979 and 1987 quakes. The magnitude 7 quake of 1940 on the right-lateral Imperial Fault near Mexicali displaced trees lined across the fault up to 5 m (15 feet). Brawley and other nearby towns were severely damaged. Rifting processes here are more similar to those pulling apart the Gulf of California than to the San Andreas Fault and other faults to the north.

Beyond the San Andreas Fault: Faults in the Mojave

Northeast of the San Andreas Fault system and south of the Garlock Fault, mountains of the eastern Mojave were built mostly along faults similar to the Basin and Range. The difference is that most of these normal faults are lower angle, curve toward the horizontal below the desert, and may even connect as "listric" faults. They are also older, more extensively eroded, and extend into Arizona and Nevada. There are exceptions. The Mannix Fault runs along the Mojave River from Yermo toward Afton; its left-lateral movement is more similar to the Garlock Fault. Similar left-slip faults are common in the northeastern Mojave.

However, the Garlock Fault is one of the most unusual structural features in California for a number of reasons. First, it trends northeast (nearly perpendicular to most structural features in California) away from Frazier Mountain, Tejon Pass, and the San Andreas Fault, before curving more easterly. Second, recent movement along the fault cuts off Sierra Nevada and Basin and Range landscapes, marking the northern boundary of the Mojave. Third, this is an active *left*-lateral fault with displacement between 10–60 km (6–40 miles). Although it is remarkably narrow (as little as 1.5 km [1 mile] wide) and only branches into two segments, it stands out on any topographic map of California.

Structural Features from the Sierra Nevada to the Basin and Range

North of the Garlock Fault is the eastern Sierra Nevada and Basin and Range with adjacent north–south trending blocks of grabens dropping down and horsts rising up along parallel faults. From the Sierra Nevada east into Nevada and along this California border to its northeast tip, such blocks were described by early researchers as looking like "caterpillars crawling north." This edge of the North American Plate is being stretched and broken as the Pacific Plate pulls away from it far to the west. As the extension tears the rocks, alternate blocks are dropped and lifted along the faults. The Sierra Nevada is lifted on its eastern side by similar types of faults.

Sierra Nevada Structures   The Sierra Nevada Fault Zone represents a series of parallel, vertical fault surfaces as steep as 70 degrees that are lifting the eastern wall of the Sierra Nevada and dropping basins to the east. The fault scarps have been eroded to still-impressive 30 degree slopes. Displacement from the basins to the crest is about 1,500 m (5,000 feet) in the north and 3,350 m (11,000

It is a dramatic drop from the top of the Sierra Nevada near Mount Whitney down into the Owens Valley. This is more evidence that recent faulting has lifted the Sierra Nevada's eastern edge and dropped the Owens Valley on the other side. Similar faults slice north–south across the Basin and Range into Nevada.

feet) in the south. The Sierra Nevada is young; most of this mountain-building has accelerated along young and rejuvenated faults during the last three million years. This activity has produced some of the most spectacular landscapes on earth. The view from the Owens Valley looking west from Hwy. 395 is an example. From about 1128 m (3700 feet) elevation near Lone Pine, 4418 m (14,495 foot) Mount Whitney (the highest peak in the contiguous United States) can be seen less than 21 km (13 miles) away.

The Alabama Hills represent slices of rock west of Lone Pine that were very recently lifted above the Owens Valley along branches of the Sierra Nevada Fault Zone. Even streams carving through them are older than the hills. A dramatic recent event that lifted this region higher above the Owens Valley may be the most powerful earthquake in California history. The 1872 Owens Valley, or Lone Pine, earthquake broke rocks along a 200 km (120 mile) line and lifted the Sierra Nevada block about 5 m (15 feet) higher above the Owens Valley. It destroyed Lone Pine and left thirty people dead in the sparsely populated valley.

Clearly, the Sierra Nevada is being lifted on the east along active vertical faults similar to the Basin and Range, while its gentler western slopes are relatively free of seismic events. In the south, the peculiar drainage of the Kern River is controlled by the 20 km (75 mile) long north–south trending Kern Canyon Fault and its valley. Lava flows 3.5 million years old across the fault indicate it is old and inactive. However, this fault and its canyon continue to divide the Sierra Nevada into two parallel ridges. Farther north, even the Lake Tahoe basin is a block dropped down by faulting, with the northern Sierra Nevada branching off to the northwest and the Carson Range on the east.

Many of the vertical and horizontal joints so common in the Sierra Nevada were caused by stress from extensional and compressional forces when the rocks were buried; the weathering of these and exfoliated rocks will be covered in the next section. Though there are other interesting structural features in the Sierra Nevada, we will return to the active Basin and Range processes, where this discussion began.

Structural Features of the Basin and Range   The crustal extension previously mentioned is breaking crust along mainly right-lateral faults, with vertical movement which also causes basins to drop between mountains. One of the most dramatic illustrations of how these structural features control topography is along the classically used transect between Mount Whitney and Death Valley. That roughly 135 km (85 mile) line drops from the highest peak in California to the Owens Valley, back up to the Inyo and Argus Mountains, down to the Panamint Valley, up over the Panamint Mountains, and down to the lowest place in North America. Three major mountain ranges, three deep valleys, and the mostly parallel faults that helped form them account for repeated elevation changes of up to 3000 m (10,000 feet). This transect defines the Basin and Range.

The Death Valley Fault Zone trends north–northwest away from the Garlock Fault, creating outstanding fault scarps; they separate the lowest parts on the eastern edge of Death Valley from the adjacent Black Mountains. Because this fault zone is currently dropping the valley faster than faults bounding the western side, the valley tilts slightly down toward the east and the Black Mountains. As the Death Valley-Furnace Creek Fault Zone trends farther northwest, it is easily followed along the fresh and outstanding fault scarps that cut alluvial fans at the base of the Grapevine Mountains. From here, it continues through the Last Chance Mountains and to the northwest, where it marks the boundary between the White Mountains and Fish Lake Valley.

Similar faulting drops Deep Springs, Eureka, Saline, Panamint, and so many other valleys of the Basin and Range. Outstanding fault scarps also commonly surround ranges such as the White Mountains, separating them from adjacent deep valleys. Active faults above the northern Owens Valley have helped raise White Mountain Peak to 4,342 m (14,248 feet). Many of these faults are capable of generating strong earthquakes, as they have in the past.

Similar Basin and Range processes and landscapes encroach into the northeastern edge of California and the Modoc Plateau. Honey Lake Valley has been dropped below the surrounding uplifted mountains. The active Surprise Valley Fault Zone separates the Warner Range to the west from Surprise Valley and the Alkali Lakes to the east, and a series of north–south trending faults separates blocks on the Modoc Plateau. These are just some examples of the familiar structural features that have built Basin and Range landscapes.

Tectonic Activity in and around the Central Valley

We end our tour of tectonic processes that build California landscapes with the Central Valley. The valley has been gradually downwarped into a long synclinal trough that has filled with thousands of meters of sediment over millions of years. Only a few structures warp or break the monotony of this valley, and oil and gas almost always accumulate in the sediments around them. The Sutter Buttes and the Stockton Fault and Arch are examples in the northern valley. Moving south, processes and landscapes more common in the Coast Ranges and Transverse Ranges begin to encroach. The Kettleman Hills represent long anticlinal folds that pop out of the western San Joaquin Valley south of Coalinga. They are examples of the many folds trending parallel to the Coast Ranges that become increasingly common to the south, such as

Elk, Lost, and Buena Vista Hills, McKittrick and Wheeler Ridges; they are all oil producers.

These folds are very young and many are growing rapidly as compressional forces similar to those building the Transverse Range impact these landscapes. Pipes and roads are buckling near many oil fields. Southwest of the valley edge, the San Emigdio Mountains were built in about the last three million years and they continue to grow remarkably fast—about 3 m (9 feet) per thousand years—as they migrate toward the valley. We end with the White Wolf Fault and its scarp which separates the valley from the Transverse Range. It broke in 1952, causing the powerful and destructive 7.5 magnitude Kern County earthquake. Notable seismic activity continued in this area into the late 1990s.

It is fitting that we have ended this section with a new and growing mountain range and a recent powerful earthquake. We have now reviewed some of the more important mountain-building processes and their landscapes. We cannot escape them because wherever we are in California, we are on or near the plate boundary. A recent study found that the most earthquake-free region of California is probably somewhere near Fresno, but any geologic map shows that faults begin to appear not far from there. Californians learn to live with tectonic forces while we admire the spectacular landscapes those forces have produced. Now we will examine the external forces of denudation and the California landscapes they produce.

◆ EXTERNAL DENUDATIONAL PROCESSES AND LANDFORMS

Weathering Attacks and Contributes to California Landscapes

As constructive tectonic processes push solid rocks toward the surface, weathering immediately attacks these rocks and breaks them down. These chemical and mechanical **weathering processes** are reducing California rocks into the loose regolith and soil on which most Californians live and work. Such unending weathering processes have also controlled the development of many California landscapes as weathered material is often eroded, transported, and deposited to form various California landforms which will be examined in this section.

Chemical weathering occurs in California rocks when culprits such as oxidation, weak carbonic and organic acids, and hydrolysis (occurs when reaction with water changes minerals) gradually attack rocks at and near the surface. Mechanical or physical weathering processes include expansion and contraction due to temperature changes, frost action, exfoliation, root pry, and the pressure caused by growth of salt crystals and hydration (occurs when water combines with and expands minerals). All of these weathering processes reduce rocks to rubble.

The role of each process changes with every California environment. For example, frost action is common in California's highlands.

Most joints and fractures in rocks form from stress when the rocks were buried deep below the surface. The joints formed from these compressional or extensional forces are often quite orderly, running in parallel and perpendicular patterns. One exception to this is exfoliation. This occurs when bedrock, once buried under pressure, is lifted and exposed by the gradual erosion or "unloading" of the rocks above. As pressure is released, blocks of rocks now at the surface are able to expand and break into onion-like sheets or slabs which are separated by curved joint patterns.

Even the largest blocks of previously unjointed granitic bedrock expand and weather into great rounded exfoliation domes. You will find them in the Sierra Nevada and many other California mountains dominated by fresh granitic outcrops. Half Dome and the domes above Tenaya Lake in Yosemite are classic examples. At Half Dome, one side of this original exfoliation dome was more extensively jointed, leaving it weaker and vulnerable to erosion by the glacial activity that helped scrape it away.

Regardless of the causes of the joint and fracture patterns, illustrations of the accelerated weathering within them abound. Some of the best examples are displayed in Sierra Nevada-like plutonic rocks around the state. Whether in the Sierra Nevada, Alabama Hills, Joshua Tree, outcrops near Riverside and the Peninsular Ranges down into Mexico, or in numerous other California landscapes, the process begins with the exposure of jointed rocks. Weathering attacks the weaker joint patterns where water often accumulates, isolating rectangular blocks of bedrock. Nature then attacks the corners and edges of the rectangles faster, gradually producing spheres of more rounded boulders. The most widely spaced joints produce the largest boulders.

In contrast, vertical jointing dominates in Klamath Mountains plutonic rocks and is weathered into the pinnacles at Castle Crags State Park south of Mount Shasta.

Surfaces of rock outcrops across the state are stained in red, brown, and darker colors by oxidation when oxygen in the air or water combines with iron, magnesium, manganese, or other elements in rocks. The rusted reddish-browns of rocks in the Marble Mountain Wilderness of the Klamaths west of Scott Valley are reflected in names of local landmarks. Red Rock Canyon on Hwy. 14 north of Mojave also gets its name from beautifully stained sedimentary outcrops. The dark streams hanging down Sierra Nevada cliffs result from trickling water which often accumulates during rain and snowmelt; this water acts as a catalyst for chemical reactions that accelerate oxidation of minerals along these streaks.

In southeastern California, desert varnish has stained many otherwise undisturbed rock surfaces brown or black. Studies have shown that over hundreds of years, wind-blown clays and various metallic elements are cemented by manganese-oxidizing bacteria that survive in desert climates. When rock debris is tumbled or overturned on the desert floor, the lighter, less-stained sides are exposed.

Differential Weathering

Weathering processes attack and decompose rocks at different rates. This differential weathering creates some of the more spectacular landscapes in California. In general, igneous and metamorphic rocks are more resistant to erosion than sedimentary rock outcrops. For instance, a block of granite or a basaltic lava flow will probably resist weathering, forming ridges next to weaker sedimentary rocks, which might form lowlands. There are many exceptions to these general rules.

Because the dark extrusive igneous basalt is more mafic with less silica (quartz), it will weather faster than the high-silica intrusive igneous granite. Conglomerates and sandstones high in quartz usually form more resistant ridges and cliffs compared to their weaker sedimentary counterparts, such as siltstone, claystone, and shale. Regardless of rock type, the fractured, crumbled, and deformed rock formations will usually weather and erode faster than rocks exposed to less stress and deformation. Such differential weathering has produced impressive landscapes throughout California.

At Castle Crags State Park in the Klamaths, long quartz dikes are most resistant, forming the ridges and peaks above the granitic rocks with less silica. But, these granites are, in turn, more resistant than the serpentines they tower over.

Crystal Caves are near the western border of Sequoia National Park. Cave tours are designed for visitors curious about how the caves and their stalactites, stalagmites, columns, and colors were formed. Calcium carbonates in the marbles combine with ground water to form weak carbonic acids that weather the rocks. Time is the other key ingredient.

Table Mountain is a lava flow in the central Sierra Nevada foothills near Jamestown. The lava rolled down a river canyon, cooled and solidified about nine million years ago. Subsequently, weaker surfaces adjacent to the flow have been denuded so that the more resistant flow now looms above surrounding landscapes. These are known as inverted landforms. Likewise, lava in the Cima Dome volcanic field in the eastern Mojave flowed into and along a valley about 630,000 years ago. Geologists can measure the rates at which the surrounding weaker weathered surface is being eroded by measuring the height of this relatively resistant lava flow above surrounding desert pediment. Meanwhile, some ten-million-year-old lava flows at Red Rock Canyon north of Mojave have covered and are now protecting older, weaker sedimentary layers below.

Differential Weathering in Sedimentary Rocks Shapes Landscapes Alternating layers of sedimentary rocks have also been differentially weathered, producing fascinating landscapes across the state. Along I-5 near the Oregon border, exposed conglomerates in the Hornbrook Formation form the ridges, while layers of sandstone and shale form the valleys. The valleys and rivers of the Santa Cruz and other Coast Range Mountains that do not follow faults and synclinal folds often cut into more easily weathered siltstones, mudstones, and shales.

Lifted, contorted, and exposed, the alternating sedimentary rocks of the Transverse Ranges display repeated examples of resistant conglomerates and sandstones. They protrude as ridges and cliffs above adjacent weaker shale and other sedimentary layers. Dipping layers of more resistant rocks at Vasquez Rocks and Devils Punchbowl in the San Gabriels, Mormon Rocks in Cajon Pass, and in slopes towering above Chatsworth and Santa Barbara are just a few examples. Some of these landscapes have provided great scenery for television and motion picture productions.

Limestone Caverns At least small outcrops of limestone and marble are found in spots in almost every California province. However, the most renowned carbonate caves are in the west-central Sierra Nevada and at Mitchell Caverns in Mojave Desert's Providence Mountains. In the foothills from southern Calaveras through Tuolumne into northern Mariposa Counties are Mercer's, Moaning, and Bower Caves. Farther south, Boyden Cave is off Hwy. 180 going into Kings Canyon, while Crystal and Clough Caves are on the western edge of Sequoia National Park.

Like the others, Mojave's Mitchell Caverns formed when underground water circulating through calcareous rocks combined with calcium carbonate to form weak carbonic acids. These acids dissolved minerals so that water could carry them away in solution, leaving the caverns. Dripping water in the underground caverns created the limestone stalactites, stalagmites, columns, and curtains that are common in such caves. When the climate dried and water tables dropped, Mitchell Caverns were left dry and inactive as we see them today.

Smaller-Scale Weathering Patterns There are smaller-scale weathering processes limited to specific California environments. They include the intricate patterns of honeycomb cavities weathered in some exposed rocks especially along the central California coast. This is sometimes known as tafoni. Finally, various types of frost action features and patterned ground are common in California's highest elevations.

Results of Weathering All of these weathering processes are responsible for producing the loose regolith and soil which has allowed life to flourish in California. Weathering also loosens the rocks that can move in landslides and other mass wasting processes on steeper slopes. Additionally, it paves the way for the processes of erosion, transportation, and deposition of materials by water, ice, wind, and coastal waves and currents. All of these **erosional processes** produce their own landforms as California mountains are denuded, delivering aprons of debris into the surrounding lowlands. We now turn our attention to the processes and landscapes resulting from the erosion, transportation, and deposition of this material. First, we will examine some landscapes made by mass wasting.

Mass Wasting

Like many other geologic processes, some form of **mass wasting** is found in every California region. Ancient landslides have left landscapes and clues which often allow geologists to assess future hazards. Active mass wasting processes add a little more excitement and danger to living on some California hillside slopes, but they also discourage many from moving to such locations. From the slower processes of soil creep to the faster earth flows and the life-threatening disasters caused by landslides and mud and debris flows, California represents a laboratory for these earth movements set in motion by the force of gravity.

Slower Movement

Soil creep is common on California hillside slopes where deep layers of loose regolith and soil are weathered from the bedrock below. Though gravity may pull the loose materials down at only around 1 cm (0.4 inches) per year, tremendous masses of debris can be delivered down slope over time. Trees adjust by bending back up and telephone poles, fences, and other structures lean at an angle downhill. If you notice these features on a California slope that does not receive heavy winter snows, soil creep may be the culprit. Over many years, soil creep has gradually destroyed homes and other structures built by those who did not look for its subtle clues. Irrigation, cutting and filling, and destroying vegetation cover frequently accelerate movement on such slopes.

Earth flows are common throughout California where loose surface materials have been saturated, lubricated, and made heavier by water and where stabilizing vegetation has been cleared or burned. The size of these earthflows ranges from a few square meters to entire hillside slopes. The entire flow may occur in a few days or in a few minutes. Typically, material breaks away along a crevice, leaving a horseshoe-shaped scarp. Gravity pulls the loosened lobe of material downhill, where it is deposited as the equally recognizable toe of the flow. Since these associated features can often be visually linked to the same event, they stand out on many slopes throughout California. Earth flows are especially common on cleared and heavily grazed slopes in the Coast Ranges after prolonged heavy rains.

Fast and Furious

A special type of earth flow is spontaneous **liquefaction**. This occurs when the supporting structure of clay soils or other loose sediment collapses, usually aided by high water tables and shaking. The material flows similar to a viscous fluid. Different types of liquefaction have been recorded, and they will occur during California's many earthquakes. The loose fill used to extend land for development into San Francisco Bay and some areas around Marina del Rey and Venice are examples of the most vulnerable types of substrate. During the 1906 San Francisco and 1989 Loma Prieta earthquakes, Bay Area residents were reminded of the dangers of building on these earth-turned-to-jello fills.

Landslides

Perhaps the most dangerous and devastating examples of mass wasting are California's frequent landslides, when entire rock masses or parts of hillsides break off and slide downhill under the force of gravity. The abundance of freshly faulted, crumbled, and weathered rock material hanging along countless steep slopes creates landslide-prone areas across parts of California.

In the Coast Ranges Landslides are especially common in the Coast Ranges where serpentine rocks of the Franciscan melange have been crushed and crumbled by faulting. Where looming on steep slopes that have been undercut by streams or human activity, especially when saturated by heavy winter rains, these rocks become very slippery. Such slopes frequently break away and

slide downhill. These slides have destroyed structures on slopes near downtown San Francisco and Telegraph Hill in the 1990s, and they have caused millions of dollars of damage in every other Bay Area county. Many of the deaths and injuries and the destruction of hundreds of homes and businesses during the downpours of January, 1982, were caused by such landslides. Though the north Coast Ranges are heavily forested, the same combination of factors may produce local conditions where landslides deliver more material down slopes than any other process, including running water.

There are many notorious Coast Ranges slides. Devil's Slide has been active for years on the steep slopes around Hwy. 1 south of San Francisco. Here, the Pilarcitos Fault has helped weaken falling rock masses. Devil's Slide presents a dangerous threat and a constant headache to road crews because it drops directly into the sea.

Residents of Big Sur are accustomed to becoming isolated by large and small landslides over Hwy. 1. In 1983, a more massive landslide broke a steep hillside from the top and crumbled it hundreds of meters down to the sea, destroying Hwy. 1 along the Big Sur coast. An impressive scar was left by this slide. It cut Big Sur off from other parts of California for months during and after the heavy El Nino storms of 1983. As expected, the 1998 El Nino brought a repeat performance of devastation and isolation along Big Sur's coast.

Farther north, Clear Lake once drained west into the Russian River until the largest landslide in California blocked it a few centuries ago. Today, most of the drainage from the now higher lake flows east into the Sacramento River.

Landslides in Southern California Landslides have impacted landscapes in parts of southern California's Transverse and Peninsular Ranges for many thousands of years. About 17,000 years ago, one of the largest slides known to North America broke away from Blackhawk Mountain at the base of the northern San Bernardino Mountains. Giant blocks of limestone slid down Blackhawk Canyon and onto the desert floor on a cushion of compressed air at speeds up to 435 km (270 miles) per hour in about eighty seconds. The more than 24 sq km (10 square mile) slide is up to 30 m (100 feet) thick southeast of Lucerne Valley. Perhaps it is no coincidence that it occurred during the peak of the last Ice Age, when the area was wetter than today.

A giant slide broke off Martinez Mountain on the east side of the Santa Rosa Mountains about 15,000–20,000 years ago. After travelling about 7.5 km (4.5 miles) and dropping more than 1,800 m (about 6,000 feet), the enormous blocks of rubble were deposited on the desert floor that is now south of Palm Desert and La Quinta.

Many of the more recent and notorious southern California slides have occurred along populated steep coastal slopes from Santa Barbara and Ventura to Los

Heavy rains and steep, unstable slopes combined to create a classic California landslide at La Conchita/Seaside along Ventura County's northwest coastline. Fresh rock exposures near the top mark where the slide suddenly broke away. Residents in homes at the base of the slide miraculously escaped without injury.

Angeles and Orange Counties. Though many have devastated some of the most famous and highest-priced seaside communities in Malibu, Palos Verdes Peninsula, and Laguna, slides are not limited to those areas. After repeated drenchings from record storms in 1995, residents of the small seaside community of La Conchita southeast of Santa Barbara heard loud rumblings. The steep slope above began to break away. As residents ran from their homes to safety, an enormous chunk of the hillside above slumped down from a widening crevice, pulverizing or damaging several homes below.

In 1926, a much larger seaside cliff at Point Fermin on the southeastern end of the Palos Verdes Hills gave way. Rock layers which dip toward the sea and were cut by waves were probably set in motion by human activity, especially excessive watering that accumulated in the expanding layers below. Today, broken chunks of San Pedro Street and building foundations destroyed by this slide hang dramatically over the cliffs above the ocean.

The much larger Portuguese Bend Landslide was mapped in 1946; it had impacted the southwestern edge of the Palos Verdes Peninsula to the ocean for at least 37,000 years. Nevertheless, houses were being built on it by the 1950s, causing the slide to expand and accelerate. Due to water from irrigation and septic systems of more than 150 homes, and the fill and vibrations from the highway at the base of the slide, dipping rock layers began to move toward the sea cliffs.

As the center of the slide's surface subsided and the base was raised up 1 m (3 feet) per year, material moved toward the ocean from the head of the slide at even greater rates. Power lines, pipes, roads, and structures have been repeatedly sheared, buckled, crumbled, and rebuilt in the slide, which usually accelerates after each heavy rainy season. Attempts to stabilize the slide include driving gigantic stakes through it.

The 1998 El Nino rains reminded some residents of southern Orange County why they should not build on unstable slopes. National media coverage concentrated on the area around the Laguna Hills, displaying graphic shots of expensive homes and condominiums teetering, then falling down steep embankments that were weakened by the storms. Because many of the developments were recently built, onlookers wondered if Californians will ever realize that those who do not learn from history are doomed to repeat it.

Malibu Slides   Of all the Malibu slides and slump blocks, especially along and near Pacific Coast Highway, Big Rock is one of the largest and most notorious. Big Rock Landslide is a 4.7 sq km (1.8 square mile) coast-facing block of the Santa Monica Mountains which is falling down to Pacific Coast Highway and the sea. After record rains in 1983, its movement was measured in cm (inches) per day as widening crevices opened, separating the head of the slide from the Santa Monicas. There was genuine concern that the slide might break away into the sea, taking the highway and scores of homes with it. Again, there was plenty of fault to be shared.

Developers were blamed for building on the slide, the county was blamed for issuing the permits, residents were blamed for the septic systems and irrigation of exotic plants that weighted and lubricated the slide, and Caltrans was blamed for cutting and other road construction at the base of the slide. All of the parties readied their lawyers as one special courtroom was designed for what might have been the greatest litigation proceeding in U.S. history. A last minute out-of-court settlement seemed to leave all the parties equally unhappy. Meanwhile, pumps were installed to pull water out of the slide, and perforated piping drained water out of its side; the slide slowed dramatically in the following years.

As this south side of the Santa Monica Mountains is lifted along the Malibu Fault Zone, Pacific Coast Highway and all who live around it and use it must look up to the freshly crumbled, weathering material lurking above. Nature sent another round of dramatic reminders of her power during the 1998 El Nino year. More than fifty inches of rain fell on the surrounding mountains that year. So many slides were reactivated that the Pacific Coast Highway was closed for more than twenty days. Clearing and stabilizing the largest slide of about 300,000 cubic meters cost $20 million during several months of work. Some residents and road workers questioned whether this section of California Route 1 between Santa Monica and Oxnard (once known as Roosevelt Highway) should have ever been built.

When will the next slide become active? This is a question that too many California hillside residents must ask.

This slide covered Pacific Coast Highway in Malibu after the 1998 El Nino storms poured more than thirty inches of rain on surrounding steep slopes. Traffic was blocked for weeks; the road was narrowed for months and not fully opened until the following November. There were numerous other devastating, multimillion-dollar slides, such as at Big Sur, along the California coast during 1998.

Watch for Falling Rocks

Rock falls accumulate as talus slopes and talus cones at the base of California's steepest slopes and cliffs, especially in the Sierra Nevada. After blocks are weathered and loosened, gravity tumbles them down. They create obvious hazards for the unknowing visitor searching for that perfect view or, on private lands, the unaware developer or future homeowner looking for the lot with the perfect view.

Rock falls are particularly common on such steep, glacier-carved cliffs as those in Yosemite and Kings Canyon National Parks. In 1980, three hikers were killed by rock slides near Yosemite Falls. On July 10, 1996, an exceptionally huge mass of weathered rock broke off from the cliff between Glacier and Washburn Points in Yosemite National Park. More than 25,000 tons of rock came cascading down 2,400 feet onto the valley floor at Happy Isles. One visitor was killed and more than a dozen people were injured as the impact from the slide toppled about one-quarter square mile of trees. The dust cloud kicked up by this slide was so thick that breathing was difficult for hours. When it settled, fifty acres of the valley floor were covered by 2 cm (1 inch) of granite dust. In June, 1999, another deadly Yosemite rock slide made the news.

Don't Go with the Flow

Debris flows and mudflows have also caused death and destruction throughout California history and have shaped many California landscapes. In northern California, water from melting ice has mobilized boulders and debris on glacial moraines in the Klamaths. These debris flows carried material several kms (miles) downstream from the moraines at Swift, Canyon, and Deer Creeks and left deposits up to 100 m (300 feet) high containing large

boulders. Debris and mudflows have raced down Shasta and other Cascade volcanoes when warm rains or sudden heat waves melt heavy snow packs. House-size boulders were carried with such a flow down Mud Creek from a Shasta glacier in 1924. Sudden heat from volcanic activity or eruptions is capable of causing devastating flows (called lahars) on these volcanoes.

More frequent and just as dangerous are the mud and debris flows shaping landscapes mostly in southern and eastern California's arid and semiarid regions. These processes that build alluvial fans and bajadas will be examined in the next section.

Mud and debris flows can also occur in wetter California climates, especially where protective vegetation has been disturbed or destroyed. Another of Nature's reminders came to northern California residents of Rio Nido (along the Russian River) in February, 1998. Record rains brought rivers of mud that devastated the community, forced evacuations, and destroyed homes.

That Sinking Feeling

Subsidence of relatively level surfaces has also posed problems for many Californians. It is usually a slow process caused by settling of loose fill or the pumping of oil, gas, or water that relieves pressure from underground reservoirs. In 1995, it was reported that Treasure Island, the military's artificial extension of Yerba Buena Island in San Francisco Bay, had subsided from about 14 feet above sea level (asl) to 9 feet asl, primarily due to the 1989 Loma Prieta earthquake. Costs to save Treasure Island were estimated at $500 million.

Thousands of square kilometers (miles) of the San Joaquin Valley have subsided more than 25 cm (10 inches), mostly due to overdrafting of groundwater reservoirs. Broken pipelines and roads are examples of the problems caused as one area has dropped nearly 10 m

(30 feet). These problems extend into the Delta region, where reclamation of wetlands and farming of peat soils has caused many islands to subside several feet below sea level. However, subsidence is not limited to groundwater overdrafts or the Great Valley and Delta.

Oil pumped from the Wilmington oil field east of Terminal Island near Long Beach since 1937 decreased subsurface fluid pressures and caused subsidence. Subsidence of up to 10 m (30 feet) in an area the same shape as the oil field being pumped damaged bridges and buildings. Engineers constructed higher dikes to block ocean waters from the industrial area now below sea level. Salt water was later pumped into the oil reservoir to stabilize fluid pressures and subsidence and to force out more oil.

There are few places in California immune from mass wasting processes set in motion due to the force of gravity. Even more important, however, is that nearly every California landscape is shaped or impacted by running water, the subject of the next section.

Landforms Made by Running Water

A view of any California landscape is a view of landforms carved or deposited by running water. These are also known as **fluvial landforms**. There are other processes working on California landscapes. Glaciers, winds, and waves have also eroded, transported, and deposited material in parts of the state. However, none of these rival the significance of running water when considering dominant external forces shaping landscapes in California.

Recently uplifted mountains across California provide streams with plenty of freshly weathered material to cut and carry downstream; energized streams carve deep, narrow, V-shaped canyons with steep slopes. Their tremendous sediment loads are deposited on adjacent valley floors, filling California basins with layers of alluvium. We will begin our discussion of California landscapes made by running water in cismontane California, which is the more moist part of the state on the ocean side of the highest crests. We will then turn to drier transmontane California on the "opposite" or rainshadow sides of the highest crests, where running water shapes very different landscapes.

Water Erodes in Cismontane California

Rivers Follow Paths of Least Resistance There are numerous examples of California rivers that have established their courses along structural weaknesses as they follow paths of least resistance. One of the best examples is the north–south path of the Kern River cutting into the Sierra Nevada along the Kern Canyon Fault. The Klamath, Mad, and Eel Rivers flow within folded and tortured

White water cascades down Sierra Nevada's steep slopes. Here, the roaring Kings River cuts a V-shaped canyon deeper, as it has for centuries. Steep slopes and fast currents indicate that this young river is in the degradational stage, while smaller tributaries cut their own lesser canyons.

structures in northwest California. Meanwhile, the Russian River headwaters in the north, the Salinas River farther south, and similar streams follow southeast–northwest structural features similar to the Coast Ranges. The Salinas River and some of its tributaries flow within the confines of parallel, elongated structural depressions. Once established, many of these rivers cut their own deep courses.

Young, Energetic Streams Degrade High-energy white-water streams continue to slice deep, narrow canyons and gorges into youthful topography of the Klamaths, Cascade volcanoes, Sierra Nevada, Transverse, Peninsular and parts of the Coast Ranges, and even through many of California's dry desert ranges. The Klamath Mountains—with their adjacent narrow ridges and canyons connected by steep slopes—are the most impressively rugged. Scott Valley is the only flatland to interrupt this Klamath topography that challenges the hardiest traveller.

You might expect thick forests of the northern Coast Ranges to quell the erosion caused by permanent streams. However, frequent landslides in weak serpentine rock formations can deliver freshly broken material to the sometimes raging torrents below. Less predictable seasonal streams more common to the southern Coast Ranges often drain bare slopes ravaged by summer and fall brush fires; they carry away the tons of loose and exposed soil and regolith and slice deeper in their brief but muddy winter rages.

Similar conditions are common during the brief winter storms which follow intense drought and fire seasons in southern California's Transverse and Peninsular Ranges. In addition to fires, other natural and human events in the mountains of coastal California provide vulnerable, fresh sediment waiting to be carved and carried away by water.

Even the more consistent rivers and tributary streams of the Sierra Nevada are cutting deep V-shaped notches into resistant granite slopes. They accomplish most of their work during spring snow melts. Standing next to raging rivers like the Kings following a heavy snow season, one can hear the sounds of boulders the size of trucks crashing below these powerful currents. Degradational streams also rule on these steep slopes. A variety of other landscapes are forming as California rivers cut through recently uplifted terrain.

Numerous California streams have continued to stubbornly flow and cut in place as renewed mountain building lifts surrounding landscapes. These antecedent streams include the Santa Margarita River northeast of Oceanside and the Santa Ana River, which is slicing through very recent uplift in the northern Santa Ana Mountains. Antecedent streams in the Transverse Ranges include the Ventura River north of Ventura and Malibu Creek, which has carved a spectacular north–south gouge into the east–west trending Santa Monica Mountains.

Several streams in the Coast Ranges first follow the northwest-southeast trend of inland valleys, then suddenly veer and cut through direct gorges to the coast. Alameda Creek through Niles Canyon east of Fremont, the Pajaro River across the San Andreas Rift Zone to Monterey Bay, and the Cuyama River east of Santa Maria are examples. Even Lone Pine Creek flowing east from the Sierra Nevada continues to slice in place through the recently uplifted Alabama Hills.

Some of California's more interesting landscapes result when deep notches are carved by rejuvenated streams into recently uplifted terraces. Especially prominent river terraces represent former valley floors lifted above the Smith, Klamath, Trinity, and Eel Rivers. Weaver Creek near Weaverville has cut a fresh channel up to 120 m (400 feet) deep since the Pleistocene.

San Diego's Coast Along the coast of San Diego County, more than a dozen marine terraces represent raised platforms now overlooking the Pacific. Recently rejuvenated streams have since sliced deep notches into those terraces as waters race west to the ocean. At the end of the last Ice Age, sea levels rose up to 90 m (300 feet). These streams abruptly slowed at their higher base levels, depositing their sediment loads into San Diego's famous coastal baymouth bars and the lagoons behind them. Similar coastal processes formed landscapes at the mouths of other California canyons. But, the combination of these features is most conspicuous next to I-5 in northern San Diego County.

Farther inland in the Peninsular Ranges, streams alternately flow gently through broad valleys on the surface of faulted block benches, then cascade and slice over bench edges through deep notches down to the next lower block to the west.

Making Deposits

Just as these streams are eroding and transporting material, the sediment they must deposit on surrounding valleys or shorelines forms very different landscapes. As soon as the fast-moving streams blast out of steep mountain canyons, their velocities slow on the subdued relief of valley floors, and they deposit course alluvium. The first materials to be deposited at the base of these mountains are the coarsest gravels, rocks, and even boulders that may overflow channels onto roads and into developments during heavy rainstorms. Such repeated events over centuries pile up fan-shaped structures at canyon mouths especially in drier areas of southern and eastern California. In wetter regions, substantial year-round stream flow cuts and carries such material farther downstream. As the slowing streams flow farther out over valley floors or to the ocean, they deposit the finer sand, silt, and clay particles that make up most of California's flood plains.

These broader flood plains contain more lethargic, meandering aggradational streams that have deposited the fine fertile sediments in California's most productive farmlands. In the Central Valley, the Sacramento and San Joaquin Rivers and their many tributaries laid thick deposits as broad areas of the valley were flooded from heavy Sierra Nevada snow melts. Fertile soils of the Salinas Valley, Los Angeles Basin, and dozens of other California valleys were formed from similar deposits.

Fluvial Processes and Landforms Common to California's Dry Climates

Ironically, some of the most dramatic landscapes carved and deposited by running water are found in California's drier regions. Here, persistent drought has left slopes barren and vulnerable to the rare heavy rainstorm. In transmontane California, sporadic and unreliable precipitation episodes can dump one year's average rainfall within hours, and such events can occur any time of year, particularly during summer in California's southeast de-

TAMING THE COLORADO

For centuries, the aggrading Colorado River dumped sediments toward the Gulf of California. This formed the delta that diverted the river away from the Imperial Valley and into Mexico. In the early 1900s, those who tried to divert a portion of the Colorado back toward the Imperial Valley were reminded of the power of running water. Their canals and diversion projects silted up from 1902–1904 until a great flood in January 1905 turned the entire river toward the Imperial Valley to fill the Salton Sea. The Colorado was not controlled until February, 1907, after it had eroded deep channels in the Alamo and New Rivers, causing damage along an 80 km (50 mile) stretch from the Salton Sea.

A classic alluvial fan pours out of the mountains and into the California desert east of Palm Springs. The most recent mud and debris flows have left freshly disturbed surfaces and deposits that appear lighter. The fan is crossed by thin, linear dirt roads.

Once the rare downpour, often generated by an isolated summer thunderstorm, forms over a drainage basin, these loose materials combine with water and rush from the steep slopes into rills and gullies. Then, they are channeled into deeper canyons. The momentum of these viscous mud and debris flows can carry truck-sized boulders out of narrow canyons only to dump them on the desert floor below.

A typical event may last only a few hours, but a series of these catastrophes over centuries has carved intricate patterns of rills and gullies onto desert slopes. The events have built impressive **alluvial fans** at the mouths of canyons, fans made of successive debris and mudflows.

From Young Alluvial Fans to Old Age Desert Landscapes   Some of the most conspicuous fans are at the bases of slopes surrounding the Owens Valley, especially at the base of the White Mountains and then moving east and south, such as on slopes around Death Valley. Visitors to these landscapes who are unaware of the consequences of sudden, violent rainstorms have been swept away by flows that roar out of canyons, damaging or burying everything in their paths. These processes and landscapes are witnessed throughout the Basin and Range and in steep terrains to the south, into Mexico.

Similar events have deposited alluvial fans at the base of southern California coastal mountains, especially during heavy winter storms that follow the drought season's wildfires. Heavily populated alluvial fans and the catastrophic events that shape them are common at the base of mountains surrounding the Los Angeles Basin and nearby valleys. Residents in canyons and on these fans live in constant danger of becoming the next victims, especially after fires ravage the slopes above.

With time, adjacent alluvial fans may continue to build until they coalesce into gently sloping bajadas (the more subdued surfaces of pediment which slope from the base of the mountains to the playas or valleys below). In the absence of recent mountain building, the rugged topography gradually yields and is denuded into the very sediment it produced. In older landscapes, only inselbergs

serts. On coastal slopes, especially in southern California, isolated landscapes are left even more barren for brief periods after summer and fall wildfires. Equally dramatic events erode and deposit tons of loose debris, regolith, and soil exposed by fires to winter rains, creating landforms similar to those described below.

Much of the spectacular scenery of the Basin and Range and the rainshadow slopes of southern California's recently lifted mountains has been etched by these processes. Weathering continues to produce abundant loose materials waiting for very rare heavy rainstorms.

(tiny remnants of eroded mountains) may protrude above vast, expanding old-age pediplains. Geographically, we have moved from the fresh gouges and fans typical of the steeper Basin and Range to the mostly gentler topography typical of the older aggrading landscapes of the Mojave.

Desert Playas Salt playas and saline lakes are common throughout transmontane California. They are found in desert basins where abundant Ice Age waters evaporated and where recent wetting and evaporation have left salts behind. Interior drainage is the rule in California's desert valleys as brief floods and shallow groundwaters are trapped with the minerals they have carried. During the Ice Ages, the Owens and other rivers had up to ten times more water than when they were discovered by Europeans; a series of streams and lakes may have flowed from the Owens to Death Valley through the Mojave Desert to the Colorado River. The water is almost gone, but the salt playas remain. Their hard clay and crusty, bright, salty surfaces are not only testimony to today's hot, dry climate, but their minerals are often mined (a topic covered in Chapter 2). Names like Badwater in Death Valley and Soda Lake near Baker give clues to the nature of these basins so important to California's desert landscapes.

Badlands Classic badlands have been cut by water in some of California's driest regions. The combination of steep slopes, loose materials, sporadic precipitation, and a lack of protective vegetation leave surfaces vulnerable to erosion by water. Intricate repetitive patterns of thousands of rills and gullies have been cut into the delicate volcanic ash around Ubehebe Crater and in the mudstones at Zabriskie Point in Death Valley during rare downpours. There are many other examples of badlands in southern California deserts, including the Borrego Badlands, best viewed from Font's Point. Even marginal areas such as the hills along Hwy. 60 between Riverside/Moreno Valley and Banning/Beaumont have been appropriately named "The Badlands." It is not surprising that streams and dry washes are choked with sediment when heavy rain finally falls.

Many dry slopes exhibit parallel retreat which produces the rugged, steep landscapes common to California deserts. Excellent examples can be found in a quick survey of the landscapes above Needles, which gave this desert town its appropriate name.

Accelerated Erosion

Accelerated erosion is destroying soil and producing higher sediment yields in streams and rivers in parts of California. Whether the cause is overgrazing, overfarm-

ing, burning, clear cutting, or extensive off-road vehicle use, deep rills and gullies and badlands topography are cutting into once productive soils across the state. These careless land-use practices may produce quick profits. However, even the briefest landscape survey reveals how the long-term productivity of these lands and the economies they support could eventually be destroyed.

Some examples of accelerated erosion include slopes within the Coast Ranges and around the Oxnard Plain. Areas of off-road destruction near Gorman and in Ballinger Canyon on the northern boundary of Santa Barbara and Ventura Counties are just a few of the many other examples. Clearly, the processes and landscapes of running water not only dominate California physical landscapes, but they are being substantially modified by Californians.

California's Glacial Landscapes

When the **Ice Ages** began (before the Pleistocene Epoch, more than two million years ago), ice accumulated on California's high mountain crests. Large glaciers advanced and cut deeper valleys into the Sierra Nevada, Klamath, and Cascade Mountains. While continental ice sheets extended from Canada into the central United States, only these local mountain/valley (alpine) glaciers carved into California highlands. Periods of cooling (glaciations) allowed the expansion of massive glaciers to lower elevations; during warmer, drier periods (deglaciations), California's ice fields retreated or completely melted away.

Today, we live in an interglacial period. Scientists are using many methods to study these glacial advances. For instance, they date glacial till (debris eroded, transported, and deposited by glaciers) and other evidence which is sometimes sandwiched between lava flows and other geologic events.

The El Portal tills may have been deposited by the most extensive ice caps and glaciers about 750,000 years ago during the "Nebraskan" Ice Age. The last glacial stage ("Wisconsin") was not as expansive as it peaked about 18,000–20,000 years ago and ended about 10,000 years ago, but it left the most recent glacial landscapes. Alternate cool and warm periods since the last ice age have caused the expansion and then the complete ablation of numerous tiny ice patches remaining in California. Today, there are about sixty tiny glaciers remaining in the Sierra Nevada. There are also patches of ice in the Klamaths and California's Cascades (including about five small glaciers on Mount Shasta's slopes). The largest ice fields include the Palisade Glacier west of Big Pine and Lyell Glacier between Yosemite Valley and June Lakes. However, the spectacular erosional and depositional glacial features represent landmarks left by cooler, wetter periods of California's very recent past.

Why and Where the Glaciers Grow

Accumulation of glacial ice in California is enhanced by cooler temperatures and increased precipitation. We would expect the following combination of most favorable geographic conditions to encourage the growth of glaciers: the highest mountain ranges with the most extensive high altitude surface areas, more northerly locations, and north–south trending barriers facing the Pacific to block moisture from eastward-moving Pacific storms. It is not surprising that the Sierra Nevada exhibits the most impressive glacial features in or near California.

Individual mountains, such as Shasta, may be farther north and nearly as tall as the Sierra Nevada, but they do not represent such massive barriers; consequently, they are not capable of accumulating as much ice during glacial periods. The Klamath Mountains are neither as tall or extensive as the Sierra Nevada; their impressive glacial features are still no match for a Yosemite, Kings Canyon, or the moraines of the eastern Sierra Nevada. The Coast Ranges are not nearly as tall, and they are located adjacent to ocean waters; marine air masses with moderate winter temperatures frequently produce snow levels above their peaks. Although nearly as high, the White-Inyo Range (several miles east of the Sierra Nevada), is not as massive and is located on the rainshadow side of its bigger brother. Though glacial landscapes are found in parts of each of these ranges, the Sierra Nevada Mountains have the best combination of conditions in California to encourage growth of alpine glaciers.

The farthest south we see any evidence of alpine glacial landscapes in California is in the San Bernardino Mountains, where there is evidence of only tiny Pleistocene Epoch glaciers. Only a few miles south, the San Jacinto Mountains—high enough, but incapable of capturing and holding much ice and snow due to less extensive high alpine terrain—exhibit no glacial landscapes. All other mountains to the south are too low, dry, and warm to support glacial activity.

Glacial Scenery in California

In the highlands of northern and central California we find spectacular erosional scars which remain from extensive glaciation. As compacted ice and snow (firn) accumulated in those highlands, it began to move downhill under gravity's force. Rocks were repeatedly plucked away from those highlands until bowl-shaped depressions (cirques) formed at the base of many peaks and ridges. This erosion transformed so many rounded highlands into a series of individual sharp peaks (horns) and sawtooth ridges (aretes).

During warmer, drier periods, melting ice filled the cirques and other depressions with glacial lakes (tarns). During cooler, wetter periods, the ice rivers advanced downhill, scraping away and plucking at bedrock surfaces. Where two glaciers merged and combined forces or where bedrock weakened, they eroded faster, creating glacial stairways. Imbedded coarser material carved grooves in the bedrock as the glaciers moved through; more widespread scouring polished other rock surfaces like sandpaper on wood.

Smaller tributary glaciers fed ice and debris to the massive trunk valley glaciers which carved much deeper U-shaped troughs from once V-shaped stream canyons. When the glaciers finally retreated and the ice melted, the smaller tributaries became hanging valleys, complete with waterfalls plunging abruptly over the vertical cliffs on the sides of the main valleys. Milky glacial meltwater carried the fine glacial flour (scoured by ice against bedrock) and filled the chains of paternoster lakes remaining behind on the now U-shaped valley floors.

Nearly all of the jagged exposed bedrock and rugged mountains of the high Sierra and Klamaths contain classic

Looking north into the Trinity Alps toward the Klamath Mountains. The Trinity Alps exhibit aretes, cirques, U-shaped valleys, moraines, and other typical glacial features.

examples of ice-eroded landscapes. At June Lakes in the eastern Sierra Nevada, the Rush Creek glacier rolled downslope only to be split by Reversed Peak. The smaller fork split to the east, carving into the valley where Gulf and June Lakes are today. The larger fork carved a deeper valley to the north, where Silver and Grant Lakes currently pour into Rush Creek. With the ice gone, today's Reversed Creek drains, oddly, directly toward the Sierra Nevada from June and Gulf Lakes. It then turns north around Reversed Peak, finally flowing through the more deeply carved canyon into Silver and Grant Lakes and into Rush Creek and then Mono Lake.

Like giant conveyor belts, the glaciers once transported glacial till (unsorted rock debris eroded into and carried by the ice). The till was deposited and accumulated in huge piles called moraines, or it was left behind in the form of erratic boulders and other debris as the glaciers receded. As a shoe would push mounds of soft sand ahead and to the side, the valley glaciers built hills of lateral moraines to their sides and terminal moraines at their toes, especially as they poured into valleys beyond the mouths of canyons. Though they are found throughout the Sierra Nevada and Klamaths, the moraines are most spectacular in the eastern Sierra Nevada, where they are hundreds of meters high. Fallen Leaf Lake south of Lake Tahoe is dammed by a moraine, as is Convict Lake southeast of Mammoth. West of Bishop, McGee Creek, Pine Creek, and other streams up and down the eastern Sierra Nevada flow east out of canyons containing impressive moraines.

Yosemite   One of the world's most spectacular and classic examples of a glacially carved U-shaped valley is the Yosemite Valley. Where the Merced River now cascades down its glacial stairway (including Nevada and Vernal Falls) in Little Yosemite Valley and merges with Tenaya Canyon, enormous glaciers once ground into Yosemite Valley. The principal glacier receded for the last time only about 10,000 years ago, but the El Portal Glacier of about 750,000 years ago was the largest of them all. Growing to 1,800 m (6,000 feet) thick and 60 km (37 miles) long, it cut Yosemite Valley more than 600 m (2000 feet) below its present level. This valley glacier extended past El Portal, where it deposited a terminal moraine. The lesser and final "Wisconsin" Glacier left a wall-to-wall lake behind its terminal moraine at Bridalveil Meadow. Typical of many California glacial lakes, it has since filled with sediment and supports one of today's meadows.

Scrapes and gouges on Yosemite's rocks are mere details compared to the spectacular cliffs, hanging valleys, and waterfalls left behind by its glaciers. The spectacular shear cliffs of El Capitan rise 884 m (2,898 feet) above the valley. Numerous joints and fractures on the side of Half Dome made the rocks vulnerable to erosional forces of the valley glaciers that carried them away. Ribbon Falls is the highest single falls in the valley at 492 m

(1,612 feet), but it dries to a trickle for much of the year. Yosemite Creek plunges over 435 m (1,430 foot) high Upper Yosemite Falls, then crashes and cascades onto the rocks only to spill over 98 m (320 foot) Lower Yosemite Falls. The upper falls is one of the highest in the world; after a wet year, the entire falls has few rivals. The many falls and hanging valleys were once capped by tributary glaciers which could never cut rock as fast as the gigantic trunk glaciers into which they merged. These spectacular glacial landscapes do not begin or end with Yosemite.

Glacial Landscapes Beyond Yosemite   To the south, the south fork of the Kings River now flows through Kings Canyon. This is one of the deepest canyons carved in the Sierra Nevada and is strikingly similar to Yosemite Valley. Splendid glacial landscapes with classic horns, aretes, and U-shaped valleys are common throughout Sequoia National Park's high country. Glacial activity diminished rapidly south of the Kaweah River and the line between Visalia and Olancha. The 11 km (7 mile) long Kern Canyon Glacier was the most southerly of any major California glacier, advancing just south of this line, down to about 1,750 m (5,700 feet) asl.

The Klamaths were also heavily glaciated with up to sixty glaciers from west of Red Bluff to the Oregon border during several Pleistocene Epoch glacial stages. Typical and dramatic glacial features are common in the granitic bedrock of Klamath's high country. The most remarkable landscapes are similar to the Sierra Nevada in the Siskiyou and Salmon Mountains, the Trinity Alps, and the most impressive glacial features of the Marble Mountain Wilderness. The Trinity Alps glaciers extended as much as 18 km (11 miles) long down to 750 m (2,450 feet) asl. Conspicuous glacial deposits and erratic boulders abound in Trinity's Coffee, Deer, Swift, and Canyon Creeks. Today, patches of ice up to only 2 hectares (5 acres) remain by the end of summer near the Thompson and Sawtooth Mountains.

Small glaciers formed only near California's highest Basin and Range peaks. This more subtle glacial topography dots highlands and a few canyons of the White Mountains. Because this region was in the rainshadow of the magnificent Sierra Nevada ice fields, the greatest Pleistocene Epoch changes brought cooler and wetter conditions. Many of today's intermittent streams and rivers became perennial as inland lakes filled with water and were connected by those streams well into the Mojave Desert. The Owens River flowed with ten times more water and Death Valley filled with Manly Lake up to 275 m (900 feet) deep during the wettest periods. Some researchers believe that a waterway may have flowed all the way from Lake Russel and western Nevada through the Mojave and to the Colorado River, into the Gulf of California.

Just as glaciers have left scars on some of California's modern landscapes, so wind has been working to erode, transport, and deposit materials. These landscapes are the focus of the next section.

California Landforms Made by Wind

Of all the denudational processes and landscapes, wind is one of the least important in California and in the world. This relative statement can be misleading unless we consider the enormous tonnage of fresh material being eroded, transported, and deposited around our state by all natural processes.

There are two general settings where wind becomes a more important agent in landscape evolution in California. Where waves are pushing sand onto California beaches, changes in tide levels and other adverse conditions may create disturbed sites where permanent plant cover is not established. Along these vulnerable, isolated coastal strips, wind can carry loose sand great distances. Additionally, in some of California's rainshadow deserts, precipitation is too sporadic to support protective plant cover. Again, wind may erode, transport, and deposit material; these processes polish desert rocks and create their own desert landscapes.

Wind Leaves Its Marks on Desert Landscapes

Throughout California deserts, patches of desert pavement have formed as weathering breaks particles into finer clays, silts, and sands which can be blown away by the wind. Additionally, clay surfaces alternately expand when wetted and contract when dried, pushing coarser pebbles toward the surface. The accumulated coarser particles are jammed together in a surface matrix which cannot be blown away by the wind. A poorly developed soil may form below this natural pavement.

Deflation denudes desert surfaces and forms blowouts and areas where sandy surfaces are carried away from the bases and roots of anchoring plants. Devil's Cornfield in Death Valley dramatically displays plants and their roots protruding above the windblown sand; numerous plants died because they could not hold on after losing their footing. New sources of windblown sand are continually weathered from exposed desert mountains and plains in California.

Dunes in the Basin and Range   In the Basin and Range, sand dunes accumulate where formerly free-moving wind and sand is finally blocked by mountain barriers. The sand is deposited in topographic traps or forced up the bases of mountains. The most impressive dunes are in or near the Death Valley area. The tallest dunes of up to 210 m (700 feet) are in the southern Eureka Valley. At the southeastern edge of Death Valley, the Dumont Dunes are 128 m (420 feet) high.

The dune fields within Panamint and Death Valley are not nearly as tall, but represent captivating lessons in natural history. Erratic winds keep the Star and other dunes shifting and changing shapes while they remain in the same place. Smaller dunes in northern Death Valley are more stabilized by mesquite, which taps into the shallow groundwater. All of these Basin and Range dunes share some striking similarities.

Low dunes have even accumulated in Saline Valley and south of Owens Lake. Following the draining of Owens Valley water to Los Angeles, thick, health-threatening alkali dust clouds rise and are swept around and away from the valley when winds are strong. More recent legal agreements with the City of Los Angeles (reviewed in Chapter 6) are designed to improve these conditions.

Mojave Dunes   In the Mojave Desert, Devil's Playground contains the tallest and largest dune field. Sand was transported to the area by the Mojave River, then blown by previously prevailing winds over thousands of years. Kelso Dunes (up to 168 m [550 feet] tall and 6.4

Winds seem to line up rows of parallel dunes in this part of Death Valley. Desert sands are often deposited in corners of the valley that are somewhat protected from the strongest winds by surrounding mountain barriers. Dune vegetation helps to stabilize the drifting sands.

km [4 miles] long) are the highest. Like most California dunes, they are composed mainly of lighter quartz and feldspars, but some heavy metals such as iron have oxidized, leaving a rusty stain to these dunes.

Southern Desert Dunes Far to the south, prevailing winds out of San Gorgonio (Banning) Pass blow sand, brought by the Whitewater River, from northwest to southeast across the Coachella and Imperial Valleys. The San Gorgonio Pass/Whitewater area exhibits some of the best ventifacts (stones and other objects shaped by wind-blown sand) in the state. Efforts to stabilize the shifting sand with trees, fences, and urban sprawl have helped. Still, high winds can blast sand against heavily abraded surfaces and create treacherous travel conditions. Active dunes occasionally threaten and actually consume parts of housing projects, such as in Cathedral City during the 1990s. Meanwhile, isolated classic barchan dunes migrate up to 30 m (100 feet) per year from near the Borrego Badlands area east toward the Salton Sea.

The Algodones Dunes (Sand Hills) on the southeast corner of California are the most expansive dunes in North America. Ridges of sand up to 80 m (250 feet) high trend perpendicular to the prevailing northwest winds. These winds have pushed this 72 km (45 mile) long dune field southeast into Mexico. Roads have been covered and canals filled with this blowing sand. At least portions of each of these dune fields have been altered by human activity. Ironically, these activities include aggressive attempts to stabilize them and to rectify the results of disturbances from off-road recreational vehicles.

Coastal Dunes

Similar problems are common to California's coastal dune fields, but there are also many differences. First, the sand in most of California's coastal dunes starts as weathered material from California's mountains that is transported by rivers and streams to the ocean. Once it is coughed out on the shoreline, usually during heavy winter and spring storms, constant wave action begins to work the sand along the coast, usually from north to south. Where weaker waves deposit sand (often in bays and protected inlets), the wind can now blow the sand inland or against the sides of protective promontories, where it is saved from further attack from the waves.

Because prevailing winds blow onshore along most of the California coast, accumulated sand dunes often migrate inland unless there is sufficient dune vegetation to anchor them down. Often, ice plant and other vegetation is introduced on these dunes to restabilize them after the native vegetation has been trampled or destroyed. Victims of migrating dunes include roads, farms, housing projects, and water reservoirs consumed by the sand.

Most sand dunes on California beaches take on light colors because they contain minerals high in silica; quartz is one of the most common minerals found on these dunes. Typically, darker minerals with less silica and more iron and magnesium are more easily attacked and destroyed by the weathering and abrasive processes encountered during the trip from the mountains to the sea. This usually leaves more resistant minerals such as quartz to dominate beach sand.

The processes that shape California's coastlines are reviewed in more detail in Appendix B following Chapter 6.

◆ SUMMARY

Where tectonic processes have slowed or ceased, weathering and erosion eventually will destroy mountains and level landscapes. In California, where there are abundant

Sand is coughed out of coastal streams and rivers, then worked along the coast by waves. Here, it is deposited as sand spit barriers, sometimes considered baymouth bars, that protect Bolinas Lagoon from pounding ocean waves near Stinson Beach. The quiet lagoon is now filling with mud carried and deposited by surrounding streams.

fresh outcrops and steep slopes, denudational processes work quickly and often dramatically. However, at this time in geologic history, California is situated on a remarkably active plate boundary, and the tectonic forces are winning the see-saw battle. Good examples are the many California mountain ranges growing faster than they are being destroyed. Most geologists agree that these mountain-building forces will continue to dominate over denudational forces in most of California into the near geologic future.

California exhibits spectacular diversity in its physical landscapes and in the geologic processes that shape them. The topographic features produced by these processes impact weather and climate, plants and animals, and hydrology throughout the state. Californians, willingly or not, also recognize their connections to these landscapes and processes. The cycles of change in our physical world are causing dramatic changes in our human landscapes and our everyday lives. These are topics for the following chapters.

SOME KEY TERMS AND TOPICS

accelerated erosion	Ice Ages	Pacific plate
alluvial fans	liquefaction	San Andreas Fault Zone
Big Bend	marine terraces	tectonic processes
denudation	mass wasting	volcanic activity
erosional processes	modern volcanic regions	weathering processes
fluvial processes/landforms	mountain building	wind (landforms made by)
glacial landscapes	North American plate	

Additional Key Terms and Topics

basaltic lava flows	geomorphology	stretching/pulling apart
composite volcanoes	geothermal energy	subduction
constructional processes	great earthquakes	synclinal troughs
differential weathering	hot springs	tectonic landforms
dunes	interglacial period	thrust fault (blind)
earthquake intervals	left-lateral fault	topography
exfoliation	limestone caverns	transform fault
folding	right-lateral fault	vertical faults
Garlock Fault	rock displacement	

Chapter 4

California's Weather and Climate

C an you find another place on earth the size of California displaying such *diversity* of climates? Depending on the classification system used, you may find examples similar to nearly every major climate group, except for tropical climates, somewhere in California. We could devote this entire book to California's weather events and climate zones and still not cover them all.

Just as California's climates significantly influence the shaping of its landscapes, the variety of geologic features and plant communities in the state (discussed in Chapters 2, 3, and 5) have significant influence on California's weather and climate. Though recognition of these and other *connections* is important, there are three major, more general geographic factors which have the greatest influence on California's weather and climate. These controlling factors are latitude (distance north from the equator), ocean air mass versus continental air mass influence (usually an east–west component, but strongly influenced by situation in relation to mountain barriers), and elevation above sea level. We begin our discussion with these three more general, dominant controls on California's weather and climate.

We will then consider many other factors that affect weather and climate and cause the numerous exceptions to our generalities. For example, gradual climate change has always played a role in shaping California landscapes, beginning long before humans arrived. However, changes in microclimates caused by people are relatively fast and dramatic. Today, there is increasing evidence that humans are changing California climates on a much grander scale. Because every Californian is impacted by these climate changes (drought, flood, heat, cold), every Californian has a stake in the results.

Cumulus clouds (only resembling smoke from a fire) boil up the windward slopes of the San Jacinto Mountains as moist air is forced to rise, expand, and cool to its dew point.

KEY ISSUES AND CONCEPTS

◆ Some knowledge of pressure systems, air masses, global circulation, and other basic concepts in atmospheric science is required to understand the state's weather events and climates.

◆ The formation and movement of dominant air masses greatly influence local and regional temperature and precipitation. Particularly noticeable in California are contrasts between moist, marine air masses (which are mild) and dry, continental air masses (with dramatic variations in temperatures).

◆ Temperatures are generally cooler and precipitation increases at higher elevations in the state. Important exceptions in California occur when stable temperature inversions trap cooler, stagnant air at lower elevations. Additionally, precipitation totals may decrease toward California's highest mountain peaks after clouds have dumped much of their moisture on lower and middle elevation mountain slopes.

◆ Summers are dominated by the East Pacific High Pressure, California's relatively cold ocean current, stable air, and coastal fog. Intense heat is common inland. With a few exceptions, summer precipitation is rare in most of the state and is usually isolated when it occurs.

◆ Autumn is a season of change in California when summer's inland heat, dominant sea breezes, and stable air become less reliable.

◆ Nearly every weather station in California (except for some in the southeast) experiences peak precipitation during winter. Though most of winter's low pressure systems are steered into the state from the north Pacific, a variety of middle latitude wave cyclones make each rainy season unique.

◆ Spring is another transitional period in California. Heat gradually returns to inland locations; winter's turbulence gives way to the East Pacific High and more stable air toward summer.

◆ The state's climates, topographic features, and human populations contribute to some of the poorest air quality and most dangerous fire seasons in the nation.

◆ Subtropical and middle latitude west coast Mediterranean climates dominate in cismontane California; dry climates dominate in transmontane California. Mountain ranges not only act as barriers to air masses, but may tower into elevations where patches of snowy forest and more isolated highland climates exist.

◆ Climographs illustrate the diversity between and seasonal changes within the state's climates. Weather extremes not revealed by climographs are common in California; they may result from unusual patterns such as El Niño/Southern Oscillation and blocking highs.

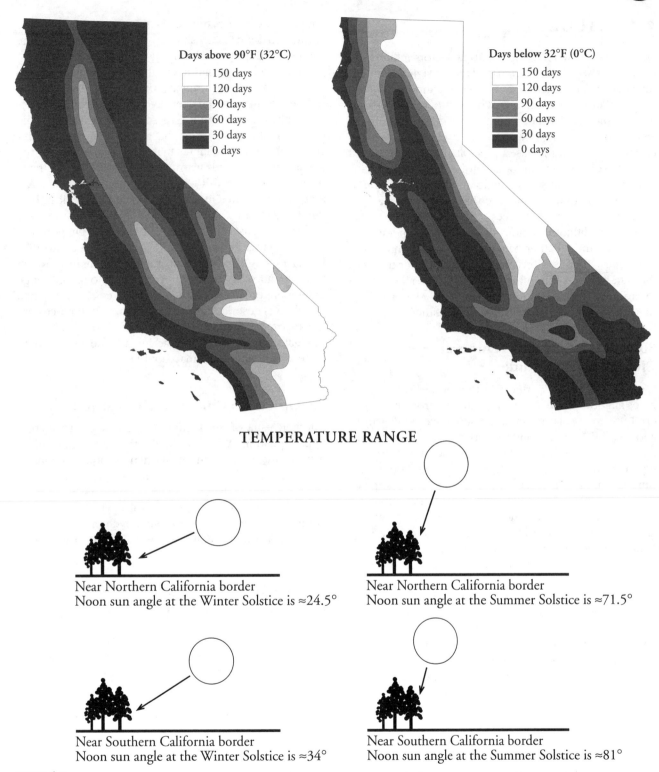

TEMPERATURE RANGE

Near Northern California border
Noon sun angle at the Winter Solstice is ≈24.5°

Near Northern California border
Noon sun angle at the Summer Solstice is ≈71.5°

Near Southern California border
Noon sun angle at the Winter Solstice is ≈34°

Near Southern California border
Noon sun angle at the Summer Solstice is ≈81°

MAP 4.1

Temperature Patterns. Many factors are responsible for temperature variations throughout
the state. Besides latitude and variations in solar radiation, the effects of ocean versus
continental air masses and elevation play important roles.

◆ LATITUDE

Like the other two major geographic factors influencing California's weather and climate, latitude significantly influences radiation, temperature, precipitation, humidity, and myriad other elements. When all other factors are equal—such as distance from the ocean, situation in relation to mountain barriers, and elevation—cooler temperatures and increased precipitation will be found as we travel north in California, farther from the equator. This is partly because sun angle and intensity decrease as we travel north during any time of the year across California's nearly 9½ degrees of latitude. However, this also leaves different regions of California vulnerable to air masses and weather patterns more common to their particular latitudes. Consequently, moving north across the state will result in more than just a general decrease in land and water surface temperatures. Map 4.1 illustrates how temperatures change with latitude.

Solar Radiation and Temperatures Change with Latitude

We start at the very northern border of the state (42 degrees latitude). Here, the angle of the sun from the southern horizon at solar noon (noon sun angle) ranges from a low of 24½ degrees on December 21 (winter solstice), to 48 degrees during the vernal (spring) and autumnal equinox, to a high of 71½ degrees from the horizon on June 21 (summer solstice). Note the dramatic change of sun angle and resulting intensity changes throughout the year. Additionally, dramatic change in the length of day and night—from very long summer days to very long winter nights—accompanies this annual cycle.

Near to and during the summer solstice, residents near the state's northern border, even with daylight savings time, see morning's twilight return by 5 A.M. After the long summer day, noticeable evening twilight remains after 10 P.M. The length of short winter daylight hours and long nights is just as dramatic, but reversed from summer, during the winter solstice.

The southern edge of the state is barely more than 32½ degrees latitude. Here, the winter noon sun is about 34 degrees from the southern horizon; it rises to nearly 57½ degrees during the vernal and autumnal equinox and to an annual high of almost 81 degrees at solar noon during the summer solstice.

The nearly ten degree difference in sun angle between northern and southern California results in increased solar radiation intensities toward the south, and it is partially responsible for differences in California's climate zones.

Still more dramatic are the seasonal changes in the length of day and night and the forty-seven degree annual change in sun angle at any one location. This en-

courages weather patterns, air masses, and temperature regimes to dramatically shift north across the state during summer and drop south during winter.

Almost all elements of weather and climate depend on sunlight for their original source of energy, and the differences in sunlight intensity have profound impacts especially on temperature. As southern California experiences higher insolation (the amount of radiation received at the surface) rates than northern California, the average temperatures warm more than 10°F as we travel from the northern to the southern California coast. Average temperatures in San Diego near the Mexican border range from about 13°C (55°F) in January to 22°C (71°F) in August; in Crescent City near the Oregon border, they range from about 7°C (44°F) in January to 13°C (56°F) in August. Therefore, California's high range in latitude and solar insolation translates into a high range of temperatures from north to south, even along our mild coastline. These latitudinal temperature differences are greatly exaggerated in transmontane California; as we investigate weather stations far inland, the north–south temperature difference may double.

Precipitation Changes with Latitude

Another result of this latitude range is a great variation in precipitation. Again, when all other factors, including distance from the ocean, situation in relation to mountain barriers, and elevation, are similar, precipitation increases as we travel north. This is because we travel away from the subtropical high pressure which dominates around 30 degrees latitude as we move north, and closer to the subpolar Aleutian low pressure and polar front.

◆ IMPORTANT LESSONS IN THE PHYSICS OF OUR ATMOSPHERE

In this section we will discuss one of the most basic and important concepts necessary to the understanding of California's weather.

Less-Dense, Low-Pressure Air Rises: Clouds and Stormy Weather

Vertical air motion is the cause of almost all periods of precipitation, fair weather, or drought in California (see Figure 4.1). We begin with the rising air which is responsible for stormy weather and precipitation. When air masses, or parcels, become less dense than their surroundings, they begin to rise. This makes sense when we recognize that less-dense air parcels contain fewer molecules per given volume than their neighboring air masses.

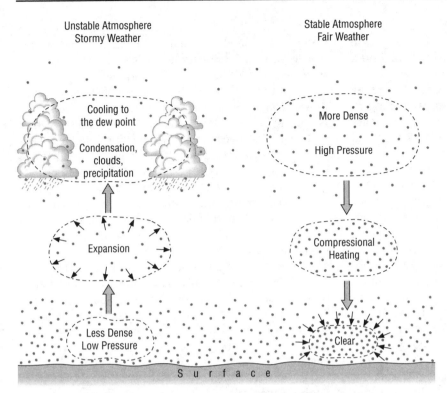

FIGURE 4.1

Rising or Sinking Air? When armed with abundant moisture, rising air masses over California may produce clouds and precipitation. Higher pressure and sinking air masses usually produce fair and dry weather, unless a shallow layer of cooler fog or low clouds is trapped in stable air near the surface.

Because the less-dense air parcels are lighter (like pieces of less-dense wood in a body of water), the surrounding fluid buoys them upward. We refer to this as *low* atmospheric pressure because there are fewer molecules per volume to exert air pressure on any surface. Therefore, less-dense air is associated with low pressure and rising air parcels. (Two common events that cause low pressure to form in California are (1): diverging air aloft draws surface air upward, causing winter-like storms, or (2) air is heated at the surface in inland valleys and deserts during hot summer afternoons, causing it to expand and become less dense.)

When such air parcels rise into more rarefied (thinner), high-altitude air, they encounter weaker forces pushing in from the outside. As a result, they expand like balloons. As these air parcels rise, they expand, pushing surrounding air away. Therefore, they lose energy and cool at the dry adiabatic **lapse rate** of 10°C per 1,000 m (5.5°F per 1,000 feet). As air cools, it loses its ability to hold water vapor (H_2O in the gaseous state). This causes relative humidities to increase as the air approaches saturation, (or its **dew point**), which is when condensation takes place. (Relative humidity measures the amount of H_2O in the air compared to the amount of H_2O the air can hold at a given temperature.) The dew point is reached when relative humidities approach 100 percent, and the air can no longer hold its water vapor. At this point, billions of the gaseous H_2O molecules combine to form liquid water drops; fog or clouds form.

Consequently, less-dense, low-pressure air masses will rise, often cooling to their dew points (if there is sufficient moisture) as condensation occurs. When the clouds form, higher-energy water vapors condense to form lower-energy liquid water drops, releasing latent heat into the rising column of air. This latent heat of condensation added within the developing clouds causes the air pockets to expand and rise even faster. As air is drawn up from near the surface, a volume of even less-dense, lower-pressure air is left below. We now have a chain of events that drive the engine of a storm. When these updrafts are strong enough, tremendous amounts of moisture are brought into the clouds, only to condense into larger liquid water drops. They eventually freeze into giant ice crystals that begin falling to the ground. Precipitation results.

This is why California weather forecasters, especially in winter, often associate a dropping barometer measurement (barometers measure air pressure) with an approaching low-pressure system. This low pressure may bring with it less-dense rising air masses, cloudier skies, unsettled weather, and possible storminess.

More-Dense, High Pressure Air Sinks: Fair Weather

The opposite of the previous conditions occurs in high-pressure systems. When air parcels become more dense than their surroundings, there are more molecules exerting pressure per volume, and so the air pressure increases. However, these dense, heavy air masses will sink like more-dense bowling balls in pools of water. Whether they start out cool or warm, if they are denser and heavier than their surroundings, they sink. As they sink, they encounter greater air pressures pushing in from the surrounding lower-altitude air. These stronger forces push the air parcels together from the outside and squeeze their molecules closer together.

This squeezing force heats the air parcels by compression at that same adiabatic rate of 10°C per 1,000 m (5.5°F per 1,000 feet) as the agitated, colliding molecules are forced ever closer together. A similar effect is witnessed when we use a hand pump to force air into a tire or ball. The work we do on the pump compresses and agitates air, generating heat. We can feel the heat from some of these forces at the base of the pump. In nature, because the fast-moving molecules of warmer air can hold plenty of water vapor (H_2O in the gaseous state), condensation of clouds is unlikely in the lower relative humidities produced by this heating by compression. Fair weather results.

It is commonly believed that hot air rises. We can now make that statement more accurate. It is true that the agitated molecules in hot air want to expand and rise, and they will, if allowed. This happens frequently in tropical air when sun-heated surfaces then heat a shallow layer of air above them. This moist, super-heated afternoon air is often free to expand and rise and expand even more. It eventually cools to its dew point, creating cumulus clouds, afternoon thunderstorms, and precipitation. With a few exceptions, such a weather event is unlikely to occur in California where unmodified tropical air is rare.

Most California heat waves are created by large domes of heavy, dense, high-pressure air aloft that sink toward the surface. As these air parcels are heated by compression, they want to expand and rise, but they are stopped by heavy, dense air parcels falling around them and squeezing them together. The dry intense heat waves that visit California are usually caused by giant high-pressure systems that move over us "aloft." Their sinking and compressively heated air masses can hold much more water vapor than they contain, so relative humidities are usually very low during these episodes. Fair, dry weather rules below these high pressure "ridges."

When the dome of high pressure finally weakens or moves away, compressional heating will cease as the air is liberated to rise. The result is usually cooler weather with higher relative humidities and more cloudiness. (Remember that temperature is the other variable that can change pressure. Very cold surface air masses are usually quite dense and also represent high pressure. This produces cold, stable, clear winter days. Again, it is important to associate stormy or fair weather with low or high pressure, but not necessarily with cold or warm temperatures.)

It follows that high pressure must be more dominant in drier southern California than to the north, and it must dominate all of California during our dry summers. Why? The culprit is our atmosphere's general circulation pattern. We are now prepared to continue our discussion of the role latitude plays in the state's weather and climate.

Global Circulation: California's Situation

A very generalized view of our atmosphere's circulation patterns begins near the equator. This is where surfaces warmed by solar radiation transfer heat to the air above, which is usually free to expand and rise. These rising air masses spread out away from the tropics at the top of our troposphere just as rising air from a kitchen stove spreads out when it hits the ceiling. As these upper air currents diverge and move toward the poles, they are cooling. They are also forced to converge into smaller volumes aloft, and they become packed closer together. They never make it far to the north. At about 30 degrees, they form the heavy and dense air masses of subtropical high pressure. As the air sinks out of these high pressure systems from aloft, stable, fair weather is the rule at the surface (see Figure 4.2).

Therefore, we expect fair weather with less precipitation to dominate as we move south in California, closer

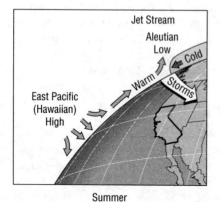

Summer   Winter

FIGURE 4.2

Seasonal Changes. When pressure patterns shift south during winter, storms invade California from the North Pacific. The East Pacific High returns by summer, pushing low pressure systems far to the north.

to 30 degrees and the subtropical high. Because the southern edge of California is south of 33 degrees, we expect the driest conditions there, but what causes the heavy precipitation farther north?

Remember that the air sinking at about 30 degrees must spread out when it reaches the surface. Some of it moves back to the Equatorial Low (as the trade winds) to fill that void, only to be warmed and lifted again. However, some of it also spreads north toward the Arctic, only to be turned to its right (due to the coriolis effect) as the westerlies. This middle latitude current is destined to collide with much colder, denser northern air masses at the surface. On the average, this collision occurs at about 60 degrees north. However, the boundary between relatively warm middle latitude air and colder polar air migrates, depending on the time of year and the movement of air masses. When the two air masses meet, the warmer, less-dense air from the westerlies glides over or is scooped aloft by the heavier, cold polar air, which remains near the surface. The warmer air now rises from the surface within less dense low pressure on the warm side of this frontal boundary.

These polar fronts (often associated with the subpolar lows) usually produce stormy weather as air is forced to rise above the collision boundary. Again, the rising air expands and cools to its dew point, causing clouds and precipitation to form. Travelling north in California, we move closer to the average location of the Aleutian Subpolar Low and the polar front, so there is more precipitation. However, the boundary of these air masses and associated frontal systems migrates across several degrees of latitude during the seasons.

Because general pressure systems are dragged north with the vertical rays of summer sun, our subtropical high (known as the **East Pacific** or **Hawaiian High**) also moves north and strengthens, shielding California from storminess during the summer. Months later, when the winter sun shifts south, so do the pressure systems. By mid-winter, our protective East Pacific High weakens and moves south, opening the door to the disturbances and polar frontal systems near the **Aleutian Subpolar Low**. This is why all areas of California, except for a few spots in the southeastern deserts, experience peak precipitation in winter, usually during January or February; this is the time of year when these frontal systems sweep through especially the northern part of the state. Southern California often experiences just the tail end of the storms that more frequently batter the north. This is also why most annual precipitation records in California are more conveniently recorded from July 1 through June 30. The rainy season develops, peaks, and dissipates in the middle of the annual record, while the break occurs in the middle of the drought season.

In summary, contrasts between winter rain and summer drought and the wet north and dry south are mainly a function of latitude and the average locations and mi-grations of dominant high and low pressure systems in and around California.

◆ OCEAN AIR MASS VERSUS CONTINENTAL AIR MASS INFLUENCE

Now we are ready to explore the second vital factor which controls California's weather and climate—the dominance of moist ocean, or marine air masses versus dry continental air masses. This is usually a function of distance from the ocean and proximity to mountain range slopes that face either toward the ocean or the dry continent. In California, this is often, but certainly not always, an east–west component.

Because local weather conditions often result from the dominance and movement of air masses, we must pause to define them. Air masses represent homogeneous masses of air with distinct characteristics (such as temperature and humidity) that are derived from where they formed. The most general classification distinguishes warm (usually low latitude) from cold (usually high latitude) and wet (often maritime) from dry (often continental) air masses. As they move over different surfaces, they are modified; they often meet along fronts.

Temperatures in Marine and Continental Air Masses

There are several reasons why land surfaces heat up faster and become hotter than water surfaces when both are exposed to equal amounts of sunlight or heat energy. Because they are better conductors of heat, land surfaces also cool off faster and get colder than water during periods of heat loss. This is one reason why inland locations experience dramatic changes in diurnal (daily) and seasonal temperatures compared to their coastal counterparts in California.

Another reason why coastal areas experience milder temperatures is that air masses near the coast tend to be more moist, keeping daytime and summer temperatures cooler, while forming an insulating blanket that traps and counterradiates heat at night and in winter. In the drier air common inland, intense solar radiation causes very hot days and summers, while allowing rapid radiation loss of surface heat into space and quick cooling during nights and winters.

Therefore, there is a direct correlation in California between the distance from and exposure to moist coastal air masses and the range of temperatures. High relative humidities and frequent fog and low clouds common along the coast contrast with drier, clearer air inland, especially during summer. Mild temperatures along the coast also contrast with extremes in temperatures farther inland. These contrasts are remarkably enhanced by mountain barriers.

In California, mountain barriers may separate some of the greatest temperature contrasts within such short distances anywhere in the world. Heavy, moist pools of marine air are often trapped in basins against the ocean, or windward, sides of mountain ranges along the California coast, resulting in moderate temperatures. In contrast, areas on inland, or leeward, sides of those mountain ranges facing toward the drier continent experience extreme temperatures in the dry air; such conditions are more characteristic of continental interiors hundreds of miles inland. The ridges of California's numerous mountain ranges often separate moist, moderate, coastal air masses from the dry, harsh climates tucked behind them. This helps define the differences between cismontane (coastal slopes and valleys) and transmontane (the inland sides of the mountains) California.

Marine and Continental Air Masses Influence Precipitation

Enormous contrasts in precipitation also occur between coastal/windward locations and the inland/leeward sides of major mountain barriers (see Figure 4.3). First, since the source of almost all moisture in California is from the Pacific Ocean, we might expect precipitation totals to gradually diminish as we move far inland. Add the mountain barriers, and there are striking differences. As winter storms carry moist, unstable air from the Pacific, they generally sweep from west to east across California.

When the air masses encounter major mountain barriers such as the Klamaths or Cascades, the Coast Ranges or Sierra Nevada, or the Transverse or Peninsular Ranges, the air is forced to rise on the windward mountain slopes. The air in these strong updrafts quickly expands and cools to its dew point. *Recall that rising air produces the thickest clouds and heaviest precipitation.* In California, the air mass is forced to rise along these windward slopes where the greatest precipitation totals are common. This is called **orographic precipitation**.

Thus, numerous locations on west-facing slopes in northwestern California receive more than 200 cm (80 inches) of precipitation per year. Some western Sierra Nevada locations average accumulations of more than 3 m (10 feet) of snow pack by the end of the winter season, while total winter snowfalls are much greater.

In contrast, on the leeward sides of California's major mountain barriers, prevailing winds must sink back down to reach the inland deserts. *Recall that sinking air is heated by compression at 10°C per 1,000 m (5.5°F per 1,000 feet) and that warmer air is capable of holding more water vapor (H_2O in the gaseous state).* Therefore, in the sinking air on leeward slopes, ice crystals and water drops tend to evaporate, relative humidities decrease, cloud formation is less likely, and precipitation is rare. These areas are called **rainshadows** and California exhibits some classic examples.

The driest place in California (and one of the driest in the world) is Death Valley, where average annual precipitation is less than 5 cm (2 inches). Here, a series of mountain ranges, starting with the Coast Ranges and then the Sierra Nevada, block the encroachment of moist air

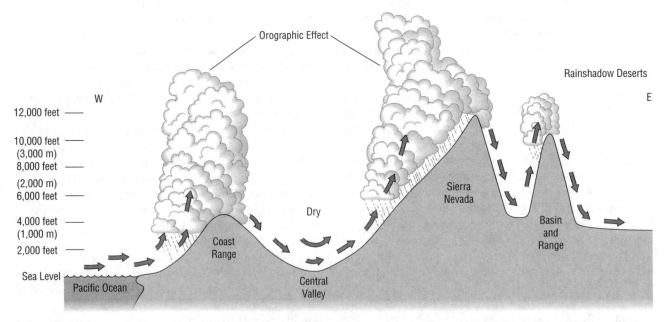

FIGURE 4.3

Windward and Leeward Climates. As winter storms move across California from the Pacific Ocean, moist air is forced to rise over windward slopes of coastal ranges and the Sierra Nevada. Condensation, clouds, and precipitation are common. Drier air must sink down leeward slopes, producing rainshadow climates.

from the Pacific. Once an air mass finally invades the region, it must sink below sea level toward the valley floor, causing compression, heating, and drying. This is why Death Valley is often left only partly cloudy or clear and dry during some of California's wettest and most powerful winter storm events. Numerous southeastern California desert locations are nearly as dry; all are on rainshadow sides of major mountain barriers.

◆ A COMBINATION OF FACTORS CONTROL TEMPERATURE AND PRECIPITATION

We are now prepared to combine the first two of the three most important geographic factors which control California's weather and climate. First, where other geographic conditions are similar, we expect to find warmer temperatures as we travel toward the south, where the land and ocean surfaces receive more direct solar radiation. We will also experience less precipitation as we move south away from the influence of the Aleutian Low and closer to the East Pacific High.

Second, we will experience hotter summer days and colder winter nights in the drier, clearer skies as we head inland (usually east) away from the mild coastal air masses, especially after crossing mountain barriers. Finally, precipitation decreases as we move east, especially after crossing those mountain barriers to their rainshadow sides.

When combining these factors, we see why, for stations at similar elevations above sea level, we record the mildest temperatures near the coast. The greatest temperature ranges are experienced in eastern California; the hottest summer temperatures are recorded in southeastern California, the coldest winter temperatures in northeastern California. Finally, we find the wettest locations in the northwest and the driest in southeastern California.

◆ ELEVATION

Temperatures Change with Elevation

The third and perhaps simplest major factor controlling California's weather and climate is elevation above sea level. With some major exceptions, which we will explore, air temperatures become cooler at higher elevations. This is a result of the more rarefied (thinner) air at higher altitudes that is not only farther from surface heat sources but is not compressed as much as lower altitude air. High-altitude air simply doesn't contain as much heat energy. The average environmental **lapse rate** is about 6.5°C per 1,000 m (3.5°F per 1,000 feet). This is the average rate of temperature change within a column of air that is *not* moving vertically; rather, we are moving through it, making measurements at different altitudes.

Therefore, the following California temperatures are typical of those recorded at the same time on a spring or fall afternoon.

- ◆ 21°C (70°F) at Redding, 8°C (47°F) at 2,000 m (6,500 feet) a few kms (miles) northwest in the Klamath Mountains
- ◆ 27°C (80°F) in Fresno, 11°C (52°F) at 2,450 m (8,000 feet) several kms (miles) east in the Sierra Nevada
- ◆ 38°C (100°F) in Palm Springs, 18°C (65°F) at 3,000 m (10,000 feet) only 10 km (6 miles) west in the San Jacinto Mountains

One of the most dramatic elevation gains and corresponding temperature changes in such a short distance anywhere in the world can be experienced during a ride on the Palm Springs Tramway from the desert floor up the fault scarps of the eastern San Jacinto Mountains and into the cool forest.

There are at least three interesting and important exceptions to this generalized rule of temperature decrease at higher elevations in California. First, because air is rarefied (thinner) at higher elevations, solar radiation is less filtered and more intense. Sunny summer days may turn surprisingly warm after hot surfaces are exposed to direct sunlight at high elevations. However, that same rarefied air is a poor insulator, allowing heat to quickly radiate out after sunset, making way for very cold nights, especially during winter. This is why California mountain locations experience greater diurnal and seasonal ranges in temperatures compared to lower elevations, especially when skies are clear.

Local Low-Level Temperature Inversions

Perhaps more important exceptions to our rule of temperature decrease at higher elevations are temperature inversions. A **temperature inversion** occurs when cooler air, which is denser, settles below a layer of warmer air, reversing "normal" conditions (see Figure 4.4a). California's mountains and valleys experience two

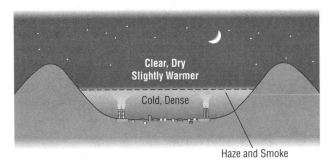

FIGURE 4.4a
Local Low-Level Temperature Inversions. Cold, dense, stable air may settle in California's inland valleys during long, clear, calm winter nights. Fog or pollution may become trapped in the local inversion by sunrise.

types of inversions. One type is the simple, low-level inversion. Local parcels of cold, denser air drain downward and settle into valleys and canyons on clear, calm nights, especially in winter. Many night and morning travellers across California's ridges and valleys notice the cold, dense air pockets that settle into low spots. Eventually, morning sunlight warms the surface, or winds may mix the once stable layers of air to break the inversion.

These local inversions are important to California farmers who plant on fields and slopes in areas with near-freezing temperatures. Frost-sensitive crops must be planted in the thermal belts just above the local canyons, basins, and valleys where cold, dense air settles on long winter nights. Many a California farmer has exploited these slightly higher thermal belts to increase growing seasons. These conditions also affect the distribution of natural plant communities with varying resistance to temperature extremes. Native plants less resistant to extreme cold may be absent where cold pockets of air can settle on long winter nights.

Widespread Upper-Level Inversions

Regional upper-level inversions cover much larger areas and affect the major population centers of California (see Figure 4.4b). Remember that California is often situated beneath a large dome of high pressure (particularly in southern California and especially in summer). These sinking air masses are often clear and dry aloft. As the air cascades down to lower altitudes, it is heated by compression. The trouble is that the air below tends to be cooler, especially when coastal air masses dominate at the surface. Frequently (usually in summer), coastal valleys are invaded by this cooler, moist, denser air from the ocean. This relatively cooler air has settled near the surface and is trapped below the warmer, drier air sinking from the dominant high pressure aloft. With very little mixing between the two layers, very stable conditions exist.

Unfortunately, California's major population centers pour tons of pollutants into the already hazy, stagnant air near the surface. Because the pollutants rarely mix with the upper atmosphere during these inversion episodes, people are forced to live with and breath unhealthy air. When upper-level high pressure strengthens, the relatively cooler ocean air is squeezed closer to the surface, resulting in shallower inversions and even less mixing.

These conditions can sometimes create a pressure cooker effect, producing the most stagnant air and the smoggiest days. Though afternoon temperatures may be heated to 38°C (100°F) in inland valleys, air on top of the inversion may be just slightly warmer. The valleys then bake in summer heat *and* smog. These conditions are common in the Central Valley in summer. On some of the hottest summer afternoons, surface temperatures may rise high enough (becoming much hotter than the air above) so that the air expands, rises, and breaks through the inversion. The haze and smog is then funnelled up heated mountain slopes and through canyons, pulling better air quality from the coast into inland valleys.

Inversions commonly cause afternoon temperatures in summer to get hotter in the mountains than in the coastal plains near sea level. Summer afternoon temperatures are often higher in such southern California mountain locations as Palomar, Julian, Idyllwild, Big Bear, Lake Arrowhead, Wrightwood, Mount Wilson, and Mount Pinos than in coastal stations to the west and south near sea level. During these periods, it is likely that mountain communities are looking down on a blanket of thick haze and smog trapped in the cooler surface air that flatlanders know as the **marine layer**.

Similar summer inversions are common in central and northern California, including the San Francisco Bay Area. Summer afternoon temperatures on nearby peaks and even in Sierra Nevada resorts commonly soar above those of the cooler, foggy coastal locations near sea level.

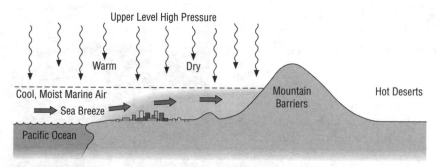

FIGURE 4.4b
Widespread Upper-Level Inversions. Particularly during summer, high pressure air sinks over California. A regional inversion develops along coastal areas when the cooler, dense sea breeze is trapped below descending warmer, drier air. Haze, fog, and smog are common in coastal valleys when the marine layer is shallow and trapped by surrounding mountains.

Passengers can easily identify an inversion when their plane pops out of the thick marine layer's haze and into nearly unlimited visibilities in the warmer, dryer air above.

Despite these notable exceptions, we know that California's mountain communities are usually cooler than the flatlands below, particularly during winter. Proof is in the impressive snow packs which accumulate at higher elevations from northern to southern California during winter. It is also proven when stations in or near the high Sierra (such as Truckee) so frequently record the night's coldest temperatures in the United States outside Alaska. Average annual temperatures along a line across central California range from near 15°C (60°F) near sea level to below freezing at the highest mountain locations (an average annual difference of more than 16°C (30°F)). The year-round, frost-free locations in California are strung along the southern and central California coast or in a few inland locations near the Mexican border, all at or near sea level. In contrast, some of the highest elevations in northern and central California may experience frost any time of year.

Precipitation Varies with Elevation

Precipitation also varies dramatically with elevation in California. We noted earlier that air masses must rise, expand, and cool (often to their dew points) as they move over mountains. This orographic effect results in increased clouds and precipitation at higher elevations; the effect is most dramatic on windward slopes. Annual precipitation increases by about 5–10 cm per 100 m (2–4 inches per 330 feet) elevation gain. This trend continues to about 2,440 m (8,000 feet) where Sierra Nevada precipitation totals average 153 cm (60 inches). Precipitation is even greater along some northwestern California mountain slopes. Consequently, higher elevations are not only cooler, but they receive more moisture. More precipitation on mountain slopes with lower evaporation rates (due to cooler temperatures and forest cover) means more water available for the soil and plants. This is usually true on all but the higher mountain slopes in California.

At extremely high elevations (above about 2,500 m [8,000 feet]), and often at or above tree lines, precipitation decreases with elevation gain. Rising air masses have already dumped much of their moisture on lower and middle slopes. Furthermore, the cold, rarefied air does not contain as much moisture when it reaches very high elevations. Drier conditions are amplified by the extreme evapotranspiration rates on slopes exposed to intense sun, high winds, and dry air even following snowstorms. This may leave little water on the exposed, highest slopes above tree lines during summer, and most runoff drains down to the forest below.

We have explained how the three major factors of latitude, coastal influence, and elevation impact California's weather and climate. We now turn our attention to a variety of more specific and often related topics.

◆ SEASONAL CYCLES

Contrary to popular myths spread beyond the state's boundaries, California weather patterns are subject to pronounced seasonal changes. Most notable are winter's heavy mountain snows and drenching valley rains that yield to summer's prolonged drought. What forces are responsible for these and other seasonal cycles, and how do they impact California?

Summer Patterns

The East Pacific High Dominates Summer Weather

Earlier in this chapter, we learned about the East Pacific High's powerful influence over California's weather and climate. Besides blocking so many storms from sweeping into California, it is also at least indirectly responsible for our prevailing winds, sea breezes, stable air, ocean currents, temperatures, and many other weather elements and events, especially during summer. As summer approaches, the East Pacific High strengthens and bulges northward, becoming the dominant weather maker for the Eastern Pacific and California.

Usually centered hundreds of kms (miles) west of California, it forms as upper level winds converge, and the air becomes dense and heavy aloft. It is often enhanced during the summer when eastern Pacific surface water temperatures remain cooler than the heated surfaces of the North American continent. Summer air above these cooler waters often becomes cooler and denser, forming higher pressure.

Like all other high pressure systems, winds flow out of it and into adjacent lower pressure systems. Then, the coriolis force pulls the air to its right as it pours out of this northern hemisphere subtropical high pressure. (The coriolis effect is produced as a fluid moves across the rotating earth.) The results are winds that blow out of the high pressure, but they are turned in a clockwise direction away from its center. Because this is the opposite direction from earth's rotation in the northern hemisphere, we call these high pressure systems "anticyclones." (Low pressure systems are considered "cyclones.")

California's Cold Ocean Current As the wind turns clockwise out of our prevailing East Pacific High, it pushes ocean currents with it. (Wind is most responsible for generating ocean currents and waves on our planet.) Because California is usually situated on the east side of this high pressure, prevailing winds curve down our coast from the northwest. Friction from these winds sets our ocean current in motion. However, the ocean is also a fluid that, once set in motion, will be turned to its right by the coriolis effect. These processes create the **California Current**, which flows from north to south down our coast (see Map 4.2).

At California's latitude, ours is considered a cold ocean current, especially during summer. Because summer air that flows out of the East Pacific High is often drawn into the hot thermal, low-pressure conditions in our deserts, it must pass over the California current before moving onshore. These winds are chilled by the current, especially in summer. By the time the sea breeze hits the coast, it is even cooler and heavier, and it has lost its capacity to hold water vapor (H_2O in the gaseous state).

The cool ocean breeze, at or near its dew point, brings the advection fog and low stratus clouds that have condensed over the cold California current. It moves in with low specific humidities (the total amount of water in the air), but high relative humidities, because the chilled air cannot hold what little water vapor it contains. This dense, stable air will remain near the surface as it moves into coastal and inland valleys and against coastal slopes. On summer afternoons, the air is heated as it moves inland, the fog and low clouds burn off, and relative humidities decrease.

California's cold ocean currents are often further chilled by upwelling. Particularly where the coastline bends more east–west, such as along the Southern California Bight (south of Point Arguello/Point Conception), prevailing northwest winds can set surface water flowing south, away from the coast. As this surface water is pushed away, cooler nutrient-rich water flows up from the depths to replace it. Summer water temperatures are typically in the upper teens Celsius (60°s) off southern California, where occasional pockets of warm water make it above 21°C (70°F) for only brief periods. Northern and central California waters are several degrees colder. This makes for great fishing in the nutrient-rich cold water, which holds more dissolved gases, but uncomfortably cold swimming conditions are the rule.

This also enhances the summer pressure gradient and the resulting sea breezes along the coast. High pressure intensifies in the dense, cooler air offshore. Because air wants to blow out of that high pressure and into the heated, expanding air of the **thermal low** over the deserts and Central Valley, summer sea breezes dominate coastal California. Especially during the afternoon, when superheated desert air is rapidly expanding and often rising, a strong sea breeze is pulled inland toward the less dense thermal low pressure.

California summers lack precipitation not only because the East Pacific High acts as a protective barrier to storms, but also because of the cold ocean currents generated by its winds that chill the air before it moves inland. If California were on the west side of the ocean and its subtropical high (such as in the eastern United States and Asia), a warm coastal current would flow from the south. The summer sea breezes would then be warm, humid, and unstable. Unstable marine tropical (mT) air masses would produce hot, muggy summers with frequent thundershowers and occasional tropical storms. Instead, our refreshing summer sea breezes are dense and stable; because this chilled air can't hold much water vapor, condensation, coastal fog, and stratus are common. Summer precipitation is rare.

Fluctuating Highs Fluctuations in the strength and location of the East Pacific High are most responsible for changes in summer weather. When the high strengthens and bulges eastward over California or combines with another high pressure system to the east, air masses cascade directly on California. Extreme summer heat waves result from the compressional heating in inland areas. Along the coast, the marine layer is pressed closer to the surface, creating shallow inversions and choking coastal cities in the smog and heat below. A thin, shallow strip of fog may hug only the beaches. Even stronger high pressure centered farther inland is rare in summer, but can squeeze the marine layer offshore, leaving coastal basins and even beaches baking in dry record heat.

When the high pressure weakens or migrates far out to sea, the marine layer thickens and stronger sea breezes

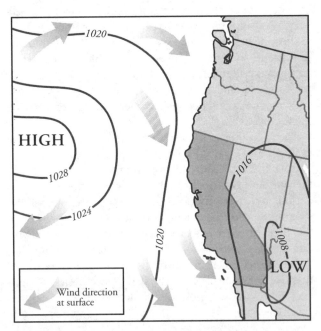

MAP 4.2

California Current and Sea Breeze. Prevailing northwest winds pour out of the East Pacific High, pushing the California Current from north to south. The cool sea breezes blow off this current into coastal valleys, particularly in summer.

penetrate far into inland valleys. These cooling breezes bring advection fog and low clouds so thick that it may not burn off in the afternoons and can even produce morning drizzle. During these weather patterns, the low stratus thickens each night as it pours into inland valleys and pushes up against coastal slopes in marine layers up to 2,000 m (6,000 feet) thick until weather conditions change.

Similar weather conditions may result (especially in late spring and early summer) when the high pressure spins winds from north to south along the California coast to Point Conception. The winds are forced to veer out to sea at this topographical boundary, only to gradually turn back toward the coast near San Diego. A large counterclockwise eddy (swirling current) may develop just off the coast, circulating and sending a thick marine layer up the coast from south to north into the California Bight. These **Catalina Eddies** may bring thick, low stratus to blanket southern California coastal valleys while much of the rest of California remains clear.

Surprise Summer Storms

A different summer weather pattern is produced especially in southern California when another high-pressure system bulges toward California from the east. Converging air aloft often produces high pressure that forms near and around western Texas. The sinking air spinning out of this summertime high also turns clockwise, picking up tropical moisture from the south in Mexico and flinging it north into New Mexico and Arizona. When this moisture-laden air begins to expand and rise in the intense summer afternoon heat of the deserts and plateaus of Arizona, it reaches its dew point, producing giant cumulonimbus clouds. Spectacular tropical-like thunderstorms erupt mostly during afternoons and eve-

nings. Arizonans refer to this as their "monsoon season" because most stations in New Mexico and Arizona receive more precipitation in late summer than any other time of year.

More rarely, this upper-level high pressure will bulge westward and settle near the Four Corners region. This sets up upper level winds from the southeast over southern California that carry moisture from Mexico and the Gulf of California across the Colorado River and Mexican border into southeastern California. Specific humidity (total moisture) in this subtropical air is high. The rising desert heat within the thermal low finally contains enough moisture to explode into afternoon thunderstorms similar to Arizona's monsoon season.

Though usually isolated, these storms can dump an average year's rainfall on one desert location in less than an hour. Dangerous severe weather and flash floods may hit one desert location while residents only a few miles away view the bright side of the cumulonimbus clouds in the hot desert sun. These summer events become more common closer to the Colorado River, the only area in California where meager precipitation totals peak during late summer.

Even more rarely, when the high pressure pushes farther west, moisture pours into all southern California desert and mountain areas from the southeast and up the spine of the Sierra Nevada. Resulting thunderstorms are more widespread and may even slip over the mountains and drift into southern coastal areas. More commonly, coastal residents are limited to viewing the sides of these towering cumulus as they build over nearby mountain slopes during summer afternoons. The cooler, stable marine air from the eastern Pacific that dominates during summer in coastal valleys contains less total water vapor (lower specific humidities), and it usually does not rise, inhibiting storm development. Even more rarely, dissipating tropical disturbances may be pulled into this

Torrential rains fall from a violent desert thunderstorm. Cumulonimbus clouds developed when moisture streaming up from Mexico was lifted over the New York Mountains near the Nevada border in the summer afternoon heat.

southerly flow from the west coast of Mexico, resulting in more widespread cloudiness and showers which contrast with California's summer drought.

Only in California's southeastern deserts and mountains and in the Sierra Nevada do these rare summer events significantly influence climates. Building clouds cast afternoon shade and higher humidities cut evapotranspiration rates at the exact time when plants need the relief most in these areas. Even the most isolated and brief summer shower is welcome relief from an otherwise long, hot summer. The more rare spectacular electrical displays, hailstorms, downpours, and ominous flash floods are peculiar oddities against a background of otherwise relentless summer heat and drought.

Unfortunately, these downpours are usually so isolated, they contribute very little total moisture to any region (even southeastern California) on an annual basis. Summer drought is so dependable, some California farmers take advantage by planting crops which fail when there is prolonged moisture. Controlled irrigation is then timed to the life cycles of special crops, such as cotton, to make them more productive. These California farmers don't worry about competition from regions that receive summer rains.

Hurricanes—An Unlikely Disaster There are at least two reasons why California has never experienced a hurricane in recorded history, and only a few tropical storms have visited even the southern part of the state. First, mainly easterly trade winds normally blow tropical disturbances that form off the west coast of Mexico away from the mainland and into the Pacific. Second, when a renegade tropical disturbance finally wanders far to the north toward California, it must travel great distances across the relatively cold waters along the Baja California coast. Because the evaporation of tropical waters of at least 26°C (79°F) provides the latent heat required for these storms to form and strengthen, they dissipate long before reaching California. Only clouds and some showers are left if a storm's remains drift into the state. Rare tropical disturbances moving north along the warm Gulf of California are also weakened as they must travel mainly over land to reach California.

During late September, 1997, powerful hurricanes formed over exceptionally warm El Niño waters off the west coast of Mexico. One of the most powerful hurricanes ever recorded in the eastern Pacific (Linda) drifted up the Baja coast, headed for southern California. In disbelief, the National Weather Service, public officials, and the media began preparing. The storm could have brought near hurricane-force winds, torrential rains, and severe flooding even as it weakened. Instead, Hurricane Linda made a last-minute left turn into the Pacific. As usual, southern California only received residual showers from the dying storm.

Fall Patterns

Autumn is the season when temperature and pressure patterns begin to change suddenly and dramatically across the state (see Map 4.3). First, the high sun angles and intense solar radiation of summer shift south. The East Pacific High weakens and follows. Second, colder air masses and storms from the Aleutian Low and north Pacific begin to trail into northern sections of California. Third, the first cold air masses of the season move inland into the Great Basin and settle on cooling surfaces inland. Ocean temperatures will take longer to cool and the pressure gradient may reverse from summer, trending from higher pressure inland to lower pressure over the coastal waters. Eventually, this cold, dense inland air builds the first strong **Great Basin High** of the season over or near Nevada.

As the cold, heavy air sinks and flows clockwise from the Great Basin High pressure center, an offshore (land) breeze develops across California to the coast. This air is eventually heated by compression as it sinks toward the coast. This is why San Francisco and other coastal cities often experience their highest temperatures of the year in September or October, but it is along the southern California coast south of the Transverse Ranges where these conditions are exacerbated.

After the descending air masses move across the deserts out of the Great Basin High, they must first pass

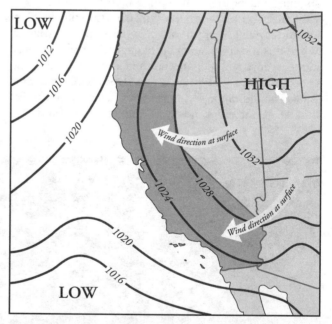

MAP 4.3

Santa Ana Winds. During autumn and winter, the Great Basin High may form when cold, dense air masses settle to the north and east of California. Average pressure gradients and wind patterns are reversed. An offshore flow may be heated by compression as it cascades down mountain slopes toward the coast.

over the mountains and then cascade down coastal slopes and canyons, where they are squeezed into coastal valleys. This reversal of average wind conditions sends winds cascading toward the coast, leaving coastal valleys on the leeward sides of mountains and passes, where there is intense compressional heating. These hot, dry **Santa Ana winds** blow the smog and haze toward the coast and often out to sea.

They often shift from the north to northeast to easterly within a few days as the high pressure drifts farther east and inland of Nevada. It is ironic that when much of the country feels that first chill of fall and winter air masses from the north, southern California may experience Santa Ana winds blowing hot from the north. Temperatures in southern coastal areas may rise above 38°C (100°F) into November during Santa Ana winds. Even in mid-winter, Santa Anas have boosted temperatures to 32°C (90°F) when much of the rest of the United States had freezing temperatures.

If the Santa Anas and down-slope winds in other parts of the state are responsible for attracting so many chilled easterners to California, they are also famous for fanning some of the most terrifying and destructive fires in the world. The fire season peaks on the heels of the prolonged summer heat and drought so characteristic of California's Mediterranean climate. Many coastal areas from central California to Mexico may experience summers when no rain falls between May and October. The annual battle of the air masses usually arrives at the end of this drought season, just when soils and plants are driest. Since the first Santa Anas and other down-slope winds often arrive before the first significant rainfall of the season, the months of September–December bring some of the most hazardous fire seasons in the world to California.

When these strong, gusty down-slope winds are heated by compression up to 38°C (100°F) and relative

During fall, the East Pacific High weakens and shifts south, the jet stream begins to move south, and North Pacific storms track farther south into California. Here, a weak front pushes just into the northern Sierra Nevada and San Francisco Bay Area before continuing east. While the series of storms drifts from west to east into the Pacific Northwest, Southern California remains dry.

humidities drop below ten percent, fires in dry grasslands, scrub, chaparral, and other woodlands are almost impossible to stop. Could you write a better script to pave the way for a disastrous fire season?

Along the Santa Barbara coast, sundowner winds may descend the southern base of the Santa Ynez Mountains as north or even cool northwesterly winds blow across most of California. These winds may be forced to sink down the south slopes of the east–west trending Transverse Ranges. Here, they are heated by compression before reaching the east–west oriented coastal valleys and can become a local version of the hot, dry Santa Anas. These very brief and local warm, dry episodes may invade valleys throughout the Santa Barbara area and even into the Ventura/Oxnard Plain. They can provide surprising breaks to normally cooler sea breezes directly off the North Pacific.

Meanwhile, in California's mountains and transmontane valleys, deciduous trees turn color and the chill in the air announces winter is not far away.

Winter's Storms

The winter season brings great changes in the general circulation patterns responsible for California's weather. As the sun angle dips ever lower and the days shorten, the East Pacific High continues to weaken and migrate south. Aloft, along the boundary where short columns of cold, heavy air meet the taller columns of warmer, expanding air, a strong pressure gradient produces the polar front **jet stream**. This high velocity core of wind meanders from west to east within the troughs and ridges known as the upper-level **Rossby waves**. All of this occurs many thousands of meters (tens of thousands of feet) high above the boundary between the shorter (cold) and taller (warmer) air masses at the surface. These upper level waves and the jet stream frequently

Santa Ana winds blow hot from the northeast, fanning flames across the Santa Monica Mountains toward the beach, devastating Malibu communities.

dip south over California during winter, along with the air mass collisions near the surface that may cause storminess.

Pools of polar air masses occasionally slip south during winter months in troughs of the Rossby waves, sometimes bringing weather from the Aleutian Low. When the cold, dense air invades south, warmer lighter air is lifted over it. Abundant vertical mixing, condensation, clouds, and precipitation result, producing a glaring contrast to the stable fair weather of summer. California's is usually not a steady and reliable rainy season, especially in recent years.

Usually migrating from west to east across California, a dip or trough in the upper-level Rossby waves and jet stream brings the battling air masses and their storms into the state. When an upper-level ridge of high pressure moves through, it pushes the upper-level jet stream and colliding surface air masses far to the north, causing fair weather. The average winter brings a splendid variety of weather; cool Pacific rains and mountain snows are followed by a few days of fair weather with clear to partly cloudy skies.

When Stubborn Patterns Set In

Occasionally, the winter troughs and ridges stop migrating across California. When these upper-level waves stall, surface weather remains stationary and records are often set. In 1977, a ridge of high pressure stalled over California. This blocking high sent storms far to the north. There was literally no snow pack in the Sierra Nevada at the end of the driest rainy season in California's history. A similar series of high pressure ridges stationed over California from the late 1980s to the early 1990s brought the longest drought in California history—six years. Both droughts devastated the state's water supply, agricultural industry, and other portions of the economy.

Antithetically, when the east side of an upper-level trough is stationed over California, warm and cold air masses clash. As the warmer air is lifted in these storms, an accelerating jet stream aloft evacuates it and pulls more air up from the surface. The great floods of 1983, 1993, 1995, and 1997 and the record 1998 El Nino rains were at least partially caused by the repeated formation of deep troughs just off the coast. The result: a jet stream aloft and clashing air masses and their storms at the surface swept over California. These stationary weather patterns are not new to California.

Two years of drought, dwindling water supplies, and devastating fires came to an abrupt end after the summer of 1889. Storms began battering California in early November. More than 660 cm (260 inches) of snow fell on Donner Pass in the Sierra Nevada by the end of that December. By January 6, 1890, more than 7 m (24 feet) of snow had accumulated in Truckee. Though Central Pacific mobilized thousands of workers and heavy equipment to keep tracks open, westbound trains were stalled

for weeks; two hundred stranded passengers died of influenza and pneumonia within one week. Western Union workers dug down 6 m (20 feet) to reach the tops of poles connecting the snapped Trans-Sierra telegraph lines. Emerald Bay residents on Lake Tahoe recorded fresh snowfall every day from December 2–January 30 as nearly endless storms battered the Sierra Nevada in January and February, 1890.

Each Winter Storm is Different

Because these winter storms may have different origins, pull in a variety of air masses, and play vital roles in shaping California's physical and human landscapes, they deserve more attention here.

Winter storms that move from west to east out of the north Pacific (or northwest to southeast out of the Gulf of Alaska) are most common in California. Because winds spin into these surface low-pressure systems in a counterclockwise direction (the same as earth's rotation in the northern hemisphere), they are called cyclones. The storms that invade California in winter are called **middle-latitude wave cyclones**; they are large and complex, some with diameters exceeding 1,000 miles.

As a storm approaches the California coast from the west, southerly winds pour warm, moist air up into the storm's east side. Often, the warm air encounters cooler air as it moves north. When the warm, less dense air is forced to gradually glide over the colder dense air, cooling causes condensation, forming mostly thick stratus clouds and often a warm front. Steady light rain and drizzle is common over a wide area of the eastern edge of the cyclone, and snow levels are usually high. As the rising air in the storm center moves toward the coast north of or directly over California, it usually has a vigorous cold front in tow.

These trailing cold fronts form in the counterclockwise spiral as cold air spins in from the north and north-

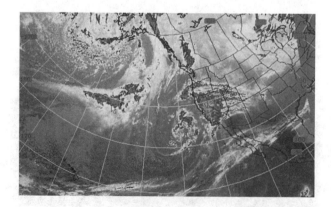

Satellite image of winter storm. This infrared image shows the counterclockwise circulation of a powerful winter storm approaching California. Warm, moist air and heavy precipitation are being pumped into the state ahead of the low pressure system as it moves east out of the Pacific.

WINTER'S RADIATION FOG

In the long, cold, clear, calm winter nights between storms, **radiation (tule) fog** often forms in inland valleys. This is very different from summertime's coastal advection fog. When cold dense air settles on moistened valley floors that have radiated heat energy into space, low-lying air finally cools to its dew point and condensation occurs near the surface. We are all familiar with the dew that forms on cold surfaces at night; this radiation fog might be considered an extension of that process into the air that has also finally cooled to its dew point. Radiation or tule fog often burns off in the next morning's sunlight, especially in southern California's inland valleys.

However, in the Central Valley during especially long winter nights, the tule fog may form and thicken until visibilities are near zero. Often, when most of California is experiencing clear winter weather, the blanket of fog in the Central Valley is so thick that it does not burn off even during afternoons. The winter sun is often not intense enough; it makes a brief appearance and stays low on the horizon. These fog episodes may last for days, when high and low temperatures near such cities as Stockton, Modesto, and Fresno never change from a few degrees above freezing in blankets of fog hundreds of meters thick.

The persistent fog creates extremely hazardous driving conditions, especially along such highways as I-5 and Hwy. 99. Accidents have involved multiple injuries, deaths, and more than one hundred vehicles at a time. This fog has also been found to impact the mental health of some Central Valley residents. Radiation fog does not form in California's inland valleys during summer, when warmer air masses are capable of holding their water vapors.

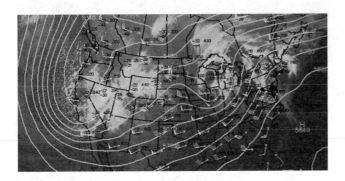

This 500 mb chart shows a deep upper-level trough of low pressure that has drifted over California, overlaid upon the corresponding satellite image (assembled at San Francisco State University's Web site). The main portion of the storm at the surface advances ahead of the trough (on the east side) and into Nevada. Behind the storm, cold, unstable air flows over California from the Gulf of Alaska, creating scattered showers and mountain snow.

west behind the middle-latitude cyclone. This denser cold air remains near the surface as it invades California and quickly lifts any warmer, lighter air in its path. The rapid lifting forms a narrow, often fast-moving but more violent cold front with vertically developed cumulus and cumulonimbus clouds. Short-duration, heavy showers and lower snow levels may also result. After most cold fronts pass, the crisp, colder, stable air eventually settles in and skies begin to clear.

When middle-latitude cyclones and their trailing cold fronts finally pass through California, they bring dramatic weather changes. Southerly winds deliver warm, moist air in ahead of the front, followed by heavy showers and erratic winds as the cold front passes. A quick shift of the wind to westerly, northwesterly, or northerly announces the passage of the front and is followed by only scattered showers of instability as the cool, crisp air finally moves in behind the storm. This is also when mountain snow levels are lowest.

Somewhat similar storms carry much warmer and moister air masses into California from the southwest. Sometimes travelling from Hawaii to California, usually in late winter or spring, these storms pick up tremendous amounts of moisture and dump it on California's coastal slopes. Some historical floods, including the great floods of 1969, were caused by a series of these storms. Even when storms originate farther north in the Pacific, they frequently strengthen as their typical counterclockwise circulation draws this energy and moisture up from the south.

At the other extreme, the colder and drier Inside Sliders occasionally slip directly south into inland California, often after moving over Washington and Oregon. Because these storms are so cold and have already swept onto land, they usually do not produce as much precipitation, but they may usher record cold air into California from the north. These Inside Sliders occasionally produce impressive but relatively dry snowfalls in the Cascades, Sierra Nevada, and Basin and Range and even into southern California mountains as they slide south along troughs through transmontane California and the backsides of the mountains. The term "Tonopah Low" is often applied when they settle over western Nevada.

Though the winter season brings the rainy season, we now recognize that this rainy season is usually characterized by alternating periods of mild weather interrupted by periodic storms of many different types and intensities. Milder weather usually dominates and lasts longer to the south, while stormier weather usually arrives earlier and stays longer farther north.

ADVECTION FOG AND THE MARINE LAYER

Advection fog in the marine layer is a more gentle and more predictable player in California's weather and climate. Along the coast, it has been romanticized, loved, and hated. Its fingers roll into coastal valleys; it pushes against, surrounds, then cascades down coastal hills. It is nearly a constant factor in summer coastal weather forecasts, especially toward the north.

We previously noted how this fog forms in the chilled air moving across the cold California current. It is not surprising that the fog becomes more persistent to the north, where colder water temperatures more commonly cool the air to its dew point. Frequently, especially along the northern California coast, the cool sea breeze brings fog which replaces air that would have been warmed in a sunny summer day.

Even in southern California, when summer afternoon temperatures approach 38°C (100°F) in the San Fernando Valley, the shallow, cool sea breeze and fog may hold temperatures below 21°C (70°F) just 16 km (10 miles) across the narrow Santa Monica Mountains barrier, along the Malibu coast. Similar summer temperature contrasts occur between the cool, often foggy Laguna coast and the hot valleys on the inland side of the Laguna Hills. Similar contrasts are also common in parts of northern and central California. The string of cities and valleys connected by Hwy. 101 north of San Francisco is often isolated in searing summer heat, while cool fog blankets coastal locations on the other side of the mountains less than 32 km (20 miles) to the west.

Advection fog can be relentless when it piles against Big Sur's coastal hills, or pours into the Salinas Valley from Monterey Bay, or envelopes Fort Bragg, Eureka, and Crescent City in a dull, grey mist. It is most impressive as it funnels through the Golden Gate (the only major, complete gap in the Coast Ranges) past San Francisco, across the bay, and sometimes even into the Carquinez Strait toward the Central Valley. Because San Francisco's peninsula juts directly into the Golden Gate, The City is famous for getting in the fog's way as it races inland through and around San Francisco, over the bay, and past Alcatraz. It pushes up and against the Oakland/Berkeley Hills. Though they are located on the east side of the bay, these cities get a direct hit from the sea breeze and fog funnelled through the Golden Gate; their summer afternoons often remain as cool as San Francisco's.

In northern and southern California, as it moves toward the normally hot, drier inland valleys during the afternoon, the mixture of fog or low stratus thins, then evaporates in the warmer air. Later, when the land cools after sunset, it marches and spreads into inland valleys, only to be burned back toward the coast by the next morning's summer sun. These diurnal advances and retreats lay the framework for the monotonous "late night and early morning low clouds and fog—otherwise mostly sunny" weather forecasts repeated throughout the summer in California's largest coastal population centers.

This marine layer and its fog and stratus delivers the cool, mild summers famous along California's coast. Particularly along the north coast, it cuts evapotranspiration rates and provides moisture for plants and animals during the summer drought. Fog drip to the soil from trees catch-

Continued

Spring Changes in the Air

As spring approaches, the sun rises higher each day, solar radiation becomes more intense, and the East Pacific High begins to strengthen and bulge farther north. Gradually, the jet stream and the waves of storms are pushed north and become less frequent in California while high pressure builds a little stronger.

Recent studies have shown that infrequent, but stubborn, late-season storms may combine with the increased spring surface heating to produce rare violent weather, even tornadoes, in California flatlands. Tornadoes are rare in California because of the dominant stable air masses. There is also the absence of extremely warm, moist tropical air to do battle with bitter cold, arctic air. The warmer maritime tropical (mT) air masses are modified because they must pass over the cold California current before reaching the state. Continental polar (cP) and arctic air masses are normally blocked and modified by mountain barriers before they reach California. However,

a few water spouts and tornadoes form each year in freak storms which bring unusually unstable air to the state. They do not rival in power or frequency the ominous tornadoes of the central United States.

While inland areas begin to heat very rapidly in the spring sun, the East Pacific High builds over ocean water still cool from winter. This sets up a strong temperature and pressure gradient as closely spaced isotherms and isobars trend nearly parallel to the coast and roughly northwest–southeast across California. The cooler, denser air moves off the ocean from the high pressure and pours into the hot, expanding air of the developing thermal low pressure inland. Strong sea breezes and thick, stable marine layers with low stratus and fog keep coastal valleys cool, often into June, except for a few interruptions from early season heat waves. Southern Californians sometimes refer to this as "June gloom."

Soils often become saturated only by late winter and early spring in California, following the cool rainy season. This paves the way for an explosion of new plant

ADVECTION FOG AND THE MARINE LAYER *continued*

Call it high fog or low stratus, it forms over the cold Pacific waters and drifts through the chilly Golden Gate, often keeping San Francisco crisp and cold during summer.

ing this moisture has been measured at more than 25 cm (10 inches) per year along the northwest coast and even along the Oakland/Berkeley Hills. Without this advection fog, many plant communities along the California coast (including the coast redwood forest) could not survive.

Summer's cool marine layers and its advection fogs are also indirectly responsible for the culturally famous California tan and some of the highest skin cancer rates in the world. In many parts of the nation, it is very uncomfortable and sometimes impossible to stay out, much less lay out, in direct summer sun; clear summer days are often just too hot. In contrast, when California's inland tempera-

tures soar during summer, people flock to coast beaches and sea breezes. Thousands of scantly clothed people lay out in and soak up direct sunlight, comfortably warm sunlight that seems less intense in the cool temperatures, sunlight that is often filtered through a blanket of advection fog. However, these conditions can deliver just as much dangerous UV radiation as a hot, sunny summer day. The sun may tan those with lighter skin, but will damage any person's skin when it is exposed for long periods. Countless California sun worshipers have been surprised when their cool summer day at the beach turned into a painful evening dedicated to soothing their burnt, dried skin.

growth from mountain slopes to coastal hills and from valley grasslands to the deserts. Depending on temperatures and the amount and timing of precipitation, spring delivers some of the most beautiful wildflower displays in the world to parts of California. Meanwhile, as winter's mountain snows melt, reservoirs fill with precious water for California's farms and thirsty residents. By late spring, weather patterns have set the stage for California's summer drought season. The annual cycle continues.

◆ AIR POLLUTION

Southern California and the Los Angeles Basin

A combination of natural factors often concentrates California's air pollution into local basins. We've already examined some of these factors. The classic example is in the Los Angeles Basin, especially where it extends into

the San Fernando, San Gabriel, and Pomona/Walnut Valleys and finally farther east into the inland valleys surrounding San Bernardino and Riverside. The pollutants come from the cars, factories, and daily activities of nearly 15 million people.

On many days, especially in summer, air sinks down from the dominant high pressure cell aloft. As it heats by compression, it forms a warm, dry lid of less dense air above the basin. Below this lid is the persistent marine layer, that relatively cooler and denser layer near the surface. This produces one of the most stable columns of air in our troposphere; the cooler, denser air remains low, and the warmer lid of air stays above. There is very little mixing or communication between the two layers. This condition is called an inversion. The pollutants from city activities—what we call **smog** (smoke plus fog)—is trapped in the denser layer of air below.

Because this dense surface air is the marine layer, the sea breeze pushes it and the smog away from the coast and into inland valleys on most days, especially during

High pressure clamps the marine layer down and the sea breeze pushes smog inland. On an average summer day, air pollution backs up against mountains ringing the Los Angeles Basin and accumulates in inland valleys.

summer. Eventually, the sea breeze and its smog is blocked by the high mountains that ring the basin, mostly the San Gabriels and San Bernardinos. On many days, the smog cannot escape up through the inversion, and it cannot move farther inland because of the mountain barriers. Prevailing winds keep it from moving back out toward the coast, and it remains trapped in the valleys.

Other natural factors may now join the drama. Remember that the high pressure aloft is associated with fair weather. Below it, there is little chance of rain that would wash the air clean, or mixing that would disperse the pollutants. Intense sun shines into the trapped basin stew and bakes it into photochemical smog. Ozone is the most famous of photochemical air pollutants; it is abundant on sunny afternoons after the fog and low clouds burn off, and it is very toxic. It nearly disappears at night, only to return with the next day's sunshine.

These conditions explain why the San Gabriel Valley and its neighbors are some of the smoggiest places in the country. However, in the last quarter of the twentieth century, remarkable progress was made to improve air quality in these basins, and air pollution was cut by more than half. The 1997 season was one of the cleanest in history despite a population of people and cars that more than doubled in the Los Angeles area since the 1960s. The smog control programs initiated by Southern California's Air Quality Management District (AQMD) and other agencies were working.

Because of more frequent inversions, 1998 was smoggier in Los Angeles and in California than 1997. Interestingly, the AQMD measured highest ozone levels during summer afternoons in a mountain community that overlooked Los Angeles' inland valleys. Apparently, a complicated stew of pollutants was drifting farther inland and up mountain slopes as it was baked into ozone. Unconvinced residents of the San Bernardino Mountain community of Crestline questioned the data. Meteorologists suggested that, at about 1,433 m (4,700 feet), little Crestline wasn't quite high enough to escape the inversion layer and accumulated smog that sloshes up mountain slopes from cities below during hot summer afternoons.

Other California Valleys Trap Smog

It is clear that most California beach cities get the first fresh blast of sea breeze during most of the year, especially during summer, and their air quality is acceptable most of the time. However, it is a different story for California inland valleys downwind from major pollution sources. San Diego County's inland valleys are good examples of pollution havens. Years ago, the city of San Diego's population soared well over one million. As it and its neighbors continue to grow, commuters and industries spew out air pollution. Most of it drifts east, accumulating in pockets many miles inland from the coast, trapped against mountain barriers.

San Jose and the Santa Clara Valley are also examples of pollution havens. The sea breeze pours around mountain barriers, through the Golden Gate, and pushes south over great Bay Area cities until it reaches the most populated—San Jose. Here, the air and its pollutants are often trapped by the surrounding hills and a familiar summer inversion. Inland valleys of the East Bay into Livermore may suffer from similar conditions as do some inland valleys of the North Bay.

In the 1990s, the Bay Area was taken off a national list (published by the U.S. Environmental Protection Agency) of metropolitan areas with major air pollution problems, and residents boasted about having some of the cleanest air of any major American population center. Unfortunately, ozone levels increased again in 1998, and

WHAT KINDS OF AIR POLLUTION
CAUSE PROBLEMS IN CALIFORNIA?

Most of the state's 34 million people are concentrated within valleys with stagnant air, and they are often forced to breath the variety of toxic pollutants produced by industries, transportation and other activities. Most air pollutants are so toxic, they must be measured in parts per million (ppm), some in even smaller fractions.

Ozone (a molecule with three oxygen atoms) is a photochemical air pollutant. Concentrations far less than 1 ppm can cause eye, nose, and throat irritation; it also irritates and impairs breathing, eats away at paint, rubber, and paper surfaces, and damages plants. Severe fatigue and other serious symptoms become evident at concentrations above 1 ppm.

Ozone can be produced in California cities when nitrogen dioxide (NO_2) is exposed to sunlight. Nitrogen dioxide, belched mostly from automobiles and power plants, is a brownish gas that impairs breathing and damages the lungs. In sunlight, atomic oxygen liberated from NO_2 combines with an oxygen molecule (O_2) to produce ozone (O_3). Remaining nitric oxide (NO) molecules react with hydrocarbons to form a host of other air pollutants.

Carbon monoxide (CO) is produced by incomplete combustion. It is an invisible gas that reduces the blood's oxygen content and can eventually cause carbon monoxide poisoning. There are several other air pollutants that Californians must endure. They range from complicated peroxyacetyl nitrates (PAN) to simpler sulfur oxides. Though acid fog episodes have been recorded in the state, acid precipitation has not been as problematic as in the northeastern United States or European locations; prevailing winds bring cleaner clouds and precipitation from the Pacific.

Particulates of all kinds are produced from natural (such as dust, salt, and smoke) and human (such as trucks, tractors, and trains) sources in the state. Anyone who has experienced the thick, dark smoke expelled behind a malfunctioning diesel engine understands the problem carbon particles represent in our cities. These particulates not only reduce visibility, but they may invade deep into the lungs and cause a range of dangerous and deadly respiratory problems. These soot clouds are most noticeable downwind of major cities in the state's inland valleys.

Following nearly ten years of research, the state Air Resources Board finally declared diesel soot a cancer-causing pollutant in 1998. Officials immediately faced a more challenging problem: how to require cleaner diesel engines without creating unnecessary hardships for diesel users. Decreasing combustion and building cleaner, more efficient engines are vital steps to remedying the particulate problems that cause air pollution. Controversy erupts when pollution control efforts focus on specific polluters, as illustrated by the trucking industry's reaction to regulations designed to increase the efficiency of California's trucks and cut diesel exhaust. Pollution control efforts and the controversies will carry well into the twenty-first century.

Another controversy erupted at the end of the twentieth century when studies revealed that recreational watercraft spewed more than 750 tons of hydrocarbons and nitrogen oxides into California's air during the average weekend. That represents about fifty percent more pollution than all the cars on California roads produce during a weekend. Local air district boards and the state Air Resources Board had finally found an explanation for the stubborn air pollution levels common near and downwind from these recreational areas. Efforts to require cleaner-burning Jet Skis and other recreational watercraft were met with opposition from manufacturers and some consumers.

the area was placed back on the EPA list of cities with polluted air. The culprits included more frequent inversions and a growing population and economy that put more cars on Bay Area freeways. Bay Area residents and officials, like their counterparts in Los Angeles, have learned that persistence is required in the battle against air pollution.

Meanwhile, the combination of population growth and agricultural activity in the Central Valley has created air pollution problems, especially in the San Joaquin Valley. As that same summer sea breeze pushes into the valley from the Bay Area, it gathers pollutants. The breeze pushes south and is trapped by the inversion and the surrounding mountains in the southern San Joaquin Valley. The big cities of the valley, such as Fresno and Bakersfield, add to the residue spewed by the agricultural industry. During the hottest summer days, when the air tries to rise and break through the inversion, the pollutants have been traced up the western slopes and canyons of the Sierra Nevada. Here, they inhibit plant growth and have damaged forest species such as Sequoia seedlings. This is nothing new to California; entire forests have been destroyed by air pollution creeping up the slopes and canyons of the San Gabriel and San Bernardino Mountains from the Los Angeles Basin during hot summer afternoons.

Even the Coachella and Imperial Valleys trap dangerous air pollutants. The mixture of urban and agricultural activities produces a host of pollutants much like the Central Valley's until hot afternoon temperatures break the inversion and vent the cooked stew.

◆ CALIFORNIA'S CLIMATES

Before we examine California's plants and animals, we should take a closer look at the different climates around the state and the factors that contribute to and control them. We will use our understanding of California weather patterns to explain why these climates exist and how they evolved.

Climate classification has always been a difficult and controversial job, especially in California. First, particular types of climate data and classifications serve specific needs. Biologists, farmers, hydrologists, tourists, architects, city planners, utility workers, and so many others are interested in different elements of weather and climate in California.

Second, it is especially crucial in a state like California to establish the scale of climate study. The larger regional climates (macroclimates) cover and connect the most general, somewhat homogeneous, climatic regions of the state. Local climates cover smaller areas and environments, such as hillside slopes, canyons, river valleys, basins, and mesas. Microclimates are the miniature environments found near the ground at specific sites next to rocks, trees, buildings, or other features that impact climate on the smallest scale.

We will use the Köppen system of regional climate classification because it is the most widely used and understood, and it uses conveniently recorded values showing annual trends of temperature and precipitation. The boundaries of these climate groups may also roughly coincide with major vegetation types, a subject of Chapter 5. The Köppen system uses a shorthand code of letters to place regions into major climate groups, then subgroups with smaller subdivisions, all based on seasonal temperature and precipitation patterns.

No Tropical Climates in California

There are no "A" (tropical rainy) climates in California because every location experiences seasons with the temperature of at least one winter month averaging below 18°C (64.4°F). Maritime tropical air masses (mT) are greatly modified before reaching California, so they only affect local areas for brief periods. Tropical air flowing from the southwest is chilled by cold ocean currents before reaching California. This air can even be cooled until it takes on characteristics of maritime polar (mP) air masses. Meanwhile, air from the south or southeast must pass over great land masses and even mountain barriers before reaching the state. It is often modified so that it resembles dry, hot (cT) air masses.

The Driest Climates: California Deserts

A variety of "B" (dry) climates exist trending toward southeastern California, where cT (dry, hot continental) air masses dominate in the summer and even some cP (dry, cold continental) air masses invade and settle in during winter. These are regions where potential evaporation rates exceed precipitation during the year (there is no water surplus) and no major permanent streams originate. Located near the dominant subtropical high and behind major mountain barriers that create great rainshadows, these are the driest places in California and North America. Any moist air mass encroaching into these regions is drastically modified and dried by the time it sinks into these low desert valleys.

In the southern San Joaquin Valley and throughout southeastern California, BWh (true hot desert climates) exist where precipitation is less than one half of potential evapotranspiration, and the average temperature of even the coldest month is above freezing. A hotter division of this climate (BWhh) exists where average maximum temperatures exceed 38°C (100°F) for at least three months. These very hot deserts are found in lower desert valleys from Death Valley to the Colorado River and in the Coachella and Imperial Valleys.

Interestingly, a few of these locations are the only places in California that often experience peak precipitation (though with meager totals) in late summer rather than winter. (The causes and dynamics of these summer thunderstorms have already been reviewed.) Regardless, summer afternoon temperatures may soar over 49°C (120°F); the hottest temperature ever recorded in California and North America was nearly 57°C (134°F) in Death Valley.

Semiarid California

Bordering the driest climates and scattered within southern California's inland valleys and along its extreme southern coastal strip are the semiarid steppe (BS) climates. Here, precipitation is more than 1/2 of (but still less than) potential evapotranspiration rates. This is an intermediate climate between the true deserts and more humid climate groups. Therefore, these landscapes often support grasslands and are somewhat wetter and often cooler than California's true deserts.

These include the higher elevation rainshadow, semi-arid deserts of transmontane California, ranging from the higher elevations of the Mojave, north into the Owens Valley and other parts of the Basin and Range. Precipitation is greater and temperatures are cooler than the hot, dry deserts below them; evapotranspiration rates are not as extreme. The BSh climate's coldest month averages above freezing, or the mean annual temperature is over 18°C (64.4°F). Still higher terrain exhibits BSk (cool desert) climates, where the average temperature of the coldest month is below freezing, or the mean annual temperature is below 18°C (64.4°F); these often trend into the colder, wetter, higher elevation mountain climates.

In inland valleys of cismontane southern California (including the southern San Joaquin), BSh climates experience occasional invasions of moist air, but summers are usually hot and dry. They are bordered by cooler and wetter Mediterranean climates. Along the coast from Orange County south, the BShn is a foggy coastal semi-arid zone. With annual precipitation around 25 cm (10 inches), it is drier than the Mediterranean coast to the north. However, coastal stratus and fog are common especially in summer as the ocean air moderates temperatures and cuts evapotranspiration rates.

Mediterranean Climates

Most renowned and widespread in California are Mediterranean climates. They are categorized under the mild, mesothermal middle-latitude "C" climates, where the average coldest month temperatures drop below 18°C (64.4°F), but remain above −3°C (26.6°F) and where precipitation is often greater than evapotranspiration. In California, all of these are more specifically "Cs" climates, or mild humid climates, where intense summer droughts give way to winter rainy seasons. In some years in southern California, more than five months may pass without measurable precipitation. These climates dominate cismontane California at lower and middle elevations from the coast up the mountain slopes, from the Oregon border to southern California. These environments typically experience severe fire seasons from summer well into fall.

When the East Pacific High builds north in late spring and dominates through the summer, it protects cismontane California from storminess and precipitation. The clockwise winds spiraling out of this high pressure then push the cold California ocean current down the coast. As these prevailing winds are pulled inland toward California's hot thermal low, they must first pass over this current, where they are chilled. The cool, dense sea breeze that moves onshore may carry plenty of low stratus and fog, but it is very stable.

This further inhibits the formation of storms or any type of unsettled weather. The monotonous "late night and early morning low clouds and fog—otherwise mostly sunny" forecast is typical of these Mediterranean coastal climates, especially during summer. During winter, the East Pacific High weakens and migrates south. At this time, the polar front jet stream slips south and low pressure disturbances invade from the North Pacific. California's winter rainy season results.

Hot summers rule in Csa climates of the inland valleys; the average temperature of the warmest month is greater than 22°C (72°F). These regions are far enough inland or protected by small topographic barriers so that summer's

cooling sea breezes are weaker and modified by the time they arrive. These often border the Csb (cooler summer) climates of higher elevations or coastal zones, where the warmest month averages less than 22°C (72°F). More distinctive are the Csbn climates along the immediate coast, where persistent coastal fog and stratus clouds keep summers even cooler. Recall that this is due to the cold California ocean current that keeps coastal air masses chilled and near their dew points during summer.

Mountain Climates

Classified as "Ds" are the microthermal (snowy forest) climates, where the average temperature of the coldest month is less than −3°C (26.6°F). These are only found at higher elevations in the Klamaths, Cascades, Sierra Nevada, and near southern California's higher ridges and peaks. Heavy snow is common and substantial snow packs accumulate during the winter storm season, due to orographic effects. However, studies have shown that most of the annual precipitation falls only within several days during winter's most severe storms.

During summer, rare North Pacific storms might sneak into the north. Isolated afternoon thunderstorms (especially toward the south) may also provide brief relief from summer drought. However, they do not produce significant or reliable precipitation compared to winter storms. This is an interesting and rare variation from the more common "D" climates around the world which usually have winter dry seasons or no dry season at all. The average warmest month in Dsb climates is less than 22°C (72°F); summers are not hot. At still higher elevations, the Dsc climates average fewer than four warm season months with temperatures above 10°C (50°F).

Finally, California's "EH" climates are the highland climates similar to the worldwide arctic or alpine class, often known as tundra climates. Average temperatures of the warmest month are less than 10°C (50°F) and winters are bitter cold. Winter's high winds and temperatures below −18°C (0°F) make these hostile places. These climates are only found on California's highest peaks and ridges above the tree line. Once winter and spring snows finally melt, the water frequently drains into forests of lower elevations, making way for short, harsh growing seasons, where weather swings between extreme conditions in the rarefied air. Brief frost or violent thunderstorms may interrupt the summer drought at any time.

◆ CALIFORNIA'S CHANGING CLIMATES

From the warm tropical climates of the Tertiary Period to the cooler Ice Age which ended just 10,000 years ago, what we now call California has experienced dramatic

EL NIÑO/SOUTHERN OSCILLATION

Many scientists blame El Niño for some of California's unusual weather events, and certainly for the 1998 episode. During average years, rising air in the Intertropical Convergence Zone (ITCZ) near the equator pulls the Trade Winds into the Equatorial Low. South of the equator, the Southeast Trades push the cooler waters from the Humboldt Current from south to north up and along the coast of South America and then along the equator toward the western Pacific. Likewise, the Northeast Trades (north of the equator) also push the remnants of the California current toward the equator and then into the tropical west Pacific.

During rare years, around December, air pressure rises in the west Pacific, the Equatorial Low weakens, and the trade winds subside. This is called the Southern Oscillation. The combined effects on the ocean and the atmosphere are often referred to as **El Niño/Southern Oscillation (ENSO)**. Westward flowing ocean currents near the equatorial Pacific also slow and back up, and the cooler Humboldt and California currents may begin to wane. Large pools of warmer water form in the eastern tropical Pacific and begin backing toward Central and South America, baking in the sun (see Map 4.4).

Sea levels rise in the warmer-than-normal water of the eastern tropical Pacific, and large masses of exceptionally warm moist air form over the water during these El Niño events. The amplified contrast between this super warm water and air and the colder water and air of the North Pacific often brings the Jet Stream farther south, sometimes directly over California. When a series of winter storms forms in the Pacific, they are often guided toward California by that enhanced jet stream. Moving toward the coast, they frequently tap the heat energy and moisture from these unusually warm tropical air masses, pulling them up into their counterclockwise circulations. Now strengthened, the storms carry this tropical air in ahead of them to California, where heavy downpours are produced as they sweep through the state.

Although many factors must come together for such storms to target California, the floods of 1983, 1993, 1995, and 1998 did occur during enhanced El Niño events. During those winters, satellite images dramatically showed pools of warm, moist air flowing into California from the heated tropical Pacific, ahead of almost every major storm. This "pineapple connection," often carried in by a subtropical jet stream, produced record downpours in California.

The 1998 ENSO was the best predicted and arguably the most substantial of all previous events. Meteorologists, climatologists, and oceanographers were already predicting it and its effects during early summer, 1997, before it fully developed. In an unprecedented show of solidarity, these scientists warned of the possible downpours. Their predictions became reality with the wettest February in Los Angeles history and the wettest season ever recorded in many communities from northern California to Orange County, including all-time records in San Francisco and Santa Barbara. Several California mountain communities added impressive snowfalls to that record. Scientists had progressed all the way from being surprised by the 1983 ENSO to predicting the 1998 event. The millions of dollars spent to prepare the state saved both lives and many more millions of dollars in private and public property damage.

El Niño does not always mean flooding in California, but it is repeatedly and more frequently blamed for many weather anomalies in the state. In contrast, a La Niña is recognized during years when eastern Pacific waters are unusually cooler than normal. As expected, this opposite of El Niño often results in very different weather patterns, including drought in southern California as torrential rains ravage the western Pacific. By the end of the 1990s, a substantial La Niña had replaced the historic El Niño of 1998. In contrast to 1998, Los Angeles received less than four inches of rain by mid-February, 1999. Drought had returned to southern California in an unpredictable cycle that can change in a day.

Recent research indicates that ENSO is one of the most important weather makers on our planet. It is blamed for weather anomalies (such as a decrease in hurricanes in the Atlantic) thousands of miles from Pacific waters. It certainly deserves the attention given to it by scientists all over the world.

climate changes. Even during the last 150 years of record-keeping, there have been impressive annual variations in temperatures, while fluctuations between intense flood and drought have been even more remarkable.

In recent years, these fluctuations have become more pronounced as anomalous weather patterns become the rule and "normal" seasonal patterns less reliable. As additional years of records accumulate, we might expect the chances of breaking records to decrease. However, there is a lengthening list of recent anomalous weather patterns and events. They include the longest drought during the six years from the late 1980s to early 1990s and the record-breaking downpours, floods, and snowfalls of 1995, 1997, and 1998. These events are catching the attention of farmers, insurance companies, biologists, flood-control officials, water departments, the tourist industry, and, of course, climatologists. There are many more examples.

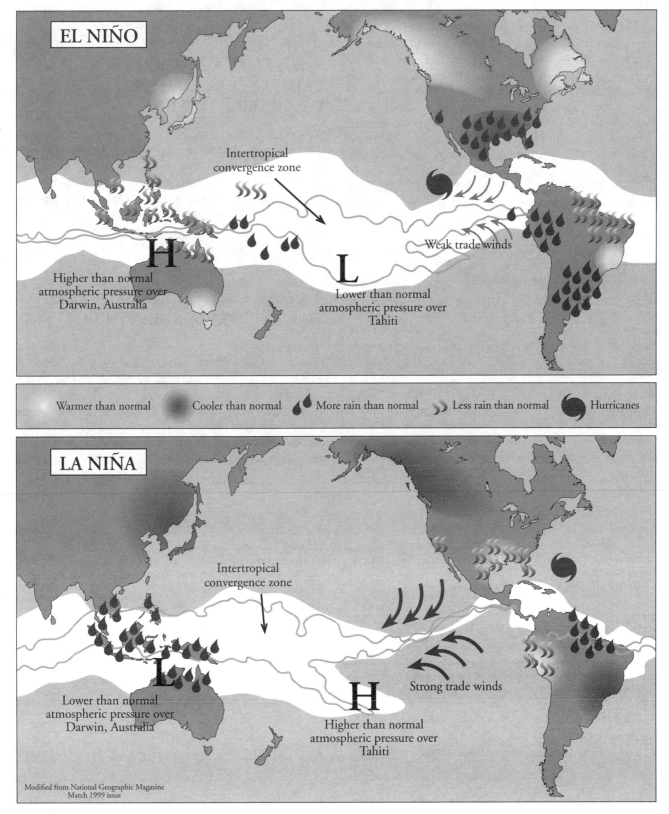

EL NIÑO

Intertropical
convergence zone

H

Higher than normal
atmospheric pressure over
Darwin, Australia

L

Lower than normal
atmospheric pressure over
Tahiti

Weak trade winds

Warmer than normal   Cooler than normal   More rain than normal   Less rain than normal   Hurricanes

LA NIÑA

Intertropical
convergence zone

L

Lower than normal
atmospheric pressure over
Darwin, Australia

H

Higher than normal
atmospheric pressure over
Tahiti

Strong trade winds

Modified from National Geographic Magazine
March 1999 issue

MAP 4.4

El Niño/Southern Oscillation. El Niño/Southern Oscillation occurs when unusually warm
water accumulates in the eastern tropical Pacific Ocean. El Niño and La Niña cycles may
have dramatic impacts on California's weather.

By the early 1990s, bark beetle infestations were devastating drought-stricken pine forests, while water rationing was required on many farms and in cities across California. Heavy rains and snows refilled reservoirs to capacity in 1993, but 1994 was about the third driest in the state's history. This was followed in 1995 with record rains, floods, and mountain snows. As residents in the Sierra Nevada dug through more than 6 m (20 feet) of snow to get to the second floors of their cabins, more than 38 cm (15 inches) of rain was recorded along many coastal slopes within a twenty-four-hour period. Parts of the Napa-Sonoma grape country were inundated by storms that delivered more than 250 cm (100 inches) of rain during that 1994–1995 season. A powerful winter storm produced heavy rain and mountain snows across the state as late as mid-June. Skiing continued until mid-August, 1996, at Mammoth Mountain.

Two weeks of torrential rains flooded northern California valleys in early 1997. The rains stopped early that year, leaving many parts of the state dry after mid-February; it did not rain in Los Angeles from mid-February until fall. It was the longest period without measurable rain in that city's history. This was immediately followed by the 1998 El Niño downpours. Several stations up and down the California coast (including San Francisco, Santa Barbara, and UCLA) recorded their wettest years in history. Several northern California communities received well over one hundred inches of rain, while well over fifty inches of rain poured over the Santa Monica Mountains in southern California. Even Death Valley experienced the wettest season on record in 1997 to 1998.

◆ DIVERSITY AND CHANGE DOMINATE CALIFORNIA WEATHER PATTERNS

Superficial assumptions about California's unchanging, mild climates are blown away when these sometimes radical spatial and temporal variations are explored. These conditions make California an ideal state for the study of so many extratropical weather events and climates. Before we use this information to make connections and explore the biogeography of California, we can interpret climate data for selected weather stations around the state.

◆ CLIMOGRAPHS REVEAL CLUES TO CALIFORNIA'S MANY CLIMATES

Climographs are used to show annual variations and trends in temperature and precipitation for selected weather stations in California (see Figure 4.5a, b, c). These and other graphics present California climate data in an organized and easy-to-understand fashion, ready for interpretation. The commonly used Koppen classification system shows the distribution of California's diverse climates (see Map 4.5).

Column One

• Max. Temp. is the average of all daily maximum temperatures recorded for the day of the year between the years 1961 and 1990.
• Ave. Temp. is the average of all daily average temperatures recorded for the day of the year between the years 1961 and 1990.
• Min. Temp. is the average of all daily minimum temperatures recorded for the day of the year between the years 1961 and 1990.
• Precipitation is the average of all daily total precipitation recorded for the day of the year between the years 1961 and 1990.
• Data are smoothed using a 29-day running average.

FIGURE 4.5a
Climates near California's north and south corners.

Column Two

• Extreme Max. is the maximum of all daily maximum temperatures recorded for the day of the year.
• Ave. Max. is the average of all daily maximum temperatures recorded for the day of the year.
• Ave. Min. is the average of all daily minimum temperatures recorded for the day of the year.
• Extreme Min. is the minimum of all daily minimum temperatures recorded for the day of the year.

Column One

Precipitation　Max. Temp.　Ave. Temp.　Min. Temp.

Column Two

Extreme Max.　Ave. Max.　Ave. Min.　Extreme Min.

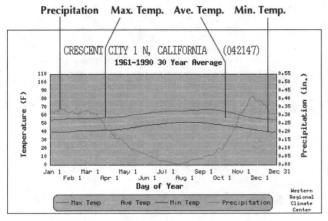

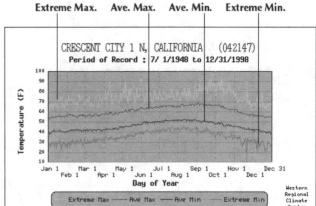

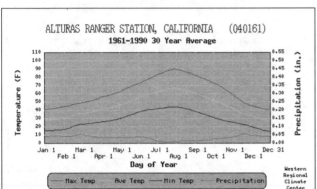

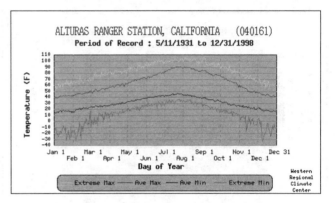

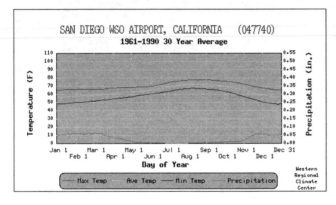

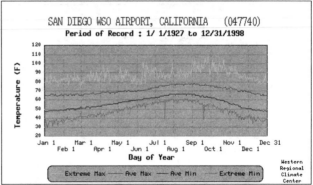

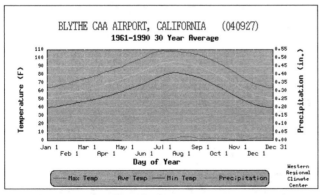

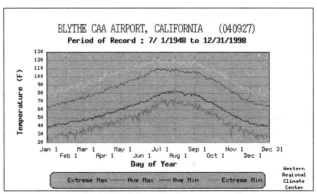

FIGURE 4.5a *continued*

Column One

Precipitation Max. Temp. Ave. Temp. Min. Temp.

Column Two

Extreme Max. Ave. Max. Ave. Min. Extreme Min.

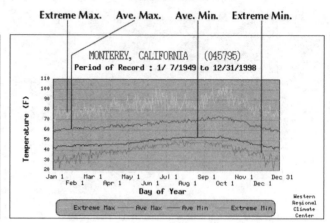

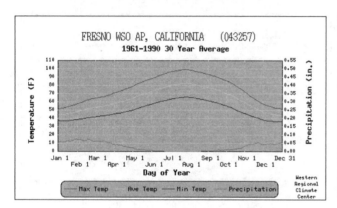

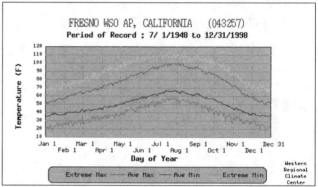

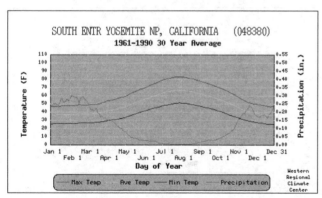

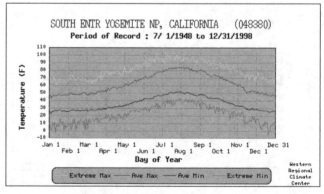

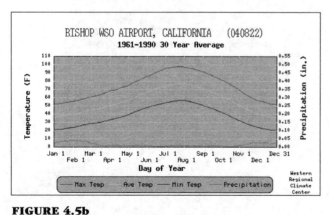

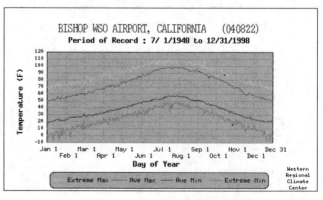

FIGURE 4.5b
Climate across central California.

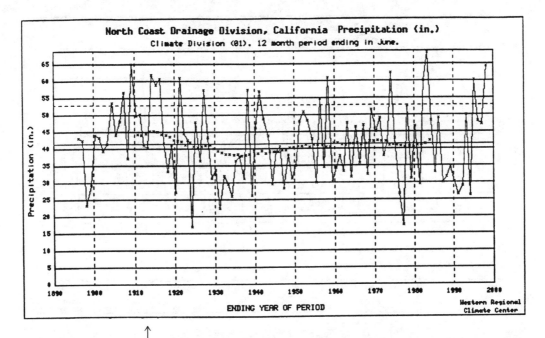

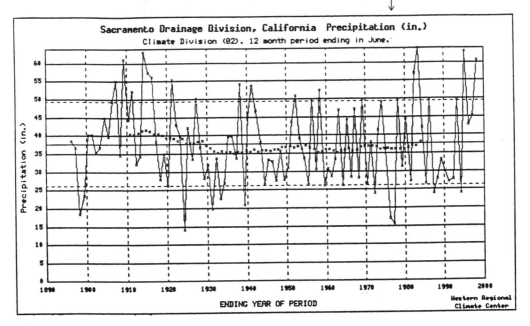

Total Precipitation		Total Precipitation	
Years: 1890–2000		**Years: 1890–2000**	
AVERAGE	41.578	AVERAGE	37.695
SIGMA (RMS)	11.372	SIGMA (RMS)	11.580
COEFF OF VAR	0.274	COEFF OF VAR	0.307
SKEWNESS	0.224	SKEWNESS	0.305
MEDIAN	41.540	MEDIAN	36.590
MAXIMUM VALUE	68.270	MAXIMUM VALUE	63.850
MINIMUM VALUE	16.870	MINIMUM VALUE	13.970
NUMBER OBS	103.	NUMBER OBS	103.

FIGURE 4.5c

Average and extreme precipitation within selected regions.

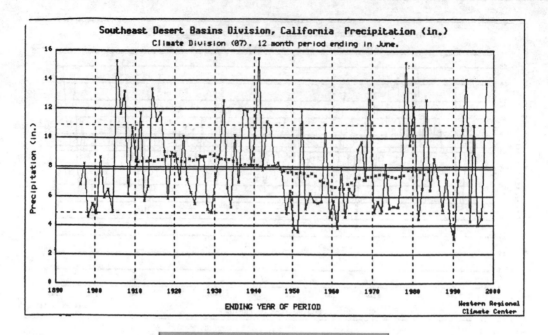

Total Precipitation	
Years: 1890–2000	
AVERAGE	7.883
SIGMA (RMS)	3.007
COEFF OF VAR	0.381
SKEWNESS	0.664
MEDIAN	7.170
MAXIMUM VALUE	15.450
MINIMUM VALUE	3.060
NUMBER OBS	103.

FIGURE 4.5c *continued*

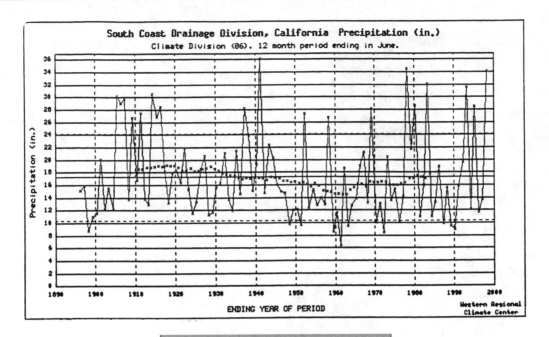

South Coast Drainage Division, California Precipitation (in.)
Climate Division (06). 12 month period ending in June.

Total Precipitation	
Years: 1890–2000	
AVERAGE	17.321
SIGMA (RMS)	6.916
COEFF OF VAR	0.399
SKEWNESS	0.914
MEDIAN	15.210
MAXIMUM VALUE	36.050
MINIMUM VALUE	6.330
NUMBER OBS	103.

FIGURE 4.5c *continued*

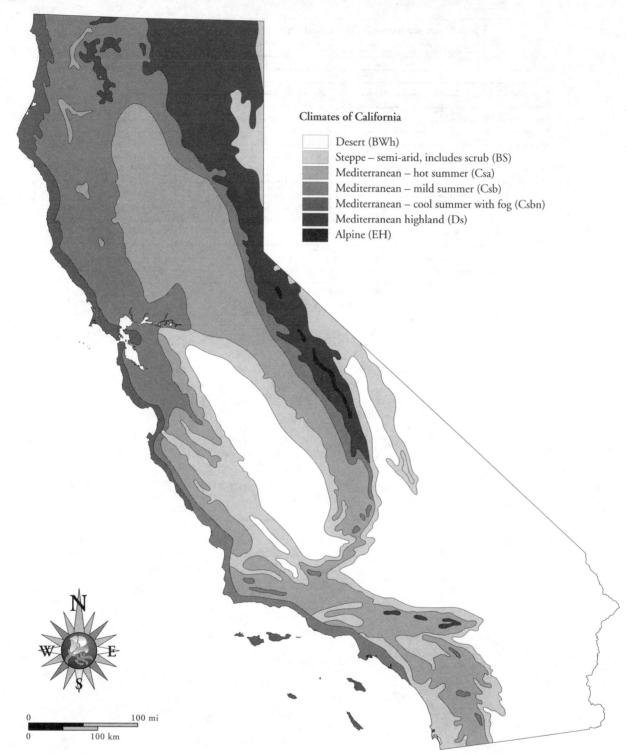

Climates of California

- Desert (BWh)
- Steppe – semi-arid, includes scrub (BS)
- Mediterranean – hot summer (Csa)
- Mediterranean – mild summer (Csb)
- Mediterranean – cool summer with fog (Csbn)
- Mediterranean highland (Ds)
- Alpine (EH)

N
W E
S

0   100 mi
0   100 km

MAP 4.5
Köppen Climate Map of California.

SOME KEY TERMS AND TOPICS

advection (coastal) fog	Great Basin High	rainshadow
Aleutian Low	jet stream	Rossby waves
California current	lapse rate	Santa Ana Wind
Catalina Eddy	marine layer	smog
dew point	middle-latitude wave cyclone	temperature inversion
East Pacific (Hawaiian) High	orographic precipitation	thermal low
El Niño/Southern Oscillation (ENSO)	radiation (tule) fog	

Additional Key Terms and Topics

adiabatic lapse rate	environmental lapse rate	radiation
air pollution	fire season/hazard	sea breeze
atmospheric pressure	global circulation	snow level, depth
climate change	humidity	solar radiation
climate classification	land breeze	stable air
climographs	latitude factors	temperature
compressional heating	marine air mass	temperature range
condensation	microclimates	tropical storms
continental air mass	mountain barriers	unstable air
coriolis effect	pineapple connection	upwelling
downslope winds	precipitation	
elevation factors	pressure gradient	

Chapter 5

Biogeography: Distribution of Plants and Animals

The state's astounding variety of biotic communities with their diverse collections of plants and animals is examined in this chapter. The living laboratory we call California is so enormous and biologically diverse that the study of it poses some problems: Where do we start? How do we organize our study? How do we classify the various living environments? Of course, these same problems confront botanists, zoologists, and biogeographers around the world. However, scientists studying California's plants and animals have engaged in exceptionally fascinating and controversial debates involving these problems and other related issues. Their debates often revolve around the diversity, connections, and change that are major themes throughout this book.

The diversity of California's plants and animals is in large part a result of the state's wide range of latitude and elevation and its position on North America's subtropical and mid-latitude west coast.

KEY ISSUES AND CONCEPTS

◆ The state's unusual biological diversity makes it a challenging place to study and classify plants and animals. More general organizational schemes that include the use of biomes, vegetation zones and belts reflect efforts to simplify these studies.

◆ California exhibits the tallest, largest, and some of the oldest plants in the world. Communities vary from thick forests to sparse deserts and from riparian woodlands to sandy dunes. Remarkable diversity is the rule.

◆ The organization of California's plants into communities is most effective, compared to other organizational schemes. These communities with their species are in various stages of succession as they evolve within specific environments. In this chapter, a general survey of each plant community's habitat and structure is followed by more detailed discussions of specific plants and animals common to each community.

◆ Water availability, temperature, solar radiation, humidity, elevation, soil, slope exposure, fire, human impacts, and a host of other factors determine the nature of each plant community.

Generally, the greatest biomass and diversity will be found in California landscapes where water is available for the longest period and year-round temperatures are mild.

◆ Most of the state's plants and animals have adapted to long summer drought, occasional fire, and other environmental conditions and events common to California.

◆ A transition of plant communities is evident in cismontane California from the coast to inland valleys and from sea level to higher elevations. The most general changes result from climatic conditions reviewed in Chapter 4.

◆ In dry transmontane California, plant communities are generally more lush at higher elevations and near oases, where cooler, moister conditions prevail. Such plants and animals yield to the more widespread, hardier desert scrub species better adapted to adverse conditions in lower deserts distant from water sources.

◆ Ecologic islands, riparian, dune, and other isolated plant communities result when local habitats differ from their general surroundings.

◆ BIOMES

Past biogeographers have sometimes tried to organize terrestrial California into general **biomes**. (Biomes are defined as the largest regional ecologic units, or subdivisions, of plants and animals.) The logic of this system is that biomes are the largest recognizable terrestrial ecosystems, and an **ecosystem** represents a group of interacting organisms and the physical environment in which they live. This simplified approach provides only the most general categories and associations of California's plants and animals. Consequently, the organizational approach based on biomes is no longer embraced by scientists who search for a realistic understanding of California's living landscapes. It only serves as a starting point in our study.

Knowledge of specific **habitats** is also critical in the study of the distribution of plants and animals. (Habitats include a combination of physical factors that represent

the environmental conditions in which organisms live. These include climate, slope, soil, drainage, and many other factors that are especially important to plants and animals of California.)

In the simplistic biome scheme, the *forest* biome is often the most productive and has the greatest **biomass** (total weight of organisms). In California, these biomes appear in more favorable habitats, where there is more water and where temperatures are not too extreme. These forests are abundant in higher elevations of cismontane California and across especially the western slopes of central and northern California's major mountain ranges. More specific forest biomes in California are the *temperate coniferous forests* (needle-leaved) and *temperate deciduous forests* (broad-leaved, often found mixed with coniferous forests in the state).

The *scrub biome* could include environments from the coastal scrub to the chaparral and even into oak woodlands. (Some biogeographers may not use the scrub bi-

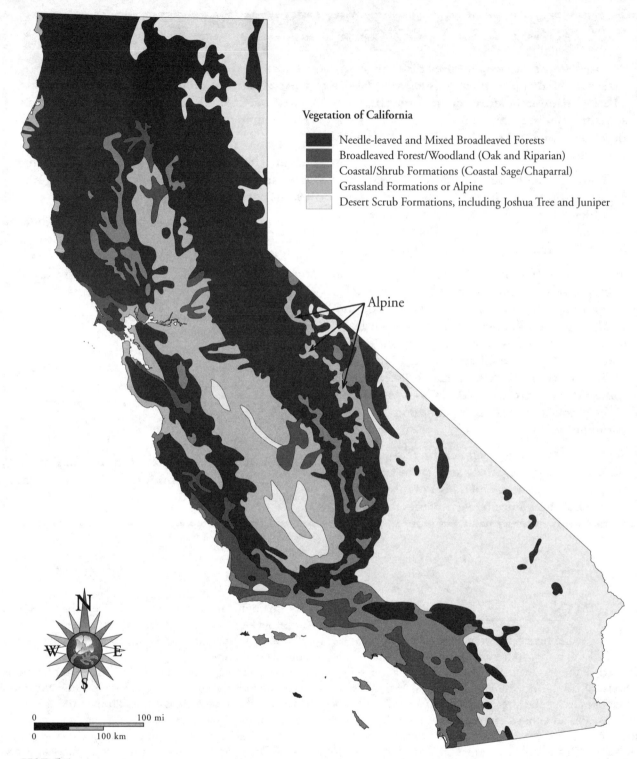

Vegetation of California

- ■ Needle-leaved and Mixed Broadleaved Forests
- ■ Broadleaved Forest/Woodland (Oak and Riparian)
- ■ Coastal/Shrub Formations (Coastal Sage/Chaparral)
- ■ Grassland Formations or Alpine
- □ Desert Scrub Formations, including Joshua Tree and Juniper

Alpine

0 _____ 100 mi
0 _____ 100 km

MAP 5.1
Distribution of Vegetation in California. Only the most general features of the state's diverse vegetation can be shown on such a map.

ome. They might consider chaparral to be a dwarf, *sclerophyll forest*, and they might consider the oak wood-land communities with their scattered trees to resemble a *savanna biome*.) Regardless, we are now considering plants and animals that suffer from considerable water shortages or other adverse conditions compared to their forest neighbors. These are typical of the Mediterranean environments of lower and middle elevations throughout much of cismontane California, especially in southern and central California.

The *grassland* biome includes most of cismontane California's inland valleys, where even drier and hotter summers may eliminate most trees and shrubs.

The *desert* biome includes most of transmontane California, where water shortages are most severe and temperatures are extreme. Only the hardiest plants and animals can survive in these environments with low biomass and less **species diversity** (number of different species).

Finally, the *tundra biome* is found only in California's highest alpine environments. Here, cold temperatures and short growing seasons are important limiting factors for plants and animals.

Some very general connections can be made when comparing California's biomes, vegetation structures, and habitats to other regions of the world (see Map 5.1). Many of these connections may have become apparent during our review of the state's weather and climate. One obvious example is how the state's Mediterranean scrub is similar to that of Chile, the southwest coast of South Africa, southwest Australia, and the Mediterranean. All five locations exhibit the typical Mediterranean climates discussed in Chapter 4—east of dominant subtropical highs, winter rain, summer drought, and most experience coastal fog. Another connection is the temperate marine coniferous forest common to northern California. Note how Mediterranean scrub often yields to similar forests in other areas of the world where climates become cooler and wetter. More specific and numerous are the similarities to other geographic locations created by a wide range of altitudes and mountain barriers.

◆ VEGETATION ZONES AND BELTS

Just as there is controversy and oversimplification with the biomes scheme, early attempts to organize California into generalized **life zones** yielded categories that are too broad. In the 1890s, C. Hart Merriam recognized a transition of **life zones** in Arizona, from the hot and dry lower deserts to the cooler and wetter forests at higher elevations. He and others after him made this simple connection: while travelling from lower to higher elevations in the southwest United States, we may encounter six major biotic zones. These zones (Merriam's **Life Zones**) resemble what we might observe if we were travelling, instead, from drier and hotter northern Mexico to northern Canada.

Although crude, this concept was sometimes applied to California in general, and the Sierra Nevada in particular, with surprisingly successful results. As we review these life zones here, we will use coinciding **Vegetation Zones** to describe them. The different, but related, concept of vegetation zonation by elevation is a little more specific and was proposed by scientists long after Merriam's Life Zones (see Figures 5.1a and 5.1b).

The Lower Sonoran Zone is identified below about 300 m (1,000 feet) on the slopes of the western Sierra

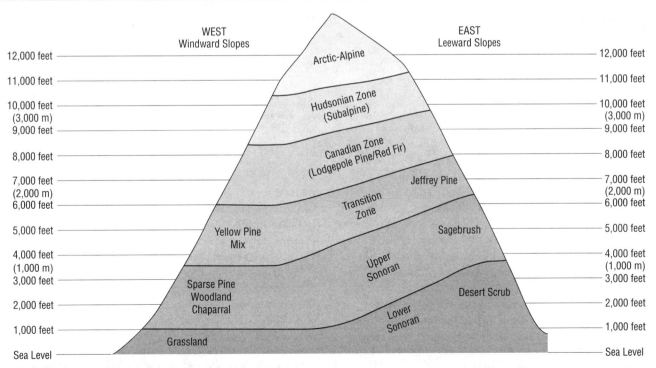

FIGURE 5.1a
Vegetation Zones and Belts. Cross section showing simplified model of vegetation zones and belts across the Sierra Nevada, from west to east.

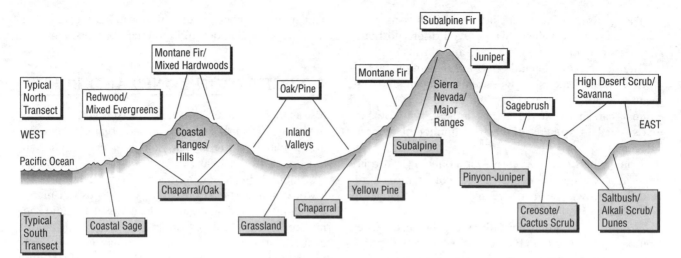

FIGURE 5.1b

Vegetation Transects. Still simplified, but more realistic, are these transects from west to east across the entire state. Some plant communities common to northern California are listed in their proper locations above the transect; several southern communities are shown from west to east below the transect.

Nevada and below about 1,200 m (4,000 feet) on the eastern rainshadow slopes where there is desert and grassland vegetation similar to the hot, dry Sonoran Desert. Below about 1,200 m (4,000 feet) on the western slopes and 2,000 m (6,500 feet) on the eastern slopes is the Upper Sonoran Zone. These higher semiarid environments are somewhat cooler and more moist. Chaparral, woodland, and even some pine forest begin to dominate on western slopes, while sagebrush rules on the rainshadow slopes of the east side.

From about 1,100 m–1,800 m (3,500 feet–6,000 feet) on the western slopes and 2,000 m–2,400 m (6,500 feet–8,000 feet) on eastern slopes are the cooler and wetter mixed forests of the Transition Zone. A mix of yellow pine forests covers western slopes, while the resilient Jeffrey Pine grows on eastern slopes. From about 1,800 m–2,600 m (6,000 feet–8,500 feet) on western slopes and 2,400 m–3,000 m (8,000 feet–10,000 feet) on eastern slopes is the Canadian Zone. Lush forests of lodgepole pine and red fir grow in this still cooler and wetter belt. From 2,600 m–3,200 m (8,500 feet–10,500 feet) on the western slopes and at higher elevations on eastern slopes is the Hudsonian Zone, home of the subalpine belt. Here are communities similar to the coldest woodlands, or taiga, around Hudson Bay, where only short, widely spaced trees are found.

Above all of these, at the highest elevations, is the Arctic-Alpine Zone with its alpine belt vegetation. Here, above tree line, organisms are under greatest stress from the very cold temperatures and short growing seasons somewhat similar to arctic tundra.

Note how these zones and belts are characteristically tilted up into higher elevations on the eastern rainsha-

dow sides of mountain ranges. This is typical in California, where you must travel to higher elevations in transmontane ranges to experience the moist conditions typical of lower elevations facing the ocean. A good biogeographer will also notice that, though these zones are easy to understand, they are still too general for California. There are just too many other factors that determine which type of community will exist at any one location—there are too many exceptions to these schemes.

◆ LIVING COMMUNITIES

Therefore, in this chapter, we use plant communities to paint a picture of California's living landscapes. We have already defined the more general biomes and ecosystems. In contrast, a community refers to the relationships among animals and plants in an area. More specifically, it might be defined as a group of plants and animals that interact with their environment within a space-time boundary. This is a more precise method of studying habitats and life forms based on dominant species. It has been widely accepted and used since Phillip Munz and David Keck developed it in 1959. (See Figure 5.1b.)

Each community and its species has evolved over time as a result of dispersal events, climate, slope, soils, fires, human interaction, and many other factors. Such ecological **succession** is a gradual, but continual process after each event or disturbance. A series of intermediate seral (non-climax) communities may eventually mature to a **climax community**. Such a climax community is considered to be in equilibrium so that it can maintain itself until the next event or disturbance. One example is how many of the state's plant communities are still evolving from the effects of the last Ice Age that ended about 10,000 years ago.

During that short ten thousand years, plant communities have adapted, and continue to adapt, to smaller climate changes. On smaller scales, ecological **succession** may follow a volcanic eruption, fire, flood, or landslide. This makes us question the concept of succession and how we might define a **climax community**. Many modern scientists argue that the whole idea of a climax community is idealistic at best and that we really should consider our plant communities to be in dynamic equilibrium. Regardless, it would benefit any biogeographer studying this state to consider each plant community's stage of succession and the time since the last disturbance. These considerations help explain the complicated montage of plant communities commonly encountered in the state's landscapes.

We will begin at the coast and sweep inland, first at lower elevations, then up to the higher mountain terrain of cismontane California. We will then break to examine some exceptions or islands in the general trends. Finally, we will look at some of the plants and animals of transmontane California, on the rainshadow sides of the mountains and in California's deserts.

Specialized botanists and zoologists may cringe at the thought of such a general survey of only the salient features of California's life forms, but it is the appropriate approach in a book searching for more general connections and relationships. Information in this chapter has been drawn from many major surveys of California's plant communities. When there was conflict among the experts, especially in the classification of specific plant communities, efforts were made to find common ground.

◆ COMMUNITIES OF CISMONTANE CALIFORNIA'S LOWER ELEVATIONS

Coastal Sand Dune and Beach Communities

Beach refers to the strip of coastline above mean tide inland to the greatest extent of storm waves during highest tides. A foredune often marks the inland boundary of this strip that is occasionally inundated and disturbed by wave action. Beach plants and animals must adapt to at least rare invasions of ocean waves. **Coastal sand dunes** may extend well inland of the beach and foredune to more stable ground. Though organisms here are protected from or elevated above wave action, they must adapt to shifting sands. Technically, the terms **coastal strand** or **littoral strip** are synonymous with beach, though they have unfortunately been used to describe both beach and dune zones.

Habitat and Structure

Marine air moderates surface temperatures and brings vital moisture to coastal dunes, unlike their counterparts in California's deserts. Winter storms may bring waves that wreak havoc on California's beaches, but they also bring frequent clouds, drizzle, and rain over the dunes. Summer fog and stratus keep temperatures down and relative humidities up, resulting in lower evapotranspiration rates on coastal dunes. Due to the marine air, summer air temperatures are rarely hot (especially on the north coast) and winter temperatures are rarely cold enough for frost (especially on the south coast). Just as ocean water temperatures may change by only a few degrees Celsius during the seasons, the difference in monthly mean air temperatures is no more than 6°C–9°C (about 13°F) at any one location. At first glance, this may seem like an ideal environment for plants.

Though air temperature extremes are not nearly as severe as on desert dunes, exposed sand surfaces even along the coast experience dramatic changes. Because many dune plants grow close to the sand surface, they may endure wild fluctuations in temperatures. As high winds along an exposed coastline keep the disturbed sand moving, they also bring sea salt spray.

Add to this the nutrient-poor substrate where water drains through so rapidly in one place only to pond in nearby hollows, and we recognize conditions that present a series of challenges to living organisms. Because the amount of disturbance and salt and sand spray varies and because soil conditions change dramatically, we expect to find a wide variety of organisms adapted to the wide variety of conditions from the harsh sandy beach to more stable dunes farther inland.

Though about 23 percent of the California coast is beach and dune, these plant communities account for less than 1 percent of California's land surface. Many of California's dune communities have been destroyed or altered, especially in the south. However, a few good examples of natural dune environments exist, especially to the north. The largest coastal dune fields are west of Santa Maria and include southern portions of Pismo State Beach. At a few locations, lines of dunes protect bays such as Morro Bay south of Morro Rock. Extensive dune communities (some undisturbed) stretch along parts of the coast from Cape Mendocino to the Oregon border. Human disturbances, such as trampling and off-road vehicles, have repeatedly destroyed anchoring vegetation and set formerly stabilized dunes in motion, especially along the central and southern California coasts, often with costly results.

Plants. Just above the high tide level, pioneer dune plants appear. These plants grow close to the ground and often have interconnected roots that form an extensive network below the sand, including deep tap roots. Such root systems also absorb available moisture and stabilize the sand. Most plants prefer the more protected leeward sides of coastal dunes. Many are perennial succulents that conserve water; light gray leaves that reflect light and reduce evapotranspiration rates are common. Introduced beach and dune grasses are especially common in the north, while salt grass and more desert-like species are more common on California's southern coastal dunes.

Other notable plants often have common names which may summarize some of their characteristics. They include Beach Bur or Silver Beachweed (*Ambrosia chamissonis*), Yellow and Beach Sand Verbina (*Abronia* spp.), Beach Pea (*Lathyrus littoralis*), with its clusters of tiny pink and white flowers, and the beautiful Dune or Beach Morning Glory (*Calystegia* or *Convolvulus soldanella*), growing from deep roots from Oregon to the Mexican border. Beach or Dune Evening Primrose (*Camissonia cheiranthifolia*) may also be common. Like many of the grasses, other aggressive introduced species have stabilized dunes but have also crowded out native plants. They include the tiny pink Sea Rocket (*Cakile maritima*), and Ice Plant (*Carpobrotus* or *Mesembryanthemum, chilensis*) covered with its tiny, shiny blisters. Hottentot Fig (*Carpobrotus* or *Mesembryanthemum edulis*) is also common, with its slender, juicy fingers pointing up out of the sand. These last few introduced plants are commonly used as ground cover on California's human landscapes.

Where coastal dunes stretch farther inland in California, there is more protection from wind and salt spray. Dunes are more stable and support richer soils that provide friendlier environments to living organisms. A wider variety of plants and animals can thrive, giving rise to a mixture of dune plants and many species commonly found in coastal scrub communities. These include Dune or Coastal Buckwheat (*Eriogonum parvifolium*), Tree Lupine (*Lupinus arboreus*) and Coastal Silver Lupine (*Lupinus chamissonis*), and showy herbaceous flowers such as California Poppy (*Eschscholzia californica*). Even stands of Coyote Bush (*Baccharis pilularis*) are established on stable sand and are often joined or replaced by California Sagebrush (*Artemisia californica*) in more southerly locations.

On many of the oldest and most stable dunes, succession has produced impressive biomass. On the north coast, the climax dune forest includes Shore Pine (*Pinus contorta contorta*) and Sitka Spruce (*Picea sitchensis*) trees. Moving toward the drier dunes to the south, undisturbed climax communities may include species common in oak woodlands, chap-

arral, and desert-like conditions farther south. Exceptions to this include hollows and traps where fresh water is ponded at the surface or is immediately below the surface, allowing dune slack communities to evolve. Marsh and/or riparian plants such as sedges, rushes, and willow thrive in these spots and phreatophytes grow where water can be tapped just below the sandy surface.

Animals. Insects, lizards, mice, and other small animal tracks on the dunes are indicators of the scarcity of food and the lack of larger mammals. Strikingly similar tracks may be found on the harsh dune environments of California's inland deserts. Larger predators on the coastal dunes are usually birds, including red-tailed hawks, kestrels and gulls. Meanwhile, various species of bees and butterflies are among the flying pollinators of specific flowers in the dunes. One of the most famous is the El Segundo Blue Butterfly (*Euphilotes* or *Shijimiaeoides battoides allyni*). It has been isolated only on the dunes just above Dockweiler Beach below the planes taking off from Los Angeles Airport! These endangered butterflies have enjoyed impressive local media attention as they feed off beach buckwheat on the last dunes remaining in this region. They have become one of the many symbols of what Los Angeles loses as it grows. They also symbolize the dozens of native dune plants and animals which have become endangered or extinct as humans modify and destroy California's delicate coastal dunes.

Coastal Scrub Communities

Coastal scrub plant communities are also known as coastal sage scrub or soft chaparral. These names correctly suggest the similarities with chaparral. However, the smaller plants with softer leaves and the more frequent sage and other aromatic species are conspicuous differences, especially in the south. These scrub communities are common along California's coast from Oregon to the Mexican border, but they often creep farther inland and to higher elevations toward the south, into the Coast Ranges, and even along the lower slopes of the Transverse and Peninsular Ranges. Coastal scrub communities are, however, restricted to elevations usually below about 750 m (2500 feet) throughout California. Most coastal scrub species are adapted to frequent fire.

Habitat and Structure

Coastal locations guarantee some of the mildest diurnal and seasonal temperatures in the world. Moist air masses pass over before being lifted by mountains, so winter precipitation is less than on nearby higher terrain. Great variations in winter rains in the coastal scrub range from and incorrectly assume that the weeds and other introduced species that thrive on the disturbed urban fringe are natural elements of these communities.

Coastal scrub communities are generally recognized by the drought-adapted, short, scrubby bushes and shrubs less than 2 m (6 feet) in height. Dense growth is common, especially on north-facing slopes and the north coast. An explosion of soft green growth and spring wildflowers is common after wet winters, especially during the first few years following wildfires. By late summer, the same communities have turned dry and dusty; shades of golden, gray, and brown dominate as some plants drop their leaves in these thorny, water-stressed environments.

Plants. On the wetter north coast, species include taller bushes such as Coyote Bush or Chaparral Broom (*Baccharis pilularis*) and Tree Lupine (*Lupinus arboreus*). Lower shrubs include monkey flowers, especially Sticky Monkey Flower (*Mimulus* or *Diplacus aurantiacus*), and wild berries, including California Blackberry (*Rubus vitifolius*). Salal (*Gaultheria shallon*), with its berry-like fruits, and Poison Oak (*Toxicodendron* or *Rhus diversilobum*) are also common.

Poison oak is common along much of California's coast, growing from close to the ground to overhead vines where vegetation and wetter conditions will support it. Its shiny leaves grow out in groups of three and often turn pink and red by late summer and fall. Even after dropping its leaves, stems contain the toxic oils which can cause severe and painful rashes. Poison oak can often be identified by its smooth stems, as it lacks the hairs and thorns of wild berry plants.

Understory herbs such as Sword Fern (*Polystichum munitum*), Bracken Fern (*Pteridium aquilinum*), and various flowering plants are indicators of wetter soils in north coastal scrub communities.

Moving south, the above species are often joined or replaced by plants better adapted to prolonged drought, especially on south-facing slopes. When their shallow, extensive root systems can gather water, soft-stemmed shrubs and herbs grow rapidly. Most lose leaves or die back during the summer drought. This is in contrast to the harder chaparral species which usually have deeper root systems and are **sclerophyllous**. (**Sclerophylls** are evergreen plants with stiff, leathery leaves.)

California or Coastal Sagebrush (*Artemisia californica*) is a classic and often dominant coastal scrub shrub. Its tiny, soft, grayish-to-light-green leaves are strongly aromatic and they have been used to make healing washes and teas. It is not a true sage but is

Coastal sage scrub and dune plant communities meet at the base of this slope along the Big Sur coast.

more than 180 cm (70 inches) in the north to less than 25 cm (10 inches) to the south. This results in a wide variety of species in areas from the wet north to the semi-arid conditions along the south coast. Summer fog and low stratus is common along California's entire coastal strip, delivering lower temperatures and higher humidities in the coastal scrub than at inland locations during the dry summer months.

Coastal scrub will gradually blend and merge into a variety of other plant communities along broad ecotones (transitional zones between two different habitats). The type of community will depend on local and regional conditions such as climate, slope exposure, and soil. Coastal scrub may invade coastal dune communities which have been stable for many years. Without disturbances, it may evolve into forest communities on the north coast. Coastal scrub species frequently blend into oak woodland, grassland, and chaparral communities, especially to the south. Semidesert species, including succulents, become common near the Mexican border.

Though only about 2.5 percent of California is coastal scrub, these plant communities are seen frequently by many Californians because large agricultural and population centers have been established among them. Unfortunately, this is also why these plant communities contain many of California's rare and endangered plants and animals. It is also why many Californians frequently in the sunflower family. True sages (*Salvia* spp.) are also common and sometimes dominate the coastal scrub. Black Sage (*S. mellifera*) has dark leaves and black stems, Purple Sage (*S. leucophylla*) has lighter leaves and purple flowers, and White Sage (*S. apiana*) has white leaves and is very common. All of these true sages have opposite leaves growing on square stems and have pungent aromas. Some plants may be draped with the parasite dodder, also known as witches' hair or broom for its rusty orange tangle of stringy stems.

The many species of buckwheat (*Eriogonum* spp.) also have tiny leaves. Their dense clusters of tiny flowers form terminal heads upon small shrubs. Pink flowers of California Buckwheat (*Eriogonum fasciculatum*) turn a conspicuous rusty brown when they dry. Other small plants common in California coastal scrub include Deer Weed (*Lotus scoparius*), a small shrub with only a few small leaves on slender stems and numerous tiny, classic pea-shaped flowers. Various monkey flowers (*Mimulus* spp.) are also common.

During long periods without fire, many woody coastal scrub species may grow a few meters (several feet) tall. They may grow into the chaparral communities. Like chaparral plants, most of these crown-sprout after fires. Laurel Sumac (*Malosma* or *Rhus laurina*) has classic taco-shaped leaves and is not frost tolerant. Lemonade Berry (*Rhus integrifolia*) grows along the immediate coast. Its red, acidic berries may be used to make a bitter drink. Its relative, Sugar Bush or Sugar Sumac (*Rhus ovata*) is usually found farther inland where summers are hotter. These last three species often grow in southern coastal scrub on north-facing slopes.

Into the Driest Coastal Scrub. Even farther south, especially on more exposed, south-facing slopes, these coastal scrub communities become southern semi-desert coastal scrub or maritime desert scrub. Plants are usually smaller and more widely scattered. Species tolerant of even drier conditions include Yucca or Our Lord's Candle (*Yucca whipplei*). With its long, narrow, sword-like leaves, it has been described as looking like a giant pincushion. California Indians weaved fibers from the leaves to make baskets and other necessities and ground the roots to make soap. Older Yuccas bloom and die after sending out roots that produce younger plants nearby. For more than 1 m (3 feet), clusters of its white flowers bloom along the top of a stalk which is even taller. These stalks become conspicuous to humans during late spring and early summer; they are even more attractive to the Yucca Moths (*Tegeticula* spp.),

whose larvae feed off the Yucca fruit which develops from the moth-pollinated flowers. Indians roasted flower stalks and ground the seeds for flour.

Prickly Pear Cactus (*Opuntia littoralis* and other *Opuntia* spp.) are common on the driest slopes. With thorns removed, their large, fleshy pads and their fruits (called "tunas") have been eaten since the Indians and Spanish discovered them. Bright yellow sunflowers of California Encelia or Bush Sunflower (*Encilia californica*) have dark brown centers and grow at the end of long stalks. Bush Sunflower is related to Brittlebush (*Encelia farinosa*), which grows only in the driest regions, especially inland, in southern California's lower deserts. Stonecrops or Live-forevers (*Dudleya* spp.) are very peculiar plants that survive on exposed coastal rock faces and cliffs; many are now rare or endangered.

Animals. Numerous animals of the coastal sage scrub are similar or identical to desert species. Insects, arthropods, lizards, snakes, birds, and small mammals account for much of the limited animal biomass, a reflection of the low productivity in these communities. Ectothermic animals are often more successful here because they are more efficient energy users; many conserve energy by becoming dormant during severe drought. Often, lizards feed on the abundant insects and spiders, snakes (fewer in number) may feed off all three, and various birds may eat any of them.

The Coast Horned Lizard (*Phrynosoma coronatum*) has a wide range across California and is closely related to the desert species. This flat, rounded, prehistoric-looking insect eater prefers ants, but has been seen eating bees. It can change its shade to match the color of its usually exposed and sandy background. Populations are rapidly decreasing as habitats are destroyed and humans harass and capture them. Numerous other lizards are common in many open areas across California, including the very common Western Fence Lizard or Blue-Bellied Lizard (*Sceloporus occidentalis*) and the Side-Blotched Lizard (*Uta stansburiana*). Both can be seen doing push-ups in the sun, probably to attract mates and to scare off potential predators.

With its alternate light and dark longitudinal stripes or circular rings, the largest banded snake in California is the Common Kingsnake (*Lampropeltis getulus*). It eats lizards, small mammals, and other snakes, including rattlesnakes, which are also at home in coastal scrub and many other California communities. The Gopher Snake (*Pituophis melanoleucus*) imitates rattlesnakes in looks and behavior, but it preys on small rodents, lizards, eggs, and birds by crushing them. It is the largest and perhaps most common snake in southern California.

Numerous small mammals live in the coastal scrub and throughout California. They include many species of small mice with large ears, which survive by eating seeds, insects, and a variety of other foods. The nocturnal Deer Mouse (*Peromyscus maniculatus*) is a common example. The California Mouse (*Peromyscus californicus*) is one of the largest mice in California. Pocket mice and white-footed mice species are also common throughout these habitats. Different species of woodrats or packrats (*Neotoma* spp.) are notorious for gathering sticks and other available or discarded debris in piles to make their large nests. They may survive extreme drought by eating prickly-pear cactus for water. Many species of kangaroo rats (*Dpodomys* spp.) are common from the coast to the desert. With powerful hind legs, they can leap to avoid predators such as different species of rattlesnakes. The California Ground Squirrel (*Spermophilus beecheyi*) is a larger rodent that is commonly seen during the day. All of these rodents are common throughout many California habitats, especially into the chaparral; many become food for snakes, birds, or larger mammals.

Without abundant food, the larger mammals are few and usually must roam through or make visits to the coastal scrub for food while birds have the advantage of being able to fly to food and water sources. Mammals become more common and include larger species in areas which are ecotones to other plant communities, especially near wetter habitats farther north. These may include ringtails, bobcats, mountain lions, gray fox, coyote, mule deer, and even black bear.

Grasslands

Originally, about 13 percent of California was covered by grasslands. These are mostly in California's inland valleys, especially those tucked behind coastal hills or mountains. They are not deserts; they are usually a part of cismontane California. These great valleys include the Sacramento, San Joaquin, and Salinas and other inland valleys surrounding the Bay Area as well as inland regions of the southern California coastal plains.

Habitat and Structure

Most grasslands receive less winter precipitation than adjacent higher terrain where chaparral and woodland may dominate. Summers are long, hot, and dry. Winter rains drain quickly through the thick, porous soils of these inland valleys, often leaving roots dry; poorly adapted plants wither by early summer. There are also coastal grasslands scattered from Oregon past the Mexican border. Though precipitation may be greater and temperatures milder, coastal grasslands often grow in fine-grained or nutrient-poor soils that may become waterlogged in winter but can dry into formidable hard-pan surfaces in summer. Most trees and even shrubs cannot survive in these adverse environments due to a lack of water or nutrients or both.

These communities are often divided into valley grasslands and the cooler, wetter northern coastal grasslands or coastal prairie. Inland valley grasses creep into higher elevation chaparral and woodland communities where soils become poor or into drier, south-facing slopes. Along the coast, they are also more common on south-facing slopes; they may grow into woodlands where more moisture is available to plants for a longer period or they may yield to coastal scrub or chaparral where soils become more porous.

Grasslands in the foreground dotted with a few trees yield to chaparral on more distant slopes in eastern San Diego County.

HUMAN IMPRINTS

The range of grasslands across California probably expanded slightly due to early human activities, but productivity has decreased more recently. Native Americans were the first to modify these marginal environments by burning them, knowing that the fresh regrowth would support more game animals. Ranchers have cleared borderline coastal scrub, chaparral, and oak woodland to introduce Mediterranean grasses and expand their grazing land for domestic livestock. Eventually, native grasslands became the most modified, destroyed, and misunderstood general plant community in California. Early pictures of land surrounding Spanish missions and Mexican ranchos sometimes illustrated the already barren, trampled, overgrazed land.

This is one reason why these parts of California that were once native grasslands have often been mislabelled natural desert. It is estimated that about 700,000 small cattle and sheep grazed California landscapes during the peak of the Spanish Period. By 1862, 3 million cattle and 9 million sheep grazed in California, many near gold rush populations. Because European grasses were adapted to centuries of this intensive grazing, they thrived in our grasslands as native grasses disappeared. Unfortunately, continued overgrazing and overfarming have destroyed about one-third of these once productive lands in California. Expanding networks of deep rills and gullies and windblown dust and sand is common evidence of the accelerated soil erosion in California's marginal lands; pursuit of short-term profits at the expense of long-term productivity is often the cause.

This is a community restricted to elevations below about 1,200 m (4,000 feet). Only about 1 percent of California's native grasslands, with their perennial bunchgrasses and other species adapted to these adverse conditions, have survived. Invasions of more aggressive, nonnative weeds and European grasses, overgrazing, farming, and urbanization have eliminated most of the original grasslands. Of the few remaining patches of native California grasslands, the Carrizo Plain (just west of the southern San Joaquin Valley) is probably the largest; it was saved by the California Nature Conservancy.

California's Kansas? In Elna Bakker's classic book, *An Island Called California*, she referred to the grassland plant community as "California's Kansas," illustrating striking similarities to the U.S. Great Plains grasslands. For example, the pronghorn antelope and tule elk, like the plains buffalo, played the role of large grazers in California's Central Valley.

Bakker also pointed out the many differences between the two environments. California's grasslands are frequently interrupted by other plant communities. Even the Great Central Valley has wide fingers of riparian woodlands, scattered vernal pools, and extensive wetlands meandering down from the Sierra Nevada and spreading across the valley. Though temperatures drop to freezing each winter, California's inland valleys never experience the prolonged hard freezes and bitter cold of the Great Plains. Finally, while California's grasslands are stressed and challenged by prolonged summer drought, the Great Plains enjoy occasional spring and summer downpours.

Consequently, California's perennial bunchgrasses are ready to explode into growth during the first warm early spring days, while plains grasses will emerge from buried roots later in the spring. By late spring, California's grasslands are already stressed in drying soils, while plains grasses thrive well into summer. California's native bunchgrasses are better adapted to the long summer drought, but the introduced European species quickly turn to brittle brown and gold in early summer heat.

Plants. Hundreds of plant species once flourished and are now scattered in California's native grasslands, some of which are often seen in bordering plant communities. They include perennial bunchgrasses, annual grasses, and annual wildflowers. The most common native perennial grasses include Purple Needlegrass (*Stipa pulchra*) and the bluegrasses (*Poa* spp.). In spring, these bunchgrasses grow quickly from tufts to produce flowers. The many introduced grasses which now dominate and are most frequently seen across California's grasslands include wild oats (*Avena* spp.), fescues (*Vulpia* or *Festuca* spp.), brome (*Bromus* spp.), and many others. Growing among the grasses, native wildflowers may produce the most remarkable displays of spring. They include California Poppy (*Eschscholzia californica*), various lupines (*Lupinus* spp.), Owls Clover (*Orthocarpus* spp.), and many sunflowers, such as Goldfields (*Lasthenia californica* or *L. chrysostoma*). Growing from bulbs, mariposa lilies (*Calochortus* spp.), amaryllis such as Blue Dicks (*Dichelostemma pulchella* or *Brodiaea pulchella*) and iris such as Blue-Eyed Grass (*Sisyrinchium bellum*) add to the brilliant spring displays.

Also common in California grasslands are the many species of mustard; most of them are introduced weeds. Black Mustard (*Brassica nigra*), with its small yellow flowers atop slender stems sometimes grows higher than 2 m (6 feet); it is responsible for turning many California hillsides into fields of yellow in spring. Franciscan padres first spread these very successful invaders with black seeds. Even the edible Wild Radish (*Raphanus sativus*) is a very common introduced member of the mustard family. Horehound (*Marrubium vulgare*) is a mint introduced as a cold remedy. It is now common in disturbed sites and fields, where its fruits turn into annoying burrs which are distributed after they have attached to animal fur or to our clothing. Many different native and introduced thistles are also common. Some introduced thistles are so aggressive that they are quickly spreading from their disturbed sites and overtaking native habitats.

In the northern coastal grasslands or coastal prairie, many different species of perennial bunchgrasses are commonly joined by sedges, rushes, perennial forbs, and species also found in valley grasslands. Because soils remain wetter for longer in these northern grasslands, foliage is also greener throughout the year.

Animals. We have already noted the impact of domestic livestock on California's grasslands. A diverse assemblage of native fauna also lived in or wandered through the many adverse conditions common to these habitats. Most of these animals thrived with the abundant moisture and fresh growth of spring, but struggled to survive in dried habitats of late summer. Classic lessons in the study of California **food pyramids** are often taken from these grasslands.

There are abundant small herbivores, or primary consumers, especially insects. Grasshoppers, ants, and crickets compete with small mammals and birds for edible new growth in spring and seeds later in the year. Meadow mice, pocket mice, kangaroo rats, gophers, and California ground squirrels share the grasslands with seed-eating birds such as goldfinches and sparrows. With fewer predators, the gopher population has exploded to more than thirty per acre in some fields. Jackrabbits, with their giant ears, may be seen darting between covers to eat native and introduced plants.

Grasshopper mice, deer mice, and lizards prey on many insects as do carnivorous birds, such as kingbirds, nighthawks, and meadowlarks. Other secondary consumers, such as snakes, coyotes, foxes and badgers, and predatory birds, such as burrowing owls and American kestrels, may eat small mammals. Some of these animals, such as the coyote, are omnivores; they consume a wide variety of plants and animals to increase chances for survival in adverse conditions.

Red-tailed hawks are frequently seen soaring above grassy areas in search of rodents or reptiles for dinner. With their light undersides and red-tinted tails, they seem to glide effortlessly in daily thermals until they swoop down on their stunned prey. Numerous burrows which punctuate these grasslands indicate efforts by smaller mammals to escape both extremes in weather and their predators. As we work our way through the **pyramid** from the producers toward the tertiary consumers, the size of the animals generally increases, but the total biomass greatly decreases.

Tule elk and pronghorn antelope were the two large grazing animals of the Central Valley grasslands. The Tule elk, the smallest elk in North America, is indigenous to California and was endangered for years. After near extinction, numbers increased into the hundreds within natural reserves in the San Joaquin and Owens Valley. Now overgrazing by increased populations is becoming a problem. A herd size of two thousand is often the number cited by those who want to maintain a healthy population in California's reserves. This Tule Elk (*Cervus elaphus nannodes*) is smaller than the Roosevelt Elk (*Cervus elaphus roosevelti*) of northwestern California.

Pronghorn antelope were also nearly driven out of California, except for the northeastern part of the state, but there are populations of this species in other states. The rare or endangered status of so many California grassland animals is an obvious result of rapid encroachment of human activities and populations and the destruction of these plant communities.

Oak Woodlands

Often referred to as foothill woodlands and sometimes grouped under the more broad, global biome, "savanna," oak woodland plant communities may contain several different types of oak trees and associated species. They are spread and scattered around cismontane California from Oregon to Mexico usually in areas wetter than grasslands, but drier than forests. Oak woodlands surround the Central Valley.

Habitat and Structure

Various oak trees may appear with or replace grasslands at higher elevations with more precipitation or where soils trap and hold water for longer periods, especially on north-facing slopes. Oak woodland may also replace coastal scrub or chaparral where porous soils become more fine-grained and are capable of storing more water, especially in cooler, shadier habitats. In contrast, the wetter California forests may be replaced by oak woodlands at lower elevations or on drier, south-facing slopes, or where soils will not support forest growth.

At least sixteen species of oaks (*Quercus* spp.) and their woodlands grow from just above sea level throughout cismontane California. They may reach higher elevations above 1500 m (5000 feet), especially in southern California. Climates are typically California Mediterranean with mild, wet winters followed by warm, dry summers. Depending on moisture and soil conditions, oak trees may be widely scattered with only grasses below. On wetter, especially north-facing sites, or near canyon bottoms, numerous large oak trees may even join pines or riparian species to form a dense woodland with an understory of shrubs. Stately oaks are often a part of the scenic photographs and paintings depicting historical and rural California hillside landscapes. Covering about 4 million ha (10 million acres) or 10 percent of California, they also provided many native Americans with the most common source of staple food—the acorn. Oak woodlands continue to provide unique shelter and food for hundreds of animal species.

The best illustration of how oak woodland communities fit into California's biogeographic landscapes is found along the western Sierra Nevada. Travelling up from the drier valley grasslands, sparse oak trees and shrubs are first noticed until, at higher elevations, denser oak woodlands and shrubs may alternate with chaparral and forest species. Gradually, the oaks give way to pines in the higher elevation ecotones between oak woodlands and cooler, wetter forests.

On coastal slopes, wetter forests may give way to oak woodland on drier south-facing slopes in northern California. In contrast, southern California's south-facing slopes are often too dry for oaks; the coastal scrub, grasslands, or chaparral only yield to oak woodlands in wetter locations, such as north-facing slopes. Travellers through the Coast Ranges along highways such as 101 are certain to pass through a variety of oak woodlands that often contribute to California's picturesque landscapes.

Plants. Oregon Oak, or Garry Oak (*Quercus garryana*) is a deciduous white oak tree common to northern California and southern Oregon oak woodlands. Growing inland from California's coastal forests, it is the only California oak tree distributed widely outside the state. More common to central California, especially on the drier, hotter inland slopes is Blue Oak (*Quercus douglasii*), actually another deciduous white oak tree. These large oaks have lobed leaves up to 7.5 cm (3 inches) long and feed numerous acorn-eating mammals. To the south, they are replaced by the less common Engelmann Oak or Mesa Oak (*Quercus engelmannii*), a semi-evergreen white oak with long, smooth leaves, restricted to slopes south of the Transverse Ranges.

Commonly found on wetter and north-facing coastal slopes from the Coast Ranges south is Coast Live Oak (*Quercus agrifolia*). As its name implies, it is evergreen and commonly grows in clusters on coastal slopes adjacent to coastal scrub, chaparral, and grassland communities. Its small, hard, spiny leaves suggest adaptations to drier climates more typical of chaparral species, such as its very similar but much smaller relative, California Scrub Oak (*Quercus dumosa* or *berberidifolia*). An even closer relative that grows on many central California stabilized sand dunes is the Dwarfed Coast Live Oak or Pygmy Oak (*Quercus agrifolia* var. *frutescens*). This dwarf variety may survive the strong, salty winds, poor soils, and other adverse conditions which rule out larger oaks.

Golden-Cup Oak or Canyon-Live Oak (*Quercus chrysolepis*), with its giant yellow cups holding each acorn, and Black Oak (*Quercus kelloggii*) are common on moist and higher elevation sites and are some of the most widely distributed oaks from northern to southern California. Large-lobed leaves of deciduous black oaks are often responsible for producing the fall colors on southern California's higher mountain slopes.

The Valley Oak (*Quercus lobata*) is California's largest oak. Growing on low hills and in valleys from northern California to the Santa Monica Mountains, it forms open savannas in drier areas and forests near riparian strips. Individuals more than 30 m (100 feet) tall with nearly equal diameter crowns and trunk diameters up to 3 m (9 feet) have been measured. They also have very large, lobed leaves and long acorns. Most of the original stands have been destroyed for firewood or replaced with grazing and agriculture. Interior Live Oak (*Quercus wislizenii*) grows mostly in higher elevations of inland California, from the Cascade and Sierra Nevada foothills to the Peninsular Ranges, where it becomes shrubby in a drier habitat.

In California, deciduous oaks are often identified by their larger, softer leaves, while evergreen oaks usually have smaller, harder leaves.

Many of the deciduous oaks are found in northern California or at higher elevations; they may drop their leaves to escape past or current winter cold. Evergreen oaks live in milder climates or have adapted to the cold. They often have extensive and deep root systems which can access water most of the year. Oaks often grow in clusters because they resprout after fires or where squirrels buried acorns and did not retrieve them. Human activity, such as trampling or overwatering the root systems, and especially habitat destruction due to agriculture and urbanization has already wiped out many of California's oak woodlands. Numerous California communities have passed laws to discourage the continued destruction of oak trees.

A Wealth of Other Plants Mix with the Oaks. Several other interesting plant species are commonly associated with oak woodlands. California Buckeye (*Aesculus californica*) is California's native in the horse chestnut family and is common in and near oak woodlands of central California. In spring, stalks to 13 cm (5 inches) long are covered with white flowers. This **drought-deciduous** small tree loses its leaves by late summer, leaving the large buckeyes, or horse chestnuts, dangling like pendulums in the autumn breezes. Native Americans shelled, ground, cooked, and leached them for a high-carbohydrate staple dish similar to mashed potatoes; they are still an important source of food for animals.

Redbud (*Cercis occidentalis*) grows on hillsides surrounding the Sacramento Valley and along the western Sierra Nevada. It is winter-deciduous, but is covered with tiny pink flowers by early spring. As a member of the pea family, its brown pea pods are another important food source for animals.

The California Black Walnut (*Juglaus californica*) becomes locally dominant in oak woodlands especially on north slopes from Santa Barbara through Orange County. Walnut woodlands are found in the Ojai Valley and in the Puente and San Jose Hills south and west of Pomona. Some stands grow in the middle of recent urban sprawl, but many have been eradicated. This California walnut can be identified by its long, opposite leaflets. Its walnuts are not commercial quality, but hungry squirrels do not seem to mind. In even wetter sites, the oaks are joined by the more widely distributed California Bay or Laurel (*Umbellularia californica*), with its dark green, overwhelmingly pungent bay leaves. This species is usually found in wetter communities, such as mixed evergreen forest. Where coastal summer fog is common, thin veils of Lace Lichen (*Ramalina menziesii*) are draped over and hanging from oak trees like delicate yellow-green hair or beards, providing surfaces where more moisture may condense.

Especially at higher elevations and on wetter sites, pines mix with the oaks. Gray (Digger) Pine (*Pinus sabiniana*) is the first to appear in some of the driest locations, where it grows in foothill woodlands surrounding the Central Valley and into the Coast Ranges in the same areas as blue oak. It is called gray pine because of its long silver-to-light-green needles. This dry, scraggly-looking pine may also be seen protruding above chaparral plants as it divides into several large branches.

Like most dry pines, it produces very large cones with seeds that were important for California Indians and are still vital to the survival of some animals. Several other pines and plants from grassland, coastal scrub, chaparral, and forest plant communities may mix with woodlands when conditions are favorable. Common understory plants such as poison oak are examined within more proper settings before and after this section.

Animals. Close inspection of oak trees reveals numerous smaller species and some of the larger species of animals making their homes and gathering food there. Excellent examples of a few of California's parasitic and plant-eating insects include tiny aphids, which suck plant juices, and the white flies, oak moths, and tent caterpillars which consume green leaves. Larvae hatch from many species of butterflies to feed on oak leaves. Millions of various borers and beetles are puncturing through the bark of oak, pine, and other trees throughout California, sometimes killing the weaker trees. Bark beetles devastate pine stands during severe drought years when trees lack the sap to encapsulate such invaders. Spotty patches of brown, dead pines grew to large clusters across the Sierra Nevada and other California mountain regions as bark beetle infestations killed thousands of trees during the early 1900s, marking the end of the longest drought in California history.

Gall insects include the cynipid wasps. Females lay their eggs on oak leaves or stems, the eggs hatch, and larvae eat the plant, making irritating chemicals which cause the tree to grow a large gall at that point. New wasps eventually emerge from the protection of these crusty, hollowed, paper-light brown galls, leaving puncture holes upon exiting. Larger galls may look like small, dried apples clinging to stems. Other parasitic insects prey on oak woodland animals, such as the bot flies on small mammals and the fleas, mosquitos, and biting flies on small and large animals.

A variety of birds eat the acorns and insects of oak woodlands. The acorn woodpecker prefers to drill its holes in softer dead trees to store the acorns it gathers. These powerful woodpeckers have distinctive red caps. Natural inner cushions protect the head from impacts caused by constant drilling. They also eat insects in the bark or in the air. Scrub jays hide their acorns in rich soil, where the forgotten morsels may sprout to seedlings. Numerous other animals, such as mule deer and squirrels, make acorns an important part of their diets. Some species, such as mice and rabbits, use oak understory for cover, while others, such as hawks and owls, use the top of oaks as observation posts. From their perches, such predators might spot one of the many amphibians, reptiles, or small mammals for dinner. Large mammals such as fox, coyote, bobcat, mountain lion and black bear may live in or wander through these woodlands, especially within ecotones merging into other plant communities.

Chaparral

Nearly 10 percent of California is covered with one of its most widespread and famous plant communities—chaparral. Throughout cismontane California, chaparral is found in drier spots with poor soils to the north. It becomes far more common to the south, especially on porous soils inland from the coastal scrub up to higher elevations where it may finally yield to cooler, wetter montane forests. Therefore, the isolated chaparral we see only in drier spots to the north becomes more widespread as we sweep south, especially into the southern Coast Ranges and Sierra Nevada. It dominates the foothill and mountain slopes of cismontane southern California to higher elevations. Areas of chaparral even spread into a few transmontane desert locations, where it begins to resemble chaparral in Arizona and northern Mexico.

Habitat and Structure

Though many chaparral species are also found in "soft chaparral" coastal scrub communities, true chaparral tends to be a taller, thicker, more evergreen community. It may receive more precipitation on higher slopes in winter, but suffer through hotter, drier summers in areas more distant from coastal fog and stratus. Typically, extensive roots penetrate through very porous soils which may be well-drained, but nutrient poor.

Chaparral is the model Mediterranean, drought-adapted plant community. Most of the dense thickets of shrubs are sclerophyllous, a term referring to the hard leaves which often are small with waxy or resinous coatings and fine hair. Leaves may also curl or be oriented to decrease direct sunlight, all adaptations to keep transpiration rates down during the long, hot summer droughts. Though productivity is relatively low, it averages six times higher than deserts. Whether chaparral is dominated by small shrubs only several centimeters (a few inches) tall, or dwarf woodlands more than 4 m (12 feet) high, these woody plants provide an almost impenetrable evergreen cover wherever they grow across California slopes.

Fire

All chaparral communities are adapted to fire. Many species crown sprout (regrow from root crowns) after fires. Some shed seeds which will only germinate after a good

scorching is followed by moisture. A greater diversity of herbs and other species follows during the first few springs immediately following fires; the diversity and numbers of animals explodes along with the spectacular displays of wildflowers and fresh growth. Some of the herbs are considered "**pyrophyte** endemics," because they only germinate and grow after fires. As the years after fire pass, species diversity usually decreases as the woody chaparral thickets grow taller at the expense of low ground cover.

After many years, only a few larger species may dominate. These mature stands often contain large openings below the canopy cover from the ground up to several centimeters (inches) high. The cavities provide passageways for small animals below the cover of chaparral, while enormous quantities of dead stems and leaves and other dried debris accumulate on and around the base of these plants. This fuel will contribute to the next wildfire, when temperatures may reach 700°C (1200°F), and the fire succession cycle will continue.

Fire plays an important role in most California plant communities, especially in those adjacent to chaparral. Fire may ravage some California chaparral and coastal scrub slopes as frequently as every fifteen years, on average. The drought-adapted plants contain plenty of fuel and relatively little moisture by summer's end. Chamise (*Adenostoma fasciculatum*), a common chaparral dominant, is known to burst into flames as a fire *approaches*, when temperatures reach 427°C (800°F). It is no surprise that this is a classic drought-adapted species that crown sprouts after a fire and produces seeds which may lay dormant for years until they are scorched. Although fires are beneficial in the long term for plant communities, humans often consider them catastrophic disasters.

Plants. In even the most thorough study of chaparral, it would be a challenge to examine the more than eight-hundred plants, including more than two-hundred woody plants that make up California's chaparral communities. Here, we focus on a few of the more common species. Many of California's chaparral communities may be distinguished and classified by the dominant species or by habitat characteristics, such as location (island versus Sierran versus semidesert, etc.) or elevation, or soils. The assemblage of plants in western Sierra Nevada chaparral is quite different from that found on California's Channel Islands; the heavier rains and snows of winter and hot dry summers in the western Sierra Nevada are not known to the plants of the islands. Another example of chaparral diversity is the persistent high humidity, fog, and stratus of the islands, which is not known to the semidesert chaparral growing near piñon-juniper and Joshua tree woodlands of transmontane California.

CALIFORNIANS AND FIRE

We have built within numerous California plant communities where fire is inevitable. Each fall, the national media displays yet another California housing tract or community burning to the ground. Many of these fires burn through several different plant communities and human settlements in one day and rank as some of the greatest fire disasters in our country's history. They often involve world-famous locations, such as Malibu, Laguna, Beverly Hills, Santa Barbara, Oakland, and Berkeley. Such human disasters are compounded by the mud flows and severe erosion that follow when winter rains pound the hillsides made barren by the fires. In nature, these events may carry away many of the nutrients deposited on the soil by fire. In built environments, the homes and structures not destroyed by the fire may be damaged or swept away in the next winter's floods. Californians have built in fire country, suppressed fires, and paid the price in the long term.

Though California Indians started their share of fires, there is evidence of frequent, smaller fires throughout California long before humans played a role. These fires were started by lightning and probably burned much smaller areas because they occurred on days with rain and higher humidities. It is also likely that smoldering logs and embers left by smaller fires erupted weeks or months later during dry, windy conditions, occasionally causing more spectacular and widespread wildfires. During much of the 1900s, humans suppressed natural fires throughout California, allowing dangerous accumulations of dried fuel near their communities. As a result, modern wildfires—sometimes started by accident or by arson—often erupt when hot, dry winds can fan flames feeding on excessive accumulations of fuel.

It is impossible to stop and difficult to direct a firestorm blazing through overly mature chaparral or other plant communities when temperatures are near 38°C (100°F), relative humidities are below 10 percent and winds are gusting over 80 km per hour (50 miles per hour). Yet, these are frequently the conditions fire fighters encounter during autumn's Santa Ana winds in southern California. Each year, these infernos return as regularly as the seasons. Because of past fire suppression, today's wildfires may burn so much accumulated fuel and reach such high temperatures, they kill native plants and animals that may have otherwise survived to quickly repopulate an area.

Consequently, from civilization's standpoint, California has one of the most dangerous and destructive fire seasons in the world and we constantly argue about what to do about it. Even in some of our most remote forests and parks, we have aggressively attacked wildfires to "save" valuable timber, watershed, or recreational lands. We have only recently learned that by allowing some wildfires to burn or by practicing control burning, we will actually restore plant communities to their natural states and decrease the threat of more disastrous fires in the long run.

These are difficult policies to implement in a state with more than 34 million people, especially when lives and valuable property and resources are at stake. The most obvious correction we can make is to stop building in fire-prone regions. In the long run, we will save lives and spend less money on fighting fires and on disaster aid. This will require more knowledgeable and careful land-use planning in the future. Unfortunately, such long-term, common-sense solutions are difficult to implement with increasing pressure from growing populations to expand farther into California's wild areas, areas often seen to preserve a part of the California Dream.

Today, developments continue to encroach upon areas destined to burn in California. The wide ribbons of fire breaks—areas where vegetation is cleared along strips connecting one ridge after another—are particularly obvious in southern California. These may serve as future battle fronts where fire crews are seen on TV, making their brave stand against the next threatening fire. On days with higher humidities and gentle breezes, fire crews may start control burns. These burns are designed to clear accumu-

Continued

Fires burn hot and fast, leaving such devastation where there was once thick chaparral. Crown and seed sprouts will quickly fill the void with fresh green leaves and colorful flowers.

lated dead fuel and return a plant community to more nat-ural conditions so that the next fire is not so hot.

After fires ravage hillsides near the urban fringe, local crews may even seed the slopes with fast-germinating, non-native grasses. These introduced seeds are often washed away with the first winter rains; they rarely pro-vide a better long-term plant cover for protection from erosion than the native species with which they compete.

The practice continues because it is seen as "doing some-thing" to protect the community. California's annual dra-mas are played out each year with the suspense, tragedy, and irony experienced by countless human populations around the world who have dared to venture into regions where the powerful forces of nature are still in control. In California, the resulting landscapes reveal fascinating inter-actions between nature and humans.

Chaparral species may also occur in locations where forest or woodland is expected, but where outcrops of poor soils such as those weathered from serpentine have created adverse conditions. In southern California, chaparral may replace oak woodland or grassland where fine-grained soils change to the very coarse, porous, and well-drained substrate favored by chaparral plants' roots. Finally, slope exposure is a major factor that determines the dominant chaparral species. A quick glance at chaparral on smaller, local hillsides within California's major landscape trends reveals the shorter, sparse plant cover on drier south-facing slopes that face direct sun. Compare this to the taller, thicker, and lusher growth on cooler, wetter north-facing slopes facing away from direct sunlight. In marginal environments, slope aspect may even produce completely different plant communities on opposite slopes.

Many of the herbs and wildflowers of adjoining communities, such as grassland and coastal scrub, are also common in chaparral; this is especially true in open areas or after fires.

Numerous species of manzanita (*Arctostaphylos* spp.) grow throughout and sometimes dominate California chaparral from near sea level to higher mountain slopes. Light green leaves grow from a background of dark red woody stems and smooth red bark, which make this an attractive species in the wild and a great ornamental plant for domestic gardens. From its attractive pink flowers develop the famous "little apples," berries which gave manzanitas their common name. Manzanita is also used in about fifty California place names. It frequently creeps into other plant communities, such as yellow pine forest, where it may dominate the understory. Except for its different flowers and lack of red bark, the Silk-tassel Bush (*Garrya* spp.) could be mistaken for manzanita.

Several species of ceanothus (*Ceanothus* spp.), with their small, green leaves, are often called California lilac. Different species grow tiny clusters of various colored flowers from white to blue that bloom in the chaparral from lower elevations in late winter to higher elevations into summer. Rubbing the flowers with water may produce a mild, sudsy soap. Nearly pure stands of ceanothus may grow higher than a few meters (several feet) to maturity within several years after fire. They may die of old age within ten years to clear the way for other species. With nitrogen-fixing roots, they help increase soil fertility for plants to follow. They are also known to throw or pop their seeds away when mature. Though they may not crack unless they land on very hard surfaces, the seeds will crack in later fires.

Mountain Mahogany (*Cercocarpus betuloides*) is another typical chaparral species that is a nitrogen fixer. Smaller plants from the pea family such as Deerweed (*Lotus scoparius*) and lupines (*Lupinus* spp.) also typically move in after fires as nitrogen fixers and restore soil fertility.

Chamise (*Adenostoma fasciculatum*) is another chaparral species found in almost pure stands. How-ever, it often grows as a lower shrub in drier sites with even more classic drought and fire adaptations (some were reviewed in the section on fire). With its tiny, hard leaves (which superficially resemble buck-wheat) and extensive root systems, it may be the most common chaparral species in California.

Red Shanks (*Adenostoma sparsifolium*) is often called ribbon bush or ribbonwood due to the dry strips or ribbons of rusty bark which peel, hang and curl off the plant. It also has tiny leaves, but it grows much taller than chamise to form dwarf woodlands, usually in very mature stands between elevations of about 600 m (2,000 feet) and 1,800 m (5,900 feet), which have not been burned for many years.

Especially common on southwestern Sierra Nevada chaparral slopes is Flannel Bush (*Fremontodendron* or *Fremontia californicum*), with its long, conspic-uous stalks of yellow spring flowers. It is commonly associated with montane chaparral, but also grows on the dry side of the Transverse Ranges. Its other name, Fremontia, was taken from the historical figure, John C. Fremont, and was adopted for the publication of the California Native Plant Society.

Various desert and scrub varieties of oak grow in the chaparral, including California Scrub Oak (*Quercus dumosa*). Its dwarfed size and its small, thick, hard, and often spiny leaves are among this plant's typical chaparral characteristics. It is important to many animals of the chaparral, especially as a source of acorns.

Other interesting and important chaparral plants were overlooked here for the sake of space. It is said that Toyon (*Heteromeles arbutifolia*), has the holly-like leaves that gave Hollywood its name. It is also known as Christmas berry, for its ripe red clusters of berries which appear in front of a green leaf background by late December. Toyon grows in many chaparral communities, including the hills above Hollywood. Man Roots (*Marah* spp.), or wild cucumbers, grow each year as vine-like plants creeping through chaparral and adjacent communities. They emerge from a giant tuber which may reach the size of a person. Its baseball-sized fruits grow giant thorns which make them resemble weapons from some science fiction movie. Once cut open in spring, they may also resemble cucumbers with their internal seeds. Various currants and gooseberries (*Ribes* spp.), other berry plants (*Rhamnus* spp.), and such species as Sugarbush (*Rhus ovata*) are also common in the chaparral.

Animals. Though productivity may nearly double after a fire, production in the chaparral still averages about 600 g per sqm per year (5,300 pounds per acre per year), compared to only 335 g/sqm/year (3,000 pounds per acre per year) of biomass in coastal scrub. Because biomass decreases by about 90 percent for every step up the food pyramid, total animal biomass depends upon such productivity. Consequently, chaparral also supports more animal life than coastal scrub and desert communities, but fewer animals than California's wetter forests. Although many chaparral communities provide abundant berries, seeds, and acorns for primary consumers, there may also be fresh herbs and flowers, especially in new growth after fires.

Because annual droughts with literally no rain may stretch from April or May into October or November, water is often the most important limiting factor for the survival and growth of plants and animals. This favors the survival of animals that can slow their metabolism to hide from drought or travel greater distances in search of water.

Many species wander into chaparral from adjacent plant communities. Most coastal scrub animals may also thrive in chaparral habitats where they will find less open space, but more protective cover.

Smaller Animals of the Chaparral. Most chaparral birds have the advantage of flying to distant water sources. Like many other animals, they are often dull brown or gray for camouflage in the dry, drought-tolerant foliage. California's state bird, the California quail, is common in many plant communities and is frequently seen scurrying through openings or cavities in the chaparral. This dark bird grows up to 39 cm (11 inches) long. It waddles through the brush, eating vegetation, seeds, and insects. California quail have a conspicuous reddish brown crown with a protruding black topknot feather that resembles a dangling miner's head lamp pointing the way for the bird. During severe drought years, some plants eaten by California quail contain larger amounts of chemicals that inhibit quail reproduction.

The wrentit is a small bird who sings "The Song of the Chaparral," a call resembling the high-pitched bouncing of a ping-pong ball after it is dropped on a tile floor, with smaller time intervals between successive bounces. It is quick and difficult to spot. The wrentit is just one of the many animals that dine on abundant berries and insects in the chaparral. Other birds with distinctive sounds include the morning dove's "coo," screeches of the cactus wren, and, at night, the deep "whoo" of the great horned owl. Along with the owls, red-tailed hawks and red-shouldered hawks are skilled and fierce predators. The list of other common chaparral birds is a long one, including the rufous-sided towhee, California towhee, California thrasher, and scrub jay. Hummingbirds, such as Anna's hummingbird, with its metallic red throat and crown and green back, are among the others.

Ants, grasshoppers, beetles, bees, and butterflies are among the insects commonly seen that play important roles in chaparral communities. Arthropods such as spiders and scorpions are seen as ferocious predators by some smaller animals, but as scrumptious morsels by others. Smaller arthropods such as ticks and mites are also sources of food for some, but are frequently annoying nuisances to many animals and humans who may unknowingly gather them by brushing against chaparral vegetation. By the late 1990s, confirmed cases of Lyme disease from ticks caused concern among some California outdoor enthusiasts.

Reptiles are far more common in these dry habitats than amphibians, and most species are shared by other plant communities, such as the coastal scrub.

The striped racer is a snake which races through the chaparral with its head held high. Its sleek, longitudinal stripes may pass at speeds up to 7 km (4 miles) per hour, as it hunts many kinds of smaller animals. As the name implies, the common gopher snake (which only looks like a rattlesnake) is one of many species helping to keep rodent populations under control.

The western rattlesnake is one of the most common of the chaparral rattlers, and it often has the typical diamond pattern on its back. After biting their prey, rattlesnakes often follow their victims to where the animals finally drop from effects of the venom. There and then, dinner is served. Contrary to myth, few Californians ever die from rattlesnake bites, except when small children or people with strong allergic reactions are bitten. The bites can cause a few days of violent illness.

Larger Animals of the Chaparral. Though larger animals are fewer and so are rarely observed, they may be seen searching for smaller animals or various edible plant parts in the chaparral. Small mammals, such as woodrats, often represent food for larger predators. The California quail can become a meal for coyotes, foxes, bobcats, or even Cooper's hawks. Where coyote may feed on almost anything at any time, the smaller ringtail cats hunt birds late at night and may be attacked by great horned owls.

Mountain lions survive by ranging over large distances of about 256 sq km (100 square miles), hunting for mule deer and other larger animals. It is no surprise that recent human encounters with mountain lions in California have been mostly in areas where there is accelerated human encroachment into wildlands. The sensationalist media has ex-

One of the most powerful predators in California, mountain lions require a large range. You will not get this close to a wild cougar, nor do they want to get so close to you.

ploited these unfortunate events. However, in California, there has been an average of only one mountain lion attack on humans every few years. As expected, the smaller bobcat is restricted to smaller ranges of about 4 sq km (1.5 square miles) and usually to hunting smaller animals, such as rodents and birds.

The bear on California's state flag will not be found in any of the state's plant communities. The California Grizzly Bear (*Ursus arctos*) is extinct. They once roamed in large numbers through many California plant communities from the coast through lower-elevation inland regions. However, they were most often spotted around grassland, chaparral, and woodland communities. Their huge shoulders and claws were rarely used to rip apart larger animals. They were more commonly used to dig for roots, tubers, smaller mammals, and colonies of tasty ants and termites.

The grizzly is now remembered as a fierce and powerful giant—its average size was about 900 pounds—that was hunted to extinction by the early 1900s. From the time of Spanish settlement, grizzly bears were seen as dangerous obstacles to the expansion of California farm and grazing lands. Accounts of famous grizzly encounters and hunts started with the Spanish and continued through the 1800s. The last grizzly in southern California was probably spotted in the Santa Ana Mountains before 1910. One report locates one of the last California grizzly bears with her cub near Kings Canyon before 1915. However, the last recorded grizzly bear killing was in Sequoia a few years earlier. Most records confirm their extinction by then, accelerated by the $10 reward received for each dead bear. The subspecies relative of this bear survives from the northern Rockies into Canada.

The California grizzly's smaller and more docile relative—the Black Bear (*Ursus americanus*)—is common today, especially throughout central and northern California's forests and in many other productive plant communities. The black bear's diet is similar to its extinct grizzly relative: various kinds of plants, berries, roots, tubers, and small animals. However, it lives in California's cooler forests and sometimes hibernates, habits that were *not* associated with the California grizzly. The several black bears introduced from the Sierra Nevada to southern California's San Bernardino Mountains since the 1930s have thrived. By the 1990s, their population had swelled to more than three hundred in that mountain range alone.

As more humans visit and settle in these marginally wild regions, more frequent bear encounters delight the sensationalist southern California news media. Each year, these black bears wander out of the forest and into the urban fringe of southern California's inland valleys. They become the stars in news stories when they are filmed rummaging through garbage and even bathing in hot tubs in the suburbs. When one young boy was mauled while camping in the San Bernardino Mountains in July, 1996, graphic pictures of the recovering youngster's wounds and film of the hunt for the renegade bear made one of the top news stories on local Los Angeles TV broadcasts for days. Increasing bear encounters in northern California are also making the news; they are also the result of encroaching developments.

These events are not new to Californians. After years of repeated encounters, nuisance bears learn not to be afraid of humans. They also learn to associate the presence of humans with food. For years, bear management programs in parks and other wildlands emphasized the identification and tagging of problem bears who had become too "tamed." These bears were usually transported back up to more isolated wildlands, where it was hoped they would return to their wild ways and natural diets. Unfortunately, many such bears have stubbornly walked great distances right back to the nearest people. These bears, who have lost their ability to survive on their own, become dangerous to humans and are usually killed.

Mixed Evergreen Forest

In transition between the drier oak woodland and chaparral communities and the wetter, more productive coastal and montane coniferous forests are the mixed evergreen forest communities. In coastal mountains of the north, these forests are usually inland from the heavier winter rains, summer fog, and coastal coniferous forests. However, they grow closer to the coast compared to the oak woodlands even farther inland that endure extreme drought and hot summers. In the western Sierra Nevada and the southern coastal mountains, they appear higher in elevation, above the warmer, drier oak woodland and chaparral, but below the cooler, wetter montane coniferous forests.

Throughout California, where wetter coniferous forests might be expected, especially to the north, mixed evergreen forests may grow in patches on drier south-facing slopes and in nutrient-poor soils. Where chaparral and oak woodland are expected, especially farther inland and to the south, patches of mixed evergreen stands may appear in wetter, more productive sites, such as north-facing slopes. Nearly 5 percent of California is covered by these mixed evergreen forest communities.

Habitat and Structure

The name, mixed evergreen forest, correctly suggests that most of the trees are hardwoods (especially oaks) that keep their leaves throughout the year. In California's Mediterranean climates outside the wetter coniferous forests, most of these trees survive with sclerophyllous (hard) leaves, which help cut transpiration rates. However, a greater variety of trees often mix in, including numerous conifers and broad-leaf, winter-deciduous trees, depending on moisture and soil conditions. Species common in the poor soils of the closed-cone coniferous forest communities may also be found here. Many understory species, such as those typical of the chaparral, commonly creep in from other plant communities. It is not difficult to imagine this plant community as a broad ecotone bridging its drier, less productive, and its wetter, more productive neighbors; it shares species and structural characteristics (physiognomy) with them.

Plants. In central and southern California, mixed evergreen forest may include or be dominated by Coast Live Oak (*Quercus agrifolia*), Canyon Live Oak or Golden-Cup Oak (*Quercus chrysolepis*), or Interior Live Oak (*Quercus wislizenii*). In the Sierra Nevada and higher elevations of the Transverse and Peninsular Ranges, the broad-leaf, winter-deciduous Black Oak (*Quercus kelloggii*) may appear at the expense of other species such as Coast Live Oak. These communities are not only denser than California's oak woodlands, but they include many other tree species.

Madrone or Pacific Madrone (*Arbutus menziesii*) and Tanoak or Tanbark Oak (*Lithocarpus densiflora*) are both evergreen trees with large, oval leaves, but Madrone's bark and flowers contribute to its likeness to a giant manzanita. Known as Oregon myrtle in Oregon and pepperwood in parts of California's Coast Ranges, the previously examined California Bay or California Laurel (*Umbellularia californica*) may have the most pungent aroma of any tree in California's mixed evergreen forest. Big-Leafed Maple (*Acer macrophyllum*) not only displays its classic, giant palmate leaves, but it is the largest maple in California and may occur in mixed evergreen forests throughout the state. A quick look at this maple (especially its large leaves) reveals why it cannot survive on California's drier, more exposed slopes.

Conifers often associated with the yellow pine forests mix in at higher elevations of the Sierra Nevada and in southern California. Coulter Pine (*Pinus coulteri*), with its long, dull needles and giant cones, thrives in these communities. Big-Cone Douglas Fir or Big-Cone Spruce (*Pseudotsuga macrocarpa*) grows only in southern California, mostly on north-facing slopes. It is far more adapted to drought and fire and has much larger cones than its relative, Douglas fir, which grows in wetter habitats to the north.

In California's northern mixed evergreen forests, species that require more moisture usually join the mix. Exceptions are found only on the driest, most exposed sites, where chaparral-like species such as Huckleberry Oak (*Quercus vaccinifolia*) are found. Also growing as shrubs among the oaks are Bush or Golden Chinquapin (*Chrysolepis sempervirens*). The leaves and structure of this member of the beech and oak family make it look right at home in drier mixed evergreen sites. However, it is also found in completely different communities, such as in high elevations of the Sierra Nevada. Its relative, Giant Chinquapin (*Chrysolepis chrysophylla* or *Castanopsis c.*) grows as a much larger tree in wetter mixed evergreen sites and even into redwood forest communities. As yellow pines become more common, they are joined by other conifers, including Sugar Pine (*Pinus lambertiana*), Knobcone Pine (*Pinus attenuata*), Western White Pine (*Pinus monticola*), and Incense Cedar (*Calocedrus decurrens*).

However, when species such as Douglas Fir (*Pseudotsuga menziesii*), Port Oxford Cedar (*Chamaecyparis lawsoniana*), Western Hemlock (*Tsuga heterophylla*), and Grand Fir (*Abies grandis*) become more common, they indicate a transition into the wet, lush coastal coniferous forest communities found only on the northwest coast. Soil chemistry may become the important factor for location of many of these species. On the wettest slopes, especially in the Klamaths, the fast-growing straight and tall Douglas fir often dominates and may even be joined by an occasional Coast Redwood (*Sequoia sempervirens*). In these ecotones between the marginal and most productive plant communities in California, species distributions are determined by distance from the ocean, soil, slope angle and aspect, disturbance from fire or logging, and numerous other factors. The truly diverse and complicated "mixed" evergreen forest lives up to its name.

Accompanying this plant diversity is an often abundant and wide variety of animals. An example of the variety of foods available to animals is the Oregon White Truffle (*Tuber gibbosum*). This tasty underground mushroom is one of many important fungi which grow in the soil and on the roots of trees below the mixed evergreen forest. They also serve as treats for rodents, such as the golden-mantled ground squirrel.

Animals. Most animals of mixed evergreen forests are quite common in surrounding plant communities. Mice, chipmunks, chickarees, and squirrels are typical small mammals here. The western gray squirrel prefers to eat acorns, so its nests are often found in oak trees. The tree canopy provides protection from hawks and other predators as this skilled climber with a large bushy tail darts up and around the trees gathering and stashing acorns. Raccoons make their homes in tree cavities and roam at night for a wide variety of food. Their comical-looking facial markings resemble masks. Even their eating habits, such as washing themselves and their food when water is available during dinner, can be entertaining.

There are numerous members of the weasel family in California, especially in different plant communities of the northwest. Many of them are fierce predators; they are usually more common near water. Rarely seen in the northwest forests are wolverines, badgers, fishers, weasels, martins, and minks. Rare river otter live in burrows out of the water. Skunk are more common; their famous scent glands and thick fur on long bodies with short legs are characteristic of the weasel family.

Mule deer graze throughout California, and they frequent mixed evergreen forests. They eat fresh sprouts and herbs and often establish noticeable grazing lines marking the upper limits of their reach. This abundant animal is the only native deer in California. Their numbers were once controlled by mountain lions, but the population is often decreased by hunting today. Like many wild animals, the behavior of these graceful deer may change as they are exposed to humans who may think they are "cute." Humans who try to befriend and feed deer and other wildlife in California put the animals at risk. The animals may turn away from their natural diets and methods of getting food, often leading to poor nutrition and more dependance on humans. This can be dangerous for people as well; even deer have, when cornered, defended themselves and kicked and killed startled tourists in places like Yosemite.

As many as one-hundred bald eagles nested in California in the 1990s, while more than six-hundred winter in the state each year. Most concentrate just south of the Oregon border, especially in the Klamath River area when salmon or steelhead are abundant. They may be seen perched on taller trees and snags near rivers and in plant communities such as mixed evergreen forests. By the late 1960s, their nesting numbers had dropped to twenty after heavy hunting and concentrations of DDT had nearly destroyed reproductive cycles. Since the protection given them with enforcement of the 1972 Endangered Species Act, bald eagle populations have dramatically rebounded so that they have been seen as far south as the Mexican border.

Coastal Coniferous Forest Communities

From the Oregon border to Big Sur, California's coastal coniferous forests represent the southern extension of some of the most impressive temperate rainforests in the world. Though these forests were and are more extensive from coastal Alaska through western Washington and Oregon, they are just as impressive and contain many of the same species where they are strung along California's north coast. Because they contain the tallest living trees in the world, it could be argued that portions of California's coastal forests are even more spectacular.

Habitat and Structure

Parts of these forests are scattered all the way to the sea, but they are usually located slightly inland from the stronger winds and salt spray coming off the beach. They grow from the western slopes of the Klamaths south into the northern and central Coast Ranges. In the north, where average precipitation may reach 250 cm (100 inches) per year, these forests cover all the slopes down from exposed ridges on fertile soils. At the southern edge of their range, near Big Sur, where precipitation drops to near 50 cm (20 inches), these forests only grow at the bases of wetter north-facing slopes and within canyons. The northwest coast also has the shortest summer drought in California; rainy seasons usually start earliest and end last here.

The effects of summer drought are also curbed by the persistent summer fog and stratus which hugs the coast. Not only does this maritime air keep summer temperatures cool and relative humidities high, decreasing evapotranspiration rates, it also results in fog drip that can actually add some moisture to the soil during periods without precipitation. Up to 25 cm (10 inches) of fog drip per year has been measured beneath forest canopies along parts of California's coast. The maritime air also moderates winter temperatures so that snow is rare and temperatures seldom drop below freezing. With abundant water and moderate temperatures, there are few limiting factors. Consequently, where soils are favorable, production is higher here than in any California plant community.

Plants. Botanists often divide these plant communities into two segments. The north coast coniferous forest communities include a wide variety of species common to the Pacific Northwest coast, but they do not usually include coastal redwoods. The coastal redwood forest shares some of the Pacific Northwest coast species, but it has its own characteristics and is exclusively Californian. We will examine the coast redwood only after looking at some of the other common species in California's northwest coastal forests.

Even the names of the species indicate that these are usually stately trees more common to the cool, damp forests farther north, forests with few rivals on earth. Grand Fir (*Abies grandis*), Sitka Spruce (*Picea sitchensis*), and Western Hemlock (*Tsuga heterophylla*) may dominate and be joined by other trees such as Western Red Cedar (*Thuja plicata*) and Port Oxford Cedar (Chamaecyparis lawsoniana). Hardwood species may grow on the fringe of or represent an understory below these forests. Big-Leaf Maple (*Acer marcrophyllum*), California Bay or Laurel (*Umbellularia californica*), Madrone (*Arbutus menziessii*), and Tanoak or Tanbark Oak (*Lithocarpus densiflora*) are examples.

Below these canopies, the ground cover must be adapted to constant damp conditions with filtered light at best. Herbs such as Redwood Sorrel (*Oxalis oregana*), shrubs such as the various wild berries, and numerous fern such as Bracken Fern (*Pteridium aquilinum*) and Sword Fern (*Polystichum munitum*) are common. A water-loving, velvety coating of green moss seems to cover every surface from rocks to trees to bare ground. Fires may clear out these understory species and logging opens the forests to successional species adapted to more light and less moisture.

The two most common trees growing in these forests are also the most important to California's timber industry. Douglas Fir (*Pseudotsuga menziesii*) and Coastal Redwood (*Sequoia sempervirens*) may be found separately or mixed together. They grow fast, straight, and tall and provide high-quality, valuable wood which has many uses. Because Douglas fir grows—along with other species such as Red Alder (*Alnus oregana*)—as a natural successional species, it is preferred by the timber industry when replanting after logging an area. Because most of northwest California's private and public forest lands are now tree farms, successional species such as Douglas fir are far more common than before logging began.

Currently, more than 90 percent of California's original forest lands have been logged at least once. This means that if you are wandering through a California forest, you are likely to be viewing at least a second- or third-growth stand. If you have the opportunity to visit the less than 10 percent remaining of our truly old-growth forests, you are in environments more

TALLEST TREES IN THE WORLD

Native stands of Coast Redwood (*Sequoia sempervi-rens*) are scattered from the southwestern tip of Oregon along coastal slopes south to Big Sur. Coast redwood is endemic to this region, but it was more widespread across the western United States during glacial periods. Ice Age fossil remains of coast redwoods have been found as far south as Los Angeles, where it apparently grew within local canyons. Today, it is restricted to the immediate coastal slopes inland to about 16 km (10 miles), except to more than 32 km (20 miles) inland where coastal fog and stratus are siphoned with sea breezes through major west–east canyons. The transition from dense coastal redwood forests to drier forests to oak woodland and even drier communities often within several km (miles) from west to east is remarkable. South of the Bay Area to Big Sur, coast redwood is usually restricted to patches in local cooler, wetter microclimates.

The tallest trees were cut decades ago before they were protected. However, remaining virgin growth is protected in today's state and national parks, and trees can reach higher than 110 m (360 feet) to become the tallest trees in the world. A young redwood's growth may average more than 0.5m (1.5 feet) per year for more than a century. In some areas, 4,525 kg/ha (4,000 pounds per acre) per year of added growth accumulates the greatest total above-ground biomass known to California—up to 346 kg/sq m (1,500 tons per acre).

Native redwood stands are dependent on many other factors besides heavy winter rains, persistent summer fog, and the absence of prolonged frost. In river valleys, spectacular floods may leave thick silt deposits, destroying other species, but the coast redwood thrives by growing new shallow root systems higher on the trunk.

Fires usually burn around the fire-resistant bark, clearing the surface of competitors and leaving open soil where new redwood seeds may sprout and seedlings thrive.

Chemicals in the thick bark also discourage insects and diseases from harming redwoods. Consequently, the world's tallest trees may live for more than 2,000 years (though the bristlecone pine in the White Mountains is the oldest and *Sequoiadendron giganteum* in the Sierra Nevada has the greatest mass). When coast redwoods finally burn or are cut, they vigorously sprout from stumps. Individual trees often grow from rings of interconnected stumps and roots.

These are some of the tallest trees in the world. These old-growth coast redwoods grow in moist, sheltered locations within Humboldt Redwoods State Park and several other moist sites in northwestern California.

---

representative of California's past. Many of these remnants are protected in California's parks and wilderness areas, but some of them are at the center of controversies pitting the timber industry against those who want to save the trees. Perhaps such controversy over so little land illustrates the enormous value of this timber and the pressures and conflicts which will continue as so many interests ask for more from our precious resources.

Animals. Termites and other insects join the fungi and other decomposers to recycle decaying organic debris in California's north coastal forests. Slimy, shell-less, bright yellow banana slugs grow up to 15

cm (6 inches) long as they ooze among and devour decaying organic debris in moist forests. Many kinds of moisture-loving salamanders, birds, and mammals, including black bear, are also found here.

Due to destruction of up to 90 percent of its preferred habitat, the Northern Spotted Owl (*Strix occidentalis caurina*) was classified as a threatened species by the federal government in 1990. These owls prefer to nest in the larger, taller trees, especially in old-growth forests, but their numbers dwindled as decades of intensive logging replaced old growth with tree farms. To environmentalists, the spotted owl was just one of many indicators of California's vanishing old-growth forests. As the owl's threatened status was used to help slow cutting, the bird represented a roadblock to the timber industry in its efforts to access remaining old-growth stands for the sake of short-term profits.

This controversy boiled over into a media-hyped and oversimplified national debate about "jobs versus the environment." It happened to coincide with a nationwide recession and retooling from labor-intensive to high-tech logging practices by larger timber firms. Instead of focusing on rational discussion and debate about long-term habitat and watershed destruction and sustainable yields for a healthy, long-lived timber economy, emotional images of lost jobs and soaring unemployment were broadcast by the media from traditional small California timber towns.

As the economies of these small California towns suffered into the 1990s, timber industry executives and employees searched for and found their perceived enemies in those who regulated cutting. There was little honest debate about the future of California's forests, while the media thrived on the simplistic war they helped create. (By the late 1990s, pairs of northern spotted owls were observed adapting to life in second-growth forests.)

With continued habitat destruction, it was no surprise that numbers of the California spotted owl, a different subspecies of the northern spotted owl, were also decreasing. It often makes its home in older, larger trees in mountain forests farther inland, such as in the Sierra Nevada. In January, 1993, the National Forest Service slowed logging in many of these forests to keep the California spotted owl from becoming threatened and to avoid renewed confrontation between timber interests and environmentalists. However, the timber industry still complained about the further loss of short-term revenue.

Once often seen foraging along boundaries between the north coastal forests and their meadows from northern California to Canada, Roosevelt Elk (*Cervus elaphus roosevelti*) numbers also declined rapidly until recently. Also known as wapiti (Shawnee for white rump), males grow spectacular antlers and may weigh up to 450 kg (1,000 pounds). These territorial bulls are famous for their violent battles, when they charge and lock horns during the fall rutting season. Dominant bulls may win control of more than ten cows. The few remaining herds are added attractions for wildlife enthusiasts among the big trees. A few members of its smaller subspecies relative, the Rocky Mountain Elk (*Cervus elaphus*

nelsoni), remain in isolated sections of northeastern California.

◆ MONTANE CONIFEROUS FOREST COMMUNITIES AND ABOVE: AN OVERVIEW

Various montane coniferous forest communities grow on mountain slopes from above about 300 m (1,000 feet) in the north to above 1,500 m (5,000 feet) in southern cismontane California. Sparser mountain forests may be found at even higher elevations in transmontane California. In northwest California, montane coniferous forests may appear between the wetter forests to the west and drier communities to the east. Such low elevations in the rest of California are usually too dry to support pine forests, but from the Klamaths to the northern Coast Ranges and from the Cascades to the Sierra Nevada, these communities are widespread. Farther south, coniferous forest communities are more restricted to patchy and isolated higher country, especially in the Transverse and Peninsular Ranges.

The various montane coniferous forest communities cover nearly 20 percent of California. At higher elevations, they grade into less productive alpine communities above the tree line.

Belts of Vegetation Zones Across California

Starting in the transition above chaparral and oak woodland communities, the first dry pines begin to appear on California's mountain slopes where temperatures are cooler and precipitation is greater. At slightly higher elevations, these trees eventually grow together to form the mixed coniferous/lower montane or what is also known as the yellow pine forests. Moving farther up, coniferous forest species more common to wettest montane habitats are found at even higher, cooler elevations.

In high country above these lusher forests, annual precipitation begins to decrease again, producing less-dense stands of shorter trees more tolerant of prolonged freezes and snowpacks. We have now passed through the red fir/lodgepole pine communities, into the subalpine forest. Finally, at highest elevations, even dwarfed trees disappear in the harsh, exposed terrain of the Alpine Zone above the tree line. In transmontane California, including the rainshadow sides of California's major mountain ranges, these plant communities or vegetation zones are usually squashed closer together and tilted up into higher elevations. Our review of these plant communities begins at lower elevations and works into the highest California terrain.

Mixed/Lower Montane Coniferous Forests

Habitat and Structure

Lower or mixed montane coniferous forest communities cover about 10 percent of California. Tree height is usually not as impressive as in the northern coastal forests. Outside the giant sequoia forests, tallest trees may grow up to 60 m (200 feet). Undergrowth ranges from sparse in drier forests and poor soils to tall, dense, thick shrubs and small trees, often with species more common to adjoining plant communities. Hardwoods such as oaks often join the pines. In drier environments, the needle-leaf tree species tend to have much larger cones and seeds, increasing their chances of survival in adverse conditions.

Most of the soils are made of porous materials weathered from especially granitic bedrock, and they tend to reflect the acidic nature of the pine needles which accumulate and decay on the forest floor. A variety of herbs, grasses, and spring wildflowers are common below breaks in the canopy, especially after fires, but they turn brittle and brown by the end of the summer drought. Fire has played an important role in determining the physiognomy and species distribution within these mixed montane coniferous forest communities.

These communities could be considered to be within the Transition Life Zone above the drier Upper Sonoran Life Zone communities and below the colder parts of the Canadian Life Zone. More generally, these forests are found above California's flat valleys and below the more exposed, steep, rocky slopes of higher elevations. This explains why they are sometimes called lower montane forests. Another common name is yellow pine forest, which technically refers to forests dominated by ponderosa, Jeffrey, and sometimes coulter pine. However, this label is often also used to describe mountain forests with similar physiognomy, but different dominant conifers. You can see why these communities are sometimes labelled as mixed montane coniferous forests. In this section, we will start with the lower, drier pines and generally work up into the higher, cooler, wetter forests. With so many different dominant species, it will become obvious why there is so much difficulty agreeing on one name for these communities.

Plants. Often growing among the chaparral and oak communities is Gray (Digger) Pine (*Pinus sabiniana*), which was examined in a previous section. Coulter Pine (*Pinus coulteri*) is especially common in open stands along the boundaries of dry pine forests from the Bay Area south into Baja. Like gray pine, it has long needles, but they are darker green. Coulter pines grow the largest cones in the world. In lower elevation open forests of southern California on wetter north-facing slopes and in protected canyons

usually above about 900 m (3,000 feet), they may grow near Big-Cone Douglas Fir (*Pseudotsuga macrocarpa*). Sometimes called big-cone spruce, this is related to the Douglas fir of the north except, as expected in the drier south, its cones are much larger.

Ponderosa Pine (*Pinus ponderosa*) and Jeffrey Pine (*Pinus jeffreyi*) look much alike and form similar forests. Like coulter pine, both are three-needle pines, but ponderosa pine has large plate patterns on its trunk. It also grows sharp spines turning out from its smaller cones, earning its other name, "prickly ponderosa." Jeffrey pine has long, narrow ridge patterns on a bark that smells like vanilla or butterscotch when sniffed. Its cones grow spines turned inward. Ponderosa is the most widespread pine in the western United States and is vital to the timber industry.

Because Jeffrey pine survives colder winters with average January temperatures less than −1°C (30°F), more severe drought, and even lightning strikes, it is more common in the challenging higher elevations to the north and drier forests into Baja. Even in the Klamaths, Jeffrey pine grows with chaparral on the driest sites and poorest soils. In the Warner Mountains in California's northeast corner, Jeffrey pine grows at lowest, driest sites. It yields to ponderosa on higher, wetter slopes, which yields to washoe pine (a rarer yellow pine of the western Basin and Range) above about 2,600 m (8,000 feet). These Washoe Pines (*Pinus washoensis*) grow here with the most extensive Quaking Aspen (*Populus tremuloides*) woodlands away from riparian habitats in California. Such impressive stands of aspen suggest environments similar to the Rocky Mountains, where there is less summer drought. They are also noted for their extensive networks of interconnected tree roots.

Shifting west, Douglas Fir (*Pseudotsuga menziesii*) is restricted to moist forests throughout northern California and was discussed with the north coast coniferous forests. Its cones hang down from drooping limbs. Sugar Pine's (*Pinus lambertiana*) numerous clumps of five needles make bushy stems. These are the tallest pine species in the world (up to 75 m (245 feet) and they grow some of the longest cones— more than 30 cm (12 inches) in length. The attractive sugar pine was named for its sweet sap. It is widespread throughout California's conifer forests. In contrast, Pacific Yew (*Taxus brevifolia*) is a rare, slow-growing conifer found in deep shade of old-growth forests only in northern California and beyond. This tree became famous when the National

LARGEST TREES IN THE WORLD

Giant Sequoia (*Sequoiadendron giganteum*) grows only in about seventy-five mostly small groves on the western slopes of the Sierra Nevada. Perhaps the most spectacular of California's numerous endemics, it is the largest (but not the tallest) living thing on Earth. Giant Sequoias only grow on the wetter slopes above about 1,350 m (4,400 feet) and below about 2,600 m (8,500 feet) in the western Sierra Nevada, often in habitats with and similar to white fir. They are also relics of a wetter period, when they grew down to about 900 m (3,000 feet) elevation and were far more widespread. They are restricted to slopes which were not carved by glaciers.

Many of the largest trees are more than 60 m (200 feet) tall, weigh more than 1,000 tons, and are more than 2,000 years old; some are more than 3,000 years old. Many of the largest are in Sequoia National Park's Giant Forest, where the General Sherman Tree stands more than 83 m (273 feet) tall. The General Grant Tree in adjacent Kings Canyon National Park is more than 81.5 m (268 feet) tall with a 12.3 m (40.3 feet) diameter base. Growth rates for some young trees are up to 60 cm (2 feet) per year, which are some of the fastest rates in the world. How have these ancient giants grown so tall and survived so long?

They thrive on moisture from winter's heavy orographic precipitation. Snow packs average more than 3 m (10 feet) by winter's end, melting into deep soils where giant sequoias' extensive shallow roots are anchored. They survive summer drought by growing in moist, sheltered sites. Their bark is up to 60 cm (2 feet) thick, and it is resistant to fire, insects and parasites, fungus, and disease.

The first branches and exposed living portions of the giants are usually near the top, high above the reach of ground fires. Heat from occasional ground fires opens cones to shed seeds, while the flames on the forest floor leave soft, nutritious soils and clearings where new seedlings can get plenty of sun. Fire is also important to clear the forest of smaller plants and trees such as white fir, which, if too tall, could direct fires in a ladder effect toward the higher living crowns of the giant sequoias. This is one reason why suppression of fire in these forests actually threatens the giant sequoias. Control burns and managed wildfires should increase the health of these forests.

Loggers began to cut these giants by the 1870s. When the giant sequoias fell, however, their wood splintered into myriad pieces. Though many trees were cut for scrap uses, the poor quality wood saved the remaining groves from destruction until conservationists were able to protect them in national parks. Most of the older trees finally die when their crowns become too heavy and they fall over. Today, the extensive shallow roots may be trampled by visitors, weakening the anchoring systems and making some of the trees more vulnerable to topple.

After measurements proved sequoias in Sequoia and Kings Canyon National Parks to be the largest trees in the world, they were given names, such as this General Sherman Tree.

Cancer Institute announced that chemicals from its bark and roots inhibit the growth of tumors.

Incense Cedar (*Calocedrus decurrens*), with its reddish bark, might be mistaken for small giant sequoia if it weren't for its branching chains of leaves that resemble flat needles. White Fir (*Abies concolor* var. *lowiana*) invades wetter and higher yellow pine forests throughout northern and southern California. This white fir may become dominant above yellow pine forests where average annual precipitation is more than 100 cm (40 inches). Its white bark and rows of short needles that point up from the stem make it easy to identify. Surprising relic stands of white fir atop the New York, Clark, and Kingston mountain ranges in the eastern Mojave are actually a Rocky Mountain variety known as *Abies concolor* var. *concolor*. These trees were stranded and then isolated on high north-facing slopes of these desert mountains with other species during the last several thousand years as California climates became warmer and drier.

To illustrate the diversity and complexity of California's montane coniferous forests, note that several of the previously discussed species are among the sixteen conifers growing within a 2.6 sq km (1 square mile) area near Russian Peak in the Klamath National Forest of Siskiyou County, southwest of Scott Valley. This may be the greatest variety of different conifer species growing naturally within any area of its size in the world.

Plants Closer to the Ground. It was previously mentioned that a number of hardwood trees, shrubs, herbs, grasses, and wildflowers common in other plant communities may mix with the conifers in these transitional montane coniferous forests. Such species as Black Oak (*Quercus kelloggii*), a common and widespread winter-deciduous tree with large-lobed leaves, adds to the fall colors and contributes to diversity throughout California's mountain forests. It often grows on drier sites and south-facing slopes adjacent to wetter coniferous forests along with species such as Canyon Live Oak or Golden-Cup Oak (*Quercus chrysolepis*).

On the mountain forest floor, about thirty-four species of paintbrush (*Castilleja* spp.) grow in nearly every California plant community; their flowers add delightful color below the forest fringe. They photosynthesize like most plants to produce food, but they are also partially parasitic as they attach to roots of shrubs to steal moisture and minerals. In many species, the bright red colors actually come from large, leaf-like bracts, which look like brushes dipped in paint, framing the much smaller flowers.

Snow Plant (*Sarcodes sanguinea*) does not photosynthesize, but it attaches its roots to and feeds off fungi which break down decaying organic material in the soil. Its peculiar bright red stalks grow up to one foot (30 cm) out of the spring snowmelt. Pinedrops (*Pterospora andromedea*) is another mycotrophic or saprophytic plant that looks like a skinny version of snow plant but has no roots and simply steals directly from fungi associated with other plants. These and other mycotrophic herb species are common in moist, shady spots below the forest floor where layers of organic materials accumulate and decay. They are also common below the canopy of red fir forests at higher elevations.

Animals. Just as these environments support intermixed plant species, they are also home to a mixture of critters that are common to adjacent lower- and higher-elevation communities. Review the animals surveyed in lower-elevation communities (such as oak woodland and chaparral) and in higher-elevation communities for a glimpse of these animals.

Red Fir and Lodgepole Pine Forests/ Upper Montane Forests
Habitat and Structure

We now move to higher elevations above the giant trees and denser montane coniferous forests to more exposed mountain slopes. In northern California mountains, we must first pass through the often cool, dense growth of the red fir forests, where annual precipitation is greater than any other mountain community. Here, the colder temperatures, heavy snows, and shorter growing seasons prohibit many lower elevation species from invading. More than 150 cm (60 inches) of precipitation may fall each year in wetter sites, with total snow falls up to 13 m (more than 42 feet) per year building snow packs more than 4.5 m (15 feet) high by winter's end.

Above about 2,500 m (above 8,000 feet) elevation, moving toward the Subalpine Zone, lodgepole pine may become more dominant, as precipitation decreases with height. Because lodgepole pine survives harsher conditions, it often replaces red fir in waterlogged soils at lower elevations or on more rocky sites exposed to the colder climates of higher elevations. At even higher elevations in southern California, more prolonged summer drought prohibits growth of red fir. Here, upper limits of montane coniferous forests often blend directly into lodgepole pine forests. Red fir often mingles with upper limits of the montane coniferous forests in northern mountains, and lodgepole pine may be common in higher subalpine communities. However, these two species often mingle in the north to form a separate plant community between the communities above and below them. Merriam may have labelled this community as part of the Canadian Life Zone; others have used the term "Upper Montane Forest."

Plants. The two varieties of California's Red Fir (*Abies magnifica*) are widespread in northern California high country but grow only a short distance into southern Oregon and western Nevada. Red fir often replaces white fir at higher northern California elevations. It has redder bark, larger cones, and more rounded, shorter needles than white fir. It is also a common Christmas tree known as "silver tip." Growing on well-drained soils usually above about 1,600 m (5,000 feet) and below 3,000 m (10,000 feet), it may tolerate cold better than any other conifer. Noble Fir (*Abies procera*) replaces it in the Klamaths; Cascade Fir or Lovely Fir (*Abies amabilis*) takes over north of California's Cascades. Both are very similar to red fir.

Red fir and lodgepole pine stands are frequently struck by lightning. Lightning-caused fires may clear patches of them so that local regrowth is usually the same age. Though lodgepole pine may grow in sunny clearings caused by recent fires, it is often replaced by red fir, which thrives in shadier habitats established many years after fire.

Varieties of Lodgepole Pine (*Pinus contorta*) are widespread throughout western North America. The variety *murrayana* grows from the higher forests of the Klamaths and Cascades as low as 1,800 m (6,000 feet) and into the Sierra Nevada up to 3,600 m (12,000 feet), usually above red fir forests or where soils are too waterlogged or dry to support the less versatile red fir. In the Peninsular Ranges, upper limits of montane coniferous forests change to lodgepole pine at higher elevations. Lodgepole's name refers to the structural support it provided for California Indian homes. It has a white bark with scales, needles in clusters of two, and small, sharp cones. The tallest lodgepole pines grow up to 30 m (nearly 100 feet) in the most mature, healthy stands. It and red fir often represent the highest elevation stands of dense, tall trees in California, but lodgepole pine grows in more adverse conditions.

Small stands of Quaking Aspen (*Populus tremuloides*) may join lodgepole pine in wetter riparian habitats. Resembling but growing above sugar pine in more rocky, exposed soils into subalpine communities is Western White Pine or Silver Pine (*Pinus monticola*). It grows square plates on its bark and its branches curve up; it grows much smaller cones than sugar pine. In contrast, stems of Mountain Hemlock (*Tsuga mertensiana*) and its cones droop down. Other trees such as Western Juniper (*Juniperus occidentalis occidentalis*) and Jeffrey pine also grow on more exposed slopes, joining red fir and lodgepole pine into the subalpine communities.

Yellow-green staghorn lichens grow on the trunks of many trees down to the average snow accumulation line, which may be more than 4.5 m (15 feet) from ground level. Dark, shady conditions, bitter cold, and heavy snows inhibit understory growth in red fir and lodgepole pine forests. Shrubs are often restricted to openings below an otherwise dense forest cover. They include mountain species of manzanita (*Arctostaphylos* spp.) adapted to cold and snow. Mountain or Bush Chinquapin (*Chrysolepis sempervirens*) is found in several other California plant communities with its spiny fruits bearing nuts eaten by squirrels and bears. Currant, mountain berry, and other shrubs are joined by herbs and summer wildflowers, which may be more common in coniferous forests of lower elevations or in subalpine communities at higher elevations. Mycotrophic or saprophytic plants, similar to those examined as part of the coniferous forest ground cover, annually spring up through late spring's melting snowpacks, below the denser red fir or lodgepole pine canopy, where abundant organic debris has accumulated.

Animals. One of the most notorious animals living within these communities is the Lodgepole Needle Miner (*Coleotechnites milleri*), the larvae of a small moth. The moths are abundant in August when they lay their eggs, which later hatch into small caterpillars that will bore into the needles of the lodgepole pine. In large numbers, they may kill the trees, leaving open patches of dead pines to be followed by more diverse species and the eventual return of lodgepole pines. Some early forest managers, seeing this as an unfortunate waste of valuable timber, unknowingly sprayed infested forests with DDT and other poisons to control the "pests." Many of the more than forty predators that kept needle miner numbers under control (including gleaning birds, such as mountain chickadees, wasps, and other insects), were also harmed by the spray; this created even more serious long-term problems.

The Mountain Chickadee (*Parus gambeli*), a small gray bird with black and white bands on its head, is just one of many birds living in these forests. It is a model gleaner, a bird which climbs up and down trees picking insects from bark. It lives in many different California forests and woodlands and requires some patience to spot. Its lonely three-note call is a familiar mood-setter in a quiet forest. Mountain bluebirds, Clark's nutcracker, sapsuckers, woodpeckers, and numerous cone crackers are among the list of birds seen and heard in these communities. Great horned and pygmy owls swoop down on rodents and other small animals for dinner.

Mice, pocket gophers, shrews, and ground squirrels populate the forest floor. There are eight different species of chipmunks in the Sierra Nevada alone. These are actually small squirrels, and each inhabits different communities. In these high-altitude zones with deep snow, gray squirrels are replaced by chickarees, which live in trees above the snow pack and feast on pine and fir seeds. Black-tailed jackrabbits are replaced by snowshoe hares, which are more skilled at hopping through deep drifts. Other larger animals include weasel, fox, coyote, and black bear. Marten or pine marten are large weasels that attack and feed on smaller mammals such as squirrels and chipmunks. These long, short-legged animals are quick and deadly hunters through the trees and deep snow; their thick fur is well-suited to long, cold winters.

Subalpine Forests

Habitat and Structure

We now venture still higher to California's subalpine forest communities. Though some of the species creep up from the red fir and lodgepole pine forests, all plants and animals must be specially adapted to the long, bitter-cold winters. Here, summer growing seasons may last only seven to nine weeks, and frost is common even then. Subalpine forests grow at elevations just above 2,000 m (6,500 feet) in the Klamaths, but they grow at higher elevations inland in the Cascades. This is also true in the Sierra Nevada, where the most extensive subalpine communities are found in California. On isolated southern and eastern high mountains, these plant communities begin as high as 3,000 m (nearly 10,000 feet). Because very little of California's topography has been lifted to such high elevations, it follows that these plant communities represent a very small percentage of the state. Due to such harsh conditions, the biomass and species diversity is limited compared to most other California communities.

In all locations, subalpine forests' upper limits mark the **tree line**, where environmental conditions are so harsh that trees cannot survive. Above the timberline, temperatures could drop as low as 40 degrees below 0°F. The harsh winter may be followed by quick snowmelt runoff and severe summer drought where poor soils are often incapable of supporting tree growth.

Hardy trees and other plants and animals in Lassen's high country must endure bitter winter cold, blowing snow, and short growing seasons as plant communities recover from volcanic activity. Lush forests are out of the question.

Below tree line, on wetter slopes to the north, precipitation may reach 125 cm (nearly 50 inches), or it may average below 70 cm (28 inches) in isolated southern and eastern highlands. Almost all precipitation falls as snow, except for the few summer showers in the north and a few summer thunderstorms in the south that break the short warm season's drought. Soil water is frozen throughout the year, except for the short summer, when snowmelt may quickly run off exposed, rocky surfaces only to be lost to lower elevations and forests. High winds are a constant challenge to life, especially during winter.

Subalpine species may be most interesting due to their ability to survive in such harsh environments. These are communities where desiccating winds drive ice pellets to form flag trees. Their windward sides look blasted, battered, and bare, with more protected branches on the leeward sides growing and pointing away from the prevailing winds. Terms like *krummholz*, a German term for bent or twisted wood, describe the tortured nature of some of these stunted species. They are often dwarfed to the height of the average snow pack. Any tree that grows above this line is exposed to the deadly, fierce, cold blasts of winter or to the violent avalanche. When soils finally thaw, some plants even photosynthesize in the dim light below the protective snow cover.

Though many trees are dwarfed to near shrub size, true shrubs are not common in subalpine plant communities. Some shrubs may be more typical of the snowy forests at lower elevations. Summer's herbs, grasses, and wildflowers must quickly spring from melting snows, grow, bloom, and return to seed before autumn's first heavy snow. Many of these species are also common in higher alpine communities and are especially dense in well-watered mountain meadows.

Plants. Mountain Hemlock (*Tsuga mertensiana*) grows mostly on wetter sites in northern California subalpine communities and is widespread throughout the northwestern states. Needles grow out from all sides of its branches; it looks like a fir but is actually a pine. Whitebark Pine (*Pinus albicaulis*) also grows in the north and into the Pacific Northwest, but Limber Pine (*Pinus flexus*) grows on drier, rocky slopes in central and southern California and into highlands of the southwestern states. Both of these trees have long needles at the ends of stems and may look like lodgepole pine, but their needles are in clusters of five instead of two.

Its common name, Foxtail Pine, describes the needle-covered branches of *Pinus balfouriana*. This species survives only where summer showers break the drought in the Klamaths and where summer thunderstorms occasionally dump rain on the southern Sierra Nevada. Evidence for the slow growth of many trees in these forests is found in a few foxtail pine measured at more than 3,000 years old. The largest junipers in the world grow in the Sierra Nevada and some species creep into California's subalpine communities, but they often become twisted testimonies to the torturous life on these exposed slopes. Several trees of the red fir and lodgepole pine forests, such as western white pine, are also found in subalpine communities.

Great Basin Sagebrush (*Artemisia tridentata*) is one example of the few hardy shrubs from other plant communities that have invaded and adapted to these adverse subalpine environments. In moist habitats, high elevation species of willow, mountain berries, herbs, and wildflowers common to alpine communities may be established.

Great Basin Bristlecone Pine (*Pinus longaeva*) is a subalpine tree growing near the timberline in California's higher transmontane mountains. It often grows near limber pine, but in poor soils weathered from dolomite. Bristlecone pine is found in the White, Inyo, and Panamint Mountains with limber pine, but it grows alone on higher and nutrient-poor dolomitic soils and in the Last Chance Mountains. Some bristlecone are the oldest trees on earth; the oldest has been growing in California's White Mountains for more than 4,600 years.

These are the harshest subalpine conditions, where extreme winter cold combines with extreme drought in the rainshadow of the Sierra Nevada. Nearly all precipitation falls as snow and much of that sublimates in the windy, dry conditions that follow. Bristlecone pine may look somewhat like foxtail pine, but even foxtails could not survive these harshest of habitats. Somehow the gnarled, dwarfed bristlecones survive. In these environments of ultra-slow growth and decay, scientists have used downed wood, Carbon 14 dating, and tree rings from bristlecone pines to trace climate and timberline variations back 8,000 years.

Animals. Many animals living in California's subalpine communities may also be found either in the lodgepole pine and red fir forests below or in the alpine communities above. Numerous species migrate out by winter to escape the deadly cold. This includes as many as thirty species of birds. Perhaps the most notorious and commonly heard is the noisy Clark's nutcracker. These are large gray jays with white markings on black wings. Because Clark's nutcrackers may store more than 30,000 seeds per season in caches of fifteen, many subalpine pines rely on these birds to disperse and plant their seeds, which may produce seedlings, which eventually grow in clumps. This is similar to the clumping of oak trees in communities at much lower elevations, caused when gray squirrels bury acorns and do not retrieve them.

Meanwhile, other birds such as bright blue mountain bluebirds may be spotted on tree tops or hovering above the unsuspecting insects that will serve as their next meals. Most of these birds migrate to lower elevations or to southern latitudes for the winter.

Mountain Juniper (*Juniperus occidentalis* ssp. *australis*) grows conspicuous nutritious fruits with seeds that may not germinate unless they have passed through the digestive systems of birds or mammals. This helps disperse their seeds and eventually seedlings into different plant communities. Just as insects, mice, chipmunks, squirrels, birds, and other animals depend on subalpine plants for survival, so do the plants often benefit from the activity of these animals. These relationships will be considered in more detail in the next section on alpine communities.

Alpine Communities

Less than 1 percent of California has been lifted to elevations above the tree line. On these isolated islands in the sky, terrible cold and wind create such harsh conditions that even dwarfed trees cannot survive. The tree line may drop down to nearly 2,000 m (about 7,000 feet) in the Klamaths, but it is a little higher on Mount Shasta, Lassen Peak, and in the Warner Mountains. The timberline continues to tilt upward from the northern Sierra Nevada south until it approaches 3,350 m (11,000 feet) in the southern Sierra Nevada. It is slightly higher in the drier White and Inyo Mountains to the east. Only three solitary spots of alpine communities emerge just above the tree line in southern California: at more than 3,000 m (10,000 feet) near and on the Transverse Range peaks of San Antonio and San Gorgonio, and on the Peninsular Ranges' Mount San Jacinto.

During the Pleistocene Epoch Ice Ages, when many of the northern highlands were covered with ice, these alpine communities extended down more than 1,200 m (4,000 feet) elevation to include nearly 10 percent of the state.

Habitat

Precipitation continues to decrease with elevation gain from the subalpine; annual totals up to 100 cm (40 inches) are common in the central Sierra Nevada, with more precipitation in the Klamaths and less to the south and east. Almost all precipitation falls as snow; even the occasional summer thunderstorm may produce hail, sleet, and snow. Winter temperatures below −18°C (0°F) are common, and temperatures frequently drop below freezing even on summer nights. Winter snows will bury plants in drifts that may not melt until late summer. Then, intense summer sun can dry and damage plants.

Fierce winds will then batter plants in exposed sites and intensify evapotranspiration rates as the dry, rarefied air blasts through. Following the summer thaw, snow-melt rapidly drains down rocks and porous regolith into the forests below. This leaves alpine communities stranded without water during the shortest growing seasons in California, ranging from one to two months. The only exceptions are in meadows and lakes where water has been dammed. Most soils are rocky, poor, acidic, and unproductive. Though trees are eliminated, an amazing variety of life forms are successful in these habitats.

Often referred to as the Alpine Zone, C. Hart Merriam placed these communities in the Arctic-Alpine Zone (above the Hudsonian Zone), while some generalists simply call it tundra. It is not surprising that plants similar to California's alpine communities grow in the far north latitudes of North America's tundra, also beyond the timberline. Other plants, adapted to summer's drought, are related to those in California's driest deserts. You may find many of the more than six-hundred species of hardy alpine plants in other California communities. About two-hundred species grow only in alpine habitats. Here, we can only begin to look at the structure of these communities and a few of the species surviving in them.

Plants. Perhaps the most hostile of California's environments are on the bare, exposed, rocky alpine slopes known as alpine fell-fields. Clinging to these surfaces with little or no soil are sometimes dense mats or cushions of growth. Lichen is found where fungus can anchor in and gradually weather rock and where algae can join to carry out its role of photosynthesis. In cracks and sheltered spots, perennial prostrate plants hug the surface but grow more extensive root and subterranean stem systems below. These plants lie ready to grow and flower as soon as the short, unreliable mid-summer growing season begins. They join annual herbs to produce spectacular wildflower displays. Many of these species have the large flowers required to quickly attract pollinators. Various grasses and sedges may join the crowd to help capture and protect finer particles from erosion.

Sunflowers, buckwheats, and lupines are among the hundreds of common plants here. Species names often reflect the nature of the plants and their habitats. Paintbrushes include Alpine Paintbrush (*Castilleja nana*). Various phlox include Coville's Phlox (*Phlox covillei*), while Pussy Paws (*Calyptridium umbellatum*), Evening Primrose (*Oenothera xylocarpa*), the bright blue flowers of Sky Pilot (*Polemonium eximium*), and bright yellow sunflowers of Alpine Gold (*Hulsea algida*) are among numerous flowers adding color to California's otherwise barren summertime alpine landscapes.

In and near alpine meadows, water is available for a longer period into the growing season and soils are usually better developed. Grasses and sedges may accumulate to form dark sod or even peat bogs in wetter locations. A few shrubs growing near these meadows include heather and willow. The edges of meadows are first to erupt in summer wildflowers, a splash of color which shifts toward herbs near the center of meadows within a few weeks. Many of these meadows were once lakes and are continuing through their successional stages. At lower elevations, lodgepole pine or other dwarfed trees may eventually encroach; in driest high country, annual grasses and sagebrush scrub may invade. But, in most of California's highest country, communities resembling alpine tundra are usually the climax. A variety of species growing in so many changing habitats demands more attention than is possible in this fleeting sweep through California's plant communities.

Animals. Many larger animals and birds are capable of migrating from the alpine to lower elevations during winter. The California or Mountain Bighorn

Thousands of feet above the tree line near Mount Whitney, you will find some of the harshest California environments, where only a few species hug the ground in late summer, then lie dormant in the cold for the rest of the year.

Sheep (*Ovis canadensis californiana*) is one of three subspecies of California's bighorns that were once far more numerous. Most mountain bighorn live in the central Sierra Nevada, but there is a small herd in the Warner Mountains. They once migrated to lower elevations, such as the Owens Valley, during winter, but human barriers and activities have impeded these migrations. Diseases, habitat destruction, and overgrazing by domestic livestock greatly reduced their numbers in California to about 350 by 1990, prompting wildlife biologists to implement programs to save them.

More abundant deer also migrate to lower slopes during winter. Birds have the advantage of migrating rapidly to feed on seeds and insects of the alpine and then leaving to escape harsh conditions ushered in by winter. The gray-crowned rosy finch is the only bird that nests in the alpine, but it will fly down the east slopes of the Sierra Nevada during harsh winter weather.

Other animals, such as most rodents, hibernate through the winter. This state of slowed metabolism helps them conserve resources and body fat accumulated during their summer and fall food-gathering frenzies. Among the mice, gophers, chipmunks, and squirrels is the approximately 25 cm- (10 inch-) long Belding's ground squirrel; it may be seen on rocks in the central Sierra Nevada, screaming alarm calls to warn of a possible incoming predator. It hibernates for up to eight months, living off body fat from summer's seeds and insects.

The largest squirrel of the Sierra Nevada is the plump and furry-tailed yellow-bellied marmot. It can grow twice as long as Belding's ground squirrel and weigh more than ten pounds just before the long winter hibernation begins. Numerous marmot heads may be seen protruding above rocks. Their loud whistles also warn of possible dangers.

A few animals remain active in winter. The pocket gopher burrows through the substrate, eating roots and other plant parts buried under the snow. Pikas, also known as cony or chief hares, are the size of rats but have rounded ears and no tail; they look like and are more related to small rabbits and hares. They collect and guard piles of nutritious herbs near their rocky shelters so that they may snack and survive through the winter. Pikas also make territorial calls when approached, unless the predator is a marten or long-tailed weasel, which are capable of navigating through the rock cavities in quick pursuit. When these skilled predators are hungry, the only way to escape being served as the next meal may be to run for it! Though the white-tailed jackrabbit is seen in drier southern Sierra Nevada and Great Basin alpine habitats, northern California's snowshoe hare usu-

ally remains below the tree line. Both of them change color to blend with seasonal backgrounds.

◆ ECOLOGIC ISLANDS

There is one big advantage of using generalists' past attempts to classify California's plants and animals into overly simplified biomes or vegetation zones—they often provided structure and organization to clarify what many saw as too confusing and complicated. Though there is still healthy controversy, in the last few decades, a confusing array of conflicting information about the biogeography of California has been studied, debated, agreed upon, and reorganized.

The old methods may be likened to grouping everyone with the same skin color or accent in California into the same culture or assuming everyone from the same culture has the same lifestyle and habits. This is where overgeneralizing may become meaningless and counterproductive. Even most generalists now agree that to understand the diverse plant and animal communities in California, we must go far beyond the few generalized biomes and vegetation zones. This section is devoted to ecologic islands because they are examples of extremely important plant communities that are too easily overlooked using those old methods of classification.

Habitats

Ecologic islands include habitats which are isolated and different from their surroundings, and they may appear in any portion of California for many reasons. They could include cliffs or talus slopes in the midst of otherwise gentle topography. They could be sources of fresh water in an otherwise **xeric** (dry, desertlike) landscape. Many such factors, and the plant communities that result, are examined in other parts of this chapter. Commonly in California, they are edaphic communities, where a sudden change in the chemistry of the soil or water eliminates some plant and animal species and allows others to successfully compete. (Edaphic refers to the nature of the soil.) Because great geologic diversity in this state has produced so many different types of adjacent rock outcrops, soil chemistry can radically change over very short distances. A good geographer or any other scientist *must* consider these factors when examining the distribution of plants and animals in California.

When more fertile soils grade into serpentine or other soils low in nutrients and high in heavy metals, or to highly acidic soils such as mountain spodosols (podzols) or clay oxisols, they present new challenges to plants and the animals that depend on them. More than two-hundred plant species and varieties are endemic on serpentine soils alone in California. In poorer soils, California's densest forests may become open, while more open forests may abruptly turn to woodlands or chaparral; woodlands may turn to grasslands or drier xeric environments in poor soils. Bald Mountain in northwest California serves as a classic example. There are so many rare and endangered species in California partly because humans have so frequently modified or destroyed these isolated, unique habitats.

These ecologic islands are scattered in tiny patches throughout the state. Because they are found in some form in every region, and because they include so many endemic, interesting, and sometimes well-known and unusual species, we can focus on just a few of them. We will lump them with some other species which were otherwise skipped in our sweep through cismontane California communities.

Plants. Closed-cone coniferous forest communities are usually restricted to poor soils where lusher forests would otherwise thrive. The cones open after many years from the heat of fires to finally disperse seeds on freshly burned soil. These trees usually form a more open canopy and often have other characteristics linking them to drier habitats. They may grow with chaparral and coastal scrub capable of surviving more adverse conditions. Most of these trees grow in relic stands which were much more widespread when California climates were cooler and wetter thousands of years ago.

Knobcone Pine (*Pinus attenuata*) is probably the most widespread example and is scattered from the Klamaths to southern California. This species survives in some of the driest climates and poorest soils of any California pine, usually inland from the immediate coast. It is often surrounded with other forest species in northern California, but with non-forest species in southern and drier sites. There is a greater variety of coastal closed-cone pines—including Shore Pine (*Pinus contorta* ssp. *contorta*), which is a

relative of lodgepole pine—growing on coastal dunes and cliffs in northern California. Other examples include Bishop Pine (*Pinus muricata*) and the sometimes twisted and scraggly-looking Monterey Pine (*Pinus radiata*) of central California and the Channel Islands. Interestingly, Monterey pine has been introduced as a timber crop to replant some southern hemisphere forests, where it grows taller and straighter than in its marginal California habitats. By the late 1990s, California's Monterey pines were proving how vulnerable they can be in such marginal environments. They were the first pines to be decimated by the spreading pine pitch canker. Some biologists warned that up to 80 percent of Carmel's pines could be wiped out by the fungus within thirty years.

Torrey Pine (*Pinus torreyana*) protrudes above the coastal scrub in northern San Diego County and is also found on Santa Rosa Island. It has that typical dry pine look but grows needles in clusters of five. It is probably saved from summer drought by the cool coastal fog and stratus. The approximately 9,000 trees only at these two sites make Torrey pine the rarest pine in the world.

Eight of the ten species of cypress (*Cypressus* spp.) in California are endemic (restricted to California). They are also divided into coastal and inland species and usually occur in isolated patches. These are the trees with scale-like leaves and fleshy cones which sometimes resemble tiny soccer balls. Monterey Cypress (*Cypressus macrocarpa*) is confined to the Monterey Peninsula on sites with granitic soil, persistent fog, wind, and salt spray. In spite of these restrictions, the contorted and tortured images of these trees appear in countless photographs and paintings as contrast to the scenic coastline.

These rare Torrey pines grow in marginal, semiarid environments along northern San Diego's coast and offshore islands where you might not expect to find pine trees. Look for different pine species struggling in other marginal habitats in California, such as the fire pines and piñon pine/juniper woodlands.

The most widespread inland cypress are the Sargent Cypress (*Cypressus sargenti*) of the Coast Ranges and the MacNab Cypress (*Cypressus macnabiana*) of northern California, which are usually restricted to serpentine soils. As the name implies, tecate cypress grows on poor soils in southern California past the Mexican border. Cuyamaca Cypress (*Cupressus stephensonii*) was originally thought to be endemic only to the southwest slope of Cuyamaca Peak in San Diego County, until individuals were reported in Baja. Regardless, it is the rarest cypress in California, and it grows into higher elevations where chaparral turns to conifer forest. Before the taller of these trees was burned, they towered more than 14 m (46 feet) high. Occasional fire is an important factor in most of California's cypress stands, but if fires are too frequent, extinction of the rarer and more isolated species may follow.

Numerous other California species occur only in ecological islands. Furthermore, shrubs common to chaparral, such as chamise, and different species of ceanothus and manzanita may be indicators of poor soils within otherwise more favorable sites. Even the California oaks include scrub species adapted to more adverse conditions, such as Leather Oak (*Quercus durata*), with its curled leaves. Because California Huckleberry (*Vaccinium ovatum*) is common on poor soils in central California, it should be no surprise that nearly pure stands of bishop pine (another dry habitat pine) grow on Huckleberry Hill near Monterey.

The Baldwin Lake Pebble Plains east of Big Bear Lake, Anticline Ridge near Coalinga, Corral Hollow Ecological Reserve southwest of Tracy, and Pine Hill in El Dorado County in the Sierra Nevada are famous for their ecological island status. All have assemblages of interesting, rare, and endangered plants and animals adapted to unusually adverse conditions. Some of the most fascinating examples are in the dwarfed closed-cone conifer forests or pygmy forests on the Mendocino County ecological staircase. Here, hardpan soils stunt tree growth and change the dominant vegetation from forest to shrubs.

Animals. As expected, numerous mostly smaller rare animal species are associated with specific soils or plants within these challenging ecologic islands. They include many insects, amphibians, and reptiles. The smaller and more unique habitats are often home to smaller and more delicate populations of rare animals. Other animals (especially larger mammals and birds) may live and are often more common in adjacent communities, but they may migrate through and sometimes settle in these patches of Cal-

ifornia. Many of them are considered in other sections of this chapter.

Monarch Butterflies (*Danaus plexippus*) could be the only insects which make lengthy, round-trip migrations; they may travel up to 4,800 km (3,000 miles), but over several generations. Up to 5 million California monarchs winter mainly on the central and southern California coast; individuals have been known to migrate more than 1,000 km (650 miles). Most California monarchs spend their winters feeding on nectar, and many can be seen in Monterey pine and eucalyptus trees. A close look at some trees at locations such as Pacific Grove and Morro Bay might reveal many hundreds of monarchs covering the trees.

They begin their journeys toward the north and east in the spring. They return to the California coast each fall. The monarch's larvae feed off milkweed, then grow to larger caterpillars, and turn to butterflies in about two weeks. Though they are immune to the poisonous milkweed, otherwise potential predators recognize them as distasteful. This is just one example of how animals may migrate into or through California's ecologic islands.

◆ RIPARIAN COMMUNITIES

Any habitat or community located on or adjacent to a river bank or other freshwater body is considered riparian. Because water availability is usually the most important limiting factor for most California plants and animals, it is not surprising to find the greatest biomass and species diversity in riparian communities. Especially toward southern California, water shortages limit the growth and survival of plants and animals; remarkable changes in the size, diversity, and density of organisms is striking along water courses.

This is where coarse-grained soils often contain abundant nutrients and organic materials. This is where plant roots and animals can search out year-round sources of surface, soil, or shallow groundwater. This is where explosive growth and successful reproduction are encouraged by the abundance of fresh water instead of being limited by its scarcity. This is where the plants and animals closer to water courses must adapt to periodic flooding and sediment deposits, and this is where wildlife will find abundant food, water, and shelter.

Riparian Habitats and Structures

There is an astounding variety of riparian communities in cismontane California. Some are narrow strips along tiny seasonal streams or in deep, narrow canyons. Some are wide, sprawling swaths of forests adjacent to major

Sycamore, oak, bay, and willow are just a few of the trees that thrive along California's stream courses, where they can access moisture most of the year. This is a winter scene.

perennial rivers that seasonally flood across broad valleys. The most impressive riparian forests were the extensive gallery forests up to 16 km (10 miles) wide that poured into the Central Valley along meandering rivers spilling out of the Sierra Nevada. Some of the largest Valley Oaks (*Quercus lobata*) grew in these forests. Today, less than 10 percent of the original 400,000 ha (about 1 million acres) of Central Valley riparian woodlands remain.

Throughout California, whether riparian communities have taller shrubs, small trees, or towering giants, they are relatively moist, cool, shady, protected habitats. Brief exceptions may be noted in winter where dominant broadleaf deciduous trees lose foliage and open the surface to sunlight. This also explains why California's brightest fall colors are seen along its riparian woodlands.

Generally, the presence of water encourages the establishment of plant and animal species typical of wetter communities, and the differences are more dramatic in southern California. In contrast to much of the state, summers are more productive in riparian zones because water remains available; winters are least productive where broadleaf deciduous trees common to riparian communities become dormant. Though humans have greatly reduced riparian communities to less than 1 percent of the state, these areas attract constant attention as they contain some of California's richest assemblages of flora and fauna and its most precious commodity—water.

Today's remaining riparian communities continue to slice and meander through every California plant community. They range from moist, dense redwood forests growing in fresh wet sediments in northwestern California to ribbons of noticeably thicker and taller shrubs lining the washes of southeastern California deserts.

Plants. Many different species of willow (*Salix* spp.) grow with their characteristic elongate leaves in riparian communities from the coast to the highest mountains back down into the hottest deserts. Depending on the species and habitat, they may grow as prostrate shrubs to dense thickets of large shrubs to tall trees up to 10 m (more than 30 feet).

The four species of alder in California may be important nitrogen fixers in nutrient-poor soils. The more common White Alder (*Alnus rhombifolia*) gives way to a shrublike Mountain Alder (*Alnus tenuifolia*) at higher elevations. Big-leaf Maple (*Acer macrophyllum*) is a valuable hardwood, while the yellow wood of Oregon Ash (*Fraxinus latifolia*) is used for furniture; both also grow in canyons up into higher elevations. Box Elder (*Acer negundo*), California Bay or Laurel (*Umbellularia californica*), several species of oak (*Quercus* spp.), and other trees may all enjoy wetter habitats found in riparian woodlands.

Western or California Sycamore (*Platanus racemosa*), like maple, has huge palmate leaves. It is restricted to riparian habitats and canyons of central and southern California. This is another relic species that was far more widespread until the warmer, drier climates after the Ice Ages stranded and isolated it in these moist spots. It can look somewhat out of place as it turns color and then looses its leaves just in time for the mild rainy seasons in lower elevation southern California canyons.

Poplars require moisture and their different species are also separated by elevation. They include the Fremont Cottonwood (*Populus fremontii*) and the Black Cottonwood (*Populus trichocarpa*), which grows into higher elevations and up to 50 m (more than 160 feet) tall with its silver-bottomed leaves. Cottonwood gets its name from the cotton-like white hairs of the female flowers that drift in the wind. Quaking Aspen (*Populus tremuloides*) may dominate higher elevation riparian communities into eastern and northeastern California and in isolated stands as far south as the San Bernardino Mountains. It is difficult to miss the white bark behind light green leaves which wave and tremble in even the slightest breeze. After dropping their leaves, aspen will survive the coldest winter temperatures California can muster; they put on some spectacular fall colors in canyons north of Bishop and in higher terrain of the Warner Mountains.

Shrubs also often include willows. Mule Fat (*Bacharis glutinosa*) somewhat resembles willow. Like willow, sedges, and some other species that grow near flowing water, mule fat easily bends during and adjusts following major floods and submersions. A variety of other shrubs found in this ecotone between dry land and water include dogwoods (*Cornus* spp.), oaks (*Quercus* spp.), gooseberries and currants (*Ribes* spp.), other wild berries, and wild grapes. Herbaceous plants are more common in recently disturbed sites; rushes, sedges, cattails, and many different wildflowers are on this long list of riparian species often growing in areas where recent floods have reworked and deposited new sediment.

Animals. When larger animals and birds become thirsty and hungry, they often venture into riparian communities from other habitats, knowing where to go for water and more abundant food. Numerous bird species migrating many hundreds of kilometers (miles) stop to rest or winter along California's water courses. They join the great diversity and biomass of animals who spend their entire lives in the shelter of these productive ecotones between dry land and water.

Many aquatic insects live their entire lives in or near water. Others, such as mosquitos, damselflies, and dragonflies, may fly away as adults. When temperatures warm, the riparian scene is busy with flying moths, butterflies, wasps and bees, and crawling with ants and other insects, caterpillars, and worms. Because there is no shortage of nectar and fresh green shoots to choose from on the plants or in the soil during spring and summer, there is no shortage of primary consumers, including vegetarian birds.

The crawling and flying bugs become food for spiders, birds, bats at night, and other predators. Even fish dine on them when they venture too close to water. Flycatchers, warblers, wrens, and flickers are among the enormous list of birds frequenting riparian communities. Salamanders, reptiles, and rodents, such as mice and woodrats, become dinner for kites and hawks by day and long-eared and great horned owls at night. Several native and introduced frog species also represent tempting morsels to larger animals.

Raccoon commonly settle in riparian woodlands, where they feast on most of the edible aquatic and land animals and plants. California's native aquatic turtle, the Western Pond Turtle (*Clemmys marmorata*) lives in and around fresh water in valleys and mountains of cismontane California and locally along the Mojave River. Because their activity levels range somewhere between lethargic and comatose, their diets are restricted to juicy plants and occasional insects or dead animals that cannot escape. If it could not withdraw into its hard shell, this species would be easy prey for California predators looking for a scrumptious dinner. This is a very different species from the Desert Tortoise (*Xerobates* or *Gopherus agassizii*) of transmontane California and the many turtles introduced into the state.

Although beaver (*Castor canadensis*) were hunted for their pelts to near extinction by the 1900s, they may be found today mostly in northern California valley and mountain water courses, where they gather and feed on native vegetation. In the mountains, they will chew and fell trees such as aspen and willow to make dams. Ironically, in lowland waterways, where they are called bank beaver, they are a nuisance when they excavate and burrow into river and stream banks designed to hold back water.

Coyotes, foxes, skunks, rabbits, and other larger mammals frequently visit riparian habitats. When it comes to animals, California's riparian communities are like bustling cities filled with busy consumers, especially during spring and summer months. Some animals take up residence in the city; others commute in from adjacent communities to do their business. If spring and summer in the riparian resemble a weekday lunch hour in one of California's downtown financial districts, could the winter lull resemble a weekend night in that same financial district? It is ironic that California's thriving cities and the agricultural land required to support their human populations have especially expanded, encroached upon, and destroyed more than 90 percent of nature's great riparian cities that once supported abundant California wildlife.

◆ TRANSMONTANE DESERTS

Here, we survey some of the most interesting and important features in the distribution of plants and animals living on the other side of California's great physical barriers. Plant communities in the rainshadow deserts of California must be adapted to at least two climate extremes. First, temperatures are not moderated by marine air. Diurnal and seasonal temperature changes are extreme, so plants must adapt to extremely intense solar radiation and hot temperatures on summer days followed by extremely cold winter nights. The difference between recorded high and low temperatures in one year at one desert location could be more than 56°C (100°F)!

Second, winter's Pacific storms drop most of their water on the windward sides of the mountains, and as the drier air masses finally flow down the opposite rainshadow slopes, they are warmed and dried. Consequently, most California deserts have no trouble living up to this oversimplified definition: true deserts receive less than 25 cm (10 inches) of rain annually, while evapotranspiration rates greatly exceed precipitation. Death Valley receives an average of less than 5 cm (2 inches) of rain per year while potential evapotranspiration rates can be more than 380 cm (150 inches). Similar conditions are common in other lower deserts of southeastern California, where more than one year may elapse without recorded precipitation.

Even in the cooler, wetter semi-desert conditions at higher elevations, dry continental air masses rule and continentality controls climates.

Poor soils (some with high salt content), fierce, desiccating winds, limited shelter, and dangerous exposure above ground—the list of harsh conditions goes on. Plants and animals must adapt or die. Somehow, many species not only survive, but often thrive in these adverse environments. However, unlike our review of many cismontane California plant communities, this section is not about great size, diversity, or biomass. It is about how hardy species have adapted to the harshest of conditions in California's spacious desert communities.

Our review of California's biogeography has already skipped or spread into transmontane California on at least four occasions. You may recall the semidesert chaparral communities that spill over to the inland sides of the Peninsular Ranges and Transverse Ranges into the edges of the Colorado and Mojave deserts. These chaparral communities include manzanita, chamise, ceanothus, sugarbush, mountain mahogany, various scrub oak, bush poppy, yerba santa, and many other familiar plants.

Some of these and other more desert-like communities also creep along the edges of the southern Sierra Nevada and west into cismontane California's western Transverse Ranges and southeastern Coast Ranges. It is interesting that this geologic pivot point (where the Garlock and San Andreas Faults, three mountain ranges, and five physiographic regions meet) is also an ecological pivot point. The result is a fascinating mix of desert, semi-desert, and cismontane plant communities with their plant and animal species. It is another example of the many connections between California's diverse geologic features and climates and the plants and animals adapted to these diverse settings.

We also surveyed the high pine forests of the Warner Range in northeastern California and the higher subalpine forests with the oldest trees in the Basin and Range east of the Sierra Nevada. Finally, we peaked at the surprising stands of White Fir (*Abies concolor* ssp. *concolor*) isolated on high north slopes of the Mojave's Clark, Kingston, and New York Mountains. These trees form an open forest with pinon pine and other species from above 1,900 m (6,200 feet) to nearly 2,350 m (7,700 feet). The total of nearly 1,200 white fir grow up to 20 m (65 feet) tall and some are more than four-hundred years old. At these lofty elevations, temperatures are cooler and winter snows and summer thundershowers are more frequent than in the hot desert communities below.

In this section, we remain mostly east of California's great physical barriers. We will gradually drop below previously mentioned and rare transmontane forests toward the warmer, drier lower elevations. Plant communities will change from desert woodlands to desert scrub as we travel from the north and/or higher elevations toward the south and/or lower elevations. Remember that moving north in California deserts usually means higher elevations and colder, wetter conditions, except for the few hot and dry deep valleys which finger north (such as Death Valley). Moving toward the southern deserts usually means lower elevations and warmer, drier conditions, with exceptions such as those isolated, high mountain forests poking up out of the Mojave.

Piñon Pine and Juniper Woodland Communities

Though less than 3 percent of California is covered with piñon and juniper woodlands, they are distributed throughout transmontane California above 1,200 m (4,000 feet) and below 2,400 m (8,000 feet). This places them below the wetter coniferous forests and above the warmer, drier desert scrub. These dwarf forests are found from the eastern Cascades and Modoc Plateau (where juniper usually dominate) south into the eastern Sierra Nevada (where piñon dominate) and into the Basin and Range, where they grow below the subalpine forests. Moving south, they are common on the eastern slopes of the Transverse and Peninsular Ranges and on those higher elevation desert slopes. They also creep west into drier portions of cismontane California's Transverse Ranges and southern Coastal Ranges, previously mentioned as an important natural pivot point, where they intermingle with species more common to cismontane plant communities.

Habitat and Structure

The trees in these dwarf forests are often mixed. They range from widely scattered stands of especially juniper less than 3 m (10 feet) tall in lower, drier locations with poor soils to denser forests of mainly piñon pine up to 15 m (about 50 feet) at higher elevations with quality soils. The latter phase of these communities is clearly a cooler, wetter semi-desert, where annual precipitation could be as high as 50 cm (20 inches) and winter snow is common. In these cooler, wetter environments, the juniper and mostly piñon woodlands have dense understories and may mix with species common in coniferous forests. In drier sites, the understory predictably consists of more widely scattered, smaller shrubs and mostly annual herbs common to California's true deserts. Regardless, it is often possible to observe from one location the forest-covered slopes above and desert scrub below; all of this standing within the usually dry, clean air of the transitional piñon and juniper woodland communities. Most of these California plant communities are related to similar communities throughout the Great Basin and Colorado Plateau to the east.

Plants. Junipers (*Juniperus* spp.) are small evergreen trees of the cypress family. They have scale-like leaves which resemble flat needles, small juicy cones commonly known as juniper berries, and aromatic, sometimes twisted and contorted wood. Different species may grow into stately trees or *krummholz* forms in some of California's highest forests; others grow as shrubs on the fringe of California's true hot deserts. Though species of widely spaced juniper are common in northeastern California and even in subalpine zones of the Sierra Nevada, they are usually associated with drier sites than piñon pine. Here, we focus on the more important transmontane species.

North of Bridgeport and often in the open, rolling countryside of northeastern California well into Oregon and Nevada, is Western Juniper (*Juniperus occidentalis* var. *occidentalis*). Its close relative, Mountain or Sierra Juniper (*Juniperus occidentalis* var. *australis*) is found on high mountain slopes especially in the Sierra Nevada. It is also found in parts of the Transverse and Coast Ranges around that previously identified pivot point. California Juniper (*Juniperus californica*) grows from the southern Sierra Nevada into southern California, and Utah Juniper (*Juniperus osteosperma*) is found in the Great Basin, Mojave, and Transverse Ranges.

The One-Needle or Single-Needle Piñon Pine (*Pinus monophylla*) is the most common piñon pine in California, growing from the eastern Sierra Nevada and Basin and Range into that pivot point again and then south into Baja. Four-Needle Piñon (*Pinus quadrifolia*) grows from the Santa Rosa Mountains of the Peninsular Ranges into Baja California, while Two-Needle Piñon (*Pinus edulis*) is found only from the higher mountains of the eastern Mojave, east into the southern Rockies. Hybrid trees with one to five needles may be found where the single-needle piñon grow with other species.

Great Basin piñon and juniper woodlands often grow with high desert shrubs such as Great Basin Sagebrush (*Artemisia tridentata*), rabbitbrush (*Chrysothamnus* spp.), and Bitterbrush (*Purshia tridentata*).

In the Transverse and Peninsular Ranges, semi-desert chaparral plants such as Desert Scrub Oak (*Quercus turbinella*) and yucca (*Yucca* spp.) are common. Moving into drier southern deserts, Joshua Tree (*Yucca brevifolia*) and even hotter desert shrubs such as Creosote Bush (*Larrea tridentata*) begin to appear in the scrubbier, sparse growth of piñon and juniper boundaries.

Animals. Animals may find fresh vegetation to browse and juniper berries, acorns, and other food in the piñon and juniper woodlands. Piñon nuts (sometimes called piñones) have been especially important for the wildlife and California Indians and are now considered a delicacy in some modern recipes. Several species of birds include hairy woodpeckers, chickadees, warblers, and nuthatches. Like Clark's nutcracker, the pinyon jay has been known to transport and bury seeds in caches more than 13 km (20 miles) from the producing trees. Unlike most jays, the pinyon jay has no crest and is duller gray and less blue. These noisy birds move in flocks between trees and are particularly important in spreading and planting piñon pine nuts that could grow to become the next seedlings in these woodlands.

Numerous rodents may live in and around these woodlands, including a typically large-eared, white-footed deer mouse called the pinyon mouse. Other mice, great basin kangaroo rats, wood rats, pocket gophers, chipmunks, and ground squirrels compete for available food. Usually nocturnal porcupines often hide in trees during the day. These spiny creatures are rarely seen, except as road kills especially in northeast California. They gnaw on young bark by winter and eat fresh buds, leaves, and herbs during summer. Gray foxes, coyotes, bobcats, and mountain lions are occasional predators in these communities, while mule deer and pronghorn antelope browse on the scrub understory. California Bighorn Sheep (*Ovis canadensis californiana*) often move down from higher Sierra Nevada terrain to escape winter cold and snow. Desert Bighorn Sheep (*Ovis canadensis nelsoni*) migrate to higher elevations to escape the desert's summer heat.

Joshua Tree Woodlands

Though a very small portion of California is covered with Joshua tree woodlands, they form some of the state's more distinct and celebrated plant communities. It is said that stands of Joshua trees (*Yucca brevifolia*) sometimes outline the boundaries of the Mojave Desert. They are scattered from the southern Owens Valley throughout the Mojave Desert and into southern Nevada and northwestern Arizona at elevations above 600 m (2,000 feet) to about 1,600 m (just above 5,000 feet). These com-

Joshua trees are often found in the Mojave below piñon/juniper woodlands and above desert scrub, though they mingle in marginal areas. Here, desert scrub creates an understory through which a coyote navigates.

munities are especially common north of the Transverse Ranges, around the Antelope Valley, and in eastern Mojave's ranges. In these cooler and wetter higher elevations of the Mojave, winter frost and some snow are common. Joshua trees do not grow in the hot, dry habitats of lower deserts to the south; they are a certain indicator of high desert in the Mojave.

Habitat and Structure

Like piñon and juniper woodlands, species from many other communities grow with them. At higher elevations, they may creep into piñon and juniper woodlands. Depending on geographic location, understory species from scrub communities such as sagebrush, blackbush, saltbush, or creosote bush scrub are common. Considering elevation and geographic location, discussion of Joshua tree woodlands should follow sagebrush scrub and perhaps blackbush scrub communities as we work our way down to lower elevations. However, because these towering, ghostly figures form open woodlands unique to the high deserts of the southwest United States, they are addressed here.

During spring, especially following a good rainy season, grasses, herbs, and sometimes spectacular displays of wildflowers explode in new growth among the brush. Within weeks, these plants die back and go to seed, dried and brittled by the summer sun. Local, infrequent, and unreliable summer thunderstorms may deliver short-lived downpours. However, unlike the gradual soaking common during winter's cold rains and snowmelt, much of the water from summer's brief storms may run off or eventually evaporate in the heat. Therefore, new growth and flowering usually peaks just when temperatures are warming in the spring.

Plants. This species of yucca got its common name, Joshua, from the Mormons, who associated its up-

lifted arms and old age with the biblical military leader. This member of the agave family is sometimes called tree lily and should not be confused with the smaller, scrubbier Mojave Yucca (*Yucca schidigera*). It also has smaller leaves than most other yuccas. The trunk, limbs and size of *Yucca brevifolia* easily qualify it as a tree.

Younger trees grow for years as single poles up to 3 m (10 feet) before they bloom or feeding insect larvae cause them to branch out. Fresh new leaves are added to the branches as the tree grows at the expense of the lower old leaves, which wither and eventually fall to the ground. The long, thin, spear-like leaves added to the length of each branch are a reminder that this is a desert tree. The largest trees grow more than 10 m (32 feet) tall and wide, making them the largest flowering plants of the Mojave. Their large, white, lily-like blossoms are more numerous when favorable spring temperatures follow soaking seasonal rains.

Numerous species of shrubs and herbs common below the Joshua trees are usually members of desert scrub communities covered in the next section.

Animals. Joshua trees are recognized for supporting a variety of small animals, some of which are totally dependent on the tree for survival. A classic example is the mutualistic symbiosis which benefits yucca moths (*Tegeticula* spp.) and Joshua trees. At dusk, the yucca moth is attracted to the Joshua tree's white blossoms. It flies from tree to tree, gathering the sticky pollen until it lays its eggs in the flower and pollinates its targeted plants. As the larvae grow and mature, they feed off some of the developing fruit. These two species must occur together.

Meanwhile, larvae of the giant yucca skipper and yucca weevil eat from fresh growth, and termite colonies recycle nutrients as they feed off of and find shelter in the dried and downed wood at the base of these trees. Beetles and other insects are also common among the Joshua trees.

The desert or yucca night lizard is just one animal which feeds off these insects under the shelter of downed wood, while wood rats (also known as pack rats) pile their nests at the base of Joshua trees. Various snakes, including the night snake, slither among the debris sensing out many of these smaller animals for a meal.

Woodpeckers also eat termites, but you will find many other birds here, including up to twenty-five species known to nest in Joshua trees. These include northern flickers, flycatchers, house wrens, and American kestrels. The colorful black and yellow Scott's oriole makes its nest from yucca fibers and feeds off the tree and its insects. On the hunt are red-tailed hawks by day and screech owls by night. Housing so many diverse, interconnected, and interdependent neighbors, the Joshua tree may display a unique microecosytem, if not its own microgeography.

◆ DESERT SCRUB COMMUNITIES

Various communities with vast, open expanses of desert scrub cover nearly 30 percent of California. Lack of water is the most important limiting factor. However, severe summer heat in the lower deserts, bitter winter cold in higher northern desert shrublands, and many other factors combine to create some of California's harshest environments. Climates are too harsh and dry and soils too poor to support even dwarf trees. These mostly transmontane communities are found in patches in northeast California, become more widespread in basins east of the Sierra Nevada, and then completely dominate the landscapes of California's southeast deserts.

These most challenging environments might be considered antithetic to California's north coast forest communities, where abundant water and mild temperatures rule for most of the year, producing relatively impressive accumulations of biomass and greater species diversity. Some desert scrub communities are also found in the southwestern San Joaquin Valley, behind the rainshadow of the Coastal Ranges.

Habitats, Plants, and Structures of Desert Scrub Communities

Sagebrush Scrub

Sagebrush scrub communities (sometimes known as Great Basin sagebrush scrub) are widespread at highest desert elevations, especially in California's northeastern

deserts. Various rather evenly distributed sagebrushes cast their dull gray-green shades across the landscapes into several other Great Basin states. In California, these communities are common on well-drained soil from above 1,300 m (more than 4,000 feet) to about 2,300 m (7,500 feet) but they locally extend much higher into the subalpine of eastern ranges.

Sagebrush survive in many different habitats, from the understory of transmontane woodlands and forests to exposed range without a tree in sight. More common in northeastern California and the Modoc Plateau and east of the Sierra Nevada crest, they become more scattered toward the south and then isolated into the Peninsular Ranges. They even extend into the Transverse Ranges around that previously identified pivot point.

Most common and widespread from Canada to Mexico and east past the Rocky Mountains is Great Basin Sage (*Artemisia tridentata*). Its long light gray leaves end with three teeth, and it may grow more than 4 m (13 feet) high, though it is usually a smaller shrub. Other sagebrush include the darker Dwarf Sagebrush (*Artemisia nova*), Black Sagebrush (*Artemisia arbuscula*), which is another dwarf species adapted to poor soils, and Silver or Hoary Sagebrush (*Artemisia cana*) in dry meadows.

Bitterbrush or Antelope Brush (*Purshia glandulosa* or *tridentata*) look like darker green great basin sage, but are often heavily overgrazed. Various saltbush (*Atriplex* spp.) become common in more alkaline soils in these communities. Also common and well-known in these communities are Rabbitbush (*Chrysothamnus* spp.), Hopsage (*Grayia spinosa*), and Mormon Tea (*Ephedra viridis*). Rabbitbush is also known as Mojave rubberbrush because small amounts of rubber can be extracted from it. It is a standout when its bright yellow autumn flowers protrude above this community. Meanwhile, stems of the leafless Mormon tea can be boiled to make a bitter drink with a stimulant.

Various bunchgrasses include Bluebunch Wheatgrass (*Agropyron spicatum*), and annual grasses are dominated by the introduced Cheat Grass (*Bromus tectorum*). Overgrazing has restricted distribution of many species, but greatly increased the abundance of less tasty sagebrush and rabbitbush, two plants that often dominate the scenery in these communities. Fire is also changing this community.

Blackbush Scrub

Blackbush (*Coleogyne ramosissima*) dominates these communities which are common at elevations just below sagebrush scrub, but above the lower desert communities such as creosote scrub (especially from about 1,200–1,800 m [3,900–5,900 feet]). Although their leaves are grayish green, these low shrubs look black from a distance, and they sometimes resemble antelope bush. Often found between high and low desert, they mix with many other communities and species, including Joshua trees. Such plants as yucca, Turpentine Broom (*Thamnosma montana*), Burrobush or Cheesebush (*Hymenoclea salsola*), Horsebrush (*Tetradymia* spp.), and Winterfat (*Ceratoides lanata*) are common. A conspicuous and interesting plant is the Paper Bag or Bladder Sage (*Salazaria mexicana*). Like Mormon tea, its skinny green stems are usually leafless, but it grows its seeds in thin, inflated, paper-like pods which easily float in wind or water.

Shadscale Scrub

These communities are also often found between the upper sagebrush scrub and lower creosote bush scrub communities. You may find them in more alkaline soils throughout the Great Basin and on higher, steep mountain slopes with rocky soils in the southern deserts. They are scattered in and north of the Owens Valley and on rocky slopes of the Basin and Range and Mojave. These communities are sometimes lumped with and considered a part of saltbush scrub communities. This is because the Winter Fat (*Ceratoides lanata*) member of the saltbush family occurs with the dominant Shadscale (*Atriplex confertifolia*). Joining them is a species common in saltbush communities, but not itself in the saltbush family—Bud Sage (*Artemisia spinescens*). Most of these species grow as small, compact plants less than 50 cm (20 inches) tall with light-colored leaves.

Saltbush Scrub

Though saltbush scrub communities are common in higher salinity soils of lower desert plains and basins, they are also established on rocky soils of higher desert slopes. Because they are found in various adverse conditions growing in poor substrates, they may occur above or below creosote scrub and other communities. We will look at them now and venture into the creosote and cactus scrub after we finish our descent into alkaline basins. Joining the previously noted shadscale shrubs and low-growing shrubs from other desert communities are other members of *Chenopodiaceae*, the saltbush family, including Allscale (*Atriplex polycarpa*) and Greasewood (*Sarcobatus vermiculatus*). Desert Holly (*Atriplex hymenelytra*) grows whitish leaves with pronounced edges resembling holly. These attractive compact bushes stand out against darker backgrounds as if planted in desert gardens. The list of *Atriplex* species which represent various saltbush is extensive. Saltbush scrub also shares a number of annual and perennial grasses and herbs with other plant communities.

Tumbleweed (*Salsola iberica*) is an introduced weed from Asia also called Russian thistle. It thrives in areas overgrazed and near disturbed and irrigated farmland. These roundish, thorny plants become dried and detached, rolling with the wind and spreading their seeds as they go. By the 1900s, they were widespread throughout the west and had become common nuisances in saltbush scrub and many other California plant communities. Annoyed California residents have used many colorful names (such as "Volkswagen Eaters") to describe these uninvited guests who roll into yards or across roads at the most inconvenient times and places.

Alkali Sink

By the end of the last Ice Age, about 10,000 years ago, California's great inland lakes were evaporating, leaving high concentrations of salt in the remaining trapped ponds and in the basin soils. Since then, floods have carried more minerals into inland drainage basins while still more water has evaporated from capillary action below the surface. Concentrations of salts are left behind and only halophytes—salt-tolerant plants—can survive.

Moving down the better-drained desert slopes toward the alkali sink, the vegetation gradually changes from saltbush scrub to the most salt-tolerant halophytes. These communities are spotty in lower basins of the Basin and Range through the Mojave and into the Colorado Desert. They are closely related to, and share species with, their coastal marsh counterparts. Although these desert habitats experience much greater variations in temperature, it is interesting that we have travelled so far across California's plant communities only to find such similar plants and habitats.

More saltbush with light-colored and scaly leaves include Allscale or Cattle Spinach (*Atriplex polycarpa*) and Wingscale (*Atriplex canescens*). As salt content rises to near 1 percent, Seepweed, Inkweed, or Desert Blite, and Sea Blite (*Suaeda* spp.) splash dark gray shades just above the salt pans and once provided much of the black ink for Native American art work. In saltiest conditions approaching 2 percent, Pickleweeds (*Salicornia subterminalis*) appear with their leafless, sectioned, jointed stems. These succulents store water and drop excess salt with their dead stems. Iodine Bush (*Allenrolfea occidentalis*) resembles pickleweed and is another common halophyte in these salty brews.

In wetter locations grow various rushes, reeds, and cattails. Where water is near the surface, phreatophytes such as Honey Mesquite (*Prosopis glandulosa*) can grow tap roots down nearly 10 m (33 feet) deep. These winter-deciduous legumes grow small leaflets during spring and long bean pods. They once represented an important staple food for California Indians and are still vital to local wildlife.

Scraggly but bushy Salt Cedar (*Tamarix* spp.) were introduced from Eurasia and have aggressively taken over near many water sources. They also have extensive roots which can tap and deplete underground water sources as their leaves transpire tremendous amounts of water. These species may also be found in or near sand dunes where groundwater may be tapped. By the late 1900s, efforts were launched to eradicate these water bandits where they were threatening local aquifers.

Creosote Bush and Cactus Scrub

The Oldest Plants Are Also Common   We now skip back above the salty basins but below the higher desert woodlands and sagebrush scrub, mostly on well-drained soils. Here, the most common shrub throughout the Mojave and Colorado Deserts grows. Because Creosote Bush (*Larrea tridentata*) survives in many different desert microenvironments, it is widespread and it may be the single plant most people associate with California's desert landscapes. It does not tolerate the extreme cold and prolonged frost of the higher desert terrain but, because it does tolerate extreme heat and prolonged drought, it is often dominant in middle- and lower-elevation deserts. This leaves it a wide range throughout transmontane southeastern California.

It also means that it may creep into and mix with other desert communities; myriad other species, including many cacti, may be associated with it throughout these various microenvironments. Creosote bush is common in areas of the Sonoran Desert, where precipitation peaks during the summer monsoon season. It also thrives into California's Mojave, where summer thundershowers are infrequent and unreliable, and peak precipitation occurs during the cool winter season.

The creosote bush grows small, dark green leaves with thick waxy coatings that provide the pungent aromas during rainfall. The plant drops many of its leaves during drought, but after about 2.5 cm (1 inch) of rain, it grows fresh leaves and numerous yellow blossoms to attract pollinators. Its roots expand out away from the plant, robbing soil moisture from new growth which cannot compete.

The results are almost equally spaced bushes resembling a well-planned park environment. It has been discovered that rings of "clone" plants sprout from these extensive root systems. When botanists consider all the cloned shrubs growing out from an original plant's root system to be the same plant, they are the oldest plants in the world. One "King Clone" in Johnson Valley was found to be more than 11,000 years old and another near Yuma is even older.

Numerous other shrub species are associated with creosote bush scrub in the Mojave Desert, including plants more common in adjacent communities. Common and scientific names often reveal characteristics of these shrubs. White Bursage (*Ambrosia dumosa*) is a short gray bush with small leaves that often grows with creosote. The peculiar inflated stems of little Bladderstem or Desert Trumpet (*Eriogonum inflatum*) often line disturbed sites such as roads like so many holiday decorations. Burrobush (*Hymenoclea salsola*) and various saltbush (*Atriplex* spp.) are other members of the long list of shrub species.

Moving into the Cactus Scrub   Other species are more common in the Colorado Desert and often associated with cactus scrub. Desert Agave or Century Plant (*Agave deserti*) grows thick leaves from its base. After about twenty to twenty-five years, it sends up a stalk which grows up to 30 cm (12 inches) per day to blossom with large yellow flowers that attract bats. Jojoba (*Simmondsia chinensis*) grow from California's lower Colorado Desert well into the Sonoran Desert of Arizona and Mexico. It has flat, waxy leaves. Female plants produce fruits with the high quality oil harvested in today's jojoba plantations scattered from southeastern California and beyond.

Brittlebush or Incienso (*Encelia farinosa*) drops its leaves and becomes brittle during drought. It grows fresh leaves and is covered with brilliant yellow sunflowers

Blooming creosote decorates these lava flows in the Mojave. Golden ground cover remains from an extraordinarily wet winter.

after heavy rains. Other *Encelia* species are common. The tall, dead-looking, thorny sticks that radiate out from the base of the Ocotillo (*Fouquieria splendens*) and point up to 5 m (16 feet) high are also **drought-deciduous**. After about 2.5 cm (1 inch) of rain, these stems erupt with small green leaves on the side and brilliant red tubular flowers at their ends to attract hummingbirds. Each ocotillo can repeat this cycle up to seven times/year.

The cactus family (*Cactaceae*) is represented so well in these California communities that many biologists place them in a separate community. They are well adapted to compete in the hot, dry conditions of the lower desert but are not tolerant of prolonged frost or severe cold. By growing shallow, widespread roots, they can gather water quickly during rare downpours. They survive by storing water, reducing leaf surfaces, and growing spines and thorns for protection from desiccating winds and intense sun. Their spines and the acidic nature of their stored moisture also protect them from hungry and thirsty animals. They are most common on rocky or other well-drained surfaces of California's lower Colorado Desert.

Barrel Cactus (*Ferocactus acanthodes*) is the largest, most robust of the common California cacti. It thrives in open, rocky locations. Various species of cholla (*Opuntia* spp.) are densely covered with spines and have common names which help describe them, such as Staghorn (*Opuntia echinocarpa*) and Teddybear Cholla (*O. bigelovii*).

Teddybear are sometimes called jumping cholla. When spiny sections break off, they might get caught in an animal's fur or in your clothes or skin. The painful barbs are difficult to pull out, but the attached cactus sections may grow to new plants after they have been transported and dropped—an effective method of dispersal. They don't really jump, but they can be annoying to careless travellers. Some of the most impressive and accessible stands of these cacti are at Cholla Gardens in southern Joshua Tree National Park, where some plants grow taller than the humans on the nature trail.

Beavertail Cactus (*Opuntia basilaris*) really grow big pads resembling beavers' tails. Different species of prickly pear cactus follow their showy flowers with scrumptious red fruits which serve as feasts for wildlife. The famous Saguaro Cactus (*Carnegia gigantea*), with its massive arms twisting majestically skyward, is found naturally only in a few spots in California just this side of the Colorado River. You will find them especially east of 114 degrees longitude in eastern San Bernardino County's Whipple Mountains. They become common on well-drained slopes in southern Arizona and northern Mexico, where annual precipitation peaks during summer. The exalted saguaro, often a symbol of the desert southwest, has been introduced into landscapes of the Coachella Valley and into films and pictures of southern California landscapes where it usually does not belong.

After it rains, most plants in these communities must display showy flowers to compete with other species for attention from pollinators. The list of ephemerals which contribute to colorful spring displays is far too long for this review. Lupine, brome, gilia, pincushion flower, desert star, fiddleneck, popcorn flower, and many other colorful names still fail to do these species justice after a wet winter. The few annuals that flower after late summer thundershowers become more numerous toward the southeast, across the Colorado River and the Mexican border.

Animals. Desert animals are presented with a series of difficult challenges including extremes in temperatures, lack of reliable water sources, and limited food production during drought. Unusual adaptations allow a surprising variety of animals to survive and even thrive in these conditions. Many desert an-

These cholla gardens grow at lower elevations within Joshua Tree National Park. "Jumping cholla" don't really jump, but it won't matter if you carelessly step into them.

imals get their moisture from eating plants or other animals and excrete very concentrated waste, saving moisture. Larger animals and birds can move to water sources, while others must escape the heat and drought by burrowing or seeking other shelter. Ectothermic animals have an advantage in the desert because they gain much of their heat from the environment, rather than by metabolism, which uses more energy. Many animals will pant to cool off after overheating. Here is a partial summary of the busy animal world in a typical California desert scrub environment.

Ants, bees, beetles, butterflies, and moths are some of the pollinating insects which become more common when their targeted flowers are in bloom, especially during spring. Tent caterpillars live in colonies behind their webs, often feeding on desert plants in the rose family. Beetles and millipedes feed off decaying organic debris at the base of many shrubs. Black stink beetles will often point their abdomens upward and emit a foul liquid when threatened. Crickets, katydids, and many kinds of spiders are also common. Scorpions wait for their prey (usually other arthropods and often other scorpions) at night, then sting and crush it. Tarantulas attack and eat prey that venture into their webbed burrows. The large, black tarantula hawk is a wasp which seeks out and paralyzes the tarantula so that its larvae may feed from the spider.

Reptiles usually eat insects and other animals, with exceptions such as California's largest lizard, the chuckwalla, which is a vegetarian. This usually dull gray or black lizard is already plump but wrinkled and it can store water under its skin. When threatened, it may lodge itself into rock cracks and inflate so that it cannot be pulled out. Numerous other lizard species are active in the desert scrub.

All snakes are carnivores. Rattlesnakes are pit vipers that sense out their prey, stun them with powerful venom, and then follow them until they drop. They can swallow mammals larger than their heads. The Mojave rattlesnake has some of the most potent venom. Though California rattlesnake bites cause painful swelling and illness, they very rarely are deadly to the careless humans who have forced snakes to defend themselves. The best advice to relieve symptoms is to get the victim to the nearest hospital.

The lethargic desert tortoise can store up to one liter (quart) of water. It is now a threatened species partially due to those who have taken them for pets, run them over and used them for target practice. However, the large aggressive raven populations that have exploded in recent decades are primarily responsible for the more than 90 percent decrease in desert tortoise populations, which occurred within fifty years ending in the late 1900s.

Various toads become active after desert rains. Couch's spadefoot toad comes out of its burrow, mates, and lays its eggs in temporary ponds. Within a month, the larvae grow into tadpoles, grow legs, then leave the water just in time to burrow—as toads—to escape the drought with their stored water. They will emerge when the thunder and rain return.

Desert wood rats gather debris, including sections of cholla, to make their nests. They rely on such plants as prickly-pear cactus for their moisture. Kangaroo rats scrape and discard the salt off saltbush leaves, which have high water content, before eating them. They can live their entire lives without drinking water; with very concentrated waste, they are one of the best water conservers in the desert. Protected in their burrows by day from the desert heat, they even eat their waste to gain the moisture back. Like kangaroo rats, pocket mice and ground squirrels often feed off seeds from shrubs and make their burrows under protective canopies of those same plants. Grasshopper mice are deadly, aggressive predators. They eat insects and attack scorpions by first biting off their stingers. They even attack and eat other rodents. Bats use their sonar to feed at night when temperatures are lower.

Jackrabbits are the hares with giant ears that allow rapid heat loss. Cottontail rabbits have shorter ears; they live in burrows and become active at night in summer to escape the heat. Coyote occasionally feed on them after running them down, as they dart from bush to bush.

Desert Scrub Birds. Several birds, such as cactus wren, have learned to make nests in spiny chollas or other cactus for protection. Hummingbirds are important pollinators of specific tubular flowers. The phainopepla is a dark bird with a large crest which often rests on the top of branches when it is not consuming seeds of the desert mistletoe. These seeds are distributed to other plants in its droppings, disbursing the mistletoe.

Many birds (including verdins, swallows, flycatchers, gnatcatchers, swifts, and wrens) feed off desert insects. Some of these are gleaners, and all of them gain moisture from their food. Common raven populations increased more than 300 percent in parts of the California deserts during the 1900s and they pose a serious threat to native species, including the desert tortoise. Roadrunners rarely fly, but these cuckoos can run and glide with their long tails up to

24 km (15 miles) per hour. They will eat berries and insects, but they may be more famous for their attacks on small mammals, lizards, and even rattlesnakes.

This is just a sample of some of the activity among the many animals living in what unknowing visitors have labelled a desert "wasteland."

◆ DESERT WASH, RIPARIAN, AND OASIS COMMUNITIES

Habitat and Structure

Limited water is most responsible for restricting biomass and species diversity in California's transmontane deserts. Therefore, it is no surprise that ribbons of larger plants and lusher growth follow dry washes. Here, water may only briefly flow, then disappear below the surface but still within reach of root systems. As expected, the growth may become dense thickets or even strips of gallery forests where surface water is found most of the year and where richer soils remain moist year-round. These conspicuous interruptions in the dry scrub represent just a tiny fraction of California's desert landscapes. They also represent vital watering holes and production zones for site-specific plant and animal species and for animals capable of commuting in from great distances from around the region.

There is great diversity in these plant communities. Where surface water flows rarely over impermeable bedrock of desert washes, there may be only subtle changes in the monotonous desert scrub, but where there is permanent surface water or thick sediment and abundant groundwater, there is an explosion of life and activity. Abundant growth is rarely established in the middle of braided channels that carry the most destructive flash floods. However, these events are often responsible for depositing rich sediment, dispersing seeds, and increasing species diversity, from the wash channel to its outer banks. The common larger shrubs and small trees are often deeply rooted and deciduous.

Desert Wash Plants. Honey Mesquite (*Prosopis glandulosa*) is one of the most common of the tall shrubs or small trees to inhabit the desert wash. Joining the Honey Mesquite is a similar member of the numerous legumes, Catclaw Acacia (*Acacia greggii*). These legumes grow long seed pods that were important food sources for Native Americans and are still vital to the survival of so much wildlife. Roots of some young plants have been known to grow up to 10 cm (4 inches) per day until reaching soil moisture. Then, the plants can safely establish surface growth, sometimes years later. Numerous sharp barbs growing on its stems also earned catclaw its other name—wait-a-minute-bush.

Other common members of the pea family include the Palo Verde (*Cercidium floridum*). It gets its "green stick" name from the chlorophyll in the bark that remains after it drops leaves during severe drought. Smoke Trees (*Psorothamnus spinosus*) rarely have leaves, but literally appear like ghostly gray puffs of smoke only along washes of California's lower, southeastern deserts. Like all the species named so far, the evergreen Ironwood (*Olneya tesota*) seeds rely on flash floods to tumble, scarify, and crack them to germinate. This further restricts them to desert washes.

There are many willows common to these communities, but Desert Willow (*Chilopsis linearis*) is often found lining washes of the Mojave, even though it is not a true willow. It does have long narrow leaves, but its pink flowers resemble snapdragons and its seed pods resemble beans.

Numerous desert wash shrubs may also be found in the open desert, but many species, such as Arrow-weed (*Pluchea sericea*) are usually restricted to these wetter sites. Arrow-weed stems were gathered by California Indians for making baskets and arrows. Chuparosa (*Justica californica*) is actually a tropical-like shrub with long, red tubular flowers. Burrobrush or Cheesebush (*Hymenoclea salsola*) produces a rancid cheesy aroma when it is crushed between the fingers. Many other shrubs, such as Broom Baccharis or Desert Broom (*Baccharis sarothroides*) grow along with these plants. This nearly leafless plant with broom-like stems may grow up to 4 m (13 feet) high in wetter habitats.

The open sediments and sands of these washes are often splattered and sometimes covered with the spectacular colors of desert wildflowers in spring. The size and density of these ephemeral herbs often depends on temperatures and especially the amount and timing of seasonal rainfall.

Plants of Desert Riparian and Oasis Communities. Diversity and biomass often increase where more reliable water sources are available at or near the surface. Different species of willow (*Salix* spp.) become common and may combine with sedges, rushes, and cattails to form thickets. Various other willow-like shrubs join arrow-weed, including the similar mulefat or Seep-willow (*Baccharis glutinosa* or *salicifolia*). Joining and similar to desert broom is a common indicator of water, Squaw Waterweed, or simply Baccharis, (*Baccharis sergilloides*). Joining honey mesquite is a similar legume growing to tall shrubs or small trees and producing twisted bean pods—Screwbean Mesquite (*Prosopis pubescens*).

Velvet or Arizona Ash (*Fraxinus velutina*) grow to small trees in riparian strips of desert mountains and into the Sierra Nevada. The larger Fremont Cottonwood (*Populus fremontii*) is a sure sign of more prominent and permanent sources of water; they even combine in strips of forests along the few more permanent water courses (such as the Mojave River) of California's deserts, where seedlings thrive in deposits of fresh, moist silt.

Introduced species, such as the previously noted Tamarisk or Salt Cedar (*Tamarix* spp.), may become problem invaders when they aggressively compete with natives for water. They were once planted as wind breaks, but one mature tamarisk can draw and transpire nearly 50 liters (14 gallons) of water per day. Their extensive roots grow rapidly. Today, aggressive thickets of tamarisk seriously deplete desert water sources throughout southeastern California. When tamarisks are removed, water returns, followed by natural vegetation.

California Fan Palm (*Washingtonia filifera*) is California's only native palm tree. It grows naturally in riparian and oasis communities from Twentynine Palms and Joshua Tree National Park south into Baja California. Some famous place names in California's deserts—including Thousand Palms, Palm Desert and the Palm Canyons of Palm Springs and Anza Borrego Desert State Park—are identified by their impressive palm oases. These relic palms were stranded and isolated along and below desert springs—with desert species previously noted—

thousands of years ago, as climates became drier. They are usually found along or downstream from faults where rocks have been crushed, ground, and weakened, allowing groundwater seeps and natural springs to erupt. Over millions of years, they have also been gradually dragged toward the northwest from Mexico on the west side of the San Andreas Fault.

Growing the largest leaves of any California desert plant, they require perennial sources of water. The seeds are distributed by birds, such as the American robin, and other animals, such as coyote. Native Americans used their fibers, ate their fruits, and also distributed their seeds. Like so many other California plants, California fan palms benefit from fires that clear the surface of competitors and allow seedlings to thrive. Along with other palms from around the world, they have been introduced especially into cismontane central and southern California, where they thrive when nurtured. The palm trees people often associate with Los Angeles, Hollywood, and the southern California coast have all been introduced into a Mediterranean region where they do not belong.

Animals of Desert Wash, Riparian and Oasis Communities. Many of the previously noted desert animals live within or frequently visit these water holes. They will not be repeated here.

Nearly half of California fan palms have tiny holes caused when giant palm-boring beetles lay their eggs. For years afterward, the larvae drill tunnels in the palm wood. Females of the southern California carpenter bee use the beetles' exit holes to raise their young.

Mule deer visit riparian and oases communities for water and fresh green meals. Coyote come for the water and the abundant smaller prey living within the protection of the dense vegetation. Desert bighorn sheep come to eat leaves and shrubs and must drink regularly.

At least eleven different pupfish and five killfish were isolated in water bodies after the end of the last Glacial Period, when transmontane California's interior drainages began to dry and disconnect. These tiny species of fish have actually adapted to different temperature, chemistry, and other conditions unique to each of the remaining ponds.

Black-chinned sparrows, Gambel's quail, gnatcatchers, and ladder-backed woodpeckers may remain in California desert oases. Other sparrows visit for the winter, and warblers and others visit in spring, while grosbeaks, hooded orioles, and flycatchers fly in during summer to feast on oasis plants and insects.

California fan palms are native to the canyons of Anza Borrego Desert State Park. They grow where water seeps out of upstream faults and flows down the canyons.

If not permanent homes, these islands of food and water serve as crossroads, rest stops, and places of congregation for numerous animals.

◆ CALIFORNIA DESERTS' ECOLOGIC ISLANDS AND SAND DUNES

Habitats and Structure

Transmontane deserts, like cismontane California, contain ecologic islands. These are sometimes islands of plenty, such as the oases communities previously outlined. Often they are islands of even greater adversity, such as the alkali sinks with their halophytes or areas of poor soils, such as those weathered from limestone and dolomite, where specialized plants such as bristlecone pine grow. The formation of stark desert pavement, lacking surface soils, was a subject of Chapter 3 on California's geology and geomorphology. Spineflower or Spiny Herb (*Chorizanthe rigida*) is a tiny, spiny buckwheat annual that turns into a prickly, dried protrusion up to a few centimeters above the hot, stony surfaces. There are few competitors in these dried infernos!

We end our journey through California's plant communities in its desert sand dunes. The formation of such great dune fields—from the Basin and Range's Eureka, Death, Panamint, and Owens Valleys, through the Mojave to the Kelso Dunes and Devil's Playground, to the Colorado Desert's Algodones Dunes—was a subject in Chapter 3. Though dune sand covers less than 5 percent of California's deserts, that is still a lot of land within such vast deserts of such a large state. Here, we examine some of the life within California's desert dunes.

It is fitting that these communities have so much—and so many plants—in common with the coastal dunes where we began our journey in this chapter. To recognize how plant communities so geographically detached can be so similar helps us to understand the connections between the many regions and diverse settings that make California such a fascinating state. Like their counterparts along the coast, many desert dune plants have fast-growing and extensive underground rhizomes which help anchor the plants and stabilize the dunes. Some are phreatophytes with deep tap roots that grow down to the water that first percolated through and was then trapped below the sand. When their roots find moisture, these normally small shrubs may grow much larger on and near the dunes. Herbaceous ephemerals may grow quickly following rare heavy rains, produce flowers, then seeds, and die back during the intense drought certain to follow.

Plants. Some of the most noticeable species also grow in other communities. They include creosote,

saltbush, indigo bush (*Psorothamnus* spp.), Mormon tea, mesquite, and desert willow in the Mojave and Palo Verde in the Colorado Desert. They are joined by perennial grasses which include endemics such as Eureka Dunegrass (*Swallenia alexandrae*), found only in Inyo County, where its expanding underground rhizomes follow shifting sands.

Most of the wildflowers are low-growing, spring-flowering, herbaceous ephemerals. These include Dune or Evening Primrose (*Oenothera* spp.), with its large white flowers, which open in evening hours to attract moths, and Sand Verbena (*Arbronia villosa*), which grows rose to purple flowers on a vine. Another vine-like plant is the Coyote Melon (*Curcurbita* spp.), which grows gourds known as Calabazilla or Buffalo Gourd. The white Desert Lily (*Hesperocallis undulata*) grows a large, deeply-buried, onion-like bulb also known as the Ajo. Desert sunflowers, marigolds, dicoria, codenia, and spanish needles are just some of the common names within the longer list of wildflowers which may appear after rare rainfall. The Algodones Dunes alone contain six plants that occur nowhere else in the world. There are at least eighty-five species endemic to all of California's deserts, making their contributions to the state's diverse and unique natural settings.

Animals. Numerous pollinating insects gather nectar from dune wildflowers. Beetle tracks and the tracks of many small mammals are common on the desert sands, sometimes with the coyote in pursuit. Most of the animals found in these communities are common in other desert habitats and have been previously noted, but there are several animal species which are particularly successful in the dunes.

Fringed-toed lizards live in wind-blown sand and are built to dive so quickly into the sand, they are said to be sand swimmers. Zebra-tailed lizards have side bands and black zebra-like bars on the bottom of their tails. Their speed has been clocked up to 29 km (18 miles) per hour as they sprint on hind legs with their tails curled behind. Various rattlesnakes are found around the dunes. They usually don't rattle unless they are threatened by a larger animal. The sidewinder is an example of a rattler perfectly adapted to the sand. It hides its body in the sand with only the head up, waiting for a potential dinner, usually an unfortunate rodent. The sidewinder can accelerate to impressive speeds with its meandering or side-winding locomotion.

A hawk may soar near the dunes in search of its next victim among the activity below, while the vulture will wait for the desert to eliminate a weaker individual. The migrant birds and other species have left

Animal tracks indicate it was a busy night on these dunes in Death Valley.

long before the days of severe heat and drought, and on those days when the sand gets blistering hot, the animals wait in shelter, mostly below the sand. At dusk, the desert again erupts in life. Birds such as poorwill and nighthawk hunt for insects well into the evening, and owls swoop down on unsuspecting prey. As the desert kit fox darts around the sand, it is certain that there will be tiny tracks leading only away from more than one little mammal's burrow. These are tracks of the latest victims of nature's grand cycle, victims that will never return to those burrows.

◆ PLANTS AND ANIMALS INTRODUCED BY HUMANS

Throughout this chapter, we have reviewed some of the **introduced species** that have invaded, competed, and thrived in California's natural and not-so-natural plant communities. As the list of intruders grows, they often place more stress on organisms already challenged. These invaders are particularly common and successful in disturbed sites, particularly where the human imprint is more pronounced.

Considerable attention has already been given to non-native invaders that have been particularly aggressive and successful in the state's grasslands. Mustards, thistles, and a mint called horehound are examples. Perhaps the most famous of all weeds is the notorious tumbleweed, another species that earned considerable attention in a previous section.

Of course, people have also purposely introduced and nurtured plants and animals that, for various reasons, they perceive as more attractive or useful than California native species. Even where invading beach and dune grasses haven't taken over our beach dunes, ice plant and other ground cover has often been purposely intro-

duced to stabilize dunes. The saguaro cactus has been transported west of the Colorado River into the Coachella Valley and beyond. California's native fan palm now decorates landscapes throughout southern and central California, far beyond the confines of its original desert oases. With a little water, other palms from around the world are thriving, but only the fan palm is native to California.

We will end this chapter by listing a few of the more common non-native species that pose problems as they squeeze out the natives in California wildlands. They range from edible figs to various European brooms, from giant reeds to pampas grass (*Cortaderia* species). Fennel, with its strong licorice smell, is another example of an aggressive non-native. Biologists estimate that up to 20 percent of the plant cover in the state's open lands consists of introduced invaders. Even California farmers are battling opportunistic weeds that cut into agricultural production and profit.

The ubiquitous eucalyptus is a good example of what can happen when a non-native species is introduced for what seems to be a good reason. When this invader from Australia failed to provide valuable wood to a growing California, it was used for wind breaks and shade. It thrived in our Mediterranean climate, but it is a ragged tree that can, without warning, drop huge limbs. In groves, eucalyptus represents a serious fire hazard. Residents of the Oakland hills learned this fire lesson the hard way.

After burros used as pack animals broke loose from early California prospectors, they quickly multiplied and populated California deserts. Burros had overgrazed and damaged thousands of square miles of California desert scrub before government agencies from the Bureau of Land Management to Death Valley National Monument (now National Park) advertised their adopt-a-burro program during the 1980s. Many of the big-eared invaders

FIRE ANTS AND KILLER BEES THREATEN

Fire ants from South America first invaded the southern United States during the late 1900s. By the late 1990s, they were established in many of the California valleys that do not experience long periods of below-freezing temperatures. From the Central Valley south, they were building mounds the size of basketballs as they crowded out established ant colonies and aggressively attacked any invaders. When disturbed, these red ants launch massive attacks that include painful stings laced with venom. They forced some families to abandon their backyards. As officials search for an efficient way to eradicate these pests, fire ants are expected to increase their range and become a greater problem in California well into the twenty-first century.

Africanized "killer" bees also arrived in southern California by the late 1990s and have colonized as far north as Los Angeles County. The similarity to the fire ant problem is striking. They first made their way north from warmer Mexican climates. Once established, they become hyper-defensive and hyper-aggressive. If disturbed or threatened, Africanized bees may launch aggressive attacks, inflicting hundreds of painful stings on their victims. Some of the attacks on humans and other animals have been fatal. They represent yet another example of how introduced species can be more than just a nuisance to Californians.

were successfully rounded up and given homes by burro lovers, allowing some desert scrub to recover for bighorn and other natives and grazers.

Wild horses have created similar problems by overpopulating and overgrazing rangelands. When non-native animals are introduced, it may be reasonable to consider any number of them as enough to overpopulate our wildlands. These are only examples of some of the dilemmas presented to those who manage our rangelands, wildlands, and wildlife each year.

The list of intruders goes on and is especially evident in or near California's waterscapes. They include crayfish consuming our California newts, habitat destruction and non-natives eating away at numerous native fish species, European green crabs munching their way along the coast, and Chinese mitten crabs burrowing in levees and clogging pipes in the Delta. Non-native frog and turtle species were considered in more detailed sections of this chapter.

One of the most notable controversies erupted after the aggressive northern pike was somehow introduced into Lake Davis in the northeastern Sierra Nevada in 1994. State wildlife officials poisoned the lake in 1997 to kill the pike before the fish could spread to threaten the state's aquatic industry. All other fish and insects in the lake—including its famous trout—were also destroyed by the poison; nearby Portola lost its water supply. The chemicals unexpectedly lingered for more than nine months, well into the summer, resulting in painful losses to local businesses.

Many of the scores of plants and animals introduced into the state by commercial agriculture are examined in Chapter 9 on primary industries. Accompanying the new plants and animals are a host of introduced pests, weeds, and diseases that threaten the state's agricultural production each year. These have also earned considerable attention in Chapter 9.

◆ HUMANS ENCROACH ON ANIMAL HABITATS

Throughout this chapter, we have examined scores of California's plant and animal species that are **threatened**, more seriously **endangered**, or even extinct. They range from some of the tiniest plants and insects to the long-extinct California grizzly bear. The introduction of foreign competitors and predators, encroaching developments, and other human activities are challenging the very survival of countless native species across the state. Debates about how to save these species involve which habitats to preserve and which developments and other human activities to curtail. Issues repeatedly fueling and complicating these debates involve private property rights and short-term economic profits.

Finally, we will focus on two more species that have not yet received the attention they deserve.

Bald eagles once soared free over California's coast and offshore islands. Their nesting numbers dropped to about twenty in the 1960s due to DDT, habitat destruction, and human encroachments, as outlined in a previous section in this chapter. Extinction was a real possibility. Successful efforts by agencies such as the U.S. Fish and Wildlife Service and organizations such as the Predatory Bird Research Group at UC Santa Cruz (with help from legislation such as the 1972 Endangered Species Act) brought bald eagle nesting numbers to over one-hundred during the 1990s.

By the late 1990s, a growing number of bald eagles were building their enormous nests near California's inland reservoirs, where stocked trout and other fish represent year-round food supplies. Up to eighteen eagles have been observed in their winter migrations to Lake Cachuma. Nesting pairs were observed at San Antonio and Nacimiento Reservoirs near the Monterey/San Luis Obispo County border and at Skinner Reservoir in Riverside County. Officials upgraded the bald eagle's status from endangered to threatened in the 1990s and, by the end of the decade, were considering removing it from the listings under the Endangered Species Act. These are substantial improvements since the 1960s, when bald eagles had entirely disappeared from southern California.

The California condor's story is a similar one, except that it edged so close to extinction that there were finally no condors in the wild. The state's most famous vultures typically grow to about twenty pounds with a wing span of 3 m (9 feet). Costly efforts to save them included raising the remaining few condors in captivity, while teaching them to fear humans and survive in the wild. These painstaking efforts involved Ventura's Condor Recovery Program, the U.S. Fish and Wildlife Service, local zoos, and other organizations.

As their numbers grew in captivity (from less than 30 in the 1980s), condors were gradually freed. As expected, some never survived due to power lines, accidental poisoning, illegal shootings, and other incidents. By 1998, 35 condors were living in the wild, 20 on the central California coast, and 15 in Arizona. Total numbers were expected to soar over 150, including up to 60 in the wild in 1999. These recovery efforts will continue into the twenty-first century.

Notice the connections that must be made to understand and solve these problems that threaten and endanger our native plants and animals. Natural disasters, changes in weather and climate, water diversion and storage projects, increasing human populations, economic activities, cultural values, technologies, and growing urban areas all play important roles; each have earned entire chapters in this book. An understanding of the varied processes, cycles, and systems that are shaping California landscapes and how they are connected becomes extremely valuable.

SOME KEY TERMS AND TOPICS

biomass	endangered/threatened species	sclerophyll
biome	food pyramid	species diversity
climax communities	habitat	succession
drought-deciduous	introduced species	tree line
ecologic islands	life zones	vegetation zones
ecosystem	pyrophyte	xeric

Additional Key Terms and Topics

alpine	desert wash	pioneer plants
arctic-alpine	Douglas fir	red fir/lodgepole pine
bighorn sheep	fire adaptations	redwood
bristlecone pine	grassland	riparian
cactus scrub	indigenous	sand dunes
California's Kansas	Joshua trees	scrub biome
chaparral	limiting factors	sequoia
cismontane communities	meadow	subalpine
closed-cone forest	Mediterranean scrub	temperate coniferous forest
coastal coniferous forest	mixed evergreen forest	temperate deciduous forest
coastal sage scrub	montane coniferous forest	transmontane deserts
coastal strand	natives	tundra biome
creosote bush	oak woodland	vegetation structure
desert biome	oasis communities	yellow pines
desert scrub communities	piñon-juniper woodland	

Chapter 6

Water Resources:
Hydrology of California

An understanding of California's complex hydrology requires some combined knowledge of how geology, geomorphology, weather and climate, and plant communities interact to produce the state's natural waterscapes. Humans increasingly impact and exploit these water resources. Therefore, we must also use the expertise of engineers and chemists to help us distribute quality water for diverse uses across the state. Historians remind us of our past mistakes and successes in water use, while professionals in the social sciences, economics, and law must plan together to solve problems related to current and future water distribution, quality, and costs.

As water continues to play a vital role in California's natural and human landscapes, geographers and hydrologists must remain knowledgeable about the connections and relationships between many different disciplines, issues, and interests under the umbrella of California's water budget. Land-use planners and policy makers must tap these water experts so that informed decisions about California's water future will be made, decisions that will improve the quality of life and living environments for all citizens. The general public must become more educated about connected water issues so that they may participate in making informed decisions about future water resources. After all, the state's diverse waterscapes—both natural and human—are changing by the day.

KEY ISSUES AND CONCEPTS

◆ Geology, geomorphology, weather and climate, plant communities, and particularly human impact and intervention influence and mold California's diverse waterscapes.

◆ There is extreme variation in the seasonal and spatial distribution of water in California, from wet winters and springs to summer drought, from the wet northwest to the dry southeast. Remarkable variation is also common from year to year.

◆ About three-fourths of the 200 million acre-feet of water that falls on and flows into California is lost to evapotranspiration. The remaining water is absorbed to become groundwater or flows through streams and rivers.

◆ Californians capture and divert about 20 percent of all water resources. More than 80 percent of those diversions go to agriculture.

◆ About 80 percent of all stream and river flow in the state occurs in north coast streams and the Sacramento/San Joaquin drainages. Relatively unreliable flows are common in much of the rest of the state, where flood control is often more important than storage for use.

◆ Californians have struggled and sometimes fumbled throughout history to survive severe and recurring droughts and floods.

◆ Californians have redistributed water across the state, building some of the greatest *water*

projects on the planet. They include, but are not limited to the following.

❖ Sacramento Valley and Delta—Sacramento Flood Control Project
❖ San Francisco—Hetch Hetchy Aqueduct
❖ East Bay Municipal Utilities District (MUD)—Mokelumne Aqueduct
❖ Los Angeles Department of Water and Power—Owens Valley
❖ Metropolitan Water District of Southern California (MWD or MET)—Colorado River Aqueduct
❖ Central Valley—Central Valley Project (Federal Government)
❖ California Aqueduct from the Feather River to Southern California—California Water Project (State of California)
❖ Peripheral Canal Proposals and Plans—control and distribution of Delta water.

◆ Hundreds of groundwater reservoirs and dozens of major aquifers, mostly below California's basins, have provided Californians with substantial water resources for many decades. Pollution, overdrafting, and subsidence have caused long-term problems.

◆ After decades of fighting over water rights and distribution and debating about costly new projects, Californians more recently found an abundant new source: protection, efficient use, and conservation of existing water resources.

◆ NATURAL WATERSCAPES

Input and California's Water Budget

Approximately 200 million acre-feet of water falls on California each year as precipitation. (One acre-foot is about 326,000 gallons, about equal to that used in an average California household of four each year.) The average precipitation across the entire state is about 58 cm (23 inches) per year, only 79 percent of the average precipitation experienced throughout the rest of the United States.

However, temporal and spatial distribution of California's precipitation is much more variable than in most of the United States. About 80 percent of all precipitation

falls from November through March, and about two-thirds of all California precipitation falls on the northern one-third of the state. Average annual precipitation ranges from more than 200 cm (80 inches) during 75 rain days on the north coast to less than 25 cm (10 inches) during 40 rainy days on the south coast. Less than 5 cm (2 inches) per year falls during just a few days of rain in the driest southeast deserts. The year-to-year variation in this seasonal rainfall can be just as dramatic. Because prevailing winds drive almost all major California storms inland from the Pacific and across California's 1,072 mile-long coastline, most of this moisture originates from Pacific Ocean waters.

Additionally, more than one million acre-feet flow into California from Oregon, more than two million acre-feet

Summer flows are modest along the South Fork of the Eel River.

are frequently overdrafted from groundwater supplies each year, and a few million acre-feet are drawn into the state from the Colorado River, depending on each year's water supply.

Because water input = storage + output, all of this more than 200 million acre-feet not stored is lost to evaporation or runoff. (Precipitation (P) = Gain or loss in storage (G) + Evaporation (E) + Runoff (R)). In California, about three-fourths (more than 150 million acre-feet) of all incoming water is eventually lost to **evapotranspiration** each year.

All of this leaves more than 50 million acre-feet of runoff in California, or about one-fourth of total incoming water, but human meddling has substantially im-

pacted and complicated California's **water budget**. Because more than one-third (nearly 20 million acre-feet) of that runoff total is actually used by humans, only a little more than one-half (more than 27 million acre-feet) flows out unobstructed and unused, often during heavy storms or in California's less accessible or wild and scenic rivers.

Today, humans interfere with California's natural hydrologic cycle by rerouting, pumping, and distributing about 40 million acre-feet of water for agriculture and urban use (see Figure 6.1). However, more than 50 percent (more than 20 million acre-feet) of all water destined for use by humans in California's water projects is lost to evaporation, mostly during transport and on irrigated

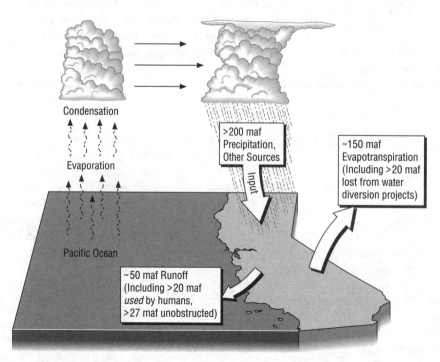

FIGURE 6.1

Water Budget. This idealized diagram models the hydrologic cycle in California during an average year. The cycle is complicated by highly variable inputs and outputs and by human water diversions.

farmlands each year. So, Californians manage to capture about 20 percent of all water sources to the state before evaporation, but our diversions lose more than one-half of that water (up to 10 percent of all incoming water to the state) to evaporation. You can see how human interference has complicated an otherwise simple water budget.

Output: There Goes the Water

California's precipitation may evaporate, or it may be stored by infiltration into the ground. It may also be stored by adding to snowpack, or by accumulating behind natural or human barriers at the surface. What remains will flow as runoff. Stored groundwater may return to the surface after it is absorbed by plant roots or erupts in natural seeps and springs or it may be exploited for human use. Before wells were drilled, a long-term balance existed between the amount of water recharging California's aquifers and that emerging from seeps and springs. Reemerging groundwater continues to contribute to the base flow of many of California's perennial streams.

On impermeable surfaces or when pore spaces become saturated, excess water must evaporate or run off. In California, water from the first autumn storms usually soaks into the pore spaces of dry ground. However, water from late winter and early spring storms often falls on surfaces already saturated by previous storms, resulting in greater runoff.

Snowmelt from California's higher terrain is also added to runoff. Each year, the accumulated snow depth and its moisture content is measured in the Sierra Nevada so that the quantity of spring runoff from this region can be estimated. Hydrologists traditionally make these annual estimates of runoff after the April 1 snow measurements to determine whether water storage or flood control measures should be emphasized. Accumulating from all these sources, water contributes to runoff as overland and then channel flow through California's many waterways.

Evaporation and Water Demands

However, up to three-fourths of all precipitation that falls on California each year is eventually lost to **evapotranspiration**. Consequently, California averages a water deficit most of the year (where the total annual potential for evaporation usually exceeds actual precipitation), except along the coast north of San Francisco. Seasonally, a net water surplus is common everywhere in the state during winter, except in the southeast deserts. A net water deficit usually occurs everywhere during summer, even on the northwest coast. The annual potential for evaporation ranges from less than 100 cm (40 inches) on the

north coast to about 125 cm (50 inches) on the central coast. However, water demand and deficits commonly range over 175 cm (about 70 inches) in southeast California and can soar above 300 cm (about 120 inches) in California's hottest, driest deserts. You can see that the time and amount of water surplus expands toward the northwest, just as the time and amount of deficit increases toward the southeast.

Groundwater

Groundwater fills pore spaces and saturates permeable and porous regolith, soil, and rocks scattered across about one-half of California. Most of these substrates are composed of sediments deposited in California's valleys, where the size of the **aquifer** is usually determined by the size of the valley and the thickness of the sediments. Some groundwater is also stored below northeast California's volcanic plateau. Substrates in the other half of the state are relatively impermeable with little or no infiltration and storage. Some of the few exceptions to this may occur when underground water is stored within the joints and fractures of otherwise solid bedrock, such as granite.

There were once more than 450 large and small groundwater reservoirs with a total holding capacity of up to 1.3 billion acre-feet of water in California. This is enough water to cover the entire state up to 4 m (13 feet) deep; it is no surprise that artesian wells and fountains were common throughout the state during early years of human settlements. Today, many of these reservoirs have been depleted, leaving about 850 million acre-feet; only about 17 percent of that is accessible. There are only about fifty substantial groundwater reservoirs in California outside the Central Valley. About forty of them are found below structural basins along the coast; all are being used.

The greatest accessible groundwater sources are below the Central Valley. Here, more than 15,000 square miles of aquifers with **water tables** ranging from above 120 m (400 feet) to about 1,200 m (4,000 feet) deep may have storage capacities up to 100 million acre-feet (equal to about one-half of the total annual precipitation that falls on the entire state each year). Many of these aquifers are recharged annually by the infiltration of runoff from winter and spring precipitation.

Theoretically, the storage of groundwater should remain constant as an equal amount of water is lost and recharged each year. However, many of these natural aquifers have been impacted by overdrafting, subsidence, pollution, and saltwater intrusion during the last century. How Californians have created and now struggle to solve these groundwater problems is a topic reserved for a later section on water developments in California.

MAP 6.1
Runoff. This map shows the major waterways in the state.

Runoff

If water is not evaporated or stored, it must run off. Map 6.1 shows the state's major waterways. Of the 200 million acre-feet per year of precipitation on California, about 65 percent evaporates directly; another 10 percent will eventually evaporate from water diverted for use by humans. Therefore, mean annual runoff directly from California surfaces averages about 20 cm (8 inches) per year, or about 35 percent of average precipitation, and some of that will eventually be lost to evaporation before reaching the ocean or inland basin base levels.

Runoff is also highly variable in time and space. More than 100 cm (about 40 inches) of runoff per year is common on the northwest coast, and more than 200 cm (about 80 inches) per year runoff has been measured on more exposed, impermeable surfaces there. Average annual runoff in drier southeastern deserts averages less than 0.25 cm (0.1 inch) per year.

When springwater, snowmelt, interflow, and overland flow finally accumulate in channels, it is easier to measure. It also becomes obvious that most of California's runoff is concentrated in its northern streams. Here is the annual average distribution of stream and river flow in California:

28 million acre-feet runoff from north coast streams = 40%

22 million acre-feet runoff in Sacramento system = 31%

7 million acre-feet runoff in San Joaquin system = 9 %

14 million acre-feet runoff in remainder of state = 20%

It is interesting to note that up to 40 percent of the state's natural runoff flows toward San Francisco Bay where the San Joaquin and Sacramento Rivers meet. The Sacramento River flows nearly 600 km (370 miles) from the Trinity Mountains to the Delta; the San Joaquin drains a larger area, but with less discharge. Both rivers meander along their silty floodplains to meet at the Delta where more than 700 miles of interconnected waterways make up less than 1 percent of the state's landmass.

Another 40 percent of California's water flows out of the relatively small but drenched northwestern portion of the state. This leaves the rest of California, including all of southern California, with only 20 percent of California's total stream flow. Also recall that about 20 million acre-feet of California's annual runoff total is lost to evaporation after it is trapped or rerouted by humans.

Gauging stations are located along all substantial California streams so that hydrographs can be used to analyze streamflow patterns. This information is needed to plan and manage water storage and flood control projects. Perennial streams are more common toward the north, while intermittent streams are the rule toward the south. Coastal streams—draining mostly direct rainfall and little, if any, delayed snowmelt—experience 75 percent to 90 percent of mean annual runoff by March 31. Streams draining the Sierra Nevada experience more than 60 percent of mean annual runoff *after* March 31, while Sierra Nevada streams most reliant on snowmelt may not experience peak flows until May. Natural springs supply most northern California streams with reliable base flow all year; throughout California, ground-

water levels are usually the last to rise after heavy precipitation and the last to drop during drought.

In southern California, the only perennial flows are in the largest rivers or in streams fed by more reliable springs. Most other southern California streams receive insufficient spring water to support any base flow during summer and fall. Here, peak discharges and flooding usually occur during the storm events responsible for them. A closer look at some major California rivers by region reveals some interesting details.

Northern and Central California Rivers and Streams It is not surprising that the greatest discharges/area flow from northwestern California rivers. The Trinity River is an example of a stream draining a mix of direct rainfall and delayed snowmelt. This causes higher discharges to be spread over a six-month period from winter through spring. However, the Trinity eventually flows into the Klamath River, which claims the greatest total area (about 12,000 square miles) and discharge (more than 68,000 acre-feet per day in the peak month of February) of any California **drainage basin**. Discharge drops to August and September lows of nearly 6,000 acre-feet per day on the Klamath. The Eel River has the third highest average discharge (peaking at nearly 39,000 acre-feet in January and February) as it drains more than 3,000 square miles. The Smith River drains only slightly more than 600 square miles, but peaks at nearly 18,000 acre-feet in January, the fifth largest discharge in California.

Rivers which drain down the western Sierra Nevada into the Central Valley usually peak later in spring. Generally, streams have later peaks and lower peak discharges per area toward the southern Sierra Nevada, especially those draining snowmelt from the highest terrain of central and southern sections of the range. The Sacramento River drains the second largest area in California (8,900 square miles, including parts of the Trinity and northern Sierra Nevada). It also has the second largest average discharge (peaking at about 49,000 acre-feet per day in February) of any California river. It usually bottoms out at slightly more than 8,000 acre-feet per day by August and September. Other rivers carry significant discharges from the Sierra Nevada. The Feather River peaks in April at about 21,000 acre-feet, fourth in California; the American River peaks at about 14,000 acre-feet, sixth in California; the Kings River peaks in June at about 12,000 acre-feet, seventh in California.

These rivers once flowed into and flooded the Central Valley each season until California's great flood control projects were built. A series of rivers, marshlands, and lakes once expanded and contracted with the seasons within this 725 km (450 mile) long and 65–110 km (40–70 mile) wide valley. The Sacramento River system seasonally flooded vast expanses north of the Delta, while the Delta itself was flooded as the Sacramento and San Joa-

The Santa Ana River after a heavy rainy season. Discharge is so slight during average years that parks and golf courses have been established in the river bed.

quin Rivers gradually flowed toward Suisun Bay and the Carquinez Strait and into San Pablo Bay.

Meanwhile, inland drainage was the rule in the southern San Joaquin Valley. There, the Kings, Tule, and Kaweah Rivers once filled the vast Tulare Lake, which once had nearly four times the surface area of Lake Tahoe and even grew to 500,000 acres in 1862. When Buena Vista Lake was filled by the Kern River near Bakersfield, it would sometimes coalesce with Tulare Lake during flood years to form one huge San Joaquin Valley water body.

Rivers and Streams in Southern California   Compare the great rivers of northern California to the Los Angeles River, which rises to a 1,000 acre-feet per day discharge in the average peak month. Even lower discharges are typical of streams along the south coast and in the deserts. The highest discharges here are more common in February and March and coincide with the storms that produce them. The Mojave River flows into the desert from the San Bernardino Mountains and usually soaks into the porous surface within fifty miles of its headwaters, before passing Barstow.

Even these southern California rivers can produce extensive flooding. In March, 1938, the Los Angeles River peaked at 67,000 cubic feet per second (cfs), while the Mojave poured 120,000 acre-feet of water past Barstow and toward Soda Lake during that year. Mojave waters have since spread across its normally dry desert channel in other flood years, such as in 1995. The Colorado is not truly a California river; it originates and gets almost all of its water outside the state and then flows along the California border with Arizona. Sediments deposited by the Colorado have cut it off from the below-sea-level farmland of the Imperial Valley so that it flows away from the state, into Mexico and the Gulf of California. We will review human endeavors to control and redirect its flow later in this chapter.

California's desert waterways have dried mostly within the last 10,000 years. During the Ice Age, the impressive Owens River filled Owens Lake to more than 75 m (250 feet) and flowed on to fill desert basins such as Searles, Panamint, and Death Valleys. These connected systems of inland rivers and lakes were testimony to cooler, wetter California deserts of that time. In the more recent drier climates, skimpier Owens River was reduced to connecting several swampy areas to Owens Lake. Water diversions to Los Angeles during the twentieth century further dried the Owens Valley and its river until Owens Lake virtually disappeared.

Southern California's dry beds and washes are in stark contrast to northern California's perennial rivers. Much of the flows of mighty northern California rivers are controlled and stored in massive state water projects. However, more than 18 million acre-feet (less than 10 percent of total incoming water but about 25 percent of California's initial runoff before any loss to evaporation) is protected in mostly less-accessible rivers under the state's Wild and Scenic Rivers program.

Lakes

Natural lakes are not as numerous in California as in more humid areas, but a few of the state's basins have filled with substantial water bodies. Though it is shared with Nevada, Lake Tahoe is California's largest natural lake. Its 191 square miles contain 122 million acre-feet of water, about four times the total storage of all California reservoirs. However, only less than 2 m (6 feet) of its surface can be used each year without depleting this source of water. Clear Lake in the northern Coast Ranges is the largest freshwater lake completely within California.

During the Ice Age, vast freshwater lakes filled numerous basins within California's inland deserts and even

Clear Lake sprawls out beyond the town of Lakeport and rural landscapes southeast of Ukiah.

in the San Joaquin Valley. More recently, Tulare Lake and Buena Vista Lake frequently overflowed during seasonal runoff from the Sierra Nevada until great flood control projects of the twentieth century encouraged farming in much of the San Joaquin Valley. From north to south, Goose, Eagle, and Mono Lakes represent substantial natural water bodies in eastern California inland basins. Goose Lake has the potential to overflow into the Pit River only during the most unusual and severe flooding events.

Evaporation normally exceeds precipitation in many inland basins such as the Surprise Valley, at Honey Lake, and especially in the mostly dry basins scattered across the deserts farther to the south. Whether they are referred to as alkaline basins, saline sinks, or playas, most only contain water during wettest periods.

Wet and Dry Cycles

Floods: Going for a Swim Again

Californians may rightfully complain about the media's obsession with the state's weather disasters. We must also admit that an exceptional number of wild weather years are scattered through California's climatological record. They go back to years like 1861–1862, when Los Angeles was inundated, and a lake sixty miles across formed in the Sacramento Valley. Consider the March 2, 1938, floods: 87 dead, 290,000 acres flooded, including the inundation of large portions of the Los Angeles Basin before the great urban developments. Some river flows were nearly a hundred times greater than average rainy season peaks; the Santa Ana River at 100,000 cfs, the San Gabriel River at 65,700 cfs, and the Los Angeles River at Main Street at 67,000 cfs are examples. These and other early flood events served as warnings about California's flood control future.

In more recent times, California's historical flood years have not been limited to the memorable deluges of 1955, 1964–1965, and 1997 in the north, to 1969 in the south, or even to the more widespread floods of 1978, 1983, or 1995. California has become a perfect laboratory for the study of how a diverse variety of drainage basins respond to periodic floods and droughts and how people have recently played important roles in modifying these drainages. The now infamous 1998 El Nino year serves as a recent example.

How Floodwaters Accumulate In California's natural landscapes, from grasslands and chaparral to woodlands and forests, precipitation gradually accumulates behind natural barriers and in the soil to recharge groundwater tables. Finally, the surface becomes saturated and slowly releases water as runoff. When this interflow turned overland flow finally accumulates in channels, peak flows are produced in streams and rivers that may lag far behind periods of heaviest precipitation.

Lag times between peak precipitation and runoff and the severity of flooding depend upon many natural variables. Precipitation duration and intensity are obvious factors that start the whole process. Small, steep drainage basins with exposed, impermeable surfaces experience more frequent flash flooding with short lag times, especially where brief bursts of heavy rain are common. Steep local canyons recently laid bare by autumn's wildfires are particularly vulnerable to these floods during heavy winter rains. These conditions have repeatedly combined to terrorize especially southern Californians who dare to build and live in such environments.

Loose, permeable soils are capable of storing excess water. However, when stripped by fire, construction, logging, or overgrazing, they are combined with the water and coughed out of canyons as devastating mudflows. Sediment loads of such California streams that drain steep slopes cleared of protective vegetation cover rank toward the highest in the world, while the erosion of soil and regolith in upstream headwaters can be remarkable. Such flooding and debris flow events may last only a few hours.

Similar to these events are the rare and brief flash floods which hit a few of California's local desert canyons each late summer. Spawned by isolated but severe summer afternoon thunderstorms (often fueled by tropical moisture from Mexico), tons of water, mud, and debris can race down desert slopes and out of desert canyons lacking protective plant cover. Conspicuous alluvial fans and lobes of debris which radiate out of California's desert canyons are clues left by these wild flows. It is no consolation to anything or anyone in their paths that these violent events only last a few minutes or hours and may be followed by months of no rainfall.

In contrast, expansive, forested drainages with low relief and permeable surfaces capable of storing large amounts of precipitation experience fewer brief floods and longer lag times to peak runoff for each precipitation event. Much of the water is gradually released from natural storage near and below the surface, while vegetation cover and low relief slow the progress of surface water running downhill. Sediment loads are relatively light in these more tranquil environments, and channel flows may peak days or even weeks after a storm.

Finally, when precipitation is stored as snow, peak runoff may be delayed by months. This is common in streams and rivers draining the Sierra Nevada, where peak discharge may not occur until May. Before California was developed, these rivers regularly poured spring floodwater into the Central Valley. Even in 1995, after heavy winter snows and a cool spring, many Sierra Nevada streams peaked during June. Discharge on most streams was high all summer; it is no coincidence that Mammoth's ski slopes remained open until August 13, and Yosemite's waterfalls were impressive and powerful through the summer of 1995. The 1998 El Nino produced a repeat performance of late spring and summer runoffs from heavy snows. Skiers, recreational water users, and consumers are typically delighted by such rare years.

Humans Seek Control

People have made enormous impacts on these natural events and on the hydrologic cycle in general in California. Land use has drastically changed California's waterscapes, especially during flood periods. In urban areas, they have paved and built countless impermeable surfaces that block infiltration and cut groundwater recharge sources; quick, explosive runoff over these paved surfaces is common during storms. With each new urban expansion, Californians must cope with the severe flash flood conditions they have created. Drops of water no longer trickle down the leaves and stems of plants toward an irregular surface covered with organic litter and into soils laced with cavities and roots. Instead, those drops may fall on a roof or parking area and be quickly channelled to a gutter, then to a small, smooth flood control channel, then to a larger one.

Now, the effort is to get that water out of the streets and away from our homes and industries as fast as possible before it interferes with our lives and economy. This requires the construction and management of more elaborate and costly flood control systems with each new development. The paradox is that the same California urbanites who draw expensive water from so many sources hundreds of miles away, then must pay so much money to get rid of the "free" water that rains on their communities. It is also ironic that some California developers who expand impermeable surfaces and create more severe flash flood conditions often complain when communities ask them to contribute to the expansion of flood control systems.

On California's cleared and irrigated farmlands, evapotranspiration rates can be staggering and costly. This helps explain why agriculture accounts for about 80 percent of all water used by Californians. And though runoff is less than in urban areas, recently plowed and exposed soils erode quickly and increase the sediment yield to local streams during storms when compared to previous natural landscapes. More than one California reservoir, basin, or mudflat has been filled by soil and sediment from eroded farmlands upstream. All of these are problems which constantly challenge California farmers and degrade soil quality, but they also impact the long-term productivity of the state and the quality of living environments for all Californians.

Today, watershed and flood basin zoning, water management, and flood forecasting are considered important nonstructural **flood control** methods. Additionally, California's structural flood controls—its diversion and storage projects—are designed to decrease peak flows and flood frequencies by expanding flows over longer time periods, sometimes stabilizing flows for years. Larger **multi-purpose reservoirs** hold about 95 percent of the flood control capacity in the state. Flood channels, levees, bypass structures, and debris basins augment these concerted flood control efforts.

There are more than thirty-one flood control districts in California, each with its own watershed boundaries. A few, including the Los Angeles County Flood Control District, became some of the most powerful agencies in the United States. Without them, chaos would rule after every major storm across the state, much as it did in the unorganized Sacramento Valley during the late 1800s and into the twentieth century.

As engineers search for new ways of storing water for use, they usually also consider flood control projects that will protect farmlands from at least the ten-year flood and urban areas from floods that occur on the average of every one hundred years. Investment in such projects saved Californians billions of dollars in flood damages during the late 1990s alone. There have also been a few exceptions, where poorly planned projects have caused their own disasters.

Some Mistakes Lead to Disaster   Just before midnight on March 12, 1928, the Saint Francis Dam north of Saugus broke away from its rock wall and sent a deadly wave of water through the Santa Clara River Valley. By the time it reached the ocean about five and a half hours later, the flood had destroyed many lives and towns, killing more than four-hundred people in its path. It also destroyed the credibility and ended the career of William Mulholland, who had just inspected the leaking dam and declared it safe.

In December 1963, the Baldwin Hills Dam failed near Culver City, forcing massive evacuations and causing $50 million in damage. There have been other close calls. In December 1964, Hell Hole Dam failed on the Rubican River as it was being constructed. The floodwaters were held downstream by Folsom Dam on the American River. When the San Fernando earthquake hit on February 9, 1971, the Lower Van Norman Lake dam was badly damaged. Only a few feet of dam was left to prevent reservoir waters from cascading into thousands of homes in the San Fernando Valley. The flood path was evacuated, and the reservoir was drained to avert what would have been the worst disaster in the history of California. Californians have learned that water projects poorly planned and built can be riskier than no projects at all.

These projects have also inundated large areas of wildland, tamed some of the state's wild rivers, and caused destruction of natural habitats. Government agencies are often charged with developing fish and wildlife management programs to mitigate some of the negative impacts of these projects, such as the devastation of waterfowl and shorebird populations due to habitat destruction.

Periods of Drought

Just as development's impacts on natural habitats and landscapes are often slower than a single flood, so are the creeping and controlling fingers of drought. As we argue about how to define and deal with floods and environmental destruction, so too do Californians constantly argue about what is drought. If it is subnormal precipitation, then how severe should it be and how long should it last before we call it a drought? Certainly, as when measuring precipitation and runoff, when the du-

ration, severity, and areal extent of subnormal precipitation expands, especially when evapotranspiration rates are high, there must be a drought. Who blows the whistle and who should make it official in a state that can experience record rains in one corner and record drought in another all in the same year? When should cutbacks in water use move from encouraged to required? Californians, with all their diverse interests, can only agree to compromise when answering these controversial questions. We have plenty of experiences to serve as examples.

Following the fourth driest year (1976) in the history of California to that date, 1977 became the driest year on record. Precipitation was 35 percent of normal statewide and less than 33 percent of normal in northern and central California, source of most of California's water. The April 1 measurements showed the lowest snowpack in history in most locations, and runoff was 24 percent of average for the year. This obvious drought caught the attention of and impacted almost every rural and urban Californian; urbanites were forced to ration water, and the agricultural economy was especially hit hard. After record production in 1975, California farmers blamed the drought for more than $510 million in losses in 1976 and about $800 million in losses in 1977. Groundwater tables were lowered to anemic levels in many parts of the state as more than 10,000 new wells were drilled in 1977; aquifers supplied more than 50 percent of all water to agriculture by the year's end.

Alternating dry and wet years (including devastating floods in 1978 and 1983) followed until the six-year drought from the late 1980s to early 1990s dragged on as the longest in state history. This drought was punctuated by a few brief periods of precipitation in portions of the state. Consequently, public perception of and official reaction to this drought was somewhat confused and less organized. The drought ended by the mid-1990s; then, the devastating floods of 1995 filled nearly every California reservoir past capacity. The floods of 1997 and 1998 kept reservoirs full.

Droughts and floods are a familiar part of California's wild natural history. Yet, the timing and length of these alternating cycles is irregular and difficult, if not impossible, to predict in the long range, even with current technological advances. What were nature's cycles are now perceived by exploding human populations to be ever more costly nuisances and disasters. Accumulated experience should help us plan for and cope with future flood and drought events.

We will now consider how people have modified California's waterways and built some of the greatest water projects in the world. First, we should examine some of the diverse plants and animals that decorate California's diverse waterscapes. The following is a very brief summary of the biogeography of California's waterways.

Biogeography of California's Freshwater Environments

Because these are the plants and animals that live either in or near water, this section appears here instead of in Chapter 5. You may refer to Chapter 5 for a review of California's riparian, wash, alkali sink, meadow, and other communities where water is often available. This section is a brief review of plants and animals more common only in California's **freshwater environments**.

Vernal Pool Communities. Vernal pools or "hogwallows" appear in small California depressions as shallow water bodies trapped by a hardpan layer at or near the surface. These pools evaporate during the summer, often toward an alkaline center of muddy clay and silt that finally turns hard and cracked. Species of plants and animals found in and near these pools are most dependent on the length of time water is available into the drought season. They may come to life in spring, only to die back during summer. These pools are found throughout California, but especially in grasslands and woodlands; they were quite common in San Joaquin Valley basins. Though native species continue to thrive in the remaining pools, agriculture, grazing, or urbanization have destroyed most of them. More than two-thirds of the Central Valley pools have disappeared.

Annual herbs and wildflowers grow around the rim of the pools and migrate inward as the pools evaporate and the wet ring closes in. Common annual herbs include the orcutt grasses or orcuttia (*Orcuttia* spp.) and other plants whose names suggest grassy characteristics, such as Hairgrass (*Deschampsia danthonioides*). Foxtails (*Alopecurus* spp.) are perhaps more familiar annual plants of vernal pools. Common perennials are quillworts, or Merlin's Grass (*Isoetes* spp.), with their large clumps of long quills.

Bogs. Bog communities are sometimes referred to as sphagnum bogs when sphagnum moss (highly absorbent, spongy masses of moss) grows in cold waters high in acid and decaying material. These nutritionally deficient peat bogs are essentially wetlands with habitats of soggy and saturated substrates containing partially decomposed plant remains. They are sometimes called fens when more nutrients are available. Typically, connected mats of mosses, roots, and other vegetation grow inward from the margins of water bodies until the entire basin is covered with a thickening accumulation of living and dead material. Shrubs and trees will sometimes eventually grow into these habitats of accumulated poor, peaty soils.

In some bog communities with poorest soils, carnivorous plants must consume insects for nitrogen. California Pitcher Plant (*Darlingtonia californica*) is also known as Cobra Lily. However, most California bogs are dominated by mosses and sedges.

Freshwater Marsh Communities. Along shallow margins of water bodies, including slow-moving streams and rivers, marshes form in higher-nutrient soils saturated for most of the year. Many California marshes are at least briefly submerged by annual runoff. The high water content and decomposing organic debris often decrease oxygen supply and encourage the buildup of toxic gasses such as methane and hydrogen sulfide. Only plants tolerant of these conditions can survive, often growing together with dense, interconnected root systems.

Because intense photosynthesis and nutrient recycling produces huge accumulations of biomass, marshes are some of the most productive ecosystems in the world. Tulare County and tule fog are examples of Central Valley names coming from the tule-like environments of these marshes. This vegetation once grew in a 100-yard (meter) thick belt around Tulare Lake. Sedges, rushes, reeds, and cattails combine to dominate these marshes. The familiar cattails (*Typha* spp.) may grow up to 3 m (10 feet) high, with their characteristic sausage-like tops. Numerous flowering species and, in the water, floating and submerged species, are also common. Various willow, mulefat and Buttonbush or Button-willow (*Cephalauthus occidentalis*), with its large, lance-shaped leaves, might be found nearby on higher ground.

California once had more than 500,000 acres of freshwater marshes and swamplands. Because they were common in flatlands with shallow depressions, marshes were most numerous in the Central Valley. There were originally more than 3,360 km (2,100 miles) of shoreline marshes in the San Joaquin Valley alone. These included the shorelines of Tulare (the largest), Buena Vista and Kern Lakes. Many of these marshes have been drained or altered for grazing or agriculture, such as rice cultivation in the Central Valley. Weeds and other introduced plants are now common. Marshes were common even in eastern and southern California along the Owens, Mojave, Colorado, Los Angeles, San Gabriel, Santa Ana, and San Diego Rivers, among others.

Right In the Water. The most extreme examples of California's hydrophytic plants grow in the water. (These are known as limnetic environments.) There are many types of planktonic algae and algae growing attached to the bottom of shallow water bodies that often give the water a cloudy or greenish appearance. Snow margin plants are adapted to higher

Water lilies, like these on the foggy northwest coast at Redwood National Park, are among the species growing in the water.

alpine environments and colder water. Snow cup red algae communities are more common in lower elevation warmer waters of the Sierra Nevada.

Throughout California, floating aquatic plants grow in smaller, calm water bodies, but they are broken up and blown or washed ashore on the turbulent, less-protected larger water bodies. Colorful common names such as water fern, yellow pond lily, pondweed, water smartweed, duckweeds, and water buttercup are used to illustrate the nature of these species. Rooted plants grow in shallower water and, on higher ground, begin to resemble plants named in communities discussed in Chapter 5.

Coastal Brackish Marshes. Salt-tolerant plants begin to appear when salt intrudes into these wet environments. California's coastal brackish marshes are alternately flooded by saline and fresh water. The coastal salt marshes found in upper intertidal zones of protected bays, estuaries, and lagoons often have even higher salt concentrations.

Saltwater rarely reaches the east Delta, as fresh water from the Sacramento and San Joaquin Rivers pushes it out. However, salt concentrations increase toward the west Delta, especially during high tide and when late summer and early fall freshwater runoff is at its lowest. The greatest tide of saltwater into California water communities flows through the Golden Gate and into San Francisco Bay, up to thirty miles into the Carquinez Strait.

Before California's great water diversions, heavy freshwater flooding would periodically bring freshwater fish into San Francisco Bay and water fit to drink into Suisun Bay. Gone are those days when such volumes of freshwater pushed so far west. Today, complex water flow control systems are required to keep saltwater from moving into the Delta's channels and to keep it from further intruding into Delta groundwater reservoirs. However, the real destruction of these coastal marshlands is a result of their direct transformation to land uses that serve humans. More than 60 percent of San Francisco Bay and Delta marshlands are gone, many converted directly into housing tracts and other urban environments. Evaporation ponds have replaced others, including Alvarado Marsh in the South Bay.

Wildlife in Water Environments. Because the abundance of water makes these plant communities so productive, it is no surprise that aquatic environments also support a tremendous variety of animals that live in or near them. Add the number of animal species that visit from surrounding communities or stop off during annual migrations, and we now have an astounding number of species who rely directly on California's aquatic environments.

The riparian forests were considered in Chapter 5. There are abundant stories of how ducks, swans, marsh wrens, rails, and geese once cluttered their skies. Abundant populations of deer, antelope, tule elk, rabbit, and other larger mammals who roamed the surrounding countryside were also dependent on these water sources.

Before the great water projects impacted their distributions, silver salmon and steelhead trout (seagoing rainbow) were abundant in most coastal streams throughout the state, but especially to the north. King salmon were common in Sacramento and San Joaquin tributaries down to 4,000 feet and in many large coastal streams. Bass thrived in warmer waters.

Rainbow trout were common in Sierra Nevada and Cascade streams; today they are found in most California lakes and streams where water temperatures remain below 70°F (21°C). The golden trout, California's state freshwater fish, is native to the Kern River high country and is now found throughout the Sierra Nevada high country. Sturgeon and perch are among the many other fish remaining in California's waters. Stickleback, chubs, and pupfish survived where sufficient water accumulated in California's deserts.

A variety of other animals flourished in California's waters before humans took control, including many kinds of burrowing species. Golden beaver, mink,

Beaver may be less common today, but are still found especially along northern California water courses.

and river otter were common, while abundant populations of fish and turtles were found in water bodies such as Tulare Lake.

The water ouzel, or American Dipper (*Cinclus mexicanus*) is an excellent example of one of California's many birds that live with water. These are small, grey birds with stubby tails. They fly only along stream courses and never move beyond about 50 m (150 feet) of the stream once they mate and build nests. Because they feed on aquatic insects and larvae, they are good swimmers capable of walking on stream bottoms, where they may remain under for up to one minute. Perhaps their habit of dipping or bobbing as they overlook a stream allows them to better see beneath the water surface. They may be found along forested streams, particularly in the western Sierra Nevada.

Ducks, geese, wrens, rails, swans, cranes, and various shorebirds are other examples of the variety of bird species depending on California's water environments. Many riparian birds, such as the now rare yellow-billed cuckoo, bell's vireo, yellow warbler, and willow flycatcher, are disappearing as their habitats are destroyed. Meanwhile, the opportunistic cowbird has increased its populations from the one spotted in 1900 in the Sacramento Valley to flocks of 10,000 surrounding today's irrigated fields.

Mono Lake is still the largest breeding ground in California for California gulls. (Only the Great Salt Lake is more important.) There will be more about troubled Mono Lake in the next section.

Human developments have destroyed most of California's aquatic environments and threatened many of the species that depend on them. Of the more than 775,000 original acres of riparian forest, only 3 per-

cent remain, while thousands of acres of wetlands and waterways have been altered or lost. Physical, chemical, and temperature changes act as barriers to many fish and other water species, such as salmon, which are now often stranded in fields and behind dams. Steelhead trout once flourished in coastal streams from Alaska to Baja California, but today are rarely seen south of Malibu.

We now turn to the modifications humans have made in nature's waterscapes. In California, these changes are truly astounding.

◆ WATER FOR THE PEOPLE

Humans' emphasis on supply, delivery, and use has resulted in the redistribution of water across the state and drastic changes in California's water environments. The variety of uses for water in California includes agriculture and other industries, domestic and urban usage, generation of energy, recreation, and landscaping. These users now exploit the majority of water available at the surface (more than 40 million acre-feet), and they lose more than one-half of that to evaporation. More than 80 percent of all California water used goes to some form of irrigation; all domestic, commercial, institutional, and manufacturing users combined account for less than 10 percent.

Today's water issues and future water policies must include consideration of appropriate and equitable distribution, consumption, pricing, and quality of water. This is especially important because water use may top 50 million acre-feet early in the twenty-first century. Past emphasis on developing expensive water projects to promote growth and water use is being replaced by modern conservation efforts that help us manage our existing water resources and projects more efficiently.

Drastic variations in the **per capita use** of water over space and time in California have been striking. Per capita use tripled between 1900 and 1975. More recent droughts and higher costs have encouraged conservation so that per capita consumption has decreased in many areas since the mid-1970s. Consumption has dropped below one-hundred gallons per person per day in many high density neighborhoods. Yet, it exceeds six-hundred gallons per person per day during summer in some warmer inland valley suburbs with single family homes.

California agriculture remains the great user. About 5 acre-feet of water is required to produce one year of food for each Californian. That is about 1,000 gallons of water for each pound of food produced, with wide variations. Production of one pound of bread or tomatoes requires more than 100 gallons; one gallon of milk requires more than 900 gallons, and it takes about 2,500 gallons of water to get one pound of steak on your table! It is no wonder agriculture accounts for up to 80 percent of all California water consumed.

California has seven major lakes and about sixty major reservoirs. If natural Lake Tahoe is ignored, the state now stores more usable water in its reservoirs than is found in its natural lakes. What events have led Californians to build more large dams with reservoirs containing greater storage capacities than any other state? The following is a combined historical and geographical review of major trends and issues in water use and the resulting projects that distribute water throughout the Golden State.

Native Americans

Most of California's Native Americans were hunters and gatherers who lived near water for convenient drinking, fishing, hunting, cleaning, and food preparation (such as boiling water and in leaching pits, where water was poured through foods to filter out acids). Native population density was proportional to available food and water supplies. The approximately 300,000 Indians who lived in California at the time of Spanish contact were scattered across the state in diverse groups, but they were clustered in villages with up to 1,000 residents along water courses. Though California Indians viewed water as something to be manipulated to improve their natural world, they tried to maintain a symbolic relationship or "balance" with nature and usually did not "develop" water resources as we do today. Most villages claimed the entire width of the stream and the riparian plant and animal communities spread out on each side. Cultural life and social events were often centered around water. Sustainable is a common term used to describe their management of water and other natural resources.

California Indians apparently experimented and developed beyond their hunting and gathering roots in only two areas: the Owens and Colorado River Valleys. Up to 3,500 Native Americans (more than 60 percent of California's desert population) practiced agriculture along much of California's Colorado River border. The Kamia, Halchidhoma, Mohave, and Quechon (Yuma) peoples planted maize, native vegetation, and, later, crops introduced from Spain in the rich layers of silt left by the Colorado's cyclic floods. The extent of flooding and meanders on the Colorado determined the location and extent of farming.

The Paiute in the Owens Valley built a dam on Bishop Creek and diverted water through several miles of ditches. The water spilled over plots of more than a square mile near what is now Bishop, irrigating local, native plants. Evidence suggests that more than 2,000 people and thirty villages were eventually supported there by what some have called irrigation without agriculture.

The Spanish introduced new crops and eventually agriculture to California's Native Americans. This Indian labor force would later play a vital role in building water systems for the Spanish and Mexicans.

The Spanish Era

Using their concept of the Christian tradition, the Spanish brought very new values to California's water, land, and people. Nature was seen as a divine gift to be made useful (subdued and exploited), and California's land and people had to be conquered in the name of God and civilization. Early Spanish expeditions recognized the lack of water in California and noted that the best places for settlements were almost always along water courses. The farming and the cattle, sheep, goats, and horses they brought were vital to the success of their new presidios (forts), missions, and pueblos (villages or towns); but they knew that none of these could be supported without reliable water resources.

Starting with the Portolá expedition in 1769, the Spanish consistently searched for and found sites with a combination of good water, farmland, and enough Indian labor to develop the irrigation agriculture to support a settlement. The first site for a mission and presidio in San Diego was selected largely because of the San Diego River's reliable water supply and its riparian environment. In 1773, Indian laborers and the padres built a dam six miles from the Mission and an aqueduct to the San Diego settlement.

The first pueblo was established in 1777 at San Jose along the Guadalupe River, again where there was abundant water, rich soil, and riparian woodland. When Governor Felipe de Neve announced the foundation of Los Angeles (El Pueblo de Nuestra Señora La Reina de Los Angeles de Porciuncula) in September, 1781, on a low terrace of the Los Angeles River, he praised the reliable source of water from the river and the surrounding rich farmland it would irrigate. Indians labored under the direction of Franciscan padres to build water detention and delivery systems for the settlement.

Even when Governor Diego Borica in 1797 selected the site for Alta California's third pueblo, Branciforte (near Santa Cruz), he noted favorable conditions along the San Lorenzo River similar to San Diego and Los Angeles. Though some Spanish missions and pueblos failed, these early settlement sites, including most of the twenty-one missions finally completed along the southern and central California coast, were usually located next to reliable water courses.

The initial missions, presidios, and pueblos proved vital to the Spanish plans for settlement. These settlement patterns served the Spanish well in previously settled areas east of California. Missions served to christianize the California Indians, presidios housed Spanish troops for military protection, and pueblos were centers for Spanish civilians. Though these settlements often evolved detached from each other, elaborate water distribution systems were often required for success. Water shortages and occasional conflicts between adjacent growing settlements searching for new water supplies became common. These were small-scale precursors of the giant water projects and water wars which would impact California development throughout and beyond the next two centuries.

The Spanish Crown officially claimed ownership of all water and other resources in California but granted temporary ownership or **water rights** to the resources. Water-use policies were developed in each growing settlement for the common benefit of the Spanish and the California Indians. Conflicts during the Spanish and Mexican Periods were to be settled with compromises equitable to all parties. Power was delegated from the Crown to the new world viceroy to the California governor down to the local presidio commander.

The local town council, known as the "ayuntamiento" usually made major water decisions. Each community elected a "zanjero," who supervised its irrigation system and water rights. After a dam (saca de agua) and main irrigation ditch (zanja madre) were constructed, the water was often lifted out of the river by a water wheel (noria), then drained into a basin for use. The water systems were often built by criminals and California Indians. Anyone who wasted or polluted the precious water could be fined or punished.

Water conflicts were most common between adjacent pueblos and missions. In 1782, the governor had to settle a dispute between Father Serra and the California Indians he supervised at Mission Santa Clara and the nearby residents of San Jose pueblo over the waters of the Guadalupe River.

Leaders at Los Angeles Pueblo and Mission San Fernando also repeatedly argued over the waters of the Los Angeles River during the early 1800s. This is when Los Angeles claimed that the growing mission upstream had to waive all water rights to Los Angeles' mostly self-proclaimed "pueblo water rights." Though a typical equitable compromise was probably reached, Los Angeles and numerous other communities would later claim that these so-called "pueblo water rights" were carried over from the 1848 Treaty of Guadalupe-Hidalgo, which awarded today's southwestern states to the United States. Los Angeles and other California communities often used this likely misinterpretation of history in the courts to expand their land and water rights into the twentieth century. The Spanish actually emphasized balance and equity over the exclusive or uncontested rights claimed by Los Angeles.

The Mexican Era

Some of the basic Spanish values toward water and nature were carried forward during control by Mexican and then Anglo-American settlers and authorities, though it took decades for many Americans to learn their water lessons. Most saw water as a source of economic gain, but some Mexican authorities incorporated years of lessons learned from natives and from developing arid lands to the south. By the 1830s, most successful Mexican irrigation projects required a combination of money, labor, and political power to back them; other projects were usually abandoned unless individuals took the initiative to maintain them.

However, a new source of competition for water had also emerged in the form of ranchos. The Spanish had awarded just a few of these grants of private property ranging from 20 to 300 acres to individuals, but the number of grants and ranchos exploded during Mexican rule to more than 800. Most of these grants were near established Spanish settlements which had priority over water rights, but the ranchos raised cattle for hide and tallow trade and did extensive farming, all of which required reliable water sources. The vaqueros and especially the rancheros who lived and worked on the ranchos often had close ties to nearby settlements.

Consequently, many rancheros, after assuring authorities that they would not harm the surrounding resources, Indians, or communities, were given permission to build their own main ditch (zanje madre) from a water source. Such was the case when José María Verdugo built a dam and water delivery system for his livestock near Los Angeles and Mission San Gabriel after being awarded Rancho San Rafael. His was just one example; unlike their Spanish counterparts, Mexican ranchos were both numerous and enormous.

In contrast, many Anglo settlers from more humid climates initially struggled without experience in drought-stricken California territory. Seeing an overabundance of resources, the Americans ignored the lessons of limitation learned and practiced by the Spanish. American settlers, at first, replaced the Spanish concepts of common good and centralized control with individual rights and minimal government. It wasn't until the twentieth century, after decades of water chaos, that they would be forced to reach back for some of the lessons left by the Spanish.

All of this would lead Californians to build some of the greatest water projects on earth. These projects would have seemed impossible to those who participated in the state's first expeditions and settlements, whether they be Native American, Spanish, Mexican, or Anglo.

Anglo Settlers Bring Water Chaos

American settlers brought new ways of looking at California's resources in general and its water in particular. Theirs was a California with inexhaustible resources and wealth that could sustain unlimited growth. They shunned organized, central authority and pushed for individual freedom and against any controls on industry and private enterprise. Once they wrestled control of the state, Anglo-American laws, or lack of them, had immediate impacts on California landscapes. Though the discovery of gold and other abundant resources reinforced these attitudes, Californians quickly ran into a giant roadblock—limited water supplies.

Water chaos was often the rule from 1848 into the twentieth century. Frustrated entrepreneurs and developers repeatedly fought over how to distribute limited water supplies during one season or expel excess water during annual flooding. As water wars spread through the land and in the courts, the winners were usually those with the greatest economic and political clout. However, when flood or drought ravaged the land, most Californians lost regardless of their economic status. Californians were recognizing tragedy of the commons, as individuals exploited their water resources at the long-term expense of everyone's resources.

That first more than fifty years of American control in California brought much more than water chaos. Many smaller, private, local and community-owned water companies and districts were actually quite successful; some gradually evolved into thriving communities and cities familiar to modern California. Much has been learned from the haphazard mistakes made during that period of trial and error in California's water history. Most importantly, it became clear that in such a large state, diverse groups of people must work together to consider multiple interests, such as those from agriculture, mining, and the state's urban centers. Only then would major problems, including water disputes, be resolved.

It was 1839 when John August Sutter was granted his large rancho where the American River joins the Sacramento River. His plans to build a sawmill, fort, and settlement on the American River required large amounts of water. However, his water needs represented only a drop compared to the millions of gallons that would be used each day, the hundreds of miles of waterways, and the massive flooding and water wars that would soon plague the Sierra Nevada foothills and Sacramento Valley. These nightmares would be played out after his foreman, James Marshall, discovered gold at Sutter's mill less than ten years later.

Hydraulic Mining

The gold rush was on and water was a vital necessity to the '49ers and those who followed. Water soon became the focus of attention a few years later, after 1853, when layers of gravels rich in gold were found on the slopes above northern gold country mines and in Nevada County. Giant hoses would be used to channel hydraulic pressure from upstream sources and blast the gravel off the slopes, making the gold accessible. These first hydraulic operations were local, private ventures with no outside supervision.

By 1857, many of the smaller companies were consolidated into enormous operations. With such concentration of capital, more than 700 miles of ditches fed giant hydraulic mines in Nevada County; by 1879, there were more than 1,000 miles of waterways. In the early 1870s, the California Water Company in El Dorado County was worth $10 million and owned 24 lakes, while the North Bloomfield Mine was using 100 million gallons of water per day. Some hoses could blast water more than one-fourth of a mile to tear through the slopes, all in the name of **hydraulic mining**. Enormous devastation is still visible in the erosional scars and cliffs at such locations as Malakoff Diggins State Park.

Hydraulic mining proved disastrous for nearly all who resided downstream. Sacramento Valley farmers already often waited well into each growing season for their fields to drain of annual flood waters. Then, the problem was exacerbated during the 1860s and 1870s when the flood of mud and sediment arrived from the hydraulic mining operations to bury and destroy many downstream farms. The Yuba and Feather River channels were clogged with about 6 meters (20 feet) of sediment, causing more serious and persistent flooding. Steamboats that once ventured to Oroville and Chico Landing could now barely make it through the debris into Sacramento. Proposals by the Army Corps of Engineers to organize the mess and clear the channels were denied.

Then, just as people initially flocked to the Mother Lode, so did the population of surrounding regions and California cities explode from 1850 into the twentieth century. The great migrations of people from around the United States and the world were often to California's cities, such as San Francisco. Water had also become vital to the farming, shipping, and trade that fueled California's new economy and to its growing cities. Though these early Californians resisted central authority and restrictions on private enterprise, the negative effects of hydraulic mining had impacted too many powerful agricultural and commercial interests. The result: in 1884, the Federal Circuit Court, in one of the first rulings to control environmental destruction, stopped all hydraulic mining in California and closed the industry.

This sweeping ruling to restore some order to California's waterscapes was an exception during more than fifty years of water chaos in California. The preferred approach usually emphasized unbridled free enterprise and a first-come, first-serve atmosphere driven by personal profit and lacking in government intervention. Victims who could afford it repeatedly dragged their cases into the California courts and the courts sometimes added to the chaos. Yet, some early California settlements did serve as small-scale models, showing how well-planned water systems were vital to the success of any California community. A few of their stories follow.

Early American Settlements Gain Water

In 1851, 500 members of the Church of Jesus Christ of Latter-Day Saints established their Mormon irrigation colony on 35,500 acres of Rancho del San Bernardino along the Santa Ana River. Representing California's first church-sponsored irrigation colony, it served as an outpost on their route to Salt Lake City. They successfully built irrigation ditches to their planted fields until troubles in Salt Lake City called them home in 1857.

In 1857, fifty German immigrants from San Francisco created the Anaheim Water Company for all water rights along the Santa Ana River in Anaheim. They turned their 1,165 acres of Rancho Juan y Cajon de Santa Ana into 20-acre tracts of successful vineyards and fruit orchards. Each settler had to pay $1,200 in assessments, which included rights to the water system. Other close-knit groups who successfully pooled their riches to establish new **water colonies** in California included the Indiana Colony at Pasadena and the Kansas Colony at Rialto. Irrigation on the Kings River Delta near Fresno began in 1858. By the 1860s, other religious colonies had established irrigated vineyards and orchards; they included the Presbyterians at Westminster and Quakers at Earlham.

In 1882, George B. Chaffey gained all rights to San Antonio Creek's water when he purchased more than 6,000 acres of Cucamonga Grant land along the Southern Pacific Railroad. He established the San Antonio Water Company and provided reliable piped water supplies to every farm and town parcel. He named the place Ontario, after his home town, and built tree-lined Euclid Avenue with its streetcar service. He used a similar model to establish Whittier, while other settlers used his mutual water company model to establish such communities as Pomona and Redlands.

Meanwhile, the 1870s and 1880s brought a wave of new land and irrigation companies to the San Joaquin Valley. The San Joaquin and Kings River Canal and Irrigation Company, the Irrigation Company of Merced, and the Fresno Canal and Irrigation Company offered subdivided lots and water rights. As the end of the nineteenth century approached, an explosion in California's irrigated acreage caused even greater competition for water resources.

By the 1870s, more than 60,000 acres were irrigated in California (more than 10,000 acres in Los Angeles County alone); that number increased to 300,000 by 1880, one million by 1890, and 1.5 million acres by 1900. California led the United States in irrigated acreage before the end of the nineteenth century. As farmers, industries, and local communities and cities competed for limited water supplies, conflicts multiplied. Because the government generally continued to take a hands-off approach, the courts were jammed with cases involving water. The following summarizes early trends in California water laws that dealt with these pressures, including interpretations which are sometimes used in the courts today.

Early Water Laws

By 1850, the California legislature had already established "Riparian Water Rights": the concept that anyone owning land along a waterway had rights to use that water to the exclusion of others. This approach dated back to east coast settlements and even to England, where water was abundant; it was already being challenged in the 1850s by those who needed water but owned no land directly on water courses. This led to the incorporation of the "Doctrine of Prior Appropriation," which allowed the diversion of water to land away from a river for reasonable use on a first-come, first-serve basis.

By 1866, the state and the U.S. Congress confirmed the rights of riparian owners *and* appropriators, but riparians often won in California court battles. As California courts tried to establish some sort of balance, a general pecking order of water rights evolved. The riparian users who first used the water were usually first in line, followed by first-in-time, first-in-right appropriators, followed by any later appropriations. During drought periods, there was often no water left for late-comer appropriators. Critics argued that "riverbank monopolists" had seized control of California water and that development would be stifled.

Interpretation of these water laws was questioned time and again, often by powerful landowners who found themselves with no water. Meanwhile, appropriators posted simple claims on signs where their water diversions tapped a river. Though California courts usually sided with riparian rights during conflicts, riparian users who later bought streamside properties had to wait in line behind those, including appropriators, who were already using water.

This complicated balance between riparian users and appropriators who diverted water was called "**The California Doctrine**." As California's population exploded through the late 1800s and into the early 1900s, pressure was mounting on the courts to favor new appropriators who represented much of California's growth and future. However, legislators often helplessly looked on as court decisions sided with the first riparian users and appropriators even into the early 1900s. These lawmakers often only added to the problems as they consistently resisted the organized planning and central control of water projects. Modern interpretations of water rights and the California Doctrine are summarized near the end of this chapter.

More Chaotic Water Policies

In 1868, a state legislature under pressure passed the Green Act. This lifted the acreage limit on land sales and allowed powerful speculators to convert huge parcels of wetlands and swamplands. Some of these parcels were more than 10,000 acres, mostly along the Sacramento and San Joaquin Rivers and Delta. Now without limits and controls, each owner raced to build competing private projects to save individual lands from seasonal floods. The result was hundreds of miles of diversions, channels, and levees that sometimes slowed the progress of floodwaters through the valley and out the Delta, causing more widespread flooding. Each landowner responded with yet higher levees until a maze of costly, chaotic channels and structures dominated the Delta and surrounded Central Valley landscapes.

An interesting twist came in 1887, when agriculture, industry, and other irrigationists and developers pushing for appropriation rights got the Wright Irrigation Act passed. For the first time, local irrigation districts could form and condemn the private irrigation companies. Modesto and Turlock were perhaps the most successful of about fifty districts created so that smaller family farms and water agencies would gain water for the people's benefit. A fresh breeze of hope was sweeping into California waterscapes, bringing 150,000 acres into irrigation in southern California alone by 1889. Then, just as some hint of order and equity was creeping into California's water laws and the orange and lemon orchards were spreading, the terrible droughts of the 1890s destroyed most of these special districts; chaos and desperation returned.

The droughts of the mid-1890s took their toll on California. There was still no organized plan to deal with such disasters. Desperate communities even looked to rainmakers to save them. (Charles Hatfield became a national celebrity when he reportedly used his foul-smelling formulas to make rain in Los Angeles. He once rode on the lead float at Pasadena's Rose Parade and, in December, 1915, was offered $10,000 by San Diego officials to make it rain there. When a disastrous flood hit San Diego the next month, the city refused to pay Hatfield unless he took responsibility for the destruction.)

Establishing Order

By the turn of the century, Californians had already grown weary of the successive droughts, floods, and the economic hardships they caused. The political tide had turned against uncontrolled and unconnected private interests and toward organized projects with state and federal support that might bring economic justice, social reform, and some sort of order. From the farmlands of the Central Valley to the urban centers of San Francisco Bay, Los Angeles, and in other California communities, the twentieth century would bring the kind of order in California's waterscapes that early settlers could only dream of; the result would be construction of the greatest water projects on the planet.

The change in the political winds swept almost simultaneously across San Francisco, Los Angeles, and other municipalities whose citizens and officials finally realized that large, organized publicly funded water projects would have to replace their dependence on smaller, unreliable private companies. It swept across the entire state when the federal government passed the Reclamation Act of 1902 and established the U.S. Reclamation Service to build new water projects with land and hydroelectric sales, fees, and other revenue.

The plan was to encourage homesteaders and smaller landowners to gain water rights from large, organized federal projects and to bring parcels of 160 acres or less under irrigation. This 160-acre limit would be fought, challenged, and manipulated by big land barons, monopolies, and speculators who once controlled and exploited resources at the public's long-term expense. The act represented one of the first large-scale efforts to organize big public water projects that would supply the state—including, ironically, its powerful landowners—with reliable water sources for the twentieth century.

This trend was fortified when, in 1928, a California constitutional amendment finally required *all* water users to be "reasonable." Cooperation within well-organized water projects was replacing the water chaos and waste of specific individual and private interests.

◆ CALIFORNIA'S MANY WATER PROJECTS

Central Valley Flood Control

The glaring need for organized efforts to bring California's waterways under control was most obvious in the Central Valley and Delta. Ordinary tides regularly flooded up to three-fifths of the Sacramento/San Joaquin Delta, and the most severe tides and floods drowned nearly all of it. In wet years, farmers had to wait months for floodwaters to drain along the Sacramento River floodplain. As previously outlined, the unorganized and often competing individual attempts to control this flooding sometimes made it worse. Other years brought severe drought, devastating the region's otherwise exploding cattle industry and wheat crops. Map 6.2 shows California's major water projects.

These waterways had also become vital shipping corridors since the beginning of the gold rush. For example, steamboats made the trip between Stockton and Fresno along the San Joaquin River three times a week. How-

MAP 6.2
Water Projects. These are California's major water projects.

ever, silt from hydraulic mining operations began to muddy other steamboat routes along the American, Yuba, Feather, and Sacramento Rivers. The 1884 court order that stopped upstream hydraulic mining was one of the first steps to restore order to these river systems.

Though these restrictions would have very positive long-term results, it took decades for the accumulated, choking sediment to wash through.

By 1905, the residual sediment from hydraulic mines had peaked at Marysville and was finally being flushed out of the Feather and Sacramento Rivers. Unfortunately, the damage had been done, and nature delivered the dramatic consequences of decades of unorganized and unregulated water management as devastating floods plagued the Sacramento River in 1902, 1904, 1906, 1907 and 1909.

These disasters further convinced Californians that an organized, concerted effort was necessary to control the state's waterways; the settled lands along the Sacramento River became the center of attention for these efforts. Consequently, by 1905, the California Debris Commission was given congressional authority to use the Army Corps of Engineers to design a plan that would help restore order and reclaim the valley.

By 1911, the California Debris Commission's chief engineer, Captain Thomas Jackson, revised a complicated plan to direct water around a series of weirs and channels to save valuable lands near the Sacramento River from flooding. Though Congress took years to fund the plan, the California Reclamation Board was given responsibility to finally regulate the large number of individual private flood control schemes that included many miles of unconnected and unorganized levee systems. By 1913, two dredges were scraping the Sacramento River mouth clean of silt, and by 1916, thousands of passengers and about 90 percent of freight were carried between San Francisco and Sacramento by boat. The increasingly productive farms of the valley were soon connected by railroads and electric cars.

Though the valley farm boom was shattered by recession after World War I, the federal government continued to expand and improve the new Sacramento Flood Control Project. Scouring of the Sacramento River system continued throughout the 1920s until the river bed dropped to normal levels in 1927; the scouring worked into upstream tributaries during the following years. Meanwhile, the gradual additions of Delta land reclaimed since the late 1800s had expanded from 300,000 acres in 1910 to 700,000 acres in 1918. By 1930, a total of 450,000 acres of Delta were completely enclosed and protected.

Even this flood control, reclamation, and farming had its costs in the Delta. The numerous newly dried and protected islands had rich, peaty soils that supported intensive farming. This farming of reclaimed wetlands caused many of the Delta islands to subside below sea level. Irrigation water that was once stored had to be quickly pumped west and out into the bay, while saltwater intrusion became common during drought. Though the previously reclaimed land continues to be productive, today's high costs may prohibit re-reclaiming many of these subsided islands if they ever flood again.

Nevertheless, by the 1930s, the Sacramento Flood Control Project was seen as a great success in saving the valley. In 1933, the Stockton deep water port opened, mostly for the export of agricultural products. By 1944—with 900 miles of levees, 438 miles of channels, 91 gauging stations, 31 bridges, 7 control structures and bypasses, 5 check dams, and 3 pump plants—the Sacramento Flood Control Project was considered an American model, the first of its kind. Political tides had shifted, and officials and citizens were sold on massive, organized public water projects. The U.S. Bureau of Reclamation carried this momentum into the planning and construction of the enormous dams and water control systems of the now famous Central Valley Project, to be reviewed later in this chapter.

Meanwhile, the valley continued to reap the benefits of successful flood control. By the 1960s, the Port of Sacramento was exporting lumber and wood chips, rice, and other farm products from California, along with products brought in on the rail and truck lines that converged on these ports from other states. By 1977, 2.5 million tons of products were carried on more than 100 ships from Stockton's port, while 1.8 million tons of goods were shipped from Sacramento on more than 120 ships. The two ports handled about 5 percent of all deep-draft shipping in the entire state, while more regular runs were made by shallower barge traffic to San Francisco Bay and out the Golden Gate. Agriculture, shipping, and recreational opportunities were enhanced throughout the rest of the century, and the valley's population exploded.

The San Francisco Bay Area

San Francisco's Presidio and Mission were founded in 1776 because of proximity to the Golden Gate, the strategic entrance to the bay. Poor soils and lack of water at the end of this rocky peninsula were uncharacteristic of other Spanish settlements in California. By the 1850s, American settlers had gained control of California; the gold rush, the economic boom, and the population explosion would rapidly make San Francisco into a world-famous city. However, water had to be shipped in by barge and six fires ravaged the new city in the early 1850s.

Mounting frustration into the late 1850s set the stage in 1862 for the new Spring Valley Water Works to take control of water sources and become responsible for water deliveries to a thirsty San Francisco. Later, The City grew impatient with the company's poor supplies, service, and high rates and, from the 1870s to the end of the century, it fought the private company for control of its water supply system, usually with little success.

Consequently, Spring Valley Water Company provided San Francisco with most of its water from the 1860s to 1900. The private company had strung pipelines from Pleasanton and Alameda Creeks in the East Bay, around the southern part of the bay and up the peninsula. Public confidence in the company, which had traditionally sold water by the bucket, had further eroded as San Francisco's population topped 350,000 by the early 1900s. Officials began searching out more distant sources to secure a reliable water supply for the growing city. Thirty years of debate and controversy and $100 million later, the first water would finally flow from the Sierra Nevada's Hetch Hetchy, 170 miles east of San Francisco, supplying The City with far more water than it could use.

San Franciscans Stumble Toward Water

San Francisco's water project plans began with extensive surveying when the city and its chief engineer targeted the waters of the Tuolomne River in the Sierra Nevada. The plans included dams on the river and its tributaries to store water, such as in Lake Eleanor. One of the most critical and controversial parts of the project would require the flooding of Hetch Hetchy, a spectacular valley considered by many observers, such as conservationist John Muir, to be every bit as awesome and beautiful as Yosemite.

Muir and other conservationists used momentum from their successful campaign to first create and then expand the young National Park System, which included nearby Yosemite. They launched a popular nationwide campaign to stop the project. Muir argued the flooding of Hetch Hetchy was like damming ". . . the people's cathedrals and churches, for no holier temple has been consecrated by the heart of man." He accused the project's planners of succumbing to the "powers of darkness" and being motivated by "the almighty dollar." This was one reason the Secretary of Interior, in 1902, denied the city's request to submerge Hetch Hetchy. But, this was only one obstacle to San Francisco's plan for a big water project.

Downstream from the proposed project, the Modesto and Turlock Irrigation Districts also claimed rights to the Tuolumne River. Then, a political scandal halted a scheme to bring water to The City from drainages north of the Tuolumne. The scandal broke when it was made public that Bay Cities Water Company had paid off the Union Labor party, the mayor, and the Board of Supervisors to drop their plans on the Tuolomne and instead consider sources to the north along the American and Consumnes tributaries, owned, of course, by Bay Cities Water. Public trust in city officials eroded. In addition, when San Francisco took a big hit from the 1906 quake and fire, city officials were forced to pour public resources into the rebuilding of the city instead of an expensive water project.

San Franciscans Finally Get Water

By 1907, the scandalous leadership had been forced out, and new city officials revised efforts to gain control of Hetch Hetchy. Despite so many formidable setbacks, San

Francisco citizens in 1908 approved a $600,000 bond to start the project after an aggressive public relations campaign. This was followed by positive engineering reports and agreements with competing water districts. In January, 1910, San Francisco voters approved another $45 million in bonds to start the project; Congress and President Woodrow Wilson approved it by 1913.

Opponents of the project, including conservationists, the private Spring Valley Water Company, and Modesto and Turlock farmers, had lost. A hydroelectric power system was added to help pay for the project, conservationist's concerns were swept aside, and construction began in 1914.

By the mid 1920s, O'Shaughnessy Dam (named after the city engineer who pushed the project forward) was being constructed to flood Hetch Hetchy. More bonds were later passed to complete the project, which included a twenty-five-mile tunnel through the Coast Range, touted as the longest ever built. By 1934, the first water flowed to San Francisco. Though project costs totalled $100 million, the city had more than enough water to sell to several other Bay Area cities. San Francisco continued to expand its water diversion projects until it had committed more than $500 million dollars. In 1961, another $115 million in bonds was approved to further expand the aqueduct and increase sales to other communities.

By the late 1970s, San Francisco realized substantial profits as about 250,000 acre-feet of water flowed from the Hetch Hetchy Aqueduct each year; the project was already paid for, and the city was selling more than half its water supplies to others. By 1980, it was selling more than $14 million of water to more than fifty other south and east Bay Area communities and generating nearly $20 million of electricity each year.

The City continues to profit from futuristic thinking and long-term investments that are beyond the resources of private water companies. Today, the aqueduct continues to drain water from the Sierra Nevada, west to the Bay Area and into Crystal Springs Reservoir on the San Andreas Fault.

MUD in the East Bay

Meanwhile, the Mokelumne drainage to the north of the Tuolumne was left to be developed for East Bay water sources. The aqueduct connecting the Mokelumne with the East Bay was built in just six years, from 1923 to 1929. By 1980, the Mokelumne Aqueduct was diverting nearly as much water from the Sierra Nevada as the Hetch Hetchy. This water was destined for the expanding populations of northern East Bay suburbs, and it was controlled by the East Bay Municipal Utilities District (MUD). MUD would become one of many California examples of how a utility with control over water could gain awesome political and economic power.

While the Bay Area was faulted for draining Sierra Nevada watersheds and destroying natural habitats for profit, Los Angeles would be condemned for seizing control of and exploiting vast watersheds hundreds of miles beyond its populated basin. While San Francisco used its water projects to generate revenue, Los Angeles would expand geographically by annexing huge land holdings and communities to gain more water rights. Los Angeles proved to be more aggressive and efficient in gaining water rights and building water projects. However, the success of these water projects changed the landscapes of both cities, supporting both growth and the thirsty nonnative plants that migrants and settlers brought with them.

Los Angeles, Owens Valley, and Mono Lake

The Los Angeles Town Council of 1850 followed water policy examples set by previous Spanish and Mexican authorities by supporting a controlled community water system. Under the direction of a "zanjero," permits were issued, and water was distributed with the taxes and fees to support the system, while Indian laborers were used to maintain it. Though irrigated land soared to 4,500 acres in L.A. by the 1870s, commerce quickly overshadowed agriculture as the most important economic activity in the growing city. By the 1880s, agricultural lands were quickly being transformed into residential subdivisions to house the fast-growing population. L.A. residents had already grown nervous about the quantity and quality of their water after suffering through several years of water problems caused by their own blunders.

In 1863, as residents continued to drink the same water that had just been used for bathing and washing, there was a deadly outbreak of smallpox. In 1868, the city incredulously granted a 30-year lease to the private L.A. City Water Company, giving the company authority over the city's water supply. Then, during the 1870s and 1880s, L.A. initiated numerous costly legal battles—as it distorted the true meaning of previous Spanish and Mexican property and water rights—to prevent upstream users from diverting what Angelenos considered "their" water. When the courts ruled that water rights came with any land annexed by the city, the stage was set for L.A.'s massive geographic expansion as it gained control of more water.

Los Angeles Takes Control of Its Water

By the end of the 1800s, Los Angeles city officials and the public recognized the limitations of depending on one private company for their water supplies. The giant wheel which once turned and scooped water up from the Los Angeles riverbed into a maze of canals and ditches had become obsolete; constantly leaking pipes created annoying mud and water holes on city streets. In 1902, the city finally bought out the private water company and built a more extensive and efficient system to serve an expected population explosion into the young century.

As the city and its citizens seized municipal control over Los Angeles River rights, nearby settlements were annexed in so that everyone could benefit from this expanding water supply. The 43 square miles that was Los Angeles in 1900 nearly doubled within four years, and few anticipated that L.A.'s population would multiply by more than five times from 1900 to 1920.

Los Angeles Looks Toward the Owens Valley

Amid this explosive growth, the city passed a $1.5 million bond in 1905 for the survey and planning of a new system to bring water from the Owens Valley; in 1907, a $23 million bond was passed to build the project. These bonds were passed despite allegations that the region's largest banking, power, newspaper, and railroad industries, headed by men like Henry Huntington, would realize enormous profits from increased land values. Voters rationalized that all Angelenos would benefit from the abundant water that would fuel the city's growth. Heading this aggressive charge for a new water project was **William Mulholland**, who was hired by the city to manage the new municipal water system.

Mulholland was a poor Irish immigrant to Los Angeles, originally hired by L.A.'s private water company to dig ditches. He rapidly worked his way to the top of that company and was noted as the only person with a keen knowledge of L.A.'s complex network of ditches and canals. City officials made a wise decision when they took control of the system; they hired Mulholland to head it, expand it, and make it more efficient. Superintendent Mulholland made a smooth transition from the private to the public sector; within four years, he had produced a new, efficient water system with meters that produced a $1.5 million profit for the city. Even so, few would have believed that his Los Angeles Department of Water and Power would become one of the most powerful public agencies in the United States.

In 1904, Mulholland proclaimed that L.A. would soon run out of water. He became the aggressive and successful advocate of a new project that would extend L.A.'s power 235 miles north into the Owens Valley. He convinced city officials, citizens, and even national power brokers that L.A.'s growth would stop at 300,000 within five years without an enormous water project. With the backing of L.A.'s most influential citizens and businessmen, he successfully fought for two bond measures totalling $24.5 million, which citizens passed by landslide votes of 14 to 1 and 10 to 1. He also lobbied Washington for the right-of-way granted by Congress and President Theodore Roosevelt in 1906, in which they declared that L.A.'s needs were more important than residents of the Owens Valley.

Aqueduct construction began in 1908. On November 5, 1913, the aqueduct opened and began draining water by gravity flow out of the Owens Valley 233 miles south to Los Angeles. As the water cascaded into the San Fernando Valley from the Owensmouth Cascades near Sylmar, Mulholland made his famous declaration to all Angelenos, "There it is. Take it." Suddenly, though only briefly, L.A. had control of four times more water than it could use, due to a project built under budget and completed ahead of schedule.

Meanwhile, the city that covered about 43 square miles in 1900 and more than 80 square miles by 1904, had grown to 285 square miles with the San Fernando Valley addition by the end of 1915. Was this the "Titanic Water Project to Give City a River," as proclaimed by the *Los Angeles Times* headline of July 29, 1905, or would it be a water project that built a titanic city?

The project was soaked in scandal that was addressed in numerous stories and books and even in the famous 1974 movie *Chinatown*, starring Jack Nicholson. It was learned that a San Fernando Valley land syndicate had purchased 16,000 acres for $35 an acre before plans to bring water to L.A. were made public. This syndicate included media giants *Los Angeles Times* owner Harrison Gray Otis and *Los Angeles Express* owner Edwin T. Earl, railway and real-estate tycoon Henry Huntington, and Union Pacific President E.H. Harriman. All of them lobbied the public for the project and for the San Fernando Valley annexation. When their friend Moses Sherman quit the Board of Water Commissioners and joined the syndicate with his inside information, there were too many coincidences; this cast a suspicious cloud over the entire project. These suspicions were largely swept aside by a public that saw more water as beneficial to all.

Still More Water for Growing Los Angeles

Though the L.A. Department of Water and Power's aqueduct was about six times larger and was built in one-fifth the time and at one-fourth the cost of San Francisco's connection to the Tuolumne River, it was quickly outgrown by a multiplying population. Between 1914 and 1923, L.A. annexations expanded its area by four times again, especially into the San Fernando Valley, where thirsty farmlands would benefit from city water. By the 1920s, the L.A. area had topped the San Francisco area's population, and Los Angeles was purchasing lands in the northern Owens Valley to control water farther upstream. Many more adjacent communities would be absorbed by the city to share its abundant water supply.

Hundreds of miles away, frustrated Owens Valley ranchers and businessmen sensed a loss of control in the destiny of their own valley. They waged a water war with the Department of Water and Power (DWP) by organizing to get top dollar from city annexations. Los Angeles' aqueduct was seized once and even blown up several times. The fears of Owens Valley residents were justified; powerful L.A. had gained control of their future. By 1933, L.A. was forced to buy nearly every farm, ranch, and town in Inyo County. By the 1930s, it controlled more than 300,000 acres from the Owens Valley into the Mono Basin. Today, L.A. is the principal land owner in Inyo County.

By 1940, ten years after L.A. had approved a $40 million bond, an extension and new aqueduct into Mono Basin was completed. This second aqueduct was built parallel to the overburdened first aqueduct to carry water from the Mono Basin along with additional groundwater reserves. L.A. (then the number one U.S. county in agriculture and already boasting the top port city on the west coast) continued to grow.

The Battle for Mono Lake

By 1980, 80 percent of L.A.'s water came from the Owens Valley and Mono Basin, only 17 percent from local sources, and the rest from the Metropolitan Water District. The city's thirsty population was more than three million, but, as more water was diverted from the drying Owens Valley, Mono Basin to the north was now being drained and Mono Lake was dropping rapidly. Amid new fears and allegations that Los Angeles had become too powerful and arrogant as it destroyed more lives and ecosystems far beyond its boundaries, a national campaign grew in the 1970s and 1980s to save Mono Lake. This coincided with a political shift in California as citizens grew more suspicious of new water projects and diversions to southern California. This trend will be reviewed later.

The lake was dropping to dangerous levels, causing a marked increase in salinity that threatened the lake's natural ecosystems. After the second aqueduct was completed, 90,000 acre-feet per year was being diverted (about 17 percent of L.A.'s total water supply), and the lake level was dropping at 1.5 feet per year. By the late 1970s, coyote were able to cross the newly emerged land bridges to the lake's islands, ravaging one of the California Gull's most significant breeding grounds.

After forty years of diversions, Mono Lake's volume had been cut in half, its level had dropped 45 feet and its salinity was 2.5 times higher than ocean water. Winds blew alkaline dust storms past the now-famous exposed tufa towers, creating health hazards from air pollution in the region. Even its brine flies and shrimp were threatened, a loss that would destroy surrounding wildlife and seriously impact migratory birds that relied on the lake.

In 1978, public and private groups formed the Mono Lake Committee, which quickly gained recognition as it fought the DWP in the courts and the public opinion

Researchers believe that the level of Mono Lake, with its exposed tufa towers, has finally stabilized. Streams draining the eastern slopes of the Sierra Nevada (in the background) flow into the lake.

arena. Studies in the 1980s showed that, with continued diversions, the lake would finally drop another 50 feet and stabilize at 6,330 feet above sea level as a dead sea in the year 2012. L.A. continued to resist, but by 1989, the Mono Lake Committee had 18,000 members and $700,000.

By the 1990s, conservationists and friends of Mono Lake had won enough court battles to force the DWP to allow sufficient streamflow to stabilize the lake level at 6,377 feet above sea level and to preserve its ecosystems and the fish populations in the surrounding creeks. Due to the work of a joint committee begun in the 1980s, a compromise was reached in October of 1991: DWP would curtail its diversions and support environmental projects to save Mono Lake. Since then, the proportion of Owens/Mono water used in the city of L.A. has decreased, while the proportion of water from the Metropolitan Water District and other sources has increased.

L.A. took another hit in the late 1990s when the Great Basin Unified Air Pollution Control District went on the offensive. Winds blowing across the bed of Owens Lake (dried since the 1920s) were carrying dangerous dust particles up to 100 miles downwind. The chronic dust pollution caused some residents in and around the Owens Valley to suffer from respiratory and other health problems. L.A. was forced to negotiate with the victims. Proposed costly remedies included spreading gravel across the lake, planting vegetation, and periodic flooding with water that L.A. was reluctant to give up.

In 1998, an historic agreement was reached between Los Angeles and Great Basin's air district. L.A. agreed to treat at least 22 square miles of the Owens Lake bed until clean air standards were met in 2006. The $120 million project would end up flooding about 10 square miles of the lake with shallow water and cut Los Angeles' water supply from the Owens Valley by 40,000 acre-feet per year.

Los Angeles Discovers Hidden Water Resources

Recently, L.A. and other southern California communities have rediscovered their own water sources. Local groundwater supplies are enhanced by water spreading basins, where southern California streams pour into the L.A. Basin from the surrounding mountains. There, water ponds over porous sediment, where it infiltrates and recharges valley aquifers. More aggressive efforts to stop the pollution of these groundwater basins are seen as vital to the water futures of many California communities. Recent conservation efforts have proven that the cheapest new sources of water are provided by cutting the waste and pollution of current supplies.

The Colorado River and Metropolitan Water District

The Salton Sea: A Mistake

During the 1800s, thirsty southern California communities were already looking toward the Colorado River to enhance their water supplies. By 1877, Thomas Blythe was irrigating about 40,000 acres of his Colorado River Valley farmland. In 1896, Charles Rockwood and George Chaffey formed the California Development Company; by 1900, Rockwood was diverting water into an overflow channel of the Colorado River known as the Alamo River. After flowing about 50 miles through Mexico, the course turned into the United States, and by 1901, silty water was flowing into Imperial Valley's 400 miles of canals and 100,000 acres of agriculture.

Suddenly, disastrous flooding struck in 1905. By August, the entire Colorado River had changed course into the diversion and was wildly flowing into and filling the previously dry Salton Sink. Southern Pacific took

Water pours into Salton Sea from pipes draining excess runoff and minerals off grape farms.

over from the now disabled California Development Company, but it couldn't route the river back into its main channel toward the Gulf of California until February, 1907. After about one and a half years of filling with Colorado River water, the newly born Salton Sea was left behind to accept irrigation runoff from nearby farms.

For decades, fertilizers, pesticides, salts, and other chemicals have been flowing into the Salton Sea from surrounding farms. As water evaporates, chemicals accumulate. Scientists and officials continue to debate the future of this contaminated pool of water that is sometimes foul-smelling, particularly when its shores are lined with dead fish and other decaying organic litter.

Imperial Valley Farmers Look to the Colorado

By 1909, George Chaffey's promotions brought more than 15,000 people, and 160,000 acres of land were under irrigation in what was now called the Imperial Valley. In the search for a more reliable source of water, the public Imperial Irrigation District formed in 1911 and proposed a new All-American Canal. By 1916, farmers of the Imperial Irrigation District bought California Development Company's assets. They continued to push for this new canal to divert water from the Colorado *before* it flowed into Mexico, in order to avoid developing problems with landowners on the Mexican side.

These events helped support Arthur Powell Davis, head of the slumping U.S. Reclamation Service and a nephew of John Wesley Powell (the famous explorer of the Colorado). For years, Davis argued that a massive Colorado River Project was required to protect all existing and future canals and smaller downstream projects on the river.

Allocating Colorado River Water

By the 1920s, L.A. and other southern California communities joined with lower Colorado River communities and the U.S. Reclamation Service to propose a giant dam upstream in Boulder Canyon. The project would include hydroelectric power and that All-American Canal. Many of the other six states in the Colorado Basin (Wyoming, Colorado, Utah, New Mexico, Nevada, and Arizona) were incensed by this proposal. They feared California's growth and claimed that the state, which contributed so little to the river, only wanted to steal it. The wave of criticism grew when the 1922 Supreme Court applied the right of prior appropriation to states; this suggested that the first state to use Colorado River water would get to keep it.

Conflict was briefly quelled by the Colorado River Compact in November, 1922. This suspended prior appropriation in the Colorado Basin and allotted half the river's estimated total flow to the four upper-basin states (Wyoming, Colorado, Utah, and New Mexico) and the other half to the lower basin's three states (Nevada, Arizona, and California). One problem was that the river's average flow of 15 million acre-feet was estimated too high, and there would not always be 7.5 million acre-feet available to each of the two basins. Yet another big obstacle was that there was no agreement about allocations to specific states within each of the basins. In 1924, fearing California's domination of the river, Arizona Governor George Hunt attacked the agreement.

Nevertheless, in 1927, the Metropolitan Water District of Southern California (MWD) was forming to encourage the control and exploitation of the Colorado River, a project that only the federal government could afford. By 1928, several communities had joined the MWD, but Los Angeles kept control by having the largest number of votes in the water agency. Also, in 1928, the Boulder Canyon Project Act was finally passed by Congress. California had reluctantly agreed to equal allotments for the upper-river and lower-river states. However, the Boulder Canyon Project Act would eventually limit California to 4.4 million acre-feet (maf) per year and half of any year's surplus; Arizonans got rights to 2.8 maf per year and the other half of any surplus (when they were ready to use it), Nevada was left with only 0.3 maf per year. The Boulder Canyon Project Act, activated by President Herbert Hoover, included a giant dam and power plant and an All-American Canal to the Imperial Valley.

Water wars continued. In 1931, MWD voters had already approved a $220 million bond to build Parker Dam and the aqueduct that would carry water from its Lake Havasu to southern California. Arizona's new governor reacted in 1933 by sending his state militia to stop construction of Parker Dam. Arizona finally backed off in 1935 after the U.S. Congress and Supreme Court were forced to avert a possible military confrontation between the two states; they officially authorized the building of California's dam.

By 1935, Hoover Dam was built in the more favorable Black Canyon (not Boulder Canyon). It was the largest dam in the world. As Lake Mead filled behind it, southern California bought most of the electricity produced there to help fund the project. On June 17, 1941, the first water was brought to California's coast along a 242-mile aqueduct across the desert from Parker Dam and Lake Havasu.

By 1942, the All-American Canal poured controlled flows of Colorado River water into the Imperial Irrigation District. This sparked controversy as the average farm in the Imperial Valley grew to about 500 acres, nearly double the U.S. average. Some farms were more than 3,000 acres. Absentee land ownership was the rule on many of these corporate farms. They benefitted not only from the cheap labor of poor farm workers mostly from Mexico, but also from the cheap water delivered from the tamed Colorado River, water that could reliably irrigate about 440,000 acres of the Imperial Valley.

Persistent agribusiness successfully lobbied for exemption from the 160-acre limitation set by the Reclamation Act. San Diego tapped in by 1947 and Colorado River water began flowing to the Coachella Valley about two years later. The Colorado River had finally been tamed to benefit millions of farmers and residents from the lower desert to the southern California coast.

The Metropolitan Water District

Colorado River water soon accounted for slightly more than one-half of all the water used by southern Californians. About 80 percent of this was used by only four agricultural districts throughout California's lower desert and most of that in the Imperial District. Meanwhile, the Metropolitan Water District (MWD) grew from just thirteen member cities in 1941 to providing water for more than 11 million people over more than 5,000 square miles by 1980. At first, there was more water than needed. But, by the 1960s, the MWD was already using all of the water flowing into the system. Even San Diego, after licking its wounds from a lost battle with L.A. to control Colorado River supplies, was forced to tap into the system. Charged with determining the distribution and cost of so much of southern California's water supply, MWD (or MET, as it is often called) became a powerful force in shaping the region's future.

By the early 1990s, the MWD served more than 300 cities, adding more than 3 million more customers since the 1970s. Meanwhile, other communities, especially in San Diego and Orange Counties, became more prominent in the MWD as once-dominant Los Angeles city's control fell to 22 percent by the 1990s. This power shift has occurred even though the Los Angeles Department of Water and Power must now rely on the MWD for much more of its water because of L.A.'s agreement in 1991 to curtail its diversions from the Mono Basin extension of its Owens Valley Aqueduct.

By the late 1990s, San Diego County had further complicated this water story and eroded MWD's power base. Local officials unveiled a deal that encouraged Imperial Valley farmers to sell water destined for their fields to San Diegans—for a profit. MWD was the potential loser as San Diego struggled to gain more control of its water future. If Imperial Valley farmers began conserving their water allocations intended to irrigate crops, could they sell their water to thirsty San Diegans? MWD officials questioned the legality of these water maneuvers.

The controversy became even more complicated when Coachella Valley farmers complained that the Imperial Valley had stolen their share of Colorado River water years ago. If there was a water agreement with San Diego, Coachella Valley deserved some of Imperial Valley's profits, they claimed. Yet another California water war threatened to carry into the twenty-first century.

Today, water is pumped and channeled through the Colorado River Aqueduct and distributed to many southern California coastal communities under the guard of the MWD; it flows to farmlands and communities along the lower Colorado River and the Imperial and Coachella Valleys. Controversy and conflict continue to surround the taming of this great river. The Colorado drains about one-twelfth of the contiguous U.S. land area and flows along a 1,400-mile course through seven states. Though it is one of the siltiest rivers in the world, we have built nine major reservoirs on it capable of storing more than 56 million acre-feet of usable water. Amid years of legal battles, California once used an annual allocation equal

The Coachella extension of the All American Canal marks a clear boundary between desert and productive farmland.

to the combined use of the other six states in the Colorado Basin. The biggest state has recently been forced to share more Colorado River water with its smaller competitors.

Colorado River Allocations Cut

Even after agreements were reached between the states to build Hoover Dam, it was discovered that original estimates of the Colorado's reliable flow were inflated; only about 14 million acre-feet/year would be available for allocation, not 15 million. Then, there were the direct conflicts between California and Arizona and, finally, the necessary agreements with Mexico to share some of this water.

Perhaps the most profound court decision on water rights was made by the U.S. Supreme Court in *Arizona* v. *California* in 1963. It confirmed the guidelines set by the Boulder Canyon Act of 1928 and limited California's allocation to 4.4 maf per year. This was still more than 50 percent of the original 7.5 maf per year allowed the lower basin states (California, Arizona, and Nevada). Arizonans got most of the rest when they opened their Central Arizona Project in the 1980s. This was a big defeat for California and the MWD. Now that Arizona was finally capable of using its "fair share," California would have to curtail its use of Colorado River water.

The result was that by the 1990s, California had cut its use to 4.4 maf, down from the more than 5.3 maf it took before Arizona's exploding population and agricultural interests finally demanded their share. This pressured southern California agencies (including the MWD) to tap other water sources, such as the State Water Project. By the 1990s, the giant MWD was distributing more than 3 maf of water from several sources each year, after being forced to trim its Colorado River allocations.

It is easy to focus on conflict when reviewing events leading to the distribution of Colorado River water. However, compromise and cooperation better describe how powerful economic and political interests finally came together to produce one of the greatest water distribution projects in the world. It certainly encouraged the dramatic growth of Southern California's population and economy.

Central Valley Project

As Central Valley agriculture expanded and farming communities increased productivity into the 1900s, farmers and officials recognized the need for a massive water project. A number of events eventually led to the construction of the Central Valley Project and its completion by the middle of the century. However, obstacles had to be overcome before the construction of a big project that could simultaneously relieve the valley's related problems of irrigation, flood control, land reclamation, drainage, navigation, and power generation.

In the late 1800s, farmers had used wind and horses for power to pump water from wells drained of their artesian pressures. Huge dry wheat farms and cattle grazing empires used far less water than many of the intensive irrigators who would soon invade the valley. By the early 1900s, California and the Central Valley was experiencing a magnificent land boom. Wheat empire ranches, sometimes ravaged by drought, were bought for $25 an acre, subdivided, and sold as prime vineyard and orchard lands for more than $100 an acre. Companies, such as the Fresno Canal and Irrigation Company, planned and built towns as the land was divided into smaller plots, which included water rights.

Public irrigation districts were even more successful. By 1922, 3 million acres were controlled by irrigation districts, and by 1930, up to one-hundred districts supplied more than 90 percent of the water in the San Joaquin Valley. As the number of wells pumping water out of San Joaquin Valley aquifers grew from 597 in 1906 to more than 23,000 in 1930, overdrafting became a major problem; groundwater levels plummeted.

Farmers Call for a Giant Water Project

By the 1920s, California had become an agricultural powerhouse, growing crops, such as fruit, nuts, grapes, alfalfa, and cotton, that often required intensive irrigation. The San Joaquin Valley was already leading the state in agricultural productivity. Though Central Valley farms continued to prosper during the nation's agricultural depression of the 1920s, several drought years in the 1930s cut the state's agricultural production. Especially hard hit were the smaller farmers in the valley who could not afford the additional $5,000 required for wells and pumps to put 60-acre plots into cultivation. Even the larger corporate farmers with holdings of hundreds of thousands of acres in the valley recognized the need for a more reliable source of water from a great, organized project. There was also that continuing problem with groundwater overdrafting and subsidence.

State officials and land owners had identified the Central Valley's need for a water project. Even by 1931, California's State Engineer, Edward Hyatt, was proposing a massive "State Water Plan" that would have extended into southern California. However, Pacific Gas and Electric (PG&E) led a successful opposition and defeated three attempts to pass the California Water and Power Act, which would have permitted the state to pay for water projects by selling the electricity generated by each project.

Finally, in 1933, the state legislature approved the Central Valley Project. This was followed by a close general election that December, when the Central Valley Project barely survived. Due to opposition from PG&E and southern California, it won by only 33,600 votes out of 900,000 cast. (Interestingly, the measure won in almost every region north of the Tehachapis and lost in southern California. Southern Californians saw no direct advantage in supplying the Central Valley with state water, and PG&E saw it as a threat to their energy monopoly. This voting pattern would be very different nearly fifty years later with the Peripheral Canal proposal.)

The Federal Government Completes the Central Valley Project

Another twist occurred when, in 1935, California declared that it could not afford to build the project it wanted. The United States Bureau of Reclamation stepped in with President Franklin D. Roosevelt's emergency relief funds. This further threatened the virtual power distribution monopoly PG&E had established in northern and central California because the federal government would only contribute to projects that were partially paid for by using public power. Also, under the Federal Government's Bureau of Reclamation Act of 1902, water from the project would be restricted to farms of 160 acres or less. Corporations and other owners of enormous acreage in the valley fought these rules and tried to get California to seize control of the project even though the federal government was forced to build it. Although there were plenty of smaller farms in the valley, 1935 statistics showed that only 10 percent of the farmers produced more than 50 percent of the crops and employed about three-fourths of the valley workforce.

It was 1951 when California finally abandoned its efforts to control the Central Valley Project (CVP). This, after owners of the larger spreads had identified enough loopholes to circumvent their limitations. Additionally, the U.S. Bureau of Reclamation agreed to send excess power to PG&E, which PG&E sold to its customers for big profits.

The CVP was completed by the U.S. Bureau of Reclamation during the struggle for control between the state and the federal government. Construction began in 1937. The Contra Costa Canal was built in the 1940s to divert water from the western Delta to Martinez Reservoir. In 1944, power was being sold from the new Shasta Dam and Lake. By 1951, water finally flowed from 600-foot high Shasta Dam hundreds of miles south to the Delta-Mendota Canal and the San Joaquin Valley.

Today, the Central Valley Project includes an enormous water transfer system, supplying irrigation water throughout the Sacramento and San Joaquin Valleys. It includes Shasta and Keswick Dams on the Sacramento River, Folsom Dam on the American River, New Melones Dam on the Stanislaus River, and the Friant Dam on the San Joaquin River. Great canals carry water from these reservoirs. They include the Tehama-Colusa Canal along the west side of the Sacramento Valley. The Delta Cross Channel and Contra Costa Canal were designed for Delta farmers and also to stop saltwater intrusion as water flows south through the Delta. The Delta-Mendota Canal moves the water south from the Delta along the west side of the upper San Joaquin Valley. Then, the Madera Canal and the Friant-Kern Canal transport water farther south, but along the east side of the lower San Joaquin Valley.

This federal project solved many of the valley's water problems identified earlier in the century. Ranked as another of the world's great water projects, it also plays a vital role in making the Central Valley one of the planet's most productive agricultural regions.

Another controversy raged into the late 1990s when federal courts ordered that some water be returned to the dried-up San Joaquin River bed downstream of the Friant Dam. Groups including the Friant Water Users Authority and more than 15,000 farmers between Fresno and Bakersfield served by the project protested and con-

Accessible Shasta Lake is a visible symbol of water diversion projects that start in northern California.

tinued to fight the decision. Their opponents celebrated the courts' recognition of endangered salmon and downstream fisheries that were destroyed by massive water diversions. Diverse groups with competing interests will continue to make water history in California into the twenty-first century.

California Water Project

Even during construction of the Central Valley Project, California continued to aggressively search for new sources of water for its growing population and agricultural industry. Corporate farmers' concerns about the CVP's 160-acre limitation and an exploding population fueled efforts to build new water projects controlled by the state. Specifically, numerous big landowners of hundreds of thousands of irrigable acres in the San Joaquin Valley included oil companies, Southern Pacific, and the Kern County Land Company. Meanwhile, California's population increased by more than 3.5 million during the 1940s and would increase by half a million per year during much of the 1950s. It is no surprise that, especially in the Central Valley, overdrafting and pollution of groundwater, and land subsidence became major problems.

Toward California's Last Major Water Project

In response to such problems, the new State Water Resources Control Board and State Engineer A. D. Edmonston proposed yet another enormous water project in 1945. It would begin at a new Oroville Dam on the Feather River and distribute water to customers all the way from the Sacramento Valley to the Delta and Bay Area, then to the San Joaquin Valley and southern California coastal communities. In 1951, the state legislature appropriated money to study this 750-mile-long project that was renamed the California Water Project. After

floods ravaged central and northern California in 1955–1956, the legislature appropriated $25 million to begin a newly refined California Water Project. However, there were many obstacles to what would be California's last major water project of the twentieth century.

First, the California Department of Water Resources had to be created in 1956 to combine and organize the efforts of all the various state departments that would be involved. Second, Californians began to argue about who would get the water and how it would be delivered. Northern Californians questioned if southern California should be allowed to move even more water south. Even southern California's MWD held its support until the last minute, trying to guarantee as much water delivery as possible.

All of this came to a head in 1959 when the State Water Resources Development Bond Act (the Burns-Porter Act) first passed the state legislature and then was ratified by only a 174,000-vote margin in the 1960 general election. Though it failed miserably in northern California, powerful political and economic support from the thirsty south and San Joaquin Valley farmers carried it. It was a huge victory for Governor Edmund G. (Pat) Brown, who put his political reputation on the line as an aggressive proponent of the project.

The resulting bonds totalling $1.75 billion were sold between 1964 and 1972 to build yet another giant project to divert and control water within the Feather River watershed. The water would be sent to areas north and south of the San Francisco Bay, the San Joaquin Valley, and to southern California. Unlike the CVP, this project would be controlled by the state.

Who Pays and Who Benefits?

The California Water Project fulfilled its first contracts by delivering water between 1962 and 1973. Alameda County received the project's first water in 1962; by 1968, its water flowed to the San Joaquin Valley. By 1971, it flowed over the Tehachapis and into southern California. It turned out that southern California got the bulk of water (about 2.5 maf per year, 2 maf per year going to the MWD), while the San Joaquin Valley received about 1.3 maf per year.

Though water users were to pay about 80 percent of the project's costs and 13 percent was to be paid from electricity generation, federal taxpayers subsidized much of the State Water Project deliveries. Furthermore, heavy subsidies allow many irrigators to pay only a small portion compared to their use. Many valley farmers used these special subsidies to expand irrigated areas, instead of slowing their groundwater pumping. Because the project was paying for itself by the 1970s, and 80 percent of the costs are paid by water users, urban users still must bear the higher rates. Farmers continue to argue that they cannot compete to produce crops without the subsidies, that many California farms would disappear without the subsidies, and that farms are good for the California economy. Critics argue that free market water prices would simply force many farmers to conserve water or to grow crops which require less water or have higher market values.

Today, California's State Water Project is also ranked as one of the world's largest. After water is distributed around the Feather River and Bay Area, its California Aqueduct carries water through the San Joaquin Valley and south. In southern California, it splits to a west branch and pours water into Castaic Lake. Its east branch continues far to the south, filling Lake Perris. From these sources, water is delivered to southern California coastal communities south to the Mexican border and even into inland valleys and the Coachella Valley.

Water from a Variety of Sources

A host of smaller state and federal projects continue to complement the State Water Project and other water projects within California. In 1964, water destined to flow into the Pacific from northwest California's Trinity River was diverted into Clair Engle and Lewiston Lakes, then through a 17-mile tunnel through the Trinity Mountains, into Whiskeytown Lake and finally into the Sacramento River. There have also been new proposals from the Army Corps of Engineers and others to divert still more water from northwest rivers and sources even more distant.

However, by the 1970s, questions about costs, priorities, water distribution, and environmental degradation soured Californians' enthusiasm for new water projects. These recent developments will be covered later in this chapter. Consequently, as California's political and economic climate forced this new shift in its water policies, the state had built its last major water project of the twentieth century; even this California Water Project would not be expanded or completed as originally planned.

Meanwhile, the water used by any Californian could come from a variety of sources that may change by the month or year, depending on which source of water is more abundant in this complicated juggling game of water distribution. For instance, California in the late 1990s had to cut its use of Colorado River water by nearly 1 maf because Arizona began taking its "fair share" for its Central Arizona Project. This is serious business because the Colorado River was the major source of water for southern California. The MWD is now making up for its nearly 700,000 acre-feet per year cut by switching to other sources, such as the California Department of Water Resources and the California Water Project. Local communities must sometimes decide on how much of their cheaper groundwater can safely be pumped without **overdrafting**, as they mix this groundwater with more expensive sources from the water projects.

Groundwater for California's People

Though there are more than 800 maf of groundwater reserves below California, less than 140 maf are accessible and usable (see Figure 6.2). Groundwater supplies about 40 percent of the state's water, but that percentage varies by region and is much higher during periods of drought. Though southern California also relies on aquifers for about 40 percent of its water, Orange County uses about 70 percent groundwater, and the percentage is even higher for parts of Riverside and San Bernardino Counties.

During normal years, Californians **overdraft** about 2 maf of water out of their more than 100 maf of accessible, usable reserves. This overdrafting increases dramatically during drought years to up to 10 maf per year, and it decreases during wet years, when less groundwater is required and groundwater basins are recharged. During the drought year of 1977, more than 20,000 new wells were drilled in the state. During that year, 9,000 of those wells were drilled in the San Joaquin Valley, where farmers rely on aquifers for nearly 40 percent of their water supply.

Overdrafting in the San Joaquin Valley

The number of wells pumping water in the San Joaquin Valley grew from just below 600 in 1906, to 5,000 in 1910, to 11,000 in 1920, to more than 23,000 in 1930. By 1940, groundwater accounted for most of the water used in the San Joaquin Valley, and there were more than 35,000 wells pumping 6 maf of groundwater before 1950. By this time, some groundwater tables had dropped three to four times lower than their original fifty feet within just twenty years.

Overdrafting, pollution of groundwater, and ground subsidence had become problems throughout California,

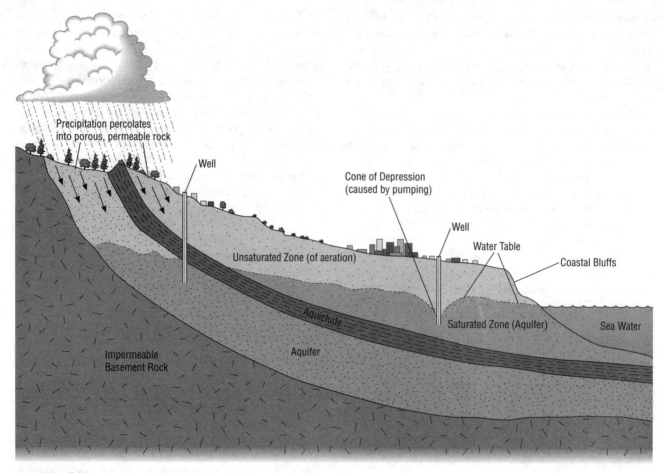

FIGURE 6.2
Groundwater. Abundant groundwater once accumulated in aquifers below the state's inland valleys and coastal basins as shown in the diagram. Diverse agricultural and urban interests now compete for groundwater that is too often overdrafted or polluted.

but nowhere were they as serious as the San Joaquin Valley. Ominous warnings of overdrafting included surface damage where entire aquifers in the western sections of the valley were collapsing and being destroyed by subsidence of up to 30 feet. By 1980, a cumulative total of more than 17 maf of water had been overdrafted from the southern San Joaquin Valley alone. Today, nearly three-fourths of the state's overdrafting (up to 1.5 maf) occurs in the San Joaquin Valley during normal years.

Who Owns Groundwater?

A simple dilemma continues in the San Joaquin Valley and across much of California—overdrafting groundwater is cheaper in the short-term than purchasing more expensive surface water; but, in the long-term, groundwater sources will be depleted. These problems have been exacerbated by a history of legislation and court rulings that have kept California in a state of groundwater policy chaos. After mixing correlative rights, appropria-

tion, and prescription into rulings on groundwater conflicts, the state has settled on "mutual prescription." This is supposed to limit all users to safe yields, or reasonable use of shared aquifers. Conflicts continue over how to define these terms for each aquifer.

This is why, to head off future competition to exploit shared groundwater reservoirs, the state's groundwater policy is to encourage local management programs for connected groundwater basins. Cooperation is required between all parties who use and share groundwater reservoirs to eliminate overdrafting, subsidence, and pollution of these resources. Safe yields must be established across the state to limit pumping to the long-term rates of recharge. If individual communities and districts begin competing for water in these shared aquifers, instead of planning ahead and cooperating to take safe yields, such water resources will be quickly depleted.

One obvious example of groundwater chaos is the water war that flared up during the 1990s in Monterey County and the Salinas Valley. By 1998, overdrafting had drawn saltwater into wells up to six miles inland. Farmers and municipalities closer to the coast had done their share of overdrafting, but farmers pumping groundwater many miles upstream in the southern Salinas Valley were also responsible for taking groundwater that could increase the hydraulic pressure that pushes saltwater toward the sea where it belongs. Who would restore the aquifer, and who would pay for it? Some still publicly pondered whether there was any problem at all as the state water board threatened to intervene in another classic battle over water. The controversy continued into the twenty-first century.

Meanwhile, holding basins continue to serve as sources for more groundwater. Where surface flows can be ponded to soak into porous sediment, groundwater basins are recharged. These efforts have proven quite successful even on the fringe of urban areas (such as the San Gabriel Valley), where mountain streams (such as the San Gabriel River) pour into flood basins. Partially treated water can also be recycled into and further cleansed within these groundwater reservoirs as they are recharged.

Current Events and the Water Future

In 1967, the U.S. Army Corps of Engineers proposed damming the Eel River so that water could be diverted through a tunnel to the Sacramento Valley into the California Water Project. Facing high costs and environmental concerns, those plans evaporated by 1971. Instead, by the early 1970s, more water was being released into the Delta to restore water quality for fish, wildlife, and the San Francisco Bay system, while the California Wild and Scenic Rivers Act was established to protect wild rivers on the north coast. Californians were beginning to change their views on water policy, and projects such as the Peripheral Canal would be caught in this political shift. When the Peripheral Canal was proposed to divert more water from the Delta toward the south, opponents built a powerful coalition; California water policy would never be the same.

The Peripheral Canal

Plans for the Peripheral Canal were released in 1965; it became a controversial issue that would finally be decided by California voters nearly two decades later. It included a 43-mile long, 30-foot deep, 400-foot wide canal that would curve around the east side of the Delta to divert fresh water south to the pumping plants near Tracy. Advocates claimed that for $179 million, 7.8 maf per year could be added to the state's water projects, while more controlled release of water into the Delta would ease the saltwater intrusion problem. Critics argued that northern California was already losing enough water to the south. They claimed that the system was too complicated, would cost far more than first estimated, and would ruin Delta farms and Delta and Bay ecosystems by seriously compromising the quality of water without any safeguards.

After gaining support from former Governors Pat Brown and Ronald Reagan, the Peripheral Canal Bill was passed by the State Senate and Assembly in 1980. Representatives from the San Joaquin Valley and southern California had the political power to push it through against the objections of almost all northern California interests. Fearing the political clout of the San Joaquin Valley farmers and southern California voters, Governor Jerry Brown signed it on July 18, 1980. However, the political winds had already shifted in California as citizens gained enough signatures to force a public vote that would take place in June, 1982, to decide the fate of the Peripheral Canal.

Opponents' ammunition included the fact that while project costs were skyrocketing to $2.5 billion, some enormous San Joaquin Valley farms were already receiving water subsidies of more than $400 per acre each year. Opponents also successfully revived and enhanced old concerns that southern valley farmers and southern California cities were already stealing enough water from northern California. Support from powerful San Joaquin Valley farmers was not enough to counter the united opposition from virtually all of northern California; voters rejected the Peripheral Canal. In Marin County, the vote was 32 to 1, and in San Francisco, it was 21 to 1 against the project.

Taxpayers, who had supported so many costly water projects since the turn of the century, had lost their enthusiasm for new ventures. Defeat of the Peripheral Canal signalled that those who saw new massive water projects as too costly to our economy and environment had become the majority.

As if to emphasize the complexity of these issues, by the late 1990s, a new (or perhaps not so new) scheme emerged to control the flow of water into the Delta. The stated goal was to simultaneously protect the quality of water in the Delta and bay and deliver more water to thirsty California farmers and cities.

Some critics claimed it couldn't be done without more destruction to water quality, fish, and the environment. They called it Peripheral Canal II and demanded greater participation in the decision making. Consequently, this time environmental groups, farmers, water agencies, and other officials tried to design a compromise project. It was decided that during the early years of the twenty-first century, California's governor and the U.S. Secretary of State would hammer out a plan that would consider all interests.

Why has the Delta become such a focal point for water issues? It may be the best example of competing interests putting the greatest pressure on limited water supplies.

POLLUTION AND WATER QUALITY

While Californians battle over limited water supplies, we are losing millions of acre-feet to **pollution**. Various impurities such as gases, dissolved solids and minerals, and organic materials are naturally incorporated into any California water source. However, pollutants such as petroleum products and additional organic matter decrease the quality and usefulness of water. Dangerous contaminants include organisms such as bacteria, viruses, protozoa, and worms, and toxins such as radioactive substances, mercury, and heavy metals. Though California water agencies have the technology to accurately measure these substances and are required by law to make their results public, Californians debate what quantities are safe and acceptable in our water supplies. The list of water quality problems has, as expected, skyrocketed along with California's population and demand for water. The loss of valuable water supplies, health hazards due to pollution, and programs to clean polluted water have cost California citizens and businesses billions of dollars.

Water Pollution in Rural Areas

One of the first and most obvious problems was increased suspended sediment from accelerated rates of erosion. This is more than a clarity problem in California. Though the devastating erosion caused by hydraulic mining during the gold rush has ceased, sediment yield in California drainages plowed, logged, or cleared for construction has been known to increase more than ten times, choking rivers, streams, and lakes with mud. Dissolved solids, such as salts, harden the water, especially when water flows great distances and drains regions where there are farming, mining, or chemical processing activities. Dangerous heavy metals may also leach into the water supply from industrial and urban areas. Some of the hundreds of millions of pounds of herbicides and pesticides used in industry, agriculture, and gardens in California also gradually leak into our water supplies.

People in the Central Valley and Delta have wrestled with these problems for years. High levels of toxic chemicals from fertilizers and pesticides have especially contaminated agricultural runoff in the southern San Joaquin Valley, particularly where there is poor natural drainage. During the 1980s, bird deformities and dead waterfowl in the Kesterson National Wildlife Refuge near Los Banos were blamed on accumulations of pollutants such as selenium.

Officials considered closing the refuge and allowing the pollutants to continue to accumulate (not popular with environmentalists), blocking runoff from the contaminating farms (opposed by local farmers), or covering the contaminated soil with dirt. Some smaller ponds in the region are so polluted, health experts warn of dangers in consuming their birds and fish. This pollution has also infiltrated and polluted many valley aquifers. The thirty-three wells closed in the Fresno area in the late 1980s alone are only examples of the thousands of wells contaminated beyond use throughout California. Ironically, it seems that the people who need water most are also most responsible for contaminating their own groundwater sources.

Pollution in Urban Water Supplies

In 1979, carcinogens from business and industry were found in the enormous 200-square-mile aquifer that supplies the San Gabriel Valley with most of its water. More than 25 percent of the valley's four-hundred wells were eventually closed, while cleaning the aquifer was estimated to take decades and cost more than $1 billion. More than 40 percent of Los Angeles, 17 percent of San Bernardino, and 13 percent of Riverside Counties' wells have been contaminated. It is estimated that nearly 50 percent of the groundwater in the Santa Ana River Basin will be undrinkable by 2015. This is a vital source not only for Orange County, but also for the San Bernardino and Riverside areas.

The effects on smaller communities can be very costly, such as when Santa Monica was forced to close most of its wells during the 1990s. A gasoline additive, methyl tertiary butyl ether (MTBE), appeared in the groundwater Santa Monica takes from the aquifer below the west side of Los Angeles. When wells closed, all of

The Delta

The Sacramento-San Joaquin Delta represents less than 1 percent of California, but accepts about 40 percent of the state's runoff along more than 700 miles of twisted, interconnected waterways. Local farmers grow more than $300 million of crops each year on more than sixty islands, many below sea level and still subsiding. Residents and visitors take advantage of recreational opportunities in these scenic waterways, such as boating, hunting, fishing, birding, and viewing other wildlife. Millions of waterfowl migrate along the Pacific Flyway and stop in the Delta or stay for the winter, while striped bass and salmon swim from the ocean upstream to spawn in the fresh water.

Additionally, about two-thirds of Californians get at least some water which, instead of flowing into the Delta and bay, is diverted to San Francisco Bay communities or to the Central Valley and southern California. This is done through the Central Valley Project or California Wa-

POLLUTION AND WATER QUALITY *continued*

these southern California communities were forced to pay for imported water which is four to six times more expensive than groundwater. Extensive research into the problem finally led to negotiated settlements with the polluting oil companies. Water users were partially compensated, and efforts were made to clean up the MTBE pollutants.

Rare, but more spectacular, chemical accidents and spills have temporarily closed California waterways and shorelines to public use. Each accident has enormous short-term costs, while long-term costs are always difficult to estimate.

The chemical quality of some California waterways has also suffered from excess nutrients such as nitrogen carried from irrigation, industrial waste, and sewage treatment plants. These nutrients cause algae blooms and accelerated growth of other organisms which eventually lead to the depletion of dissolved oxygen, especially in warmer, more stagnant waters. Such eutrophication can destroy fish and other organisms that rely on oxygen for survival. San Francisco Bay suffered from such conditions during the 1960s until the quality of runoff into the bay improved.

Wild swings in acidity are not usually as common in California waterways as in northeastern sections of the country where acid rain was once a greater problem.

An ominous pattern of dangerous water pollution followed California's dramatic development into the 1940s. Contaminated runoff and chemical and petroleum spills caused more frequent quarantines on eating shellfish, the closing of large stretches of beaches, and the pollution of groundwater reservoirs. San Francisco and San Diego once sent minimally treated to untreated sewage into surrounding waters. San Diego Bay was once quarantined by the State Health Department.

By the late 1940s and into the 1950s, new state and federal laws finally had enough teeth to begin to discourage many polluters, and money was made available to assist research and antipollution programs that would improve future water quality. These efforts had to be fortified in the 1960s and 1970s with the rapid growth of California's population and industries. Well into the 1970s, San Francisco's overtaxed system sent tons of raw sewage directly into the ocean during heavy rainstorms.

From Large to Small Polluters

Past efforts to control water pollution often focused on sewage and other large, "point source" polluters. It is hoped that all future California sewage will experience primary treatment (removal of solids, trash, and oils in screens and settling ponds) and secondary treatment (where aeration and microorganisms speed the breakdown of chemical and biological impurities, and chlorine or other chemicals are added to kill bacteria). However, the removal of suspended material and pathogens and preliminary chemical treatment does not produce safe water. This is achieved in a third step of treatment that removes viruses and disinfects the water for reclaimed uses and also removes excess nutrients to fight eutrophication. We finally have a new source of water! The problem with this ideal attack on sewage and other point-source pollution is money. Even in the twenty-first century, some Californians still refuse to pay the costs necessary to chemically treat and sterilize their own wastes so that new sources of water can be delivered to the state.

The problem is even greater for the attack on non-point sources. These pollutants come from smaller farms, mining and logging industries, and urban runoff. A look at the tons of garbage washed from Los Angeles' streets onto Santa Monica Bay's beaches after the first heavy rain of the season illustrates the problem. This is more than an aesthetic and health problem. It not only cuts into the quality of California living environments, but it leaves a negative impression with tourists who spend billions of dollars visiting California.

It will require exceptional cooperation between public and private sectors to convince so many Californians that their individual polluting activities have at least indirect negative impacts on everyone. California is the perfect setting where these interests could, and should, be merged with successful results.

ter Project. Annual high-water flows, which once flushed out the Delta and bay and restored healthy natural habitats, have been diverted, and saltwater intrusion has become a problem. So many private and public interests and local, regional, state, and federal agencies must cooperate and compromise to conserve the limited water that must be shared.

Diking and filling of the Delta started in 1850 and continued into the mid-1960s. By then, the California Water Project was making its impact there because the Delta is the pivotal point where water stored from northern rivers is diverted to southern California. One specific pivotal point is where Delta waters are drawn south toward the Clifton Court Forebay, where sediment is allowed to settle out. The water is then pumped up about 200 feet at the Harvey O. Banks Delta Pumping Plant, where it will be sent south to be further pumped into the California Aqueduct.

Some of the Delta water must be first allowed to flow into the Suisun Marsh, toward the west Delta and the bay.

Where the Delta ends and the bay begins is not clear in this view of water channels, salt ponds, and housing projects. The answer is somewhere around the nearby Carquinez Strait, depending on tides and river discharge.

This is the largest remaining brackish marshland on the west coast. A delicate balance must be maintained between fresh and saltwater for wildlife survival and for the general health of the Delta and bay. To accomplish this, salinity control gates have been built at the entrance to Suisun Marsh to let fresh water flow west during high runoff and low tide; they are then closed to block the intrusion of saltwater during high tides and low freshwater flows.

Delta water issues include the competition with the Central Valley Water Project allocations. There are also the many islands with productive farmland that continue to subside well below sea level, protected from floods only by aging levees. It may have become too costly to reclaim many of these islands if the levees ever fail. And, numerous residential developments, such as Discovery Bay, encroaching into the Delta from East Bay suburbs have swelled the population to about 300,000. The balancing act to satisfy so many competing interests in the Delta is getting more and more complex. There is also that nagging problem of pollution not only from salt, but selenium and other contaminants from agricultural and industrial discharges into the Delta.

The American River and Auburn Dam

Another stellar example of struggles resulting from increasing pressures on California's water systems is the continuing controversy concerning flood control and water supplies along the American River. Flood control standards usually call for planning to handle at least a 100-year flood for urban areas and a 10-year flood for farmlands. The basin along the American River that extends from the base of the Sierra Nevada through Sacramento was far more vulnerable to flooding before Folsom Dam was completed in 1955.

The dam was ready in the nick of time. Folsom Reservoir was expected to fill within about three years, but the entire reservoir filled to its capacity of about 1 maf within just seventy-two hours during a flood in 1955. The stored water is used during summer drought. Although the dam has saved much of Sacramento and the basin below the dam from disastrous flooding since its construction, the basin is now considered to be protected from only a 63-year flood.

Consequently, the Auburn Dam was proposed as another multipurpose dam along the American River in 1965. The 508-foot dam would be built just below the confluence of the North and Middle Forks of the American River and would flood more than 5,000 acres in the Auburn Recreation Area 35 miles northeast of Sacramento. Like its predecessor, the Folsom, it was originally planned to supply stored water during summer's drought and enhance flood control during winter and spring runoff. But, after the site was cleared and prepared for the new dam in 1967, its construction was held up for years by safety and environmental concerns. When an unexpected 5.7 earthquake rocked the area ten years later, the design had to be changed to address those safety issues.

Then, the 1980s–1990s federal budget cuts stopped the $1 billion project, in which three-fourths of the cost was to be paid by the federal government and the rest covered by state and local taxpayers. Because it is recognized that the American River has the potential of carrying five times the amount of floodwater as the Sacramento River and because it funnels into a basin whose population has recently grown to more than 400,000 people, a compromise must be reached.

Many options are being considered. More flood control could be accommodated at Folsom Lake, but at the expense of water that otherwise would have been stored for summer irrigation. Folsom's flood gates could be lowered on the dam to increase flood storage capacity in the reservoir, and higher levees could be built downstream. Or, instead of another large, multipurpose dam, a smaller flood control detention dam, or "dry dam," could hold water only during brief periods of flooding.

On June 27, 1996, the U.S. House Transportation and Infrastructure Committee once again killed the project, but approved $57 million to fortify the existing levees in the system. This was clearly not the compromise that disparate groups could live with, and proponents vowed to push the issue again in the coming years. Meanwhile, more developments in the floodplain are creating a greater flood threat, while development and other land uses upstream will deliver floodwaters more quickly to the river system in the coming years.

Some federal and even state taxpayers are asking why they should help pay to protect the hundreds of thousands of people who continue to settle in a basin notorious for its disastrous floods. Many fiscally conservative groups are forming unlikely coalitions with environmental organizations who argue that there are already too few rivers and riparian environments remaining in California to save. They also argue that this project will support further development of the floodplain below. All of this led some lawmakers, in June of 1996, to proclaim, "The day of big multipurpose dam projects is over."

Dam opponents across the state continue to accumulate data to back their arguments. Such data often include hazards posed by what scientists call reservoir-induced seismicity, earthquakes that can affect some areas (such as at Oroville) after dams are built and reservoirs are filled.

Efficiency and Conservation

Many citizens have launched other campaigns to save portions of those few wild rivers remaining in California. By the mid-1980s, federal programs protected portions of seven California rivers, including the American, Eel, Feather, Klamath, Smith, Trinity, and Tuolomne Rivers. In 1989, California included portions of seven rivers in its wild and scenic system. These are further examples of the new era of water management, **efficiency, and conservation** ushered into California during the 1970s that continue in the twenty-first century. Modern water conservation and efficiency programs have already saved California taxpayers billions of dollars that would have been thrown into the construction of new projects. And, this "new source" of water has also kept water prices from skyrocketing above what many Californians consider to be already high rates.

Numerous businesses, schools, and municipalities have already proven that water use can be cut more than 50 percent from previous wasteful practices without sacrifice. Simple retrofitting of existing water systems and changing landscaping and irrigation methods has made the difference. Meanwhile, some of California's remaining wild rivers and pristine water ecosystems have been at least temporarily spared from development and de-

struction. Trends in growth and technology and Californians' willingness to use that technology will dictate the future of California's waterscapes.

As the host of issues still being debated includes who gets water and at what cost, California's greatest water users—its farmers—can also liberate the greatest sources of "new water supplies" by making their diversion, delivery, and irrigation systems more efficient. In the past, inexpensive water supplies provided California farmers the stability to compete with rain-fed agriculture from other states and countries. Now these farmers must be expected to invest in water efficiency and conservation programs that will lead to a stable water future for the entire state.

Water Projects Shape Landscapes

Today, California continues to manage some of the greatest water diversion and storage projects in the world. There are more dams and reservoirs (more than 1,300) than any other state. Most are designed to control flooding during peak flows and then gradually release water from supplies maintained year-round. However, these projects often have unwanted consequences. Sediment accumulation in calm waters behind dams decreases the long-term carrying capacity of California reservoirs, and erosion of sediment-starved channels and beaches downstream from these dams is a recurring problem throughout the state.

Some of the dams are earth and rock fill, and must be maintained and protected from percolation and erosion damage. Hydraulic-fill dams are usually more reliable because they are constructed with layers of sorted materials. Most impressive are California's giant concrete dams, built as arches to direct reservoir water pressures toward natural bedrock walls. These monuments to California's changing human populations and activities have made their own remarkable changes in California's landscapes.

Swimming, surfing, boating, water skiing, steelhead fishing on the north coast and trout fishing in the Sierra Nevada are some of the major reasons why more than 60 percent of Californians' recreational activities involve use of the state's waterways. The percentage is even higher if the number of birders, campers, picnickers, and hikers who follow California's water courses is included. Since the 1940s, Californians gained leisure time and mobility. Artificial water environments replaced natural waterways, and millions of dollars have been spent by local governments and state agencies to improve water recreational opportunities. Water for recreation has become big business in California. Meanwhile, there is growing conflict between recreational users and those who want water projects for more "traditional" uses.

Californians have learned how these water projects can change cultural, economic, and political landscapes,

WATER RIGHTS AND POLICY

Early American settlers in California should have paid more attention to earlier Spanish water policies. The Spanish were accustomed to developing dry lands; they anticipated water shortages, and they planned for them. In contrast, many early Americans came from climates where excess water had to be drained and pushed aside. They were not as comfortable dealing with California's water shortages and its long, dry summers. This inexperience contributed to more than a century of bitter disputes and debates about water rights and distribution, debates that continue to this day. The problems were also fueled by an early sense of rugged individualism that drove many toward private monopoly of land and water for profit, resulting in flood control, irrigation, and reclamation chaos.

Today, California has the world's largest and most complicated water projects, and it receives 40 percent more federal dollars than any other state to operate those projects. California landowners do not own the water, but they can own the rights to use it. More than 3,700 agencies have been established in the state (many by legislative acts) with authority to supply, deliver, use, and treat water. Nearly 1,000 of these are community, county, and state water utility districts, and many cover very small areas and only have a few members. They include reclamation districts from the 1860s, irrigation districts from the Wright Act of 1887, and the municipal and county districts that have proliferated since the early 1900s.

To qualify as a voting member, some districts require land ownership, so corporate land owners are frequently in control. (About four corporations have traditionally controlled the Westland Water District, while four corporations also controlled nearly 85 percent of Tulare Lake Basin farms.) Examples of other powerful agencies abound; the Kern County Water District and the Metropolitan Water District are examples. Regardless of size, each water agency and individual has restricted rights based on water laws that have helped shape California's cultural, economic, and political landscapes.

Riparian rights are claimed by those who own land bordering any stream or other water course. Any responsible use which first benefited the riparian landowner is considered ahead of others. However, most of California's water is distributed, or appropriated, away to lands not adjacent to the water source. This is allowed if the water was not first used by riparian owners and if the water is also used for a reasonable purpose. This appropriation doctrine allows those who first reasonably use the water the first right to divert it. When the courts eventually settled on this balance between riparian users and appropriators, it was known as the California Doctrine. Battles over what is "reasonable" use and "who was first" have dominated recent California water law. These are now the key issues to

be determined during conflicts. With so much at stake, courts have dealt with conflict and controversy over competing uses since California became a state.

It is clear that the California Doctrine and other state mandates have long since taken control of what was once a more chaotic water policy. The state requires all water uses to be reasonable for the beneficial use of the land, and such uses must be for the general welfare and for the public interest. Because most uses of California water, especially appropriated water, must be considered "public uses," they are subject to state control.

Perhaps the intended result in a growing state has been the evolution of water laws away from technicalities and toward a more balanced use of water based on social and economic realities. By necessity, area-wide resource planning began eclipsing individual water rights, and public and municipal corporations wrestled control away from private owners and investors. As enormous cities, such as Los Angeles and San Diego, gobbled up more land, they also took vital water rights away from local owners.

This trend spread to the use of precious groundwater, when the California Supreme Court's Rule of Correlative Rights restricted owners only to groundwater below their land. When overdrafting and saltwater intrusion threatened to ruin such groundwater reservoirs as in the western Los Angeles Basin, municipalities were forced to agree on "mutual prescription" to restrict their pumping to only a "safe" amount of water. By the late 1990s, saltwater intrusion into Monterey County and the Salinas Valley became a critical problem. The State Water Resources Control Board threatened to intervene and allocate water if the county failed to find ways to stop saltwater that had been drawn inland up to six miles by overdrafting.

What is "safe" and how do we protect our aquifers from those who would deplete them? Just as individuals once engaged in chaotic local battles over water, so do regional and local governments now clash over these rights, especially regarding groundwater. It is hoped that cooperative politics and wise water management policies are replacing these costly conflicts. With so many users, complicated negotiations between powerful private and public interests and government agencies are often necessary to produce a modern water management program. Many of these groups and alliances bring a wide range of interests to each debate.

Today, the State Water Resources Control Board reviews applications and issues water-use permits, hopefully in the name of fairness and future prosperity rather than power politics. However, the powerful members of the board are appointed by the governor and confirmed by the state legislature. Across California's political spectrum, it is acknowledged that water policy decisions are too often controlled by money and politics.

and they have witnessed their obvious physical impacts. This is why, since the 1950s and 1960s, when officials and planners consider the feasibility of new projects (such as diverting water from the Colombia and Snake Rivers and other Pacific Northwest sources), a series of important issues are addressed. New projects must be economically justified and financially feasible, and they must include sound engineering. They also must be environmentally sound and operate efficiently. Most of California's most efficient storage and development sites have already been claimed. Consequently, the billions of dollars and extended time periods required, modern seismic and other safety concerns, and environmental constraints have become common roadblocks for new projects.

Future Technologies

Is it possible that future technology will bring new water supplies to the state? In places like Catalina Island and the mothballed plant in Santa Barbara, desalinization of sea water is a proven technology. But, the cost of such water is still more than double the cost of water from California's diversion projects. This is why Santa Barbara officials chose to connect to California's water projects and not use its desalinization plant into the twenty-first century.

Future improvements in long-range forecasting of precipitation may help us plan ahead. There is continued success with cloud seeding, especially in the Sierra Nevada, but who will claim responsibility if a catastrophic flood follows such experiments or if farmers and ranchers in Nevada claim that California is stealing water destined for their state? Until we learn more, cloud seeding could lead us down a dangerous road to litigation.

With nearly nine-hundred wastewater treatment facilities in the state, only about 10 percent are designed to treat water for reuse for irrigation and groundwater recharge. Reclaimed water should and will become more available as the number of wastewater reclamation plants grows into the twenty-first century. There are many other practical examples of how the efficient management of existing projects and the water they supply continue to provide the most promising new sources of water for California's future.

Future Allocation of Water

Agriculture accounts for about 80 percent of California's water consumption; this leaves less than 20 percent for the more than 80 percent of Californians who live in urban areas. Most of this urban use (about two-thirds) is consumed in homes, particularly by single family residences with lawns and gardens, and by multi-family residences indoors. Industry is a distant second, using water for steam, cooling equipment, and sanitation; petroleum

refineries, smelters, chemical plants, pulp mills, and food processors such as canneries also require large volumes of water. Commercial users are a distant third on the urban list; they include restaurants, car washes, laundries, and water for landscaping. A much smaller proportion is used by government for landscaping parks, fire fighting, sanitation, and other activities.

The road to equitable distribution and pricing of California water continues to be rutted with historical and geographical problems. Regulation of this utility is necessary because water is a monopoly, and users are restricted to whatever is available in their geographic region. Pre-existing water rights, subsidies, and political clout often determine who gets the water and at what price. Many Californians, especially farmers, argue that California's economy can only grow when water supplies are high and costs low.

As outdated laws and pricing programs often continue to discourage conservation, Californians are asking some important questions. Should we continue traditional subsidy programs to farmers that can total up to $1,100 per acre for CVP water? Can we afford to use about one-half of all agricultural water to grow livestock? The very subsidies that discourage more efficient use of water are paid by federal and state taxes, hydroelectric sales, and higher urban water bills. (In 1990, growers were paying between $2.50–$19.31 per acre-foot for CVP water and $22–$47 per acre-foot for State Water Project water. The MWD was paying $233 per acre-foot for the same untreated water. However, agriculture accounts for only about 2.5 percent of California's modern economy.)

Off the farm, more equitable water rates are often set with break points, or signals, to encourage efficient use in urban areas. Basic meter fees are shared by every customer in the same class to pay capital or fixed costs for maintenance of the water delivery infrastructure. Any additional commodity or marginal costs include the additional purchases, pumping, energy, laboratory work, and other efforts required to deliver the water. In communities throughout California, two- or three-tier pricing systems have successfully regulated water use because customers who consume above certain breaking points automatically pay more for each additional unit of water. This also requires users who exhaust water sources and place the greatest burden on the system to pay the highest price. When such pricing systems become more widespread on California farms, farmers will be forced to switch to more water efficient irrigation systems and crops.

There are too many examples of how much water Californians unnecessarily waste and could save. Estimates in 1990 showed that the MWD could save about 100,000 acre-feet per year by lining channels, fixing leaks, and making other repairs. The Imperial Irrigation District had preventable losses of up to 400,000 acre-feet per year. (Will their proposed sales of conserved water to San Diego encourage more efficiency?)

As citizens and policy makers realize that someone must pay, water efficiency programs and conservation efforts become ever more popular methods of finding that "new source" of inexpensive water. California's water future and its waterscapes will be determined by these efforts.

◆ TRANSITION FROM PHYSICAL GEOGRAPHY TO HUMAN GEOGRAPHY

We have reached a transitional stage in our survey of the geography of California. This is an approximate halfway point between the physical geography chapters and the chapters that examine the human geography of the Golden State.

This halfway point in the book is an ideal place to consider the importance of soils that form from many of the processes we have previously reviewed, but that are also vitally important to agriculture and other human activities we are about to review. Appendix A is designed to introduce the reader to some very general concepts related to the distribution of soils in the state.

More lengthy is Appendix B, a survey of coastal landscapes and the processes, cycles, and systems that are changing them. Appendix B is our opportunity to consider the dynamic natural processes and human impacts shaping the California coast before we launch into the sweeping analysis of the state's human geography that is the focus of the last half of this book.

SOME KEY TERMS AND TOPICS

aquifer	groundwater	water colonies
California Doctrine	hydraulic mining	water pollution
drainage basin	lag time	water projects
efficiency and conservation	multipurpose reservoirs	water rights
evapotranspiration	overdrafting	water table
flood control	per capita use	William Mulholland
freshwater environments	water budget	

Additional Key Terms and Topics

hydrologic cycle	porous	water delivery systems
inland drainage	reclamation	water diversions
irrigation	runoff	water history
Native Americans	Spanish Era	water pricing
peak discharge	stream flow	watershed
permeable	water allocation	

California Soils

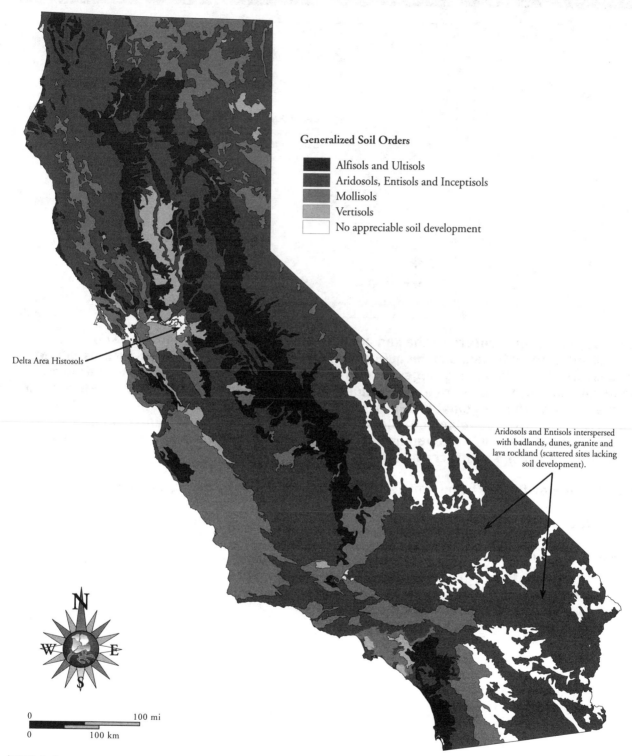

Generalized Soil Orders

- ■ Alfisols and Ultisols
- ■ Aridosols, Entisols and Inceptisols
- ■ Mollisols
- ■ Vertisols
- □ No appreciable soil development

Delta Area Histosols

Aridosols and Entisols interspersed with badlands, dunes, granite and lava rockland (scattered sites lacking soil development).

N
W   E
S

0   100 mi
0   100 km

MAP A.1

Distribution of major soils in California. Grouping soils for such a map is not easy. Alfisols (moderately weathered) and Ultisols (highly weathered, often from Alfisols) are often found below forests. Soils lacking maturity include Aridisols (poorly developed, often in recent desert deposits), Entisols (undeveloped youthful soils), and Inceptisols (weakly developed adolescent soils). Mollisols are often dark, highly organic and found in grasslands, while Vertisols are swelling and cracking clays, and Histosols are organic peat or bog waterlogged soils.

THE SAN JOAQUIN SERIES
California's State Soil

California State Soil
San Joaquin Series

Generalized
Distribution of
San Joaquin
Series

May 1998

The name San Joaquin refers to the San Joaquin Valley which comprises the southern half of the Great Central Valley. San Joaquin soils are used for irrigated crops such as wheat, rice, pasture, figs, almonds, oranges, and grapes. Where the soils exist in their natural, unmodified condition, they are used for livestock grazing and wildlife habitat. More than 500,000 acres of this soil exist in California, mainly on the east side of the Central Valley. With increasing urban development along the east side of the Great Central Valley of California, many areas of San Joaquin soil are being used for the expansion of cities and towns, such as Fresno and Sacramento.

The soil is one of the first four soil series recognized in California by the Division of Soils, USDA 1900. Over the years, the initial concept of the San Joaquin soil has been refined, but it is the oldest, continuously recognized soil series within the State. It is one of California's Benchmark Soils. A profile of it is displayed in the World Soil Museum in Wageningen, Netherlands.

The legislation designating the San Joaquin Soil as the official State Soil of California was the culmination of perseverance and hard work of students and teachers from Martin Luther King Jr. Middle School in Madera, CA, and a partnership formed by the students with the Natural Resources Conservation Service (NRCS), Professional Soil Scientists Association of California (PSSAC), State universities, legislators, and many others.

The San Joaquin series consists of moderately deep, well drained and moderately well drained, very slowly permeable soils underlain by a silica cemented hardpan. They formed in alluvium from dominantly granitic rock. In their natural condition these soils are on old valley terraces with a hummocky topography locally known as "hogwallow" microrelief. Slopes range from 0 to 9 percent.

Setting

The San Joaquin soils are on hummocky, nearly level to undulating terraces. They formed in Pleistocene-age alluvium, derived from glacial and stream action, carried and deposited by streams that originated high in the Sierra Nevada Mountains. Average annual precipitation is about 38 cm (15 in.). Average annual temperature is about 16° C (61° F).

Profile*

Surface: 0 to 6 inches – brown loam
Subsoil: 6 to 16 inches – brown loam
Subsoil Claypan: 16 to 26 inches – brown clay
Subsoil Hardpan: 26 to 48 inches – nearly continuous brown, light brown, and strong brown indurated duripan with more than 90 percent silica and sesquioxide cementation
Subsoil Hardpan: 48 to 60 inches – brown indurated duripan with 70 to 90 percent silica and sesquioxide cementation.

*Textures from lab data reflect slightly different values than field estimates.

Classification

Fine, mixed, active, thermic Abruptic Durixeralfs San Joaquin soils are in the Alfisol soil order. Alfisols are mostly soils of intermediate age which are well developed. The term "Abruptic" indicates an abrupt and pronounced textural clay increase. The term "Durixeralfs" indicates the presence of a duripan (hardpan) and a climate where winters are moist and cool and summers are warm and dry. The term "fine" indicates that the subsoil zone of clay increase averages between 35 and 60 percent clay. The term "mixed" indicates that the mineralogy is not dominated by one type of clay mineral. The term "active" indicates that the ratio of the cation exchange capacity to clay is 0.40 to 0.60. "Thermic" refers to an average annual soil temperature of between 15° to 22° C (59° to 72° F).

Data**

Some Chemical Properties of the San Joaquin Soil

Horizon	Depth Inches	pH	Organic Carbon	CEC meq/100g
Ap	0-6	6.4	.84%	9.8
Bt1	6-10	5.8	.57%	9.8
Bt2	10-16	5.9	.29%	9.8
2Bt3	16-21	6.1	.21%	20.7
2Bt4	21-26	6.6	.19%	21.5
2Bqm1	26-29	7.8	.06%	17.4
2Bqm2	29-48	7.7	.05%	15.4
2Bq	48-60	7.8	.04%	13.3

Some Physical Properties of the San Joaquin Soil

Horizon	Depth Inches	Sand	Silt	Clay	Bulk * Density
Ap	0-6	30.3	56.3	13.4	1.45
Bt1	6-10	30.9	56.0	13.1	1.65
Bt2	10-16	31.9	52.3	15.8	1.68
2Bt3	16-21	28.4	33.8	37.8	1.53
2Bt4	21-26	31.7	31.6	36.7	1.56
2Bqm1	26-29				1.72
2Bqm2	29-48				1.75
2Bq	48-60				1.66

*g/cc at 1/3 bar

** Analysis by the Soil Survey Investigations Staff, NRCS, Lincoln, NE, sample #S83CA-077-042
For additional lab data and analysis procedure contact the USDA, NRCS State Office in Davis, CA

For an official series description of the San Joaquin soil, go to the Official Series Description Data Access Facility, and type 'san joaquin' in the request box.

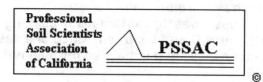

Professional Soil Scientists Association of California   PSSAC ©

Martin Luther King Jr. Middle School, Madera, CA
Cal Poly State University, San Luis Obispo
California State University, Fresno
University of California
USDA Natural Resources Conservation Service

Source: Authors: Kerry Arroues and Steve McShane. Layout/Design: Greg Manifold.

Applying Geographic Concepts to Explore California's Coast

◆ SHORELINE GEOGRAPHY

Among a remarkably rich assemblage of landscapes, the state's cherished and celebrated coastlines may best represent all that is Californian (see Maps B.1 and B.2). An interface where land, atmosphere, fresh water, and ocean meet, the coastal strip is an ideal place to recognize profound connections between natural and human processes that are shaping California. From coastal bluffs covered with forests to delicate sand dunes, from wide sandy beaches to some of the most modern and dense human developments, the California coast is an excellent example of the themes that run throughout this book—connections, diversity, and change.

These shorelines may appear—as backdrop, setting, or star—in more films than any other landscapes on our planet. It is no surprise that most Californians and visitors consider the state's shorelines unequaled and irreplaceable jewels.

Coastal Geomorphology

Such a fascinating story must begin with cycles of matter and energy that have shaped the coast for thousands of years. Internal, mountain building forces have folded and faulted coastal landscapes above the sea. There are countless examples of dramatic, steep landscapes that result when mountains are lifted vertically out of the ocean; you will find them from the Oregon border to the northern Coast Ranges' King Range to Big Sur's Santa Lucia Range, and from Point Conception to the Mexican border. No doubt, these modern events and landscapes are evidence of greater processes that have gradually, for millions of years, lifted California out of the water, first from the east, and that continue pushing the Pacific Ocean farther out to the west. Rather than falling into the sea, most coastal Californians are gradually rising above it.

Mass wasting processes deliver many of the steeper slopes directly back into the ocean, where waves can reshape and carry the debris out to quieter waters or other distant shorelines. Rocky coasts, bluffs, and cliffs are left behind to precariously dangle until the next landslide. However, the majority of sand grains and other material along California beaches have more complex histories capable of captivating any beachcomber.

Most of the sand on our beaches originates in the very coastal and inland mountains that have long been raised well above the sea. Exposed rocks are weathered into smaller particles, allowing external denudational forces, particularly running water, to carry them down the slopes, into rivers and streams and eventually toward California's shoreline.

These forces are working not only in coastal mountains, but in the Sierra Nevada and even northeastern California. For instance, follow the Sacramento River upstream into northern California and notice the tributaries that branch out toward the state's northeast corner. All of these areas have been potential sources for material that can be carried by rivers and streams eventually to their base level—the sea. The only barriers to this ageless process are today's dams and other obstructions built by humans. Whether coughed out of the Smith River in the north, the Golden Gate, the Tijuana River in the south, or hundreds of streams in between, these sediments meet another energy source when they reach the coastline.

Rivers of Sand

Wind at sea causes ocean swells to form and then travel hundreds, even thousands, of miles from their sources. These swells travel in parallel wave patterns as they represent energy passing across the ocean. The largest swells with the most energy are produced by the strongest winds which blow over the greatest area (known as fetch) for the longest period of time. In other words, big powerful storms that last a long time generate the largest swells.

The most consistent and powerful swells that approach California's coast usually, especially from late fall through winter and spring, originate from storms in the northern Pacific and Gulf of Alaska. Less frequently, especially during our late summer, the southern hemisphere's winter storms (such as off the coast of New Zealand) or hurricanes off Mexico might send powerful swells up toward California from the south. As all of these swells approach the coast, they will become major players in working material and shaping landscapes previously mentioned. This is a meeting place—a complex interface—with few rivals on our planet.

As the swells move across the sea to eventually approach shallower water along California's shoreline, they agitate surface water and anything on it to rotate and bob in a circular motion. Wave bottoms then drag along the shallow floor of the shoreline, causing them to slow down and bunch up. As the wavelengths decrease, wave heights increase. Eventually, the top of the wave, with its inertia, spills over the dragging bottom and the wave

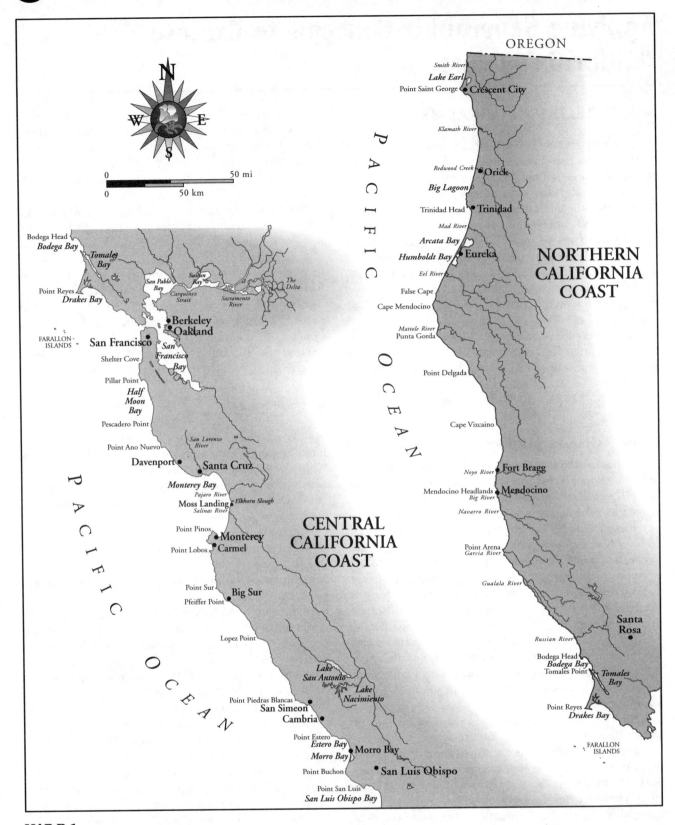

MAP B.1
The Central and Northern California Coasts.

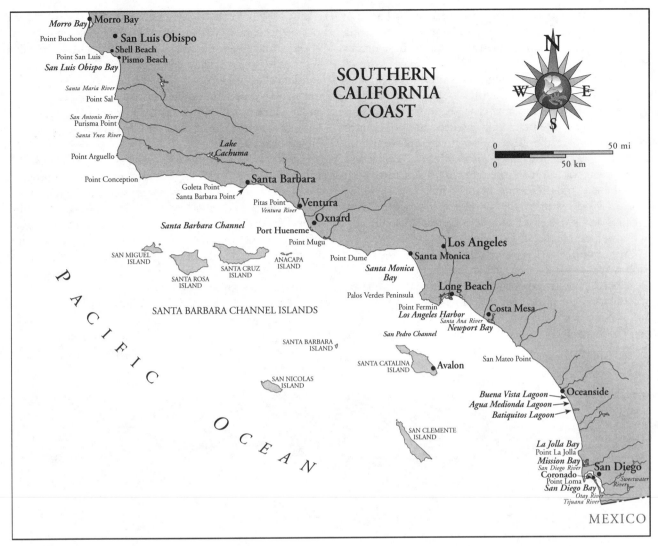

MAP B.2

The Southern California Coast.

Waves refract into this cove just north of San Simeon. Kelp beds wave in the surf and elephant seals rest on the sand below a classic marine terrace.

breaks on the beach. Anyone who has ever had a wave break on them or just in front of them on a California beach has witnessed the tremendous energy these breakers carry.

Now imagine being caught as a rocky cliff or sand grain in this surf zone, repeatedly clobbered and pulverized every eight, ten, or twelve seconds. California's rocky points are the first to experience the onslaught of these waves. As the waves first slow and bunch up around the points, they also bend, or refract. This wrapping effect concentrates the greatest wave forces on coastal headlands, creating high energy environments where erosion is king. Cliffs and rocky beaches result because any loose sand and other debris is usually carried away (see Figure B.1).

As wave refraction continues into coves and bays, each wave's energy is spread out over a greater area. As these waves finally break on beaches within these coastal indentations, they are gentler and tend to deposit sand rather than erode it away. This is why you will usually find the widest sandy beaches within the protection of the state's inlets, coves, and bays.

A series of coastal cells can be found along California's shorelines, where sand is first delivered from streams and rivers and even distant upstream shorelines. As the refracting waves break at angles, they push this sand up at an angle along the beach. This uprush of wave and sand is sometimes called "swash." Gravity eventually pulls water remaining from the spent waves back, but straight down the beach face. This backrush is sometimes called "backwash."

You can watch repeated swash and backwash sloshing water up and down at angles and carrying tons of suspended sand as longshore drift rules along most California beaches during any given day. A longshore current develops in shoreline waters to aid in the transport of suspended sand originally agitated and pushed along by the waves. Because most of this wave energy comes from the north Pacific, sand is usually transported from northwest to southeast along California's coast.

If you still don't believe in the power of these forces, do some body surfing or paddling around in the surf zone. On most days, you will notice how *you* are being transported by the waves and currents along the shore-

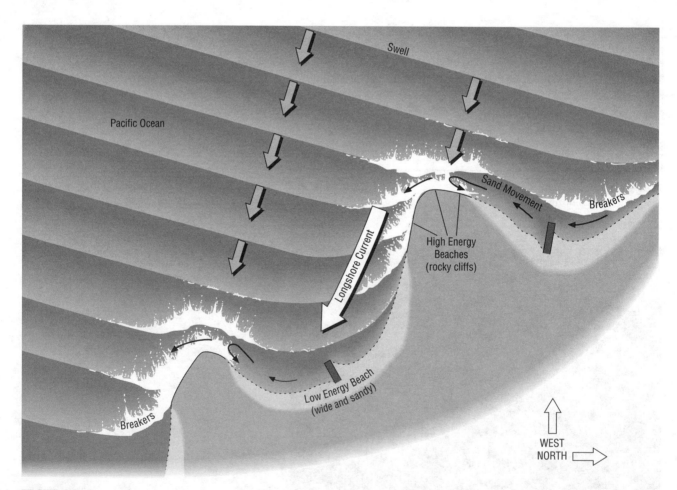

FIGURE B.1

Rivers of Sand. Waves are refracted as they approach shallow waters along the California coast, often transporting sand from northwest to southeast.

line. Imagine the fate of those little sand grains that are so easily suspended in turbulent water. Sand that is not finally stranded along lower energy beaches (and sometimes blown inland by prevailing winds) will eventually be carried into deep submarine canyons and deposited in deeper waters, completing the coastal cell cycle.

Wave Action Shapes the Coastline

The extent of wave erosion is often controlled by three general factors. First are the very long-term changes in sea levels relative to coastal elevations. On the California coast, marine terraces and benches are common; they represent old shorelines and wave-cut platforms and some depositional surfaces now elevated high above the sea. Some of the most dramatic in northern and central California are at Crescent City, Trinidad, Cape Mendocino, Davenport, Santa Cruz (where there are five terraces up to 260 m [850 feet]), Point Lobos to Point Sur, San Simeon, Cambria, Morro Bay to Point Buchon, and Shell and Pismo Beaches. Central coast terraces support a variety of land uses, from grazing, to artichoke and Brussels sprouts farming, to housing developments and resorts.

Marine terraces are also common along the Southern California coast from Santa Barbara to the Mexican border. (Palos Verdes Peninsula is surrounded by several.) They are even evident on offshore islands such as San Clemente and San Nicolas. The opposite effects of coastal subsidence or higher sea levels may be less common in California, but examples are found in drowned coastal marshes and estuaries such as Humboldt Bay, San Francisco Bay, and San Diego County's lagoons.

Second, wave erosion is controlled by California's daily tide range (about 2–3 m [6–10 feet]), less than many of our planet's other coastal regions. This exposes only a narrow coastal strip to erosional processes. Third and finally, wave height is an obvious factor in wave erosion; it is determined by exposure to prevailing wave patterns, an important consideration along California's jagged, lengthy coast.

There are some interesting details that help explain the nature of California beaches and the changes that are evident from place to place and time to time. During winter, especially on exposed beaches north of Point Conception, storms in the north Pacific send out enormous waves that crash on California beaches. Erosion of sand creates narrow "winter beaches" or carries all the sand away, leaving larger rocks and boulders, steeper beaches, or naked bluffs. The sand is often deposited in longshore bars in calmer waters just beyond the surf zone.

During summer, the gentler waves push and redeposit sand back up on the flatter, wider, finer sand "summer beaches." These seasonal cycles are usually less evident in more protected areas of the Southern California Bight south of Point Conception. Notable and historical exceptions to Southern California's relative calm include some classic El Niño/Southern Oscillation (ENSO) years when exceptional storms pounded the coast.

Humans Modify Local Shorelines

Humans have also played roles in working with or battling nature to encourage the formation of local shorelines that serve their interests. Piles of rock or other debris or vertical walls are built out perpendicular to the shore to catch sand flowing along the beach. These groins act as barriers; sand is deposited on their upstream sides, building wider, sandier beaches.

Breakwaters are sometimes built parallel to the beach just beyond the surf zone to intercept and exhaust most of the wave energy that would otherwise pound the beach. Not only are coastal waters often calm enough to anchor boats on the shoreline side of the breakwaters, but resulting gentler waves tend to deposit sand and build wider beaches. Sometimes these perpendicular and parallel structures are joined into giant T-shaped jetties, resulting in greater protection from waves and even wider beaches.

Remember that most of the state's beaches are steep, with deep water close to shore. Consequently, sediment carried to the ocean by flooding streams is often deposited onto submarine deltas well below sea level, while remaining sand is worked along the shoreline by waves. This is one reason why dramatic deltas (such as the Mississippi or Nile) are rare along California's coast. They are often limited to small bouldery deposits (such as at the Ventura River) stranded and only occasionally disturbed by the very forces just discussed.

Now that we are armed with these general concepts and rules, we must also recognize that every California

Anacapa Islands' rocky terraces fade into distant haze. Powerful forces are shaping these exposed cliffs and shorelines.

beach is unique; there are specific physical factors and processes that contribute to the landscapes we observe along each shoreline.

From Monterey Bay to Points North and South

You will find dramatic examples of previously reviewed processes and landscapes around Monterey Bay. A classic coastal cell extends from Santa Cruz south to Monterey. The Salinas, Pajaro, and other rivers and streams cough sediment out to the bay's beaches. Refracting waves push the sand away from the points and toward the protected beaches near Moss Landing. Here, sand that is not stranded above high tide or blown inland gets caught at the head of Monterey submarine canyon. This magnificent canyon in the middle of the bay trends southwest and drops to near 3,000 m (>10,000 feet) below sea level. (It is more than one-half mile deep only three miles below Cypress Point.) Evidence of the effectiveness of this giant sand trap is found on the enormous submarine delta that radiates out from the canyon bottom just offshore. This is sand carried all the way down from these shorelines, filtered through the canyon, and deposited in the abyss.

Interestingly, it was near here that scientists first discovered some of the processes that were shaping California beaches. Even before 1950, researchers had recorded growth of beach berms in Carmel at rates of up to 2 m (6 feet) per day, with summer beaches measuring more than 200 feet wider than winter beaches. They also noted how protected beaches, such as the one tucked behind Pillar Point in Half Moon Bay, were flat with fine sand grains. Moving south along the bay, away from the protection of Pillar Point, the beaches were steeper with coarser sand.

Each coastal strip is full of surprises, and we can review only a few here. Bodega Head, once an island, has been connected to the coast by a sand spit deposited by longshore currents. Then, wind and vegetation created dunes that are now aligned with the northwest winds. Today, a curving sandspit encloses the coastal inlet on the protected side of Bodega Head. At Point Reyes lowland's northern coast, northwesterly winds have driven dunes inland as much as 1,200 m (4,000 feet). At Morro Rock, you will find a tombolo (sand deposits linking the rock to the mainland) that resulted from beach and dune deposition on the rock's landward side. The human imprint (as reviewed in Chapter 3) is also evident there.

The San Francisco Bay system is not only one of the world's finest harbors, it is also the only place along that section of coast where streams from interior California reach the sea. The bays are structural depressions that were repeatedly flooded during Pleistocene Epoch glacial cycles. These depressions extend into valleys trending north and south of San Francisco. A superimposed Sacramento River cut the narrow channel of Carquinez Strait to connect Suisun Bay to San Pablo Bay. Though sections of the channel are now up to 60 m (200 feet) below sea level, 85 percent of the water area of the bays is less than 10 m (30 feet) deep. Currently, sediment pouring in especially from the Sacramento and San Joaquin Rivers is gradually filling the bays. Like many coastal locations, such as Morro Bay, human activities (such as grazing, farming, and developments) have increased sediment load delivered by rivers and accelerated the rate of fill.

The South Coast

You will also find a variety of processes shaping landforms along southern California's coastline. You might observe the Newport Bay estuary, a water-filled valley slicing through the elevated Costa Mesa block. It was cut by the now diverted Santa Ana River. Today, most of Newport Bay's islands are made of sediments from the bay floor, dredged to clear boat passages. The sand spit extending out from the bay results from lower wave energy at that point; deeper water in the nearby Newport submarine canyon and deposition of sand transported along the beach by longshore currents are the culprits.

Farther south, San Diego Bay is the only sizable natural harbor on the California coast south of San Francisco. Point Loma (nearly 120 m [400 feet] above sea

Here's what happens when storms fueled by El Niño attack the beach. This is Venice Beach, 1983, after waves up to 10 m (30 feet) eroded and carried sand along the shore and out to sea. The rest room is about 3 m (10 feet) above what is left of the beach.

level) forms an effective barrier west of San Diego and north of the bay against waves and wind from the northwest. To the south of Point Loma, a long, curving sand spit crept northward from the mouth of the Tijuana River. It finally extended from the mainland to connect what was once South Island (now the city of Coronado) and North Island (the site of the Naval Air Station). Spanish Bight was the inlet that once separated the islands; it is now filled.

By now, sediments from the Otay, Sweetwater, and San Diego rivers should have naturally filled San Diego Bay, and the northward drift of beach sand should have blocked the harbor entrance. However, San Diego River's diversion into a channel on the south side of Mission Bay and breakwater, channel maintenance, and tidal action prevent such natural filling.

Along San Diego's coast, especially in North County, are numerous marine terraces occasionally sliced by streams flowing into the ocean. The nature of these coastal landscapes was reviewed in Chapter 3. After the last Ice Age, rising sea levels invaded the mouths of these stream channels. Within them, today's quiet estuaries are still being filled by river sediment, while coastal currents straighten the shoreline, depositing baymouth bars. On inland sides of the baymouth bars, some lagoons remain, but many are filled with salt marshes and sediment.

A growing population has spread developments across San Diego County's terraces and threatens to further impact these lagoons and estuaries. San Diegans, from developers to preservationists, continue heated debates about the future of their cherished and valuable coastal landscapes.

Ocean-Atmosphere Interaction

The cold, north-to-south flowing California Current earned some attention in Chapter 4. However, this current is more than a weather maker; it regulates the nature of ocean water off the state's coast and the marine life living in it. The California Current represents the east side of the enormous North Pacific anticyclonic gyre. Pacific Subarctic water flows from west to east with the West Wind Drift and Subarctic Current, across the North Pacific toward North America at high latitudes. It turns south along the North American coast at about 48 degrees latitude to become part of the California Current. This water is known for its low salinity and temperature and high oxygen content. Comprehensive samples and studies of the California Current system, begun in 1949 with the California Cooperative Oceanic Fisheries Investigations (CalCOFI), have included thousands of reporting stations and, more recently, an avalanche of satellite data.

The speed of this dominant north-to-south offshore current averages less than 25 cm per second (<0.6 miles per hour), with highest speeds about double the average.

This is a surface current flowing along the coast with maximum depths of about 300 m (1,000 feet), extending out as far as 900 km (560 miles). In other words, it is a relatively shallow current with maximum flow near the surface. It is also a very complex current with seasonal fluctuations, and it contains and is surrounded by giant eddies.

The California Current is usually strongest during spring and summer. Take a dip in the Pacific off California's central coast to prove it; the water can be colder than 10°C (<50°F) in May. However, a coastal counterflow toward the north often appears along a narrow stretch against the coast, especially during fall and winter. This Inshore Countercurrent hugs the shoreline over the continental shelf and slope, rarely extending more than 100 km (about 62 miles) offshore.

In very deep waters, the California Undercurrent may also transport water in a countercurrent toward the north. This deep current is also the exception to the prevailing California Current and is not apparent to the average observer. Such countercurrents are amplified within the massive Southern California Eddy that often forms in the Southern California Bight. This giant counterclockwise swirl of coastal waters forms south of Point Conception. Why?

The Southern California Bight is defined as the area of coastal waters south of Point Conception to Cape Colnett in Baja California and west out to the California Current. Like most of the Bight's coastline, its bumpy bottom topography trends northwest to southeast. Consequently, these waters are often protected from direct hits by the California Current and storm swells from the north Pacific. For centuries, sailors and fishermen have feared the dangerous high seas and punishing cold currents and winds north of Point Conception; in contrast, notably calmer, warmer waters are the rule along the protected coast south of Point Conception.

This coastline at Point Conception and Point Arguello—the edge of California's widest cross section—represents a definitive boundary between northern and southern California waters and marine life. Ocean temperature, density, salinity, dissolved oxygen, waves, weather, and sea life change radically around the point. North of the point, an abundance of plankton and other sea life thrive in the cold waters that contain higher concentrations of dissolved gases and nutrients. South of Point Conception, you might find mackerel and barracuda in the warmer waters.

The Southern California Bight also contains some of the most interesting subsurface features off the state's coast. Southern California's continental shelf (the shallow platform less than 100 m [300 feet] deep) surrounding the continent is relatively narrow. Its width averages about 6.5 km (4 miles) and locally narrows to just 1.5 km (about 1 mile) before it drops steeply seaward down the slope. A number of erosional terraces are found on the shelf, probably submerged by rising sea levels after the Ice Ages. Additionally, numerous submarine canyons support currents that carry sediment farther out to a series of deeper basins, which, in turn, are frequently interrupted by shallower ridges.

Marine Life

California waters represent one of four recognized eastern boundary regions. These regions are narrow strips of coastline about the same distance from the equator on the eastern edges of the Pacific and Atlantic Oceans in both the southern and northern hemispheres. Some researchers argue that these areas produce more than one-third of all fish, though they represent only about one-thousandth of our planet's ocean surface.

Here, upwelling cold currents bring nourishing nitrates and phosphates to the lighted surface. After prevailing northwest winds give coastal currents a budge, the ocean water veers to its right (due to the Coriolis effect) and is often pulled away from land. Cold waters are pulled up from the depths, bringing nutrients that cause the explosion of life in the boundary region. Although it is particularly noticeable between Cape Mendocino and Point Conception (where water temperatures are cooled down to 3°C below average compared to outer waters at similar latitudes), this upwelling has attracted the best fishing fleets from around the world to the California coast.

From sardines to oysters, overfishing has combined with natural wild swings in California marine life populations to create alternating periods of economic boom and disaster in the fishing industry. California's Sardine (*Sardinops sagax*) industry peaked around 1936 to 1937, when the annual catch exceeded 700,000 tonnes. By the 1950s, the catch was anemic, and by the 1960s, devastated populations had to be protected from total destruc-

tion. The Northern Anchovy (*Engraulis mordax*) is an example of one of many other species which has played a major role in California's cool current fisheries. Interestingly, both of these species tend to thrive in the Southern California Bight, away from the strongest upwelling currents.

In the Intertidal Zone

The intertidal zone is yet another place to discover diverse life forms. From surf grass to various species of kelp, the producers (plants) are responsible for making food and providing shelter. In tide pools along rocky shores, you will find different species adapted to fluctuations in sea level and wave action. High in the splash zone, above high tide, are organisms that endure long dry periods. They include rock louse, barnacles, and various limpets.

Moving down into the high tide zone, you might find more limpets, hermit crabs, shore crabs, and tube-building snails. A few chiton might be seen attached to the rocks. Many of these life forms survive in the violent surf zone by anchoring on or into rocks. Still lower, in the middle tide zone, you will see a greater variety of creatures, from barnacles and mussels to sea stars and anemones and crabs. Toward the lower tide zone are organisms that remain under water except during very low tides. There, you might notice green abalone, octopus, and spiny lobster.

Organisms on sandy beaches face very different challenges. Annoying beach hoppers (beach fleas) attack sea weed washed ashore. Look in the sand for sand crabs and sand dollars. Dig deeper and you might find a variety of clams, including the giant Pismo clam. Look toward the water or on isolated rocks for harbor seals or barking sea lion, out beyond the surf for dolphins and sea otter, or farther out for migrating whales, including the California Gray Whale.

Dashing along the beach's tide zone are willets and curlews searching the sand for food. Look for larger shoreline birds, such as gulls, pelicans, and cormorants. All of these creatures are either adapting to or are victims of the geography of the California shoreline.

Kelp

Algin, which is found in the cell walls of kelp leaf blades, allows the kelp to bend and twist with the waves. It is used as an emulsifier and stabilizer in more than seventy foods, medicines, and other products, from lipstick to beer to paint. Some of the brown kelp frond canopies that grow to the surface are worth up to a million dollars per square mile. By the 1960s, a company named Kelco (its workers started harvesting kelp in 1929) had established itself as California's kelp-harvesting powerhouse, taking more than 150,000 tons per year.

An elephant seal pup, surrounded by stranded kelp, looks up and toward the telephoto lens on a central California beach.

During the 1950s, the kelp-harvesting industry was in trouble. This came after sea urchins, thriving on sewage outfalls, grazed in record numbers, destroying the state's kelp beds. They were also unchecked by their natural predator, the sea otter. By the late 1950s, California's kelp harvest disappeared. An aggressive attack was mounted against the spiny kelp eaters, from divers with hammers, to tons of quicklime. Since those kelpless years, control of sewage outfall and growing markets for sea urchin harvests, especially in Asia, have allowed California's kelp industry to thrive. The only exceptions have been during unusually stormy El Niño years, when higher waves and water temperatures have taken their toll.

Environmental Issues on California's Coast

Throughout this book, we consider human/environment interactions and the public controversies they provoke. Some of the celebrated environmental controversies of our time involve development and use of our coastline. A few of our historical mistakes could be comical if they weren't so shameful. They include a small pocket beach at Fort Bragg composed of tin cans from a nearby city ocean dump, all arranged like any other beach material. As late as the 1960s, you could stumble through Tin Can Beach along the north coast of Orange County.

DDT

By the 1970s, scientists had discovered that large concentrations of dichloro diphenyl trichloroethane (DDT) in pelicans caused the birds to lay eggs too thin for offspring to survive. DDT is a powerful insecticide. Pelican populations dwindled so rapidly, it threatened the species. Simultaneously, sea lions with concentrated DDT suffered premature births and stillborns in record numbers. Interestingly, mussels have helped scientists identify and deal with the problem.

Mussels are bivalves that filter food from the enormous amounts of water drawn through their systems. Scientists have used them in such programs as Mussel Watch to monitor the amount of pollutants drifting in ocean waters. Mussels helped scientists determine that DDT pollution was far more extensive and damaging than originally believed in Southern California, especially off Los Angeles. Unfortunately, the resulting DDT ban did not immediately solve this problem.

Though the Montrose Chemical plant was shut down in 1971 (after dumping more than 19 metric tons of DDT in the White Point outfall off Palos Verdes), large concentrations of DDT were still measured in mussels and other organisms into the 1980s. Up to 70,000 pounds were gradually being released as residue from pipes and land dumps. Furthermore, fish eat mussels and other marine animals eat those fish, further concentrating DDT and other poisons until a dead animal settles to the ocean bottom. There, the animal decays amongst bacteria, where bottom feeders may consume the poisons that were not brought back to the surface by upwelling currents. This is why it took decades to control levels of DDT in marine animals living along California's coast.

Petroleum Pollution and Natural Seeps

Oil spills and accidents caused gradual and sometimes catastrophic environmental destruction along California's beaches during the twentieth century. A few were so ghastly that California citizens and lawmakers were shocked into regulating the pumping and transport of petroleum along the state's coast. Entire environmental movements were born after oil companies reacted with indifference to particular oil spills and resulting environmental and wildlife destruction.

El Niño's heavy rains run off city streets into storm drains and wash Los Angeles' trash into the surf zone. Santa Monica Pier with its now-famous solar-powered Ferris wheel and Pacific Palisades are in the distance.

However, chances are good that the annoying tar you pick up on your feet comes from natural sources. California, especially the Santa Barbara Channel, has some of the most active petroleum seeps in the world. From natural gas, to light and crude oil, to tar, hydrocarbons seep to the surface through faults and other natural structures. You can see it on land at the La Brea Tar Pits right along Wilshire Boulevard in Los Angeles. However, one of the greatest natural oil seeps in the world is about ten miles west of Santa Barbara at Coal Oil Point, where 50–70 barrels of oil per day have been estimated to escape.

Not only is this oil part of California's natural history, it was recognized and used by California Indians long before the European invasion. Tar that washed ashore was a handy resource to seal boats and waterproof containers. Of course, petroleum eventually became a vital resource for the state's modern industries and car culture. During the twentieth century, oil and gas fueled the engines that encouraged California's mobile populations to pave landscapes and spread their settlements, searching for more independence and the California Dream. Later in the 1900s, dependence on petroleum came with a price—traffic jams and pollution of our air, water, and soil.

◆ CONCLUSION

California's coast is a meeting place for nature's energy, matter, and resources, for human energy, and for ideas and dreams. It continues to earn extraordinary attention. Within each chapter of this book, throughout the sections on physical and human geography, you may notice references to these coastal landscapes and the processes, cycles, and systems shaping them. There may be no better place to survey the exceptional diversity, profound connections, and rapid changes that define California.

Chapter 7

Human Population and Migration in California

INTRODUCING HUMAN LANDSCAPES AND CULTURES

The focus of the first half of this book was on natural processes and the physical landscapes they have produced. You have discovered how California's natural landscapes provide clues to the dynamic natural processes that have been at work long before people arrived in the state. Likewise, California's more recent human landscapes (human imprints on the land) are products of the people and cultures that have shaped them; it is no surprise that these human landscapes also provide clues about the natural resources and technologies available to the people who have created them. Additionally, these human scenes reveal much about the cultural preferences of Californians and our methods of developing and working with those resources and technologies.

From the clear-cut forests of the northwest, to the expansive farm fields of the Central Valley, from the sprawling suburban neighborhoods and malls, to the towering skyscrapers of its great cities, California's wealth of human imprints must be as diverse as its people. These people and their landscapes represent more than fascinating subjects for study. They provide lessons about past failures and successes, and they are examples, both good and bad, of the kinds of communities and living environments we will choose to build in the twenty-first century.

In the last half of this book, which focuses on California's people and their human landscapes, we continue to emphasize a systematic, topical approach, while we use descriptions of some of California's regions to serve as practical examples.

One of the most famous modern geographers, H. J. de Blij, cited at least three major twentieth century developments in the field of cultural geography that will help guide us as we try to understand California's human landscapes. First, he noted how Carl Sauer (professor of geography at UC Berkeley in 1927) defined cultural landscapes as "forms superimposed on the physical landscape by the activities of man." Second, the phrase, "**sequent occupance**" was developed to describe successive stages in the evolution of a region's cultural landscapes. Third, more recent definitions of the cultural landscape include "a composition of man-made or man-modified spaces to serve as infrastructure or background for our collective existence."

Regardless of specific variations in the definition of cultural landscape, it is clear that California's cultural landscapes include tangible qualities, such as land-use patterns, industries, architecture, and transportation features. However, they must also include the intangible qualities, such as the smells, sounds, moods, and atmospheres cast by each human landscape. How can we make our human landscapes more livable and functional? These are the kinds of issues and problems addressed in the following pages and chapters.

California's people and their landscapes constantly remind us of the major themes of this book—diversity, connections, and change—that help make the study of geography so fascinating and applicable to the issues of modern life.

KEY ISSUES AND CONCEPTS

◆ A growing number of diverse people and cultures continues to shape California's landscapes. As these human imprints spread across the state, they also represent clues to how Californians live and work and the resources and technologies available to them.

◆ Demographers are challenged to study these diverse and changing populations that have grown rapidly in every decade since statehood. The state's population continues to explode, partially due to natural increases, but particularly due to massive immigration. However, percentage rates of increase are not as great today due to the large population base already established.

◆ California is unique among states as, for most of its history, the state has consistently experienced positive international *and* interstate migration, with few exceptions. These migrations have reshaped the state's population, cultures, and human landscapes.

◆ Numerous factors, including powerful push-pull factors and chain migrations, have led to, and continue to, encourage mass migrations to California.

◆ Immigration during the end of the 1900s increased the disparity between economic and cultural groups in the state.

◆ The source of immigrants has changed over the decades. During the last several years, Latino and Asian immigrants have dominated the immigration stream, establishing in California some of the largest populations and settlements beyond their homelands.

◆ Modern Californians are some of the most mobile people on the planet.

◆ All of the state's great population centers are growing fast, including the Los Angeles, San Francisco Bay, and San Diego areas and several Central Valley metropolitan areas. Most newer, emerging cities are growing farther inland.

◆ The state's population is expected to increase rapidly well into the twenty-first century. These growth trends will continue to fuel debates concerning congestion, overpopulation, immigration, and environmental degradation.

◆ THE HISTORY AND GROWTH OF CALIFORNIA'S DYNAMIC POPULATION

Where are California's more than 34 million people? Where did they come from, and how did they get here? How has this population been widely distributed and locally concentrated and at what densities? When these questions are addressed, the rapid growth and mobility of California's dynamic populations stand out; this has been particularly true since the Gold Rush. This study of population characteristics known as demography follows. Who are these people and what cultures do they represent? The exceptional diversity that has always dominated California's populations continues to this day. These issues are addressed in the more lengthy sections on California ethnic groups, cultures, and lifestyles which follows our discussion of population.

A Brief History

By the end of the twentieth century, California had a population of 34,000,000 and it controlled one-fifth of the 270 electoral votes cast in the presidential elections. No other state in the foreseeable future will even approach this population and the political power it carries. One out of every eight United States residents lives in California. It took over a century to achieve these remarkable numbers. During each decade from 1850 to 2000, California grew faster than the national average; it is the only state that can make that claim.

Native Americans

We know that people have lived in California for more than 10,000 years. It is estimated that about 300,000 Native Americans lived in California when the Spanish finally began settling the region in 1769. Although there were entire regions where the densest populations may have averaged only about one person per square mile, California Indians were often clustered by the hundreds in local coastal canyons, plains, and inland valleys with abundant food and water. The harshest deserts and mountain peaks had no permanent settlements.

We know that California Indians actively traded resources, but developed somewhat smaller social and political organizations compared to some other North American tribes. They included approximately six language stocks, fourteen language families, nearly one-hundred different languages and more than three-hundred dialects within what is now California. Diverse physical environments and numerous large natural barriers encouraged this exceptional diversity of Native American cultures. Research of these people has pro-

This is Chief Kientpoos, or "Captain Jack," the Modoc leader who resisted attempts to herd his people into unfamiliar reservations. He and his warriors used their knowledge of the lava tubes that are now tourist attractions at Lava Beds National Monument to avoid capture.

duced scores of volumes that hardly begin to unravel the mysteries they left behind (see Map 7.1).

Beginning with the Spanish, settlers brought European diseases that killed thousands of natives. By the 1830s, about 50,000 California Indians had died. The political and economic changes brought by the Mexican ranchos and, later, the Gold Rush further devastated the native populations. Only about 125,000 American Indians remained in California by 1845, and by 1900, the census counted only 15,000 California Indians. By the early 1900s, vast areas of California's coastal and inland valleys typically contained less than 1 percent of their original Native American populations. Entire groups of California Indians and their cultures had vanished.

The Spanish Period

The Spanish began to explore the California coast as early as 1542, when Juan Rodríguez Cabrillo became the first European to reach Alta California. By the early 1600s, explorations along the California coast included the efforts of Cermenho and Vizcaíno and other adventurers, including the British Sir Francis Drake, who harassed Spanish ships.

In 1769, Spain finally moved to settle California. Captain Gaspar de Portolá and Franciscan Father Junípero Serra landed in San Diego with soldiers to take formal possession of Alta California. This led to the series of presidios and missions and then pueblos that highlighted

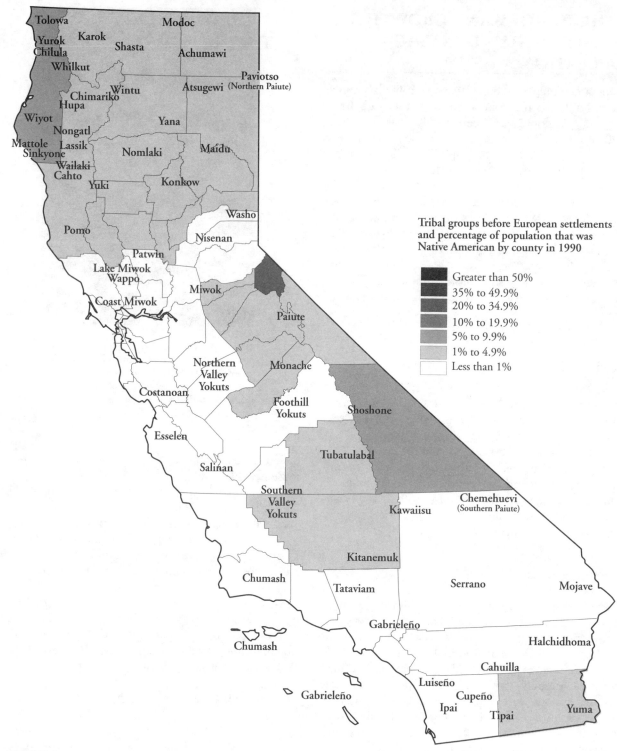

MAP 7.1

California Indians. This map illustrates the great diversity of Native Americans in California, past and present.

Spanish plans to create self-sufficient settlements with Indian labor. By 1823, the last of twenty-one missions was completed at Sonoma (see Map 7.2).

The Spanish located many of their California missions near some of the largest populations of Native Americans. They forced these American Indians to become a part of mission life. The total number of people living at each mission varied from less than 500 to more than 4,000. After Mexican Independence in 1821, central authority and the importance of the missions waned, causing populations to decrease at several missions during the 1820s.

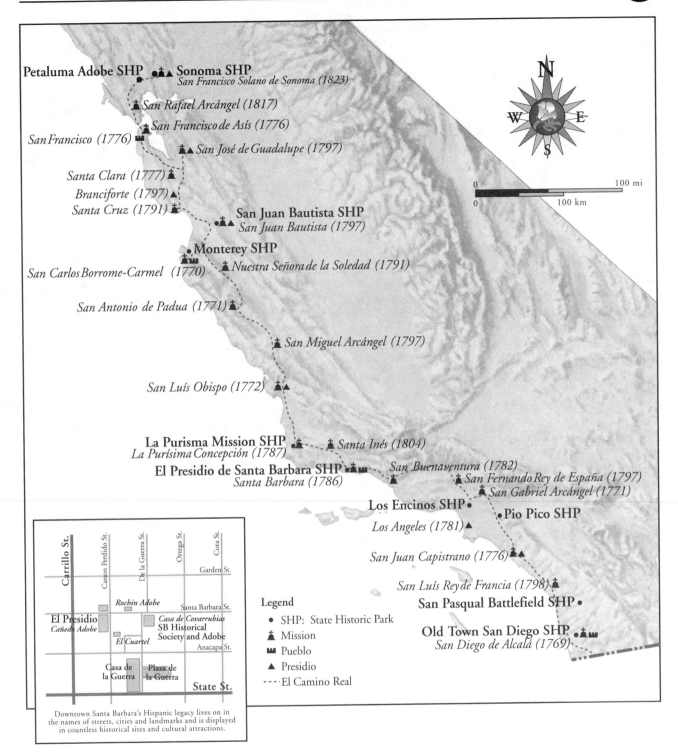

MAP 7.2
Spanish California. The Spanish and Mexican Periods left outstanding imprints on California landscapes.

The Mexican Period

In 1822, the Spanish transferred authority to Mexican officials in California. Eventually, the missions were secularized, while hide and tallow trade became increasingly important to California's economy. Enormous land grants led to the establishment of huge ranchos, up to 800 by the mid-1840s. Extensive Mexican ranchos made very different use of and impressions on the landscape, compared to the Spanish missions and pueblos. They also encouraged the now romanticized California rancho lifestyles.

During the years after 1822, California hosted a growing number of pioneers from the American frontier. Jedediah Smith made the first recorded Sierra Nevada crossing. He was followed by other immigrants into California, eventually including John Sutter, who received a land grant in the Sacramento Valley.

The American Period

During the 1840s, as their numbers grew, conflicts between these American pioneers and Mexican authorities also increased. Finally, during the U.S. war with Mexico, John Fremont, John Sloat, Robert Stockton and others helped lead the Bear Flag Revolt in California. American forces wrestled control of California from Mexico, and Andrés Pico, commander of the final Mexican force, signed the Treaty of Cahuenga in January, 1847. Just more than a year later, the U.S. war with Mexico ended with the Treaty of Guadalupe-Hidalgo: California and the Southwest now officially belonged to the United States.

In January, 1948, James Marshall discovered gold at Sutter's Mill on the American River. When news got out, thousands swarmed into California and its Mother Lode. California would never be the same. The 49ers were just the beginning of a population explosion that has continued, in waves, ever since.

The state's total population soared faster than the rest of the nation for each decade since 1850 (see Figure 7.1). From a total population of less than 100,000 in 1850, to 380,000 in 1860, to 560,000 in 1870, to 865,000 in 1880, to 1.2 million in 1890, to nearly 1.5 million in 1900, the people came. When the Gold Rush boom deflated, thousands settled in the growing urban landscapes of the San Francisco Bay Area, while farming communities sprang up in the Central Valley. Though many Mother Lode counties lost population after the initial rush, northern California was the focus of the most dramatic population growth during those first few decades of statehood after 1850.

American settlers first fortified and extended the trails and then brought the railroads. By 1863, Central Pacific Railroad (with Leland Stanford, Collis B. Huntington, Mark Hopkins and Charles Crocker in the lead) used Chinese laborers to build the first tracks east over the Sierra Nevada. By 1869, they met Union Pacific tracks in Utah; a one-week route between New York and Sacramento was established. California's Central Pacific had become Southern Pacific Railroad and railroad owners quickly became the most powerful landowners in California.

By the 1880s, Southern California had joined the California population explosion; the southern part of the state became the leader in attracting people throughout the twentieth century. Word spread that there was a lot more than gold in California's hills. Mild weather, open spaces, manufacturing and other fine jobs, Hollywood, and cutting-edge lifestyles pulled in millions from all over the country and the world throughout the 1900s. By 1920, the state's population was nearly 3.5 million, nearly 7 million by 1940, and it passed 10 million around 1950. It had soared to more than 15.5 million by 1960 and nearly 24 million by 1980. It sailed past 34 million in 1999 and headed toward 35 million for the year 2000.

Joining the American settlers from the east in the decades after the Gold Rush were waves of British and Irish, German, and Chinese immigrants. (From 1860 to 1890, the Chinese and Irish were the two leading foreign-born populations in California. However, the Chinese Exclusion Act of 1882 cut Chinese immigration by the end of the nineteenth century. Chapter 8 highlights experiences of these and other groups in California.) The British and northern European invasion into California continued during the early 1900s. However, Italian immigrants began to dominate the stream and Russians soon joined them in the mid-1900s.

Thousands fled the tragedy of the Dust Bowl, bringing only what they could carry to California. Those from the Plains, particularly Oklahoma, were labelled with derogatory names such as "Okies." (They are considered in a

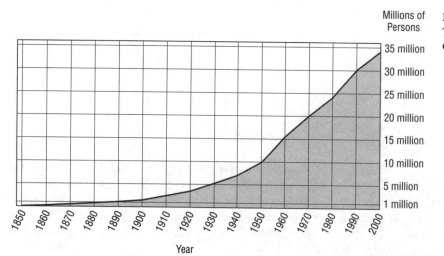

Millions of Persons

FIGURE 7.1

The history of population growth in California.

Year

section to follow.) Each year during and after the Great Depression, more immigrants flowed in from elsewhere in the United States, seeking better-paying jobs; this was most notable during World War II and Cold War military and aerospace buildups. So many flocked in from the Plains, Midwest, and South that loyalists from each state would celebrate with their own parades, barbecues and picnic reunions. All of these groups brought their cultures and often built landscapes more reflective of their homelands than the Mediterranean lands they were invading.

By 1950, Canada had become a major source of immigrants, but Mexican immigration had soared to the lead and would remain there for the next several decades. Immigrants from other Latin American countries joined the wave of Mexican immigrants during the last part of the twentieth century, along with surges from Asia and the Pacific Islands. As the twenty-first century approached, California's rapidly evolving faces, cultures and landscapes were being repeatedly transformed and remade.

The Nature of Population Change

It is easier to calculate California's population trends than to understand the reasons for them. Predicting future trends is even more difficult. The **demographic equation** provides a simple method to calculate population change affecting any region:

TP (Total Population) = OP (Original Population) + B (Births) − D (Deaths) + I (Immigration) − E (Emigration). The **natural increase** in this population equation is even more simple: births − deaths.

Natural Increases

The period after World War II into the 1960s was known as the **baby boom** due to high natural increases in the state's population. Later, the baby bust dropped natural increases from the late 1960s into the mid-70s. In 1970, there were 358,000 births and 165,000 deaths within California, for a natural increase of 193,000; in 1980, there were 390,000 births and 180,000 deaths, for an increase of 210,000; and in 1989, there were 505,000 births and 216,000 deaths, for a natural increase of 289,000. Do you notice the trend? That period since 1980 is known as the baby boomlet. It continued well into the 1990s, as natural increases remained at record levels. Thus, even without immigration, California's population will continue to rise into the twenty-first century.

There are other ways of examining the births and deaths that contribute to California's increasing populations. Crude birth (natality) rates are the number of live births per 1,000 people each year. They range from 10 per 1,000 in more developed countries to up to 50 per 1,000 in the poorest countries of the world. Crude birth rates in California were just more than 20 per 1,000 into the 1990s. That is lower than most poorer countries, such as in Latin America, Africa, and South Asia. However, it is higher than nearly every developed country in the world, including the Canadian and U.S. averages.

Crude death (mortality) rates are the number of deaths per 1,000 people each year. Worldwide, they range from less than 10 per 1,000 to more than 20 per 1,000 in the most troubled nations. California's mortality rate dropped from near 7.6 in 1988 to about 7 per 1,000 by the early 1990s, lower than many developed countries. California's birth rates are higher and mortality rates slightly lower than the U.S. average. This is another reason why our population is increasing so rapidly compared to the rest of the nation and other developed regions of the world.

Finally, total fertility rates are used to estimate the average number of children that will be born to each woman based on the current year's birth rates. Demographers recognize that a total of 2.1 children per woman is required to replace the present population. The current world rate is 3.2, but that number drops to near 1.7 in some more-developed countries. According to the State of California, fertility rates dropped to that 1.7 figure briefly in California during the baby bust in the mid-1970s. However, fertility rates jumped to nearly 2.5 children per woman since the 1970s. California's fertility rate continues to be considerably higher than that required to replace its current population.

Life expectancies are also slightly greater for Californians than the rest of the nation. During the 1990s, men were living an average of more than seventy-two years, while women's average life expectancies were nearing eighty years. As we analyze more specific trends and statistics, such as infant mortality rates (deaths of children age one or less per 1,000 live births per year), we recognize some disturbing trends.

Recent studies show an alarming range of births, deaths, and health conditions between Californians in different income groups and neighborhoods. Your chances of living a healthier, longer life are much higher if you have a high income and live in one of California's safer neighborhoods. In contrast, you will almost always find substantially higher birth and fertility rates, higher mortality rates and lower life expectancies in California's poorest neighborhoods, especially those with the most recent immigrants. This has been the case for decades, as much of California's natural population increase comes from California's poorest communities. Vital statistics in these neighborhoods sometimes resemble those of the less developed countries that are the homelands of the most recent immigrants.

It becomes clear that, especially in California, births and deaths and other statistics showing *natural* population change are not the most significant parts of the state's demographic story. After all, the state's population more than tripled during the ten years between 1850 and 1860. It increased by more than one-hundred times in the century between 1850 and 1950. More than 8 million people were added to more than double the already impressive population during twenty years from 1940 to 1960.

The world's population "doubling times" due to natural increase, typically projected at forty to fifty years, are almost meaningless when compared to California. It is a state that increased its numbers by 2,000 per day, a 25 percent increase during the 1980s. And when the population increase "slowed" to 1,500 per day (10,000 new people per week) during the recession of the early 1990s, some California officials expressed concern. They often cited statistics showing the slowing **percentage population increase** without noting that the masses were still coming, but were being added to an already incredible population base.

Migration Complicates the Story

Whether the subject is California's past population trends or projections for the future, the most important factor was, and continues to be, migration.

Age-Sex Population Pyramids   Even when **population pyramids** are used to analyze and predict California population trends, massive immigration creates the most dramatic change. These age-sex population pyramids are snapshots of the distribution of California's population by age groups. They show the number of dependents in our population (those younger than fifteen and older than sixty-four who may not be in the work force) so that

we can adjust our society's social services and infrastructures to serve them.

These pyramids also reveal the productivity and purchasing power potential of certain age groups that will be targeted by advertisers and businesses marketing their products. Particularly in California, age-sex pyramids have been radically changing, brief snapshots of a mobile population (see Figure 7.2).

Back in 1850, the crowd that rushed to the California Mother Lode was predominantly male in a huge age block between eighteen and fifty. Some of these immigrants stayed in California to grow old. However, the 1880 pyramid showed that these early pioneers had vanished or were absorbed within the continuing waves of younger immigrants. (New immigrants were still a majority of males between eighteen and fifty, but now followed by females and younger children). Interestingly, those young males played an important role in getting the railroad to complete a line to the new state. To them, California was a lonely place without women and families. They correctly believed that the railroad link to the east would allow females easier and safer access to the west coast.

By 1910, the group between eighteen and fifty once again represented a huge bulge in California's population pyramid (still dominated by males), overshadowing the elderly population that remained in the state. Even in 1940, that younger adult age group showed an impressive bulge in the pyramid, although the ratio of men to women was more balanced.

Clearly, California's promise of opportunity made im-

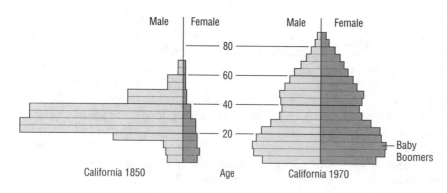

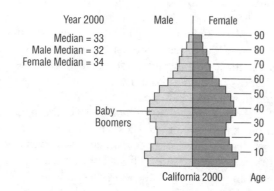

FIGURE 7.2

California age-sex pyramids. Dramatic male majorities during the gold rush were gradually balanced by the mid-1900s. By the beginning of the twenty-first century, baby boomers were graduating into middle age. *Sources*: California Atlas (Donley), U.S. Census, and California Department of Finance.

FLAWS IN THE TRADITIONAL DEMOGRAPHIC TRANSITION

Massive migrations and mobility have made population projections in California problematic at best. But, if you think models relying on age-sex pyramids make predictions rough, don't even try to understand or predict California's population trends using the traditional demographic transition; without considering immigration, you'll be doomed to failure. Stage one of that model applied to California's Native Americans for centuries. High birth and death rates kept populations relatively controlled by limitations of natural resources and technologies. During this first stage of the demographic transition, populations probably stabilized in the long-term.

Many of the new Californians flooding in during the 1800s brought a population in transition, with lowered death rates (due to increased knowledge and technology), while the birth rates remained high or only slowly crept down. This is similar to the second stage in the demographic transition. Then, just as women and children be-

gan to balance the population during the 1900s, birth rates for people born in California plummeted. That's when the population story became very convoluted in California.

By the late 1900s, there was dramatic disparity between birth rates and family sizes of native Californians—from second-generation families on—and recent immigrants from poorer regions of the world. Most California natives are participants in the final stage of the demographic transition, where births and deaths are low and the population is growing very slowly, if at all. Recent immigrants bring the transitional (middle) stages of the demographic transition to California, where death rates have been driven down, but birth rates are still high; their high fertility rates are not yet reflective of modern cultures in a highly developed economy. Estimating the number and nature of these future immigration waves further complicates reliable predictions of California's future populations.

ELDERLY MIGRATION PATTERNS

The importance of migration and mobility cannot be overstated in California. The elderly serve as a great example. According to the American Association of Retired Persons (AARP) and census data, by the mid-1990s, California had more people age 65 or older than any other state. The elderly population was more than 3.3 million and the number had increased by about 6 percent within three years, but all those elderly people represented only 11 percent of the total California population, which is a lower percentage than most other states. About 16 percent of older men were still in the work force compared to about 7 percent of older women. About 5 percent of el-

derly persons were in nursing homes, though those percentages rise dramatically with older ages.

As people who reach age sixty-five have an additional average life expectancy of eighteen years and the baby boomers graduate into this age group between 2010 and 2030, how will California change? Much of this will depend on where they decide to retire. Will they be pushed out of California to other states with lower living costs and less crime, congestion, and pollution? Or, will they simply migrate to more rural parts of the state as locations convenient to employment opportunities become less important to them?

migration the driving factor behind these population trends. However, by 1970, California's post-World War II baby boomers made a most impressive bulge on the pyramid in younger age groups ranging up to their early twenties. By 2010, this now-productive bulge will approach retirement age; their offspring, the second-generation boomlets, will assume responsibility for production in our society.

Here is a summary of California's population by age going into the 1990s, according to the U.S. Census: about 8.5 percent below 5 years old, more than 14 percent at 5–14, more than 14.5 percent at 15–24, more than 34 percent at 25–44, about 18 percent at 45–64, and nearly 11 percent at 65 and older. The percentage population

below five years old was slightly larger in California than the rest of the nation, while the percentage of older people was slightly less than the national average.

For decades, poorer, less educated, more recent immigrant families, whether they were from other struggling states or other countries, have been larger than the California average household size; they brought with them higher birth and fertility rates. These birth and fertility rates and family sizes usually drop to the state average for second-generation families in California. Consequently, new immigrants have had profound short-term impacts on California's population pyramid, impacts that are very different from native-born populations. Today, immigration continues to play a major role in changing California's age distributions. Immigration is notably changing the percentage of ethnic groups that contribute to the state's modern population pyramid.

Age-sex pyramids may also vary widely by location. Consider the dramatic bulge created by college-age groups migrating in and around UC Berkeley, UC Davis, and other college towns. Traditional military towns and cities (such as those around the Monterey and Oceanside areas during the Cold War) have had unusually large percentages of young males in their population pyramids.

◆ A CLOSER LOOK AT MIGRATION PATTERNS AND THEIR EFFECTS

The questions of mobility that change California landscapes are not restricted to one group. Will the gap between rich and poor continue to grow as it did during the 1980s and 1990s? Will low-paying service and laborious manufacturing jobs attract poor, unskilled workers, while well-educated, high-income professionals flock in to fill jobs in high-tech, trade, and entertainment? In this section, we explore this important and controversial issue of immigration into California in more detail. This may only give us a hint of future population trends in the state, but it will certainly unveil some interesting details about the people who come to California.

Demographers define **migration** as the permanent relocation of one's residential place and activity space. This rules out the daily, weekly, and monthly commutes to work, school, appointments, and meetings and the less-frequent visits, vacations, and temporary lodgings we may seek during the year. There are several different types of migrations that occur into, out of, and within California that continue to have profound effects on the state's populations and landscapes.

Considering Net Migration

To more accurately evaluate changes in California's population, we add net migration into the previous calculations for natural increases in 1970, 1980, and 1989. See

the equations illustrated in Figure 7.3. The increase in population slowed a bit during the recession of the early 1990s (down to more than +300,000 per year), but it accelerated again as the California economy surged ahead into the twenty-first century.

Migration to and from Other Countries

International migration (to and from other countries) is sometimes loosely referred to as migration from "abroad" or "overseas," but it includes the Latin American countries. California has received an enormous influx from several countries since the 1800s, but has lost relatively few emigrants to most of those countries. Millions settled in California in the decades after the Gold Rush, first mainly from European and Asian nations and the Pacific Islands. Since the mid-1900s, newcomers from Latin America have ruled the immigrant stream, and by the late-1900s, Asian immigrants were competing for the lead. Millions have also returned to Latin America, and particularly back across the border to Mexico, but the net population change for California has been overwhelmingly positive each year (see Figure 7.4).

The Primary Destination for Immigrants from Other Countries   From 1901 to 1920, a great wave of 4.5 million immigrants, representing nearly 30 percent of all immigrants into the United States, settled in New York. The majority were from Italy and eastern Europe, Russia, Great Britain, Ireland, and Germany. From 1980 to 1996, a new great wave of 5 million immigrants, representing about 33 percent of all immigrants into the United States, settled in California. The majority, in order, were from Mexico, the Philippines, Vietnam, El Salvador, China, and South Korea. You can see that not only has the primary destination of immigrants to the United States shifted toward California, but the source regions of those immigration streams have also shifted dramatically (see Figure 7.5).

During the 1900s, the percent of California's population that was foreign born first peaked around 1910 at

	California Births	−	California Deaths	=	Natural Population Change	+	Net Migration to California	=	Net Population Change
1970	358,000		165,000		193,000		101,000		+294,000
1980	390,000		180,000		210,000		303,000		+513,000
1989	505,000		216,000		289,000		377,000		+666,000

FIGURE 7.3
Demographic Equations.

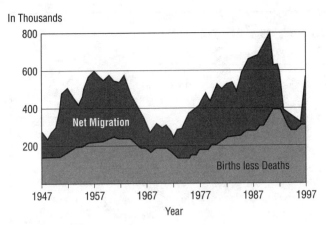

FIGURE 7.4

California Population—Annual Growth in Thousands. *Source*: California Department of Finance.

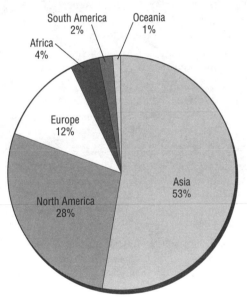

FIGURE 7.5

Legal Immigration to California by Region of Birth, 1995. (Note that this is *legal* immigration for 1995 only.) *Source*: California Department of Finance.

nearly 23 percent. According to a U.S. Census Bureau report, by 1997, one-quarter of the state's population (about 8 million) was foreign born, the highest percentage of the century and nearly triple the 1970 figures. Among the state's total immigrant populations into the late 1990s, 42 percent were from Mexico and 9 percent were from other Central American countries, with immigrants from El Salvador in the lead. Additionally, census data and other studies revealed that about 33 percent of California immigrants during the late 1990s were from Asia, with the greatest numbers from the Philippines, then Vietnam, and then Korea.

The effects of specific migrations into California depend on the source of migration, the direction, and the size of the migration stream. By the 1990s in the United States, states with large immigrant streams from other countries already had large established settlements of earlier immigrants particularly from Latin America and Asia. California led the nation in this pattern.

Migration to and from Other States

Interstate migrations (between California and other states) were also overwhelmingly positive from the Gold Rush years until 1990. Numerous states east of the Rocky Mountains lost people to California throughout the 1900s; imprints left by these Midwesterners, Southerners, New Yorkers, and New Englanders are still evident across the state. During the recession of the early 1990s, there were finally short periods when California lost more people to other states than it gained from them.

In the late 1990s, as the California economy rebounded, interstate migration turned positive again. By 1996, the net inflow of people from other states to California exceeded the outflow by about 25,000. That positive trend continued to accelerate in the late 1990s. Many of those people were turning back to California after finding more adverse conditions in those other states and new opportunities in the Golden State.

◆ CALIFORNIA'S NEW FACE

What do these recent economic and population trends have in common? They show us that the California whose power was based on manufacturing jobs, a white middle class, and a generation who dominated a growing state since World War II is gradually fading away. The new California is the result of no less than an economic, population, and cultural revolution—a restructuring of major proportions that has set the stage for the state in the twenty-first century.

In 1970, nearly 80 percent of all Californians were white. By the end of the 1900s, the California Trade and Commerce Agency's Office of Economic Research reports the following racial breakdown: 53 percent of California residents were white, 29 percent Hispanic, 11 percent Asian/Pacific Islander, 7 percent African American and 1 percent Native American. Asian and Latino populations—in numbers and percentage of the total—continued to soar through the 1990s in California, while thousands of lower- and middle-class residents were lost to interstate "white flight." Hispanic births outnumbered white births in 1992 for the first time since the 1800s.

MIGRATIONS FROM OTHER STATES MAKE CALIFORNIA UNIQUE

One pattern that most states with high international immigrants share is a net loss of people to other U.S. states, but statistics show that California does not share this trend. Of the five states receiving the most immigrants from abroad from 1985 to 1990, California was the only state that had positive net migration from other states. It ranked seventh nationally in its ability to attract these interstate migrants. In 1989 to 1990, this net domestic migration was still positive by more than 200,000 in California.

Then, according to state figures, California finally began losing more immigrants to other states during the early 1990s. From July 1, 1992, through June, 1993, 390,000 people left California, and only 290,000 people entered the state from other states. From July, 1993, through 1994, California lost about 250,000 more people than it gained from other states. As that trend continued into the next year, the state posted a net loss of people to other states for each year in the first half of the 1990s. Experts cited several reasons for this change in tradition: a sagging California economy, high unemployment, the high cost of living, crime rates, and natural disasters.

In contrast, Colorado led the nation in attracting people from other states by 1994, with its low unemployment and crime rates and lower housing prices. Other western states successfully exploited California's bleeding interstate migration stream during that period; some even launched public relations campaigns to attract escapees from wounded California. Specifically, nearby states such as Nevada, Arizona, Idaho, Utah, Oregon, and Washington were gaining new arrivals from California. By 1997, California's economy and image were remade, and the state was again experiencing a net gain in interstate migration, and this trend continued into the twenty-first century.

INTERSTATE MIGRATIONS ALSO REMAKE CALIFORNIA'S POPULATION

The specifics of these trends since the mid-1980s are fascinating. According to the University of Michigan Population Studies Center and census data, California has been gaining international immigrants who represent minority groups when they arrive in the state. At the same time, there was a net loss of lower- and middle-income whites to other states during the recession of the early 1990s.

This may indicate that less-skilled, working-class whites were finding better opportunities in nearby states where there was less economic and cultural competition from California's newer arrivals. However, California ranked second in its ability to attract white college graduates during the late 1980s to higher-paying jobs requiring more skills and education. The result was that California

still ranked ninth in the nation in its ability to attract all white immigrants, even into the early 1990s recession. From the late 1980s well into the 1990s, whites dominated interstate **immigration** (people moving in) and **emigration** (people moving out) to and from California.

This clarifies California's trend toward a dual economy, which has become typical of regions with large, modern financial centers. Many high-paying information-economy jobs requiring education and skills are available, as well as abundant low-wage service and labor employment requiring little education and few skills. During the early 1990s recession, an extraordinary number of middle-income workers vanished as the middle-class manufacturing jobs were replaced by these extremes.

This certainly was the trend from the 1980s well into the 1990s in California. During the late 1980s, as California lost less-educated, particularly lower- and middle-income whites to other states, it gained more than 100,000 white college graduates and a large number of minority college graduates. This was all preparation and restructuring for the new dual economy that would catapult California into the 21st century.

There are substantial cultural implications in these trends. With emigrating poor whites being replaced by poor minority immigrants from other countries and a gain of high-income whites, California's gap between the rich and poor threatens to become even a greater gap between white and minority (especially recent immigrant) groups. The economic and cultural stratification does not stop there.

Traditionally, young college graduates are more mobile as they respond to job opportunities, while elderly residents are usually less capable of moving. California trends are just the opposite. As college graduates remain in California, net emigration of elderly whites was even greater than for younger whites in California into the 1990s. With high living costs and perceived adverse living conditions that conflict with elderly lifestyles, California experienced a net loss of 37,000 elderly white residents from 1985 to 1990; many of them moved to nearby states, such as Oregon, Nevada, and Arizona. By the 1990s, California no longer shared mass immigrations of elderly with other sunbelt states.

Interestingly, some of the trends reviewed in this special section during the late 1990s. As the state's economy rebounded and surged ahead, middle-class jobs, such as in manufacturing and construction, returned and so did many of the middle class workers and families. However, the restructuring of the 1990s left lasting imprints on California's economy and population.

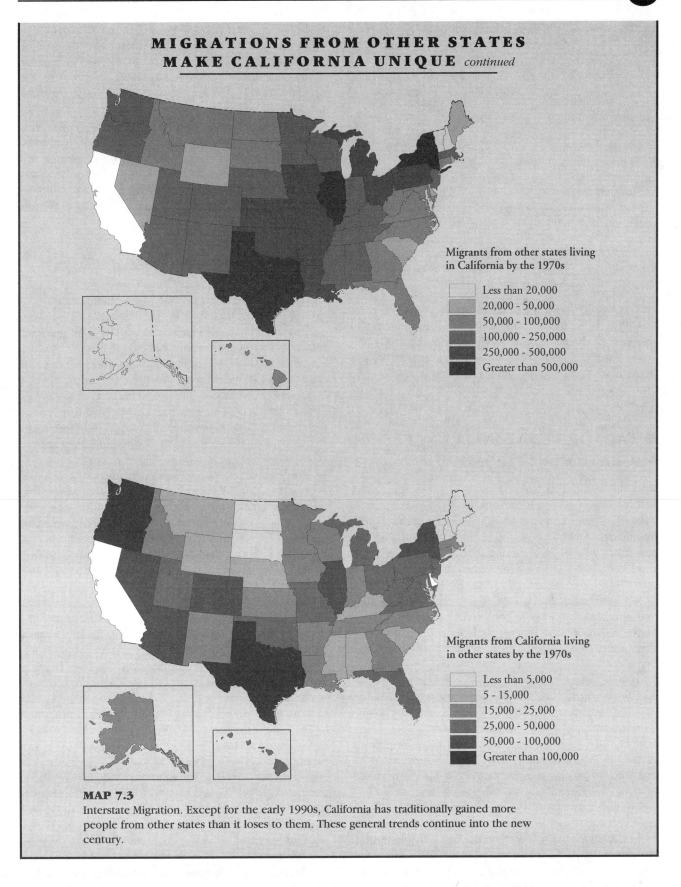

MIGRATIONS FROM OTHER STATES
MAKE CALIFORNIA UNIQUE *continued*

Migrants from other states living in California by the 1970s

- Less than 20,000
- 20,000 - 50,000
- 50,000 - 100,000
- 100,000 - 250,000
- 250,000 - 500,000
- Greater than 500,000

Migrants from California living in other states by the 1970s

- Less than 5,000
- 5 - 15,000
- 15,000 - 25,000
- 25,000 - 50,000
- 50,000 - 100,000
- Greater than 100,000

MAP 7.3

Interstate Migration. Except for the early 1990s, California has traditionally gained more people from other states than it loses to them. These general trends continue into the new century.

California Racial and Ethnic Composition

	Population July 1996	Percent of Population
White	17,130,800	53
Hispanic	9,330,800	29
Asian/Pacific Islander	3,452,600	11
African American	2,275,300	7
Native American	193,500	1

The new California is seen in the faces and cultures that work in so many of the new industries and live in so many of the transformed neighborhoods; they combine to make a new population of Californians, largely divided between wealthy and poor, that is ever-changing and ever-mobile.

◆ FACTORS THAT INFLUENCE MIGRATION PATTERNS

Why do so many people continue to migrate into and within California? **Push factors** are the adverse conditions that cause people to leave an area. Overpopulation, natural disasters, poverty, and economic and political instability have pushed millions to emigrate away from Europe, Asia, Latin America, the eastern United States, and other locations toward California during past decades. Why California? It had the more favorable **pull factors** that attracted the masses: gold, rich farmland, mild climates, open spaces, diverse and beautiful natural settings, more freedom, and the promise of better jobs and living conditions. All of these factors add up to the California Dream.

Thanks to these combined push-pull factors, California has consistently been located in a classic position where complementarity encourages increased immigration. For millions of immigrants to California, exceptional employment opportunities have cut the financial costs involved in making their moves. Once here, the state's diverse, desirable living environments have decreased emotional costs and further eased transferability. There are plenty of exceptions to these generalizations, and there are many who have left the state in frustration. However, the past and continued positive net migration rates are remarkable and speak for themselves.

Intervening opportunities have not interfered as much with movements to California as compared to many other great migrations; the state's boosters have traditionally done a splendid job playing up the California Dream. It is difficult to stop or be diverted for what may be a good opportunity when you are on the way to the land of milk and honey, where there is always fresh produce to harvest and devour, where the streets are paved with gold, where a star is born every day in Hollywood, the sun always shines, and the beautiful lights on San Francisco Bay beckon each newcomer. These myths have usually towered above the natural and cultural barriers and great distances that may have otherwise kept the immigrants from making it all the way to California.

Barriers to Migrants

Whether they were motivated or desperate, California's immigrants were often pushed, then pulled tremendous distances across formidable barriers against enormous odds. American miners and settlers looking for gold and productive land crossed the vast grasslands of the Great Plains, the expansive Rocky Mountains, and the desolate deserts only to meet the great wall of the Sierra Nevada. Legendary accounts of the busted wagons and the miserable, sick travellers starving for water and food and either dying from exposure in the desert or being frozen in the snow, have captured the hearts and imaginations of millions.

However, Asians and Pacific Islanders who made it across that huge Pacific barrier, Mexicans who penetrated through the porous border, and African Americans who came with other American settlers found new barriers within California when they arrived. These were the political, cultural, and economic racial barriers constructed by those who took control of the state after the Gold Rush. When transportation technologies began to bridge the geographic distances and obstructions to California, those cultural barriers remained. This was particularly true for people who did not fit the narrow definition of the ideal California citizen according to those who made the rules; it has been the case throughout the 1900s for those who did not speak English.

Judgments were not only made based on skin color or native language. When waves of poor immigrants flocked to California to escape the devastating droughts of the Great Plains (the Dust Bowl) and the Great Depression, they were labelled "Okies." Their sheer poverty and desperation led them to become the latest exploitable work force as they were shunned by the majority of Californians. This is yet another act in the drama that has been played out repeatedly in California, but with different disadvantaged groups during different time periods.

Place utility describes whether people are satisfied or dissatisfied with the place where they live. If so many people suffered so much hardship in California, why did they stay? The answer is probably that they saw their new home as having more place utility—and offering more hope—than their old one. So, as some of the most homesick and disenchanted immigrants practiced, and still practice, counter or return migration, most stayed, or tried to stay, or were forced to stay.

Forced to Move

Voluntary migrants are usually more likely to return to their homelands. In contrast, there were, and are, the involuntary emigrants, those that were forced to emigrate away from their homelands. At the least, they became reluctant immigrants to California due to the perception or actual threat of starvation, violence, or persecution against them in their homelands.

How California and the nation defines a **refugee** often determines who can stay. Were the "Okies" refugees from a land consumed by raging dust storms and from a life that would have meant certain starvation if they had stayed there? Which government would have killed which political refugee during the Cold War: El Salvador or Nicaragua or both? The government of El Salvador was supported by the U.S. government; the Nicaraguan government was supported by the Soviet Union. Did the immigrant from Nicaragua have a better chance of achieving "refugee" status here? How do we set policies that will impact the refugee status of future immigrants from Latin America, Asia, Europe, or Africa? All of these factors help determine how we welcome new immigrants to California and whether they stay or return to their homelands.

The Final Destination

California has become famous for being the last in a series of transitional steps that many immigrants take. People from Central America and rural Mexico often try their luck in Mexico's urban areas, such as Mexico City or Tijuana, before they take that giant leap into California. Southeast Asian refugees were placed throughout the United States during the 1970s and 1980s after our involvement in the Vietnam War. Within a few years, most of them relocated to and settled in California, including those who clustered into what became the two largest Vietnamese communities in the nation (Westminster and San Jose). You can see that California rarely becomes one in a series of transitional, less extreme steps for immigrant groups moving elsewhere; it is more likely a final destination, where steps may then be taken to different regions within the state.

Chain migrations have also played crucial roles in bringing significant numbers of immigrants to California. Since the Spanish and Mexican Periods, one individual or family would often move to California and set up a stable foundation to welcome other family members and friends. More recent illegal immigrants from Latin America and Asia, when quizzed about why they tried to move to California, note the job and shelter that a friend or relative had waiting for them. These are not usually wandering risk takers. They more often know exactly where they are going, how they will get there, and who and what is waiting for them. This is made possible by the chain of communications and support established by other immigrants from their homeland, who have already moved to California.

Finally, most immigrants arrive in California along channels already established by past migrations. Immigrants from Asia typically arrive by boat into certain California harbors or by plane at specific airports. Illegal immigrants from Mexico once flocked across openings in the porous border between San Diego and Tijuana. After Immigration and Naturalization Service (INS) reinforcements plugged those holes, new paths for channelized migrations were established by the end of the twentieth century in the remote mountains and deserts farther inland along the eastern sections of the San Diego County and the Imperial County/Mexico border.

We now turn our attention toward more specific migration streams, immigrants' experiences, and their effects on California.

◆ SPECIAL FOCUS ON IMMIGRANTS AND THEIR EFFECTS

Immigration trends and policies have sparked debate in California for decades. Everyone seems to have an opinion about these controversial issues. The following section is for those with a special interest in more facts and details about recent immigration in California.

According to data from the California Department of Finance, 5.5 million immigrants in California were legal, foreign-born residents during the mid-1990s. Many of those were once illegal residents who became citizens under the rules of the 1986 Immigration Reform and Control Act. Meanwhile, according to the U.S. Census Bureau, the approximately 2 million illegal immigrants remaining in California into the late 1990s represented nearly half the nation's total.

Disparity Between Recent Immigrants and Citizens Born in the United States

The following data from the U.S. Census Bureau, various state and federal agencies, and the *Los Angeles Times* shows the disparity between Californians born in the United States and Californians born in other countries in household size, income, and education for all races.

1996	U.S.-Born Californians	Foreign-Born Californians
Household size	42% have 1–2 members 16% have 5 or more	22% have 1–2 people/home 41% have 5 or more people
Household income	21% < $20,000/year 46% > $50,000/year	31% < $20,000/year 30% > $50,000/year
Education at 25 or older	10% < high school	42% < high school

Successive waves of immigrants took the place of cheap California Indian labor, which ran dry in the 1800s. Typically, the most recent immigrants to California, especially the illegal immigrants, have always been more easily exploited in the workplace. Cultural barriers make them hesitant to complain about working conditions in jobs that require less education and fewer skills. As you review the following data, note that these jobs are far removed from the growing high-paying, high-tech, entertainment and trade industry positions that require more education and training. Also note that wage claims and other complaints against employers to the state labor commissioner's office were falling; they dropped 35 percent between 1990–1995.

Percent of Jobs Held by Foreign-Born Workers Statewide

	1980	1996
Construction labor	20%	64%
Janitor	26%	49%
Farm worker	58%	91%
Maid/houseman	34%	76%
Electronics assembler	37%	60%
Household child care	20%	58%
Restaurant cook	29%	69%
Gardener	37%	66%
Drywall installer	9%	48%

Sources: U.S. Census Bureau, State Labor Commissioner's Office, and the *Los Angeles Times*.

The New Immigrants: Where Are They and Who Are They?

Approximately 37 percent of all new immigrants into the entire United States in the 1990s planned to live in one of seven California metropolitan areas. An even larger percentage (about 42 percent) of the nation's undocumented workers planned to live in one of those California urban areas.

The San Francisco Bay Area and Beyond

For decades, San Francisco has had a reputation for attracting refugees, asylum seekers, and other immigrants escaping discrimination and persecution. The City has absorbed a mix of southern Europeans, Asians and Pacific Islanders, Mexicans, and others from Latin America. Immigrants from Russia are one of the latest new groups to arrive. Many of these new immigrants seem to be more easily absorbed within this diverse, cosmopolitan city.

According to reports in the journal *Population*, between 1975 and 1990, more than 35,000 people from Southeast Asia settled in San Francisco; ethnic Chinese from Vietnam were quickly absorbed by The City's acclaimed Chinese community. Other Southeast Asian groups, most notably Vietnamese, Laotians, Hmong, and Cambodians, made their start in The City. Many then moved on to other north/central California locations where they found lower living costs and already-established ethnic enclaves.

By the 1990s, San Jose was home to the second-largest Vietnamese community (about 70,000) in the nation. Only Orange County's Little Saigon in Westminster had more. Vietnamese businesses and media, cultural celebrations, and educational events have transformed the economy and cultural landscapes of both San Jose in the north and Westminster in the south. Communities of lowland Laotians were established in the East Bay, while

From Asians to Pacific Islanders to more visible Latinos, you will find a mix of recent immigrants, natives and countless ethnic groups in San Francisco's Mission District.

highland Lao and Hmong had settled in the Fresno area, and more than 5,000 Cambodians had moved on to settle in the Stockton/Modesto area.

By the early 1990s, resettlement organizations in the Bay Area that had served primarily Asians expanded to serve a wide variety of immigrants, including eastern Europeans, Afghans, Iranians, and Ethiopians. Joining the new immigrants were Jews, Pentecostals, and Baptists fleeing former Soviet Union lands. Following tradition, most of these immigrants, particularly those who could not speak English, settled in poorer San Francisco communities until they gathered the resources and acculturated enough to move on into neighboring suburbs.

Large numbers of refugees from Central America who settled in San Francisco faced similar language and cultural barriers. Many were less educated and had fewer skills, but faced the possibility of deportation when asylum was not granted. Lacking the benefits of many other immigrants, they remained in poorer neighborhoods and relied on legal aid and other assistance from students at Stanford, UC Berkeley, and the University of San Francisco.

Los Angeles and Southern California

When the results of studies were released from the 1990 census and other sources on a 56-square-mile area around downtown Los Angeles, they made headlines in national newspapers. Why? It wasn't because this one area had a population of more than 1 million (about 11.5 percent of Los Angeles County) and was growing 36 percent faster than the county average. It wasn't because it could stand alone as the seventh-largest city in the United States. This 56-square-mile area received so much attention because eight out of ten residents were born outside the United States, most of them in Latin American countries, Korea, China, or the Philippines, respectively.

More than six of ten residents within that 56-square-mile area had arrived in the United States since 1980.

From 1980 to 1990, the area's foreign-born residents increased by more than 50 percent; the non-English speaking population increased by 45 percent, and the Latino population increased more than 46 percent. More than 62 percent of the area's adults were not U.S. citizens, and more than 51 percent of the total population were not citizens.

As city officials and neighborhood groups continued the traditional debates about the meaning of these trends, this part of southern California was labelled the New Los Angeles or Nuevo Los Angeles by some in the press. Were these immigrants hard-working people who were being exploited for the cheap labor they represent, adding far more to a society that returns very little to them? Or were they mostly poor immigrants desperate for the educational opportunities, health care, and other benefits that were placing strains on an already burdened infrastructure? Controversy and debates about the ramifications of these great migrations will continue in the twenty-first century.

Latino Immigrants

Californians often consider their state as the place where the United States ends. (Alaskans and Hawaiians would disagree.) In contrast, Latino immigrants especially view California as the place where the United States begins; many consider both the United States and Mexico to be like one North America, where people might move freely between latitudes. Consider the plight of some of the Latino immigrants in the following stories.

Immigrants from Central America   Nearly one of every five Salvadorans fled their country's political storms particularly during the 1980s. Many of these immigrants settled in California enclaves. Though Central American immigrants settled in visible San Francisco barrios during the late 1900s, Southern California is home to a much greater number of Central Americans, especially from El

In Los Angeles, you may not only find Indian, Mexican, and other food and cultures on the same block, but in the same restaurant!

Salvador and Guatemala. Up to 500,000 exiles in Los Angeles represent the largest Salvadoran community in the United States. Some of them are illegal, some have temporary permits to remain and work in California, and some have become citizens.

After more than thirty years of political turmoil in their country, people from Guatemala found it even more difficult to qualify for protected status and to remain in California legally. Victims from the Guatemalan highlands made up a large part of the immigrant stream into the 1990s.

The Central American Refugee Center is located in the Pico-Union neighborhood of Los Angeles, the heart of this immigrant community. It and other organizations serve as advocates for the immigrants who have established family and roots in California and fear returning to their homelands.

On the other side of the spectrum are the illegal rackets set up in the immigrants' barrios that prepare counterfeit documents for people who cannot get legal ones. Government officials during the 1990s began enforcing strict laws against such operations as they fortified the U.S. border with Mexico to curtail illegal activity. Advocates who consider Central American immigrants as refugees simply seeking political asylum continue to clash with those who seek to seal the United States border and deport anyone who is here illegally. Meanwhile, fearful immigrants are either forced to apply for protected status in the United States, live here illegally, or return home.

By the mid-1990s, reports in *The New York Times* and other media exposed a new source of immigrants from Latin America; Indians from Central and South America had become the largest group of immigrant farm workers in California. They were considered the latest exploitable work force on California's farms.

Mexican Immigrants and Return Migration   So much has been said and written about Mexican immigration into California since the mid-1900s, it is impossible to even summarize in this short writing. Since the 1970s, immigration from Mexico has surpassed previous mass migrations into the United States from Italy, Ireland, and other nations. It now represents the greatest mass migration in history from any single country into the United States.

By the late 1990s, California was home to more than half of the 6.7 million immigrants born in Mexico who now live in the United States. These trends encouraged consideration by the Mexican government to allow immigrants who have established citizenship in the United States to continue as citizens of Mexico. Such a dual citizenship opportunity could fortify the bridges that have been built between the cultures and economies of California and Mexico; the loyalties Mexican Americans feel toward both countries are often evident.

Because Mexican Americans have dominated the immigrant stream into California for decades, some might argue that the cultural calendar has been moved back to the early 1800s when California was part of Mexico. However, today's Mexican-American communities in California are almost as diverse as the state itself, just as the newest immigrants come from many different rural and urban Mexican landscapes. Due to their numbers alone, modern Mexican-Americans have assumed responsibility for much of California's agricultural and industrial production. Those who have stayed are also advancing to make clear marks on California's cultural and political landscapes.

According to the Public Policy Institute in San Francisco, most Mexican immigrants in the mid-1990s entered California illegally. Half of all Mexican immigrants return to their homelands in less than two years; more than two-thirds return to Mexico within ten years. Generally, poorer immigrants return even sooner than the average as government benefits play very minor roles in such decisions. Various surveys have shown for years that

Across the Tijuana River, on the Mexican side, is a whole different world . . . or is it?

more than nine out of ten of these immigrants enter California to work, so it is not surprising that job prospects drive their decisions and behavior once they are here. The Mexican immigrants who stay the longest usually have more skills and education and have gained security by becoming legal citizens and landing higher-paying jobs.

Illegal Immigrants from Mexico   From the mid-1980s to the early 1990s, the Tijuana metropolitan area's population doubled to more than 2 million. People from rural and interior Mexico were flocking to jobs at the maquiladoras (border factories) or using the city as a stepping stone into California. Tijuana has struggled under the pressure of so many immigrants in such a short time as Mexico's economy faltered. Shantytowns and cardboard shelters with no services (such as water, electricity, sewage, or roads) littered the outskirts of the city and became tragic media photo opportunities. On the edge of this otherwise prosperous city, twenty-three people—mostly children—froze to death in the cold of December, 1992.

By January, 1993, more than 5,000 immigrants were camped in colonias (neighborhoods) in once-scenic Piedra Canyon near Free Road between Rosarito and Tijuana. When the rains hit, the debris these migrants had accumulated blocked the natural flow of water through the canyons; thousands were flooded out. Within Piedra Canyon and nearby Laureles Canyon (both tributaries of the Tijuana River), fifteen people were killed and more than 5,000 were left homeless by the floods. Tijuana officials spent more than $50 million of their limited budget to relocate more than 2,000 people after this much-publicized tragedy. Assistance flowed in from California to the north, but poor immigrants continued to flow into Tijuana from the south. In 1998, floods and mudflows caused more misery in many of these areas.

Spanish language radio stations became leaders in the Los Angeles market during the 1990s. Here, one station advertises at the festival that will celebrate Latino cultures in downtown Los Angeles, billed as the largest Cinco de Mayo celebration in the world.

Tijuana colonias have long been the staging grounds where Mexican illegal immigrants start their venture into San Diego. However, this activity shifted away from the western extremes of San Diego County after 1994, when the U.S. federal government initiated Operation Gatekeeper, designed to stop illegal border crossings. By 1996, San Ysidro had become the world's busiest land border crossing, but many illegal immigrants had been forced far east into the remote mountains bordering eastern San Diego County and Mexico. Making their annual trek back to California after the holidays in January, 1997, more than thirteen people died after prolonged exposure to wet and cold weather. As hundreds of other immigrants crammed Tijuana's shelters unable to complete their crossings, the U.S. and Mexican governments sent warnings to would-be migrants about the dangers they faced. In what seemed to be a tragic repeat performance, more storms in 1998 and 1999 claimed new victims.

Immigrant camps certainly have not been limited to the Mexican side of the border. For years into the 1990s, smoke could be seen rising through the chaparral and oaks in canyons on San Diego's urban fringe as migrant workers prepared their meals. Many of the same people who knowingly hire undocumented workers are the most startled and first to complain when they see people emerge from the brush, leaving their temporary shelters for a hard day's work.

Rancho de los Diablos became famous as one of California's longest-lasting and largest immigrant camps until it was destroyed and the remaining families relocated. Publications including *L.A. Times Magazine* reported on the history of the camp and its final destruction in November, 1994. Up to 2,000 people once lived in this northwestern San Diego camp in the 1970s; it sprawled for more than one-half mile. The people worked in surrounding neighborhoods, developments, and agricultural fields.

When it was bulldozed, there were about four-hundred shelters made of scrap wood and metal, plastic and cardboard. The settlement included a water delivery system, portable toilets, electricity, restaurants, and several fields and courts for various sports activities. Its own town council also looked over the medical clinic, flea market, church services, and the check cashing and credit, trash pickup and toilet cleanup services. People had erected new illegal camps in surrounding landscapes even before Rancho de los Diablos disappeared.

This drama is played throughout Southern California communities where illegal and some legal workers are exploited for their cheap labor. It was repeated in Ventura County's upscale Thousand Oaks in April, 1997. Local residents were "shocked" when up to fifty immigrant workers and their children were discovered living in a shantytown of metal toolsheds and temporary huts. The small community was declared a safety hazard, and the people were evicted. Nearby residents of Thousand

PERCEPTIONS OF LEGAL AND ILLEGAL IMMIGRATION

During the 1990s, two enormously important events changed California's approach to immigration and our relationship with Mexico. Californians passed Proposition 187 by a 60 percent plurality to bar illegal immigrants from government services and schools. Some saw it as an anti-immigration backlash, others as an anti-illegal measure. Supporters pointed to the perceived burden on government services caused by illegal newcomers, while many opponents cried racism and pointed to historic and intangible benefits of immigrants. Both sides were still arguing their cases as the courts were determining Proposition 187's constitutional legality into the late 1990s. Regardless, such **illegal immigration** was perceived by the majority of voting Californians as a problem.

Also by the late 1990s, the full effects of the North American Free Trade Agreement (NAFTA) were being experienced across the state. This agreement will be reviewed in Chapter 10 on modern economies. It paved the way for an explosion of maquiladoras (industries that locate on the U.S./Mexico border). These industries ship parts in from around the world, make products using cheap Mexican labor and U.S. technologies, then ship them across the border into the United States without the previously expensive and often prohibitive tariffs.

Economies on both sides of the California/Baja border have been electrified ever since. There was a wide variation in public opinion before NAFTA passed. Those who thought immigrants into California were hard working and contributed to the health of the economy generally supported NAFTA. But, those who thought immigrants were a drain on government resources and destabilized communities and the economy were most fearful of these closer ties to Mexico.

What effect did these events have on illegal immigration? Apparently, very little. In early 1997, the U.S. Immigration and Naturalization Service (INS) released the results of one of the most comprehensive, systematic studies ever done on illegal immigration into the United States. California led the country with about 2 million illegal immigrants, or 40 percent of the U.S. total. Undocumented residents represented more than 6 percent of the total California population, almost double that of Texas, the number two state.

Mexico was the source of far more than half of all illegal immigrants to California, followed distantly by El Salvador and Guatemala. The number of illegal immigrants had previously peaked just before about 3 million immigrants nationwide were granted amnesty in 1986 by the Immigration Reform and Control Act. The number crept up again since then into the late 1990s. These statistics count only the number of illegal immigrants who stay for at least one full year.

California is living up to its well-established image as the main attraction for illegal immigrants. Many government officials and immigration experts used the figures to show that government crackdowns at the border do not work to solve this problem. They argue for more aggressive enforcement of laws designed to stop California employers from hiring and exploiting illegal immigrants in California industries and other workplaces.

Not all illegal immigrants are from Latin America. Asians make up a large percentage of illegal immigrants into the state. They can be just as vulnerable to exploitation because they are in a foreign culture with an unfamiliar language. It is difficult to engage in debate about U.S. quotas for legal immigration or to discuss the effects of the brain drain on foreign countries due to immigration into California when we can't even decide on what to do about or how to control illegal immigration.

Oaks (where household incomes averaged $60,000 and average homes were worth nearly $250,000) were forced to ask how this could happen in their community.

Much farther east, on the opposite side of the coastal mountains, very different settings are attracting poor immigrants. In the desert settlements from Mexicali and across into Calexico, the productive farmlands of the Imperial Valley beckon. Here, immigrants will find plenty of competition for the many jobs among the harvests in this hot valley with its year-round growing seasons. They will also enter one of the poorest regions in the state, where masses of poverty-stricken laborers contrast with the few who own the land and grow and manage the crops.

◆ MOVING AROUND IN CALIFORNIA: MIGRATION WITHIN THE STATE

Intrastate migration between and within California regions has also transformed California's populations, cultures, neighborhoods, and landscapes in dramatic ways. Interregional migrations (between regions within the state) and intraregional relocations (from place to place within specific regions) occur as Californians frequently move in search of improved working and living conditions. Today's Californians are more unstable than the land under them. According to studies from moving

IMMIGRANTS PROVIDE SKILLED LABOR FOR MODERN INDUSTRIES

Much of the publicity about immigrants to California paints a stereotypical picture of desperate, poverty-stricken people. By the mid-1990s, a very different picture had emerged from the Silicon Valley and other high-tech centers throughout California. Studies showed nearly one-third of all engineers, programmers, and other high-tech professionals in the Silicon Valley were born in other countries. They came mainly from Asia (particularly China and India) and some European countries. Corporations complained of shortages of qualified professionals from the United States, including trained individuals from Stanford and other universities in California. High-tech companies were reaching out to foreign countries for employees. They brought in skilled professionals who were the best in their fields, noting that the new foreign immigrants would add a diverse mix of talented people and ideas to the industry.

A skeptical global community watched as still another trend enhanced the brain drain of talent from other nations (mostly less developed) and the resulting brain gain of talent and innovation into powerful California. Others cited studies showing that corporations were paying foreign-born computer professionals salaries that averaged about $7,000 less per year than U.S.-born professionals for the same work. They claimed there was more U.S. talent out there, but companies were cutting costs by hiring from abroad.

This was not the first time, nor would it be the last, that California citizens cried foul when immigrants were invited to compete in the state's job market. The increasingly influential global economy would see to that. However, the great majority of high-tech jobs in California and the Silicon Valley were filled by U.S.-born and trained professionals, while natives also filled a much larger majority of related jobs. In the midst of these trends, California companies and universities continue to sponsor and train foreign-born high-tech professionals. Walls and barriers continue to tumble, economic and cultural bridges are growing stronger, and geographic distances are less relevant as the new communication and information revolution shrinks the globe. What will this mean for the future of immigration in California?

companies such as Allied Van Lines, California continued to have the most mobile populations in the nation during the 1990s. More remarkably, Californians continued to rank as some of the most mobile people on the planet.

Where the Immigrants Settle

What happens to immigrants who remain in California? The state's major cities often serve as transitional stepping-stones. Once they gain more resources and assimilate, many immigrants move to suburbs or even farther away from their original host city. Recent Chinese immigrants, some of whom do not speak English, may blend into San Francisco's renowned and compact Chinatown neighborhoods. However, English-speaking Chinese-Americans who have adjusted to, or fully adopted American cultures, are mixing with other Asian-Americans and ethnic and cultural groups farther away from Chinatown. They are now found in some of San Francisco's outlying districts and even beyond The City into surrounding bedroom communities. In other sections of this and the next chapter, we've investigated immigrant populations from Southeast Asia that have spread out and away from the Bay Area: the Vietnamese community of San Jose, the Cambodians in the Stockton/Modesto area, and the Hmong in the Fresno area.

The trend is clear and it dates back to past experiences of most immigrant groups who have come to California.

Poorer newcomers with less education and skills face language and cultural barriers; they are often left behind in low-income enclaves, barrios, and ghettos. Those who have acculturated and gained education, skills, and reliable employment can move away from the protection of those environments and closer to the California Dream. These trends are most conspicuous in the sprawling Los Angeles area.

According to studies at USC's School of Urban and Regional Planning released in 1997, Los Angeles and other major cities are gateways for the poorest immigrants. They eventually move out to the suburbs and clear the way for the newest wave of poor, disadvantaged newcomers. This leaves communities closer to central L.A. burdened with a constant flood of poor, disadvantaged immigrants. Meanwhile, the suburbs reap the benefits of immigration as they gain those who have become more stable and successful. During the mid-1990s, 40 percent of all families in Los Angeles and more than half the families below the federal poverty line in L.A. were headed by immigrants. Many of these immigrants were legally joining already established family members.

About 27 percent of the new immigrants to L.A. were Asians, who assimilate and move out faster than other groups. They often move out to Monterey Park and other communities farther from central L.A., particularly into the San Gabriel Valley. About 60 percent of the new immigrants were Latino; they took longer to assimilate and move away from East L.A., mostly farther east to Montebello and beyond. By the 1990s, several communities in eastern L.A. County had overwhelming majorities of Latino residents. Again, those with the most education and highest incomes moved out faster. Similar stories are told by successful members of various immigrant groups in San Diego who have filtered out and assimilated into surrounding suburbs.

California's recent migration trends are similar to past decades, though they may involve different groups within more congested and competitive urban environments. They are a part of more general events that have transformed the very nature of California's urban landscapes since World War II. Though these landscapes will be examined in Chapter 11 on urban landscapes, they have earned a review here, because they are products of immigration and population trends.

Mobile Classes and Cultures Create Urban Landscapes

Despite all the open spaces and rich natural resources, Californians were already packing into urban centers during the late 1800s, particularly after the Gold Rush. San Francisco had become the west's greatest city and it held that honor through the early 1900s. Other Bay Area cities and Sacramento kept the focus of energy and activity on northern California's more compact urban centers. By the mid-1900s, Los Angeles and other Southern California communities took the reins, building more expansive and dispersed urban settlements at an astounding pace.

Northern California had not stopped growing, but Southern California had raced ahead at astonishing speed, and its leaders had different ideas about where and how people should live. Los Angeles' plan to spread

out was successful although scholars of traditional city planning ridiculed L.A. as having no plan at all.

L.A. linked its dispersed communities with a brilliant light rail system, setting the stage for the freeways and cars that would replace it, especially during the post-World War II economic and population boom. The result was that L.A. and Southern California led the counter-urbanization trend that was also evident throughout the state and the nation. People were moving from urban to suburban neighborhoods and even returning to some rural environments with the freedom gained by their automobiles and freeways. These migrations (which peaked from the 1950s to the 1970s) were often labelled "white flight" because the middle class fled the cities with their money. Poorer, disadvantaged, often minority residents were left behind.

By the 1980s, gentrification (another form of return or countermigration) began changing urban landscapes again. Weary of long commutes and bored by the cultural deserts of distant suburbs, young, urban, upwardly mobile professionals (YUPPIES) began flooding back to California cities and restoring neighborhoods once devastated by white flight. In some cases, poorer minority residents were displaced to the very distant suburbs that had previously absorbed young, successful professionals.

By the 1990s, a rich, complex mix of ethnic groups, cultures, and lifestyles had evolved and spread across California's urban landscapes. The old rules of lily-white suburbs and freeways jammed only in one direction (in to town during the morning and out of town during the late afternoon rush hours) are being shattered. California's population patterns—whether they are urban, suburban, or rural, or white, black, Latino, Asian, or Pacific Islander—have become astonishingly complex, due to decades of evolving, and sometimes feverish, migration patterns within the state.

These suburbs spread south of San Francisco from Glen Park into Daly City, where large numbers of Filipinos, Pacific Islanders and other cultural groups mix in the "little boxes" strung on the hillsides.

MIGRATIONS OF AFRICAN AMERICANS

African Americans in California's traditionally black communities have received plenty of attention in recent decades. You may be familiar with the historically large African-American populations in Oakland, Richmond, or the Fillmore in San Francisco, in Central Valley cities such as Sacramento, Fresno, and Bakersfield, or in South-Central Los Angeles (now predominately Latino) and Inglewood.

It is no secret that, like most ethnic groups, upper- and middle-class African Americans have relocated away from many poorer neighborhoods to surrounding, more upscale communities during the late 1900s. Crenshaw's Leimert Park in Los Angeles is sometimes called Holly-Watts for its location between Watts and Hollywood. Others consider Leimert Park the most affluent African-American community attached to the most vibrant African-American community (Crenshaw) in the nation. Its village atmosphere and renowned artists' community is recognized particularly among African Americans living in nearby Windsor Hills, Culver City, and Inglewood.

However, some may be surprised to find established African-American neighborhoods in Southern California's Inland Empire east of Los Angeles. There have also been more recent migration waves of African-Americans to those and other distant suburbs (such as the high desert communities of Palmdale and Lancaster) since the 1980s. Statistics show that African-American neighborhoods and businesses have long been established in Inland Empire cities, such as Riverside and San Bernardino. More recent changes are evident, according to U.S. Census Bureau and *Los Angeles Times* data. During the period from 1980 to 1990, while the Inland Empire population increased by 66 percent to more than 2.5 million, its African-American population increased by 119 percent to nearly 170,000. By 1990, Rialto's population was 20 percent black and in Moreno Valley, African-Americans represented 13 percent of that city's 133,000 population. These trends continued through the 1990s.

The Inland Empire African American Chamber of Commerce was organized in 1990 with six members; by 1997, it had nearly one-hundred members. They range from shops and restaurants to larger industries and car dealers. San Bernardino has a small black-owned business district on E Street. A weekly newspaper, *Black Voice News*, is published in Riverside.

People now travel from the Los Angeles area to visit friends and relatives and to support black businesses in the Inland Empire, and some are staying. Though it started with a very small group, immigration from surrounding regions has built thriving and influential African-American communities in today's Inland Empire. This is just one example of a region in California that has changed due to an increasingly mobile African-American population. You may see the results of similar trends in the Bay Area (such as toward Vallejo and Solano County), Central Valley, and other California suburbs.

Once again, it is clear that migration has been and continues to be *the* most important factor in determining the distribution and concentrations of California's populations. In the next section, we will examine some of the major population centers that have been created by these immigration streams. Then, we will end the chapter with a review of some population projections and try to determine how immigration will change the future of California.

◆ POPULATION DENSITIES

According to the Population Research Unit at the California Department of Finance, California's population density soared to about 70 residents per sq km (over 180 residents per square mile) by the late 1980s; by the end of the twentieth century, it was more than 80 residents per square km (more than 200 residents per square mile) and steadily increasing. Why is this crude (or arithmetic) density important? It does confirm that California is becoming dramatically more crowded, but the state does not stand with the most or least densely populated states or nations. The figures reveal little about how the population is distributed and concentrated within various California regions. (These population clusters were reviewed in Chapter 1). Here, we have an opportunity to briefly investigate some of the more important details about California's population centers.

California's population densities vary remarkably across the state (see Map 7.4). Within entire counties (Alpine and Inyo), population densities were less than 1 resident per sq km (below 2 residents per square mile) by the end of the 1990s. Modoc, Mono, and Sierra Counties were sightly more densely populated, while Trinity and Lassen rounded out the bottom seven. All of these, except Trinity, share a border with the state of Nevada.

In the 1990s, California's most densely populated county was, by far, San Francisco, with about 6,278 people per sq km (16,260 people per square mile). Orange County was a distant second at nearly 1,150 people per sq km (3,000 people per square mile), followed by Los Angeles, Alameda, San Mateo, Santa Clara, and Contra Costa Counties. All of the top seven had densities well above 386 per sq km (1,000 per square mile). Note that all are in the Los Angeles or San Francisco Bay areas and

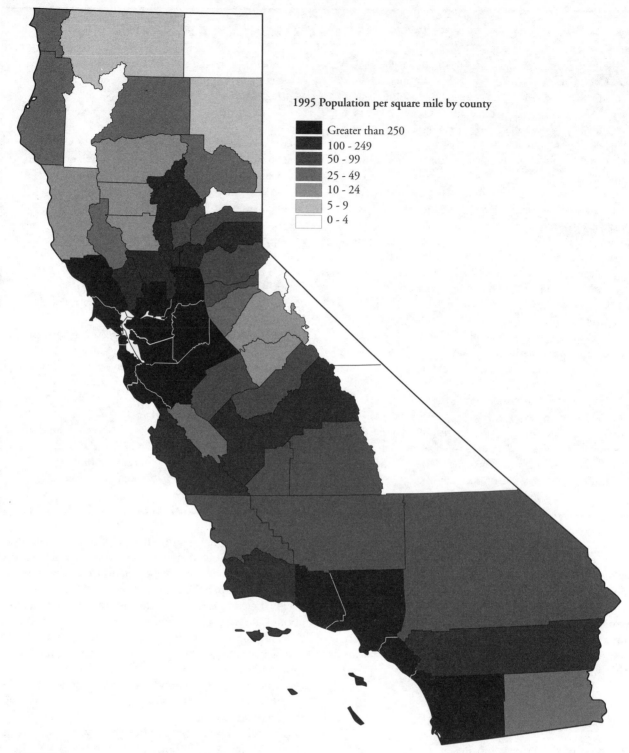

1995 Population per square mile by county

██	Greater than 250
██	100 - 249
██	50 - 99
██	25 - 49
██	10 - 24
██	5 - 9
☐	0 - 4

MAP 7.4

Population Densities. A tremendous variation in human population densities exists across the state.

all are coastal counties—the top three have shorelines directly exposed to the Pacific and the others have at least Bay shorelines. (Sacramento County, due to our state capital, ranked eighth in density. San Diego County ranked a very distant ninth; its enormous area kept it down on the list.)

Landscapes, Land Use, and Living Conditions

Leaving political boundaries aside, more than 50 percent of the state's total land areas have densities less than 1 person per sq km (less than 2 people per square mile).

Today, less than 15 percent of California landscapes are urban, even when using the broadest definitions of urban areas. Some consider that percentage of urban area closer to 5 percent. In contrast, since 1970, more than 90 percent of Californians have been urban, living in cities larger than 2,500 people. Such concentrations are typical of a modern society with highly advanced economies. (This compares to the 7 percent urban populations in 1850, 52 percent in 1900, and 81 percent in 1950.) You can see how California has developed with such contrasts in landscapes, land use, cultures, and living conditions, particularly as we travel between rural and urban areas.

◆ POPULATION CLUSTERS IN CALIFORNIA

Nearly two-thirds of the California population is clustered in the greater Los Angeles and San Francisco metropolitan areas. By the mid-1990s, the greater Los Angeles area had about 15 million people, ranking second in the nation behind New York. The San Francisco Bay Area had about 7 million, ranking fourth behind Chicago's metropolitan area. The greater San Diego Metropolitan Area had surged above 2.5 million, but ranked much lower on the U.S. list. (Attaching Tijuana would have roughly doubled that total.)

Here is a list of the top eleven California *counties* and their rounded total populations (not densities) near the end of the 1990s, according to census data and the state Department of Finance. All were continuing to grow.

Los Angeles	9,750,000
San Diego	2,850,000
Orange	2,800,000
Santa Clara	1,700,000
San Bernardino	1,650,000
Riverside	1,500,000
Alameda	1,430,000
Sacramento	1,180,000
Contra Costa	915,000
San Francisco	800,000
Fresno	795,000

You can see that little San Francisco County and Fresno County were virtually tied for tenth place going into the twenty-first century. Remember, San Francisco County was, by far, the most densely populated county in the state. Furthermore, among the county leaders, only Sacramento (just barely) and Fresno Counties are separate from the population clusters of the state's three largest metropolitan areas (Los Angeles, San Francisco, and San Diego).

Here is a list of California's top ten *cities* (within official city boundaries) and their populations at the start of the twenty-first century. Figures are rounded from California Department of Finance and census data.

Los Angeles	3,775,000
San Diego	1,250,000
San Jose	900,000
San Francisco	800,000
Long Beach	450,000
Fresno	415,000
Oakland	400,000
Sacramento	397,000
Santa Ana	313,000
Anaheim	305,000

Riverside (256,000), Stockton (245,000), and Bakersfield (228,000) rounded out the cities with far more than 200,000 people by the start of the twenty-first century. A few others were near 200,000.

All of these cities experienced modest growth into the mid-1990s, except Los Angeles (its population fluctuated) and Long Beach (where the population was dropping, mostly due to recent military and aerospace job losses). Even the lethargic trend for those two anomalies reversed into the late 1990s; the Los Angeles area, and particularly Long Beach, emerged from the early 1990s recession with transformed and rejuvenated economies and renewed population growth. Extraordinary growth of more than 5 percent during some years in Bakersfield made it the fastest-growing of the pack (in percentage) during most of the 1990s. With a growing economy, Bakersfield represents trends for most California cities into the twenty-first century.

Let's move away from the Los Angeles and San Francisco metropolitan areas that usually get so much attention and look at some of the population clusters in other parts of the state.

San Diego

Some interesting patterns have developed in the growing and remarkably dispersed San Diego County populations. Chula Vista (168,000) is narrowly the second-largest city in the county. It and its neighbors, such as National City (55,000), are joining to form the southern expansion of San Diego that is gradually connecting (both economically and culturally) to Tijuana. This area between San Diego and Tijuana is becoming a major population and economic center as many of the boundaries between the United States and Mexico fade.

On the other side (north) of San Diego is Oceanside (158,000). It barely trailed behind Chula Vista in the race for San Diego County's second-largest city. As populations merge, it is teaming up with cities like Escondido (125,000), Vista (85,000), Carlsbad (75,000), and San Marcos (52,000) to become the great population center of northern San Diego County. El Cajon (96,000) anchors the eastern extension of the San Diego area's expanding population. Cities like La Mesa (59,000) and Santee (57,500) are growing with it to create a smaller version of the Los Angeles area's inland valleys.

Southern California Deserts

Sweeping from high to low deserts, northern Los Angeles, southwestern San Bernardino, and western Riverside counties have their own population clusters that are now only separated from the greater Los Angeles and Inland Empire cities by major mountain barriers. CA 14 and I-15 and I-10, respectively, connect these high and low desert communities to the Los Angeles conurbation and to one another. In the Antelope Valley, Lancaster (130,000) and Palmdale (120,000) are struggling with what to do with their images, their relationships to Los Angeles (there are large numbers of commuters using Hwy. 14), and their remaining Joshua Trees. Similar issues haunt the people and landscapes in the communities along I-15. This is more notable around Victorville (62,000), previously tiny Hesperia (61,000), and Apple Valley (55,000). Late 1990s census studies predicted rapid growth into the twenty-first century.

Population clusters in the lower Colorado Desert are mainly in the Coachella Valley along I-10 and Hwy. 111 and the Imperial Valley. They represent mixtures of resort (mainly Coachella Valley) and farm (mainly Imperial Valley) communities. Indio (45,000) and Palm Springs (43,000) compete for the highest populations, but Cathedral City (36,500) and Palm Desert (36,000 and growing rapidly) are not far behind. Together, they and nearby Coachella Valley communities are filling the valley with more than just tourist and resort opportunities. To the south, El Centro (38,000) leads the Imperial Valley, where there is more of an agricultural focus.

The desert communities along CA 62 (such as Morongo Valley, Yucca Valley, Joshua Tree and Twentynine Palms) have not yet approached the populations or status of the previously reviewed cities.

The Central Valley

California's latest and possibly least-expected population explosion has been in the Central Valley. Among California's top thirteen cities with populations well over 200,000, four (Fresno, Sacramento, Stockton, and Bakersfield) are in the Central Valley. Most of these and other Central Valley cities are growing faster than the state average, and some are, or have recently, been among the fastest-growing cities in the state. Farmland is being paved over at a record, and sometimes reckless, pace.

Bakersfield is building bedroom communities for commuters who work as far away as Los Angeles. Residents of the valley's largest city, Fresno, complain that Los Angeles-style crime, congestion, and pollution have invaded their once productive farmlands. Some cite the expanding communities (such as Visalia) between the two cities when they predict that there will some day be one long conurbation only dotted with farmland between Bakersfield and Fresno along both sides of CA 99.

Draw a triangle using Sacramento as one point, Modesto as the other point, and the Carquinez Strait *or* the Pittsburg/Antioch area as the third. In and around this triangle (much of it is the Sacramento/San Joaquin Delta) are also some of the fastest-growing cities in California. Communities in and around Stockton and Modesto are growing into one another, while Sacramento continues its expansion. Particularly the area across the Delta to Stockton is filling with bedroom communities for those who dare to attempt the long commute to work in the Bay Area. Some futurists predict that this area will soon be one continuous and connected conurbation with the Bay Area.

The Sacramento area is now spreading populations especially northeast into Sierra Nevada foothill communities. Though there are no major cities north of that, one must wonder what will happen to growing communities like Yuba City and Marysville (which have about 50,000 when combined). Farther north in the Sacramento Valley are Chico (55,000), Redding (80,000, just on the northern edge), and smaller communities. There is every reason to believe that these and the growing towns to their east, in the Sierra Nevada foothills, will continue to fill with people trying to escape the crowds in the south.

The Central Coast

To the dismay of many who value the Central Coast as a retreat, this is another area realizing its great potential for population growth. Part of the reason is its situation between the state's two largest metropolitan areas. Significant urban areas and activities have erupted in the

Monterey Bay Area alone. Salinas (130,000) is the largest city in the region. Although it is inland of the coastal cities, it has exploited its agricultural history and is diversifying its economy. Hugging the northern edge of Monterey Bay is the region's second-largest city, Santa Cruz (56,000). This has been a traditional resort destination and college town, but has also grown and diversified recently. Watsonville (37,500) is just to the southeast.

Like many California cities, Monterey's official population (35,000) would be larger if it included some of the surrounding communities and resorts often associated with it, such as Pacific Grove (18,000) and even Carmel. Along the bay to the north, the economies of Seaside (31,000) and Marina (19,000), lacking vital diversity, were victims of military downsizing and the closing of Fort Ord. These two cities were losing people in the mid-1990s, while exploring ways to change their images and rejuvenate their economies. These efforts helped create more positive trends by the start of the twenty-first century.

To the south, closer to L.A. and more obvious along Hwy. 101 (where it touches the coast and branches to Pacific Coast Hwy.) is a new, growing cluster of cities. None have impressive populations except San Luis Obispo, at 43,500. It is the combined populations of these communities—from El Paso de Robles, Atascadero, and Morro Bay, through San Luis Obispo, to Pismo Beach and Arroyo Grande—that make up the bulk of more than 245,000 people in San Luis Obispo County.

Ranches on some of these rolling hills are sprouting housing developments. Perhaps the biggest surprise along the central coast is even farther south in Santa Maria (72,000). It would seem too far away from major economic activity to attract commuters, while lacking the serene, picturesque landscapes that attract urban escapees. Nevertheless, there it is with its generic housing tracts and urban problems more familiar to an L.A. suburb.

Heading Back Toward Southern California

Now that we've stepped into Santa Barbara County in our search for population clusters, we must venture farther south into the growing Santa Ynez Valley. Here, we find Lompoc (43,000) with its Vandenberg Air Force Base, little Solvang, and Buellton. All you have to do is look at this valley and its situation to guess that it is ripe for more growth.

However, it is the famous Santa Barbara coast even farther south that is moving into high-tech industries and diversifying, setting the stage for moderate growth into the twenty-first century. Santa Barbara (92,500) and Carpinteria (15,000) were the largest incorporated cities along this thin coastal strip in the mid-1990s. Growth is confined along a thin section between steep mountains on one side and the Pacific Ocean on the other, but it has powerful connections with the Los Angeles conurbation to the south.

Finally, we can travel even farther south to the Ventura/Oxnard Plain where farmland is being gobbled up by encroaching housing tracts and industries that ran out of room in the Los Angeles Basin. Looking inland from Oxnard (158,000), it is not difficult to imagine a continuous urban landscape linked to the San Fernando Valley and L.A. along Hwy. 101. Large and expanding communities are already making the link. Isn't it appropriate that we finally end our search for California's people near the edge of its largest city?

Less Populated Regional Centers

We left out the less significant population clusters. The budding towns of the western Sierra Nevada foothills, led by growing communities like Paradise (27,000) were mentioned, but there are other areas farther up and east. South Lake Tahoe has exploited skiing and other resort activity and the gambling across the border to grow to more than 23,000. Yet, the well-known resorts of Mammoth Lakes (5,500) and Bishop (3,550) are still no match for the state's other great population centers.

Throughout northeastern and far north-central California, the largest city is Susanville (17,200). In the northwest, people have clustered around Arcata Bay in communities like Eureka (28,000) and Arcata (16,600), as they rebuild and diversify their economies. Though all of these cities act as population, economic, and cultural centers for their regions, their populations are insignificant compared to the state's urban giants. Many of these diverse human landscapes will be explored in the chapters ahead.

◆ RECENT TRENDS AND THE FUTURE

The recession of the early 1990s temporarily slowed California population growth. Consider these data compiled by the Center for Continuing Study of the California Economy. The first year in history when California lost population to other states was 1991; that trend continued until 1995. In 1993 to 1994, Los Angeles lost 127,000 residents to other states. In 1994, the entire state lost 16,000 to Washington state alone, though that number had already dropped below 6,000 by the next year. Remember that the state's total population continued to increase throughout that period—about 300,000 during the slowest year—due to births and immigration from other countries.

Californians quickly swept that period of slow growth away. By 1995, the San Francisco Bay Area, Sacramento, and San Diego areas were already experiencing net gains from other states, a sign that their economies were the first to recover. By 1997, net interstate migration had become positive again for California, a trend that was expected to carry well into the twenty-first century.

If "The Big One" doesn't hit first, and perhaps even if it does, the population of California will continue to grow, and grow dramatically, into the twenty-first century. How much growth will there be, and where will it occur? Which California landscapes, economies, and cultures will be further transformed by this growth?

According to the U.S. Census Bureau, the state's population was growing faster than 1 percent per year into the late 1990s, faster than the national average. In 1996, 320,000 people were officially added for a total of 32,380,000. The greatest numerical growth was occurring in the most populous counties, such as L.A., San Diego, and Orange. (L.A. County's additional 44,200 people in 1996 represented only a 0.47% increase). However, for the entire period from 1990 to 1996, the Los Angeles metropolitan area added 963,626 people—more than any other metropolitan area in the nation. San Francisco's metropolitan area (including Oakland and San Jose) came in ninth nationally, adding 355,547 people in that 1990 to 1996 period.

By 1997, the state's population growth was more than 500,000 per year, by far the nation's leader in numerical growth. According to the Department of Finance, the state gained more than 580,000 people in 1997. Total population soared over 33 million by 1998 and 34 million in 1999.

The highest percentage increases were in rural counties with lower base populations. Lassen County was the leader in 1996; its additional 32,650 residents (due to its new state prison that nearly doubled inmate populations) represented an increase of nearly 14 percent. Madera (3.67 percent), San Benito (3.17 percent), Placer (2.80 percent), and Imperial (2.77 percent) Counties were also percentage leaders. (Due to a new state prison which added 3,011 inmates, little Corcoran in Kings County was California's percentage leader [22 percent] for California cities in 1997.) During the entire period from 1990 to 1996, 57 of the state's 58 counties experienced an increase in population as nearly 2-1/2 million people were added.

In 1996, the U.S. Census Bureau predicted that California would be the third-fastest growing state in the nation behind Texas and Florida, adding 932,000 residents between 1996 and 2000. (By the end of the century, that prediction was proven to be too low.)

By the summer of 1996, more than 300,000 jobs were created in California within one year, with average salaries of $25,000 per year. The state's unemployment rate dropped below 7 percent. By 1998, more jobs were being created at even a faster pace, and unemployment dipped below 6 percent, a trend that continued to the end of the century. Demographers are using these and other signals to make predictions.

In 1997, The Center for Continuing Study of the California Economy noted the increasing job opportunities and incomes across the state. They predicted that the California population and number of households would increase twice as fast as the rest of the nation into the next century. They forecast increases of more than 18 percent from more than 32 million people and 11 million households in 1996 to more than 38 million people and 13 million households by 2005.

Yet another study from the Southern California Association of Governments (SCAG) released in 1998 supported these projections for growth. The six southern California counties excluding San Diego were expected to absorb more than 22 million people during about 25 years (from 1995 to 2020). That 43 percent increase would be equivalent to adding the population of two Chicagos to those six counties alone! Much of the percentage growth was expected in high desert and Inland Empire communities, though great additional numbers were also expected in the largest cities. Similar trends are catching the attention of residents and officials in San Diego, the Bay Area, and the Central Valley.

In a final blow to those who have trouble accepting these remarkable projections, demographers at the U.S. Census Bureau expect about 18 million people to flood into California from the late 1990s to 2025. That increase is more than the entire population of the state of New York! There is obvious concern about how to build and improve infrastructures and services for the additional people so that California's working and living conditions will improve, not deteriorate.

Population Projections by Race/Ethnicity

U.S. Census Bureau projections that are confirmed by nearly every study involve the continuing transformation of California's cultures and ethnic groups. The number of Latinos in California will double from the late 1990s to 2025, when one-third of the U.S. Latino population will live in California. As immigration continues strong, more than 40 percent of the country's Asian and Pacific Islander populations will live in California in 2025. Because their numbers only increased slowly to nearly 2.5 million by 2000, the percentage of African Americans is decreasing as new immigrants and other minority groups' numbers soar.

According to the California State Department of Finance, California's Latino population will surpass the number of white residents by about 2020, after both have pushed over the 20 million mark. The number of African Americans is expected to increase more slowly, topping 3 million within a total statewide population of about 49 million in 2020. The geographic distribution of these ethnic groups may be even more remarkable.

After 2000, Hispanics will outnumber whites in the following counties: Fresno, Imperial, Los Angeles, and

---

''CRUNCHED IN CALIFORNIA''

James D. Houston wrote in 'Crunched in California' in the *San Jose Mercury News* on September 12, 1993, that California's population was still growing at 1,500 per day, even during that period of recession. He asked, what is the saturation point? Houston wrote that California was the Land of Immigrants with a real and profound crisis of conscience. He emphasized that newcomers looking to change their fortunes are really us or our ancestors.

Nonetheless, at that time many citizens were feeling the pressures of population in their communities; they included congestion, traffic, pollution, and other problems. Houston noted how the population increased from about 1.5 million in 1900 to six million by the early 1930s. He recalled the huge counter on the Oakland-San Francisco Bay Bridge where we celebrated our 17,393,134 population that finally surpassed New York on November 24, 1962. Then, the population grew at 1,000 per day until the rate of growth peaked in the mid-1980s at 2,000 per day. By 1993, the rate dropped to 1,500 per day. That's still five people every five minutes, or 10,000 extra people every week!

James Houston argued that disasters such as major traffic accidents are getting more attention because there are simply more people to be in harm's way. In 1977, there were 22.5 million people and less than one registered vehicle for each licensed driver in the state. By the end of 1991, the population topped 30 million, and vehicles outnumbered licensed drivers by several million. He argued that this is just one example of how we are approaching the carrying capacities of our environmental systems as there is more demand on water, land, housing, and infrastructure to serve all these people. He warned that we will experience social disaster if we do not develop some new strategies for limiting the statewide rate of population growth.

Houston pointed out that in the early 1900s, fear of Asian immigration encouraged laws that prevented Asians from owning land and from becoming naturalized as American citizens in California. Deep-seated racists used the label "Yellow Peril" to describe their fears. Such derogatory terms have been used to label new immigrants from other states and countries since California became a state. He argued that elitism or racial hatred should not be used as excuses to control population growth, but they must not be used as scapegoats to do nothing.

During the 1980s, the U.S. population grew by about 10 percent, the world population by about 20 percent; California grew by 25 percent, one of the fastest rates on earth. Houston pointed out that in 1991, there were 395,000 more births than deaths in California. At these rates, if *all* immigration into California stopped, the state would still grow at the 1940–1985 average of 1,000 per day.

What do you think? What do you consider to be **overpopulation** in California? At what point are there so many people that it causes decay of our living standards and quality of life? Everyone will have at least slightly different answers to these questions.

Tulare, while the ratio in San Benito County will be very close. Agriculture is vital to the economies of all of the counties on this list, except Los Angeles, which is rich in urban industries offering low-wage, entry-level employment. This has helped make L.A. the immigration capital of the nation. The Hispanic population in L.A. County alone soared above 4.5 million by 2000, larger than many states' entire populations. The proportion of Latinos is even more impressive in Imperial County. Agribusiness rules in this border county, one of the poorest in California. Throughout the 1990s, Hispanics outnumbered whites by more than 2 to 1 and represented more than two-thirds of the entire population.

According to U.S. Census numbers and the California Department of Finance, the state's Latino population soared from 4.5 million in 1980, to 7.7 million in 1990, to 9.3 million in 1996. Counties leading in Latino populations (in order) are L.A. (more than 4 million by the late 1990s), Orange, San Diego, San Bernardino, Santa Clara, Riverside, Fresno, Alameda, Ventura, and Kern.

There are also counties with very few Hispanics. The following counties are expected to continue to have less than 10 percent Hispanics even past 2010: Alpine, Amador, Calavaras, Humboldt, Marin, Mariposa, Modoc, Nevada, Placer, Shasta, Sierra, Siskiyou, and Trinity. All of these are northern California counties. All of them are primarily rural and mountainous (seven include Sierra Nevada high country) and lack agribusiness, though smaller farms and ranches may be common.

Near the turn of the century, there were only about 200 Hispanics among the 3,400 people in Sierra County and only about 600 among the 15,000 Trinity County residents! Marin County made the list of least because it is a series of mostly upper-class enclaves populated by commuters and others who have escaped urban congestion. They aggressively slowed growth, development, and, of course, immigration in past years. Each of those counties with fewer Hispanics also have very small African-American populations.

Hispanics outnumber African-Americans in every California county except Alameda. By the late 1990s, the African-American population inched up to 250,000 in Alameda County, representing nearly 20 percent of that county's population. But, the number of Hispanics is expected to move ahead of African-Americans by 2010 even there. Both the percentage and numbers of African-Americans were particularly low in Napa, Nevada, Plumas (just more than 100 out of more than 20,000 people), San Benito (about 200 out of more than 40,000), Santa Barbara, Santa Cruz, Sonoma, and Tehama Counties. The people of these and other California ethnic groups, cultures, and lifestyles will be reviewed in the next chapter.

Public Perceptions of Overpopulation

California has experienced and continues to undergo a population explosion of historic proportions; that fact is not debatable or controversial. The controversy rages about how to react to these dramatic changes. Should we try to slow or control population growth? If so, how? Where do we allow new growth and development to continue, and where do we limit it? How do we build the state's infrastructure to provide services for new and native residents so that we improve the quality of our living and working environments? All of these questions and controversies go to the heart of how each of us perceives the California Dream and how we can bring that dream within reach of more of our citizens. James Houston approached many of these issues so eloquently in a California newspaper article, which is reviewed in the box on page 255.

There are only a few basic ways to increase the quality of our living and working environments. We can use our technology to increase the amount of resources supplied to the people. Or, we can increase our efficiency so that we need fewer resources. Or, we can stabilize or decrease populations so that there are more resources per capita. It is easy to predict that if we do not practice sustained yields in our own state, we will run out of resources.

What is California's carrying capacity (the number of people we can support given our current size, resources, and technologies)? How do we judge the impact Californians have on other places and cultures of the world? Even so-called experts cannot agree on the answers to these questions.

This is why we have countless advocates with contrasting views of the ramifications of population growth in the state today. Some will argue for zero population growth, some even for negative population growth. Others still argue that personal profit should rule, and there should be no controls on, or even planning for, future population changes in the state. The latter are the traditional winners in these clashes; these trends may continue as disparate groups with different perspectives and agendas debate what to do about California's increasing populations.

SOME KEY TERMS AND TOPICS

baby boom	interstate migration	population clusters
chain migrations	intervening opportunities	population pyramid
demographic equation	migration	pull factors
emigration	natural increase	push factors
illegal immigration	overpopulation	refugee
immigration	percentage population increase	sequent occupance
international migration	place utility	

Additional Key Terms and Topics

barriers to migrants	foreign born	natality
census data	history of population	net migration
density of population	life expectancy	population explosion
doubling time	Mexican immigrants	projection of population
economic stratification	minority groups	race/ethnicity
fertility	mobility	white flight
forced migration	mortality	

Chapter 8

California's Ethnic Groups, Cultures, and Lifestyles

Understanding California's **human landscapes** (human imprints on the land) requires knowledge of the people who have built them. Because modern California populations have become remarkably complex, defining and categorizing the state's people is a difficult and fascinating task.

Ethnicity refers to the combination of a people's racial ancestry (physical characteristics) and **culture** (includes customs, language, and religion). In this section, we will venture far beyond the confines of ethnic categories to identify some of the rich mixtures of races (those people who share distinctive and inherited biological characteristics), cultures, and lifestyles that characterize California's population.

One of the countless definitions of **culture** refers to the total knowledge, attitudes, and habits shared and passed on by members of a society. Such mental and spiritual manifestations lead to more visible forms of behavior and social structures that produce even more tangible material and artistic items and landscapes. Modification and change occurs as these culture traits are passed from one generation to the next. Because cultural landscapes are tangible physical records of a culture, California exhibits outstanding examples of how a multitude of imported cultures—experiencing constant change—can evolve to produce incredibly diverse human landscapes.

Flowing in from around the world are scores of belief systems (or mentifacts) that have contributed to California's complex social organizations, technologies, and their artifacts. California culture has always been defined by adaptations, modifications, and integration within and between the many ethnic groups and cultures pouring into the state. Today, California is a world leader in independent invention and innovation partly because it has managed to capitalize on the diffusion from around the world of what is now this rich assemblage of interwoven cultures.

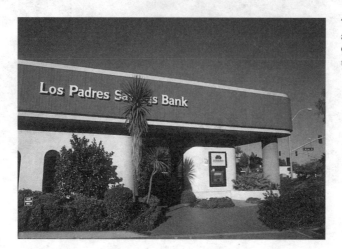

This modest bank in Santa Maria is just another example of how modern Californians celebrate—and exploit—their history and cultural traditions.

The bulk of this chapter surveys some of California's specific ethnic groups, cultures, and lifestyles. Note how the major themes of this book—diversity, connections, and change—play such powerful roles in our understanding of these cultures and the landscapes they have created.

KEY ISSUES AND CONCEPTS

◆ Diverse ethnic groups, cultures, and lifestyles are interacting and changing California in profound ways. Californians are increasingly aware of the challenges and opportunities presented by this cultural diversity.

◆ The study of the state's *ethnic/cultural groups* is organized within the following broad categories: American Indians (Native Americans); Latinos; European Americans; African Americans; and Asian/Pacific Islander Americans. All general groups exhibit their own cultural diversity and have substantial impact on California and its landscapes.

◆ Native Americans (California Indians) are making progress to revive their diverse cultures that were nearly destroyed.

◆ Latino cultures have historically played major roles in shaping the state's cultural landscapes; they have recently become more visible and influential.

◆ Transplanted European and U.S. cultures have dominated California since the days of the Gold Rush and the "Wild West."

◆ Like many of the state's minority groups, African Americans have worked to overcome stereotypes and discrimination. They are becoming increasingly geographically dispersed and economically and culturally diverse.

◆ Asians and Pacific Islanders in California represent a multitude of cultures and play increasingly important roles in the state's economic and cultural trends. Much credit goes to California's position on the Pacific Rim.

◆ Extremely diverse religions, languages, age groups, and lifestyles have always shaped, and continue to mold, the state's people, cultures, and human landscapes.

◆ Do the many elements of California's cultures come together in a giant salad bowl or melting pot? This is a matter of individual perspective and preference. Communities and organizations throughout the state are dealing with these issues of diversity.

◆ California has become a modern culture hearth (a center where advanced cultural characteristics develop and are diffused around the world). Popular cultures are overwhelming many traditional cultures and exaggerated stereotypes earn unusual attention. Many Californians toil to preserve traditional cultures and landscapes as modern, popular cultures drive us into the twenty-first century.

◆ SPECIFIC ETHNIC GROUPS, CULTURES, AND LIFESTYLES

How impossible it would be to examine every affinity group in California even in a series of volumes, much less in this next section. However, all of the general ethnic and cultural groups that make up the majority of Californians are considered here. We certainly will consider enough ethnic groups, cultures, and lifestyles to paint some broad pictures of the state's cultural landscapes.

It is also unlikely that any two people could ever agree on the order in which to present these groups or even which groups should get the most attention. The purpose here is to paint the clearest picture as quickly as possible. Toward the end of the 1900s, researchers, anthropologists, human geographers, and social scientists recognized five of the most general U.S. ethnic/culture categories:

American Indians (Native Americans)

Latinos (sometimes considered with "Hispanics" in census surveys)

European Americans (including "Anglos," sometimes generalized as "white")

African Americans (formerly labelled "Black Americans")

Asian/Pacific Islander Americans (often including South Asians)

Those same general U.S. ethnic categories are the focus of numerous ethnic/cultural studies programs and ethnic/cultural diversity course requirements in educational institutions across the state. (They include UC Berkeley and other UCs, CSUs, private universities, California's community colleges, and K–12 schools). Students are finally being encouraged to learn about diverse cultures and the vastness of the world around them. More Californians are recognizing the importance of knowing about the diverse people we mingle and work with every day. California's economic power, social stability, the quality of its living and working environments, and its very future will be at least partially determined by our ability to understand and work with these very different kinds of people.

The organizational approach of this chapter is a methodical, almost cyclic, survey of the general groups listed. Chronologically, we must begin with California's Indians, who were here for thousands of years before any other group. Hispanic people and cultures first invaded and, after 1769, built substantial settlements in California. Then, non-Hispanic European-American people and cultures played increasingly important roles until they took control in the late 1840s. With them came a mix of African-American and Asian people and cultures that have played vital roles in California ever since the 1800s.

Interestingly, we end our discussion of ethnic groups with Asian and Pacific Islander Americans to make an ironic, if not arguable, connection. Remember that the first settlers (Native Americans) in California were descendants of people who originally came from Asia. Today, Asians and Pacific Islanders not only represent some of the fastest-growing populations in the state, but they also represent powerful connections to the modern Pacific Rim and the growing global market—yet another reason why Californians must become more knowledgeable about these diverse cultures.

Special boxes in each section are designed to highlight specific issues or personal stories relevant to each group. It is important to learn from the formal research about each ethnic/cultural group; you will find such information here. Still, nothing can substitute for the personal accounts of experiences that reflect peoples' dreams and goals, their struggles and accomplishments, and their successes and failures. Though names were changed to protect privacy, each of the individual stories (in this chapter) are firsthand accounts taken from one-on-one interviews.

All of the following sections represent at least small threads that combine to weave the incredible diversity of California cultures and their human landscapes.

Native Americans (California Indians)
Some History and Heritage

Before the Europeans arrived, nearly one-third of all the Native Americans who lived within what we now consider the United States were in California; that is more than 300,000 people with more than one-hundred languages. Some of this Native American history was reviewed in Chapter 7. Historically, California had the greatest population and diversity of native people compared to other states, due to abundant natural resources and diverse landscapes. Although modern California continues to lead the nation in these attributes, its Native-American people and cultures have suffered devastating setbacks.

The Spanish and Mexican treatment of the California Indians is well documented. The state's Native-American population had already dropped by 50 percent before the Gold Rush. After California became a state in 1850, statewide publications encouraged the extermination of California Indians, and bounty hunters were paid for body parts of Native-American people they had murdered. Californians stopped several attempts by Congress to establish reservations; they claimed that California's Indians were more primitive than other Native Americans. Though a few small rancherias were established by the government for some tribes, the Hoopa Reservation in northwestern California was the only reservation in the entire state for many years.

The California Indian population had dropped to about 30,000 by 1870. In the late 1800s, J. D. C. Atkins, the federal commissioner of Indian affairs, suggested that the "barbarous dialect" of American Indians be blotted out and the English language be substituted. All of this made it too easy for many American settlers since the mid-1800s to label California's Native Americans as desperate, poverty-stricken individuals who could not control their drinking or fend for themselves. These settlers were barely familiar with only the scattered remains of native cultures that had long since been destroyed.

In the 1950s, when the U.S. government broke up and redistributed native lands, it left many tribes further divided and in chaos. More than twenty indigenous California languages were lost during the 1900s, and only about fifty remained by the end of the century, according to linguistics Professor Leanne Hinton at UC Berkeley. In this state, which has been called the third most linguistically diverse region in the world (behind New Guinea and the Caucasus), all California Indian languages are endangered.

California's American Indian Cultures Revived

Today, some call it a reawakening, some a rebirth, others a renaissance. Regardless of the label, a clear trend had developed among numerous Native-American groups in California by the end of the 1900s; they were reviving many of their customs (such as language) and rebuilding their tribes and cultures (see Map 8.1). Elderly Indians in the state were teaching younger relatives native languages and sharing stories and songs with nieces, nephews, and grandchildren in what some considered to be a race against time. Many of these languages were also being recorded.

Native Americans in California are establishing new sources of income to finance these movements, income that often comes from gambling, or what they call "gaming." By the end of the 1900s, more than thirty of the one-hundred official tribes in California operated casinos. Some tribes were too isolated to establish such profitable enterprises, while others shunned gaming and what it might do to what remains of their cultures.

Northwestern California

Most California Indian languages have rich verbal traditions that were never written, making their preservation more difficult. Each of these languages reflects different views and perspectives of our world. Loren Bommelyn studies linguistics and is only one of six people who speak the Tolowa language of the Crescent City area. In an interview by Mark Leibovich of the *San Jose Mercury News*, it was noted that there is only one word for both arm and wing, "gwa-neh." According to Bommelyn, this exemplifies the connection to, and under-

standing of, the animal world in native languages. It also shows how, when a language disappears, an entire culture—a unique way of looking at our world—is usually lost with it.

Northeastern California

At Lava Beds National Monument, visitors can tour structures rebuilt to depict life in the area's American Indian villages into the 1800s. The Modoc earth shelter winter lodge was held up with lodge pole rafters for the tule reeds and the one foot of earth cover placed on top. The Modoc sweat lodge has willow pole frames covered with birch bark, skins, or tule mats.

In November, 1872, Modoc leader Keintpoos (Captain Jack) led his people off the reservation they were forced to share with Klamath Indians. When U.S. troops tried to force them back, a war broke out that lasted from 1872 to 1873. Captain Jack and his Modocs became famous for their resistance and warfare among the maze of lava tunnels that wind below the landscape here. This is a classic example of tunnel and trench warfare in landscape that was a home familiar to the California Indians, but foreign and confusing to U.S. troops. In the long run, it just meant a long and agonizing delay in the inevitable destruction of another native culture.

In stark contrast to the past, we move ahead to the end of the 1900s near Burney. The Pit River Indians claim to have the largest land base of any California American Indian group, and they claim sovereignty from the United States. They have taken in three different language groups, including Indians from the Modoc. They argue that hundreds of thousands of acres of their land were wrongfully stolen.

In 1972, when they claimed ownership of land in a demonstration at a nearby location called Four Corners, police moved in and arrested every adult. Indian children were left without care overnight, and nearby pig farmers stopped by and fed and cared for them until the adult Indians were processed out of jail. It was a bizarre twist in the history of relations between newer settlers and American Indians on California's harsh northeastern plateau, but the Pit River Indians were grateful to those pig farmers.

The Indians opened the Pit River Casino in the summer of 1996. They hired a manager to run it and hoped that word would spread and bring the crowds that could generate much-needed revenue for the area.

Southern California Native American Cultures

The Chumash were especially devastated by the arrival of new immigrants and settlers in California; some observers once even pronounced them extinct. Today, thousands of Chumash descendants are proving the skeptics wrong. The Chumash once lived along a broad

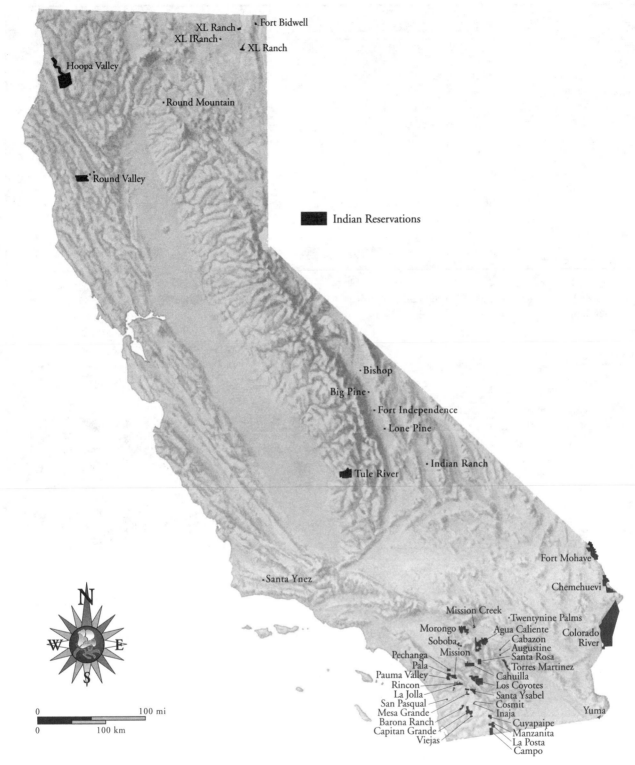

XL Ranch · Fort Bidwell
XL IRanch ·
XL Ranch

Hoopa Valley

· Round Mountain

Round Valley

■ Indian Reservations

· Bishop

Big Pine ·
· Fort Independence
· Lone Pine

Tule River
· Indian Ranch

N
W E
S

0   100 mi
0   100 km

Santa Ynez

Fort Mohave

Chemehuevi

· Mission Creek
· Twentynine Palms
Morongo   Agua Caliente   Colorado
Soboba   Cabazon   River
            Mission   Augustine
Pechanga   Santa Rosa
    Pala   Torres Martinez
Pauma Valley   Cahuilla
    Rincon   Los Coyotes
    La Jolla   Santa Ysabel
San Pasqual   Cosmit
Mesa Grande   Inaja   Yuma
Barona Ranch   Cuyapaipe
Capitan Grande   Manzanita
        Viejas   La Posta
                            Campo

MAP 8.1

Indian Reservations. Only the largest and most substantial California reservations are shown
here. Smaller rancherias and tracts do not appear. The distribution of larger tracts may reflect
the quality and value of land during the American Period.

area of the coastal mountains from the Morro Bay region
(in central California) south to Topanga Canyon in the
Santa Monica Mountains. They established some of the
densest populations and largest villages of any California
Indian group. The reasons for their success are evident

at the sites where they once clustered, which are sites
with mild climates, diverse habitats, and abundant food
(such as acorns) and water. They also found plentiful
seafood in productive Pacific waters that were navigated
in their seaworthy plank canoes.

THE HUPA AND KAROK TRIBES

THE HUPA

In the Hoopa Valley on the Trinity River in northern Humboldt County, the Hupa people are trying to save their Hupa culture and language. (Hoopa refers to the place, Hupa refers to the people.) For many years, they had the only true reservation, established in 1864. Many decades ago, Jimmy Jackson was sent to the notorious government boarding school in Riverside and was punished for speaking Hupa. By the late 1990s, he was in his late 80s. By then, Jackson and other tribal leaders were trying to preserve their language and dances in order to save their culture.

The Hoopa-Yurok Settlement Act of 1988 made the reservation in the Hoopa Valley the exclusive province of the Hupa Indians. *The Nation*—a Native-American publication—claims that local Indians are still denied their federal Indian rights in this valley with its valuable stand of trees.

THE KAROKS

The Karoks (also spelled Karuk) once had established about forty villages along about forty miles of the Klamath River to the north of the Hupa. The Kurok culture was nearly destroyed when they were scattered across northern California for years after the U.S. government broke up tribal lands. They lost the center of their culture, the sacred village known as Katamin, which is a place named Somes Bar today. The Karok tribe earned federal recognition in 1979, reorganized in 1990, and became officially self-governing by 1994. They were one of only four self-governing tribes in the state, which means they can use their annual federal grants as they wish.

Toward the end of the 1900s, there were only about ten fluent speakers of the Karok Indian language. All lived around Orleans along the Klamath River to the north of the Hupa. However, about 5,000 people have Karok ancestry and there were 3,000 official tribal members by the late 1990s. The Karok are considered to be one of the more successful groups of California Indians in rebuilding their culture by reviving their customs. Thanks goes to many of the elderly, such as Violet Super, who, approach-

ing 80, was trying to teach her two young nieces the Karok language.

On a hill above the Klamath, just upstream from Somes Bar, they are also reviving religious ceremonies that were practiced for centuries. Here, the Karok practice their Jump Dance with traditional headdresses, deerskin skirts, and abalone necklaces. The ceremonies gained so much attention, they were reported in publications as far away as the *Los Angeles Times*.

How do they finance this revival? The Karoks first accepted the slump in the timber industry as another change they must adapt to. They also shunned the casino trend followed by numerous other tribes. Instead, they started construction projects and health centers, began manufacturing furniture made from local wood, and they opened new stores. They have purchased private land around Orleans and Yreka and now own about half of Happy Camp, home of their main offices. Today's Karoks are working with the National Forest Service to manage surrounding lands; they are boosting the local economy and providing needed services for surrounding communities.

Sweat houses and redwood bark shelters are reconstructed in a village to inform visitors at Point Reyes National Seashore about the Miwok culture. The Miwok represent yet another example of exceptionally diverse Indian cultures in northern California.

Today's Chumash are preserving some historic and artistic sites through organizations such as the Satwiwa Native American Cultural Center. Chumash leaders are working to educate the public and keep their traditions alive. Various Chumash groups gather at annual celebrations featuring dances, food, artwork, and other cultural attractions that draw thousands of mostly non-native people.

Some of the groups are even in conflict about how to interpret and save Chumash traditions. This became most evident during the Autumnal Equinox weekend of 1996. As Richard Angulo of the California Indian Council led his eighth annual powwow, Paul Varela of the newer Chumash Interpretive Center and the Oakbrook Chumash organized their own competing celebrations, all in Thousand Oaks.

MODERN STRUGGLES, LIMITED RESOURCES

Disagreements and conflicts are typical within most California ethnic groups and cultures as people debate how, and to what extent, they will save their traditions, and to what extent they will become a part of the modern California experience. It is particularly difficult for California's remaining Native-American cultures that have been so devastated by more than two centuries of immigration and disease from around the world. Assimilate or resist? Compromise in ways that will increase economic success or embrace only the traditional ways at all costs? These are some of the conflicts faced by every group.

The Kumeyaay Indians have responded by trying to restore ecological balance in their territory near San Diego where the first Spanish explorers landed. Other groups have aggressively competed for the economic rewards that often result from exploiting the latest California trends.

In 1988, the Indian Gaming Regulatory Act was passed by Congress after the U.S. Supreme Court ruled that states could not regulate gambling on reservation land. By the late 1990s, thirty-five California tribes had gaming (gambling) operations pulling in about $2 billion of gross revenues. This represents the most important economic development on many California tribal lands, and it is being called their "new buffalo" (though there were no "buffalo" in California when the Spanish arrived). Near San Diego, the Sycuan Band of Mission Indians used gaming profits to buy medical insurance, provide services, and build fifty houses and other infrastructure projects. One of their members was chairman of the California Nevada Indian Gaming Association.

During the 1990s, battles raged between some state officials (who claimed that slot machines and some other forms of gambling were illegal) and many Indian groups who argued that it is none of the state's business. State leaders who were getting contributions and support from American Indian groups clashed with politicians receiving contributions from Nevada casinos. Some Nevada interests wanted to squash any California Indians' activities that might compete with their revenue.

These conflicts led to statewide demonstrations by Indian groups—such as the 3,000 who gathered in downtown Los Angeles in March, 1997—to protest a proposed government shutdown of their casinos. Some American Indians, interviewed on radio and TV, claimed that it was another example of injustice and oppression against them.

They also noted that Indian gaming activities accounted for at least 15,000 jobs and $450 million in the state's economy into the late 1990s. California Indians won an important round when this issue was put before and passed by voters in a 1998 statewide initiative.

Another type of competition has led to conflict between the Torres-Martinez and Cabazon Tribes in the Coachella Valley. The Torrez-Martinez Tribe (of the Cahuillas) was granted 25,000 acres in the early 1900s. However, half of it was inundated by the Salton Sea, and much of the rest was considered unproductive wasteland. Their bad luck in geography left them to harvest cactus, mesquite pods and yucca roots, hunt wood rats, and grow squash and corn. They tried mining salt, and they leased some lemon groves. By the late 1900s, the unfortunate two-hundred members of the Torres-Martinez Tribe had no major industry or jobs, lived in mobile homes on the northwest edge of the Salton Sea, and were considered some of the poorest American Indians in the United States.

This is when local irrigation districts and the federal government stepped forward. They agreed to compensate these Indians with $14 million and permission to buy nearly 12,000 acres of land (all above water) in the surrounding communities. Yet, when the Torres-Martinez Tribe announced plans to develop a casino near I-10 on their new land, the nearby Cabazon Tribe did their best to stop them.

The Cabazon Tribe, with only seventy members, had already built the first Indian card room in 1980. By the late 1990s, their Fantasy Springs Casino was one of the most profitable in California, and their "gaming" included bingo, satellite wagering, and video slot machines. The Cabazons were clearly trying to keep the Torres-Martinez Tribe from competing for the reliable source of income they had developed and nurtured. Other Cahuilla Indian groups in the Coachella Valley expressed concern that the Cabazons had taken the unprecedented step to keep another tribe from being justly compensated.

The Cabazons (with their nearby casino on I-10) were not alone in trying to deny the Torres-Martinez their new lands. It is no surprise that Marriott International (with three nearby resort hotels) and the two senators from Nevada (where gambling is such big business) also helped to stall the agreement into the late 1990s.

Modern Issues and Problems

Modern American Indians throughout the state are demolishing past stereotypes as they aggressively compete for a piece of the California Dream that they believe belongs to them. Their challenge is to make these changes and improve living conditions without losing more traditions and further destroying their cultures.

There is a long list of Indian groups seeking official recognition from the U.S. Bureau of Indian Affairs. Such

MODERN HEALTH CONCERNS

California Indians have struggled with devastating health issues ever since the Spanish first arrived. Even by the late 1900s, more than one-third of all Native Americans died before the age of 45, partially due to poor access to health care. According to a study published by UC Davis student Teresa L. Dillinger in 1996, Native Americans' access to health care in California is irregular at best, and it is determined largely by geography and community ties.

Though there were more services offered in Sacramento through the Sacramento Urban Indian Health Pro-

ject, Indians faced transportation and cost barriers and so received less attention in the urban area. At the Round Valley Indian Health Center, Indians within this more isolated reservation received free health care, while stronger community ties resulted in better access to transportation. The result was that California Indians in the more isolated reservation had better access to health care than those in Sacramento's urban areas.

---

recognition allows establishment of a reservation with schools, housing, and health care. According to most experts, including those at the Bowers Museum in Santa Ana, the Juaneño Indians should be near the top of the list. Originally called the Acjachemen people, their culture once thrived from what is now Anaheim to Camp Pendleton. As a separate tribe, they had their own language, religion, and social identity, and they have a rich archaeological history dating back several centuries. They consider themselves Orange County's indigenous people. They were named Juaneño by the Spanish.

During the late 1990s, many of the approximately 4,500 people who claim to be descendants of the original natives continued the search for tribal status that began more than 150 years ago. Jane Uyeno of the Native American Cultural Center in Tustin and David Belardes were among the advocates working for official recognition. Juaneño tribal lands were first seized by the Spanish at Mission San Juan Capistrano in the 1770s; these lands have since been developed into some of the densest and most attractive urban environments in California.

The Gabrielino Indians to the north dispute the Juaneño claim to territory in substantial portions of Los Angeles County. Making matters worse, the Juaneño's own conflicts surfaced; they split into two separate councils in 1995. The U.S. government then faced the major problem of which Juaneño group to officially recognize.

Today's Native Americans in California are torn by countless other fundamental issues, including religion. The Native American United Methodist Church in Anaheim is the only one of its kind in Southern California. The church includes many tribes and is even multicultural. One of its lofty goals is to build stronger ties between different religions and cultures.

In the late 1990s, the Reverend Marvin Abrams was working to help members of his congregation not to choose between Native-American religious beliefs and Christianity, but to maintain a balance between them. Cultural and spiritual Native-American traditions, such as caring for the earth, were incorporated into the Christian

services there. One problem is that many American Indians link Christianity to those who dismissed their religious beliefs and destroyed their cultures.

Those are just a few examples of the host of modern issues and problems California Indians are carrying into the twenty-first century. They are exploring new ways of living while they incorporate their traditions into ever-changing California cultures. How will future California Indians carve their own niches into the state's rural and urban landscapes?

Hispanic Heritage Evolves to Modern Latino Cultures

Hispanic Heritage

Considerable attention has been given in other sections of this book to the rich Hispanic tradition in California developed since 1769, and the massive Latino migrations of the 1900s. There are so many examples of this ubiquitous culture's impact on California, it is difficult to find a starting or ending point. Of course, we are addressing not one culture, but groups of very diverse cultures as they mold the state's human landscapes.

We could start by identifying a short list of a few California State Parks with Hispanic influence, as described by the California Department of Parks and Recreation (refer to Map 7.2 on p. 231). Get out your maps. From south to north, there is Old Town San Diego State Historic Park, with exhibits of Mexican and early American life in California. San Pasqual Battlefield State Historic Park is just south of Escondido. Here, visitors can see where General Stephen Kearny's American forces and Andrés Pico's Mexican forces fought a bloody battle—both sides claimed victory. El Cuartel is the oldest existing building in Santa Barbara; at El Presidio de Santa Barbara State Historic Park, visitors can see all that remains of the last four Spanish Royal Presidios. La Purisima Mission State Historic Park northeast of Lompoc claims the most complete restoration of any California mission with exhibits describing mission life and the Spanish period.

Monterey State Historic Park marks the capitol of Mexican California. Guided tours of the historic structures will take you back to the early 1800s. North of Salinas and west of Hollister is San Juan Bautista State Historic Park, where the mission founded in 1797 is still owned and operated by the Catholic Church. Just east of Petaluma is Petaluma Adobe State Historic Park. Here, life on the early California rancho established by General Mariano Vallejo is displayed. Sonoma State Historic Park was not only the most northerly Franciscan mission in California, but was once the home of General Vallejo, one of the most famous early settlers in the area. Mission paintings are displayed there. Nearby are several historical structures, including the Sonoma Barracks, home of the Mexican garrison and site of the Bear Flag Revolt. You can't miss this one; it's on Spain Street!

The point of this list is to illustrate the geographic extent of early Spanish and Mexican culture in California. Around and between the mentioned sites, from the Mexican border to the northern Bay Area, there are scores of related historical landmarks. They are a testimony to the state's Hispanic heritage that swept Native-American cultures aside as it spread through coastal and inland valleys.

They recall Mexico's struggle for independence from Spain and the secularization and dismantling of the Spanish missions after Mexico took control in 1822. The Mexicans established a flourishing animal hide and tallow industry in the 1820s and 1830s, products they exchanged for furniture, clothes, and other goods in a growing trade-based economy.

Then, in the 1840s, Mexicans lost their struggle with the American settlers to maintain control of California's ranch lands and settlements. However, many of the first prospectors that flooded to the Mother Lode came from Mexico or by boat from Chile and Peru. (Gold mining was foreign to "Americans," and Hispanics were often the only ones who knew about it; some taught early American arrivals how to pan for gold.) Even the state constitution was bilingual as influential Mexican Americans were among those who drafted it. The state's Hispanic legacy lives on in the names of streets, cities, and landmarks, and it is displayed in countless historical sites and cultural attractions.

Increasing Numbers and Political Influence

What has become of modern Latino cultures in California? There are new issues and new heroes. There are those activists who follow in the footsteps of the late Cesar Chavez. Beginning in the 1960s, he fought to improve conditions for the working-class in general, and for Latinos on farms in particular. His organized boycott of non-union grapes gained national attention and the

scorn of California's agribusiness. Cesar Chavez's United Farm Workers and similar organizations struggled on into the late 1990s without him.

Chicano (a term many use to identify U.S. residents of Mexican descent) movements and organizations grew especially out of the 1960s and spread across the state. Some represent focal points for the culture and support groups for Mexican Americans. Many have since branched into a wide variety of Latino political and cultural organizations.

Decades of great migrations had finally brought Latinos to threshold numbers by the late 1990s; they were noticeably flexing their political muscle. The number of Latino voters in California jumped from nearly 1.4 million in 1992 to more than 2 million in 1996. The total number of elected Latino officials in California grew from 572 in 1990 to about 800 by 1995. By 1997, California voters sent five Latinos to the U.S. Congress, four to the state Senate and 14 to the state Assembly. A few were serving on some of the most powerful committees in state government and the U.S. Congress.

Representing at least 30 percent of the California population near the end of the 1990s, Latinos are expected to account for more than one-third of the population early in the new century. Perhaps more impressive is the dispersal and suburbanization of Latinos in California (see Map 8.2). They have not only moved into suburbs and districts formerly dominated by whites, blacks, and other ethnic groups across the state, but larger percentages of Latinos are visible in community and political organizations.

Politics and Power in the Latino Community

Many experienced observers were not surprised when the same diversity, conflicts, and debates that characterize so much of California surfaced in the Latino community. Which way California? You will find a wide range of opinion in Latino communities, from San Francisco's famous Mission District and Central American enclave, to Central and Salinas Valley cities and agricultural service towns, to the great urban centers of Southern California, to the sprawling farmland of the Imperial Valley.

The Latino advocacy group Hermandad Mexicana Nacional is a political organization helping thousands of Latinos. It was formed in San Diego in 1951 and has about twelve different national chapters. Its most visible and largest chapter is in Orange County. There, the organization has been praised for helping mostly poor Spanish-speaking immigrants, but it has also been criticized by some who say they manipulate their clients for political gain. Hermandad Mexicana Nacional has coached hundreds of students to become citizens; they were involved in the controversy over whether noncitizens were voting in California, a controversy that flared up during the November, 1996 election.

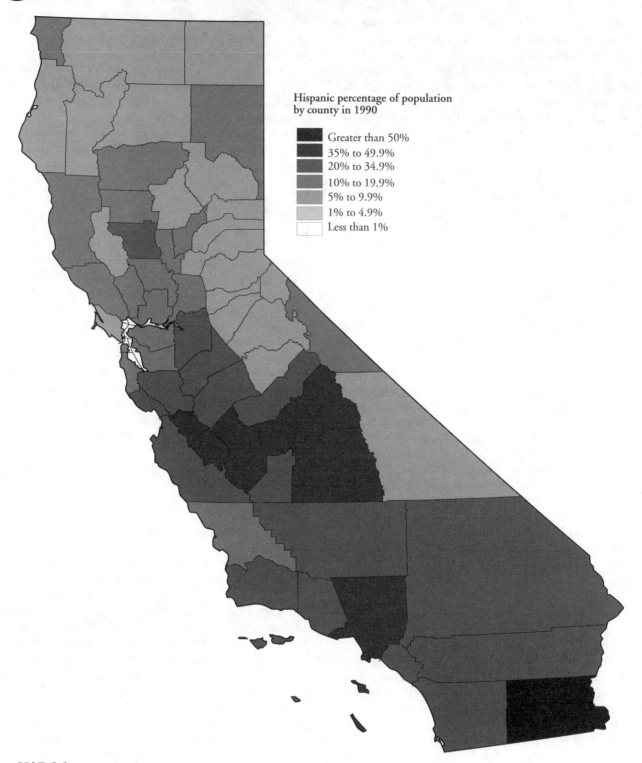

Hispanic percentage of population
by county in 1990

- Greater than 50%
- 35% to 49.9%
- 20% to 34.9%
- 10% to 19.9%
- 5% to 9.9%
- 1% to 4.9%
- Less than 1%

MAP 8.2

Latino populations are becoming more numerous and dispersed throughout California. More shading will be required into the new century.

Several other political groups (such as the Southwest Voter Registration Project) have gained the attention of Latino voters. There are also individual political leaders such as Gloria Molina. She was the first Latina elected to the California State Assembly and the Los Angeles City Council. By the late 1990s, she was the first Latina to be elected to the powerful Los Angeles County Board of Supervisors.

In December, 1996, Assemblyman Cruz Bustamante from Fresno became the first Latino speaker of the California Assembly. After term limits ended that experience, he won the race for Lieutenant Governor in the November, 1998 election. He is the grandson of Mexican immigrants. He worked his way up from difficult jobs that included picking cantaloupes. Cruz Bustamante is often quoted as saying, "Work hard and good things will come." The winds of change even blew into conservative Orange County before the twenty-first century, sweeping Loretta Sanchez into the House of Representatives.

The political and cultural influence of Latinos in California and around the nation is evident in their sheer numbers. On October 12, 1996, about 30,000 Latinos from around the United States attended a peaceful rally and march in Washington. The purpose was to show unity and bring attention to some of the issues facing their cultures. It is no surprise that a Los Angeles activist (Juan Jose Gutierrez) organized the effort. And it is not surprising that many of the diverse groups (especially Mexican Americans, Salvadorans, and South Americans) were led by Californians.

In California, Latinos represented about 39 percent of public school enrollment by the end of the twentieth century, more than 29 percent of the total population, yet only about 10 percent of the teachers. In the Los Angeles Unified School District's 774 schools, Latino students represented about 67 percent of students into the late 1990s, while only 10 percent of the teachers were Latino. California was keeping with its traditions; changes in the workforce come very gradually compared to its fast-changing populations. However, Latinos were finally finding their political power by the late 1990s. The state's Latino voting turnouts more than doubled from 1994 (6 percent) to 1998 (13 percent). For the first time in the century, four Latinos were competing for statewide offices in 1998, when even more gains were made.

Business Responds to the Latino Community

The business community is responding more rapidly to the changing demographics. California has more than twice the number of Latino entrepreneurs than any other state. By the late 1990s, California had more than 250,000 firms owned by Latinos with more than 11 percent of the state's business and about $20 billion in annual receipts. That is about one-third of all Latino businesses in the entire United States. Los Angeles alone had more than 110,000 Latino-owned businesses. Along Broadway in downtown Los Angeles, you will find one of the most vibrant Latino business districts in the world. A powerful rival continues to grow in the area east of downtown. Statewide, most of these businesses were very small and not in the high-tech sector, but concentrated in manufacturing, retailing, transportation, and construction.

Major corporations have profited from using common sense to woo Latino consumers. Communications companies recognize telephone traffic between Mexico and the United States is the second-highest in the world. Restaurants and other businesses are tuning in to the Latino community with such tactics as Spanish-language adver-

L.A.'s Pico-Union is home to thousands of recent immigrants from Latin America.

tising. Magazines such as *Hispanic Business* based in Santa Barbara attract Latino readers, and mainstream publishers and media companies such as Newsweek, Time, and Essence Communications have also entered this market. You will find Spanish-language publications in California that target specific genders, lifestyles, and politics. In the meantime, California residents are tuning in to more Spanish-language radio and TV stations. For several years during the 1990s, the number one radio station in the Los Angeles area had a Spanish language format.

Latinos Celebrate Their Cultures

Each year, scores of colorful cultural parades, festivals, and other celebrations in California mark Mexican Independence Day. This is the anniversary of the Mexican revolt against Spanish rule on September 16, 1820. The traditional parade in Los Angeles alone attracted more than 100,000 people at the end of the twentieth century.

Latino culture has flourished since the 1940s at the corner of First and Boyle Streets in Boyle Heights as mariachis gathered to entertain. This finally led to the November, 1998 festive dedication of Mariachi Plaza at that site during Los Angeles' eighth annual Mariachi Festival, attended by thousands. There, sculptor Pablo Salas successfully created more than just a dignified stage for the musicians; he used quarry stones from Mexico to build a plaza with a 40-foot high domed structure that has become an L.A. landmark.

Another parade in the Pico-Union neighborhood marks the independence of Costa Rica, Guatemala, El Salvador, Nicaragua, and Honduras. Numerous other customs and celebrations (such as Cinco de Mayo and the preparation of delicious Mexican foods) have become so institutionalized and modernized in California from Sonoma south to the Mexican border, they seem to have drifted from some of their traditional roots and into

INDIVIDUAL STORIES: THE LATINO EXPERIENCE IN CALIFORNIA

Carmen represents one of the more recent immigrants from Mexico City to California. She came to California six years ago with her husband and two of her three children and is now in her forties. They came to California for work and still believe that the economy is much better here. They now consider California their home, but they continue to celebrate many traditions, such as Mexican Independence Day and Cinco de Mayo. They celebrate Christmas but continue the Mexican tradition of exchanging most of their gifts on January 6. Carmen notes that birth control is not as readily available in Mexico, and divorce is uncommon compared to California. She observed that, in general, women (especially in rural Mexico) have larger families and less freedom than in California.

The second of three children, Oscar was born in California, but his parents migrated here from Guatemala City in the early 1970s. Though they were not poor, they moved here, as did many of their friends and family, to escape the poverty, poor job opportunities, and overcrowded conditions in Guatemala City. After about a year living with his uncle, Oscar's parents moved the family into their own apartment and took classes to augment their college educations.

When his family visits Guatemala on vacation, Oscar recognizes a beautiful landscape and people who are generally friendlier and more willing to share than most Californians. Guatemalan families are more important units in social and economic affairs than in California, and the family unit often extends beyond the parents and their children. Some Guatemalans in California are struggling to adjust to a new language, laws, and customs, especially those which clash with their traditional holidays and other customs.

There are countless other Latino stories that splash color across California's cultural landscapes. There are homesick immigrants who write renowned poems, such as "The Wrong Latitude," about the perils of living in a foreign place like California, with a foreign language and people, where individualism is the law.

There are people like Joe, who was born in Fresno in the early 1940s, after his parents came to California from Chihuahua, Mexico. He, his four brothers and sisters, and his parents worked in the fields around Fresno. His parents always stressed the importance of getting an education and only allowed their children to work in the fields during summer vacation. Joe eventually graduated from high school, joined the Army, and later worked for a California city for more than twenty-five years. His children have since earned educations and gained solid skills that enhance their success in, and contributions to, California's competitive economy.

Espy is a twenty-year-old college student. As she gains more education, she acknowledges that there appear to be more opportunities for Latinos in California than in past years. Espy notes that, like so many of her Latino family and friends, she is a proud native Californian. Her strong family bonds and Hispanic cultural pride are also evident. She is concerned that unfair stereotypes about Latinos being uneducated and working class still flourish. She notes that many Latinos in California today are professionals and community leaders. As Espy works to join them, she shows concern about some recent political movements that seem, to her, anti-Latino, which she says threaten to reverse recent progress made by Hispanics in California. She draws some analogies to the repression of California Indians under Spanish rule.

---

the "Anglo" culture. You might not be surprised to learn that Los Angeles boasts the largest annual Cinco de Mayo celebration in the world.

Although the great migrations of Cubans into the United States that accelerated during the late 1950s through the 1960s had greater impacts on other states such as Florida, there were already about 72,000 Cuban Americans living in California during the 1990s. The first migrations were mostly upper- and middle-class Cubans (often educated in the United States) escaping Fidel Castro's rule. Later migrations included more working-class people struggling in Cuba's troubled economy.

Cuban Americans continue to gather throughout California to celebrate traditions that are vital to their culture and to savor memories of their homeland. Celebrations such as "Sweet 15" parties can be as formal as any Amer-

ican wedding, with music, dancing, catering, and gifts. The importance of strong community and family ties are noticeable within Cuban American enclaves such as in Culver City.

From European to Middle Eastern Americans

Early Invaders Represent Diverse Groups

While the Spanish were the first European invaders to officially settle and secure organized rule over much of California, explorers and immigrants from other nations and cultures were showing interest. They included Sir Francis Drake, who claimed to establish England's sov-

---

THE DONNER PARTY

In 1846, the Donner Party tried an unknown "shortcut" to California through rugged mountains and the Utah desert that turned out to be longer. After alternating rugged terrain, thick mud, and salt flats broke many of their wagons and killed their animals, they nearly starved for water and food before even reaching the eastern base of the Sierra Nevada in the fall. Just about one day before they made the summit to descend down the west slopes to Sutter's Fort, the first of a series of snowstorms hit. It was the start of one of the worst winters in Sierra Nevada recorded history, and it would strand most of them for the entire winter and into the spring. One by one, they froze and starved to death. All but one of the surviving families were forced to eat the victims of this tragedy to stay alive.

Though many men and children died, most of the women survived, demonstrating the incredible tenacity and strength required to protect their families. Only half of the members of the Donner Party survived.

When word of the dangers facing new American settlers to California spread, a brief chill was cast over California fever. Even then, surviving members of the Donner Party wrote back home about how the beauty they found in California made up for the nightmare they experienced getting there. One survivor eventually wrote back east to her family with prophetic words of encouragement that seem to call from California to this day: "Never take no cut offs and hurry along as fast as you can."

---

ereignty when he spent about a month in California fixing his ship in 1579. Nearly two centuries later, rumors that Russia might extend its settlements into California finally forced Spain to act.

The Russian invaders were mainly fur traders from Alaska. By the time the Russian-American company founded Fort Ross in 1812, the Spanish were well-rooted in central and southern California coastal areas. By 1841, after they had obliterated fur seal and sea otter populations, the Russians sold Fort Ross to another kind of immigrant, John Sutter, and pulled out of the state.

For the rest of 1840s California, the mission period was already just a memory. Mexican ranchos had spread across central and southern California coastal and inland valleys, but even at this late date, there were few settlements or even explorations beyond these regions once dominated by Spanish missions, presidios, and pueblos. Some northern and eastern California Indian cultures were still relatively isolated and hardly affected by these changes.

By the mid-1800s, the Spanish culture had already left its marks on California landscapes throughout coastal central and southern California. These Europeans brought their technologies, language, Catholic religion, and other elements of their culture that were completely foreign to the American Indians. Spanish culture would continue to thrive in a state where immigration would be a dominating force in shaping landscapes for more than two centuries.

New and very different European cultures became even more apparent in California *after* the Spanish had yielded to Mexican independence. By the 1840s, this new group of mainly non-Hispanic immigrants from Europe and the United States ("Anglos") were invading California in such large numbers, they would soon gain control.

Non-Hispanic European and U.S. Cultures Arrive

These new European and American immigrants first infiltrated in large numbers during the romantic Mexican Rancho Period. The state's great ranchos with their vaqueros and caballeros were dispersed, if not isolated from central authority. American ships, trappers, and explorers were making frequent visits to California. They were welcome trade partners, and some returned home with stories of California's potential and leisurely lifestyles. Others settled and even established and managed some of the rancheros.

By the 1840s, busy trails and chain migration routes from the states were established. Wagon trains filled with eager American settlers lined the trail to California. They endured unthinkable hardships after leaving their homes in the spring and heading west across the Great Plains, Rocky Mountains, along the Humboldt and Truckee Rivers, and finally up over the Sierra Nevada. Most survived the trip, arriving in late summer or early fall. Others were not so lucky.

A Time of Transition The tide of American settlers, with their new attitudes, cultures, and power structures, had already overcome California. By 1846, American forces were seizing parts of the state in the war with Mexico. By June, 1847, after only a few struggles within the state, California had become a captured military province of the United States; during this transition period, its first U.S. military governor was Colonel Richard B. Mason.

Long after fighting had ended in Mexico, the Treaty of Guadalupe Hidalgo was signed in February, 1848 and ratified the next month. This effectively ended the drama over where to draw the new border between the United States and Mexico. With that treaty, the United States took about 40 percent of Mexico, including California and

New Mexico, and the Texas border was set at the Rio Grande. News of the final agreement did not reach the state until August, 1848, and the state's constitutional convention was finally selected more than a year later, on September 1, 1949. California was officially part of the United States; it became a state of the Union in 1850. (The rich Latino cultures which evolved from these early years before statehood and the remarkable immigrations that have since molded them are reviewed in the previous section.)

The Wild West After news spread in 1848 that James Marshall stumbled upon gold as he worked for John Sutter along the American River, California would be transformed by a wave of migration never seen before in North America. California's Gold Rush exploded in 1849 and, although gold production peaked in 1852, many thousands were already pulled in from the United States and the world. They flocked mainly to the Mother Lode, but the impact was felt throughout California.

They included not only the diverse American cultures with European ancestry, but African Americans, Asians, and people directly from Europe. The names of settlements and boom towns reflected the new Anglo dominance, but they also reflected the diversity of cultures and their origins: Yankee Hill, American Camp, Taylorsville, Jamestown, Scott's Flat, Indian Hill and Diggings, Cherokee, Spanish Flat, Irish Hill, French Flat and Corral, Dutch Flat, English Mountain, Chinese Camp, Canada Hill, Plymouth/Jackson, Georgetown, Washington, Iowa Hill, Michigan Bluff and Bar, Jerseydale, Mormon Bar, and myriad others.

Other Mother Lode settlements were named to reflect the buoyant, wild west atmosphere within this emboldened Anglo-dominated movement: Rich Bar, Rich Gulch, Brandy City, Poker Flat, Eureka, Rough and Ready, Last

Chance, Placerville, Fairplay, and Fiddletown. When the Gold Rush subsided, some of the new people would disperse with their cultures and settle throughout California, especially in the Bay Area and other coastal plains. During the 1850s, Anglo-Americans were sweeping away Spanish traditions in much the same way the Spanish had, for decades, assaulted Native-American cultures in California.

The stage was set for waves of American immigrants so diverse that some of today's historians are kept busy trying to understand them. For decades, their origins would be traced from the Atlantic states, then the Midwest and South. Depending on the year and the latest opportunity and trend, they might arrive as miners, business people, or farmers, and they would flock to the coast, then inland, and back to the coast.

European "Anglo" American Cultures Take Over An aggressive, profit-driven immigration stream brought rugged individualism that ruled the American West. These Anglo-dominated, competitive cultures brought their technologies and took quick advantage of the abundant resources they found in California. Though many had European ancestry, they had long ago adopted the free pioneer spirit of the American frontier, viewing California as a land with unlimited resources and opportunities.

Once again, cultures that seemed foreign to this newly established majority were often dismissed, and the people who seemed foreign were often excluded from participating in what was becoming the California Dream. These attitudes and cultures dominated for more than a century as California experienced some of the fastest population growth, development, and modernization the world has ever known.

From the mid-1800s through the 1900s, European immigrants flowed into California, some using eastern states as stepping-stones. They included Irish immigrants who fled the disease and starvation of the potato famine that killed about 1.5 million during the 1840s and 1850s. Though the number of Irish immigrants peaked before 1900, increasing and record numbers of immigrants came from Sweden, England, Wales, and Russia and even greater numbers from Italy and Germany well into the 1900s.

They first joined the American pioneers, and in subsequent years, they followed U.S. citizens simply migrating west for the better job opportunities, climate, and living conditions. Some religious and other affinity groups worked together to form water companies and productive farming communities that would years later be subdivided into suburbs and urban neighborhoods.

These newcomers included some of the most famous Californians, such as William Mulholland, a poor Irish immigrant who once worked as a ditch digger in Los

The Columbia stage line transported miners and others around the gold country when this was part of the Wild West.

This Irish pub in the Gaslamp Quarter, San Diego, may celebrate as many imaginary traditions as real ones, but that is typical of transplanted cultures in California.

Angeles. They included John Bidart, who moved to California from the French Pyrenees in the late 1880s; by the early 1900s, he was known as one of the most powerful sheep ranchers and farmers in Kern County with his giant alfalfa and corn farm. By the 1930s, they were joined by a desperate parade of "Okies," people who were fleeing Oklahoma and other Dust Bowl states after losing their farms, traditions, and some family members to the depression. After World War II, the European invaders also blended with the wave of U.S. migrants from the South and Midwest into California cities and especially suburbs to search for plentiful jobs and the California Dream. All of them folded their cultural traditions—whether from Italy or Iowa, Germany or Georgia—into the California experience.

Modern Diversity in European-American Cultures By the late 1900s, many of California's competitive, profit- and consumer-driven Anglo cultures continued to evolve and dominate. However, by the early 1990s, a recession was impacting every culture in what had grown to be a remarkably diverse state. The latest immigration streams from Latin America and Asia were truly phenomenal and the proportion of whites, and blacks, in the state was dropping steadily. Competition for limited resources intensified, and this brought many conflicts between cultures to the surface.

The new California is more than a state so diverse that there will be no majority ethnic group by sometime early in the twenty-first century. It is made of people who are learning to celebrate their ancestries and rich cultural traditions. It is a state that is exploiting its image as having the most diverse population in the world. By the end of the 1990s, California had again gained the spotlight and competitive advantage by recognizing these strengths in diversity.

What has become of those diverse European-American cultures in California? Oversimplified images of a privileged class with a generic culture are just as unrealistic and unfair as any other stereotyped culture in California. Some of the state's poorest immigrants in the late 1800s escaped from adverse living conditions in Ireland and then from places like Italy during the early 1900s. Many of them eventually blended in or dispersed. Others continued to concentrate; San Francisco's Italian North Beach, Santa Monica's noteworthy English communities, and a few scattered Mormon enclaves are examples.

Various ethnic groups fled from Europe's devastating wars and hate groups after being persecuted because of their ancestry or religion. Today's "white" population in California is still as diverse as any in the world, both economically and culturally, and it is still difficult to define (see Map 8.3).

Russians in California At the 1996 California Geographical Society Annual Meetings, Susan W. Hardwick gave a paper on Russian immigration and crime in California. It is a story about people who lived in a crumbling socialist society and moved to a competitive capitalist system in the midst of a recession in the early 1990s. She pointed out that more than 50,000 emigres from the former Soviet republics had settled in the United States within eight years; most of those settled in California cities. Many had difficulty adjusting to the unfamiliar, less regimented culture and the lack of economic opportunities, especially during the early 1990s recession.

One result was an increase in Russian organized crime, including tax, insurance, and medical fraud, extortion, auto theft, money laundering, and even murder. It has become problematic for law enforcement officials especially in the state's largest cities, including Los Angeles, San Diego, San Jose, San Francisco, and Sacramento. Some of the Russian crime networks based in California were connected with other criminal organizations around the country. Majority members of the Russian immigrant community are obviously concerned about those oversimplified stereotypes that could be used to label them.

Jewish Californians Jewish immigrants came to America before there was even a United States. As decades, and then centuries, rolled by, some came to California to escape prejudice and discrimination. Others came to escape the scourge of tuberculosis or for other health reasons. Still others moved to California to escape the sweatshops on the east coast. Many Jews came to California for a combination of these reasons, but like many recent immigrants, they were looking for better lives for themselves and future generations. At times, Jewish immigrants found the same kind of prejudice and discrimination they had fled. In response, they formed tight

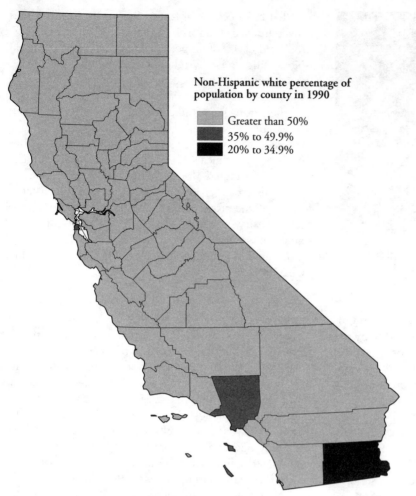

Non-Hispanic white percentage of population by county in 1990

- Greater than 50%
- 35% to 49.9%
- 20% to 34.9%

MAP 8.3
The distribution of California's non-Hispanic white populations in 1990. Massive migrations of Latinos and Asians kept this map changing into the new century as the percentage of whites decreased.

communities in California (such as in San Francisco and Los Angeles) for survival.

By the 1860s, Jewish families were settling in large numbers in San Francisco. Even before that, in 1855, the Hebrew Benevolent Society acquired more than three acres in Chavez Ravine near today's Dodger Stadium and established a community cemetery. The first official Jewish congregation in Los Angeles was established in 1862, and the first L.A. synagogue was dedicated in 1873 on what is now Broadway. The Los Angeles Jewish community had become an active, vibrant, vocal part of Los Angeles. Then, increased discrimination during the late 1800s slowed progress and forced the community to draw more inward.

By the early 1900s, Jews from Eastern Europe streamed in and brought the expansion of welfare and other support organizations within the community, many of which continue to thrive today. As the Jewish community struggled for acceptance and fought prejudice displayed against non-Christians through the early 1900s, it fanned out mostly south and west from downtown L.A. They transformed neighborhoods with their delicatessens, bakeries, grocery stores, and shops. Many Jews

struggled past entry-level jobs to become builders and developers, and into industries such as real estate. Some became pioneers in a developing motion picture industry.

Large migrations followed World War II and the Nazi Holocaust; thousands of Russian and Iranian Jews were added, and L.A. soon had the largest population of Iranian Jews in the United States. As recently as 1966, California had about 500,000 Jewish residents. Today, there are nearly 900,000 Jews living in California, and more than 500,000 of them are in the L.A. area. They represent a variety of income groups, classes, and diverse lifestyles.

Along Fairfax in L.A. are especially working class, Orthodox, German, and Hasidic Jews (a neighborhood that will get more attention later in this chapter). In the Pico-Robertson neighborhood, small Jewish-owned businesses represent the modern center of the community. Nearby you will find the distinguished Museum of Tolerance, dedicated to the triumph of knowledge and understanding of different cultures over ignorance and racism. Wealthier Jewish residents are clustered farther west from Beverly Hills and Westwood to Santa Monica and Malibu.

FROM BAKERSFIELD COUNTRY TO RIO LINDA

Some trends and older stereotypes may still be found if one searches. Around Bakersfield are farming communities that evolved from groups such as the Basque. They came to California from Europe's Pyrenees in the late 1800s. They brought their sheep ranches to the San Joaquin Valley. The area was later known for its traditional farming and ranching cultures and conservative politics that emphasized private property rights.

The Bakersfield area earned a reputation as "Nashville West" after World War II, when local country western clubs developed the honky-tonk music that became known as the "Bakersfield Sound." When performers such as Merle Haggard and Buck Owens toured the nation, fans hardly believed this music was from California. By the late 1990s, Buck Owens was still playing at his lucrative nightclub and restaurant each weekend night to a packed house, but Bakersfield had become as diverse as most of California and was shedding oversimplified images of past years.

Dennis Dingemans exposed the truth about another one of the state's perceived lower-income, mainly white neighborhoods. He wrote in the Spring 1996 edition of *Pacifica*, an Association of Pacific Coast Geographers publication. He focused on the small community (20 square miles and 21,000 residents) of Rio Linda north of downtown Sacramento and called it "Sacramento's Redneck Neighborhood." It was still more than 85 percent white into the 1990s.

Dingemans wrote about oversimplified and insensitive popular images that were exploited, such as old sofas and junk cars littering a landscape among uneducated and uncultured white people. There were few college graduates or professionals and a large number of workers competing for manufacturing and military jobs. Local media even sensationalized the very small white supremacist groups in the community.

It was subdivided on a hardpan soil that occasionally flooded; even the name Rio Linda was changed from the original Dry Creek. Its first major settlers were disappointed and angry Midwestern farmers. After relocating, they found the land to have unproductive soil. Later, yet another wave of immigrants, mainly from the southern United States, followed the military there. Although it has developed beyond the poultry and egg production center of past years, there are still hundreds of horses, cows, goats, and other livestock in the community. Most of the people live in single-family houses on large lots with limited services. Though Rio Linda has a vibrant, traditional main street, there are also large numbers of junkyards, deteriorating structures, and few franchise retailers.

Recently, a sense of pride in past struggles and tough times has galvanized the community, partially thanks to an active business community and local historical society. Rio Linda has successfully broken away from the unfair, oversimplified generalizations about its residents. It is advertising a community of positive, diverse, hardworking, forward-looking people who enjoy more space and less congestion offered by their rural/suburban lifestyles.

This traditional Jewish neighborhood along Fairfax in Los Angeles now exhibits a mix of cultures, including Ethiopian.

Celebrations of Jewish cultural pride are common in Los Angeles, from the Jewish Arts Festival to the Jewish Yiddish Culture Festival. Jewish foods and holidays have blended into L.A.'s diverse cultures. More recent Jewish immigrants are struggling with the same issues that have haunted past immigrants to California—which Jewish traditions to cherish and save while learning a new language and culture, and how to deal with lingering prejudice. Meanwhile, Israelis (Jews from Israel) are living between both worlds, not fully integrated into either. Some of them eventually return to Israel.

The Anti-Defamation League reported that the number of anti-Semitic acts throughout California and Los Angeles was finally decreasing into the late 1990s. They credited educational outreach programs, enforcement of hate crime laws, and an overall drop in crime rates, but cautioned that these trends can change within months. By the turn of the century, new technologies allowed electronic distribution of such messages of hate.

JEWISH EXPERIENCES IN CALIFORNIA: PERSONAL STORIES

Sarah is an older Jewish female from Princeton, New Jersey. Her grandparents came to the United States from Russia during the late 1850s, ahead of most Jewish immigrants. She, all of her siblings, and most relatives are college educated. Education was the most important value in her youth and she still craves knowledge. She has experienced considerable anti-semitism in California, even in the job market; she now considers this "a condition of life in America."

Joseph is a younger college student who observes that older Jewish people generally practice more traditions than their children. He notes how some Jewish youth in California might participate in early celebrations (such as Bar Mitzvah) to satisfy older family members, but carry on with few Jewish traditions thereafter. He and his friend, who is not Jewish, occasionally confront oversimplified or false stereotypes about Jews; they note how the uninformed label them as all being from New York City, valuing money, and working as lawyers, bankers, comedians, or in the TV and movie industry. He has heard anti-Semitic remarks from people who are unaware he is Jewish and has confronted friends to get their reactions. He notes that most Jews respect California and cherish the role they play in the state's economic and cultural landscapes.

Armenian Americans Armenia was once a kingdom of Southwest Asia. It and its people were eventually divided between the former U.S.S.R., Turkey, and Iran as the Soviets attempted to suppress their nationalism within tightly controlled republics. Many Armenians (most are Christian) resented being forced to mix with people of Turkish descent, who they blame for slaughtering more than one million of their ethnic kin during World War I.

Following the breakup of the U.S.S.R., Armenia became an independent state in December of 1991, and Armenians experienced a rebirth of ethnic and nationalist pride. However, many Armenian groups were stranded outside Armenia, especially within nearby Azerbaijan, when boundaries were drawn; when they revolted to join Armenia, the violence claimed thousands of lives into the early 1990s.

This is just one example of the historical conflicts and struggles that were experienced by so many immigrants, and the ancestors of immigrants, to California. Since the 1800s, from Europe to Latin America to Asia, such suffering has pushed immigrants toward the state. These people brought their horror stories as baggage to California; unfortunately, some also dragged their conflicts along with them. Like other ethnic groups, Armenian Californians also have plenty of success stories. George Deukmejian, Governor of California during the 1980s, is certainly one of them.

Today, California is home to about 500,000 people of Armenian descent. Because there are more people of Armenian ancestry in other countries than the total population of Armenia, Armenian citizens in America with valid passports were allowed to vote in Armenian elections in the 1990s. It is estimated that half of the 3,500 registered-to-vote Armenian citizens voted in that country's presidential elections on September 22, 1996, in Los Angeles alone. They voted at the Armenian Society of Los Angeles' headquarters in Glendale and at the Armenian Consulate in Beverly Hills. Many of these people had already left Armenia before that country became independent from Soviet rule in 1991; they exhibited strong emotions and pride in their culture while voting. (It is no surprise that Mexico also considered allowing Mexican immigrants the right to U.S. dual citizenship after they settle here.)

Persian Americans California is the state and Los Angeles is the city with the largest concentration of Iranian, or Persian, Americans in the United States. Many of them came during the mass migrations following the 1979 Islamic Revolution. That was an especially difficult time for Persians in California as hostages were taken at the American embassy in Iran, causing many Americans to express strong resentment toward anyone Iranian. This is another example of how one group was stereotyped though its people are ethnically and religiously very diverse. Unlike the more homogeneous Iranian communities on the East Coast, each Iranian-American subgroup especially in California has its own history and culture and has made different contributions to the state's cultural landscapes.

Many modern Persians in California are products of earlier revolutionary changes that took place in Iran from about 1925 to 1979. During this period, Iran shunned its most fundamentally conservative Muslim traditions and embraced a host of modern, western ways. The government's organized efforts to modernize dress codes, improve the economy, fortify the middle class, build a military, and boost its image in the western world were remarkably successful. That government eventually, and violently, collapsed when religious fundamentalists, fueled by growing frustrations and resentment, took control. There were a large number of Iranian students and other visitors in California and the United States when the Islamic revolution changed everything in the late

PERSIANS FLEE TO CALIFORNIA: A PERSONAL STORY

Mike was born in Iran in the early 1970s. After the Islamic revolution, his father was shot at and threatened with death if he stayed. Mike's mother and father sold their house and assets in one day for almost nothing; the three fled without a chance to say goodbye to friends or other family members. They made their daring escape with nomads on a truck through long stretches of hot desert.

They eventually flew to Greece to meet with a lawyer who might arrange for their legal immigration. When the lawyer didn't show up, they flew to Mexico City and eventually stayed in Tijuana for four months waiting for someone to help them. Finally, two Persian men transported them to the border, where they paid a total of $3,000 to farmers on the Mexican and American sides for safe entry and eventual transportation to a relative's house in Southern California.

At first, Mike had to attend private school, where, at age 13, he was enrolled in the third grade because he did not speak English. His father was granted asylum after making clear his close ties to the Shah, the former leader so hated by the new fundamentalist Islamic Republic. In time, Mike had worked quickly up and through the school system in the San Fernando Valley.

His mother and father were, and are, active in the arts. His mother eventually gave up her citizenship in California and returned to Iran, where she was happier; his father could not safely return, and so he built his new life in California. Mike still remembers some of the poetic stories and classical Persian music he left behind. He particularly recalls the traditions and celebrations associated with the Persian New Year around late April.

1970s. Some returned to Iran to join the new revolution; others, less comfortable with and fearful of fundamentalist rule, remained behind. Many had access to financial resources that subsidized chain migrations of family members and friends to California.

Many of the new immigrants from Iran were Armenians and Jews fleeing the new regime, seeking political asylum and permanent residency in California. Iranian religious minorities brought their traditions with them to California. The area just south of Westwood Village in Los Angeles became known as Little Tehran. In this relatively expensive place to live and do business, Persian script is seen on storefronts and Iranian restaurants. Jewish Iranians may be found in wholesale and retail trade districts around downtown Los Angeles, while Armenian Iranian businesses are common in Glendale.

The Persian population in California and especially Los Angeles includes a relatively high proportion of educated professionals and business owners. There are close ties within individual affinity groups, such as various Muslims and Kurds, Armenian and Assyrian Christians, Jews, Bahais, and Zoroastrians. There are even a few hundred supporters of Iran's fundamentalist Islamic revolution who have created even more divisions within this diverse culture.

African Americans

Forced migration occurs when an outside group makes the decision to relocate another group of people. Many ancestors of Californians once faced horrific hardships that pushed them to America. No other ethnic group to settle in the United States shares the humiliating and torturous past of African Americans' ancestors who were forcefully and physically moved and sold as objects in the shameful slave trade. From the late 1500s to the early 1800s, 10–12 million Africans were captured, chained, and shipped as slaves to the Western Hemisphere. Most were shipped to the Caribbean and Latin America, but nearly one million made it to the United States. African Americans in California did not arrive on slave ships from Africa. Most of them were descendants of slaves and their offspring who took a series of steps in relocating to California from other states since the 1800s.

Blacks and mulattos (those with mixed ancestry) played important roles in California cultures since the Mexican ranchos ruled the state. Then, after the Gold Rush, many new American settlers encouraged segregation and institutionalized racism. In the face of laws prohibiting blacks from voting, migrating to, and becoming citizens of California, San Francisco blacks started the Franchise League in 1852 and later the convention of Colored Citizens of California. These groups lobbied the California State Legislature for their civil rights.

These efforts and struggles continued well into the 1900s, when great African-American migrations occurred into California along with other groups especially from the Midwest and South. It is true that many of these immigrants settled in the state's largest cities and eventually established, and were often confined to, renowned African-American communities, such as Oakland, San Francisco's Fillmore, and Los Angeles' South-Central. However, there are many exceptions to these generalities.

Allensworth

One grand exception was the creation of a "race colony" in the San Joaquin Valley by five African Americans in the early 1900s. The leader was Colonel Allen Allensworth. He was born into slavery in Kentucky in 1842. He broke slavery laws by educating himself; he learned to read and write and eventually escaped slavery to fight in the Civil War. After the war, he studied theology at Roger Williams University in Tennessee, became a minister, and was a Kentucky delegate to the Republican National Convention in the 1880s. After launching an aggressive campaign and rallying support from a host of respected citizens, he was finally appointed chaplain of the 24th Infantry as captain. He served this African-American infantry company for twenty years, successfully educating his troops until he retired to Los Angeles in 1906 as Lieutenant-Colonel Allensworth.

In his retirement, Allensworth went on educational and inspirational speaking tours. He encouraged African Americans to be thrifty, value education, and plot a long-term strategy to uplift the race by relying on black self-help efforts and "doing for themselves." He met another gifted black teacher, William Payne. Payne had been an assistant principal and then a professor at the West Virginia Colored Institute, before relocating and finally settling in Pasadena, California. Weary of struggles for inclusion into white society, they followed the paths of some Swedish, Finnish, German, and other religious and

affinity groups before them; they planned a separate racial colony. The big difference is that this would be the first black colony in California.

Allensworth, Payne and three other prominent African Americans founded Allensworth in 1908 along with its farming and water company. It was founded as an agricultural settlement at a small depot on the Santa Fe line in southwestern Tulare County between Bakersfield and Fresno. The site was also selected for its perceived rich farmland and, at the time, abundant water. The settlement grew as African Americans from around the country flocked to the only town in the United States that was planned, built, settled, and governed by African Americans.

Businesses such as stores, shops, bakeries, and the Allensworth Hotel thrived. All of this activity was within what became a separate 35-square-mile school district and voting precinct with its own county library and post office. (As usual, Colonel Allensworth's wife played important roles, such as chairing the local school governing board.) By 1910, the once uninhabited land had been developed into eleven black-owned farms totalling nearly 7,000 acres. Allensworth helped make Tulare County one of the top agricultural counties in the state.

In 1914, Colonel Allensworth was killed when a motorcycle struck him in Los Angeles. New leaders took over, and the town continued to thrive well into the 1920s. By then, groundwater supplies were diminished and deliveries of irrigation water were unreliable. Experiments with new businesses and new methods of drilling wells and farming were not enough; by the 1930s, people were leaving Allensworth to look for greener pastures. The final blow came when arsenic was found in the drinking water in 1966.

The ghost town was restored as a California State Park in the 1970s and it remains today a symbol of African-American heritage in California. The remaining buildings stand hauntingly in the quiet haze of the San Joaquin Valley west of Earlimart, the peacefulness interrupted occasionally by the passing of nearby trains. Allensworth is a tribute to all hardworking citizens of California who fought racism and toiled for a piece of the California Dream. Annual celebrations regularly interrupt the calm—Black History Month in February, Old Time Jubilee in May, Juneteenth Celebration, Founder's Day in August, and the popular Rededication in October.

Some African-American History in Los Angeles

John Alexander Somerville sailed from an integrated Jamaica to San Francisco in 1902. He loved the natural beauty of the Bay Area, but after being denied food, shelter, and employment because he was black, he was lured south by pictures of orange groves below snow-capped mountains. He saved money and enrolled in USC's dental school, where he confronted more discrimination. Even-

Born out of hope and despair, Allensworth (north of Bakersfield) is now a historical landmark honoring the struggles of hard-working African Americans who built a farming community there.

WORKING TOGETHER TO SOLVE PROBLEMS

Even in the midst of the pain left by the 1992 riots, the Southern Missionary Baptist Church in the Crenshaw District had more than 2,000 members. Then, the 1994 Northridge earthquake destroyed it. Church leaders used this new disaster as an opportunity. Church members and the community responded by building a new modern sanctuary at a time when some black churches around the nation were being burned by vandals.

The 30,000-square foot, $2.8 million church was built from federal earthquake recovery loans and donations from the community. It was completed in the summer of 1996, thanks to time and resources donated by local construction workers and companies. Community members even brought homecooked food for them. Participants agreed that they were rebuilding L.A. and helping the neighborhood recover from the 1992 riots and 1994 earthquake, while teaching everyone how to work together.

Members of organizations such as the New Leaders in downtown Los Angeles are also working to turn L.A.

around. The New Leaders is an organization of about 120 primarily African-American young professionals who have joined forces to empower the African-American community. The group started in 1995, but developed from the Young Black Professionals that started in the 1980s. Members know the New Leaders as TNL; it is a post-civil rights movement of successful African Americans. Business seminars, youth development, tutoring, and field trips are among the activities organized by the group.

Field trips have included a visit to the Museum of Tolerance (a memorial to Holocaust victims), followed by discussions of Jewish and African-American relations. The organization aims to "provide a forum for personal, economic, and community development for the existing and future leadership within the African-American community." Members are from business, finance, medicine, law, news, and entertainment.

---

tually, he became the first black person to graduate from USC's School of Dentistry in 1907; he was at the top of his class and then passed the state dental board exam with the highest score ever. Somerville opened a practice at 4th St and Broadway in the center of L.A.'s African-American business district and bought a house. In 1912 he married Vada Watson who became the second black person to graduate from the USC dental school and the first African-American woman certified to practice dentistry in California.

Though the African-American population in L.A. tripled from 2,131 in 1900 to 7,599 in 1910, racial discrimination confined them to overcrowded neighborhoods. This led the Somervilles to found the Los Angeles Chapter of the National Association for the Advancement of Colored People (NAACP) in 1913. Then, the housing shortage became even worse by 1920, when the African-American population soared over 18,000. Somerville responded by building his own 26-unit apartment house; it opened in 1925. That same year the Golden State Mutual Life Insurance Co. opened at 14th St. and Central Avenue; it was the nation's largest black-owned business.

Since L.A.'s best hotels did not allow blacks, Somerville built the Hotel Somerville at 41st and Central Ave. In 1928 the hotel hosted the NAACP's first West Coast convention. Famous celebrities and performers stayed there, barred from other parts of town. However, Somerville was hit hard by the market crash of 1929 and had to sell the hotel. It was renamed the Dunbar and continued as the center of L.A.'s blues and jazz music scene for more than twenty years.

Los Angeles' African-American population nearly doubled during the 1930s, due to continued massive immigration. Restricted housing and segregation confined blacks to the area along Central Avenue south of downtown. Housing surveys and death certificates from the 1930s indicate the black tuberculosis epidemic that swept the nation was concentrated in parts of this Central Avenue district where the oldest dwellings had the highest room density ratios.

After Somerville recovered financially, he served in 1936 as California's first black delegate to the Democratic national convention. He and his wife, Vada, died in 1972 after their sixtieth wedding anniversary. This was long after he became the first black to be appointed to the Los Angeles Police Commission and after the Queen of England had declared him an officer of the Order of the British Empire for his contributions to Anglo-American relations. (Much of the preceding history about the Somervilles was featured in the December 23, 1996, edition of the *Los Angeles Times*.)

More Recent Triumphs and Trends

The Ebony Showcase Theatre, located on West Washington Boulevard near La Brea in Los Angeles, was opened by the famous entertainer Nick Stewart and his wife Edna in 1950. It soon became a celebrated showcase for African-American talent and finally became known as one of the longest continuously running African-American theaters in the country. The Ebony helped thousands of young people get their start in photography, dance, writing, video, and TV production, especially when **seg-**

regation and discrimination barred blacks from most of the established entertainment industry.

At one time, nearly every renowned black actor worked at least briefly at the Ebony Showcase Theatre. Next door was Mimi's Restaurant, a venue for blues and jazz musicians run by Edna Stewart. By the mid-1990s, the theater had lost its edge and was disintegrating in financial disaster. Residents and politicians banded together in a controversial attempt to gain control and save the landmark. The *Los Angeles Times* and other publications reported its bailout in September, 1996. As part of the Mid-City Recovery Redevelopment Project, the Community Redevelopment Agency approved $3.1 million to buy, renovate, and save the deteriorating theater and its surroundings for the future of the community.

Communities Recover from Disaster California's African-American communities—like too many other groups—have been repeatedly challenged by disasters, both natural and human. The African-American community was especially hard hit by random violence and destruction during the 1992 three-day riots following the first results of the world-famous court battle of *Rodney King* v. *The Los Angeles Police Department*. Images of King being beaten by L.A. police that were repeatedly shown by local and worldwide media did more than embarrass L.A. They eventually changed to images more reminiscent of the deadly civil rights battles of the 1960s and the devastating Watts Riots of 1965.

Los Angeles was in the world spotlight again, but this time in one of the worst displays of civil violence the United States has ever experienced. As people debated whether to call it a revolt, uprising, or riot, Los Angeles had suffered yet another devastating blow to attempts to improve race relations and to its world image.

This friction between portions of the African-American community and L.A. police flared yet again from 1995 to 1997, as every detail of the O. J. Simpson investigations and trials opened new wounds and accusations of racism. Again, headlines and lead stories focused on the negative and the divisions between ethnic groups. Overshadowed by this repetitive and shameful media competition to produce the most sensationalist news stories, a majority of people in the community had been, and still are, quietly working to rebuild race relations in L.A.

Destroying Stereotypes African Americans in California are not only destroying stereotypes about who they are, but also about where they are. Conventional images might place them only in traditional settings, such as San Francisco's Fillmore and Hunter's Point, Oakland, Richmond, parts of Berkeley, and South-Central Los Angeles. Yet, like other groups, many African Americans have fanned out from the Bay Area's inner cities to more distant suburbs. Large African-American communities are

Leimert Park in Los Angeles was originally planned as an all-white, upper-class neighborhood off Crenshaw. During recent decades, it has been the heart of African-American culture in Southern California, and some would argue, in the United States.

also found in the Central Valley, from urban and suburban Sacramento to Fresno and Bakersfield. The trend to suburban and even rural environments is especially noticeable in Southern California's inland valleys and even up into more distant high desert communities like Palmdale and Lancaster (see Map 8.4). (For more details, refer to Chapter 7.)

Today, many members of California's diverse African-American communities are debating how they can best discover their roots and plot a positive course for the future. There are organizations such as the California African American Genealogical Society. This support group, started in 1986, encourages family members to consult census data, visit research libraries, and gain information from the elderly about their family histories. The California African American Museum in Exposition Park, Los Angeles, features noted work by African-American artists.

Role Models Open Doors to the Future California's dispersed black populations and its African-American enclaves are testimony to past progress, and they offer hope for the future. The list of successful black business and political leaders and role models is growing. They include the likes of the late Mayor Tom Bradley, who was repeatedly reelected to lead Los Angeles, and Willie Brown, the controversial politician who ruled over the California legislature for years before becoming mayor of San Francisco. They are being followed by a growing list of African-American women who are assuming leadership roles as doors slowly open in business and government.

They are joined by sports heroes such as Pasadena's legendary Jackie Robinson, who broke baseball's color barrier by playing for the then Brooklyn Dodgers. His wife was honored at Dodger Stadium in April, 1997, in a

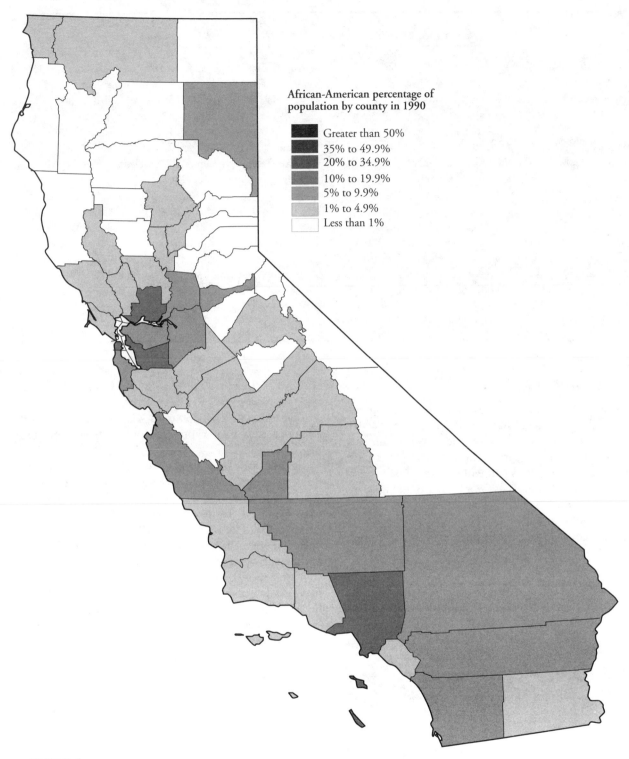

MAP 8.4

California's African-American populations are becoming increasingly dispersed and integrated with other ethnic groups.

fiftieth anniversary celebration that included the president of the United States. Others follow in his footsteps, for example, L.A. Laker-turned-businessman Magic Johnson who continues his efforts to build economic opportunities in the Crenshaw District. Many of these traditional movers and shakers of L.A.'s African-American community continued to congregate at the nearby Boulevard Cafe into the last years of the 1990s. Just down the street, you will find the African-American poets and other artists who helped put Leimert Park on the map.

MODERN CONTROVERSIES: EBONICS

Controversy is no stranger to California's African-American communities. One example is when Oakland School District officials announced in December, 1996, that they would incorporate black English into their curriculum to help African-American students learn proper English. The district was trying to increase the performance of black school children. Counted at 28,000, African Americans were a slight majority of Oakland's 50,000-student district. About 71 percent of the black students were in special education classes, and 64 percent were held back a grade. Yet, African Americans represented only 37 percent of the students in special programs for the gifted.

Ebonics refers to black English; it is sometimes known as the "dialect" spoken by some African Americans. The word comes from the fusion of ebony and phonics. Many African Americans have learned to speak in traditional English in public, but speak the dialect in casual environ-

ments. Proponents of the Oakland plan noted that the dialect developed when people from the Niger-Congo African language systems were forced to learn English as slaves. They also cited that Filipinos, Chinese, Hispanics, and others get funding to support their learning of proper English.

Some Latinos have compared Ebonics to "Spanglish," which adds Spanish words and phrases into the English language. A few Los Angeles schools have offered special programs to African-American students who speak nonstandard English, but the proposal by Oakland school officials stirred emotional opinions from people across the country, both in and outside the community, into the late 1990s. Critics argue that teaching with Ebonics only reinforces stereotypes and slows young African Americans' progress. Consequently, most attempts to use public funds to teach it in schools have been squashed.

South Asian Californians

It is amazing that even more immigrants haven't come to California from Pakistan, India, and Bangladesh, which are areas with exploding populations over an already staggering number of people. The three countries have been rocked by religious battles between Muslims and Hindus since the 1940s. These conflicts claimed millions of lives and forced millions more to migrate, especially Muslims to Pakistan and Hindus to India. As the world's developed countries were turning away from nuclear weapons during the 1990s, India and Pakistan tested and threatened each other with theirs. Single cyclones in Bangladesh killed hundreds of thousands during the final

This Hare Krishna community in Culver City claims to be the largest congregation of Hare Krishnas in the United States. The sign and gardens interact with other cultural signs here.

decades of the twentieth century. It would be difficult to find two places on our globe with more contrasts in landscapes and cultures than South Asia and California; perhaps that is why more people from South Asia have not moved here.

By California standards, Pakistan is a very poor country. It was originally carved out as the Muslim-controlled West Pakistan in the 1940s. An enormous population explosion has caused overcrowding throughout the country's rural and urban landscapes. Most of Pakistan's employment is in agricultural products. There are few middle-class citizens, and a very low average per capita GNP (just more than $400 per year). There is widespread malnutrition, a shortage of housing, poor sanitation and health care, and high mortality rates among a population lacking education and skills, while leaders throw huge proportions of their budget away on military spending. These are all indicative of a less developed country.

California must seem very foreign to those from South Asia who settle here. There are scattered clusters of people with Pakistani (mostly Muslim) and Indian (mostly Hindu) heritage throughout California, especially in the Los Angeles and San Francisco areas. The ongoing conflict between Muslims and Hindus in Pakistan and India has claimed millions of lives in those lands over the years, so it is no surprise that there is friction between members of these groups in California. Nevertheless, where people with roots in both of these countries have settled, you may find grocery stores and shops offering spices and other food, music, and videos from both India and Pakistan. You will also notice publications in these neighborhoods, such as *Pakistan Link*, with news from Pakistan and California and even a dating service.

FROM PAKISTAN TO CALIFORNIA: A PERSONAL STORY

Mr. and Mrs. Lar are from Karachi, Pakistan. The Pakistan they left was an openly conservative Muslim country where mosques dotted the landscape and where women had a strict, formal dress code. They moved with their families and settled here just before their adult years.

They remarked that many Californians seemed too eager to display feelings of affection in public and that society in general is more promiscuous here. They noted that

Californians seemed larger and frequently overweight compared to people in Pakistan. California is less crowded and congested and has much better housing than the jammed shoe-box houses in Karachi, a seemingly neverending metropolis that is more chaotic than L.A. The Lars have met other Pakistani and Indian families in the area through the Islamic Center in Thousand Oaks.

Asian Indians tend to be scattered throughout the state. You may find many Indian families following in the footsteps of earlier immigrants by investing in California's hotel/motel industry. However, they are far more diverse than this stereotype would suggest. There are concentrations, such as in Little India in Artesia. This business district has developed in a linear pattern along Pioneer Boulevard, where there were nearly twenty-five Asian-Indian businesses into the 1990s. Few changes in architecture have resulted from this transformation, but storefront signs announce the Asian-Indian culture. These landscapes are in stark contrast to a crowded India where population pressures continue to threaten that country's attempts to develop.

East Asians, Southeast Asians and Pacific Islanders

History

The history of Asian settlements on the West Coast has included triumph and success, repression, and displacement. In the years following the Gold Rush, Chinese populations settled and clustered along Sacramento Street in San Francisco. Chinese-American merchants built successful businesses there and at other places like Rincon Point, a focus of the fishing industry. Eventually, San Francisco's Chinatown gained international recognition, claiming to be the largest Chinese settlement out of Asia.

Charles Crocker recruited Chinese laborers—first from California, then from Asia—to expand and improve the growing railroads. By 1869, there were more than 10,000 Asian immigrants working on the Central Pacific line. They were valued in industries offering some of the hardest work and longest hours, but lowest pay. In 1870, the U.S. Congress granted naturalization rights for whites and African Americans, but omitted Orientals (or Asians).

After Chinese workers completed the transcontinental railroad, they branched away from distasteful railroad work and competed for other jobs. They had to face hostility that included race riots and the Immigration Exclu-

sion Act of 1882, which cut off Chinese immigration. During the early 1900s, a new group of second-generation Chinese Americans were growing up in public and Chinese-language schools as native Californians. Though many were learning American ways and earning college educations, powerful racial barriers often barred them from employment outside their communities.

Fear of Asian immigration during the early 1900s brought national and state laws that prevented them from owning land and naturalizing as American citizens. The term Yellow Peril emerged from this atmosphere of fear and discrimination. Many Asians who became frustrated with these limitations took their skills and moved to China. Those who stayed were often limited to jobs in laundries, shops, restaurants, and the garment industry.

Other Asian groups were carving their own niches within the state's cultural and economic landscapes as the 1900s progressed. Japanese Americans were establishing some thriving businesses and were especially successful in California's agricultural and fishing industries. But, when World War II erupted, Japanese Americans were driven into detention camps and allowed to keep only the belongings they could carry. They were forced to sell or give away all their other possessions.

By the end of 1942, more than 110,000 people of Japanese ancestry had been moved from the West Coast to inland detention camps after being declared threats to the U.S. war effort. Manzanar Camp in the Owens Valley was the first permanent camp to open. Writings and recordings of the plight of these people include the classic, "Farewell to Manzanar" written by Jeanne Wakatsuki Houston.

Attitudes, stereotypes, and laws regarding Asian Americans began to change after the war. In 1952, Congress finally granted Japanese residents the right to become naturalized citizens. By the late 1900s, diverse Asian and Pacific Island cultures in California were less likely to be lumped into one group. With the twenty-first century approaching, some of the fastest-growing immigration streams to California were from China, Japan, Korea, southeast Asia, and the Pacific Islands. First, second and third generation Asians and Pacific Islanders were celebrating their diverse cultural traditions while dunking into California cultures. They were also making major contributions to the state's economy, especially in areas of high technology and international trade.

Modern East Asian, Southeast Asian, and Pacific Islander Landscapes

From the Central Valley and Bay Area to the Mexican border, there are Chinatowns, Koreatowns, Japantowns, Little Tokyos, and Little Saigons that aren't so little any more. Burgeoning populations of Pacific Islanders have brought their cultures from places like Samoa, Guam, and Hawaii. Add to this the Filipino populations, which have grown to claim the greatest numbers of all these groups in California. Now, we have, by far, the largest Asian and Pacific-Islander communities in the United States, and some of the largest settlements beyond their original homelands, right here in California (see Map 8.5).

San Francisco's Asian population often receives deserved recognition. However, the most visible landscapes associated with Asian cultures in the Los Angeles area were already being examined by students like James A. Tyner in the 1993 publication of the California Geographical Society. He documented with photographs the business concentrations, signs, and building styles associated with Asian communities.

He noted that L.A.'s Chinatown and Little Tokyo have concentrated, well-defined central cores with businesses side-by-side. The most impressive Chinese community is in less concentrated Monterey Park and is now spreading farther out into the San Gabriel Valley. Koreatown is scattered along thoroughfares such as Vermont Avenue and Olympic Boulevard. The Vietnamese population is heavily concentrated and visible in Westminster, Orange County. Its Little Saigon thrives with shopping centers such as Asian Village and Asian Garden Mall on Bolsa Avenue.

Though Filipinos are the second-largest Asian population in the area, they are dispersed and less visible within places like West L.A. and the San Fernando Valley. A more noticeable linear Filipino district has developed along Santa Fe Boulevard in West Long Beach. (Far more noticeable clusters of Filipino Americans are found in Daly City and other San Francisco Bay communities.)

Some older, established Asian-American communities, such as San Francisco's Chinatown, contain distinctively ornate, pagoda-style architecture typical of Asian tradition. In contrast, L.A.'s Chinatown and Little Tokyo have only recently adopted these stereotypes to attract tourists. Many other modern Asian-American communities in California are not using this traditional architecture. In Southern California's Monterey Park, Koreatown, and Little Saigon, more practical, modern structures are

often simply decorated with elaborate Asian entryways. Business signs in these three communities tend to be bilingual, while signs in the Filipino communities are mostly in English.

The above discussion serves as a reminder; you will know when you are in California's Asian neighborhoods, but do not expect to find duplications of human landscapes from Asia's stereotyped past. Most of these communities are cutting edge, forging ahead culturally and economically into the twenty-first century. Many are led by highly educated, skilled, and successful populations with close ties to other Pacific Rim countries, due to cultural traditions emphasizing education, achievement, and ambition.

Cultural and Economic Trends

By 1990, more than 10 percent of California's population was Asian, but they made more than 12 percent of the state's university enrollment and about 21 percent of the UC Berkeley population. All of these percentages were increasing steadily into the twenty-first century. According to the U.S. Census in the early 1990s, Japanese Americans and Asian Indians (considered in a previous section) had the largest average family incomes among all ethnic groups, including whites. By 1990, 36 percent of all Californians earning more than $200,000 per year were Asian; that percentage is expected to rise above 55 percent by 2005. This is enhancing the income gap between Asians and other Californians, especially Latinos (the other fastest-growing ethnic group in the state).

According to U.S. Census Bureau data, about one-third of all Asian and Pacific-Islander businesses in the nation were in California during the early 1990s. They accounted for more than 10 percent of all the state's firms, and the number was growing at two times the national average. California had more than 230,000 Asian/Pacific-Islander businesses; five of the ten leading Asian business metropolitan areas in the nation were in California. They were Los Angeles/Long Beach, Orange County, San Francisco, Oakland, and San Jose. They accounted for more than $30.1 billion in gross sales in 1992 and substantially more by the late 1990s. Researchers listed reasons for this impressive growth in the state's Asian/Pacific-Islander-owned businesses: increasing migration, Asian politics, language barriers, glass ceilings, entrepreneurs and funding available without dependence on U.S. bank loans.

Some researchers, such as UCLA's Paul Ong, gave credit to thousands of well-financed Asian entrepreneurs, many of whom were anticipating Chinese rule in Taiwan and Hong Kong and shifting their focus toward California. Others (such as Victoria Chang, executive director of Asian American Economic Development Enterprises Inc. in Monterey Park) also noted the professional Asian immigrants who brought enough money to estab-

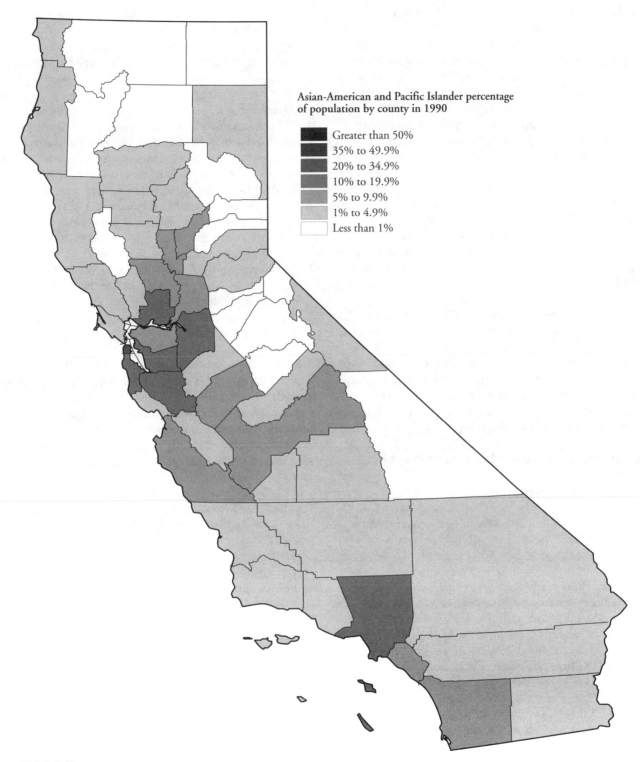

Asian-American and Pacific Islander percentage of population by county in 1990

- Greater than 50%
- 35% to 49.9%
- 20% to 34.9%
- 10% to 19.9%
- 5% to 9.9%
- 1% to 4.9%
- Less than 1%

MAP 8.5
Asians and Pacific Islanders include some of the fastest growing ethnic groups in California.
This map will require more shading into the new century.

lish businesses in the state. However, she also blamed language problems and cultural barriers for encouraging some Asians to limit their ventures to small businesses within the Asian community. She further commented on the number of U.S.-born Asian Americans who had started their own businesses after hitting glass ceilings in outside firms. Many of these new Asian firms used overseas connections or family savings for funding.

There is growing evidence of California's financial and cultural links to Asia. When the Loma Prieta earthquake hit the San Francisco area in 1989, Wall Street hardly reacted, while markets in Hong Kong, Taipei, Tokyo, Manila, Singapore, and Bangkok tumbled. By the 1990s, Asia had replaced Europe as the leading foreign source of U.S. engineers, doctors, and technical workers. Asian computer engineers are flocking to the Silicon Valley, while the multibillion-dollar computer industry in the San Gabriel Valley thrives on its trading connections with Asian countries. Many of California's Asian connections remained bountiful after numerous Asian markets tumbled and faltered through the late 1990s. However, local economies with the strongest connections sputtered during the Asian economic crisis, including the Silicon Valley slowdown that spread through the Bay Area.

Evidence of Asian cultural influence is spreading across the state. The curved eves of Buddhist temples are popping up in suburbs, while some Asian church services are held in English, Korean, and Chinese. Signs in English and Spanish are now being joined by those written in Vietnamese, the Korean Hankul alphabet, and Chinese ideograms. You can buy sea cucumbers at Asian shopping malls for nearly $1,000 per pound. In the face of such success, outsiders often label Asians as California's "model minority." Such sweeping generalizations have contributed to resentment shown by some, and they ignore the obvious diversity of communities, cultures, and goals that are Asian.

Changing Stereotypes; Changing Attitudes

Generally, Asian groups have been the least active, least vocal, and often the least visible of all affinity groups in state politics. By the late 1990s, they represented more than 11 percent of the state's population and the fastest-growing ethnic group; 40 percent of all U.S. Asians lived in California. Yet, there were only two Asians on the state's 54-member congressional delegation. Many city councils and county boards in areas with large numbers of Asian Americans (Asians outnumber African Americans in L.A. County) had no Asian representatives. Language and cultural barriers, nonvoting immigrants, and Asian diversity and cultural traditions are often blamed. (For more than 150 years, Asian families have lived in San Francisco's Chinatown without learning English.)

Asian communities in California also have their share of problems. Family fragmentation, Asian gangs (now including Koreans, Vietnamese, and Filipinos), low skills and education levels, and racism are troubling especially some Indochinese groups. Among the more than 40,000 Southern California Cambodians who live mostly in Long Beach, low skills and wages dominate the work force. In Central Valley communities like Stockton, school officials must deal with conflicts between Cambodian and Hispanic students, anti-Asian graffiti, and other forms of prejudice. Conflicts between African-American communities and Korean business owners have received repeated attention especially in L.A.'s sensationalist media. As their success became more visible, isolated acts of violence against Asians in California increased during the 1980s. Many Asian Americans blame this on the "otherness" factor (such as when some Americans hear English spoken with a strong Chinese accent).

Asian communities and organizations are responding positively and making new progress. Some of the effort comes from activists and young Asian professionals who call themselves "yappies." The Chinese American Voters Education Committee in San Francisco and the Asian Pacific American Legal Center of Southern California are among the support groups encouraging Asian Americans to stay active in politics. Rallies and demonstrations are organized to unify the diverse Asian and Pacific Islander efforts. (One example was at Los Angeles City Hall on September 10, 1996, where fifty-three Pacific Rim organizations were represented by the Asian Pacific Policy and Planning Council.) These events show a mix of cultural pride and patriotism and also serve to energize voter registration drives.

Chinese Americans During the 1990s, the Chinese-American population experienced some of the highest growth rates of any ethnic group in California—about 5 percent per year. By the late 1990s, there were more than 900,000 people of Chinese ancestry in the state. Chinese Americans had settled throughout northern California and into cities and suburbs far beyond San Francisco's famous Chinatown (which has traditionally been the largest Chinatown in the United States and The City's number two tourist attraction). In Southern California, they accounted for more than 50 percent of the population in Monterey Park, and their populations were spreading throughout relatively spacious suburbs.

Examples of this culture's influence abound, such as in 1996, when the state's Public Utilities Commission redrew 818 area code boundaries in the San Gabriel Valley. Officials were reminded that the number 8 and especially two eights so close together suggest good fortune in Chinese tradition. There was also the conflict that erupted in San Francisco's Chinatown during the 1990s between traditional Chinese and some modern American cultures.

Within The City's vibrant Chinese community are more than twelve food stores selling live animals that include lobsters, crabs, fish, birds, and even turtles and frogs. They serve some traditional Chinese consumers who believe that fresh meat is healthier and tastes better. These merchants have existed along Stockton and Grant Streets since the 1800s, and they have spread to San Francisco's Richmond and Sunset Districts in the last few decades. A smaller number of these merchants were scattered within Asian communities across southern California.

Local animal rights groups from outside the community were pressuring San Francisco officials to close the stores or place stronger regulations on these merchants.

THE CHINESE AMERICAN EXPERIENCE: PERSONAL STORIES

The Chinese-American experience in California is illustrated by professionals like Gloria. Her father moved to San Jose, where he overcame discrimination, opened his own business, and started a family. She reflects on her experiences as a native Californian. She believes that drugs have become a drag on progress in American society much like opium once slowed China's development.

Charles remembers some of his experiences after moving here from China ten years ago. One of the first things he noticed was that California had so many different cultures compared to China's more homogeneous society. He remembers how rural China—with its villages of up to two-hundred families each with their own farmland, animals, and simple three to four room farmhouses of stone and clay—is so different from California. Most families owned bicycles, radios, and sewing machines, but only the wealthier farmers could afford motor scooters, TVs, or washing machines. Charles also lived in Shanghai and noted that the crowded apartments, often housing two families, had modern conveniences compared to their rural counterparts. Still, when Charles moved to California, he was impressed with the spacious housing and modern conveniences offered to the average family.

Charles first struggled with the language barrier, but he noticed that the American educational system was not as rigorous as in China and there was less respect here for schools and teachers in general. He also noticed that the common meals in China of rice, wheat, pork, poultry, seafood, soup, and noodles eaten with chopsticks and soup spoons were replaced here with hamburgers, french fries, and soda. Incapable of pronouncing his Chinese name, friends began calling him "John Wayne," and he eventually adopted an American name. He also grew fond of baseball, football, basketball, and volleyball. Charles is proud of his new American citizenship *and* his bicultural experiences.

At sixteen, Dong Sai-Fat arrived in San Francisco by boat in 1919 from Canton, China. Nearly broke, struggling with the new language and culture, and armed with a fake ID, he worked in low-wage jobs in several U.S. cities, including Sacramento. He changed his name to Frank Fat. By 1940, he had opened Fat's Restaurant two blocks from the Capitol in Sacramento. Thanks to its delicious food, it eventually became a famous meeting place and hangout for political officials and those who followed them.

Frank's son took control of the successful family business in 1971, and his grandson took over in 1990. Fat's changed and remodeled with the times to keep its fame and success. Frank visited China only once after arriving in California. When he died at age ninety in 1997, he left his wife of seventy-two years and a rather wealthy family, including six college-educated children.

Chinatown in San Francisco contrasts with most modern California landscapes.

These protesters claimed that many animals suffered from cruel treatment and that some customers did not use humane methods to kill their animals. Some in the Chinese community reacted with disbelief. They noted how popular the animal stores were with tourists. They also claimed that the protesters were outsiders who did not respect or understand Chinese traditions and should mind their own business.

Traditions and Controversies Then, there are the herbs and other traditional Chinese treatments and remedies that are not tested as drugs in the United States and some-

KOREAN CALIFORNIANS
BRIDGE CULTURAL GAPS

Korean-American merchants, especially liquor store owners, have fallen into some notorious conflicts with American culture, particularly in California's African-American and Latino communities. Many follow the formal, traditional Confucian code of conduct. This includes avoiding eye contact, rarely expressing thanks, and placing change on the counter instead of in the hands of customers. Some traditional Koreans believe that displaying a more informal approach to others might reflect shallowness and thoughtlessness. However, many Americans consider this an insult.

This has led to educational programs sponsored by organizations such as the Korean-American Coalition, the Korean-American Chamber of Commerce and the Korean-American Grocers Association. As especially younger Korean Americans reach out to bridge these cultural gaps, it has created another gap between them and older conservative Koreans. The community has already shed its old stereotypes; Korean-American students, professionals, and successful women (rare in Korean tradition) are playing out these new roles.

After the 1992 L.A. riots devastated the community, today's Korean media, management experts, and sensitivity trainers are breaking cultural walls and encouraging acculturation. Training sessions help teach American business etiquette, such as smiling, shaking hands, and looking a person in the eye. American history and constitutional concepts are taught. The importance of speaking English is stressed, and many Korean business signs have been replaced with English translations.

times contain parts of endangered animal species. Many Californians even outside Asian communities have found natural and effective treatments for everything from arthritis, insomnia, and nervous disorders to coughs, asthma, and indigestion. They prefer these remedies over impersonal and expensive Western medicines. These traditional Chinese herbs and other medicines may emphasize the balance between yin and yang and other Asian traditions.

A few more radical and untested superstitions have led to the smuggling of endangered Siberian tiger parts, rhinoceros horns, and bear organs into California. Many Asian health groups, such as the Oriental Herbal Association, are working with state officials to identify and weed out those products that unlawfully use parts of endangered animals. They are also working to stop false labelling and to warn consumers about dangerous products that could cause illness or even death.

Such controversies are certainly overshadowed by events such as the colorful parades that drew tens of thousands across California in February, 1997, to celebrate the Year of the Ox. This included nearly 20,000 who came to L.A.'s Chinatown to witness its ninety-eighth annual Golden Dragon Lunar New Year Parade. "Gung hay fat choy" commonly resounds across California landscapes each year.

Korean Americans Though Korean American populations are also scattered about California and growing fast, L.A.'s Koreatown is world famous as the Korean capital of the United States. The majority immigrated, or are descendants of those who immigrated, to California as Protestant Christians and have established more than five-hundred Korean Protestant churches in Southern California.

Nearly half of the one million ethnic Koreans in the United States live in Southern California, and about 300,000 Korean Americans live in or near L.A.'s Koreatown, spreading from Olympic and Vermont. Near densest concentrations, ubiquitous minimalls display busy Korean signs and storefronts. Thousands of businesses with their storefronts include multinational banks as well as stores selling pine needle rice cakes, sesame leaves, lotus roots, and Korean pears.

The Korean Times is one of the many popular publications you will find. This area of Los Angeles is affectionately referred to as a Seoul suburb by Koreans and leaders from Korea who depend on the community for financial support. South Korean officials frequently stop here to greet hundreds of supporters, influential business leaders, and some demonstrators from the Korean community.

Japanese Americans Since the late 1800s, Japanese who emigrated directly from Japan were known as Issei, while their children were known as Nisei (the second generation). Sansei were the third generation of Americans with Japanese ancestry, born mostly after World War II. The first immigrants met fierce racism in California and were often confined to primary industries or urban domestic jobs. Groups such as San Francisco's Asiatic Expulsion League created an international crisis in the early 1900s when they proposed segregating the schools and forcing all Chinese and Japanese people to leave.

Previous sections have included a brief summary of the plight of Japanese Americans in California. After being forced into detention camps (such as California's Manzanar) during World War II, they were able to claim only about 20 percent of their previous possessions

THE JAPANESE EXPERIENCE IN CALIFORNIA: A PERSONAL STORY

Emily's father moved to the United States when he was nineteen; he worked for the railroads for a dollar a day and a loaf of bread. After ten years, he sent for a wife from Japan. At that time, this was a common practice among Japanese males in California. She also moved to California for a better life.

Emily was born in 1918, and her family first lived near Stockton until they moved to a sandy farm near Turlock in Merced County when she was four. The farm was part of a colony of Japanese pioneers. Their community stuck together and celebrated together on special occasions. Her family helped found the Turlock Holiness Church, the only ethnic Japanese Christian church in the United States at the time. The entire church and family moved near Modesto during the Depression in 1931 and worked the farm from dawn to dusk to survive.

When Emily started school, she could not speak English until she was in the third grade. She taught her younger brothers and sisters the language before they entered school so that they would not experience the same difficulties, but they struggled with being different. Emily remembers that she was most isolated during the eighth grade. Despite these struggles, she worked hard and eventually graduated from UC Berkeley before World War II.

Jobs for Japanese Americans were scarce, so she worked as a lab technician until the war broke out. After Pearl Harbor was bombed, she was fired and forced to return home. From there, she and her family were bused to the Merced County Fairgrounds, which was converted to a detention camp surrounded by barbed wire. They were ultimately moved by train to Colorado for much of the war.

Eventually, Emily learned about educational opportunities on the East Coast and was accepted to graduate school at the University of Maryland. The family used all of their savings to send her there, where she also worked, taking care of a family's children for room and board. Her parents and sisters eventually followed her to the East Coast, where they lived until the war ended.

Finally, they were allowed to return to California, settling in Los Angeles near today's Convention Center. In the early 1950s, Emily's parents finally gained their American citizenship after passage of the McCarran Act. Emily worked as a lab technician for a local hospital while her husband became a research scientist at UCLA. They raised their own family in a predominantly Japanese-American community in Culver City, where they lived into the late 1990s.

Little Tokyo is a sleek, modern, bustling patch of downtown Los Angeles.

upon their return. These have become painful memories that many Japanese Americans have worked hard to forget. Today, they represent one of the most educated, hard working, and successful ethnic groups in the state.

During the 1990s, the number of Japanese Americans in California capped 320,000, but was growing very slowly. This was only 1 percent of the state's population

and 11 percent of the total number of Asians and Pacific Islanders. Visible concentrations exist around Little Tokyo in downtown Los Angeles, the Japanese Cultural and Trade Center in San Francisco, and smaller centers in the Central Valley, but the population has dispersed into communities across the state. Within the Los Angeles area are the largest concentrations of Japanese Americans in America.

Traditionalists worry that low rates of immigration and birth rates and intermarriage leaves their culture in jeopardy in California. Meanwhile, advocacy groups such as the Japanese Americans Citizens League (organized in 1930) and other leaders represent strong voices for the Japanese-American community in California.

Vietnamese Americans   The second-largest Vietnamese community in the nation (in the San Jose area) was briefly mentioned in a previous section. It is notably overshadowed by its counterpart to the south. By 1990, more than 80,000 refugees made Little Saigon in Westminster the center of one of the largest Vietnamese enclaves outside Indochina. During the 1990s, more than 50,000 Vietnamese were flocking to the two-mile strip along Bolsa Avenue each weekend to visit about 1,000 shops and restaurants. Here, where Westminster and Garden Grove meet, you will find Buddhist ceremonies and temples, herbal medicine and snail-tomato-rice-noodle soap. The Vietnamese signs, entryways, and storefronts resemble pictures from a far-away land.

Today's Little Saigon is a foreign landscape to someone who expects to find the old Orange County. It is a landscape and culture that evolved primarily as a result of American involvement in the devastating Southeast Asian war during the 1960s and 1970s. This was a war that left lasting scars on the American psyche and brought desperate refugees; most of them eventually settled in California.

The first wave of beneficiaries of three years of refugee status came in 1975 and have since been studied by researchers such as Steve Dewilde at CSU Long Beach. Why did they settle in Orange County? During the 1980s, thousands of Vietnamese helped boost the state's total Asian population from 1.5 to 3 million. A Vietnamese snowball was rolling, attracted by proximity to other Asians and their businesses and low housing costs. Po-litical attitudes also played a key role. Orange County had become famous for its staunch conservative, anti-Communist politics. These Vietnamese were fleeing a feared Communist regime, and many were also virulent anti-Communists.

Though they were hemmed in by a small Korean-American neighborhood to the north, Latinos to the east, and Anglos to the southwest, Vietnamese populations grew four times over during the 1980s. More than 50,000 Vietnamese were living around Little Saigon during the 1990s, and they accounted for more than one-third of the population in many surrounding neighborhoods. The result is an energized landscape of bustling businesses that is now the largest settlement of Vietnamese beyond Vietnam. It serves a more dispersed total Vietnamese population soaring over 150,000 in all of Orange County.

Orange County's cultures and institutions are responding to these changes. At UC Irvine, you will find the most extensive Southeast Asian Archives in America; they are devoted to Southeast Asian refugees' experiences. By the late 1990s, these archives already included more than 2,000 publications for students and community members studying the histories of Vietnamese, Laotian, and Cambodian cultures. Many of the firsthand accounts were donated from businesses and homes in Little Saigon. Even UC Berkeley's famous Asian American Library is sending students to UC Irvine for research.

Hmong   One of the oldest tribes in the world, the Hmong were persecuted in China for clinging to traditional ways. After being forced to migrate to the Laotian highlands in the early 1800s, they became an isolated tribe with no written language, practicing slash and burn agriculture. Some of their most important traditional values included freedom, independence, and self-sufficiency. During the 1960s, the U.S. Central Intelligence Agency recruited them to help fight the Viet Cong during

Do you recognize Orange County? Several blocks of Westminster are designated Little Saigon for good reason.

the Vietnam War. By the 1970s, they had suffered some of the highest casualty rates of any group in the war and were flooding into Thailand's refugee camps.

Thousands eventually fled Southeast Asia to the United States; they represented some of the most disadvantaged refugees that ever immigrated to America. According to U.S. Census Data and local media, by the 1990s, more than 125,000 Hmong lived in the United States and about 88,000 were in California. Approximately 60,000 settled in the San Joaquin Valley (though smaller communities may be found in the Sacramento Valley and San Diego). Most live in or around Fresno, Merced, and Tulare, where you will find the largest concentrations of Hmong in America. Specifically, Fresno is the city with the world's largest concentration of Hmong. The more than 18,000 in Fresno County during the 1990s included members of each of the original nineteen Hmong clans, 98 percent of them living in urban Fresno.

A neighborhood known as "Ban Vinai" in southeast Fresno was named after the refugee camp in Thailand where many Hmong spent years of their lives. It is located adjacent to the Asian Village shopping center with Hmong shops and service agencies. Also nearby is the Fresno County Fairgrounds, where the Fresno Flea Market provides opportunities for bartering reminiscent of Asian markets. Hmong have impacted these urban landscapes with their intense use of any small plots (including window boxes) where they can legally cultivate native Asian fruits, vegetables, and other spices. They were even featured in a May, 1997 article in *The Professional Geographer*.

Hmong Adjust to California   Many Hmong had trouble adjusting to their new surroundings, partly because of their isolation and partly because some felt the United States owed them for their past suffering. (A few joined the March 19, 1997, demonstrations in Sacramento to protest cuts in welfare programs for immigrants. Some of their signs included "Paid the price, 40,000 Hmong dead for America" and "I rescued your son in Laos." Hmong welfare dependency rates were the highest of any immigrant group—about 70 percent. For some twenty years, many remained isolated in low-income San Joaquin Valley ethnic enclaves. Their traditional customs—including shamans sacrificing puppies, arranged marriages for girls in their early teens, and fertility rates of 9.5 children per mother—were gaining little acceptance from people in the San Joaquin Valley.

Hmong adults continue to create living environments that reflect the unsettled, seminomadic conditions they experienced in Southeast Asian refugee camps. This is seen in their apartments and in their selection of furniture and other possessions. Recently, according to the Lao Family Community Agency in Fresno and Merced, some Hmong repeated the refugee tradition of picking up and leaving with little notice. Thousands were fleeing the

poverty, unemployment, gangs, violence, and tougher welfare laws they found in California; most of them were being pulled to the Midwest. During the summer of 1996, Merced's Hmong population decreased from 13,000 to 11,000, and more losses were expected into the late 1990s.

The Hmong who stay are quick to point out the dangers of stereotypes. Along with some conflicts with California cultures and problems with gangs, they also include some of the brightest students in schools and the highest achievers. Younger Hmong who do not share refugee camp memories are marrying later and speaking "Hmonglish," a mixture of English and Hmong languages. The number of successful Hmong college graduates (including women) is growing rapidly. Contrary to tradition, Hmong youth are finding time for popular forms of recreation, and women are taking on more leadership roles. Assimilation is accelerating as Hmong and American cultures blend.

Filipino Americans   The approximately one million people with Filipino ancestry in California now represent the state's largest Asian/Pacific Islander ethnic group, though increasing numbers of Asians with mixed ancestry make counting more difficult. Recent Filipino immigration rates into the United States have soared up to 50,000 per year and most come to California. What has brought these culturally and economically diverse Filipino groups to California?

The first large immigrations developed during the 1920s, when Filipinos were brought in to replace cheap Japanese labor that had been eliminated, especially on the farms. Many Filipinos later became unemployed during the depression, but could not, or would not, return to hard times in their homeland. Responding to new immigration laws and the promise of jobs, more than 250,000 Filipinos immigrated to the United States from 1966 to 1976. Again, most came to California.

Many of these immigrants planned to leave after they earned better educations or made enough money here. However, the state's booming economy contrasted with the economic and political instability in the Philippines. Eventually, chain migrations produced impressive Filipino communities, while increasing tolerance of different ethnic groups and cultures in the state encouraged most to become permanent citizens.

Pacific Islanders   Scan a map of the Pacific Ocean. It is difficult to find a major island chain that is not homeland to some transplanted Californians or their ancestors. California's position and stature on the Pacific Rim has drawn thousands from Samoa to Guam to Hawaii. Moreover, U.S. military presence, especially during and after World War II, in these strategically located islands has strengthened the state's ties with these cultures. This also helps to explain the large numbers of Pacific Islanders

THE FILIPINO EXPERIENCE IN CALIFORNIA: A PERSONAL STORY

After an application process that dragged on for ten years, Mary's parents moved to California in the late 1960s to escape the turmoil in the Philippines. They brought enough money to start successful lives in California and they also brought many cultural traditions. Mary was forced to take music and dancing lessons and to excel in school by studying long hours without breaks. When she did not live up to her parent's strict standards, she was severely punished. This was punishment that might raise eyebrows in America, but was accepted in traditional Filipino culture. Her parents stressed that one can never work too hard or too long.

She and her sister excelled in school. However, she remembers when some of her Filipino classmates at UCLA ridiculed her for being too American. They called her a "coconut": brown on the outside and white on the inside. She experienced the internal struggles familiar to new Californians for decades. How many traditions can one cling to while adapting to the modern cultural hearth we call California? Common Filipino traditions range from emphasizing the family as the most important unit, to strong ties to the Catholic Church, to cooking meats well done. Which traditions will survive and which will fade away in California?

who have concentrated around traditional California Navy centers such as in the Bay Area, Long Beach, and San Diego.

Did you know that Hawaiian workers (known as "kanakas") were processing hides on California ranchos for trade long before the Gold Rush? They were also among the state's first gold miners. Hawaiian Californians continue to play important roles in the state's modern cultures.

American Samoans began migrating into California during the 1940s. The first groups were young males who settled near military bases or dock facilities in San Francisco, Long Beach, and San Diego for employment. They were later followed by females, young couples, and families. The latest migrations have included older Samoans who have joined their offspring. It is a classic example of the kin-linked chain migrations that have had major impacts on California and most of the Pacific Islands.

American Samoans bring a tradition of extended, loosely defined families that work and prosper or suffer together through good or bad times. Traditional Samoans do not share the more defined and confined boundaries typical of smaller American families. Occasionally, unknowing California law enforcement officials have mislabelled these extended families as gangs because they form such tight social circles.

These misunderstandings may be exacerbated by the sheer size of many Samoans and the male tradition of displaying a tough and courageous image while defending family. (Check the rosters of football teams in local high schools near Samoan communities.) Disillusioned younger Samoans who have formed isolated gangs in the San Jose and Los Angeles areas have not helped this image problem.

Diabetes and other health problems have almost become epidemic among Samoans and other Pacific Is-

landers. This is often a result of sudden changes in diets (such as more meats and fats) and more sedentary lifestyles here in California.

Other Pacific-Islander groups in California have their own stories to tell. These include the annual festivities in Long Beach where Guamanian Americans celebrate their Chamorro culture. The emphasis on family and traditional camaraderie among Guamanians is evident. Challenges created when traditional Chamorro and modern American cultures clash or blend are also apparent.

Religion

In the most general sense, **religion** could be defined as a personal or institutionalized system of worship. It usually includes belief in a divine or superhuman creator(s) or ruler(s) to be obeyed and worshipped. People's value systems are considered religious when there is worship and faith in the sacred and divine. Religion is a vital element of most cultures; it is often recognized by human geographers as a symbol of group identity and a cultural rallying point.

In a state as diverse as California, you will find myriad belief systems that help define religion. In a book this broad, we can only begin to consider the most salient features of the state's religious landscapes. Some have already been mentioned as they fit into previous sections, but not all can be covered.

A Very Brief History of Religion in California

For thousands of years before the Europeans arrived, ethnic Native American religions ruled in California. These tribal or traditional religions included animism. Hundreds of different religions reflected the varied languages and cultures in California and the diverse natural environments that Native Americans called home. They believed that life existed in all objects. Mountains and other land forms, objects in and from the sky, running water, and plants and animals could all be sacred. This is a far cry from the universalizing religions brought by the Europeans. Nearly every natural and human event and element of culture had religious connotations for Native Americans, from hunting and gathering, to celebrations and dances, to myths, relationships, and eating habits.

As waves of Europeans and others from around the world migrated in, only a few immigrants to California—mostly those from less developed economies—brought their tribal or traditional ethnic religions. More frequently, they brought universalizing religions, such as Islam, Buddhism, and especially Christianity. Most of these belief systems worked nearly as well in California as in their homelands; they now dominate the state's modern religious landscapes. Spanish missionaries first carried the Catholic religion to California. Though the Mexican government later secularized the missions and the American settlers and other immigrants would bring Protestant and other belief systems, the Roman Catholic

Church has maintained a powerful presence in California.

Modern Belief Systems

Various surveys of Californians during the late 1900s reflect some changing attitudes and incredibly diverse religious belief systems. They show that about two-thirds of Californians consider themselves very or fairly religious, while nearly one-third are not too religious or not religious at all. Less than 20 percent have no religious preference. General religious preferences of the population are more than 40 percent Protestant, more than 25 percent Roman Catholic, less than 5 percent Jewish, while less than 10 percent prefer other faiths (see Map 8.6).

True Adherents: Mostly Christians and Jews However, only less than one-third of California's people are true adherents (followers, supporters, and churchgoers) of a specific religion. Catholics combine to make the single largest denomination of adherents in California, because Protestants are split among various denominations. The

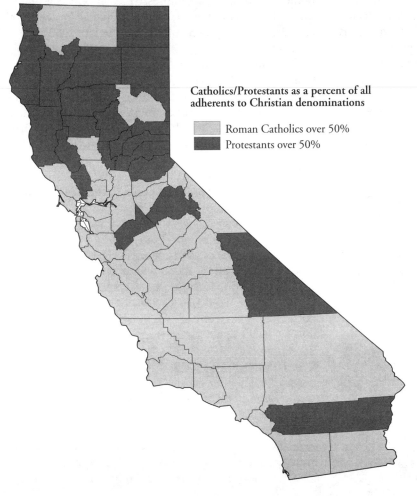

Catholics/Protestants as a percent of all adherents to Christian denominations

Roman Catholics over 50%
Protestants over 50%

MAP 8.6
Incredibly diverse religious belief systems are found throughout California. Christianity is the reported religious preference of well over half of all Californians. This map shows patterns among the much smaller group of true adherents to Christianity only.

combination of various Baptist groups ranks a distant second in specific denominations. These include diverse churches from traditional, conservative Southern Baptists, especially in rural and suburban California, to African-American Baptist groups in the inner cities. Lutherans and Latter Day Saints (Mormons) are not far behind in numbers.

If all Jewish residents are considered, they would be the second-largest specific single religious group in California. They certainly qualify as a cohesive socio-religious group, though many are not registered members of synagogues. There has even been disagreement within the Jewish community about who can be considered truly Jewish.

Numbers and Concentrations of True Adherents Obviously varying definitions (by the researchers and those surveyed) make analyses of statistics regarding religion in California problematic and subjective at best. However, there are some clear trends, especially in geographic distributions. Roman Catholic adherents are found in greater percentages (more than 25 percent in some counties) in Southern California up through the Bay Area and into the San Joaquin and southern Sacramento Valleys. These include regions where early missions and Hispanic settlements were first established and, more recently, where proximity to chain migrations from Latin America have had the greatest impacts.

Catholics represent far more than 60 percent of all true adherents in the mostly urban counties of San Francisco, San Mateo, and Alameda in the Bay Area and in Los Angeles County. They are well over 60 percent of all adherents in more rural San Benito, Merced, and Imperial Counties. There is strong Catholic tradition in all of these areas, but especially where large numbers of immigrants

This Ferndale church was experiencing a major remodelling after being damaged by an earthquake and getting the attention of townsfolk who wanted to save their traditions. Churches are often the most visible structures within rural California towns.

have flowed in from Latin America to satisfy the demand for cheap labor in urban industries or on rural farms.

Imperial County's population is not only overwhelmingly Latino, but has the greatest percentage of Catholic adherents (more than 70%). Catholics from Pacific Rim regions (such as Filipinos and Pacific Islanders) have fortified these numbers in coastal areas of the state. Considering these past and present trends, it is no surprise that you could find traditional Catholic cathedrals in California during the 1900s in Santa Rosa, Sacramento, San Francisco, Oakland, Stockton, Monterey, Fresno, Los Angeles, Orange, and San Diego.

The majority of northern California counties' adherents are Protestant. There and across California, these Protestants are split between (from largest to smallest proportions) Baptists, Lutherans, Methodists, Presbyterians, Episcopalians, and smaller denominations. However, more than 400,000 Latter Day Saints (Mormons) are scattered throughout California and make up the greatest percentages of all adherents in the northeastern and eastern parts of the state.

Remember that these numbers only reflect true adherents of specific denominations, not general religious preferences of the entire California population. The total numbers are still quite impressive; California had more than 10 million adherents and somewhere near 15,000 churches of all denominations into the late 1990s.

Other Religions Contribute to Diversity Recent migrations (especially from Asia and the Middle East) and stronger global ties have also resulted in a rise in popularity of major non-Christian religions in California such as Islamic, Hindu, and Buddhist belief systems. Their mosques and temples are peppered across California's human landscapes.

Like ethnic groups, cultures, and lifestyles, you can pick almost any religion and find it in this state. Natives, visitors, and newcomers are finding an atmosphere of tolerance for their religious beliefs, or lack of them, that can only come with knowledge of and mutual respect for the diverse people and cultures of California. This has created a rich atmosphere where congregations who welcome and bring many belief systems together to find a common good (such as Unitarian Universalists) are especially popular. Here are just a few examples of trends in California's religious landscapes.

Other Belief Systems

Islam According to Islamic leaders and the Council on Islamic Education in Fountain Valley, there are 1.3 billion Muslim adherents in the world; about one million of them lived in California into the late 1990s, mostly in Southern California. Celebrating the end of the month-long fast of Ramadan, more than 15,000 people have

CATHOLICS AND OTHER CHRISTIANS
BRIDGE THE PAST AND FUTURE

Workers hurried in 1996 to complete earthquake repairs and renovations on the San Gabriel Mission and surrounding landmarks for its 225th anniversary. It was founded in 1771 to start the oldest European settlement in the L.A. area. The mission was moved after floods; most remaining buildings date back to the early 1800s. A restoration committee was determined to get its six bells ringing as they had for decades to signal school children and church services.

Within months of that event, Cardinal Roger M. Mahony rededicated the St. John Eudes parish church in Chatsworth after a $5.3 million redesign and rebuilding followed the 1994 Northridge earthquake. Its modern design and construction reflected what Cardinal Mahony wanted in his proposed $50 million Cathedral of Our Lady of the Angels to replace the earthquake-damaged St. Vibiana's in downtown L.A. By 1997, plans were unveiled and the property was purchased to build this new cathedral in downtown L.A. Like San Francisco's famed modern cathedral (resembling a washing-machine agitator from the outside), L.A.'s new cathedral is situated for sweeping views and will be easily visible from many surrounding locations. Meanwhile, preservationists were still struggling to save the old St. Vibiana's as an historical landmark.

These projects reaffirm the powerful influence of the Roman Catholic Church on California's human landscapes. Migrations from around the world have brought other religions (especially American settlers and Protestant denominations since the mid-1800s) to compete with those first Christian invaders and their Catholic landscapes. You will find evidence of these other religious belief systems (especially Protestant, as addressed in previous sections), sometimes tucked away in inconspicuous spaces and, at other times, conspicuous on crowded street corners.

---

worshipped in morning prayer sessions at the Los Angeles Convention Center. Up to 10,000 Muslims from around the world have gathered for morning services at the Islamic Society of Orange County in Garden Grove.

The Islamic Shura Council of Southern California counted fifty-five mosques (masjid in Arabic) in the area in 1994 and seventy-five in 1997. Many are located in converted buildings. In contrast, Masjid Abu Bakr in San Diego and the $8.5 million Masjid Omar Ibn Al-Khattab near USC in L.A. were built to serve as mosques. The latter has highly visible traditional architecture with dome and minarets. More than half of those who attend Friday prayers there are African American and most of the rest are ethnic Muslims with Middle Eastern and South Asian roots. In 1998, an $8.1 million mosque was dedicated in Culver City, complete with a 79-foot minaret.

When another $2.2 million mosque was constructed, with local money, in Granada Hills (in the northern San Fernando Valley), the community imposed forty-four building restrictions on the structure. It is interesting that the prohibitions included loudspeakers, bells, chimes, and alcoholic beverages because none of these are common in mosques, and alcohol is prohibited in Islam.

Muslims are hoping for more understanding and tolerance from the community in the future. Though some Christians are unfamiliar with Islam, there are similarities. The belief in one God (Allah), the messenger (Mohammed), and Islam's Holy Book (the Koran) may be examples. Many Muslims are much more strict about the importance of regular prayer, dietary restrictions, and dress codes than most Christians. Muslims throughout California are seen weighing their traditional belief systems against the state's popular cultures.

Buddhism and Other Eastern Belief Systems Tibet's written language was started to disseminate the teachings of Buddha. Buddhism was introduced to Tibet from India in the seventh century. Isolated Tibet eventually became a center of Buddhist thought and teachings. Since China invaded in the late 1950s, it has made every effort to eradicate the entire culture and writings of these people.

After a Buddhist meditation center was founded in Berkeley in 1969, it evolved into the Nyingma Institute, offering classes and retreats to introduce Buddhism locally; it became a ray of hope for preserving ancient writings. Volunteers such as Sylvia Gretchen started Dharma Publishing. While searching the globe, they rediscovered and recovered many teachings of Buddha (some of which were thought to be lost forever) and printed more than one hundred copies of hundreds of volumes.

Printing and detail work is done at Dharma Publishing in Berkeley. Thousands of these religious books and art works have been sent to Tibetan lamas, especially those who made a pilgrimage to Bodh Gaya, the northern Indian village where Buddha attained enlightenment. Some of the collected works have been translated into English at a California temple called Odiyan, on the coast about one-hundred miles north of San Francisco. These translations are also published in Berkeley for a more general audience. Dharma Publishing has taken the next step beyond saving and preserving the writings and culture; it has opened its collections to the public and even sponsored travelling exhibits.

A majority of the estimated 800,000 Buddhists in the United States are in California. Due mostly to Asian immigrants, up to 40 percent of that total are estimated to be in the L.A. area. The state hosts more than one-hundred versions of the religion. This is one reason the Dalai Lama (the Tibetan spiritual leader) visits and conducts religious seminars in the state. Despite protests from China, participants come from around the world, and the Dalai Lama has been greeted by thousands of Buddhists. In one visit to Pasadena during the summer of 1996, he was issued a key to the city, while Pasadena's Pacific Asia Museum hosted a traditional sand painting.

Buddhist temples can be found in northern and southern California; the Nishi Hongwanji Betsuin (L.A.'s Buddhist Temple in Little Tokyo) is an example. The Hsi Lai Temple in Hacienda Heights claims to be the largest Buddhist monastery in the western world. It is a showy symbol of the influence Chinese-American upper classes have in the San Gabriel Valley. Traditional Chinese architecture includes tile roofs that curl upward at the edges and colorful paper lanterns hanging from every gateway. Like the Christian churches that dominate so many human landscapes in towns and cities throughout California, it announces the presence of a thriving culture.

Traces of Hinduism are even found among the other eastern religious belief systems evident throughout California. They include the colorful festivals in Venice and other celebrations familiar especially to the state's urban populations. Their influence was evident among the approximately 150,000 Hindus that lived in the Los Angeles area in the late 1990s.

Image and Controversy

California's more experimental and controversial religions and cults have sometimes put the state in an undesired spotlight. There was extensive media coverage of the tragic mass suicides of members of the Jim Jones cult in 1978. Although the event took place in Guyana, the cult was based in San Francisco. More recently, thirty-nine members of the Heaven's Gate cult participated in the worst mass suicide in U.S. history in March, 1997. The cult members had rented a home in a tranquil, upscale neighborhood in Rancho Santa Fe. This area was northern San Diego County's Beverly Hills, with huge estates separated by expansive orchards, lawns, and country club settings.

After the Heaven's Gate episode, even writers for the *Los Angeles Times* worried about what the circus atmosphere caused by California's latest human tragedy would do to the state's image. In one article, the *Times* recalled what various writers had to say about California culture. One of the pieces quoted was journalist Bruce

Bliven's 1935 critique of California cultures. "Here is the world's prize collection of cranks, semi-cranks, placid creatures whose bovine expression shows that each of them is studying, without much hope of success, to be a high-grade moron, angry or ecstatic exponent of food fads, sunbathing, ancient Greek costumes, diaphragm-breathing. And the imminent second coming of Christ."

The *Times* also reflected on mid-1900s writings by poet-historian John Steven McGroarty. "Los Angeles is the most celebrated of all incubators of new creeds, codes of ethics, philosophies—no day passes without the birth of something of a nature never heard of before. It is a breeding place and a rendezvous of freak religions. But this is because its winters are mild, thus luring the pale people of thought to its sunny gates."

This was followed by Curt Gentry's theories in his 1968 classic book, *The Last Days of the Late, Great State of California.* "According to one, in moving to California people wanted a new start; they shopped not only for a new job, new house, new furniture, new auto, new friends, but also for a new religion. . . . Another explanation had it that California was so democratized, so lacking in a clearly defined society, that people craved something extra-exclusive. Still another thesis claimed there were so many other distractions in California life that religion, to compete, had to be startling, sensational, different."

With all this controversy, it may surprise a newcomer that the same mainstream Christian religions found throughout America continue to dominate the religious landscapes here. It is illustrated each year when record millions from countless Christian denominations flock to Easter sunrise services on hilltops and in churches and cathedrals throughout California. Meanwhile, when minority religious belief systems and their landscapes emerge, they are usually accepted and tolerated in California more easily than any other place in the world.

Other Components of California Cultures
Language

There are myriad other pieces that come together to make up California's cultural puzzle. The state's dozens of languages are examples. **Language** is the most important method by which culture is transmitted, and it certainly helps distinguish cultural groups in California.

California school districts are struggling to recognize the significance of these languages, while encouraging all students to master English. About 110 languages are spoken in L.A. and San Francisco Bay Area schools, and 80 are spoken in the Sacramento area. Debate continues to rage between residents with opposing views on how to deal with this problem.

Predominantly progressive-leaning groups who may advocate bilingual education clash with traditional-lean-

WOMEN'S STORIES OF FAILURE AND SUCCESS

That growing gap between California's wealthy women and those stuck in poverty was evident even in the late 1990s as the government cracked down on welfare mothers. A few citizens and leaders were working to help poor women get on their feet to become self-sufficient. San Francisco's Homeless Prenatal Care program was started in 1989 by women who wanted to get homeless mothers off the street and rehabilitated. It gained steam well into the 1990s. Private donations from foundations and individuals were being used in this unique program mostly run by women volunteers to empower some of the state's poorest mothers to become independent.

There are also many stories of successful women entrepreneurs. When former management consultant Vivian Shimoyama approached major retailers with her "Glass Ceiling" jewelry to symbolize the **glass ceiling** that prevents women and minorities from rising to the top in business and politics, she was usually rejected by those who said her product was too political. She started selling her own products through her own company (Breakthru Unlimited) in Manhattan Beach during the early 1990s, and she became so successful that her annual sales grew toward $150,000 during the mid-1990s. Women from around the country were wearing her jewelry, including leaders in both political parties. She was riding a wave that had become very popular particularly in California—pins, T-shirts, and other products with a message.

Pamela Meyer Lopker attended school in Cupertino since the eighth grade and later enrolled at UCSB in 1972, where she majored in math and economics. After graduating, she stayed in the Santa Barbara area and used money from her first job as a programmer to invest in real estate. Eventually, she founded and became president of QAD, Inc., a Carpinteria software company. By 1997, she ranked on the *Forbes* 400 annual list of wealthiest people in the United States; her company was making $159 million per year and was worth about $1 billion. *Forbes* considered Lopker the richest self-made businesswoman in their survey. When negotiating with foreign companies that do not accept high-ranking women, she still had to rely on her husband, Karl. Otherwise, she felt that customers had reacted positively to her and her company.

---

ing, anti-bilingual groups who advocate total immersion in English classes first. As parents and citizens complain about inefficiencies in both approaches, state lawmakers and petitioners have been quick to introduce dueling legislation originating from their affinity groups. As of 1998, California voters were leaning toward the anti-bilingual approach.

The struggle to recognize Ebonics in the Oakland and L.A. schools and the evolution of Spanglish and Hmonglish are among the many issues involving language in California that have been addressed in previous pages.

Gender Equity

The status of women is an important measure of development for most societies. An understanding of women's roles in California can lead to clues about the state of our culture and its progress. California has long had a reputation as a progressive state where women have made great strides toward equality (compared to other regions). Do the statistics support the image?

It is difficult to measure progress based on subjective observations. Various formal and informal women's support groups have organized since before California was a state. Recently, recognition of women and their contributions to California culture have become more commonplace. The annual International Women's Day Celebration held every March 8 during the 1990s at the Museum of Tolerance in L.A. is an excellent example. Perhaps women's status is more objectively measured by economics.

During the ten years since the late 1980s, the number of businesses owned by women in California increased by nearly 80 percent. By the late 1990s, California led the nation with about 1.1 million firms owned by women, nearly double the number two state (Texas). Los Angeles was one of three national locations where a program was started to increase the number of women-owned businesses. (This was a cooperative effort between the L.A. chapter of the National Association of Women Business Owners and the Women Business Owners Corporation in Palos Verdes.) According to 1990s studies by the Institute for Women's Policy Research, California women were faring better than the national average, owning more than 35 percent of all firms. All of the statistics were not so bright.

Women working full time had mean annual incomes of just more than $30,000 by the end of the 1990s, about 73 percent of men's salaries. This ranked California fifth among states in women's annual incomes and sixth in the ratio to men's salaries. Though the study showed women doing generally better than the national average, there was a huge and troubling gap between the rich and poor. More than 16 percent of California women had no health care. An earlier study of 1989 U.S. Census Bureau information by the *Los Angeles Times* showed women ranked even lower. This study especially noted the large gap between men's and women's salaries when they worked in the same jobs, even in fields traditionally dominated by women.

Alternative Lifestyles: Gays and Lesbians

One of the most tragic historical events for homosexuals in California was the murder of San Francisco's gay activist and city council member Harvey Milk in the late 1970s. After former city council member Dan White was convicted of murdering Milk and San Francisco's Mayor George Moscone in their City Hall offices, he was given a light sentence on the grounds that he was emotionally upset, partly due to eating too much junk food with a high sugar content. When news spread that White would soon walk free, San Francisco erupted in violence. There were no winners in yet another unfortunate event that brought California even more unwanted attention, but the drama helped to electrify gay communities and their supporters in San Francisco and throughout California.

The devastation left by the spread of AIDS during the 1980s first shocked and then further galvanized these communities. Education, prevention, and research efforts had already slowed the spread of AIDS during the 1990s among gay populations. (However, reflecting a pattern established in many developing nations, it spread within California's general population during the 1990s, especially among lower income and minority groups.)

An evolution in California public opinion was becoming clear. By the late 1990s, every major California city hosted annual pride parades and gay community centers. Assemblywoman Sheila Kuehl was then the state legislature's first openly gay member. California's legislature debated bills banning discrimination and violence against homosexuals in California public schools, discrimination against gays and lesbians in housing and employment, and the controversial legal recognition of same-sex marriages. Some more conservative religious and other groups were still opposing such legislation and liberalization, while other religious and more progressive groups supported it.

The debate was, and is, typically Californian. Many different people have thrived in or moved to California as the state offers some relief from discrimination for those who practice alternative lifestyles. Since the Gold Rush, California has attracted those who were ostracized for their less traditional beliefs and lifestyles. On the other side are those who are uncomfortable with the cultural mixes and experiments that are modern California. Some progressives might say that - in California - these traditionalists have always attempted to cling to the past on a runaway train bound for an uncertain future.

In recent decades, gay and lesbian communities have become increasingly visible throughout the state. One specific example of acceptance was when the gay-oriented Metropolitan Community Church (headquartered in West Hollywood) was admitted to the Southern California Ecumenical Council in 1997. This followed a unanimous vote by the Sacramento-based California Council of Churches (representing United Methodists, Presbyterians, Episcopalians, and other mainline Protestant churches) to admit the MCC.

Like many other cultural groups, some community members have clustered in protective enclaves. In Southern California, they range from San Diego's Hillcrest, Orange County's South Laguna Beach, and Coachella Valley's Palm Springs/Cathedral City, to Los Angeles County's West Hollywood, Long Beach, and Silver Lake.

Though northern California cities (including Sacramento) have their own gay and lesbian enclaves, none is more famous than San Francisco's Castro District. This is the heart of one of the most visible and vibrant gay communities in the world; it has become a must stop for many tour guides and bus companies. An outlying extension of this community even popped up several years ago in Guerneville resorts along the scenic Russian River in Sonoma County more than an hour north of The City.

Elderly Californians

Regardless of age or gender, ethnic or income group, religion or lifestyle, all Californians share at least one reality—they are growing older. The state's mild weather and leisurely lifestyles attracted elderly, retired populations into the mid-1900s. That trend had reversed by the end of the 1900s, as older citizens fled the state's perceived crime, crowds, pollution, and higher real estate costs. Some were retiring especially in neighboring states with lower living costs. Recent statistics (reviewed in the previous chapter on population) reveal the nature of California's elderly population. There are still more people 65 or older here than in any other state among the population of more than 34 million.

Many Californians are looking to their future as they examine ways to make the state more senior friendly. Examine the human landscapes and services in your community. Do they represent environments that you would prefer when you grow older or are they hostile to those who may be slowed or limited by their age? The thriving retirement communities throughout California are ripe with examples of how living environments can be built to better serve our senior citizens. Like many other cultural groups, seniors retreat into these enclaves for safety and camaraderie. (Some of these unique human landscapes are examined in Chapter 11.)

Must we confine our elderly to these guarded forts when they can no longer compete in our fast-paced society? If we encourage continued segregation of our seniors, what is to become of the many other cultural groups throughout California that may not seem to fit in with recent trends? What kinds of sterile communities will result if we try to build them only for the most successful, the most productive citizens in their primes? How we answer these questions will reflect upon the sensitivity and stability of our modern culture.

◆ IN THE MIX: SALAD BOWL OR MELTING POT?

Perhaps more than any other time in history, California's cultures are in transition. Are we a **salad bowl** where individual cultures are emphasized, clinging to their identities among a larger mix? Or, are we becoming a **melting pot**, where everyone is encouraged to turn away from their roots and blend into mainstream culture? Examples of both of these trends abound.

Joe Hicks, who directed the Southern Christian Leadership Conference and then the Los Angeles Multicultural Collaborative (a coalition of eleven community-based groups formed after the 1992 L.A. riots) was one of many leaders addressing these issues into the late 1990s. He was concerned about "**tribalization**" that occurred as some of the cultural groups reviewed in this chapter splintered away from one another. From Latinos to Korean Americans, from African Americans to white power organizations, fear and suspicion has made some groups reluctant to integrate, and they retreat into their own enclaves to preserve their identities. Hicks noted that though separatists were still a minority in each group, people seemed to be less curious about one another.

This ignorance fortifies fears that encourage "tribalization"—the formation of interest-based groups competing for limited resources. As some of these citizens

Kosher Burrito has attracted the hungry and the curious in downtown Los Angeles for years.

and groups regress to looking out for number one, there emerges a cultural version of tragedy of the commons.

More Diverse People Competing for the California Dream

All indications are that the state's populations will continue to become more diverse into the twenty-first century. California maintains a commanding lead in new citizens and applicants to become new citizens compared to any other region in the country. When government officials threatened to cut off services to those who were not citizens in the 1990s, a new flurry of applicants responded. More than one-fourth of the surge in national citizenship applicants were in Southern California into the late 1990s.

According to government, local media, and school district data, the Los Angeles Unified School District was the nation's largest provider of citizenship instruction during the 1990s. Future citizens were enrolling in English and other courses to gain skills so that they could compete more successfully and earn voting and other rights enjoyed by U.S. citizens. Applicants especially included people from Mexico and other Latin American countries, Southeast and East Asia, Europe, and the Middle East.

Community groups, businesses, and government all wrestle with how job opportunities, services, and other resources are divided between the diverse groups that are already settled and those that are new to California. Some skilled workers complain about high-tech companies bringing educated immigrants in from Asia and Europe to undercut their wages. Communities argue about what to do about day laborers (legal and illegal) who wait on street corners for low-wage construction and other jobs.

However, the greatest scorn and condemnation from all sides is usually reserved for the state's notorious sweatshops, where illegal workers are transported into California and exploited under the threat of being returned to poverty-stricken homelands or exposed to the INS.

Fierce Competition and Inequity Create Conflict

There is no doubt that such rapid change and fierce competition has created tension and friction between different groups and communities in California competing for space and limited resources. There are many examples, especially in poorer, multiethnic cities across the state, such as Compton. This renowned African-American community and its leaders have been challenged to address the needs of a growing Latino community. By the mid-1990s, Latinos made up more than half of Compton's approximately 92,000 residents, but no Latino had ever held a seat on the city council. There were only fourteen Latino police officers on the 127-member police force.

The new Latino community demanded more representation, while some African Americans complained that Latinos did not vote. Then California voters passed Proposition 187, requiring schools to identify and expel undocumented students. Amid racial conflicts between black and Latino gangs, Compton school officials were concerned that the vote would touch off a round of violence on their campuses. By the late 1990s, Latino leaders continued to pressure Compton officials to become more sensitive to the needs of the most recent majority.

There was also a rise in anti-Asian hate crimes reported in California going into the late 1990s, according to law enforcement officials. California was home to a quarter of the anti-Asian hate crimes reported nationwide. During one year in the mid-1990s, 91 anti-Asian hate crimes were reported in northern California and 113 in southern California (53 in the L.A. area alone). The crimes ranged from harassment and vandalism, to robberies and assaults, to two racially motivated murders. These acts were against Chinese, Vietnamese, and Korean victims who were often mistaken by the perpetrators as members of other races.

Asian-American leaders searched out reasons for these acts. Their large and growing numbers and perceived economic success within an atmosphere of anti-immigrant attitudes, xenophobia, economic instability, ignorance, and fear were blamed. Across the state, law enforcement officials and leaders from nearly every California affinity group are combining efforts to make sure such acts of ignorance, fear, and hate remain isolated and rare in the state.

The struggle for resources and turf extends far beyond ethnic lines. Even surfers are practicing "localism" as the state's waves become more crowded. Local surfers select beaches for their local "breaks" (the manner in which waves peel down the beach). A few practice intimidation tactics against visiting surfers, which include heckling, vandalism, and even violence to keep them out. Tragedy of the commons rules once again as these clueless surfers often become victims when *they* attempt to visit distant California beaches. Law enforcement officials have also been cracking down on these scoundrels.

Such intense competition and conflict and resulting divisions have gained the attention of research groups such as UCLA's School of Public Policy and Social Research. Their studies showed that L.A. was changing from Iowa-on-the-Pacific to a multicultural metropolis from 1980 into the 1990s. As the percentage of white and black populations dropped, Latinos and Asians gained rapidly. At the same time, the gap between rich and poor in all races widened. Ethnic job networks were bringing more new immigrants in to fill entry-level, low-paying positions offered by employers looking for cheap, flexible labor.

Then there are the variety of politicians and political groups with their initiatives. Are they attempts to exploit the ignorance, fear, and cultural divisions or to soothe and settle them as we move into the twenty-first century? Your personal perspective will determine your answer.

Recognizing Cultural Diversity, Connections, and Change

Some might consider all of this intense competition, while others have written it off as complete and hopeless chaos. But, in the midst of all the change is a rich mix of cultures and organizations working within their communities to create more livable, workable environments throughout northern and southern California. They are people fighting ignorance, fear, and tribalism as they celebrate diversity and encourage communities to work together to solve problems. They are businesses who recognize such diversity as an opportunity for expansion as they build a vibrant economy. They are church, neighborhood, and community groups who recognize the importance of tolerance and understanding in such a diverse state. Here are just a few of their stories.

Businesses Build Bridges

They include business groups such as the California Association of Life Underwriters (CALU). *The National Underwriter* reported CALU's volunteer efforts in the early 1990s to increase ethnic membership and involvement in local and state life insurance underwriter associations. The idea is to find more minority insurance agents who could better serve the needs of California's increasing ethnic populations; the intended result is more business and better profits.

The healers also include responsible media. KBLA-AM became known as "Radio Korea" in L.A. during the 1990s. They included a radio talk program, "Listening to African-American Voices," to bridge communication gaps and neutralize friction between the African-American and Korean-American communities. Members of the traditionally more reserved Korean-American culture were reaching out to leaders in the more outgoing African-American culture. Similar attempts to bridge such gaps have been successful in other parts of California, especially in the Bay Area.

Individual Communities

Perhaps the greatest signal of change in California can be found in Orange County, once ridiculed by some as a bastion of intolerance with a stubborn monoculture. In 1945, the Westminster School District openly **segregated**

CARSON'S STORY

Another model of diversity—perhaps the state's greatest—may be found evolving south of L.A. Carson's tract housing boom hit during the 1960s. Today, you will find it sandwiched between other South Bay cities and surrounded by three major freeways. Its approximately 90,000 residents make it the eighth largest city in L.A. County. In the 1990s, that population was almost evenly divided between whites, Latinos, Asian/Pacific Islanders, and African Americans. Though the great migrations after World War II brought Samoans and other Pacific Islanders to Long Beach, Wilmington, Hawaiian Gardens, and other South Bay Navy towns, Carson ended up with more Samoans (about 2,500) by the 1990s than any place outside Samoa. It became famous as the heart of the Samoan community.

Carson's people celebrate their diversity within more than three-hundred community watch organizations and other neighborhood groups. The city continues to attract new businesses (including the new Metro Mall, one of the largest outlet malls in the L.A. area) in addition to the more than 3,000 businesses that already exist. The city motto is "Futures Unlimited."

On July 7, 1996, Carson dedicated its first mural, "Roots and Wings," to celebrate its mix of cultures. The mural was painted by Eliseo Silva, who emigrated from the Philippines seven years before. The mural is on the side of the Manila Business Center at 22030 South Main Street and contains images and symbols representing multiethnic Carson. The theme is about nurturing one plant with different roots, a theme that might apply just as well to the entire state.

---

students into either all-white or all-Mexican-American schools. This was the final blow that forced a class-action suit on behalf of 5,000 Orange County Latino children against the Westminster, Garden Grove, and Santa Ana School Districts. The courts ruled that separate schools violated rights of equal protection under the Constitution.

By the late 1990s, Westminster schools were considered models of integration. Its sixteen kindergarten through 8th-grade schools were about one-third Latino, one-third Asian and one-third white. The old, stereotypical visions of Orange County culture are fading.

Cultures Mix Within California Communities

After what has happened in Orange County, it is not surprising to find communities throughout California experiencing increased integration and diversification. Even once segregated San Diego County neighborhoods are being transformed, especially by spreading Latino, Asian-American, and Pacific-Islander cultures. The effects are noticed as far as the northwest coast timber towns, where large timber companies have been criticized for encouraging Latino immigrants to compete with locals for dwindling jobs and lower wages. Central Valley neighborhoods are now witnessing the changes, especially as a growing Latino middle class takes its place in sprawling housing projects.

Perhaps the best and most traditional examples of mixing neighborhoods and cultures are found with the people who have been crunched together on the tip of San Francisco's Peninsula. A brief walk in this compressed city can take you through dissimilar neighborhoods and cultures squeezed side by side. Even the cultures that fled into **segregated** Bay Area suburbs are now being mixed and integrated. In contrast, especially in some rural, higher-income, and gated neighborhoods in suburban California, this mixing is often less evident.

Emerging from these social upheavals are diverse community and neighborhood organizations that are learning how to work together in crime prevention, neighborhood watch, and other programs that encourage everyone to get involved to improve the quality of life. Standouts include the neighbors on 36th Street west of Vermont in South-Central L.A.. They joined together in a Kid Watch program in the 1990s. By working together, they hoped to rid the area of gangs and violence and protect children on their way to school.

In the Fairfax District across town, a different kind of evolution was taking place in the 1990s. Fairfax Avenue between Melrose and Beverly Boulevard once gained a reputation as the center for Jewish culture even for Orthodox Jews in L.A. Today, the traditional Yiddish language, the Jewish delicatessens, kosher meat, bread and book shops are increasingly sharing their neighborhood with modern cultures and businesses.

A younger crowd (led by modern YUPPIES) is flowing down from the crowded Sunset Strip. They are bringing cafes, science fiction bookstores, and a hip night life that includes cutting-edge music. Local publications were recognizing this as yet another trend that has transformed an eclectic neighborhood.

Human landscapes in communities throughout the state bear evidence of struggles with acculturation and cooperation *between* groups on the one hand and solidarity and cooperation *within* immigrant and ethnic groups on the other. Researchers (such as in a 1994 article in the *International Migration Review*) have repeatedly shown that social and economic cooperation *within* ethnic and other affinity groups leads to growth of ethnic **enclaves**. As they pool resources to build communities and influence politics, these groups also overcome discrimination and employ newcomers. Each of these affinity groups and ethnic communities builds distinct human landscapes that relate to and affect the larger society and economy of California in different ways.

A more recent report in the *Social Science Research* quarterly revealed a Los Angeles caught between the effects of past prejudice and stereotypes and a mature city that can wholeheartedly celebrate its ethnically diverse neighborhoods. In a survey of more than 4,000 L.A. County residents, it was discovered that prejudice, especially against African Americans, was still a major cause of housing segregation. Latinos and Asians expressed the greatest preferences for living in communities where their own groups were the majority, especially when they were foreign born.

This comfort with **segregation** within ethnic **enclaves** is often a consequence of housing costs, language, religion, shopping, and other cultural preferences and lack of knowledge about others. Tolerance levels fell noticeably when whites, Asians and Latinos were asked about living in majority black neighborhoods.

The general results of the survey, however, confirmed a much wider trend that has been observed throughout most of California for several decades—today's Angelenos are more at ease with ethnically diverse neighborhoods than they have ever been, especially compared to previous generations. (Cultural groups crunched together in San Francisco and other Bay Area cities are likely to be far ahead of southern Californians when it comes to tolerating differences.)

Generally, more Californians are apparently, if only gradually, becoming comfortable with the idea of living in mixed neighborhoods. These evolving attitudes and trends should continue to transform and mix California's cultures, communities, and human landscapes into the twenty-first century.

◆ TRADITIONS, POPULAR CULTURES, AND THE FUTURE MOSAIC

Now that we have reviewed individual ethnic groups, cultures, and lifestyles, it is important to see how they all fit into the California mosaic. In this section, we will explore this mix of California cultures—past, present, and future—from a different and far more subjective perspective. This could be considered the "culture lite" version, except it exposes some of the cultures (both real and imagined) that combine to make the images and myths that are California. After all, Californians who still believe that image is everything continue to help shape not only the state's cultures, but its diverse, changing landscapes.

California is certainly not lacking in **folk cultures**. (They are the remaining traditions left by more homogeneous, isolated, static social groups.) During the Native American, Spanish, Mexican, and early statehood periods, unique and isolated cultures developed and thrived within the state. Later, during the 1900s—especially after modern communication, transportation, and Hollywood's role became so influential—older California traditions were often swept aside in the name of progress.

Innovations that sprouted in California during and after the mid-1900s were immediately scrutinized by a curious world. These once novel cultures and lifestyles continue to be adopted and emulated by those fascinated with the California experiment. Many of California's material and nonmaterial innovations and cultures are now quickly mass produced for and by the mass media to become a part of **popular culture** (produced by urbanized, heterogeneous, nontraditional societies).

In some isolated pockets of California, people may still cling to their folk cultures. In a few smaller timber, mining, ranching, and farming communities (especially in northern California and in counties hugging the border with Nevada), you will find those who still identify with traditional customs and lifestyles more typical of rural parts of Oregon, Idaho, Nevada, Wyoming, or Mexico. These are exceptional people in modern California; they and their landscapes with their unique personalities are gradually disappearing. These folks are quick to express fears of losing traditional values, and they distrust the sweeping popular cultures that threaten to dominate. This is especially the rule in communities that now find themselves ever closer to California's urban centers (such as in Gold Rush country) or linked to them by major transportation corridors (such as along I-5 through northern California).

There are myriad examples where popular cultures' generic landscapes have been allowed to overshadow or even trample the unique folk cultures and landscapes that gave some California communities unique personalities. In each place, the battle between those who attempt to preserve their uniqueness and those who would sweep it away in the name of modernization and/or quick profit is being fought over and over again. California residents repeatedly act out this same drama with a nearly identical script, only in different settings and communities.

The results are that cutting-edge urban populations celebrating their popular culture make up the vast majority of today's Californians. Examples since the mid-1900s include cultures and lifestyles associated with the beach, captivated with the automobile, and obsessed with staying young, fit, and healthy in a stressful, high-tech urban environment. These images may be California stereotypes—sometimes more imagined than real—but they have already been flung around the world from California like so many frisbees. Such popular lifestyles and technologies have now settled in some very unlikely places on our planet.

Many more recent communications, computer, and multimedia technologies have also originated in such places as California's Silicon Valley or in the Los Angeles area. California's recent cultural changes are even more astounding; there is no place on earth where such a variety of people from so many different ethnic groups and lifestyles have been thrown together. This great experiment is being scrutinized by other nations and communities recently impacted by the new global marketplace with its modern transportation and communications technologies that build bridges between once isolated cultures.

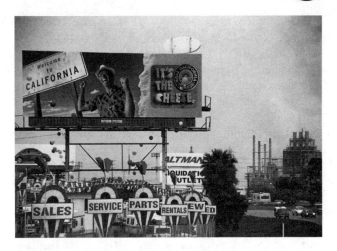

What do car dealerships, traffic jams, and refineries along the San Diego Freeway in L.A.'s South Bay have in common with the California Dream?

◆ A MODERN CULTURE HEARTH

Consequently, as we leap into the twenty-first century, California, especially within its ever-evolving urban environments, defines the modern **culture hearth**. It is a center where advanced culture traits, innovations, technologies and their landscapes develop and are then diffused around the world. The world sometimes looks on in disbelief and sometimes follows, but it is constantly anticipating the results of this great experiment in diversity and rapid change we call California.

And what is becoming of all those ethnic groups who converge on California with their myriad cultures? Once within the state, many individuals stubbornly resist the powerful forces pushing these modern technologies and popular cultures into their lives. Others have clung to as many traditional homeland values as possible while also experimenting with the new California cultures and lifestyles with which they are most comfortable. Still others have flung their traditions aside and completely immersed themselves in the new trends, technologies, and lifestyles that represent California's modern **popular cultures**.

Additional biological mixing of races and ethnic groups and acculturation within the state have made defining and categorizing various groups and individuals and their ancestries even more difficult and sometimes unrealistic. The result is that individuals within these various ethnic groups, cultures, and lifestyles have fascinating and often unique personal experiences; they combine to make up portions of this complex population of over 34 million people comingling in California. Each individual has become connected in his or her own way to the land and people of California.

◆ STEREOTYPES: EXAGGERATING CALIFORNIA CULTURES

The popularization of California cultures, both real and imagined, became big business with global implications many years ago. The problem is that people's percep-

tions of California cultures and lifestyles are often contorted or exaggerated as these innovations diffuse into different societies. What do people from other places think about Californians?

One typical answer to that question was revealed when a UC Riverside doctoral student polled more than three-hundred people who live in Oregon about their "Caliphobia." Many described Californians as superficial, impersonal, competitive, and calculating. When asked about Californians who migrate to Oregon, 68 percent said Californians cause negative change in their towns and 53 percent believed Californians would ruin their environment. The same group had much more positive perceptions about people from the state of Washington.

If these stereotypical perceptions are so pervasive, why do so many outside of the state attempt to embrace California? When *The Wall Street Journal* introduced a new section devoted to California in the 1990s and called it "California Journal," it was a response to the 280,000 (nearly 16 percent of the 1.8 million total) copies of this national and global publication that were being sold in California. Because an established political publication out of Sacramento was already using the same *California Journal* name, *The Wall Street Journal* was forced to change the name of its special section to "California." This was just one example in 1996 of how publications around the world were competing for a slice of the California pie.

California Culture Invades the World

This clamoring to keep up with California trends and cultures is evident in many other countries. Toward the end of the 1900s, Japan's fashion industry was struggling to satisfy Japanese youths' craving for California lifestyles, often exhibited by loose clothes and California-style caps. Thousands of Japanese young people had adopted surfing and skateboarding, while the number of snowboarders soared over 800,000. Where Japanese natural settings were not close enough in distance or likeness to California's, artificial resorts were built around Tokyo. They included a giant water park with waves for surfing and a giant indoor ski dome where skiers and snowboarders celebrated these sports so closely associated with California.

Perhaps a more bizarre example is how inner-city L.A.'s top export to Japan in the 1990s became customized lowrider cars. Lowrider styles began in the 1950s mostly among young Latinos in Southern California. Decades later, their classic cars gained international status as 1960s Chevy Impala convertibles sold in East L.A. for more than $10,000; they were then repaired, decorated, and sold in Japan for more than $30,000. By the late 1990s, Japanese dealers could be seen cruising throughout tough East and South L.A. and other Southern California neighborhoods looking for additions to the more than 3,000 lowrider cars in Japan.

From those who deal with House of Lowriders in Buena Park and members of lowrider clubs such as Lifestyles, there is concern that their decorated Chevys and lowrider lifestyles could be exhausted as the demand in cities like Yokohama increases. There is now even a Japanese-language version of the culture's most popular magazine, *Lowrider* (published in Pomona). Japanese lowrider shows were first organized in the early 1990s. This is just one more example of how some Japanese youth try to emulate California lifestyles. Rap music, "gangsta" videos, hats labelled "East L.A.," "Inglewood," and "Compton," and other California clothing and styles were increasingly popular in Japan well into the 1990s.

Countless examples of other popular California cultures and lifestyles are seen invading cities all the way to the East Coast and nations from Europe to Asia. There were at least twenty-five different Hong Kong companies using the state's name by the late 1990s. They included popular clothing stores, nightclubs, schools, and even the California Fitness Center. Whether these symbols of California culture are ridiculed or embraced, they are often exaggerated, if not completely transformed, to suit the imaginations and needs of the enthusiasts—or victims.

Music

There are literally dozens of songs about California that became nationally and globally popular and even top-selling hits during the 1900s. Add the songs about specific California places, especially within the San Francisco and Los Angeles areas, and you have more evidence of real and fabricated California cultures and lifestyles receiving global attention. Chances are, the power of suggestion has one of those songs floating through your head as you read this. It might be a classic such as "I Left My Heart in San Francisco," "California Dreaming," or a more recent best seller. It is *not* an exaggeration to say that the focus of popular music finally shifted from New York to the fresh sounds coming out of California during the 1960s.

Within a stew of creativity, emerging rock bands tested their sounds in San Francisco's old Victorian ballrooms. Janis Joplin, the Grateful Dead, and Jefferson Airplane were once neighbors in a Haight-Ashbury that was the center of this new music and culture. Record company executives were seen on the streets cutting deals with budding rock musicians. Northern California acts such as Creedence Clearwater Revival and Sly and the Family Stone also emerged, as the north made connections with Southern California's rhythm and blues artists.

The Southern California sound extended far beyond the popular Eagles, Doors, Jackson Browne, and Linda Ronstadt. Some groups (such as the Beach Boys) exploited the California Dream, or myth, to the limit in their music. By the 1970s, more than six of the world's major record companies were based in Southern California. The unique, diverse, and eventually popular music flowing from California has since gained recognition and countless awards from publications, critics, and the music industry.

Cars and New Technologies

California's love affair with the automobile and new technologies is one of the most visible elements of our culture. Stereotypical images of neighbors driving their cars to visit just two doors down and people who treat their cars and freeways as living companions during their hours on the road each day have been embraced by Hollywood. Comedian Steve Martin's movie *L.A. Story* was a classic parody of these lifestyles.

Such stereotypes are sometimes supported by facts, including the remarkable demand for new telephone numbers in California, partially due to the thousands of new cell phones that are ordered by commuters. Already with more area codes than any other state in the late 1990s, California requires more than twenty-six area codes to handle new demand to start the twenty-first century. This seems to be the perfect combination for Californians—high technology in their expensive cars. Even a study released in 1997, showing that drivers who are using their car phones are as likely to cause accidents as drunk drivers, hasn't stopped them. By the early 1990s, average rush-hour speeds were down to 34 mph and falling in L.A., but the commuters drove on as California had more automobiles than registered drivers.

The Valley

Valley culture was promoted as another popular California experience during the 1980s, and the image stuck through the 1990s. This San Fernando Valley lifestyle was modeled time and again by seemingly cloned white, middle-class teenage girls who hung out at San Fernando Valley malls. Its images and sounds were exposed in Hollywood movies and popular music; it was quickly dispersed and mimicked in suburban neighborhoods across the nation. Again, there are practical geographic reasons that this behavior became so scrutinized and popular. The San Fernando Valley was a growing, mostly white, middle-class suburb of Los Angeles since the mid-1900s, and it was close to, and then a part of, the Hollywood entertainment industry.

By the late 1990s, this image was no more than an exaggerated myth. Particularly in the east San Fernando Valley, populations and cultures had become just as diverse as the rest of L.A. Only vestiges of the valley stereotypes endured and spread west and north of the valley. Some of those valley boosters who have led the succession movement to break away from L.A. gradually realized that they were more like L.A. than they ever dreamed possible.

Obsessed with Health and Trendy Foods?

Californians are also often portrayed as being obsessed with eating expensive, exotic and/or healthy foods and with staying physically fit. In a state with climates and natural settings that lure people to stay outdoors and remain physically active most of the year, there is some truth to this myth. Some of the best displays of these lifestyles are along the Boardwalk from Venice to Santa Monica and at the Marina in San Francisco during most afternoons, especially during weekends. You will find further evidence in countercultures thriving from northwestern California to Berkeley and in higher-income YUPPIE cultures from Santa Barbara to the San Diego coast.

Like the Bay to Breakers run in San Francisco, the annual L.A. Marathon is especially important to Southern Californians, where fitness is king. The twelfth annual L.A. Marathon in 1997 was planned to not only feature some of the world's best runners and cyclists, but in-line skaters were invited to join for the first time. Some Californians may be accustomed to these padded and helmeted risk-takers maneuvering down streets and sidewalks. The perceived obsession with fitness is fortified by these images in a state where some fitness clubs are open 24 hours each day of the year. California, with all its people and diversity, still ranks in the top five for the number of health clubs per capita.

Many of California's trendy restaurants and markets (especially those promoting exotic, popular, or healthy diets in an entertaining atmosphere) have become world famous. Trader Joe's is one of the more trendy food markets that has flourished in California and is now spreading its wings across the country. The grocery chain was started and owned by former students at Stanford Uni-

versity and is based in South Pasadena. With its specialty and health foods that include trendy snacks such as exotic trail mixes, and its frozen entrees at discount prices, it is considered a fashion statement food store. It represents the quintessential California YUPPIE food chain.

By 1997, Trader Joe's had grown to ninety-one stores and approached sales of $1 billion per year. As it opened fifteen new stores on the East Coast, the company targeted the same kind of neighborhoods that made it successful in California—health-conscious, upscale communities with highly educated populations. Employees' trademark Hawaiian shirts and California managers with California attitudes were being welcomed in places like Cambridge, Massachusetts and Scarsdale, New York. By the late 1990s, first sales figures from the east indicated that Trader Joe's needed to work on its image. We will see if the new stores experience the wild success of their California parents. Numerous other California health food chains are also testing the winds for expansion.

Californians and Their Pets

This discussion of real and imagined California cultures could not be completed in several volumes, so we will end with the myths about Californians' relationships with their pets. Even rural Californians are amused by the stories of how their urban counterparts care for their dogs and cats. Urban California has pet cemeteries where burial costs for your dog or cat can approach the average costs of burying humans, depending on how extravagant you want to get. Before their pets die, many urban Californians spend as much as in any other society to keep them healthy and out of trouble.

Densely populated cities such as San Francisco impose pooper-scooper laws with stiff fines to force reckless owners to clean up after their pets in public places. (Fines ranged from $25 in some cities to $1,000 in Beverly Hills toward the end of the century.) In efforts to clean their streets and Santa Monica Bay, there were pooper-scooper sting operations in Marina del Rey neighborhoods, while Hermosa Beach was the only city in the South Bay to allow dogs in parks. Dog owners in Venice reacted in 1997 with a march and demonstration to encourage officials to open part of the beach to their canine companions.

The struggle for control of Dog Beach at the mouth of the San Diego River is just another example of what happens when too many people with so many diverse interests clash. Dog Beach was one of the last places dog owners could take their pets and allow them to run freely, as dogs love to do. However, it was not a place where you would want to walk, run, or swim unless you enjoy feces-contaminated sand and surf. Proponents of dog control laws are hoping to make our urban environments less smelly and our walking paths a little safer and cleaner. Dog lovers are concerned that crowding urban landscapes and demand for land are putting the squeeze on their pet cultures.

Today, California has high-tech 24-hour pet hospitals with top medical and surgical specialists who can do brain and back surgery, hip replacements, DNA testing, root canals, and orthodontia. You can even get Prozac for your depressed dog. Veterinarians dedicated to offering the same care for animals that is available to humans are armed with millions of dollars of modern high-tech medical equipment.

Like countless other stereotyped California fashions and trends, this care is only available to the wealthiest Californians who are willing to pay top dollar. Most of the state's residents cannot, or will not, participate and can hardly afford the same care for their families. Still, it is another example of a popular trend that may seem foreign and even ridiculous to rural Californians and people from other states and nations. It also stretches to the limit the range of images outsiders may have of the real or imagined Californian.

From Myth to Reality

Whether these images include hippies in San Francisco's Haight or the beatniks before them, religious cults or experimental lifestyles, inner-city gangs or racial tensions, they have all played at least small roles in California's cultures. Rural Californians and those who live in the state's more sterile suburban landscapes may be as removed from these images as people from out of state, but they are constantly reminded of them by the sensationalist media.

Meanwhile, many Californians are tracing the roots of their individual cultures and landscapes. As more residents across the state uncover the past, they are working to preserve some of these landscapes that more realistically represent California and its cultures.

◆ PRESERVING PAST CULTURES AND LANDSCAPES

Preserving Hispanic History

The Spanish and Mexican Periods brought relatively sudden and dramatic change to many of California's native cultures and landscapes. Once the Spanish began settling California by 1769, they brought their religion, language, technologies, architecture, and many other elements of their culture that thrive in California to this day. When the American settlers took control in the mid-1800s, they first tried to sweep the state's Hispanic legacy aside, much like the Spanish before them attempted to destroy Native-American traditions.

By the early 1900s, Hispanic culture was being romanticized and a dramatic renaissance was under way.

Spanish history and architecture have been preserved at the restored Santa Ynez Mission.

(Much of the credit goes to popular publications such as *Ramona*, written by Helen Hunt Jackson in 1884.) Increasingly during the 1900s, communities openly encouraged the use of Spanish names for geographic landmarks and embraced Spanish-style architecture as they celebrated their Hispanic heritage. Many of the crumbling missions were remodeled or rebuilt. Great immigrations from Latin America since the mid-1900s and proximity to Mexico are continually fusing California with its Latino cultures. These cultures caught the spotlight in a much more extensive previous section.

During the late 1900s, missions throughout the state were celebrating their 200th anniversaries while their surrounding communities often organized and led the ceremonies. Organized festivals and other activities celebrating Latino cultures are common from the Bay Area and Central Valley south. Today's ubiquitous Spanish architecture, names, language, and Hispanic cultures play important, and sometimes dominating, roles in almost every California landscape.

Rural and Traditional Cultures

California's **traditional rural cultures** are still celebrated and are even being revived in areas where they are threatened. Thanks to community efforts like those of the Surprise Valley Rotary Club, historical buildings from the area were reassembled at the Modoc District Fairgrounds. The collection of buildings is called Louieville, and it gives the visitor a sense of life in old northeastern California. Just next door, a world-class rodeo returns to town each year, all of this within the little community of Cedarville.

There are plenty of other old Wild West or mining towns that have been reconstructed or preserved in California. The settlements of Laws north of Bishop and Bodie east of Bridgeport are just two examples. Local

CALAVERAS COUNTY PRIDE

Residents have displayed pride in their rural heritage and landscapes in many ways. Calaveras County had only one superior court judge in the 1990s. In 1985, when police found nineteen murder victims buried near a cabin just a few miles from the little Mother Lode town of Wilseyville, at least two local concerns became obvious. First, the county did not have the financial or human resources to prosecute the killers, so they received assistance from the state. (Due to lack of local facilities, the suspect had to be bused fifty miles from Folsom Prison to the court in San Andreas.) Second, residents of this little town wanted to distance themselves from the sensational tabloid stories that left outsiders with bizarre impressions of their otherwise quiet, isolated community. This is not how rural communities want to get on the map. There are plenty of rural residents who are there because they want to be left alone and off the map!

groups and public agencies have dedicated tremendous amounts of volunteer time and effort to preserve these links to California's past.

Festivals and other activities in the renovated gold rush town of Columbia make it a center of attention in California's Mother Lode. You can still pan for gold, tour displays of old fire trucks, and even participate in the bailing competitions (if you don't mind getting soaked). Nearby Jamestown and Sonora are other examples of communities throughout the Mother Lode that have revitalized and exploited their wild west, Gold Rush heritage.

In Trinity County west of Redding, Weaverville is another Gold Rush town, but it continued to thrive as a timber industry town during the 1900s. When industry retooling and upheavals threatened in the late 1900s, it was kept alive by history buffs and recreational activities such as hiking, fishing, and river tourism. The town was still proud that it had no street lights into the late 1990s.

Central Valley cultures centered around farming versus encroaching developing economies and lifestyles have also received increasing attention since the 1800s.

Logging and other rural traditions mix and sometimes conflict with modern, more urban activities and landscapes in northern California towns like Willits.

Literary works by Steinbeck, Joan Didion, William Saroyan, William Everson, and Philip Levine have featured rural life and landscapes in the valley. Stan Yogi's *Highway 99, A Literary Journey Though California's Great Central Valley* was added to the list in the 1990s.

Preserving Urban Traditions

Larger cities around the state are also rediscovering their roots. In addition to exposing a wealth of history about past triumphs and failures, urban soul searching has paid off economically. Old Towns in San Diego, Pasadena, and Sacramento are just a few examples. Efforts to revitalize historical districts and to preserve historical architecture and cultures are unfolding in urban landscapes across the state.

One example includes efforts by neighborhood groups to preserve old downtown theaters and neighborhood movie palaces that have lost customers to today's modern multiplexes and malls. Proponents of preservation note the local cultures that often form around independent art cinemas and how these independent theaters offer unique opportunities for downtown districts.

There are several examples within California cities. One standout is the heralded Castro in San Francisco. Joining the list are Los Angeles' classic Wiltern Theatre, the Art Deco Alex Theatre in Glendale, and now the Warner Grand Theater in San Pedro.

Recently, the Bijou Cinemas that served Hermosa Beach since the 1930s, but closed late in 1996, were targeted for renovation by neighbors. The original Art Deco columns and archways of the Bijou are a part of the only art cinema remaining in the L.A. area's South Bay, and it is the oldest building in downtown Hermosa Beach.

Neighbors worry about the few historical buildings remaining anywhere in the South Bay after most were demolished to take advantage of higher property values. They note the agony experienced by preservationists and historians in nearby Redondo Beach as they helplessly witnessed the destruction of nearly their entire downtown district, including classic Craftsman-style structures.

A TRIBUTE TO HERB CAEN

Herb Caen often wrote of our bridges to the past, the diverse cultures that have combined to build California, and the radical upheavals that continue to change our society and landscapes. He was San Francisco's, and probably California's, most acclaimed columnist ever. His popular newspaper column exposed and dramatized the people, cultures, and lifestyles of San Francisco and the Bay Area for more than fifty years until he died of cancer in 1997. His columns featured so many of the ethnic groups who have settled in The City since the Gold Rush, including the Chinese, Irish, Italians, Latinos, African Americans, and Jews. He conveyed his love for The City with his magical, mystical, and poetic images, and he often (to the delight of San Franciscans) showed his contempt for what non-San Franciscans had done to California.

Columnist Al Martinez wrote in the *Los Angeles Times* that Caen once stated how Oakland was the only city that could make a square out of Jack London (referring to Jack London Square, of course). Caen also wrote that you should take a box lunch if you go to L.A. because there are no decent restaurants south of Santa Barbara. Herb Caen and his San Francisco were inseparable, just as we Californians cannot be separated from our rich heritage.

These trends became so controversial that even Redondo Beach was using its new preservation program in the 1990s to save its few remaining historical buildings.

Linking Past, Present, and Future Cultures

Links between the state's urban cultures and human landscapes, and its past, present, and future were most evident as San Francisco remodeled its New Main Library in the 1990s. This project was an important part of The City's restoration and renaissance of its Civic Center. When it opened in 1996, the New Main received national acclaim for its modern architecture and technologies.

Study sections focused on ethnic and other affinity groups, from Asians, Latinos, and African Americans to gays and lesbians. Patrons flocked to computers linked to the Internet in rooms plastered with names of corporate donors. Tour buses stopped for a look at the library of the future. As visitors increased by 300 percent in the entire San Francisco library system, more than one-hundred new library cards were issued each day in 1996.

In spite of this positive response, and in San Francisco tradition, other residents expressed concern and even fear that an entire traditional library culture framed by quiet, accessible stacks of dependable books and other publications was being destroyed. They protested what they called a cultural center with a mall atmosphere that had replaced the traditional research library. Especially when it comes to libraries, they said, we should always have room for the old and the new. However, the unfortunate state of our urban economies and the lack of civic responsibility that grew into the 1990s has required some painful belt-tightening. Too often these decisions involve compromising our past cultures, architecture, and human landscapes far beyond the downtown theater or library.

Of course, San Francisco simply led the high-tech library trend and controversy that eventually swept across the state.

When McDonald's announced it would abandon one of its first drive-ins, after closing it in 1994, community and historical groups in Southern California waged emotional protests. It is located at Lakewood Boulevard and Florence Avenue in Downey. Historical preservationists argued that this first McDonald's, opened in 1953—with its original architecture, Speedee the Chef logo and milkshake makers—symbolized so much California culture that it should never be destroyed. The National Trust for Historic Preservation declared it "an authentic icon of contemporary American life" and one of the country's eleven most endangered landmarks.

McDonald's responded by using its resources to rebuild and upgrade the building. The previous look, including the 60-foot high neon Speedee the Chef sign and the original architecture with arches, slanting glass, and colors to fit Southern California's sunny environment, was restored. An adjacent museum and gift shop were also planned. One article in the *Los Angeles Times* noted that architectural historians labelled the structure as modern, high-tech/high-energy, bold, exuberant, and optimistic—all that represented Southern California during the 1950s. It reopened to an enthusiastic crowd in December, 1996.

An even greater cultural and preservation controversy erupted in the 1990s. The Catholic Church announced it would destroy the decaying St. Vibiana's Cathedral in downtown Los Angeles, after it was damaged by the Northridge earthquake. The L.A. Conservancy fought for years to save the structure. Meanwhile, the city and the church quickly agreed on a more lofty site for the new, modern cathedral that would be completed around the turn of the century.

Down by the Beach

Coastal amusement parks have also played key roles in the state's history and culture. From San Francisco to Santa Cruz and Santa Monica south, boardwalks and

LONG BEACH AND THE PIKE

One of the coast's greatest losses was the famed Pike Amusement Park, which opened in 1902, along Ocean Avenue in Long Beach. Through the 1940s and Long Beach's golden years, it was the largest amusement park west of the Mississippi. Its Majestic Dance Hall and various rides (which included the mile-long Cyclone Racer, the world's largest roller coaster which eventually achieved speeds of 80 mph) attracted more than 50,000 people on some weekend days.

However, The Pike couldn't keep up with some of the state's growing attractions, such as Disneyland. By the 1970s, The Pike was also fading in the sun of this Navy town; it finally closed in 1979. Decay of The Pike was just a symbol of the beginning of some hard times for that section of Long Beach that was once a prime cultural attraction in California. By the late 1990s, Long Beach was working hard to restore its image as it expanded its port, built one of the world's greatest marine aquariums, and redeveloped its waterfront and downtown. After suffering such pain in the recession of the early 1990s, Long Beach was one of the latest California cities to turn its back on the past and on preservation. Nevertheless, the beckoning coastal strip continues to be the modern center of attention there.

California beach cultures thrive on the Venice Boardwalk during another bright, sunny day.

piers have served as foundations for some of the most popular theme parks and memorable cultural attractions the state has ever known. Even in the 1990s, the old Santa Cruz Beach Boardwalk continued to serve escapees from the hot Central Valley and the crowded urban environments of the Bay Area. Venice Beach Boardwalk was the number two single tourist attraction (and one of the best locations to view avant-garde people and cultures) in the state during the 1990s. Nearby Santa Monica Pier had undergone a stunning renaissance, complete with the largest Ferris wheel on the coast (and probably the smallest roller coaster).

It is puzzling that, with so many cultures seemingly focused on the beach, there have been even more failures of California's coastal parks. They range from San Francisco to Santa Monica Bay and south. They include only memories, such as the once-famous Pacific Ocean Park, where screams of roller-coaster riders and music from popular dance clubs have long since disappeared. Nothing was preserved of the entire park and pier.

Some Californians cling to traditional beach cultures to the bitter end. This is true for the more than one-hundred residents on the beach at Crystal Cove State Park between Corona del Mar and Laguna Beach. Though they were only leasing state-owned property and cottages and were served four times with eviction notices from 1979 into the 1990s, they fought to stay. They cherished their lifestyles at the expense of taxpayers, while the state relished the opportunity to convert Crystal Cove into a more upscale tourist resort. This was seen as a unique opportunity along some of California's most beautiful, but increasingly crowded, coastline. Along that same coastline, developers and the city of Laguna Beach unveiled plans in 1998 to replace Treasure Island trailer park with a 275-room high-end resort, with adjacent estate homes and condominiums.

The age of inexpensive beach cottages and the cultures surrounding them in California has vanished, increasingly replaced by a coastline that only the wealthy can afford to buy, rent, or lease. Particularly from Santa

Barbara to San Diego, a wave of upscale hotel developments are being planned to rise along the shoreline into the twenty-first century. Most preservationists can only watch as the coast's historical landscapes are often the victims.

◆ MODERN AND FUTURE CALIFORNIA CULTURE

Perhaps within California's great urban landscapes are clues to the state's future cultures. USC's Southern California Studies Center in 1996 ranked the Los Angeles area second in the country (just behind New York) and San Francisco third in the number of cultural assets, including theater groups, classical and ethnic radio stations, and library holdings. But, when cultural assets per capita were ranked, San Francisco leads the nation and Southern California drops below the fifth spot.

Nurturing Culture

Those are impressive rankings. However, the study also emphasized the unfortunate chaos that is especially common within the support services and infrastructures of

Thousands were jammin' at this 1997 version of Reggae on the River. Billed as the largest Reggae gathering in North America, it filled the South Fork of the Eel River in redwood country with an unlikely mass of humanity.

the Los Angeles area. It found that cities, communities, and cultures were not yet communicating or cooperating in ways that would encourage cultural development. Many of the state's cultural assets and attractions have apparently evolved independently with little common consensus or concerted effort.

Culture in Los Angeles and Southern California

Modernist architect Richard Meier may have best summarized this problem after he won the American Institute of Architects' Gold Medal Award and designed the $1 billion Getty Center in L.A. that was completed in 1997. He complained about the lack of cohesion among L.A. architects and said that there is need for some camaraderie and interest in the work of others. He argued for a form of architectural permanence that might replace the transitory environment in Southern California. As an example, he applauded the selection of Rafael Moneo to design L.A.'s new cathedral, because he might better relate to L.A.'s Spanish-speaking population and culture.

Richard Meier added that culture is an enormously important aspect of a city and it should be displayed in architecture. His design of The Getty Center looking over L.A.'s West Side and Sepulveda Pass makes his point in flamboyant style. He sees it as an expression of the relationship of space to the landscape, as it deals with L.A. not as a city of the moment, but as a more permanent place. One thing is clear—the new J. Paul Getty Museum, research, and educational facilities are no longer cramped into a tight space as they were for so many years above Pacific Coast Highway. They will call out to Angelenos and visitors from around the world for decades.

Interestingly, Austrian chef Wolfgang Puck was registering similar complaints about a fragmented and dispersed Los Angeles during the 1990s. His fame grew to global proportions after he followed his successful Spago Restaurant on the Sunset Strip with several other restaurants. He argued that the wave of restaurant downsizing and boring chain restaurants that swept into L.A. during the 1990s further fragments cultures and diminishes the aesthetic and cultural experiences that are a part of dining. In contrast, numerous unique and exciting restaurants were appearing in San Francisco where people could walk and participate in the city experience.

For years, people have been working to build L.A. cultural attractions that will encourage residents to interact with their city. A critical mass of artists that have flourished since the 1950s have made L.A. one of the world's few major players in contemporary art. Though L.A. artists are still considered far ahead of its museums, the Los Angeles Contemporary Museum of Art (LACMA), Museum of Contemporary Art (MOCA), the J. Paul Getty, and other museums bring a "civilized cosmopolitan" atmosphere to the city that is now recognized in major publications.

Partially due to the California car culture, former suburbs of Los Angeles have become more independent and have established their own cultural assets. The Orange County Performing Arts Center in Costa Mesa was completed in the mid-1980s and had achieved great success by the mid-1990s. San Diego and other California cities were also stepping up to the cultural plate during the 1990s, establishing their own identities as they added to the state's cultural assets. Several are reviewed in Chapter 11, but it is no secret that San Francisco and its Bay Area have owned and earned the traditional crown for cultural assets per capita.

Culture in the San Francisco Bay Area

Since the Gold Rush, San Francisco has earned its reputation for absorbing and accepting asylum seekers and refugees. Since quickly becoming the financial and cultural center of The West in the 1800s, it has repeatedly defined the cosmopolitan, sophisticated city. Throughout the 1900s, it moved well beyond mixing ethnic groups to become a rich, evolving stew of cultures and alternative lifestyles. From its ethnic groups to its beatniks, hippies, counterculture, gays and lesbians, traditional and alternative religious groups, historical cultures, cutting-edge technologies, fast-paced lifestyles, and sophisticated professionals, The City has offered and continues to offer something for almost everyone.

Music is just one example. Successful sounds and musical groups blossomed out of the Bay Area since the mid-1900s as it competed with Los Angeles to define the California sound. During the fourteenth annual San Francisco Jazz Festival in October, 1996, San Francisco was gaining the title "Jazz City" because music is easily accessible in this compact city. There are many ranges of jazz styles, attitudes, and local clubs where uniqueness and individuality are encouraged. Today, jazz performers are featured in several locations throughout The City and Bay Area; they even include Asian-American jazz.

Food is another example. Alice Waters is considered the mother of the California Cuisine which has recently caught on as the New American Cuisine. Her Berkeley health-food restaurant, Chez Panisse, became famous in the 1970s. She has helped to make health foods in California stores (such as gourmet pizzas and salads) popular and has been a major proponent in the spread of farmer's markets around the state. She encourages the consumption of locally grown, organic, fresh food in season whenever possible. Her idea of the Edible Schoolyard (first tried at Martin Luther King Jr. Middle School in Berkeley), where students grow some of their cafeteria food, has gained national recognition. Leave it up to a Californian like Alice Waters; she gets back to basic common sense while observers describe her approach as unique and revolutionary.

During the 1990s, yet another more elitist version of northern California culture was celebrated. Cruise ship companies began sailing into the Napa Wine Country for spa, hot balloon, and wine tours and to Old Sacramento from Pier 40 in San Francisco. Most of the ships were small and offered a relaxed experience, up to three nights and four days around the Bay and along the Napa and Sacramento Rivers. Tickets ranged to more than $1,000 per person for better cabins. Some apparently considered it a small price to pay for a piece of the California Dream in a weekend.

Celebrating Culture Throughout California

In the midst of all the previously mentioned problems festering and creating confusion within California cultures, there are also these diverse atmospheres that nurture developing culture and encourage its evolution. From the annual celebrations in San Diego's Gas Lamp Quarters to the Logging Jamboree in Calaveras County, from the jazz and other music and art festivals that tour the state to Grass Valley's Nevada County Fair, you don't have to look far to find Californians celebrating their cultures.

Want to attend just about any professional sports event? If it's in season, you will probably find it in California. Want to try the latest form of ostrich meat or use virtual models to design your own home? There seem to be many more choices of just about everything in California. Perhaps that is why there are so many extremes, countless Californians willing to dangle on the edge and experiment with the unknown.

◆ A FINAL VIEW OF CALIFORNIA'S FUTURE CULTURES

Dan Walters has been a journalist for California newspapers since the 1970s. His daily column on California politics and public policy was appearing in nearly fifty California newspapers going into the late 1990s. From his *Sacramento Bee* office, he writes and speaks about, among other things, the radical changes taking place in California cultures. He notes the increase in Latinos and Asians in California as the percentage of white and black Californians decreases. He also shows concern about the further polarization of our society.

Walters argued that change was evident within the new California by the 1990s, but the state's politics were locked in the past. Too many conflicting social, economic, and political issues kept important decisions from being made. With all these controversies, it was still a state where in a city like Huntington Park (population more than 60,000), so few people voted that 1,000 votes could get you elected mayor. It was still a state where perceived differences between north and south drove campaigns to break California into two or three separate states, where differences within L.A. threatened to break that city in half. Can we transfer social consensus into political policy consensus when there are such gaps? Can there ever be consensus in a society so complex? Is California becoming a tribal society of gridlock that is making *no* decisions while allowing problems to fester?

These difficult questions drive right to the heart of this great cultural experiment in modern California. In the midst of dramatic cultural and economic revolutions rocking the state at the end of the 1900s, was California losing its sense of identity? There seemed to be too few statewide media or other organized attempts to galvanize the remarkably diverse cultures and special interests that would all benefit from compromise and concerted efforts to plot a common course for our state. The ripple effects travel far beyond California. An anxious world looks on to see how California deals with these issues and problems before more powerful cultural and economic ties are made with the state. Many of these nations also use California as a gauge to measure how they will cope with the inevitably increasing diversity and rapid change in their own societies.

There is plenty of hope and common ground in California. The state's northern and southern connections are growing stronger. Some residents of rural northern California are beginning to realize that by breaking away from the most powerful state, they would create one of the poorest states in the nation, a sort of "Appalachia West." California's rural edges and border areas (from north to south) share many issues, including how to deal with poverty and obsolete economies. Urban regions such as the Bay, L.A. and San Diego areas are also recognizing their common ground; they too share similar issues and problems.

Fortunately, the remarkable differences within California and between Californians—the state's unequaled diversity—is more frequently valued as a strength, a common theme that can actually bind the state together. If the state can use this diversity to exploit its strategic position on the Pacific Rim, it will become not just a global model, but one of the most influential cultural hearths the world has ever known. Only exceptional natural disasters, the further recoiling and polarization of special interest groups, and archaic leadership that would toss California's future out for short-term gain can slow the state's progress toward such a glorious destiny.

SOME KEY TERMS AND TOPICS

culture	glass ceiling	religion
culture hearth	human landscapes	salad bowl
enclave	innovation	segregation
ethnic/culture group	language	traditional culture
ethnicity	melting pot	tribalism
folk cultures	popular culture	

Additional Key Terms and Topics

African Americans	gender	lifestyles
American Indians	ghetto	Pacific Islanders
Asians	hate crimes	preserving culture
beach culture	Hispanic heritage	race
competition between groups	human imprints	rural traditions
cultural history	inequity	stereotypes
elderly	integration	urban cultures
Europeans	Latinos	

Primary Industries and Rural Landscapes

INTRODUCING CALIFORNIA'S ECONOMIC ACTIVITIES AND HUMAN LANDSCAPES

Economic geography is the study of how people make their living and how their economic systems are spatially related and connected. Another definition includes the spatial variation of activities related to producing, exchanging, and consuming goods and services. Once again, you can see how our approach in geography is different from most other fields of study. It incorporates so much from a wide range of disciplines, but it has a location and space perspective. This is why an understanding of California's diverse rural and urban populations and landscapes requires knowledge of the economic geography within these regions.

Like most economic systems, California's is based on the production, exchange, and consumption of goods and services. These economic activities are divided into stages or categories of increasing complexity. **Primary activities** are associated with the harvesting or use of commodities from nature, usually in the outdoor environments of rural land-scapes. They include forestry, mining, fishing, hunting and gathering, grazing, and subsistence and commercial agriculture.

In California, hunting and gathering and subsistence farming gave way long ago to agribusiness, the undisputed king of the state's primary industries. Additionally, many other primary activities, such as the timber and mining industries, have lost much of their economic and political clout to the explosion of advanced and complex industries concentrated in the state's urban areas. The classification and examination of these secondary, tertiary, and more complex industries, along with the economic opportunities, people, and landscapes associated with them, are subjects of Chapter 10.

In this chapter, we consider the state's primary industries and the people, natural resources, rural landscapes, and trends associated with them. It is easy to see how the themes of this book weave a common thread throughout this section. California's primary industries and rural landscapes are extremely diverse, they are connected to other activities, trends, and landscapes in and beyond California in profound ways, and they are experiencing rapid changes that are transforming the state's people and landscapes.

KEY ISSUES AND CONCEPTS

◆ California's diverse economic systems can be categorized into primary, secondary, tertiary, and even more advanced industries. This chapter focuses on primary industries and the extensive rural landscapes where they are often found.

◆ Thanks to farmers' ability to exploit a host of factors, including site, situation, and market forces, California is, by far, the most diverse and productive agricultural state in the nation.

◆ Fruits, nuts, vegetables and melons, field crops, floriculture, livestock, and dairy products round out the general categories of farm products that make California an agricultural powerhouse. The state is the leading, or exclusive producer of, numerous specific agricultural products.

◆ Though farm lifestyles and rural landscapes stand in sharp contrast to those of the majority of urban Californians, they are increasingly impacted by modern trends and technologies and the global economy. Farmers must cope with modern issues and problems, such as encroaching developments, marginal profits, new technologies, natural disasters, and increasing resistance to their use of toxic chemicals.

◆ California is consistently ranked among the leading fish producing states. A variety of commercial and recreational fishing industries account for more than $200 million of the state's economy.

◆ The timber industry continues to play major economic (though diminishing) roles in towns within the state's forested lands, particularly in northern California. Though mining is still big business in the state, the relative importance of mining industries (reviewed in Chapter 2) continues to diminish compared to more advanced industries. Managing these natural resources has become more challenging and controversial as the demand for them and for multiple uses in our open spaces increases.

◆ Rural people and landscapes continue to evolve and adjust in the face of mounting pressures on their lands and resources from diverse interests. Though the state's spacious rural landscapes are extensive, exploding populations and expanding urban areas are increasingly encroaching upon and transforming them. There are scores of examples of these trends in nearly every corner of California.

◆ PRIMARY INDUSTRIES

The Demise of Hunting and Gathering and Subsistence Farming

Although recent studies indicate that people were developing agriculture as much as 10,000 years ago in Central America, there is little or no evidence that this activity spread into California's Native American cultures. The only exceptions were the native farmers who cultivated fields along the Colorado River. Most researchers agree that, except for these Colorado River farmers, occasional diversion of stream and river flow and the use of fire highlighted California Indians' attempts to enhance the resources provided by nature each year. Consequently, hunters and gatherers ruled throughout

The Farm Site

Limiting site factors, such as climate, soil, and slope, also place obvious restrictions on agricultural productivity. Technological breakthroughs have helped overcome some of these limitations. Water projects have had the greatest impact in California. Because about 80 percent of the water used in California goes to agriculture, it is no secret that many farmlands would not exist without the water projects. One need only view the dry land above and the lush, green farmland below the canals in the Imperial/Coachella and San Joaquin Valleys for proof. Fertilizers to improve poor and eroded soils and chemicals that inhibit diseases and pests have further improved short-term productivity.

Consumer Preferences

Finally, past agricultural practices and current agribusinesses in California are obviously controlled by which foods people choose to eat. The most important agricultural products reviewed in the following section have gained popularity due to cultural beliefs, traditions, and other customer preferences. More and more frequently, these are the preferences of the global market rather than only the California consumer. Profits are also controlled by modern trends, such as the growing demand for organic farm products. When California farmers sense declining interest in their products, they revive them with popular advertising campaigns.

Agriculture and the California Economy

Leading the nation for fifty years, the value of California farm and ranch products topped $24.5 billion per year by 1996. The **multiplier effect** was even more substantial—more than $70 billion per year in related economic activity was generated. As a result, nearly one of ten jobs in the state is at least indirectly related to agriculture. According to the California Department of Food and Agriculture (CDFA), eight of the top ten agricultural counties in the nation were in California (Fresno, Tulare, Monterey, Kern, San Joaquin, Merced, Riverside, and Stanislaus). Each of the state's top ten counties produced more than $1 billion of agricultural products each year. Nearly one-third of the state's landscapes were producing agricultural products.

California also led the nation in agricultural exports, which soared over $12 billion into the late 1990s, representing more than half of California farm products and nearly 20 percent of all U.S. agricultural exports. The state was sixth among the world's largest agricultural exporters. Pacific Rim countries accounted for more than half of the state's exports, Canada 18 percent, Europe 9 percent, and Mexico 5 percent. The top export countries

were Japan (consuming more than 25 percent of the state's agricultural exports), Canada, European nations, Korea, Hong Kong, Mexico, Taiwan, Singapore, Indonesia, and China. Beef and cotton were the top export commodities. Grape products, almonds, fish, and oranges were also high on the list.

A world population soaring past 6 billion is seen as an even more promising future market than California's own growing consumer population. An estimated 27,000 jobs were created for every $1 billion in agricultural exports. This has encouraged delegations of state political and agribusiness leaders to visit especially Pacific Rim countries to promote California agricultural products. It is no wonder that California's annual agricultural production continued to grow into the twenty-first century.

A Wide Variety of Products

Diversity and balance best describes the incredible variety of agricultural products produced in California. Each of the following three general categories of farm products represented more than 24 percent (over $5.5 billion per year each) of the total farm marketings in the state into the late 1990s: vegetable crops, fruits and nuts, and livestock and poultry sales. California continued as the leading dairy state, and it produced 55 percent of the nation's fruits, nuts, and vegetables. Additionally, field crop sales totalled about $3.5 billion, while nursery and greenhouse products increased to more than $2.2 billion per year cash receipts.

Specifically, California produces more than 250 agricultural products and leads the nation in more than 75 crop and livestock commodities. According to the CDFA, the following U.S. crops are grown only (at least 99 percent) in California: almonds, artichokes, dates, figs, kiwifruit, olives, persimmons, pistachios, prunes, raisins, and walnuts.

Going into the late 1990s, the top twenty farm products in California, with export rankings and annual values, are listed at the top of page 316.

Rounding out the top twenty export list of commodities that did *not* make the state's top twenty products list are prunes (8th in exports), lemons (10th), cherries (13th), onions (16th), grapefruit (17th), and wheat (18th). (Fish and seafood products, when included with these commodities, ranked as the number 5 export.) The fastest growing exports in percentage were poultry/eggs, pistachios, fish/seafood, dairy, and lemons. Though there was some fluctuation in the rankings of products by the end of the century, nearly all had increased in value.

Where in California are these products grown? The bottom chart on page 316 is a list of the most important commodities produced by each of the state's top ten agricultural counties in 1995 with their annual values.

Rank	Farm Product	Value ($) (millions)	% Total	Export Rank
1	Milk and cream	3,078	13.7	6
2	Grapes	1,839	8.2	3
3	Nursery products	1,500	6.7	
4	Cattle and calves	1,290	5.7	1
5	Cotton lint	1,064	4.7	2
6	Lettuce, head	987	4.4	7 (lettuce)
7	Almonds	858	3.8	4
8	Hay	847	3.8	15
9	Tomatoes, processing	672	3.0	14
10	Flowers and foliage	672	3.0	
11	Strawberries	552	2.5	11
12	Oranges	458	2.0	5
13	Chickens	384	1.7	12 (poultry)
14	Rice	318	1.4	
15	Broccoli	318	1.4	19
16	Walnuts	314	1.4	9
17	Eggs, chicken	288	1.3	
18	Carrots	287	1.3	
19	Celery	246	1.1	
20	Cantaloupe	237	1.1	

Rank	County	Value ($) (millions)	Leading Crops
1	Fresno	3,167	Cotton, grapes, poultry
2	Tulare	2,610	Milk, oranges, grapes
3	Monterey	2,028	Lettuce, broccoli, strawberries
4	Kern	1,978	Grapes, cotton, citrus
5	San Joaquin	1,223	Milk, grapes, tomatoes
6	Merced	1,220	Milk, almonds, chickens
7	Riverside	1,163	Milk, grapes, eggs
8	Stanislaus	1,115	Milk, almonds, chickens
9	San Diego	1,049	Nursery products, avocados
10	Imperial	1,009	Cattle, alfalfa, carrots

Source: California Department of Food and Agriculture.

In 1996, there were only slight changes in this list: the top five counties, in order, were Fresno, Tulare, Kern, Monterey, and Merced. Weather anomalies and market fluctuations caused some further reshuffling into the late 1990s, though nearly every county reported increased values over these figures by the end of the century.

Fruits and Nuts, Vegetables and Melons

Especially cismontane California is famous for its astounding variety of **specialty crops**. Its fruit, truck, and specialized crops are sometimes known as commercial gardening and fruit farming. Particularly where vegetables are grown to be marketed, **truck farming** might be used to describe these highly mechanized activities, except large numbers of migrant workers have also traditionally been used. Furthermore, citrus, grapes, olives, figs, dates, and certain vegetables are often considered mediterranean-type agriculture. This includes tree crops and horticulture, crops usually grown for human consumption rather than animal feed.

Regardless of the various (and sometimes confusing) labels and traditional categories used, these crops help identify the uniqueness of California agriculture. Where these specialty crops are grown, you will often find popular images of the state's famous rural landscapes. California's mild climates, dry summers, and impressive irrigation projects have helped especially the mediterranean-type products flourish. Much of the success of the state's agribusiness is due to these mild climates and long growing seasons, favorable soils, extensive irrigation, efficient, highly mechanized corporate farms, and effective marketing and distribution systems for its products. Without irrigation, many of the more intensive vegetable, fruit, and nut farms would return to more extensive grain production or rangelands.

Partly due to that irrigation, California is king of vegetables, fruits, and nuts. About 30 percent of California farmland is devoted to fruits and vegetables, a more intensive land-use than grains and ranching. For decades, California has led the country in vegetable production, particularly from the Central Valley; the state has traditionally led in production of asparagus, cauliflower, spinach, tomatoes, and strawberries. Specifically, more than half of U.S. lettuce, broccoli, and cauliflower has traditionally come from California. It also has led in growing fruits such as peaches, plums, apricots, lemons, avocados, figs, dates, various grapes and melons, and in nuts including almonds, pistachios, and walnuts.

More than half of U.S. fruit and nut production and of canned and frozen fruits and vegetables comes from California. Some of those agricultural products are featured here, using the California Department of Food and Agriculture organizing scheme.

Non-Citrus Fruits

The orchard industry began in California when wheat farmers started planting fruits and nuts in the 1860s. Farmers' indigenous methods helped make orchard farming a major industry in California by the turn of the century. This also allowed fruits and nuts that were previously considered food for the wealthy to become affordable and popular with low- and middle-income Americans. Alphabetically, apples and apricots start the list, but they often do not receive the attention given to California avocados.

Avocados Avocados are technically fruits and they contain more potassium than bananas. After Rudolph Hass from La Habra accidently developed the creamy-textured Hass avocado in 1935, it became the favored avocado for growers and consumers. Today, this represents about 85 percent of avocados grown in the state. The other varieties include Fuerte, Bacon, Reed, Pinkerton, Zutano, and Gwen.

Approximately 6,000 growers and 60,000 acres within California produce about 338 million pounds of avocados worth up to $250 million per year. Because avocado trees are very sensitive to cold weather and frost, they are successfully grown only in central and southern parts of the state and south into Mexico. Their placement can be tricky, but they are successful on coastal slopes exposed to milder marine air masses and elevated just above the inland valleys where damaging colder air settles on long, clear winter nights. (Such local inversions are considered in more detail in Chapter 4.) A frostbitten avocado tree, with its burnt, dried, brown leaves is not a pretty sight.

Unfortunately for avocado lovers, these trees thrive in the same climates that attract millions to Southern California. Consequently, they are regularly bulldozed for the housing tracts that sprout in their places. That is one reason you can now find them pushed to unlikely, more remote undeveloped sites where they are perched on steep slopes with poorer soils. Avocados can provide as many lessons in land use and geography as just about any California farm product.

Before trade agreements with Mexico took effect in 1997, about 95 percent of all avocados consumed in the United States were grown in California, and most of them were eaten in Pacific or Southwest states. Greatest sales occur around Super Bowl Sunday and Cinco de Mayo celebrations. California avocado growers have their eyes on potential markets beyond the western states.

Against the will of California avocado growers, NAFTA and other trade agreements encouraged the U.S. Department of Agriculture to lift the eighty-two-year-old ban on avocados from Mexico in 1997. California growers within the California Avocado Commission voiced their concerns that pests such as the fruit fly and seed weevil might invade their orchards with these imports from Mexico. Ventura County, which produces approximately $50 million of avocados per year, had already been invaded by a tiny, little-known insect that causes leathery-hard scars on avocados as it feeds on them. Persea mites also damaged the foliage of some avocado crops. Avocado growers in the region have traditionally used nontoxic methods to control such pests.

Cherries In 1991, Mexico banned U.S. cherries because of pest problems that might be introduced into their country. But, when the U.S. Department of Agriculture allowed Mexican avocados into the United States in 1997,

FALLBROOK

With 6,000 acres of avocado and citrus trees, Fallbrook (in northern San Diego County) has traditionally been considered the avocado capital of the world. Although avocados are produced in other California communities, it would be difficult to find a place beyond Fallbrook's historic and quaint Main Street where avocados are more important. There you will find the Del Rey Avocado Company warehouse. Farther out of town you might find the Chateau des Avocatiers (Manor of Avocado Trees) bed and breakfast. Pests and global competition are on the minds of avocado growers in many of these communities.

Mexico also lifted its ban on cherries. This added a market worth a few million dollars for California cherry growers. Japan has been the largest traditional export market for California cherries.

Profits from California's cherry crops usually depend on competition from Washington state and especially on weather conditions. As an example, only 550,000 packages of cherries were produced during 1995, as a result of disastrous weather; this was a reduction of 85 percent from the previous year. There are about ten counties that produce the four varieties of sweet cherries in California. San Joaquin County is the traditional leader.

Table Grapes California dates and figs are also famous, but they will never achieve the stature of the state's grape harvests. Grapes help define our Mediterranean agriculture, and they have been at the center of some of the state's most controversial labor disputes. We have already referred to Cesar Chavez' struggles to organize the United Farm Workers Union during the 1960s (in Chapter 8). This hero of the grape workers became the enemy of many grape growers searching for the cheapest labor. Hauntingly similar conflicts between UFW strawberry workers and growers in the 1990s are reviewed in the section on strawberries.

Table grapes ripen on these vines near the Salton Sea. Late spring's hot sun will speed the process.

Table grapes ripen first in late spring in the Imperial/Coachella Valley. San Joaquin Valley table grapes are ready slightly later, so there is little competition between these regions. Like most grapes, the timing of temperature and weather conditions is the key to color and sugar content. As an example, the early hot spells of 1996 and 1997 led to early crops during those years.

The California Table Grape Commission earned advertising competition awards with its "So Sweet, So Irresistible, Everybody's Picking California Grapes" campaign during the mid-1990s. This radio, TV, and mail campaign also promoted unattended sampling in produce departments. Sales increased by 33 percent where sampling bins displayed these table grapes. Some of these efforts were designed to repair damage done to the industry after it entered into that lengthy and bitter labor dispute with the United Farm Workers.

Raisins Selma, California (pop 18,000) is just south of Fresno. Locals have labelled it the Raisin Capital of the World. Selma residents show pride in their raisins during the annual Selma Raisin Festival. They acknowledge that their product doesn't get the fame or respect shown for other farm products. Nevertheless, farms around Selma produce at least 85 percent of all California raisins, which are most of the nation's raisins.

Selma's Thompson seedless grape vines bloom in the spring, the grapes mature in summer, and are harvested in August. Some are placed on paper trays to bake in the sun for up to three weeks; they become dark raisins. When placed in hot water, treated with sulfur, and dried in a special oven, they become golden raisins. The Selma Chamber of Commerce organizes the Raisin Festival as one of their promotional events. The festival is more like most county fairs, though unique desserts and other dishes with raisins are featured. Residents call it "nature's candy." The California raisin was also celebrated in the 1980s in a comedy TV series called "Fresno," a spoof about raisin barons at war.

Wine Grapes California's wine grape harvests soared over 2.2 million tons during the mid-1990s. Grape juice shortages pushed prices higher as wineries around the state could not expand fast enough to meet increasing

GROWING GRAPES

The Anderson farm consists of four 40-acre tracts growing red flame seedless table grapes along the north shore of the Salton Sea. (Grapes are typically grown on 10-acre plots.) These grapes ripen by May and June in the hot desert sun. They are preferred by consumers and, therefore, by the grower. (Most Thompson grapes are grown in the Central Valley.) Tim Anderson is the owner. His manager is responsible for producing the best harvests and profits. His crew forewoman is usually a Latina who supervises the pickers.

Plants are not watered during the three months of the cold season. During December, the plants resemble dead brown sticks. As the cold season progresses, they are pruned down to the spurs and sprayed in January with cyanamide from rigs pulled by tractors. This makes them "break" consistently during March. After the canes (branches) grow out from the spurs, hermaphroditic white blossoms appear. Many of these flowers must be combed off to protect the future grapes from clustering that might encourage mildew. Another chemical is sprayed with a nutrient mix to enhance the growth of the grapes, and another is finally used to evenly redden the fruit. The herbicide Roundup and pesticides are also used. Cuts are made in the plants' cambium layers to keep sugars from migrating down.

A local packing plant supplies the picking crews, and the grape harvest is sold to that packing house. The better harvests are shipped overseas. (England pays up to $6 per pound for these grapes, though they will reject any shipments contaminated with black widow spiders.) After all supermarket accounts are in, a check is finally sent to the owner in September.

Growing profitable grapes requires more than one million gallons of irrigation water on many days and up to 1.5 million gallons per day in mid-summer for the 160 acres. Various nutrients are mixed with the water, depending on the time of year. Tiles below the surface drain excess water to inhibit root rot and take out excess salts and other chemicals. The nutrients and other chemicals drain off the land through these clay tiles and into the Salton Sea. Many of these nutrients help produce the algae blooms that eventually die off and decompose, leading to the fish kills and rancid smells that became characteristic of the Salton Sea during hot summers. These grape vines, meanwhile, should be productive for up to sixty years.

---

demands. Many wineries, such as Grgich Hills Cellar in Napa Valley's Rutherford, cater to domestic clients to take advantage of lower transport costs and no tariffs. However, much of the growth has occurred since the California wine industry finally nurtured long-term markets abroad by supplying them with consistent quantities of quality wines.

California wine exports to other nations increased more than 430 percent during the decade between 1986 and 1996. By 1996, exports totalled $327 million for more than 47 million gallons shipped to 164 countries, according to the Wine Institute in San Francisco. Top markets were Britain, Canada, Japan, and other European countries. Here is just one example of the growing market—Ferrari-Carano Vineyards and Winery in Healdsburg, while already selling to at least seventeen countries, was under pressure to double their exports.

Additionally, California sparkling wines have gained more respect. During the 1990s, they were recognized for their more consistent, outstanding flavor and lower prices than French champagne. Good quality California sparkling wines were selling for less than $20, while higher quality labels were less than $50. Equal or lesser-quality French champagne was far more expensive. Experts predict that California sparkling wines should continue to take a larger share of the domestic market.

Vineyards and wineries have dominated bucolic landscapes throughout the picturesque Napa and Sonoma Valleys for decades (see Map 9.1). A combination of cool, wet winters and hot, dry summers (away from the coastal fog belt), rich soils, and other factors combine to make this the traditional heart of California's legendary wine country. High-quality wine grape varieties—from Chardonnay and Cabernet, to Sauvignon and Merlot—are common household names if you are a wine lover. The highest quality and priced wines are even recognized by the specific location where grapes are grown, such as the Oakville District in Napa County. However, especially in recent years, these landscapes have spread far beyond the Napa and Sonoma areas into some unlikely rural communities.

Into the late-1990s, a root louse called phylloxera forced some growers to rip up their vines. During bad weather years, California wine prices were on the rise. Vinters across the state were under pressure to grow more grapes to keep a competing import market under control. Though acreage was decreasing in some areas, the Central Valley was adding vineyards to make up for it. Vineyards in Southern California were also helping to fill the void.

By the late 1990s, vineyards were replacing vegetable farms and grazing land in valleys across the state. This grape planting craze approached an additional 50,000

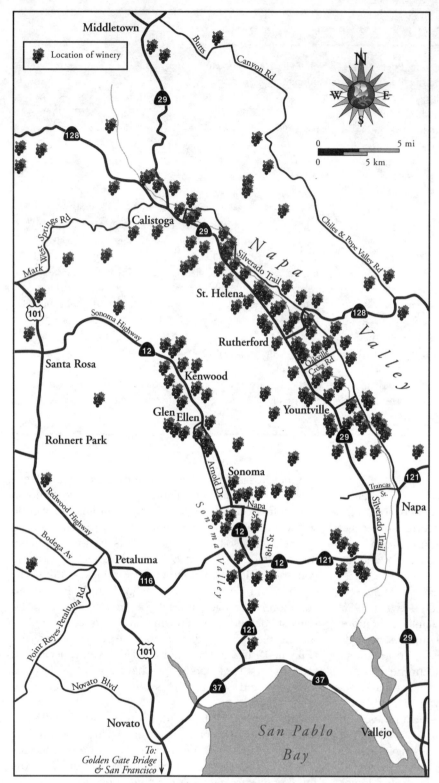

MAP 9.1
Traditional wine country has become a major tourist attraction.

acres per year and was especially noticeable along the central coast and in the Central Valley. Around Lodi, along the Mokelumne River Basin, past grape harvests produced cheaper wines or juices to be mixed with Napa, Sonoma, and Mendocino wines.

More recently, vintners have exploited summer's hot days and cool nights in the Lodi-Woodbridge area to produce their own high-quality wines in greater quantity than anywhere in the United States, including California's traditional grape-growing valleys. Vineyards were

CALIFORNIA WINERIES

EXPERIMENTING WITH NEW TECHNOLOGIES TO PRODUCE BETTER WINES

As they compete, California grape growers are experimenting with methods to improve the quality of their product. The Mondavi family's Opus One Winery in the Napa Valley is famous for emphasizing natural farming techniques and natural production of wine. They were the first in California to return to a partial gravity flow system in wine production. By the mid-1990s, other California wine producers had caught on. In the hills of northern Santa Barbara County (above the Santa Maria Valley 75 miles north of Santa Barbara) is Byron Vineyard & Winery. After harvesting, the topography is used to allow the grapes' juice to flow downhill, rather than be pumped. It is an extreme example of efforts and competition to produce the best-tasting premium wines in California.

Byron Kent Brown has experimented there by replanting at different densities and cloning vines from France, Oregon, and California. The density of vines has been increased to up to 4,300 vines per acre, producing smaller grapes and more intense fruit. New north–south orientation of the vines allows more sunlight on both sides of the canopy. Movable wires push leaves and grapes up higher, ensuring maximum sun exposure and circulation in this otherwise cool grape-growing area.

When pumps replaced the natural gravity flow of the grapes' juice, it accelerated wine making, but quality was compromised as pumped wine becomes more bitter with the harsh tannins released. Gravity flow results in a smoother, sweeter product. Some consider this state-of-the-art wine making a back-to-the-future technology.

HIGH DESERT WINES

The Antelope Valley Winery in Lancaster relied more on grape varieties from other regions as it doubled its production during the first six years of the 1990s. Only two of their thirteen wines were made from the two acres of Antelope Valley grapes, but, they are hopeful that an additional 150 acres of Cabernet Sauvignon wine grape vines will change all of that. The alternating hot days and cold nights were expected to produce a special blend of sugars and acids in a new variety of Antelope Valley grapes.

Antelope Valley Wineries would also like to get out of the official "South Coast" wines designation once given every vineyard south of the Tehachapis. They were hoping to get the U.S. Bureau of Alcohol, Tobacco and Firearms to designate their wines as from a special region due to the unique microclimates and soil conditions. After all, these highly variable growing conditions have created the variety of wines that helped make California vinters famous.

---

sprouting even in the Salinas Valley and into the Paso Robles area. In the Santa Inez Valley in northern Santa Barbara County, residents were complaining not about the vineyards, but activities at the wineries. By the end of the 1990s, large parties and even musical concerts were becoming commonplace at some Santa Ynez wineries, frustrating many neighbors who settled there to escape noise and crowds.

Nectarines   Our alphabetical survey of California's non-citrus fruit crops continues. California is the only state where there is substantial kiwifruit production and it also leads the nation in nectarines. Peaches, plums, apricots, and nectarines are all examples of popular stone fruits, or drupes, where seeds are protected by a thick shell or stone.

California produces nearly 95 percent of the nation's nectarines, or nearly $100 million worth. Most of these are harvested in southern Fresno and northern Tulare Counties in what is known as the Fresno District. This area has been the world's leader in nectarines since the late 1800s. Originally, small towns grew as markets only every 7 to 8 miles along the railroads in these flatlands. This was the greatest distance farmers could then haul their crops and get home in one day.

Cold winter fogs chill the trees for dormancy, while hot, dry summers provide the perfect ripening environment. Each of the eighty major varieties is grown to produce certain textures, colors, tastes and shipping qualities. There must be a balance between these factors, but looks and handling quality often take on more important roles than taste. The tastes change by the year as new varieties are developed.

By the mid-1990s, the entire top five varieties of nectarines had yielded to new ones within five years, so growers did not replant the same varieties they once had. Each variety comes into season within ten days to two weeks. White-fleshed nectarines were the 1990s most recent craze, but red was making a comeback. The better-tasting varieties may not look as pretty, so they sold for only $8–$10 a box compared to their poorer-tasting $12–$14 a box nicely-colored relatives. Taste, however, was also making a rebound in importance. Most of the fruit must be picked only within three days of it being fully ripened.

A few growers are into their third generation in family businesses begun up to 100 years ago. They are actually growers, packers, and shippers. Their packing houses are as big as football fields, and they now have high-tech assembly lines with scanners and computers. California's nectarine production increased by four times within the twenty years from the mid-1970s to the 1990s until it totalled two-thirds of the state's peach production.

Other Non-Citrus Fruit   This brings us to the end of our review of major noncitrus fruits. We must note that California also leads the nation in production of olives, peaches, pears, plums, pomegranates, and prunes. Long after the Spanish introduced olive trees to the state, a boutique olive oil industry finally blossomed in the Napa and Sonoma Valleys by the 1990s. With the recent popularity of olive oil, olive orchards are popping up in other regions. Members of the California Olive Oil Council and new olive farmers are hoping to make California olive oil a gourmet export into the twenty-first century. Elsewhere, California's clingstone and freestone peaches and its bartlett and other pears are famous examples of the exceptional productivity within the state's orchards.

Citrus Fruits

Raising citrus fruits is a form of truck farming that requires extensive irrigation in California's Mediterranean climate. California traditionally leads the nation in lemon production, is second to Florida in oranges (though California rules in fresh oranges, while Florida's are grown mainly for juice), and is third to Florida and Texas in growing grapefruit for market. It is also second in tangerine production, producing about $30 million of tangerines per year, representing approximately 20 percent of the nation's total. California plays a vital role in making the United States a world leader in the export of citrus products.

Early images of Southern California citrus groves full of ripe oranges and framed by distant snow-capped mountains were more real than imagined. The seedless

The state's salute to citrus is in Riverside and is open to curious visitors.

navel orange was born in Riverside. Valencia, California, shared its name with the juicy orange with seeds. There is Orange County and its City of Orange; the list goes on. The fact that most productive orange groves were located in the mildest climates led to their demise; bulldozers replaced many of them with developments.

After many citrus groves moved out to the San Joaquin Valley and other marginal climates, they were ravaged by occasional freezes. One more recent, notable cold snap destroyed up to 100 percent of the citrus crop in Fresno, Tulare, and Kern Counties during December, 1998, and cost farmers more than $500 million. South of the Tehachapi Mountains, particularly in Ventura County, most citrus groves were protected from that freeze and remained productive.

Lemons   California is the largest lemon producer in the United States and Ventura County is the largest producer in California. In 1995, there were 26,630 acres of lemon groves in Ventura County alone. Value of the state's lemon exports soared over $125 million. Only Argentina produces more lemons, but their quality is not as good. Ventura's mild coastal climate is perfect for lemon orchards. California's warm days and cool nights bring out the color in lemons and oranges because we are on the northern fringes of the citrus latitudes.

About 97 percent of all lemons sold in Japan came from America during the 1990s. The vast majority of flawless lemons in the produce sections of Japanese markets also came from Ventura County. The Japanese demand perfect size, shape, and color and are paying for them. Because Japanese are often said to first eat with their eyes, the presentation of food is considered a work of art. Consequently, thousands of cartons of lemons from orchards in Santa Paula and other Ventura County locations are marked "sunkisto remon" (sunkist lemon) to go to Japan.

Many are shipped from the Limoneira Company orchards, the largest lemon grower in the region. Only the highest quality, perfect lemons are marked "Santas" to go out to Japan. These are often known as first choice or sunkist. The second-grade lemons with a few spots or imperfect shapes are marked "Paulas" to stay in the states. They are often called "choice," or second-grade lemons. Next down the line are the nicked, scarred, or deformed "products" that are squeezed into juices.

The lemons must be picked when they reach choice sizes because they can eventually grow to the size of grapefruits. They are sorted and washed using a combination of cameras, machines, and people. They are classified by color and quality and stored in a giant refrigerator until they ripen to yellow, or they are sent out immediately if they are already ripe. The good ones are packed in boxes and loaded on ships at Port Hueneme for their twelve-day journey to Japan in a 41°F refrigerator. Packed at about 22 cents per lemon, the best are sold in Japan for nearly $1 per lemon. At the highest class fruit stands, they can go for nearly $2 per lemon.

The Limoneira Company was one of the first members of the enormous Sunkist marketing cooperative. In the 1890s, Japanese picked the lemons in Limoneira's orchards. Today, wealthy Japanese businessmen can be seen touring the Limoneira plant. Sunkist ships nearly 4 million cartons of lemons to Japan each year, almost all first choice. That's nearly the same amount that is consumed in the United States.

Nuts

Some people from out of state might eagerly agree that California produces more nuts than any other state. Seriously, did you know that California leads the nation in the production of almonds, pistachios, and walnuts? California produces three-fourths of the world's almonds and 99.5 percent of the nation's English walnuts. Top almond counties are Kern, Stanislaus, Merced, Fresno, and San Joaquin. Top English walnut counties are San Joaquin, Stanislaus, Butte, Tulare, and Sutter. The state's total annual nut production surpassed $1 billion several years ago.

Almond Growers Blue Diamond Growers (BDG) is a Sacramento, California-based cooperative of nearly 5,000 almond farmers. BDG had almost $470 million in sales in 1990. They distribute almonds internationally to consumers. The group recently implemented an electronic data interchange (EDI) system linked to its bank and carriers to decrease processed documents, reduce the number of staff, and become more efficient. Competition mainly comes from other types of nuts or other foods.

Berries

California is also a leader in producing many small, juicy, fleshy fruits we call berries. Botanically, this includes tomatoes, though we have lumped tomatoes as they are used, with the many vegetables. The state produces boysenberry, olallieberry, and raspberry crops, but they do not begin to approach the importance of the dominant strawberry.

Strawberry Fields Forever About 80 percent of the nation's strawberries come from California farms. These strawberries are produced from more than 23,000 acres and were valued at more than $500,000,000 per year during the 1990s. Ideal soil, moisture, and especially climatic conditions have made six regions in California the leaders, responsible for almost all California strawberry production: Watsonville, Ventura, Santa Maria, Orange County, San Diego, and the San Joaquin Valley.

Modern technologies are being used to grow larger, firmer varieties (such as the Camarosa) that are hardier. Because the tough Camarosa varieties can be shipped greater distances without being crushed, they replaced the tastier, but more delicate, Chandler variety during the 1990s. (California's stone fruits farmers are making similar decisions.) Unfortunately for California strawberry lovers, commerce and trade won over taste and quality in the 1990s.

Growing strawberries requires plenty of manual labor, patience, and intensive land use. This is why so many Japanese farm worker immigrants were right at home on California farms earlier in the 1900s. Even before they were legally allowed to own land in California, they established some of the most successful strawberry farms. (At one time, about 80 percent of Los Angeles County's strawberry growers were Japanese Americans.) First-generation farmers could only lease the land they worked. After Japanese Americans were placed in internment camps during World War II, the California strawberry harvest dropped from more than 27 million pounds to just over 7 million pounds per year. After the war, Japanese Americans returned, and California strawberry harvests soared to record levels into the 1950s and beyond.

Per-acre yield from strawberries has always been higher than most other crops. This is one reason that strawberry farms average only about one-tenth the size of other California farms (just about 36 acres) and that some Japanese Americans quickly recovered from the war years. Glen Hasegawa's family in Oxnard is a good example of how important Japanese Americans have been in the state's strawberry harvest history. Like his grandfather and father, he grows strawberries. They

They don't look like much, but these little strawberry fields and stands serve a large urban population during the season in Orange County. Transporting is not an issue because the farms are already surrounded by cities—the same developments that will soon consume them.

WORKING IN THE STRAWBERRY FIELDS

Today, California's strawberry industry is still depending on large supplies of cheap migrant labor, often provided by illegal immigrants from Mexico. Low wages and backbreaking work continue to dominate, and some workers even face exploitative sharecropping schemes.

Enter the United Farm Workers (UFW) in the 1990s. Watsonville claims to be the strawberry capital of the world and celebrates with a big strawberry festival each June. During the 1990s, the United Farm Workers Union, under President Arturo Rodriguez (son-in-law of the late Cesar Chavez, who helped start the union), was trying to recruit all the area's 15,000 strawberry pickers in what some called the largest labor campaign in America. With only about 25,000 members, the UFW targeted some of the region's most abusive growers, accusing them of paying slave wages and creating cruel working conditions.

They claimed that some growers were taking advantage of desperate labor pools by not adhering to state laws requiring minimum-wage pay and drinking water and bathroom facilities in the fields. Some pickers complained about making $35 per eight-hour day with no benefits such as medical insurance or disability pay, all while facing arbitrary dismissal. They claimed they were living in houses with more than ten other pickers rented at $1,000 per month. Others complained about working conditions that included direct contact with dangerous pesticides. Almost all the pickers were from Mexico.

The U.F.W., in a drama that has been played countless times on California's farms throughout the 1900s, handed out printed information and organized meetings about their union. They noted that for every $5 of strawberries sold in the market, the pickers only received about 45 cents. Growers countered with their own information campaign to discourage organizations. They pleaded that they were going into deep debts and taking huge financial risks and that the big profits were going to the cooler owners and marketers. In 1995, on the first farm where the workers voted to join the union, the grower shut down the farm and plowed under his strawberry crop.

State inspectors and even some concerned growers tried to identify and eliminate the abusive growers. Many other growers meet or exceed state standards. The U.F.W. reported that some growers responded by improving working conditions (such as giving the first increase in wages in ten years, and providing more portable toilets and drinking water in the fields). Union organizers say strawberries offer them an unusual opportunity for organization, since they must be picked within about two days ripening time or they are lost.

In April, 1997, about 20,000 UFW union members and supporters from around the nation marched in Watsonville in what leaders claimed was one of the biggest marches ever for the state's workers.

---

moved their farms to the Ventura/Oxnard Plain to escape encroaching housing tracts in Orange County. He is now an agricultural school graduate who manages two farms with his brother. He and other Californians watch as housing tracts continue to expand, squeezing the little, productive strawberry farms into smaller and smaller plots.

Vegetables and Melons

California leads the nation in production of scores of various vegetables and melons. Some of these major crops include, but are not limited to, artichoke, asparagus, broccoli, Brussels sprouts, Chinese cabbage, peas, carrots, cauliflower, celery, garlic, lettuce, onions, bell peppers, and spinach. The state also leads in production of these fruits which are grown and harvested similar to vegetables: processing tomatoes (traditionally considered and used as vegetables), cantaloupe, casaba, and honeydew melons. Other important products in these categories include snap beans, cucumbers, watermelon, mushrooms, and miscellaneous other vegetables

and melons that are also shipped as fresh or processed products.

Garlic   Nearly 90 percent of the nation's garlic is produced in California. Central California growers produce about 130 million pounds per year worth $90 million. It is the second-best selling herb in the United States and per-capita use is growing fast. Christopher Ranch in Gilroy is the largest single fresh garlic producer in the world.

After China dumped huge imports of cheap garlic on the United States market in the early 1990s, the International Trade Commission imposed a hefty dumping duty to protect California farmers in 1994. Though smaller amounts of Chinese garlic continued to enter the United States illegally, mainly from the Ports of Los Angeles and Long Beach, California garlic producers depend on officials to keep illegal dumping in check.

Tomatoes   Tomatoes are, botanically, fruits, but they are grown, harvested, and consumed like many vegetables. California is the leading producer of tomatoes for pro-

GROWING AND PICKING TOMATOES

Harry Singh and Sons is Southern California's largest tomato grower, with 700 acres and 400 to 900 workers on their Oceanside farm in San Diego County. They were given an award by the U.S. Dept. of Labor for building a $2.5 million housing project with dormitories for 325 field workers in 1990. It was celebrated as one of the most modern farm-worker housing projects in California, where thousands of workers had otherwise gone homeless, sleeping in bushes and temporary shelters.

Unfortunately, state labor officials and groups such as the California Rural Legal Assistance also claimed the same farm owed workers up to $1 million in overtime pay. These allegations brought confusion to the award ceremonies, but they underscored the significance of ongoing conflicts between California farm workers and growers seeking cheap labor, this time to pick tomatoes.

cessing such foods as ketchup and tomato paste. Over 10 million tons were harvested in 1994 and 1995 and more than 11 million tons were produced in 1996. The state's tomato crops were growing into the twenty-first century.

Field Crops

Into the late 1990s, the state produced about $3.5 billion dollars of field crops each year. Highest valued field crops were Upland cotton at more than $900 million and hay at more than $800 million per year. California ranked second in the nation in production of both, with more than 2.3 million bales of cotton and 9 million tons of hay each year. Unlike some states where cereal and other edible grains dominate, California's leading field crops are not grown for human consumption.

In contrast to some more traditional midwestern mixed crop and livestock farms, many California commercial grain farmers may specialize in one crop. In regions with inadequate irrigation, dry grain farms may share boundaries with even less productive rangelands. Modern combine machines are used to reap, thresh, and clean the product. Because these grains and other field crops often have high values per unit, are stored easily without spoilage, and are not costly to ship long distances, they may be quite profitable even when grown far from urban markets. Farmers do rely on convenient access to transportation by truck, railroad, or boat. Following California's rainy season, after the grains are grown and harvested, another crop may follow if water for irrigation is available.

The state's major field crops include alfalfa, barley, beans (including lima, blackeye, kidney, pink, and garbanzo), corn, cotton, hay, oats, potatoes, rice, sugar beets, sweet potatoes, and wheat. California even leads the nation in a few of these products.

Cotton Cotton is a special type of field crop that is sometimes grouped with specialty crops. It is an indus-

trial crop. It is the number five California agricultural product and the state's number two agricultural export. Since nearly 100 percent of California's cotton acreage is irrigated, the state might lead the nation in production when weather is especially poor in other states. Grain crops often compete with cotton for the same land on California farms. Cotton farming has been the leading agricultural activity in the southern San Joaquin Valley. Imperial Valley yields are also impressive.

In 1896, the mechanical cotton picker was adopted by cotton growers in Southern Piedmont, California, to increase farm productivity. Productivity rates on cotton farms especially increased from 1920 to 1970. Mechanical cotton pickers reduced picking time and lowered the chance of weather damage.

In 1993, China imported very little cotton. However, in 1994, Calcot Ltd., the largest California cotton cooperative, agreed to sell 240,000 bales of cotton to China. In 1995, bad weather and bollworm infestations crippled China's cotton crop, causing world cotton prices to rise to their highest since the 1860s. Imperial Valley cotton farmers, who export 80 percent of their crop, had a record year. Because U.S. exports to China were expected to soar with that country's growing economy, California cotton producers were looking across the Pacific to markets with incredible potential. Instability in Asian markets during the late 1990s threw a wild card into the forecasting of future cotton exports.

Rice Rice is an aquatic cereal grass, requiring intensive land use and lots of water. So, why is it grown in California? Hardy varieties of rice are being produced especially where abundant mountain runoff can be trapped in places like the Sacramento Valley.

To the delight of California rice growers, Japan first opened its rice market in December, 1993, after their domestic crops failed. Low-key advertisements in Japan for California rice are building as the Japanese market opens further. Meanwhile, the value of California long, medium, and short-grained rice varieties soared over $300

GENETICALLY ENGINEERED COTTON

More than 60 percent of American clothing is made from cotton, so when Davis-based Calgene Incorporated developed genetically-engineered cotton that controls color pigments, you'd think the industry would be ecstatic! By growing cotton with different tones of black, brown, blue, and red, textile industries could save more than 50 cents per pound on dyes and eliminate fading problems. However, when companies such as B.C. Cotton Inc. in Bakersfield tried to expand their breeding and growing of colored cotton, they met stiff opposition during the 1990s.

White cotton is a $1 billion industry in California. Opposition to the growing of colored cotton mounted from a range of farmers, including the California Cotton Growers Association and Calcot Ltd. They were concerned that colored seeds and lint would contaminate their Acala and Pima varieties. Consequently, the San Joaquin Valley Cotton Board enforced a strict "one variety" rule. This forced farmers to grow only the Acala variety, prized for its long, strong fibers that are easy to spin into thread. Unusual weather in 1998 forced cotton growers to relax their one variety rule; some growers began to successfully experiment with other varieties.

---

million by the mid-1990s. That's a pretty good reason to grow rice.

Floriculture

Nursery and greenhouse products accounted for nearly 10 percent of California's farm income during the 1990s. Values soared over $2 billion per year by the mid-1990s. Floriculture (cultivation of especially decorative flowers, or simple flowers and foliage) production was worth more than $600 million per year wholesale. These include cut flowers, potted plants, and bedding/garden plants. Here are a couple of examples.

Poinsettias During the early 1900s, the Ecke family grew poinsettias in outdoor fields along Hollywood, Sunset, and Sepulveda Boulevards in L.A. They moved to Encinitas in northern San Diego County (where there was a good climate, water supply, and a railroad) after developing a plant that could be grown indoors in pots.

Today, more than 70 million poinsettias of different colors are sold in the United States each year. And more than 80 percent of the world's poinsettia sales start in pots in one of the greenhouses on the 40-acre Paul Ecke Ranch. This is known as the poinsettia capital of the world. They are shipped to florists, garden centers, and markets and are especially popular during the holidays.

Roses California grew more than 269 million roses commercially, worth nearly $69 million in 1995. That was more than 68 percent of all roses sold in the United States. Colorado was a distant second with less than 26 million roses. The greatest sales occur on Valentine's Day. The greatest celebration of roses in California culture occurs each New Year's Day at Pasadena's Rose Parade.

Livestock and Dairy Products

During the 1990s, California livestock and dairy farms produced more than $5.5 billion of products per year. Their importance is revealed when ranked among the state's top agricultural products: milk and cream (1st), cattle and calves (4th), chickens (13th), and eggs (17th). More than 25.3 billion pounds of milk and 2.1 billion pounds of red meat (nearly 2 billion pounds beef) was produced each year. Annually, more than 1.7 billion pounds of poultry and 6.4 billion eggs, but only 88.6 million pounds of pork and 60 million pounds of lamb and mutton, were produced. Add more than 39 million pounds of honey and 5.2 million pounds of wool, and you can see the vital role played by farm animals in California agriculture.

Dairies California is by far the leading milk-producing state—about double any other single state. Extraordinary amounts of manufactured dairy products include more than 1.2 billion pounds of nonfat dry, condensed skim milk and yogurt. California is also number one in ice cream and frozen dessert industries. At more than 920 million pounds per year, it even surpasses Wisconsin as the number one cheese-producing state! More than 340 million pounds of butter are also produced in California each year.

The high cost of milk cows (nearly $1,300 per head) and dairy land reflects the labor-intensive, high maintenance nature of the state's dairy farms. Specific locations of these farms are often determined by the type of milk product emphasized. Dairies producing milk to be shipped directly to market are often closer to urban areas. This has produced the milk sheds (previously mentioned) surrounding the outskirts of major California cities. However, industries producing other dairy products are often located progressively farther from the mar-

COMPETITION FROM LATIN AMERICA

Cut flowers from Latin America began flowing into the United States in the 1970s; this meant new competition for many California growers. U.S. growers especially lost to flower ranchers in Ecuador and Colombia after the U.S. government passed the Andean Trade Preferences Act in the early 1990s. This legislation encouraged imports of flowers and other legitimate products from Ecuador, Colombia, Peru, and Bolivia, as an incentive to stop cultivation of drug-related crops. This is a bizarre twist in international politics that impacted California growers.

The bad news is that these flowers are cheap. The good news for California growers is that they are not as fresh. More than 60 percent of flower sales in the United States now come from imports. The main countries exporting to the United States are Colombia (65 percent), the Netherlands (more than 11 percent), Ecuador (10 percent and growing fast), and Mexico (nearly 4 percent). Even though flowers were the tenth most valuable agricultural product in California, it is estimated that domestic growers were going out of business at the rate of about 10 percent per year in the 1990s. Many of these traditional flower growers complained that they were paying the price for a U.S. Government war on drugs that wasn't working.

---

ket because these products require large quantities of milk—1 pound of milk makes 1 pound of ice cream, 10 pounds of milk makes 1 pound of cheese, and 20 pounds of milk makes 1 pound of butter.

Beef On the opposite side of the land-use scale from dairies are beef cattle. By the 1860s, there were more than 1.3 million head of cattle and calves in California. During the 1990s, there were more than 4.6 million, while nearly one million head of cattle and calves were being slaughtered each year under federal and state inspection guidelines. Today, one out of every eight cows in the nation is a Californian. In contrast to dairies, livestock grazing, or ranching, involves the commercial grazing of livestock over an extensive area. Such activities are usually in more semiarid or arid lands with poor soils and sparse vegetation, farther from urban markets. On fertile, more valuable lands where water is introduced, grazing usually yields to more intensive farming practices.

This livestock grazing affects huge areas and produces landscapes resembling traditional western stereotypes, complete with cowboy and wild-west cultures. Such landscapes, along with grain farms, would be far more extensive in California if not for great water projects that paved the way for the more intensive farms, orchards, and housing projects that replaced them. Enormous expanses of ranch lands are required for grazing, especially in the state's dry regions. Here, lower yields and incomes per area and lower operating costs are complementary.

During the 1800s, there was plenty of open land for the state's cattle ranchers. By the turn of the century, the state's crop-growing farmers had bought substantial amounts of government land. Conflicts broke out between ranchers and the farmers who were then able to restrict grazing by enclosing their land with barbed wire. During the early 1900s, ranchers who did not own their own land had to lease the public lands they used. They were also grazing more tasty breeds of cattle, such as Herefords, that required greater care and water than the

Anyone who has passed this cattle yard on I-5 in the Central Valley can appreciate the smell of the farm. It is conveniently located along the interstate, halfway between San Francisco and Los Angeles.

OSTRICH

Ostrich meat is much more expensive than beef, but it tastes as good and has much less fat, calories, and cholesterol. It sells best in health-conscious California. Several popular stores and even fast-food restaurants started to offer it during the 1990s. Ostriches require only an eighth the acreage of cattle. Though this tasty meat became popular in the 1990s, it will take many years before we know if it is a passing fad or a lasting addition to California agriculture.

Ostrich Farms in Torrance opened in 1995. Within one year, it was supplying more than eight-hundred stores and restaurants with more than $60,000 of ostrich meat each month. Owner Howard Freiberg operates ostrich farms in Modesto, Hemet, Santa Ynez, and Louisiana and has a second store in Atlanta. Startled visitors (such as along the main road to Solvang) have been entertained by these new additions to California's landscapes.

Ostrich became the choice meat for many health-conscious Californians who could afford it during the 1990s. This ostrich farm is near Solvang.

longhorns before them. Though more permanently-rooted fixed ranching resulted, leased public lands still represent the majority of grazing acreage.

Ranchers pay fees to graze their cattle on Bureau of Land Management (BLM) and National Forest Service public multi-use lands. Opponents of overgrazing argue that grazing would be substantially reduced if these fees were set to reflect the long-term impact of cattle on public lands. They argue that overgrazing on public lands is subsidized by the federal government.

After growing and maturing on vast pastures, beef cattle are finally sent to more intensive farms and feed lots for fattening. These lots are often located along major transportation routes, where meat processors are easily accessible. One of the more visible examples is found midway between the Los Angeles and San Francisco Bay/Sacramento areas, in the Central Valley along I-5. These feed lots and their notorious odors (more like offensive stenches to urban passersby) have no trouble capturing the attention of travellers on the nearby interstate.

Other Farm Animals More than one million sheep and lambs were raised in California during an average year of the 1990s. Each year, about 700,000 or more sheep were shorn for wool production with wildly varying values from less than $3 million to about $10 million per year. Annual income from total sheep and lamb production approached $70 million. There were also more than 200,000 hogs and pigs on California farms; they ac-

counted for more than $40 million per year income during most of the 1990s.

Poultry and Eggs Also during the 1990s, there were more than 250 million chickens and 22 million turkeys on California farms. Together, they generated annual incomes ranging over $380 million and $200 million, respectively. Well over one billion pounds of chicken and nearly 500,000 pounds of turkey were produced annually in California. California ranked sixth among states in turkey production, accounting for about 7.5 percent of the nation's total.

More than 6 billion eggs were produced annually, generating nearly 300 million additional dollars per year. There is very strong correlation between locations of egg-producing chicken farms and the urban areas so that the perishable eggs are delivered fresh and at relatively inexpensive prices to consumers.

On California's poultry farms, site factors are not as important as on other farms because chickens can be raised indoors on cheap land with poor soils. Recently, strong ties have grown between those who grow chicken feed (commercial feed corporations), many broiler and other chicken farmers, and distributors to the markets. Smaller "contract" farmers become dependent on commercial feed corporations who develop direct transportation links to get their feed to the farms. Because these smaller contract farmers are often at distant and marginal locations, they clump together so that the transport of feed in to the farms and the transport of chickens out to

THE SUPER BOWL OF FARM SHOWS

During the 1960s, Colusa organized the first formal farm equipment show in the Central Valley. Tulare took their idea and demonstrated how it could really be done during the 1990s; they hosted the largest annual farm equipment show in the world. Called the Super Bowl of farm equipment shows, it spread across 170 acres by 1997. The approximately 1,300 exhibits included just about every kind of farm service and equipment imaginable from around the world, from tractors, to clippers, to nut shakers, and even high-tech farming methods.

Attendance topped 100,000 and participants included farmers from about fifty other countries. Displays, country music, and barbecues contributed to a country fair atmosphere. The Tulare Chamber of Commerce was very proud.

the markets is more convenient and efficient. Economic geography thrives at the expense of these tasty production-line chickens!

Honey More than 400,000 honey-producing commercial bee colonies in California averaged more than 90 pounds of honey production during better years in the 1990s. This not only represents more than $20 million during peak years; many of these bees are cherished by farmers as they play vital roles in pollinating flowers for their future crops.

Trouble loomed on the horizon for beekeepers in southeastern California during the 1990s. It came in the form of dangerously aggressive Africanized bees. They had spread north from Mexico and colonized more than 18,000 square miles by 1998, according to state agriculture officials. Swarms of these "killer" bees were infiltrating California's traditional honeybee (also nonnative bees) locales, posing danger to beekeepers and farmers especially in and around Imperial County. By 1999, these unwanted guests had advanced as far north as Los Angeles County.

California Farms Are Different

The average modern California farm is indeed a long stretch from the stereotypical image of small family farms in the Midwest. Those Midwestern farms might include traditional images of mixed farming. There, feed (such as soybeans, corn, or drier grain) is grown for the animals and the market, and then the animals themselves are grown for the market as they provide manure for soil and more crops. On modern California farms, year-round revenue is more often provided by long growing seasons and specialized farming. The state's approximately 80,000 farms represent less than 4 percent of the nation's total, but account for nearly 12 percent of the national gross receipts from farming.

Many of today's farmers are using modern geographic information systems (GIS) to improve their profits. Colored satellite images and air photo interpretations are being used not only to display the distribution of grape varieties, but also to indicate when certain crops, such as cantaloupe, are ready for harvest. These modern techniques can also reveal drier fields that require more irrigation than others. Maps showing pH and other soil conditions help determine which crops can be grown for the greatest profit in each field. These modern global position systems (GPS), remote sensing, and other GIS techniques are improving the efficiency of what is known as "precision farming" or "site-specific farming."

One result is that water, fertilizers, and pesticides are being applied more efficiently, and harvests are better timed to increase profits and improve the quality of the crop. Environmental Research Systems in Redlands is just one company working with farmers to develop software that will help increase production. The potential for these consulting companies to help commodity speculators and investors, lenders, insurance companies, and chemical suppliers is enormous.

California farmers are concerned about the costs of these technologies that potentially enable them to micromanage to the extreme their relatively small fields and large variety of crops. However, those who do not use precision farming technologies are worried about becoming obsolete, or at least less competitive. Each year, a host of new satellites and more accessible technologies are being introduced.

Farm Life and Landscapes

Slogans for many California towns might reveal the importance of a particular crop. We have already reviewed Selma's raisin slogan. It replaced their "Home of the Peach" slogan in the 1960s. Town festivals also celebrate the historic importance of certain crops. There's the Stockton Asparagus Festival, Gilroy Garlic Festival, Escondido's Grape Stomp, Dixon's Lambtown Cook-Off, Courtland's Pear Fair, Petaluma's Butter and Egg Day Parade, and the annual strawberry festivals, such as those in Oxnard and Garden Grove.

The timing of harvests can also transform an otherwise tranquil town with a flurry of activity as a ripened crop is picked, processed, and shipped to market. We have already reviewed some of these seasonal crops, such as grapes. Peach, plum, and nectarine harvests peak during mid-to-late summer. California peach and nectarine harvests peaked at 400,000 packages per day during

Summer's green, bucolic landscapes will turn bitter cold during harsh winters in the Fall River Valley, northeastern California.

summer picking seasons in the 1990s, but dropped to about 40,000 per day by September. Nectarines are usually gone by October, while plums last about four weeks longer because there are late-harvest varieties. Even a few late-harvest peaches last until early November, such as the Last Chance variety, grown in mountains above the Antelope Valley.

The center of melon production is the Westside area of the San Joaquin Valley around Mendota. These melons also peak out by late summer, but the Imperial Valley produces melons during winter. All of this also plays an important role in transforming market shelves and produce displays.

An especially hot summer can ripen so many crops so quickly that farm workers are pushed to the limit. This was the case in the Central Valley in 1996 and a few other years of that decade. Cantaloupes, grapes, nectarines, plums, peaches, tomatoes, onions, and garlic were being harvested at frenzied paces. In Raisin City, the table, wine, and raisin grapes were all ripening at the same time. Workers, growers, and even newspaper reporters were calling it "A Harvest in Hell."

These rural landscapes of the Central Valley reflect the industrial farm; they are not scenic like those in the Napa Valley or other parts of California. During such hot summers, the **migrant workers** (mostly from Mexico) can't work hard enough to keep up with the harvest. Many of the workers have second or third seasonal jobs during the off season.

International Trade

California farmers are increasingly looking to other countries (especially Pacific Rim nations) as potential markets. California produce is showing up in Japanese markets at cheaper prices than some Japanese produce. A combi-nation of Japanese market deregulations, changing Japanese tastes, and California farmers more willing to produce products for Japanese appetites is helping.

Japan already buys more than $2.7 billion of agricultural products from California annually, more than one-half of all agricultural products exported from the United States to Japan. California broccoli from Salinas, beef, and fresh and processed fruits are especially popular. On some California farms, products such as cherries and pumpkins may be grown specifically for Japanese markets. Even rice is being exported from California to Japan.

Sales of U.S. beef to Japan totalled more than $2.1 billion per year and were increasing during the 1990s. Much of that export is from California. Because U.S. beef demand is sluggish, the California beef industry exports are crucial to the industry. The U.S. Meat Export Federation and the California Beef Council work to "educate" Japanese consumers about high quality U.S. beef.

Just as California farmers look to other markets, producers in other countries are competing for their share of the U.S. market. Mexican fruit and vegetable imports into the United States doubled in ten years from 1979 to 1989 to more than $1 billion, all before free trade agreements. Even with high tariffs, imports of Mexican frozen broccoli and cauliflower soared 500 percent during the 1980s, cutting the U.S. share of the market by nearly half. About 5,000 frozen-food industry jobs that relied on those crops were lost in Santa Cruz and Monterey counties.

California's growers, including some of the largest (especially those who have farmed in the Salinas and Imperial Valleys), began investing in Mexico. Particularly in northern Baja and other Mexican border states, California growers were pouring money into broccoli, lettuce, celery, onions, zucchinis, tomatoes, and other crops long before free trade became reality.

FAMILY- AND COMMUNITY-SUPPORTED FARMS

Tremendous variations in the nature and sizes of California farms produces diverse agricultural landscapes. Pete Andrew is a third-generation family farmer whose father first bought and then added acreage to their farm on the west side of the San Joaquin Valley. It is now 4,500 acres of wheat, cotton, almonds and table, raisin, and wine grapes—big enough to be considered a corporate farm, but still family operated. The entire family works the farm. Pete Andrew uses modern survey techniques, including a tripod and laser, to keep his land level. These efforts especially came in handy after the New Year's flood of 1997. The grapes survived, but he and other farmers were worried about almond trees susceptible to root rot.

A new kind of family farm is becoming important in California agribusiness. The **community-supported agriculture** (CSA) idea was probably imported into California from Japan in the 1980s. Full Belly Farm in Guinda, California, is north of Sacramento. During the mid-1990s, its 100 acres fed about 500 families, mainly from Berkeley and Oakland. Nearly 150 families were on the waiting list to become members of this CSA farm. For a weekly fee, they will get one bag full of baby beets, broccoli, carrots, cilantro, cauliflower, red Russian kale, lettuce, and red onion and one pound of potatoes. During open-house weekends, members are invited to visit the farm, tend to the crops, and even help with chores. In 1990, there were only two CSA farms in California; by 1997, there were seventy and that number grew toward the twenty-first century.

By supporting these family farms, a growing number of Californians were expressing their concerns about generic products flowing in from corporate farms. Others were supporting local farmers' markets that offer products grown on local family farms.

CALIFORNIA AND MEXICAN WINES: A RICH HISTORY

Spanish missionaries were already making wines in the Valley of Santo Tomas in Baja, California, during the late 1700s. The Santo Tomas winery was founded there in 1888 to take advantage of the cool evening ocean breezes. This $12 million Ensenada winery, Mexico's second-oldest winery, has embarked on a joint venture with California's Wente Vineyards in Livermore Valley, which is America's oldest family-owned winery, founded in 1883.

Wente Vineyards managed nearly 3,000 acres on the Central Coast and produced about 400,000 cases of wine annually in the 1990s; about half was exported to such countries as Switzerland, Canada, Russia, Lithuania and Ukraine, and even Israel and Chile. Now, this first Mexican-American ultra-premium wine will blend equal parts of Baja and Alta California grapes and sell in both countries.

Agricultural companies in northern California have also moved many U.S.-owned factories south of the border to maquiladoras, where American raw products are assembled into finished goods and sold to U.S. consumers. Crinklaw Farms Gourmet Decoratives of King City was shipping garlic and flowers 500 miles south to Baja, where they were made into decorative braids and wreaths by workers making much lower wages than their California counterparts. These garlic and flower wreaths were selling for up to $50 in the United States. Products ranging from Frito Lay's Munchos potato crisps to Foster Farms gourmet chicken drummettes were also prepared in Mexico for the U.S. market.

Many farmers are supporters of free trade with Mexico, but are afraid of losing their industries at home; these fears have been expressed by members of the Western Growers Association. Their approximately 1,500 members in California and Arizona produce about one-half of all fresh fruit and vegetables in the United States. These produce growers wanted preferential treatment in any pact with Mexico, though the forty Western Growers Association directors were also in some way involved in Mexican agriculture. While California's fresh vegetable farms may need protection, millions of Mexico's inefficient rural grain farmers will also have to be protected from American growers; some consensus for phased-in free trade developed from these pressures.

Problems on the Farm

Disease, Pests, and Poisons For more than a century, wars have raged against the long list of potentially devastating diseases and pests that have threatened California agricultural products. One example is the leaf-damaging bacterium injected by tiny insects known as sharpshooters. Once called California vine disease, its modern name is Pierce's disease. Other recent names reflect its threat to so many plants: alfalfa dwarf, almond

A CHEMICAL WAR

For decades, controversy has erupted over how to control disease and pests on California farms. Biological controls are often considered safer and more efficient in the long run than other methods. California's first large-scale biocontrol started during the 1880s, when a fly and beetle were introduced from Australia to keep the Vidalia beetle from destroying the state's citrus industry. Various species of whitefly continued to threaten crops, especially in Southern California into the twenty-first century. The introduction of a small stingless wasp successfully controlled an outbreak of ash whitefly in the early 1990s. Meanwhile, research scientists and entomologists were searching for parasites to control the spread of silverleaf whitefly.

Extensive crop dusting to control disease and pests has received increasing scrutiny, especially near California's expanding housing developments. Nearly 80 percent of the pesticides used in California agriculture are sprayed from the air, where they may drift five times farther than ground spraying. Every year, new stories of farm workers and residents accidently sprayed and sickened by drifting poisons make headlines in California.

Yet, crop dusters are often required to work long hours when spraying conditions for herbicides, pesticides, and fertilizers are favorable, and they sometimes must fly within five feet of orchards at speeds up to 140 mph. This is hazardous work! The days of using ground spotters and flashlights for accurate spraying are being replaced with GPS (using satellites) and other modern techniques, larger planes, and helicopters. Perhaps this explains why the number of crop dusters in California dropped from more than 1,000 to less than 500 from the mid-1980s to the mid-1990s. Larger crop dusting companies with more capital and insurance were dominating the industry, reflecting a trend in farm size and California agriculture in general during the last half of the 1900s.

Some citizen groups have organized to fight aerial spraying and to cut the use of poisons on California farms. Citizens Against Pesticide Exposure encouraged San Diego County to impose spraying restrictions within 50 to 200 feet of homes during the 1990s. Similar restrictions have become common in other communities.

One less conventional response to these problems and demands became more popular into the twenty-first century. "Bug bombers" were being introduced in the San Joaquin Valley. In these efforts, "good bugs" or their eggs were sprayed on fields. These were predators of pests that consumed and damaged crops. Perhaps more interesting was the method of spreading these predators—small "model" planes, flown by remote controls from the ground, were used. This is yet another innovation that encourages more precise pest control without the use of dangerous poisons.

Some consumers are using their purchasing power to change the nature of California agriculture by purchasing certified organically-grown farm products. Organic agriculture has become a multi-$100 million industry in the state. These products are now available to nearly every Californian from local farmers' markets, cooperatives, health food stores, and even traditional supermarkets. The UC-Sustainable Agriculture Research and Education Program is just one example of the research invested to meet these consumer demands and produce foods using fewer poisons.

---

leaf scorch, and even oleander scorch. Regardless of the name used, Pierce's disease has made grape growing in Los Angeles County virtually impossible since the 1880s. It forced northern California grape growers to destroy more than $18 million of vines during the 1990s.

University and government researchers were teaming up with farmers and Caltrans to control the sharpshooters who carry the bacteria. (Caltrans estimated that their oleanders lining California highways were worth up to $100 million during the 1990s.) Planting sticky traps, eliminating host plants, planting more resistant crops, and introducing predator beetles, bats, and birds helped the problem. A few farmers received special permits to apply costly, powerful, and controversial pesticides considered by many as desperate, short-term measures. Losses due to sharpshooters followed the destruction caused by the root louse, which ravaged grape vines during the 1980s. By the 1990s, though grape and wine demand were up, production had decreased, causing a sharp rise in prices.

Nevertheless, acreage planted in grapes expanded rapidly during the 1990s.

Encroaching Developments Transform Landscapes   For decades, California's multiplying populations have gobbled up some of the richest and most productive farmland in the world. Concerned observers have repeatedly seen their warnings about disappearing farmland bulldozed by the latest development. Since the mid-1900s, activists and leaders have even passed legislation to encourage farmers to hold on to their land in the face of impending urban encroachment. The Williamson Act may have been the most ambitious of these efforts. California farmers were guaranteed lower property taxes if they promised to continue farming and not sell out to developers. Unfortunately, the success of such laws suffered from the realities of geography.

The farmers who benefitted most from the incentives were too far from urban areas or developments to even

Farmland and ranches between San Luis Obispo and Morro Bay are being gobbled up so quickly, changes are evident from year to year. Along the central coast, you know that the next development is coming to a farm or ranch near you.

consider selling out. Those who were next in line for development and were the targets of such farmland conservation efforts had properties worth too much to keep. These trends continued through the 1990s. Developers in the San Joaquin Valley were offering up to $30,000 per acre for cotton farms worth about $4,000 per acre as agricultural land, while cotton prices wildly fluctuated each year. It is not surprising that many farmers sell out and take the big profits rather than continue their struggle to earn relatively insignificant financial rewards on the farm.

The Central Valley (which has about 7 million acres of productive farmland), gets much of the attention in this controversy. According to the California Department of Conservation, more than 20,000 acres of some of the most fertile Central Valley farmland is being consumed by developments each year. Within a ten-year period between 1984 and 1994, the San Joaquin Valley lost more than 153,000 acres of farmland and gained more than 65,000 acres of urban areas. The Sacramento Valley lost more than 100,000 acres of farmland and gained more than 35,000 acres of urban sprawl. That totalled more than 261,000 acres of farmland lost in the valley and more than 100,000 acres of urban areas added from 1984 to 1994.

All of this encroachment continues in the valley that produces about 25 percent of the nation's table food and after the country has spent billions throughout decades reclaiming the land for agriculture. About $2 billion of U.S. tax money has been spent just to build the valley's irrigation projects for agriculture; many more billions have subsidized the industry to keep it productive.

Transformation of farms to urban land has been especially quick in Kern County in general and the area around Bakersfield in particular. Kern County lost about 90,000 acres of agriculture and gained about 20,000 acres of urban space in one decade before the late 1990s. The

county even dissolved its planning commission so developers could take full control of the process.

More than 12 percent of original cropland has already been converted to urban uses in the Central Valley; another one-third of it (about 2.5 million acres) is expected to be lost during the next four decades. Los Banos is a good example; it is a cotton and dairy town that doubled in population from the mid-1980s through the 1990s to more than 20,000.

Numerous California towns and cities are adding distant housing tracts for added tax money to pay off growing debts. Unfortunately, many of the new developments are so far from the center of town, they are costing more in services than they produce in tax revenues. Some of the fastest growing cities had some of the fastest deteriorating economies during the 1990s. A few were so poor (including Wasco and Arvin), they considered disincorporating.

Many experts predict that there are only a few ways to solve the problems—develop closer to the urban centers with higher densities, or increase fees to developers or taxes to residents to pay for distant infrastructures. Increasing developers' fees is unlikely to happen because developers can go elsewhere, pitting community against community. Developers can easily skip over communities with long-term planning or growth controls and go to those without; after all, there is so much land for the picking.

Many problems have resulted from rampant development. Devaluation of homes was the result of overbuilding and the early 1990s recession; huge estates were purchased for around $200,000 even into the late-1990s. Some new homeowners complain about the lack of services, including sewers. Others worry about the "Los Angelezation" of the valley. Much of the land being developed belongs to absentee corporate land owners. Finally, once the housing tracks spring up, the residents

LOSING THE FARM OVER AND OVER AGAIN

CREEPING URBAN SPRAWL

The *Los Angeles Times* reported in late 1996 about the Tevelde family dairy farm just outside Modesto along the Stanislaus River. George Tevelde, Sr., had to sell the family dairy in Paramount and move to Chino in the 1950s when developers moved in. The Teveldes sold their family farm in Chino during the 1970s and moved to Modesto for the same reasons, only to watch Modesto grow toward them during the 1990s.

In the little town of Patterson (the apricot capital of the world), a new subdivision was approved in the mid-1990s. It would be built by Kaufman and Broad and would double the town's population, then at 10,000. Developers were confident they could draw on populations over the hills in the Bay Area to the west. Nearby is Grayson, where homes in similar subdivisions were sold to commuters who got tired of the drive and moved out, some labelling it "Grayslum." Owners complained that promised services never appeared. Today, some of the very urban problems people were trying to escape are invading the valley.

Repeated patterns of lost farms and growing developments within the most fertile valleys have become an expected part of the California story and its landscapes; they are almost as reliable as seasonal cycles. Much of the most productive coastal valley soils—from the San Diego and Los Angeles areas, to the Ventura/Oxnard Plain, to the Salinas Valley and into the Bay Area—have already been paved. Dates may be different, but the story lines are hauntingly similar.

FROM CROPS TO COMPUTERS

Today's computer industry center, the Santa Clara Valley, serves as one of the most dramatic examples of productive farmland lost to industrial development and associated home development. Before the 1970s, vegetable farms required relatively small, skilled permanent labor forces to run the farms, tractors, and irrigation systems. Up to ten times more migratory workers were required for brief periods to seasonally weed and harvest the crops. By the 1970s, vegetables were yielding to fruits and nuts on land that had nearly doubled in value. By the 1990s, engineering and high-tech industries and their housing developments had consumed almost the entire valley. Engineers, entrepreneurs, and business executives are now running the valley, and large numbers of low-income workers, many migratory, still provide services for these new industries.

---

complain about farmers spraying or the smell of nearby dairies.

Flood and Drought Historical floods and droughts have impacted all Californians, but farmers have been especially hard hit. The 1997 floods were just another reminder of the vulnerability of California farmlands. (Today's new, adjacent, growing developments are also vulnerable to these flood events.) After only several days of heavy mountain rains, about 100,000 acres of crops worth more than $250 million were damaged or destroyed by flooding in early January that year. Small farmers, dairies, and those raising livestock, wine grapes, alfalfa, and broccoli were most affected.

Ten feet of water in the Danna and Danna packing house in Yuba City drowned tractors and other equipment. One beekeeper lost $150,000 of hives that floated away. Tons of rice straw were carried away, and farmers were forced to relevel rice and row crop fields, fill in channels, and remove debris. Cleanup costs ranged up to $500 per acre. Tens of thousands of cows had to be evacuated. Cows that did not drown lost the routines that are so vital for milk production, and farmers lost stored feed and feed crops in the fields. Nearly 150,000 acres of winter wheat were also affected. Once again, Tulare Lake reappeared over farmland in the San Joaquin Valley. It briefly began to resemble those centuries before reclamation when Native Americans and early explorers navigated its waters.

All of the 1997 flood destruction still had little impact on the monstrous and diverse California agricultural output. Yet, it is clear why so many California water stories deserved the attention they received in Chapter 6. About 80 percent of the state's water is used by agriculture, and there is growing competition between agriculture and encroaching urban communities for water resources. Agriculture typically uses 27 million acre-feet annually, while Los Angeles city uses about 500,000 acre-feet. Urban agencies are pushing for the creation of a statewide water market in California to allow farmers to sell their irrigation water to cities.

Agricultural interests and farming communities fear negative impacts as more farmland is left fallow by these policies. Demands for fertilizer, seeds, machinery, and other goods related to crop production and jobs in agriculture might decrease. Meanwhile, groups such as the MWD and Bay Area Economic Forum are often leading proponents of water sales. They say impacts will be far less than the 700,000 acres voluntarily left fallow in 1991 under the federal price support program. Some environ-

---

FROM FLOODS TO FARMS IN THE SAN JOAQUIN VALLEY

Prior to flood control, The Tule, Kaweah, Kings, and Kern Rivers naturally flooded the San Joaquin Valley with more than 1,200 square miles of water between what is now Corcoran and Kettleman City. Yokut Indians fished from rafts and canoes made of tule reeds while women dug for clams and mussels. The Spanish first called it La Laguna de los Tulares. White settlers called it Mussel Slough as commercial fishermen caught turtles for delicacies sold in California cities. It was considered the largest fresh body of water west of the Mississippi.

In the late 1800s, the government sold much of the land to "sandlappers" who would farm it. They were re-

funded $2 of their $2.50 per acre price if they built levees to reclaim the land. By the 1930s, all of the basin had been reclaimed except during the greatest flood years. Colonel James G. Boswell from Georgia and Clarence Salyer from Virginia eventually bought up most of the land, then engaged in a notorious feud (mostly over water) that divided Corcoran for decades. Eventually, the families settled after the two died, and Corcoran continued its claim as the "Farming Capital of the World." Even with the great water projects (especially the Pine Flat Dam on the Kings River), surrounding rivers have briefly flooded and refilled the lake, such as in 1983 and 1997.

---

mentalists and others claim it will encourage water conservation in rural areas. We can only wait to see the results of these trends.

Illegal Crops The "**Emerald Triangle**" within moist northern California forests gained a reputation as California's marijuana-growing capital during the 1970s and 1980s. Some local residents feeling the pinch of the timber recession opted to secretly cultivate this illegal crop. Marijuana growing and selling eventually became one of the most lucrative economic activities for some of these communities. This helps explain why, for several years, marijuana became the number one cash crop in the state. Stereotypes of laid-back hippies growing pot in quiet northern California forests were first shattered when some small battles broke out, not only with law enforcement officials but between growers and thieves.

Then, in September, 1996, federal and local law enforcement agencies seized more than 500 marijuana plants worth $2 million in the Angeles National Forest in the San Gabriel Mountains. This action, coinciding with raids on homes in the Los Angeles area, busted the largest one-family cartel in the state. Modern plantations were found camouflaged on public land and protected by guards with high-powered weapons and modern communications systems. A new kind of agribusiness had invaded California, and by the 1990s, most of the illegal plants seized were actually from Southern California mountains.

Though marijuana grows as a weed, it requires some irrigation and great care to grow a commercial quality crop. Marijuana growers often cut trees and slaughter wildlife that gets in their way. Many of the farmers dam, reroute, and pollute water courses, use fertilizers that kill native plants, and use poisons to kill rats, rabbits, and other animals that might eat the plants. The Forest Service calls the farmers "dopers." This adds to the drama

in the nation's most used national forest landscapes above Los Angeles, where stories of gang fights and dead bodies made the news during the late 1900s.

Fishing Industry

California (along with Alaska and a few Gulf of Mexico states) has traditionally been among the leading fish producing states in the United States. The commercial fish catch in California peaked in 1936 at about 800 million kilograms (1.76 billion pounds). The majority of this catch was sardines, 70 percent came from California waters, and most were landed at northern California ports. After sardine production crashed in the 1940s, northern canneries were left in decline, and southern ports took the spotlight. By the 1970s, less than half of the catch came from California waters, especially due to the tuna caught off Mexico.

The state's catch oscillated around 227 million kg per year (500 million pounds) during the 1960s. During the 1970s, the state's catch soared to more than 408 million kg per year (900 million pounds). Then, during the 1980s, 227 million kg per year (500 million pounds) could be considered a banner year. According to the California Department of Fish and Game, value of the state's total catch hovered around $200 million per year going into the 1990s. Fluctuations in pounds and value of the annual catches continued into the 1990s. The 1997–1998 El Nino that devastated commercial fishing is a dramatic example.

Los Angeles area landings (where boats load and unload), which include L.A. and Orange Counties, accounted for nearly half of the total annual catch during the 1990s. These District 2 ports include L.A., San Pedro, Dana Harbor, Long Beach, Malibu, Redondo Beach, and Santa Monica. Here are the other California ports

RECREATIONAL FISHING

The San Diego charter boat industry claims to be the oldest, largest, and most experienced fishing fleet on the West Coast. Bass, large tuna, barracuda, and marlin are typically hauled in as favorites. During warm water years (such as 1997–1998), one of the most prized catches appears—yellowtail. Excitement on the docks can quickly fill charter boats from San Diego headed south off Ensenada (which has declared itself the yellowtail capital of the world). Before populations dropped so dramatically that limits were imposed, San Diego even sponsored an annual Yellowtail Fishing Contest to see who could catch the most. Yellowtail has earned a reputation as a stubborn fish that will fight to the finish. It has also earned a special place in the hearts of recreational anglers.

Recreational fishing on California streams, rivers, and lakes has fueled another multimillion-dollar industry. Bait, tackle, and other fishing gear, recreation and transportation equipment, and food and lodging are all required for a successful fishing adventure. Trout fishing alone is a multi-million dollar industry in California. People working in the state's sporting goods stores and in local rural economies near fishing holes are grateful.

arranged according to the California Department of Fish and Game by district (a list of traditional locations follows each district).

District 1: San Diego Area
   San Diego, Imperial Beach, Mission Bay, Oceanside

District 3: Santa Barbara Area
   Santa Barbara, Oxnard, Port Hueneme, Morro Bay, Ventura, Avila Beach

District 4: Monterey Area
   Monterey, Moss Landing, Santa Cruz

District 5: San Francisco Area
   San Francisco, Princeton, Half Moon Bay, Bodega Bay

District 6: Eureka Area
   Eureka, Fort Bragg, Crescent City

The fishing fleet at Noyo Harbor, Fort Bragg, displays the fishing industry's importance to local economies of the northwest coast.

There is also considerable fluctuation in marine species that lead the state in weight or value in any given year. Tuna and salmon were far and away the leaders in value (more than $40 million per year) going into the 1990s. However, greater amounts (in weight) of mackerel and squid were taken to California ports than any other catch. Then, the El Nino of 1997–1998 changed the industry again and devastated the squid catch. Other very important species included sea urchin, groundfish/rockfish, sole, dungeness crab, swordfish, shrimp/prawn, and Pacific herring. Note, again, that the order of these top California catches changed radically during the 1990s (see the sections on sea urchin and squid).

There were more than 14,000 professional fishers working on some 8,000 commercial fishing boats in California into the 1990s. Additionally, about 5,000 people worked in California fish processing and wholesaling industries. This is a far cry from the sardine boom of the 1930s, but it is significant. It is so significant that exports of fish and other seafood products (after processing) totalled more than $400 million, ranking fifth among other California agricultural exports during the mid-1990s. Recreational and other anglers on California's commercial passenger fishing vessels also played important roles in port economies. They hauled in more rockfish, bass, mackerel, and bonito than any other fish.

In this wildly fluctuating market, modern fish farmers who are establishing fisheries may hold the key to the future. Catfish and trout have been the favorite products among California's more than three-hundred freshwater aquaculturists; there are also more than fifty saltwater fish farms in the state. The California Aquaculture Association estimated in the late 1990s that about 70 percent of the state's aquaculture production was in the Coachella and Imperial Valleys. Is it possible that aquaculture businesses could take control of the state's fishing industry much like agribusiness now dominates farming? These fish farmers are increasingly impacting California's landscapes.

Tuna

Many historians have written about the famed sardine industry and canneries that thrived in northern California earlier in the 1900s, but did you know that the Terminal Island Canneries once covered nearly 10 acres and employed up to 10,000 people next to Fish Harbor in Southern California? It started in 1903 when A. P. Halfhill experimented by canning tuna that at that time were not popular for eating. Taste tests at the L.A. County Fair in Pomona were so positive that tuna canneries grew around Fish Harbor and then spread to San Diego.

Thousands of workers eventually flocked by ferry from San Pedro or over the Henry Ford Bridge. Canneries included Starkist, Bumble Bee, and Chicken of the Sea until the early 1980s, when all had moved to cheaper labor pools in less developed economies. Pan Pacific Fisheries was the only one left until it closed in September, 1995. Many Latina workers who had been canners for twenty years were left with no jobs.

Tri-Marine International bought the Pan Pacific factory, formed partnerships with canneries in Thailand and San Diego, and started shipping out tuna again in July, 1996. Many of the same Latina workers returned. It is located at Cannery and Barracuda streets. Only 250 workers are needed today at the cannery, but the tuna comes from boats fishing off the California coast. The frozen fish are unloaded into the cannery's freezer, cooked and steamed, cleaned and separated into white meat for human consumption and red meat for pets, then canned. S&W is one of the labels canned there. Major publications such as the *Los Angeles Times* have highlighted this turnaround.

Lobster

Rocky reefs along the Southern California coast make great habitats for numerous species, some endangered and depleted. Fishermen harvest squid, urchins, mackerel, and lobster from these coastal waters. About 300 fishermen harvested approximately 500,000 pounds of lobster in California waters worth about $3.6 million each year during the 1990s. Many of these are large lobster operations with big boats and hundreds of traps. Some small lobster fishermen still thrive with a few hundred traps. A few smaller-scale lobster fishermen sell their catches to downtown L.A. wholesalers, who often then sell to Asian markets. Many were worried about the Malibu City Council's move in 1997 to make their 27-mile coastal strip a marine refuge of no-take zones.

Abalone

Nearly all the abalone harvested in the nation comes from California. It is a one-shelled mollusk related to clams, scallops, octopuses, and squids. It attaches itself to submerged rocks in shallow water and feeds off plants. Indians ate abalone and used its shell. Japanese fishermen dominated the abalone industry near the Monterey peninsula from about 1900 until the Japanese were interned during World War II and their boats impounded after 1942. It is said that abalone was first pounded to become thin and tender for an abalone stew in Monterey, where the dish became famous.

In California, the peak abalone harvests were in the 1950s, when 5 million pounds of wild abalone per year were harvested. The numbers were dropping quickly after the 1960s. Recently, the harvest dropped to only 260,000 pounds per year, and some abalone species are near extinction. Over-harvesting, poaching, sea otters, coastal pollution, and development (habitat destruction) are to blame, which led to necessary restrictions on abalone harvesting. Prices are skyrocketing, as live abalone in the shell has sold for up to $25 per pound wholesale. The result is a boom in abalone farming.

U.S. Abalone operates a 4-acre farm north of Santa Cruz. Tons of abalone are raised in fifty plastic tanks. They are fed kelp. U.S. Abalone was the first California aquaculture company to sell stock to the public, though aquaculture in the rest of the nation has become big business. By the late 1990s, Abalone Farm in Cayucos was nearly ten times larger than U.S. Abalone, and there were about five other competitors in California.

The State Department of Fish and Game estimates that total California aquaculture ventures are worth about $60 million. They often involve large investments of time and money and lots of patience. Red abalone is the largest native to California and best suited to aquaculture. However, growing at one inch per year, it requires three-and-a-half years to reach desirable sizes. Most abalone sold in the United States goes to Asia or to upscale restaurants. Asia consumes the greatest amount of the world's abalone harvests.

Sea Urchin

According to officials at the State Department of Fish and Game, there are about five-hundred urchin divers in California, mostly in Santa Barbara and Ventura Counties. They are in a class known as marine harvesters, which includes those taking abalone. Fatality rates are much higher than for recreational divers, often a result of divers staying down too long to increase their profits.

Urchins are relatively easy to harvest, but you must first buy a permit from the California Department of Fish and Game and be an experienced diver. Divers navigate boats into kelp beds where the urchins feed and dive into about 45–60 feet of water. The urchins are placed into baskets and hauled to the surface. The winter harvesting season runs seven days a week from November through March.

ECONOMIC FORCES IN THE TIMBER INDUSTRY

During the construction and economic boom of the 1980s, California timber harvests increased again to more than 4.5 billion board feet—valued at more than $650 million—per year. (A board foot, the standard measure of timber, equals one square foot of lumber one inch thick. About one million board feet is required to build one-hundred homes.) During many of these years, timber harvests exceeded the rate of regrowth. In prior years, harvesting on private lands had gradually decreased, leaving public forest lands to fill the void. By 1988, timber harvests only from California's U.S. Forest Service lands soared to nearly 2.2 billion board feet valued at about $233 million. Nevertheless, private lands were still producing more timber than the state's public lands.

Unfortunately, the 1980s boom in timber cutting brought insignificant employment opportunities to timber-dependent economies. By the 1990s, revolutionary changes in the industry, a deep economic recession, and environmental concerns about overharvesting had taken their toll on timber production and timber economies throughout the state.

Storms frequently keep divers on land, but they can harvest from $500–$1,000 per day of sea urchins in favorable conditions. The Santa Barbara Channel supports near-perfect environments for urchin, where water temperatures are ideal and kelp is abundant. Urchins are the biggest cash crop for commercial divers in Santa Barbara and Ventura Counties.

California once encouraged urchin destruction because these spiny creatures eat so much valuable kelp. However, by the 1990s, Japanese markets had helped increase their value up to $2 per pound. The Japanese are using the urchin's roe for sushi. Urchin fans are quick to note that since the 1980s, the value of sea urchin harvests has frequently topped the salmon and crab industries in California, making it the largest fishery in the state. Up to 10,000 people (from marina operators to truck drivers to airline personnel) realize some economic benefits from this industry in California, which may be valued at up to $75 million each year.

Enthusiasts also remind us that the sea urchin population grew so large in the 1960s that they were destroying kelp beds in Southern California. Harvesting sea urchin helps prevent this problem by keeping their populations in check. Healthy kelp beds provide food and shelter for many other marine species.

Squid

Here is yet another example of the powerful connections between California's natural resources, its people, and their economic activities. By 1997, squid had moved ahead of sea urchin as the state's number one cash catch from the ocean. This mollusk has a cylindrical body, eight "arms," two tentacles, and powerful suction cups. Calamari had become very popular especially among Pacific Rim nations such as China; more than 175 million pounds worth more than $33 million were caught off California in one year.

Conflicts erupted as commercial fishing fleets from Oregon, Washington, and beyond began invading California waters to compete with the state's fishing industry. These out-of-staters parked their boats especially off Monterey, Santa Barbara, Ventura, and points south and were catching about 30 percent of the squid harvest by 1997. California's fishermen were worried that overharvesting would quickly deplete squid, much like other overzealous harvests had destroyed past seafood resources. Industry lobbyists were battling for legislation to limit annual squid catches.

Then, the 1998 El Nino devastated the squid industry. As squid fled from warmer waters, many commercial fishermen were returning home with almost no squid catch. The California fishing industry's economic roller coaster ride continued.

Forestry

California is second only to Oregon in the production of forest products. Nearly one-third of California is naturally covered with some sort of forest. About half of those forests grow on federal government lands and about 45 percent are on privately owned land. However, only about half of all the state's forests—or less than 18 percent (18 million acres) of all California lands—are productive forests. These are considered capable of producing at least 20 cubic feet of usable wood per acre each year.

Most of those productive forests (just under 17 million acres) are considered commercial timber acreage. Within those productive forests, about nine million acres are federally owned or managed. (Eight million acres are supervised by the National Forest Service, whose role is to manage multiple uses on its lands, including sustainable timber harvests.) Nearly 7.5 million acres of productive forests are in private hands.

The timber industry estimates that more than 100,000 people in the state are employed in industries that are at least indirectly related to forest resources. These range from private landowners, loggers, workers in sawmills, paper, and other manufacturing industries, and professional foresters and wildlife biologists. However, these jobs represent only a tiny percentage of California's economy and total workforce. Combined wood product, paper, and pulp industries typically account for less than 5 percent of the state's manufacturing employment.

Where Is the Timber?

Most timber production is concentrated within northern California's mountainous territory, which is a southern extension of the Pacific Northwest timber belt. The leading counties are usually Humboldt, Mendocino, Siskiyou, Shasta, Trinity, Del Norte, and Plumas. It is within these rural landscapes where local economies may rely on the timber industry.

Within these rural populations and landscapes, debates continue to rage. How much timber can be harvested each year while sustaining the long-term productivity of our forests? Should we be concerned only with short-term profits or should we establish sustainable yields and long-term productivity? Should we protect and preserve what is left of our forests in their natural conditions? Each landscape reveals how local and regional populations and private landowners have answered these questions. These landscapes also reflect the attitudes Californians have about their forests and rural treasures. Today, these landscapes and their resources are subject to increasing pressures from growing populations and global corporations with diverse interests and values.

The Most Valuable Trees

Which trees were most valuable to the timber industry during the last decades of the 1900s? More than 80 percent of all sawtimber in California came from softwoods (conifers). The greatest *volume* of timber and largest *number* of logs came from Douglas fir. Different species of true firs ranked second. They were followed by ponderosa and Jeffrey pines, coast redwood, sugar pine, and incense cedar. Hardwoods (deciduous trees, especially oaks) accounted for less than 20 percent of the state's timber production volume. Rankings change when the *value* of those harvests are considered. California's most valuable saw logs came from ponderosa pine and coast redwood (see Map 9.2). They were followed by Douglas fir, sugar pine, and the true firs. These statistics especially underscore the exceptional quality and high per volume value of redwood lumber.

Coast Redwood (*Sequoia sempervirens*) grows only along the northwest coastal slopes where there is heavy winter rain, persistent summer fog, and rich soils. Some old-growth redwoods are well over 1,000 years old and have been measured as the tallest trees in the world. New redwoods quickly sprout from old trunks even after they have been cut. More hardy Douglas fir (*Pseudotsuga menziesii*) grow from moist coastal to inland locations well beyond the fog belt that confines coast redwood. Under proper conditions of sun, soil, and moisture, both of these trees grow fast, straight, and tall and are prized by the timber industry. Less common redwood is famous for its natural beauty and resistance to decay and pests even after it is cut. This is very different from the Sierra Redwood (*Sequoiadendron giganteum*), which splinters into myriad pieces when cut and is not as valuable to the timber industry.

Valuable true fir include White Fir (*Abies concolor*), with its light-colored trunk and blue-green needles that point upward from the stem. Sugar pine have the longest cones and sugar-like crust that seeps from scars on the trunk. Incense Cedar (*Libocedrus decurrens*) has flat branchlets and a reddish trunk some might mistake for redwood. Finally, Ponderosa Pine (*Pinus ponderosa*), with its long, yellow-green needles, is the most famous of the "yellow pines." It is common in drier forests throughout the western states. More information about the nature of California's forests and other plant communities is found in Chapter 5.

Managing Our Forests

How can we use our forests to benefit the greatest number of people and diverse interests, while we assure that these resources will be available to future generations? You will get a wide range of answers from each interest group. The debate about clear cutting versus selective cutting is just one example. **Clear cutting** is preferred by many timber companies and foresters for most species. An entire stand of trees is cut down within an area at one time. Easy access to one clear cut will provide a large volume of timber from a small area that can make a very profitable harvest with the least effort. Great devastation over that area may cause accelerated soil erosion, mass wasting, and other problems, but it also opens that area to sunlight, hopefully for quick regrowth.

With **selective cutting**, trees are chosen by their species, age, and condition as the forest is thinned out. Though there is less total devastation in one area, access must be provided to loggers. Logging roads and other disturbances are less intense, but they are spread over a wider area and so are the profits from the harvest. Soil erosion and environmental degradation is extended along and near these access routes. The decision to do

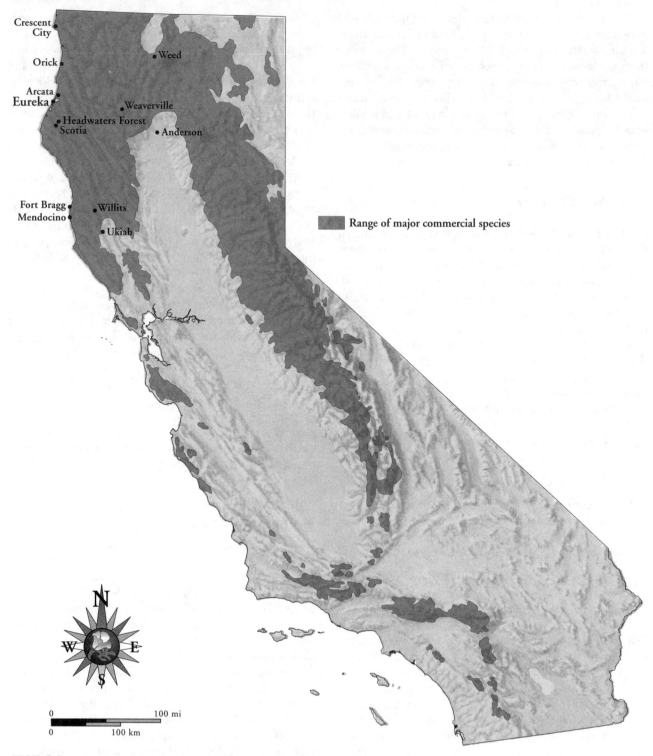

Crescent City

Orick

Weed

Arcata
Eureka

Weaverville

Headwaters Forest
Scotia

Anderson

Fort Bragg
Mendocino

Willits

Ukiah

Range of major commercial species

N
W   E
S

0   100 mi
0   100 km

MAP 9.2
California's productive timber country is concentrated in the north.

selective or clear cutting often depends on the type of forest and species, physical factors (such as climate, slope, drainage, and soil conditions), access to the area, surrounding land uses, and, of course, who owns and manages the land.

Processing Timber

Most of today's timber industries are equipped with modern technology that uses every part of a tree. Logs are first debarked. Bark is used in decorative landscaping or

WHAT ARE SUSTAINABLE HARVESTS?

Today, most of the state's forests are tree farms. The timber industry is correct in pointing out that 35 million seedlings were being planted each year during the late 1900s and that there were actually more trees growing in California than in past decades. However, these new seedlings are susceptible to insects and feeding animals, droughts and other brief weather extremes, fire, and competition with other vegetation. Most do not survive, and it takes many decades, and sometimes centuries, for a forest to return to its "natural" state after it has been logged.

Furthermore, the nature of most of California's productive forests has changed. Single species of denser and faster-growing seedlings have replaced most of the ancient giants and diverse species. Consequently, except within smaller acreage covered by national and state parks and wilderness areas, the forest landscapes you view and visit in California are probably at least second- or third-growth tree farms. The nature of those landscapes is often determined by whether the trees are cut within thirty, forty, fifty, or more years. Foresters and other concerned citizens still debate at what intervals a forest can be harvested to guarantee sustained yields and abundant resources for future generations.

---

potting soil or it is burned to generate energy. The logs (most are 32 feet long) are cut in sections for specific processing, often by extremely sharp blades that create less waste. They are sometimes first scanned by laser to determine the highest efficiency cuts.

Larger logs are sawed into lumber. Planing typically cuts boards ranging from 2″ × 4″ up to 2″ × 10″ and from 4″ × 4″ up to 4″ × 12.″ Other softwoods may be shaved into thin sheets of veneer that are glued together to make plywood. Leftover cores are used to make smaller wood products.

Sawdust and shavings from this processing are often used to make particle board. Smaller logs and wood pieces are chipped for engineered wood products and for pulp and paper. To make paper, the chips are first cooked with chemicals to separate fibers from lignin (their natural chemical glue). Water is drained and dried from sheets of the fibrous pulp, which is then rolled into paper. Even the leftover lignin may be burned for fuel or used in cosmetic or medicinal products.

All of these processes are parts of a California timber industry that has become more high tech and mechanized and less labor intensive. Such modernization continues to produce economic shock waves that are rippling into job markets and cultures across California's timber country landscapes.

Priorities in Our Forested Landscapes

Less than 10 percent of the original old-growth forest (and a much smaller percentage of old-growth redwood) remains in California. Signs of the battles over these remaining ancient forests and how to manage the larger expanses of productive timberlands are hard to miss. They are displayed in most northern California counties. The Trinity BioRegion Group is one example. It was organized by Trinity County residents to protect the area's plant and animal biodiversity and to end economic dependency on timber. Lost jobs resulting from international trade and industry automation have given more ammunition to such critics of the timber industry.

When unprocessed logs were being placed on ships to Asian manufacturing plants, locals argued that jobs were going with them. The level of pain was turned up a bit when Portland-based Louisiana Pacific opened a timber processing plant in Ensenada, Baja California, in 1989 in the midst of California's timber jobs recession. Ensenada workers were paid about $1.25 per hour for the same work that was once done in timber country for $6 per hour. California redwood logs were cut into lumber in Mexico and shipped back north, while Louisiana Pacific cut its northern California operations and work force. Eventually, the scarcity of redwood even sliced into the Ensenada operation.

Christmas Tree Farms

Though about three million Christmas trees are shipped from Oregon and Washington each year, there remain about three-hundred Christmas tree growers who sell choose-and-cut trees in California. These California growers sell about 600,000 choose-and-cut Christmas trees worth more than $14 million each year. The California Christmas Tree Growers, a choose-and-cut trade group based in Merced, is concerned about recent trends. Christmas tree lots, nurseries, and other green belts are being lost to more profitable parking lots and storage spaces, especially in Southern California.

Edison Company in particular has been gradually converting thousands of acres of its rights-of-way below power lines. The results may be that Christmas trees will more frequently be shipped from Oregon and Washington and bought at corner lots and urban markets. Here is yet another example of the connections between the state's changing land uses (or landscapes) and changing demographics and economies.

TWO STORIES OF THE MODERN TIMBER INDUSTRY

WEED

Nestled at the foot of Mount Shasta in the town of Weed, the conspicuous Morgan Veneer plant is just one example of the many timber employers that have played such important roles in the region's economies and landscapes. Weed was founded at the end of the nineteenth century by Abner E. Weed. With its consistent winds, he saw Weed as a good location to dry freshly-cut lumber. Weed Lumber Company was eventually bought out by International Paper in 1957 and then shut down in 1982. Employees who had worked for the plant, some for more than forty years, were forced into early retirement.

The owner of Roseburg Forest Products then bought the site with the intent of building a complete timber processing plant to match their big operation in Ritter, Oregon. Unfortunately, federal officials found dangerously contaminated soil left behind at the old Weed site. Plans for the new plant were stopped when its new owner could not afford the clean-up price. Nevertheless, Roseburg Forest Products continued to invest in Weed's school and other town projects, leading locals to speculate that its owner had not yet totally abandoned his plans or the town. Little Weed Historic Lumber Town Museum is an example of how community leaders are trying to sell recreation and attract tourism that might revive the economy within this picturesque landscape.

HEADWATERS FOREST

Southeast of Eureka and east of Fortuna and Scotia grow some of the tallest and most extensive redwood forests on private land. Family-owned Pacific Lumber Company had previously preserved the most sensitive forests and tallest trees until 1986, when Texas financier Charles Hurwitz orchestrated a hostile takeover of Pacific Lumber. He announced that all of the old-growth redwood would be cut by 2007. His critics argued that these majestic giants would pay for the junk bonds required to finance his deal, and the money would go to his Houston corporation.

Opponents tried to limit logging in the greatest old-growth redwood forest remaining in private hands (about 76,000 acres). Hurwitz responded by filing suit against the federal and state governments for hundreds of millions of dollars. At stake were spectacular trees more than 1,000 years old and up to 10 feet in diameter and 300 feet tall. Some publications claimed that the largest trees were worth up to $200,000 each. State and federal officials, environmentalists, and the company soon worked out a land swap that would save about 10 percent of the Headwaters' most spectacular trees.

During negotiations, environmentalists claimed that the corporation was given too much compensation for too little forest saved. The company claimed it should be able to do whatever it pleased on its land. Many biologists argue that saving Headwaters could be vital to the survival of rare or endangered species, such as northern spotted owls, marbled murrelets, and coho salmon. Public concern waned with the compromises, but those closest to this controversy continued their debates. Pacific Lumber compounded their problems in late 1998 when the California Department of Forestry cited them for gross negligence and willful violations of state forestry regulations. After their northern forests logging license was temporarily suspended, the company apologized for illegally clear cutting and using heavy equipment on protected land.

The timber industry played a vital role in Weed's economy throughout the 1900s. This 1910 photo of Weed and its lumber company was on display at the town's historical museum.

Mining

In and around California mountain ranges are some of the most celebrated gold, silver, and other mines, especially in Sierra Nevada's Mother Lode. The largest and deepest mercury (quicksilver) mines in the world have operated in the Coast Ranges. These just begin a long list of examples. The distribution and discovery of these and other abundant and valuable earth resources in California is not coincidence; it reflects a dynamic and tumultuous geologic history reviewed in earlier chapters.

California's major earth resources and mining operations were investigated in a more lengthy section in Chapter 2 and also in connection with other topics, such as water resources. Because the state's fossil fuels, nonfuel minerals, and other valuable earth resources were formed in place during millions of years of geologic processes, that section on earth history is the appropriate place for such a review. Here, we will focus more on the economic implications of these earth resources.

Those past geologic events eventually changed California's human history. Since 1848, local landscapes and mining towns have been completely remade and then abandoned in waste within months, all at the mercy of one mineral's abundance. These legendary mining operations also transformed California landscapes on a much broader scale; they brought hundreds of thousands from around the world who wanted to share in the riches. Hundreds of thousands more followed to make profits off the goods and services demanded by these miners and their mining economies. Once again, we can recognize the obvious connections between the state's natural resources and landscapes and human populations, activities, and landscapes.

Discovery of some of the most productive and high quality oil and gas fields in the world also transformed the state's economy and human landscapes during the 1900s. California quickly became one of the nation's leading producers of oil, accounting for more than 10 percent of production and proven reserves even into the late 1900s. Though the shoulder-to-shoulder oil derricks were already disappearing along the southern California coast during the mid-1900s, new discoveries (especially Elk Hills and other southern San Joaquin Valley fields) were making impacts.

A modern map also shows a few concentrations of gas fields below northern California valleys. Still more apparent are the impressive oil fields scattered about southern California coastal and inland mountains and valleys well into the Los Angeles Basin. Again, you will find more details about the formation and distribution of these resources in Chapter 2 on geologic history.

It may surprise some that mining in California today only represents a tiny percentage of the state's economy, but this is not because these earth resources are not valuable or vital to the nation's economy. (Our more extensive survey of earth resources in Chapter 2 reveals the extent of their value.) It is a result of incredible growth in other sectors of the state's economy that have outpaced and overshadowed the mining industry for more than a century.

During the 1990s, nonfuel raw mineral production in California topped $2.5 billion per year. According to the U.S. Bureau of Mines, California ranked third in the United States, producing more than 7 percent of the nation's total. Interestingly, up to 85 percent of the state's nonfuel mineral production was in industrial minerals, such as portland cement (a kind of cement that hardens with water), other construction materials, and boron. Even during the early 1990s recession, California led the nation in the production of portland cement and construction sand and gravel.

The other 15 percent mineral production came from (in order of importance) gold, silver, tungsten, and copper. California continued as the only state producing boron and tungsten. It led the nation in the production of rare-earth concentrates, diatomite, natural sodium sulfate, and asbestos. It was the number two state in production of gold, magnesium compounds, soda ash, and titanium (ilmenite).

The state's nonfuel mining industry accounted for more than 8,500 workers each year into the 1990s. California progressed through the 1990s with about thirty-five major mining companies. Of the more than one-thousand active mines, about 65 percent were sand and gravel operations, more than 25 percent were industrial mines, and less than 10 percent were metal mines. Specifically, portland cement (valued at more than $500 million) was the state's leader in nonfuel raw mineral production, followed closely by sand and gravel for construction and industry. Gold, boron minerals, and crushed and dimension stone also made the top five most valuable minerals. However, plummeting global gold prices into the late 1990s put the squeeze on California's gold mining operations.

As the state's economy and population grows ever larger and more diverse, the relative importance and influence of mining industries continues to wane. It is impossible to accurately predict the future of mining in California or its impact on the state's citizens and landscapes. It is certainly true that energy resource extraction must play a crucial role. Certainly, hydropower and petroleum and natural gas production will continue to be the major energy sources for the near future. Indicators in the late 1990s show nuclear power (due to exorbitant costs) and coal (little is found in California) will play relatively minor roles. Cleaner "alternative" resources such as solar, wind, and conservation of existing resources will likely fill the voids left by traditional sources. Deregulation of California's energy industries accelerated these changes into the twenty-first century.

CLEANING UP THE WASTE

Even as the exploration for gold and other minerals continued, some Californians engaged in debate over the impacts of mining operations. Numerous mines were having obvious negative effects on the quality of life for many modern rural and urban dwellers. In one example, the East Bay Municipal Utility District (EBMUD) filed suit to recover costs from water pollution caused by the abandoned Penn mine. This mine along the Mokelumne River in Calaveras County produced zinc and copper during the 1940s under direction of the U.S. War Production Board. During the late 1990s, mining wastes continued flowing into the river toward the Comanche Reservoir, a major water source for the East Bay.

Due to the demand for construction materials, city councils and county boards have issued permits for new sand and gravel operations throughout the state. In some communities, they met opposition through the 1990s. Such conflicts forced Granite Construction Company to withdraw its application to mine seven miles along the Santa Clara River in Ventura County. Yolo County blocked an interim-use permit to stop a company from processing gravel along Cache Creek. San Luis Obispo County stopped sand and gravel mining in the Santa Maria River. After thirty-two years of sand, gravel, asphalt, and concrete mix production, Southern Pacific Milling Company was forced to clean up and restore its 153-acre Ventura River site.

Ecotourism

Ecotourism, as defined and reviewed in other sections, has played an important role in California's rural economies since the 1800s. California's natural resources, scenic attractions, and open spaces offer endless opportunities for recreation, leisure, revitalization, education, and discovery of worlds far beyond the urban chaos. Though these activities require natural, rural, and wilderness settings and resources, they are often grouped under more advanced economic activities which include services.

The number of visitors searching out California's more famous open spaces and tranquil environments is increasing. Millions are coming from around the nation and around the world. They require lodging, food, and transportation. These are the gasoline services, eating establishments, motels, and related retail (GEMS) also referred to in other sections. Ecotourists also pay for myriad other services while they are here, and they are important parts of the state's multi-billion dollar tourist industry. Look for GEMS. You will sometimes see such services replacing other struggling industries to revitalize smaller towns. And you will sometimes notice rural communities struggling over whether to harvest their natural resources for immediate profit or to preserve them for the impending invasion of tourists from an ever-more-crowded world.

◆ THE NATURE OF CALIFORNIA'S RURAL LANDSCAPES

Rural or Urban Landscapes?

The most general survey across California will reveal enormous contrasts between rural and urban landscapes. Exactly how do our rural and urban landscapes and their people differ? Subjectively, California's rural areas represent the countryside, and the people who live there have very different, and often more traditional, cultures and lifestyles compared to those of urban populations.

Our mental images of these **rural landscapes** often include extensive, sweeping vistas covered with grasslands, scrub, or forest, often supporting grazing animals or farmland. These extensive landscapes represent the vast majority of California's land areas as they contrast with the more confined, intense concentrations of urban activities and populations in California's great cities.

There are more objective ways to distinguish between the state's rural and urban landscapes. Land values and population densities increase dramatically as we approach California cities from the countryside. As we move yet closer to the urban core, primary economic activities yield to more advanced and complex economies, and a dramatic concentration of capital becomes evident. These are not only spatial trends, but, in California, landscapes are also rapidly evolving in time to transform former rural communities into urban environments.

Rural People and Resources

The story of rural California cannot, and will not, be told only with numbers. True, it is important to know which crops are grown or which species of trees are being harvested or which mining operations produce the greatest profits and employment. These numbers can be vital to the livelihood and the very survival of every rural town. But these numbers change annually in California, depending on the amount of natural resources available and the demand for them. Though rural communities have considerable control over how they use these resources, they are increasingly impacted by changing demands from a volatile world market.

This productive pumpkin patch in Ventura is a lively place during October, but it is being squeezed on all sides by new developments along Hwy. 101. The rural atmosphere is rapidly disappearing and so are the gourds seen here.

Outside populations will also place greater controls and restrictions on the use of natural resources from these rural communities. As exploding populations consume more resources and rural lands, people are naturally becoming more concerned about the loss of our remaining national and state heritage. The result is increasing demand and competition for the remaining rural landscapes and their resources from a growing multitude of concerned groups with very different interests and agendas.

When we ask what we want future California landscapes to look like or offer, there are few California residents who will say smaller forests, less open space, and fewer farms. But that is precisely California's future. Because rural California communities have so much to offer to these many diverse interests, they will continue to take center stage in controversies and emotional battles over how to use what remains of our valuable natural resources and open spaces.

Consequently, the story of California's rural landscapes is really a story about people and the resources they will exploit or protect. With nearly one-third of California covered by some type of forest and another one-third used for some form of agriculture, this is also a story about vast amounts of land. Furthermore, because more than half of California's land is owned by the public, this story is frequently about how the citizens of California, and even the nation, plan to use or develop those public lands. Why is so much especially rural land in California owned by local, state, and federal agencies, and what is the nature of this land? This question deserves some more attention.

Rural Land Ownership and Use

Almost all of the state's historically most productive, valuable, and intensely-used land is in private hands (see Map 9.3). This includes most of its coastal areas and in-

land valleys. This is most of the land where concentrations of Native Americans lived and most of the land cherished by the Spanish, Mexican, and early American settlers. Almost all of the modern urban and suburban areas, productive farmlands (such as in the Central, Salinas, and other valleys), and even some of the most productive forests (such as along northwestern coastal slopes) are privately owned. Much of the other half of California was not as accessible or potentially productive during the state's early history, so it continued within the public domain.

Public land dominates the state's higher, rugged landscapes and most of arid transmontane California (inland of the major mountain barriers). This includes one-fifth of the state designated National Forest and another one-sixth under the U.S. Bureau of Land Management (BLM). These are the classic multi-use lands, which are maintained to serve the greatest number of diverse economic and public interests.

Typical activities in our national forests include timber production, mining, grazing, hunting, fishing, off-roading, and many other recreational activities, such as camping, hiking, birding and other wildlife viewing. You may witness similar activities on BLM lands, ordinarily with less intensive use and usually without the timber production. You can see how many of these are conflicting interests; this may explain the battles raging across the state about how we can use our public lands for the greatest benefit of such a fast-growing, diverse population.

Another approximately one-sixth of California belongs to the people as National Park Service, State Park, or Department of Defense lands. These have more restricted uses. National and State Park lands are usually set aside to preserve and display a part of the state's natural or cultural heritage for the greatest public benefit today and in the future. In contrast, the Department of Defense operates military bases which include weapons

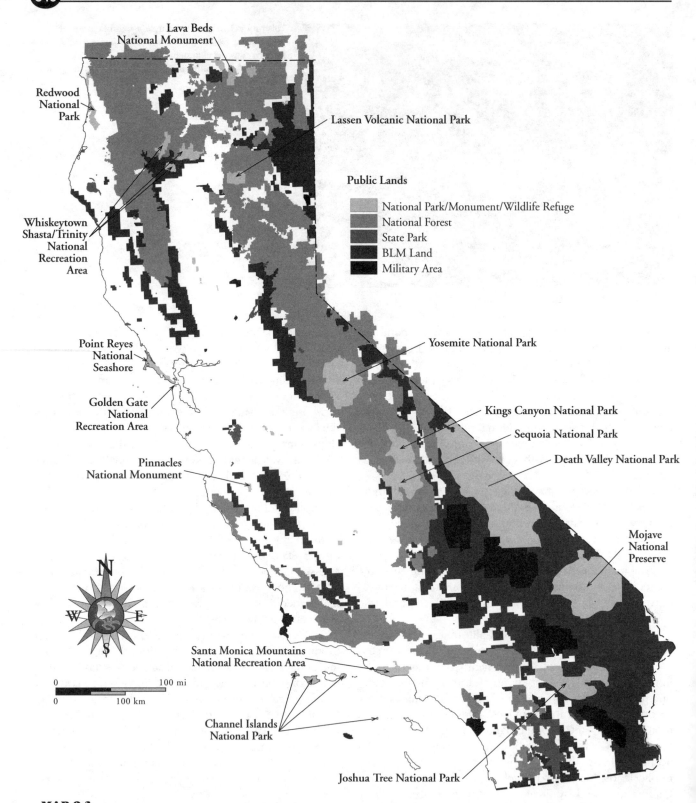

MAP 9.3
Public lands in California. National parks, monuments, and recreation areas are labelled.

and training centers that are especially extensive in inland Southern California and are mostly off-limits to the public.

Consequently, the distribution of land ownership in California falls into two very distinct patterns. Historically less-productive land, located mainly in rugged highlands and deserts, is mostly public property punctuated with private lands. Traditionally more productive and valuable lands are concentrated in cismontane California and are mainly private, sprinkled with bits of public land.

These patterns of land ownership help us understand our rural landscapes. Because more than half of California is publicly owned, there is a better than 50/50 chance that the rural landscape you view is managed by a public agency. However, if that rural landscape is intensely used, such as in productive farmlands, chances are good that it's private.

Rural Families to Global Conglomerates

We again stress the stories about people within California's rural landscapes. Many of the western myths about the family farm or ranch or timber company or mining operation have been lived out in California. Families and small groups were often responsible for settling, "reclaiming," and "taming" the land. Many of these people made their living off the land while they took sustainable yields that would assure long-term prosperity or at least productivity.

These were pioneers and settlers, hard workers, and risk takers. They built and nurtured many of the smaller towns and communities you see scattered about rural California even today. These timber, mining, and agricultural services towns survived and even prospered when dedicated individuals came together to use their natural resources wisely. However, when there was waste and shortsightedness, the towns died; there are many scars on California's rural landscapes to bear witness.

You can still spot some family operations on our rural landscapes, but they have become more rare and they never dominated the state's landscapes as some would like to believe. Instead, it was often the mammoth corporations who came to California to mine gold, cut timber, and lay railroad lines. Through most of the twentieth century, railroads owned, by far, the greatest amount of private land in California. They and the giant land and farming companies often controlled who had access to transportation and water. In other words, they decided which land would be profitable and where towns would grow. Even today, such large corporations are joined by giant timber, oil, and utility companies as the greatest private landowners in California.

Therefore, even if that rural landscape in California is privately owned, it is more likely that the labor is done by employees working for a larger corporation. Often, these are workers who are allowed to farm or harvest other resources if they pass some of their profits on to the absentee landowner. Usually, they must also sell their harvested product to a corporation. Frequently, these corporations are not based in California or even the United States. The modern-day reality about California's rural populations, cultures, towns, and landscapes is that they have become more and more dependent on the global marketplace and powerful outside forces beyond their control.

This has added to the frustration you may sense in rural California. More than 50 percent of the state's agricultural product is exported to other countries. That indicates great markets out there for California agricultural products. How can today's farmers accurately predict profits from cotton, tomato, rice, or beef products when they may depend on the value of the dollar compared to the yen, or on the year's production of these crops in other countries? Though there may be long-term profits, the year-to-year risks could be too great for a smaller family operation with seasonal debts and no influential global connections. California's fishing, mining, and timber industries face similar challenges as they link into global markets.

Tourism

Though they may visit to experience nature and the open spaces, ecotourists and other escapees from urban settings must find these isolated, bucolic landscapes somewhat accessible and user-friendly or they may not return. This has helped make GEMS vital to some of the state's rural communities; these activities have even saved smaller communities when their other resources disappeared or were in lower demand. The problem is defining who "ecotourists" are and what they want. They are a strange breed for economists and business people to identify because they may seek the most natural, pristine experiences, but require some of the comforts offered by a wide range of modern technologies and products.

For decades, numerous California rural communities have advertised and even modified their landscapes to compete for such tourist dollars. However, natural landscapes and associated activities are sometimes in direct conflict with many of the economic activities that harvest natural resources. The result is increased tension, controversy, and debate concerning local use of these resources and how to stabilize rural economies.

Additionally, these tourist, sightseeing, naturalist, and various other recreational and educational activities are also impacted by outside economic quirks far removed from California's remote and scenic landscapes. Like the resources they demand, the number of visitors who venture into California's wild and scenic landscapes often depends on employment rates, the price of fuel, and travel services in other countries and urban areas.

The Global Marketplace

There is a bit of irony when you first experience California's often picturesque rural landscapes and communities; the scenes seem so remote, so isolated from the urban chaos and economic and global competition that increasingly dominate our state and our planet. Scores of visitors flock to these rural hideaways just to escape such intense competition and fast-paced lifestyles, but the reality is that you are looking at results of participation in that global marketplace even when you view California's sweeping rural landscapes.

Californians in general, and rural Californians in particular, must come to grips with the powerful forces that are changing their lives and their landscapes. We have the ominous task of using and managing our natural resources in a responsible, sustainable fashion so that we assure a future California with productive lands and improved working and living conditions. Our cities cover only about 5 percent to 15 percent of California, depending on how "urban" is defined. Whether our rural lands are private or public, the decisions we make today will determine the future quality and productivity of the vast majority of California landscapes.

◆ CALIFORNIA'S RURAL LANDSCAPES AND LIFESTYLES CONTINUE TO EVOLVE

Scanning many of California's rural landscapes, you may find traditional farms separated in dispersed patterns typical of rural land occupance. These patterns are partly due to the rectangular land division scheme known as the township-and-range system, once designed to disperse settlers evenly across farmlands in the United States. It certainly worked in California's relatively level floodplains, especially in the Central Valley, to create that checkerboard pattern of land use that is so noticeable.

As in most Western cultures, farm buildings reflect permanence and functional differentiation. Farm houses, ranch houses, barns, storage buildings, workshops, sta-

bles, and silos for grain storage may take up considerable space on one single farmstead.

California has even produced its own rural architecture. The ranch-style house has its roots on the California farm, though it spread throughout the state's suburbs during the 1900s. Practical advantages of the ranch-style house, sometimes called the California bungalow, eclipsed traditional two-story and other architecture. The California bungalow, suburban-style, evolved into a home with the typical low-angle roof, screened porches and patios, pool and deck, and barbecue pit. It retained some of the efficiencies of the original farm home but added other space-demanding, energy-consuming qualities. This architecture seems a good match with the state's mild Mediterranean climates.

Though modern California farmlands are sometimes distinguished by the dominance of specialization and agribusiness, they do share characteristics with traditional American rural landscapes. Nearby agricultural service, mining, or timber towns come in a variety of sizes and forms. They usually include small stores, schools, churches, traditional town halls, and medical clinics. Larger towns will offer a wider variety of services and activities; residents include a larger number of professionals, such as shopkeepers, mechanics, educators, and medical specialists.

People followed the migration of rural jobs to the cities during the late 1800s through the mid-1900s, draining vitality from some rural communities. During the late 1900s, a new breed of urban professional and retirees were fleeing those same cities and rediscovering rural lifestyles. These modern invaders were changing the nature of rural communities throughout California into the twenty-first century. Here are just a few stories of how some of California's rural communities are coping with modern changes and pressures as they move into the twenty-first century.

Fields of artichokes are a common sight along the central coast. This artichoke farm is in Pescadero, where you can get artichoke soap and omelets and other unusual dishes made from this thistle.

MODERN TRENDS SWEEP INTO CARMEL

Carmel has long had a reputation as a quaint artists' colony, tourist attraction, and hideaway. For years, residents and civic leaders have argued over how much development will spoil the atmosphere, and restrictions are a hot topic in local elections. Movie star Clint Eastwood won election as mayor on a platform urging more development.

As if to underscore Carmel's uniqueness, Hyatt's famous Highlands Inn underwent a $40 million renovation during the 1980s. Though some of the rooms were priced at more than $600 per night and were used by California's richest and most famous celebrities in the 1990s, the inn was turning into a time-share operation. Taking advantage of an expanding and popular time-share market revival, Hyatt was planning to ask $14,000–$35,000 per room (with sweeping ocean views) for one week per year ownership. This is only one example of how Carmel's and the Monterey Peninsula's rural roots continue to yield to more urban activities, lifestyles, and landscapes.

Central Coast

For decades, California's central coast, from Morro Bay to Big Sur and Monterey Bay to Half Moon Bay, has touched the hearts of writers, film makers, and others who were impressed by its misty moods and natural beauty. Today, it is dotted with tourist towns and attractions that exploit these well-known virtues.

Moving north of Monterey Bay, Captain John Davenport was a winter whaler along the central coast who founded Davenport in the 1860s. The town was moved about one-half mile south next to its cement plant in 1906. Today, the beautiful hidden coves and agriculture are still there, but it is evolving more as a tourist stop with a few shops, restaurants, and places to lodge. Nearby attractions such as Año Nuevo State Park and local seal and sea lion populations help keep it on the map.

Traffic is relatively light along this stretch of Pacific Coast Highway, particularly during weekdays and winters, and especially farther north near Pescadero and San Gregorio. To the north, Pescadero has a few antique shops and clothing stores. Pescadero's famous Duarte's Tavern was started in 1894 by Frank Duarte and is still run by the same family. It became famous for its artichoke dishes and soup. When Bank of America decided to close its lonely branch there, it created one of the biggest controversies of 1997 for this little, misty town surrounded by artichoke fields.

Farther north is Half Moon Bay (locally known as HMB) with its annual October Pumpkin Festival. Such events are guaranteed to attract tourists and other visitors to its shops, restaurants, and lodges. Some of the award-winning pumpkins at this greatest annual event in HMB have been weighed at over 800 pounds. Many members of this community of 13,000 cherish their historical buildings (some more than 100 years old) and Main Street and have resisted development. An arsonist even burned down a new obtrusive three-story hotel and condominium project near the beach in 1996, apparently to protest this coastline's evolution toward modern, generic architecture and lifestyles.

Solvang

Solvang was established in 1911 in the western Santa Ynez Valley as a Danish colony. Though they experienced difficulty adapting to the dry summers, the colonists eventually established alfalfa, legumes, sugar beets, and winter wheat on the valley floor and grazing on surrounding hills. Vegetable crops became more extensive with expanded irrigation techniques. A Danish-theme town emerged that was purposely built to replicate the home country, complete with windmills and buildings with half timbers and tile or thatched roofs. By the late 1900s, the population soared over 5,000. Tourists were pouring into the shops, restaurants, and bakeries of this town that was looking less and less rural.

Controversy and conflict erupted when Solvang citizens and officials agreed to buy California Water Project water from the Department of Water Resources in 1991. Solvang's City Council recommended state water, and the voters approved it in 1991, during the worst of drought conditions. However, local groundwater from the Santa Ynez Upland Basin was five times cheaper, and by the late 1990s, the city was going broke paying for the new, expensive sources of California Water Project water. Faced with a total water bill of more than $80 million over the next few decades (a devastating blow to such a little town), the city went to court to block the required payments, while residents ripped up water-using landscapes.

Corcoran

Corcoran (between Fresno and Bakersfield) became one of the centers of California agribusiness after giant water projects tamed Sierra Nevada rivers and eased Tule Lake's periodic inundations. The Boswells and Saylors became the leading and rival cotton producers, adding improvements to Corcoran landscapes. Then, by the mid-1980s, due to an economic slump and competition from the Chinese mass production of cotton, Corcoran's economy faltered. Consequently, Corcoran bid for a prison and got it in 1988, including some of the most dangerous and famous criminals in California. As California built the largest number of correctional facilities ever, Corcoran became a prison town. It was still an agricultural service town, but with services for the prison and its employees and visitors. Residents and leaders have been concerned about its reputation ever since.

Tehachapi

Tehachapi (in the mountains southeast of Bakersfield) is a small city of about 7,000, but is surrounded by a dispersed population of about 21,000. The largest employers in Tehachapi are a cement factory and a nearby state prison. Conservative Christians are visible and active in the city's culture and there are about fifteen churches in the town.

By the 1990s, a New Age culture was also evident with the many herbalists, acupuncturists, a New Age store, and nearly two dozen trained massage therapists. Many have been inspired or drawn to this town by the spiritual energy offered within its scenic landscapes. Some even see it as another potential Sedona, Arizona. The different groups have usually tolerated one another, although there have been signs of friction; this includes efforts to keep a city ordinance banning fortune-telling.

Transforming Sierra Nevada Landscapes
Sonora and the Mother Lode

Californios (persons of Hispanic heritage who were born in California) first settled Sonora in the western Sierra Nevada foothills northeast of Modesto before the Gold Rush. When gold was discovered along the creek that runs under the town's main street, American 49'ers pushed the Hispanics out. (Today's Washington Street sits directly on the Mother Lode vein and shaft, and the town's red church sits where the Bonanza Mine made the town famous.) By 1852, more than 17,000 people had already flooded into Tuolomne and nearby Stanislaus Counties. Sonora was even a candidate to become the capital of California.

Sonora had earned Wild West status. Strict punishment was used to keep law and order; criminals were often marked. Serious violators lost an ear or were whipped on the back by each member of his jury. There were even a few hangings. Soon, the rush was over and for decades, Sonora was a sleepy Mother Lode town. The entire area's population didn't reach 17,000 again until

In Sierra Nevada's Sonora, you will find cultures clashing and debates raging about how much growth and popular culture can be absorbed before the town's personality is lost.

the 1960s. Traditions were hanging on in this rustic rural community where the *Union Democrat* ruled as the town newspaper for more than 140 years.

By the late 1990s, Sonora's population topped 4,200 (within city limits) and was growing fast. More than 20,000 people were visiting each day, including those taking care of business at this Tuolomne County Seat. Within ten years, the number of stoplights had increased from one to twelve. A new economic and population boom was sweeping across Mother Lode country as people fled from California's expanding urban giants. Some of these towns allowed the blight of generic retail chains and malls to destroy their characters. Others protected their uniqueness by banning such developments, only to watch adjacent communities steal the tax base and economic growth that came with them.

Sonora chose the middle ground. They allowed retail chains and malls to develop within city limits, but away from Main Street and the historical district. By the mid-1990s, this town that was recently near bankruptcy took the 7.25 percent sales tax of new retailers and malls as it ran up a $1.2 million surplus and spent $763 per resident. They used some of the money to restore and improve historical Washington Street, which attracted more tourists. As the town pulled away from its traditional rural roots, some worried that local merchants had made their fortunes as new retailers and were only adding low-paying and part-time jobs to the community.

Land Use Change in Rangelands of the Western Sierra Nevada

Sonora is just one of the many centers of growth as landscapes of the western Sierra Nevada are transformed into the twenty-first century. According to research by Sharon

Johnson at UC Berkeley, the number of Sierra Nevada foothill subdivisions grew by 130 percent from the mid-1970s to the mid-1990s. The result is a loss in large ranches, especially within hardwood rangelands of counties like El Dorado and Amador east of Sacramento.

According to interviews with local ranchers, the economic benefits of ranching have waned while their land values have soared. As many traditional ranchers grow older and die, the land is distributed among a pyramid of heirs. Higher estate taxes and inflexibility of assets encourage the many who inherit their portions of these ranches to sell. Developers and speculators have lined up to grab these increasingly valuable lands. They are often subdivided into individual estates which may later be further subdivided into more intense developments.

From Truckee to Lake Tahoe

At 5,820 feet in a valley fourteen miles northwest of Lake Tahoe, Truckee became an official stage stop in 1863. The railroad and logging industry brought a Wild West atmosphere with brothels and gunfights in the streets. Like many other early Sierra Nevada boomtowns, Truckee lost its edge and became rather unkempt until the mid-1900s. During the 1960s, a revival was made possible by tourism. The last lumber mill closed in 1989, making the tourist industry even more important to the town.

Though modern technology has helped, exceptionally tough winters continue to play a role in Truckee life. (Chapter 4 on weather and climate details some of these harsh winters.) This is a town where outsiders travelling along the main highway are still referred to as flatlanders.

Just to the south, the spectacular Lake Tahoe beckons. At more than 6,200 feet, the lake and its surrounding attractions offer one of the most unique mountain settings in California, if not the most glorious high-mountain lake environment in the nation. On the California side, South Lake Tahoe developments have especially grown in response to the giant casinos and entertainment centers across Nevada's state line. Ski and gambling resorts, golf courses, and peak use traffic jams have cut through the once pristine atmosphere along the lake.

Today, the Lake Tahoe region has a $1 billion tourist industry. The importance of California visitors to the local economy is underscored during periods of exceptionally bad or good ski conditions. During January, 1997, another reminder came when floods and slides blocked major roads to the area (including U.S. Hwy. 50), and businesses were briefly devastated during the height of the ski season. All of this activity is concentrated around a lake continually threatened by crowds and pollution. Battles have been fought to control growth and development so that people do not destroy the very environment that attracted them to the lake in the first place.

Traditional Wine Country

In the Napa Valley, you will find a mix of urban and rural lifestyles and architecture. Old structures have been converted into art galleries, studios, and offices. Due to its proximity to Bay Area cities, it exhibits typical urban fringe environments. This valley is now experiencing the same pressures from development that have gobbled up rural landscapes throughout the state.

Napa Valley wines gained respect in the 1970s when they started winning contests around the world, including France. Today's Napa Valley has more than 250 wine businesses; many are world famous. Some vineyards are worth up to $50,000 per acre. Thousands of wine tasters crowd the region, especially during weekends, as a growing competitive atmosphere invades this once sleepy valley. Cabernets are especially popular with those growers who sell only to selected, prestigious customers. Other wineries blend reds and whites. Robert Mondavi is one of the oldest vinters in the valley. During the 1990s, this winery produced more than 450,000 cases per year of different varieties of famous Mondavi wines.

There are now more than fifty wineries spreading north in the area along CA 29, between the city of Napa through St. Helena to Calistoga. Lodging is offered from low-cost bed and breakfasts to expensive, extravagant inns. Calistoga has become famous for its bottled mineral water and hot springs. Calistoga's Indian Springs Resort and Spa claims to be the oldest continuously operational thermal pool and spa in California. A mud bath involves mineral water mixed with hot volcanic ash up to the neck. You can follow it with a steam bath and towel wrap complete with cucumber slices over the eyes.

Just north of St. Helena is the Culinary Institute of America, housed in a former winery. It is a famous training ground for professional chefs. Shops in the area selling antiques, pottery, and furniture reflect what some refer to as northern California's "urban-country-sophisticate" image. Whether you consider this a rural or urban landscape, there is no arguing that it is a land in transition, becoming more urban by the year.

Desert Lifestyles and Landscapes

It is about the size of Switzerland. While training there, General Patton's World War II soldiers called it the place that God forgot. During many years, it produced the majority of the world's boron and rare earth minerals and most of the nation's sand and gravel. Since 1970, mining has been a billion-dollar industry there, while some estimate that there are more than a trillion dollars of minerals remaining. These are just a few examples of the resources offered by California's vast Mojave Desert.

Baker lies along I-15 with its few 24-hour garages and towing services, coffee shops, gas stations, markets, mo-

Settlements spread in the area north of Joshua Tree National Park, from Yucca Valley to Twentynine Palms. Desert communities are filling with people who establish landscapes similar to the ones they fled.

tels, and the world's largest thermometer. It is a stop between Las Vegas and L.A. with about 450 residents. The *Los Angeles Times* made famous two San Bernardino County deputy sheriffs who use it as a base as they drive long distances to calls. Aside from a few Highway Patrol units, there may be only one sheriff unit within a more than 100-mile radius.

Specifically, a 6,000-square-mile area across the open spaces of eastern San Bernardino County to the Nevada state line is shared by only two sheriff's deputies who are on duty at opposite times of day or night. This area's entire population is about 2,500 ranchers, retirees, and others escaping from urban life. Pranksters and those who are trying to distract sheriffs away from a particular area make crank calls that cost several hours of time. It may take two hours for a deputy to respond to a call; the deputies may not visit some desert hamlets for months if they are not called.

California's remote desert areas have attracted criminals, hermits, survivalists, drug lords, and the anti-social. You can see some of the old homesteader's tiny shacks scattered across the Mojave. Some were built by those who had to build on their land and maintain residence for five years to qualify for the now obsolete homesteading laws, or Small Tract Leasing Act. Homesteaders abandoned their shacks years ago. They can be found tattered, looted, and vandalized in places surrounding Yucca Valley, Landers, and other Mojave locations.

People are now moving back to these remote locations, trying to escape the urban chaos, but bringing much of their urban comforts with them. Though they must have their water delivered in huge trucks, they enjoy the quiet and remoteness. Some commute long distances into towns or cities like Palm Springs, Barstow, or the Antelope Valley for work. Some fight against the urban encroachment that might bring paved roads and

other signs of human development to intrude upon their own solitude.

Until the late 1900s, these open spaces were far removed from more regulated land uses near the state's great population centers. They attracted war exercises, toxic chemical manufacturing, and dumping operations. However, as people have escaped toward and into the Mojave, many have become less tolerant of those who would trash their remaining open spaces. Their views are in direct conflict with those who continue to see the Mojave as a huge dumping ground.

During the 1990s, four monumental dumps were planned in the Mojave. They included an enormous abandoned iron mine at Eagle Mountain near the border with Joshua Tree National Park and a 2,000-acre portion of a dry lake bed a few miles west of Cadiz in San Bernardino County. These dumps would receive tens of thousands of tons of waste per day carried on trains from Southern California's coastal valley population centers. Controversy also continued to rage around plans to bury a nuclear waste dump below the desert in Ward Valley some 20 miles west of Needles. Another toxic dump was proposed for an area near Ludlow (between Barstow and Needles). A few communities desperate for any kind of development (such as the town of Mojave) were even trying to attract toxic and heavy industries by promising fewer regulations.

By the end of the century, these wide-open spaces were also catching the attention of investors from all over the world. These included corporate farmers. Amazingly enough, isolated attempts at farming are not new to remote areas of the California desert. Early examples include a Chinese-American farmer who grew vegetables during the 1800s at the base of Darwin Falls. He sold them to the miners around the booming town of Darwin, near Panamint Springs.

During the 1990s, the Catellus Development Corporation (formerly a real-estate arm of Southern Pacific Railroad) was reported to own the most private land in the California desert, about 800,000 acres. They planned to use groundwater to produce tons of crops worth millions of dollars, while creating 1,000 jobs, especially in their Fenner Valley. Meanwhile, Cadiz Land Co. was transforming 10,000 acres of desert just south of old Route 66 in the Cadiz Valley to citrus, grape, and melon farms. They will use the aquifer that accumulates at the base of the Marble Mountains and flows toward the valley bottom.

These two companies were already in competition for a groundwater source that some suggested was not enough for either one of them. Victor Valley and Antelope Valley had already drained their wells, causing vegetation to die and dust storms to become more frequent; they now have to import state water. This caused other state water agencies to question whether there is enough water in the desert for such huge corporate ventures.

By the end of the 1990s, Catellus Development Corporation was also questioning the merits of developing the desert; they were negotiating to sell more than 400,000 acres to the Wildlands Conservancy for more than $50 million. These acres around Joshua Tree National Park and the Mojave National Preserve could then be transferred to the Federal Government and protected as wilderness.

The Southern California Council of Governments predicted that populations in the two fastest-growing areas of the Mojave will nearly triple in the twenty-five years following the mid-1990s. The 230,000 Victor Valley residents could increase to 670,000, while the 300,000 in the Antelope Valley could grow to more than 700,000.

Predictably, environmentalists and others express concern about such growth trends. This is why a coalition of groups teamed together to press Congress to create the 1.4-million-acre East Mojave Preserve. Although some of the Mojave was protected by this act during the 1990s, opponents made concessions to several conflicting interests and industries, and little financial support was allocated to maintain the preserve.

It is interesting that General George Patton was a native Californian, born and raised in San Gabriel. He used his knowledge of the Mojave to train one of the greatest armies the world has ever known to fight in World War II. Occasionally, visitors to today's Mojave, seeking the same open spaces he exploited, may still stumble upon live ammunition left from those training sessions. They represent haunting links between the past and present use of our desert resources.

Tourists, naturalists, wildlife enthusiasts, and others have discovered the solitude and natural beauty of the Mojave Desert. Will local leaders finally recognize the enormous contributions these activities make toward long-term sustainable economies?

California's Northwest Forestlands

Contrasting with the exposed expanses of open southeastern California landscapes are the moist, confining, shadowy forests of the northwest. It would be difficult to find more dissimilar rural settings within the boundaries of any other state.

Mendocino County

We will use a journey through the heart of Mendocino County to explore the nature of these landscapes. We start in Ukiah, nestled in an inland valley along the upper Russian River and Hwy. 101. Ukiah (more than 15,000 population) has been ranked as one of the most livable small towns in the United States. It is the largest town in Mendocino County (nearly 90,000 county residents), and it serves as the County Seat. Rows of pear trees and grape vines spread across this valley where the winters are cool and rainy. Thanks to the Coast Ranges, which block coastal fog, summers here are warm and dry.

With companies such as Louisiana Pacific operating in Mendocino County, the timber industry is still important to the town's economy. However, by the 1990s, downsizing in timber and manufacturing industries had impacted middle-class job opportunities. They were gradually being replaced by service jobs, an expanding wine industry, and even some high-tech firms.

Ukiah exhibits considerable diversity and culture for such a small town, a characteristic shared by much of Mendocino County. You will find a host of theaters and religious groups, including an active Buddhist community. Large celebrations such as Cinco de Mayo bring diverse groups together from around the region.

We take Hwy. 253 west out of Ukiah and then Hwy. 128 to the coast. We start where annual rainfall averages only 35 inches, but we will eventually drop down to coastal slopes that receive up to 80 inches per year. At first, hardwoods such as tan oak share drier inland slopes with a mix of conifers, madrone, and grazing cattle. More exposed slopes with poor serpentine soil outcrops open into patches of grasslands. We drop into Anderson Valley and Boonville, a hamlet that apparently is so isolated, the people here reportedly developed their own dialect. Like several other California valleys, rows of wine-producing grape vines are spreading fast here.

There is an old saying in this country: "Where the fog goes, redwood grows." As we head northwest along Hwy. 128 toward the coast, we are entering the heart of redwood country. Louisiana Pacific logging trucks pass, full of coast redwood and Douglas fir logs. Up to 60 percent of these logs come from the corporation's private land holdings within Mendocino County (about 300,000 acres). We stop at the company's demonstration forest, which was first clear-cut more than a century ago and was last cut just nine months before our visit. Following heavy winter rains, remaining redwood stumps are already sprouting new growth a few feet high. One older redwood tree here is worth more than $5,000 to the timber industry.

Travelling on to the misty coast, we approach the scenic and artsy community of Mendocino. This coast was one of the largest sheep-growing areas in California during the early 1900s. Loggers once climbed local barroom walls with their spiked boots. More recently, tourists and bed-and-breakfasts have overshadowed agriculture and timber economies. The setting for television's beloved "Murder, She Wrote" was here in Mendocino. The Heritage House stands as the town's first major bed-and-breakfast.

We travel north to Noyo and Fort Bragg, built on one of the several marine terraces that overlook the ocean. Noyo Harbor claims to be the only safe, sheltered harbor between San Francisco and Eureka and is home to an active fishing community. Along the wharf, you can view fishing fleets and the Noyo River. Boats with the tall poles troll for salmon. Larger boats with bright lights are "draggers," netting petrale sole, Pacific red snapper, cod, and other seafood. Small boats with divers and air compres-

sors harvest sea urchin, mostly to be shipped to Japan, where their "roe" is a delicacy.

Fort Bragg (population about 6,500) is the largest town along the coastline between Eureka and San Francisco. Here, you can catch a ride on the Skunk Train, from Fort Bragg to Willits. On your way to Willits along the Skunk Train route, you will be hauled up through the moist redwood forest first along Pudding Creek and then along the Noyo River. You will eventually travel farther east and inland through drier terrain with extensive oak woodlands (the reverse of our earlier drive to the coast). This train ride has become famous among tourists as one of the shortest and most scenic in the country. Parts of the treacherous route with 381 curves and thirty-one bridges and trestles are sometimes closed by flooding and slides.

The first tracks for the Fort Bragg Railroad were laid in 1885 to haul timber. It was gradually lengthened to carry redwood and other logs until the forty-mile track between Fort Bragg and Willits was finally completed by California Western Railroad in 1911. California Western's Skunk Train was given credit for opening this part of redwood country and linking population centers in Mendocino County. It remains a tribute to the history and rural cultures of northwestern California.

Transforming Rural Landscapes of the Northwest and Beyond

By the 1990s, northern California towns had lost hundreds of timber jobs to recession, downsizing and automation, overlogging and environmental degradation and regulations. Similar hits to the commercial fishing industry dropped personal incomes, pushed unemployment over 10 percent, and left a high percentage of residents on welfare. Marijuana continued to be the number one cash crop in some areas. California's three most northwestern counties became known as the Forgotten Coast or the area behind the Redwood Curtain. After all, the entire region that includes 20 percent of the state's land and 25 percent of the state's coastline has just more than 230,000 people. Little Crescent City (less than 8,500 residents) is the largest California town north of Arcata.

The decline in the timber industry hit the little town of Orick (along Hwy. 101 in northern Humboldt County) especially hard. Three of four sawmills were shut down as the town's population plummeted from 3,000 to just over 300. This downturn closed the only movie house and left only one active church and one year-round restaurant. In the early 1990s, a Eureka pulp mill closed, taking more than 260 jobs. As fishing and logging industries slumped throughout the region, some residents blamed government and environmentalists for restricting harvests. However, environmentalists point to the loss of those resources due to overharvesting, noting that 90

A trip on the modern Skunk Train out of Ft. Bragg through redwood country is for tourists, not timber.

percent of the forests have already been cut, causing erosion that contributed to the destruction of salmon habitat and the fishing industry.

Searching for Solutions While some pointed fingers, other residents and leaders were searching for solutions. In Trinity County, the growing of herbs and gathering of pine cones and moss for interior decorations is an expanding industry. But, in this region that became too dependent on logging and had difficulty attracting other industries, some traditional loggers resisted the painful transition away from their "way of life." The result was that Weaverville's unemployment rate soared over 15 percent, and figures were even higher within isolated sections of Trinity County.

New immigrants are now working with those who stayed to take economic advantage of their setting. They are targeting ecotourists, retirees, and entrepreneurs with new innovations, and they have gained the attention of the state's growing prison industry. Help also came from the federal government with money to retrain loggers and grants to communities suffering from recession during the 1990s. To offer jobs to former loggers and millworkers and recent urban immigrants, the isolated communities are starting "incubator" businesses. They are often lower-paying. They include the Arcata Economic Development Corporation that amassed $1.4 million to build the 20,000-square-foot Foodworks Culinary Center (for specialty foods).

Pelican Bay State Prison opened in Crescent City and was soon the area's number one employer, housing nearly 4,000 of the state's most dangerous criminals. The prison added more than 1,300 workers; many were former loggers. Crescent City's unemployment dropped from a high of 26 percent to down below 14 percent by the late 1990s. Many other businesses were saved, and typical problems with growth soon developed. Most of the remaining and new businesses were small, such as retail shops and restaurants. In Del Norte County, the percentage of workers in the timber and paper industries fell from more than 50 percent to about 3 percent by the mid-1990s. Unemployment eventually fell from 24 percent to less than 10 percent by the late 1990s.

In 1972, one of three Humboldt County jobs was in the timber industry; the ratio is now less than one in ten as the economy has become much more diverse. Arcata has Humboldt State University and is attracting special and small businesses, such as innovative products for cars, bikes, and boats and recycled products. Eureka is more blue collar, but it has created a 56-block redevelopment area in its formerly deteriorated Old Town. The $50 million Victorian port restoration project includes restoration of Victorian and brick historical buildings dating back to the 1800s. Eureka is now negotiating with cruise lines to become a stop between Los Angeles and Alaska.

In more accessible Mendocino County, only 4 percent of the jobs are now in timber or paper, while tourism jobs were increasing by about 7 percent per year during the 1990s. The more than fifty wineries and additional bed-and-breakfasts are popular with visitors from the San Francisco Bay Area. The community of Mendocino has a population of only about 1,000, but is swamped during summer weekends with tourists enjoying art galleries, shops, and cafes. An art colony has flourished since the 1950s in the village; the county has more people employed in the arts per capita than any other place in California. Fort Bragg was once the largest salmon-producing port on the Pacific Coast, but it is also now catering to the tourists. Wineries are also pulling tourists farther inland, away from the coast.

California's three northwestern-most counties were gaining more recognition during the 1990s, including feature stories in newspapers across the nation. In the entire region, population is growing steadily, becoming more diverse, and unemployment rates are dropping. The population of the three counties is more than 80 percent caucasian, about 11 percent Hispanic, nearly 4 percent Asian/Pacific Islander, and 3 percent American Indian. The *Los Angeles Times* reported that leaders and officials throughout the region were asking, "Where are we going?" Some want to return to days of old, but most recognize that the world has changed.

Residents of Orick worked together to produce a plan they called "Taking Control of Orick's Economic Future." They want Orick to be a destination for the more than 200,000 annual visitors to little Redwood National Park. They eventually want to become the "Gateway to the Redwoods." They are working with park officials to concentrate more attention on Orick as the center of tourist activities. These efforts are typical of rural communities across northern California and beyond the coastal counties. In Anderson, Shasta County, a factory outlet mall opened to replace timber jobs, as the area was having trouble drawing light or any other industries. These problems kept unemployment in nearby Redding, which also once relied heavily on timber, at 13 percent into the late 1990s.

California's rural recession spread throughout the Central Valley, which never enjoyed the economic recovery of the late 1990s. The more than 200,000 jobless kept unemployment rates over 12 percent in many areas, more than double the state average near the end of the decade. Eleven Central Valley counties were among the fifteen in the state with highest unemployment rates. A poorly trained work force, farm products that are exported for processing, and a population explosion far exceeding job growth were all considered factors.

Where are we going? The answer is different in each California rural community. Is the future in tourism, light or heavy industry, and prisons or in traditional reliance on logging, fishing, mining, and agriculture? Almost any of these options seemed better to many residents than a reputation for poverty and welfare. How we answer these questions will determine the very nature of California's rural landscapes and cultures. One thing is certain—many of these economies, cultures and landscapes will continue to evolve with less rural and more urban characteristics.

SOME KEY TERMS AND TOPICS

agribusiness	Emerald Triangle	selective cutting
biotechnology	migrant workers	specialty crops
clear cutting	milk shed	sustainable harvests (timber)
community-supported agriculture (CSA)	multiplier effect	transportation corridors
economic geography	primary economic activities	truck farming
ecotourism	rural landscapes	von Thunen model

Additional Key Terms and Topics

commercial agriculture	geographic information systems (GIS)	productive forests
corporate farms	global market	rangeland
desert lifestyles	global position systems (GPS)	recreational fishing
disease, pests, poisons	harvests	rural land use
economic system	hunting and gathering	rural lifestyles
encroaching developments	international trade	sandlappers
farm life	land ownership	specialized farming
farm workers	mineral production	stone fruits
field crops	mining industry	subsistence agriculture
fish catch	natural resources	timber industry
floriculture	old growth	vegetable crops
forest management	perishable products	wineries
forest products		yield per acre
genetic engineering		

Chapter 10

California's Modern, Advanced Economies

In the previous chapter, we surveyed the state's primary industries and the people, natural resources, rural landscapes, and trends associated with them. In this chapter, we examine the evolution, geographic distribution, impacts, and trends of more advanced industries in California. As in the previous chapter, we will recognize the diversity of economic activities and gain a better understanding of the profound connections and rapid changes that dominate within our economic landscapes.

This is not designed or intended to be "grocery list geography," but a serious overview of the many industries that are vital to millions of Californians. Economic upheavals during the last decade alone have proven that living standards, working conditions, and events in the everyday lives of all Californians (and millions outside our state) are often determined by intertwined national, state, and local economic trends. California's very role as a world leader will depend upon its economic health. Its landscapes will evolve as a direct result of these trends. An understanding of the diversity, connections, and change within these industrial activities and landscapes is vital to our understanding of the geography of California and is crucial if we are to anticipate future economic trends in the state.

KEY ISSUES AND CONCEPTS

◆ Diverse secondary, tertiary, quaternary, and other more complex, highly advanced industries combine to make California the greatest economic powerhouse in the nation, and seventh in the world. California ranks high in nearly every measure of economic development.

◆ The state's economy continues to evolve and diversify at accelerated rates as its industries become more advanced and complex. Spatial transition to more advanced industries is also evident when travelling from rural landscapes toward urban centers.

◆ Manufacturing, aerospace, and military spending were among the activities that fueled California's economy through much of the twentieth century. By the 1990s, a restructured economy was growing more complex, stratified, and diverse, often at the expense of manufacturing and the middle class.

◆ The state's economy returned to a period of rapid economic expansion after the deep recession of the early 1990s. Entertainment, high-tech manufacturing, services, and international trade were among the activities fueling the new economy; construction, tourism, and other industries followed, but the gap between rich and poor grew wider.

◆ The state's manufacturing industries have grown within its urban centers. New manufac-turing centers continue to erupt in suburbs on the urban fringe; others have shifted to maquiladoras just across the Mexican border or to more distant countries.

◆ Today's interconnected, advanced industries are thriving within expanding urban landscapes. High-technology information and computer services, entertainment, tourism, retail, trade, real estate, housing, government, and related economic activities are expected to lead the state's economic growth well into the twenty-first century. Vital infrastructure and high- and low-end services also extend their threads through every complex urban population, economy, and culture.

◆ Economic cooperation and partnerships are bringing capital and jobs into urban areas to replace past cuts in defense and manufacturing.

◆ Most projections anticipate continued economic growth well into the twenty-first century. Such factors as the state's economic and cultural diversity and its geographic position on the Pacific Rim are considered vital assets. However, unstable Asian and other global markets at the end of the 1990s added uncertainty to some of the more optimistic forecasts.

◆ CLASSIFYING THE STATE'S INDUSTRIES

Moving a step beyond primary industries, **secondary** production **industries** increase the value of a commodity by changing its form. These include "blue-collar workers" in small and large manufacturing industries. Food processors who mix, cook, can, and freeze various farm products, textile and apparel industries, petroleum refineries and other power producers are also secondary industries. The construction industry, defense and civilian aerospace, and shipbuilding industries are other important examples in California. Some of today's economists argue that modern agribusiness has become so advanced and complex—as fertilizers, water, pesticides, and heavy machinery are brought to the fields to produce food—that such farming should, in some cases, be considered a secondary industry in California. As we learned in the last chapter, the fine line between various stages of economic activities is often blurred.

Tertiary economic **activities**, instead of producing tangible goods, provide services. These may include personal, clerical, professional and business services, and wholesale and retail trade. This category is growing rapidly in California, often at the expense of primary and secondary activities. Additionally, tertiary activities are divided into more specific, advanced and complex industries that are growing just as rapidly in California.

Industrial landscapes rule in El Segundo and other Los Angeles South Bay cities. Here, tankers hook up to pipes for the transfer of oil to storage and refineries on land.

Highly Advanced Industries

Quaternary industries may include financial, insurance, real estate and health services, entertainment, education, information, data-processing, research, management, and administrative services. These "white-collar" industries are further augmented by the "gold collar" **quinary industries**. They include high-level management, administration and executive decision makers, scientific research and development, and similar services. There are fewer of these jobs, but they are some of the highest-paying and visible positions in the state; their numbers are also growing fast.

Transportation, distribution, and communications cut across and link all these categories of economic activity. These exchange services and infrastructures are critical to the success of every California industry.

◆ INDUSTRIES EVOLVE TO BECOME MORE COMPLEX

As we travel spatially in California from rural toward urban landscapes, we will encounter more advanced and complex economic activities. Modern Californians are also advancing in time away from reliance on primary and secondary production of goods and increasingly toward providing services. The California economy has long since passed that turning point away from dependence on natural resources. It more recently passed the turning point away from World War II and Cold War economies. Today, we are making another turn, creating changes within economic landscapes that may rival the industrial revolution.

Put simply, California's economy and workforce evolved during the twentieth century from the labor of hands in the fields to the labor of hands in the factories to today's labor of minds. Most economic indicators from the 1980s and 1990s in California clearly show that traditional middle-class primary and manufacturing industries and jobs have been overshadowed by services in the tertiary industries and beyond.

The state's modern economic growth is especially focused on the extreme ends of the services—low-skill, low-paying jobs and high-paying jobs requiring advanced skills and education. As California leaped out of its early 1990s recession, foreign trade and high-tech exports, services, entertainment and tourism were fueling its rejuvenated economy into the twenty-first century. Interestingly, manufacturing and especially construction jobs and industries were following those cutting-edge economic sectors by expanding again toward the twenty-first century.

These economic trends continue to impact California's people and landscapes in profound ways. California moved from a subsistence economy to a commercial economy in the 1800s, and it had firmly established its leadership in secondary economic activities and manufacturing industries by the mid-1900s. Consequently, its population and urban centers swelled.

California's Latest Economic Revolution

Today, the state is undergoing another economic and social revolution. The growing industries are less dependent on the physical environment and more likely to modify it; they are even sweeping away traditional cultural barriers. Newer industries are more dependent on high levels of technology and a skilled and educated workforce. They are also more dependent on competitive economic factors of supply and demand in a freer world market.

As we continue to move our economy away from reliance on primary and secondary activities and toward more advanced, complex industries, each individual and each landscape must also adapt to these changes. How are we dealing with the loss of middle-class jobs and industries and the increasing gap between the rich and poor, the haves and have-nots? How do we respond to overcrowded, poverty-stricken communities that resemble less developed nations adjacent to some of the wealthiest people and neighborhoods in the world, all in a state that would rank up to seventh among nations in world economies? It is difficult to miss these contradictions and dilemmas while travelling through any California town or city, although it is hoped that the recent economic expansion will continue to pull construction and other middle-class industries and jobs along into the twenty-first century.

In a state with such powerful commercial economies, to what extent should political decisions and more planned economies play a role? How might government and industry work together to ease the social and cultural stresses and conflicts that result from such economic upheavals? As these questions are debated, the focus is on California. Once again, these changes are taking place in other parts of the nation and the world, but the change is faster and more extreme in California. More and more frequently, when the nation and the world look toward California, they look into the future.

The California experiment continues, and geographers should, and are, playing key roles in shaping it. They can help identify the proper sites and situations so that new industries are placed in optimum locations that result in the greatest efficiency and success for businesses and communities. Those with a geographical perspective can also assist government and industry in locating future trouble spots and in creating better living and working environments for all Californians.

◆ THE NATURE OF CALIFORNIA'S MODERN ECONOMY

Tumultuous upheavals and rapid change have repeatedly transformed California's economy since the Gold Rush. Except for a few ruts and dips, the road has always led toward astounding economic growth that has produced one of the most powerful economies in the world. Economic diversity (an important theme in this chapter) is one of the main reasons the state has become such a powerhouse. Previously, we noted how growth of secondary and tertiary economic activities outpaced primary industries, including agriculture, throughout the 1900s. By the mid-1970s, manufacturing accounted for 32 percent of California's payroll and 27 percent (1.6 million jobs) of the state's workers (see Map 10.1). Manufacturing continued strong into the 1980s, when new, radical changes became evident.

The recession that stretched through the early 1990s was an unusually difficult one for Californians. Historically, national economic downturns were not as severe in California, but, due to the state's dependence on military spending (especially in aerospace), military cutbacks affected California more than any other state. This and industry restructuring resulted in a net loss of manufacturing jobs during the late-1980s and early 1990s. The number of aerospace jobs alone dropped from 337,000 to 191,000 between 1990 and 1994. This had a negative ripple effect on construction and many other industries.

Meanwhile, the service and trade industries continued fast growth into and through the 1990s. The services added more than 200,000 jobs between 1990 and 1994, during the recession! By 1993, the state reported that more than half of all jobs were already in services (29 percent) and trade (23 percent). What were the results of this restructuring? Through the recession, California dropped from ninth to thirteenth in the nation in per capita disposable income. (This still was more than 5 percent above the national average.)

The New California Economy

Into the mid-1990s, many middle-class workers in manufacturing fled the state, while the highly educated and skilled and least-skilled, lowest-income workers continued to flow in. As the gap between rich and poor widened, California's population began to match the new economic trends. These trends helped set the stage for the new California population and economy, which was steaming ahead by the late 1990s.

Today, California is home to more than 12 percent of the U.S. population and provides more than 13 percent of the U.S. Gross Domestic Product. Its gross product soared over $800 billion per year during the mid-1990s. That is 60 percent more than the next largest state economy (New York) and $340 billion more than all twelve of the other Pacific and Mountain states combined. Foreign trade imports and exports through the state's ports skyrocketed past $200 billion per year during the mid-1990s as 40 percent of all U.S. trade with Asia went through California. (An imbalance between the high number of imports and the lower number of exports was exacerbated by the Asian economic crisis in the late 1990s as Asian countries lacked the money to buy U.S. products.)

More than 850,000 increasingly diverse businesses created the foundation for this new and dynamic economy. Depending on the measuring stick and timing, California's economy ranks seventh in the world, according to California government data. We are dealing with an economy that competes with countries like the United Kingdom, Italy, and France in economic power.

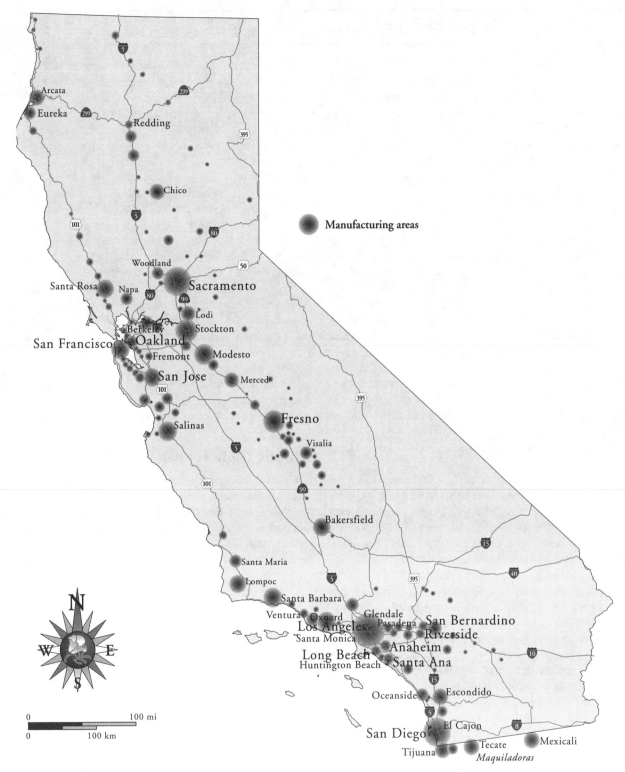

MAP 10.1
Clusters of manufacturing centers are located in and around the state's urban centers.

From the Deepest Pit

During the early 1990s, California's economy dropped into the worst economic recession since the Great Depression. Painful restructuring redistributed the wealth and growth into different economic sectors and geographic locations. By the late 1990s, the state's industrial landscapes were already remade in what resembled an economic ride from the bottom of Death Valley to the top of Mount Whitney. Is such rapid change and explo-

THE DOWNTURN HITS SAN DIEGO

Negative impacts on normally upbeat San Diego indicated the extent of California's economic gloom in the early 1990s. During previous years, as San Diego grew, it was recognized for its economic strength and diversity. Its tourist industry thrived with the success of the San Diego Zoo, Sea World, its scenic coast, and other attractions. Its proximity to Mexico and its construction industry reinforced the economy, but the military-industrial complex played a dominant role in San Diego's economy for decades. Shipbuilders and defense contractors such as General Dynamics, Rohr, and National Steel employed thousands. Consequently, corporate and military downsizing hit San Diego especially hard.

The number of uniform personnel stationed in San Diego dropped. Hotel occupancy rates fell to 65 percent in 1992, below the required level for profit. The number of construction permits and developments plummeted, causing construction employment to fall 25 percent in two years. Within three years, San Diego's only three home-based savings and loan institutions had failed.

The inflow of highly-paid and skilled professionals into San Diego during the 1980s stopped in the early 1990s. Younger, less-educated, and often foreign-born workers accounted for the population increases. San Diego's gross regional product shrank for the first time since the Great Depression. San Diego lost 50,000 jobs in 1991, a 5 percent drop in employment, and the trend continued into 1993; average annual income declined in 1992 for the first time since World War II. All of these were symptoms of the broader economic slump that had spread across the state. Just a few years later, however, San Diego would help lead California in an historical economic comeback. Expansion brought about by economic diversity lifted San Diego and California into the twenty-first century.

---

sive economic growth sustainable in the new economy? Did this transformation really take less than ten years, or was it the beginning of a lasting trend of economic uncertainty and chaos? To gain better understanding of these issues, we must examine the state's industrial landscapes more closely.

During the late-1980s to early-1990s recession, California lost nearly one million jobs, about the same number needed to employ its large streams of immigrants, mostly from other countries. Between 1987 and 1992 alone, California lost about 400,000 jobs, including 162,000 defense-related jobs; about 100,000 manufacturing jobs moved to other states. The deep recession that had already devastated many timber towns and other rural communities had infiltrated into urban areas, and into secondary and more advanced industries. Response to these hardships in primary industries and rural communities was outlined in the previous chapter. By the early 1990s, advanced industries and business leaders in the state's cities faced similar hardships.

In 1992, business failures in California rose to 19,590, a 33 percent jump from the previous year and more than one-fifth of the national total. Financial, construction, insurance, real estate, and service industries were all hit hard. Leaders blamed the aerospace/defense cuts and corporate downsizing. Business failures were up 73 percent in Los Angeles as Angelenos suffered through the worst riots in California history. The state's foreclosures doubled in 1992 to 37,557, 81 percent of them in Southern California. Economic uncertainty and fierce competition for jobs eroded living standards of those in the middle class who were lucky just to remain employed. Near the end of the recession, less than 13 per-

cent of the state's work force was union, down from nearly 40 percent in 1952. Our economy was in a tailspin and, for some, there seemed to be no end in sight.

To the Highest Peak

Within a few years, clear signs of recovery and renewed growth emerged, then quickly accelerated into the late 1990s. A restructured stage had been set for a glorious economic renaissance that would propel California into the twenty-first century. It started around 1993, when early signs of a renewed economic upswing in California were suggested by several major national publications. Some of these publications correctly predicted the nature of the new California economic recovery.

According to the *Institutional Investor* in December, 1993, California's leading industries were agriculture, tourism, entertainment, high-tech, real estate, and defense. Tourism and entertainment first showed signs of strength. However, defense (with its 1.4 million employees in 1993) remained weak, slowing the state's recovery. This publication emphasized the factors that helped pull California out of recession: world-class technological skills, vast pools of cheap labor, a site on the booming Pacific Rim, and that old reliable standby of ideal weather.

By August, 1994, *Money Magazine* encouraged stock buyers to consider companies with large shares of profits from California because they would experience substantial earnings and share-price gains in future years. By January, 1995, *The New York Times* reported that the California economy had hit bottom in 1993 and was surging ahead. Leading the recovery were business services, tourism, entertainment, export trade (strengthened by NAFTA, then weakened by the Asian economic crisis), and construction. According to the *Wall Street Journal* in February, 1995, exports, jobs, and per-capita personal income were finally increasing (though exports dropped in the late 1990s due to economic troubles in Asia and Mexico).

The Economist noted how California's share of the fastest-growing industries in the nation was expanding rapidly in 1995. In that same year, median household income increased to over $37,000 in California, while the number of people living in poverty dropped to 16.7 percent of all residents. The State Board of Equalization reported taxable transactions of $73.6 billion during the first three months of 1996, up $6.1 billion from the same period in 1995. Recession was just a memory, and the new California economy was officially moving full steam ahead. During 1996, unemployment fell below 7 percent as more than 30,000 jobs were created during individual months. Thousands more jobs were created until unemployment dropped below 6 percent into 1999.

Economic Growth Sectors: A New Foundation

California sailed through the late 1990s and into the twenty-first century on the winds of economic expansion. As of this writing, California is again drawing investment and people (nationally and internationally); its skilled labor force and Pacific Rim location are powerful catalysts. Entertainment, high-tech manufacturing, services, and international trade are the leaders and the new foundations of the California economy. Manufacturing and especially construction followed this economic upswing by rebounding toward the twenty-first century.

Motion pictures are the main component of **entertainment**; they added about 120,000 jobs in Los Angeles County alone from 1990 to 1996. That is about equal to the number of jobs lost in aerospace layoffs in the county during the same time period. Shortages of sound stages and skilled labor were the only problems slowing entertainment growth. (By the late 1990s, some economists believed that this industry had finally reached an impressive plateau in California.)

High technology is based on semi-conductors, computers, software, and multimedia produced in Silicon Valley, medical instruments and computer peripherals in Orange County, and biotechnology and telecommunications in San Diego.

One of the greatest categories of economic growth was in services. This was especially true with educational services provided by private schools and business services, particularly when software developers and consultants are included.

Exports from California grew by 19 percent in 1995, and substantial growth continued into the late 1990s. Ja-

pan's improving economy and the devaluation of the Mexican peso and lowering of tariffs on products helped. Then, the Asian economic crisis of the late 1990s caught almost everyone off guard. It put a dent in the projected trade between California and Asia even as the state's economy steamed on. Today, California exports frequently go to places like Japan, China, South Korea, Taiwan, the Philippines, Malaysia, and Latin American countries.

The California economy became healthier because it was more diverse and broad-based as it headed into the twenty-first century. Growing companies are taking a global view. As corporations and investors return, the office building market is strengthening throughout the state. By the late 1990s, office vacancy rates were even falling in Los Angeles County, which was slower to experience recovery.

Though commercial investment in California increased more than 21 percent in 1996, it improved less than 3 percent in L.A. County. Leaders expressed concern that L.A.'s new jobs were mostly lower-paying retail trade and business services, and were filled by the flood of less-educated, low-skilled immigrants. However, scores of new expansion projects began to change all of that. They included the ports of Los Angeles and Long Beach, Universal Studios, Disney, DreamWorks SKG studio, and the Alameda Corridor.

Statewide, residential construction also recovered. Median housing prices were finally rising through the late 1990s and had soared over $200,000 by the end of the decade. Those housing prices also rose sharply in most of the state's major urban areas, signs of the economic and population growth that continued through the final months of the century.

Leading into the Twenty-First Century Today, California is the leader into the twenty-first century economy, with strength in motion pictures, multimedia, and foreign trade. Long-term growth sectors include services, high-tech exports, foreign trade, entertainment, and tourism. Much of this job growth is in high-wage fields, which have replaced the aerospace losses. However, there was considerable variation in strength of specific sectors from year to year as California headed into the twenty-first century. One example was the drop in high-tech exports to Asia during the Asian economic crisis of the late 1990s.

Corporations are staying or moving back to the state to take advantage of the talent pool and brain power. According to a survey of more than 1,200 California industrial companies, corporate profits have grown fastest in technology, basic materials manufacturing, consumer goods, and health care industries. Even manufacturing was growing into the late 1990s, though it slumped in much of the rest of the nation. Within two years after the early 1990s slump, California created more jobs than it lost during the entire recession.

It is estimated that for each new job, state and local governments get $6,000 to $7,000 per worker. This is why California had quickly accumulated billions in surplus revenue by the late 1990s. California's general fund pays most state programs, and it is part of the more than $81 billion California state budget. Most of it comes from income taxes, corporate profits, and retail sales. The general fund was expected to grow by more than 5 percent per year toward the twenty-first century. Public schools and corporate tax cuts consumed much of the growth.

Growing Discrepancies

Some trouble spots still exist in this otherwise rosy economic picture. According to Deborah Reed, author and research fellow at the Public Policy Institute of California, a dwindling middle class and growing gap between rich and poor were trends that continued well into the 1990s. From 1967 to 1994, household income for a family of four in the lower 10 percent bracket in California dropped 24 percent (after inflation adjustments) down to $11,205. The top 10 percent household incomes rose 35 percent during that same period to average more than $110,000. She and other economic experts blamed restructuring and defense cutbacks during the recession, massive immigration, and new technology for California income gaps that grew faster than the national average.

Many of the new low-wage jobs are in apparel manufacturing, warehousing and retail trade within manufacturing, and service and retail sectors. These industries offer jobs especially where large concentrations of immigrant populations compete for them, particularly in Southern California.

In contrast, some high-paying industries, such as high-tech and entertainment, are finding labor shortages in the state. Geographically, many of these higher-paying positions were created in the Bay Area as the northern California economy grew faster than in Southern California. As an example, the San Jose area created nearly 25,000 new manufacturing jobs during 1996 alone. This resulted in geographic accentuation of income gaps within California. By the end of the century, Southern California's economy was creating more jobs. As corporate downsizing and restructuring continued, experts stressed the need for education to help bridge the gap between rich and poor Californians.

A closer look at the nature and geographic distribution of California's industries can reveal more about its economic landscapes.

Secondary Industries

From processing food and other natural resources to making computer parts, California has been the leading manufacturing state for decades. These **manufacturing** industries also include textiles and apparel, furniture and fixtures, paper, printing and publishing, and the making of chemicals, building materials, and petroleum products. They include the making of metal products, machinery, electronic and transportation equipment and instruments. It was difficult to miss these economic forces that dominated nearly every California urban landscape into the 1980s. They require the concentrations of labor and capital that only a city can offer.

Manufacturing Clusters

Even some of the most attractive California cities still have their stark, utilitarian-looking industrial landscapes to add economic diversity. They are clustered within California's larger cities, and they are noticeably strung out along major railroad and truck transport routes. Manufacturing centers have grown around the string of cities through the Central Valley, especially from Bakersfield, north past Sacramento. They have also erupted in smaller cities, especially along the California coast. However, manufacturing centers are particularly prominent within California's three largest metropolitan areas.

Manufacturing in the San Francisco Bay Area   In the Bay Area, manufacturing centers are linked into an elongated U-shaped formation hugging the bay. They stretch from San Francisco south through Daly City, San Mateo, Redwood City, and into the Silicon Valley past San Jose. The clusters then bend radically north into Fremont, Hayward, Oakland, Berkeley, and Richmond. They have more recently appeared in the East Bay and toward the Delta.

Southern California Manufacturing Centers   Six Southern California counties represent the greatest manufacturing belt in the United States, employing more than 1.1 million people. The largest manufacturing clusters

Long Beach Naval Shipyard employed thousands and boosted the city's economy for decades. Long Beach scrambled to diversify its economy in the 1990s after the shipyard shut down.

SAN GABRIEL'S ECONOMY EVOLVES

The history of trends in industries within the city of San Gabriel is typical of economic evolution within numerous California urban areas. San Gabriel claims to be the first European settlement in the L.A. area. Franciscan fathers first used the work of Gabrielinos (local Native Americans) to build their economy. By 1818, they produced the olive oil, tallow, soap, hides, shoes, clothing, and wine that helped support Los Angeles. San Gabriel was incorporated in 1913 after the railroad lines came through, and long after the mission was in ruins. It was known for its orange groves and tiny airport.

Following World War II, Wham-O Toys grew and prospered there. It shipped the sling-shots, Slip 'N Slides,

Frisbees and Hula Hoops (an invention that made Wham-O famous) that became popular symbols of California culture. When the Wham-O warehouse finally closed in 1994, the location was rezoned for modern development. During the same year, San Gabriel had earned the National League of Cities award for urban enrichment after redeveloping its mission district. By then, this city, with a diverse ethnic population nearly equally divided among Asian, Latino, and white, looked to more advanced industries for prosperity. Toward the 21st century, its median household incomes and home values remained considerably higher than the Los Angeles County average.

extend especially south and east of downtown L.A., and they are evident again in Long Beach. They extend noticeably southeast parallel to railroad tracks and I-5 from San Fernando through Burbank, East L.A., Norwalk and through the traditional Orange County manufacturing centers of Anaheim and Santa Ana. Here, an abundance of smaller high- and low-tech companies especially employ immigrants in low-wage jobs. These immigrants are improving their financial status, but wages are being held low within their industries.

Additional manufacturing clusters are strung out, veering west along tracks through the San Fernando Valley. Two noticeable manufacturing strings cut east–west through the L.A. Basin, linking the West Side to the San Gabriel and San Bernardino Valleys. Additional important manufacturing centers are found on the southern edge of Santa Monica Bay and in southern Orange County.

Southern California's traditional manufacturing landscapes share many similarities with other urban centers in the state. They once included mass production. These car, petroleum, tire, steel, and other industries only represented about 8 percent of employment during their heyday. Today, they are almost gone. Another category is craft specialty production, still going strong in some urban locations. Such industries include apparel, textile, furniture, printing, and other operations. In these landscapes, you will find small units of subcontractors networking and using mostly unskilled workers.

Finally, you will find the high-tech manufacturers, including makers of parts and equipment for offices, electronics, and computers. These manufacturers have played increasingly important roles in California's economy. However, a troubling Southern California Business Climate Survey conducted by USC's Marshall School of Business was published by the *Los Angeles Times* in 1998. It found that 1,700 small businesses could not find skilled

labor, and one-sixth of all businesses claimed that lack of capable workers was their biggest problem. A better skilled workforce was required to sustain economic growth in these industries.

Manufacturing in San Diego San Diego's traditional manufacturing centers followed patterns similar to L.A.'s until the explosion of maquiladora industries along the border. By the 1990s, hundreds of thousands of jobs were being added by these borderline industries. **Maquiladoras** are located where they can exploit cheap labor pools to manufacture products on the Mexico side of the border, then conveniently ship their products (free of burdensome tariffs) especially to enormous U.S. markets.

Manufacturing Fades

It would seem that people and industries who make needed products form the foundations for a stable and reliable economy. However, manufacturing took a big hit during the California recession and **restructuring** that carried through the early 1990s. Total jobs in manufacturing in California had soared above 2 million by the mid-1980s, only to drop below that mark by the mid-1990s. (By the mid-1990s, total jobs in both services and trade were well over 2 million, while government service jobs just broke through the 2 million mark.) The result is an economy that is less reliant on making tangible products and has greater emphasis on services and trade as it evolves into more advanced and complex stages.

Products from Natural Resources

Food processing, related industries, and other products directly derived from natural resources have always played major roles in the state's economy. From pro-

SWEATSHOPS

California's notorious **sweatshops** continued to make headlines through the 1990s. They have been discovered in places like the hidden corners of San Francisco's Chinatown for decades. California often leads the nation in garment industry labor offenses. In one three-month period in 1996, federal investigators recovered more than $350,000 in back wages for more than 1,000 workers. When state and federal labor investigators raided Southern California's garment-manufacturing industries, they repeatedly found numerous sweatshops. Throughout Los Angeles and Orange Counties, serious health and safety violations and childhood labor laws were broken.

Then, in August, 1996, sixty Thai nationals were freed from modern-day peonage within an El Monte apartment complex converted into a sweatshop. Confined behind a barbed-wire fence, these illegal immigrants were forced to work up to twelve hours per day, seven days a week for about $1 an hour. Increased pressure from consumer, government and retail groups has been placed on the apparel industry—from manufacturers to retailers—to locate and eliminate such illegal sweatshops. Though this may have forced some of the larger firms out of California, a few major retailers (such as Sears) have taken aggressive action to stop selling apparel originating from sweatshops.

Despite all these efforts, California continues to lead the nation in labor violations; the U.S. Labor Department issued seventy-two violations to the state's garment industries during another three-month period in 1998.

cessing and manufacturing timber and mining products to recycling, most of these more basic manufacturing industries are strongly dependent on natural resources. Consequently, individual examples were considered in the previous chapter on primary industries.

Garment/Apparel Industries

You may be surprised at the size and extent of California's garment industries. Clothing manufacturers have played important roles in nearly every major city's economy. In a state where popular fashions radiate out to the rest of the world, you will find many interconnected levels of clothing design and manufacturing. They range from high-end fashion designers to laborers sewing these fashions into reality in cramped cubicles.

The world's largest apparel manufacturer, Levi Strauss & Co., originated and is still headquartered in San Francisco. During the 1900s, Levi's established the standards for practical, casual, and comfortable popular clothing. By the late 1990s, the company's annual sales soared over $7 billion, including $2.8 billion in international sales. It employed more than 25,000 workers in the United States alone. Competition from other clothing manufacturers forced Levi's to finally downsize and cut its workforce by the late 1990s.

Nevertheless, the nation's largest garment industry is in Southern California. During the 1990s, this economy employed more than 120,000 workers in up to 5,000 factories within the L.A. area. This industry, which accounts for more manufacturing jobs than any other in L.A. County, took advantage of the geographic proximity of its various interconnected layers. Portions of this garment industry, especially where fashion designers, skilled craftspeople, and sales personnel are needed, pay well and require skilled labor. However, it also includes sweatshops that sell through ethnic marketing channels or downtown cut-rate outlets. Consequently, the industry employs 70 percent Latinos, mostly recent immigrants. The California Fashion Association estimated that 30 percent of their Los Angeles-area industry workers were illegal during the 1990s.

Some analysts, such as Richard P. Appelbaum at UC Santa Barbara, argue that this has created a pyramid of haves and have-nots divided by class and ethnicity. Certainly, there are tremendous discrepancies between the masses of minimum wage workers on the bottom and the few multimillionaires at the top.

As larger firms moved out to exploit cheaper labor pools in Latin America and Asia during the late 1900s, the approximately 5,000 smaller contracting firms—from textile suppliers to designers, craftspeople, and salespeople—stayed. Quick adjustments to changing fashions cut turnaround times down to two weeks within these smaller industries bunched in L.A. The result is improved quality control. These remaining industries may also represent an opportunity for the less skilled to work their way up the economic ladder. Unfortunately, they also included illegal sweatshops.

New Technologies Transform the Garment Industry
Modern technology is changing the nature of California's garment industry. There is new demand for trained workers with high-tech skills. As processes are automated, computers are now plotting factory production flow and sizing garments. Salaries for technology-trained workers are much higher. Groups like Rebuild L.A. have responded to these changes, and schools such as L.A. Trade Technical College are teaching these new skills.

Some private corporations are helping to sponsor the training programs. The result should be a California that becomes more competitive in the garment industry while creating more high-paying jobs, such as designers, pattern makers, graders, and production managers.

Furniture

There are fascinating similarities between California's furniture and apparel industries. Furniture industry employment in the Los Angeles area grew ahead of San Francisco in the early 1900s. In places like South-Central L.A. and Vernon, early furniture companies found the industrial infrastructure required for success, including access to suppliers and rail lines. Later in the twentieth century, large immigrant (especially Latino) populations provided a source of cheap labor. California also established its own distinctive style of furniture, more adapted to outdoor lifestyles and Mediterranean climates.

However, foreign competition and air quality regulations drove many companies out of California to cheaper labor markets during the late 1900s. The recession had an even greater impact; employment in the industry was cut by nearly half from 1987 to 1993.

By the late 1990s, about six-hundred mostly smaller household furniture makers represented a $2.6 billion industry in L.A. County alone, the nation's second-largest furniture manufacturing center. This industry's success is closely tied to new housing starts, as Californians often choose local styles of furniture to fill their new homes. Consequently, the industry recovered into the late 1990s. Younger entrepreneurs are being attracted to this industry as they link up with fashion-minded consumers looking for the latest styles. New designs not sold in California's trendy stores are being shipped especially to Asia.

Construction

According to the California Legislative Analyst's Office, about 4 percent of all California workers are in construction. As with other economic activities, construction indirectly generates income and jobs in other sectors, perhaps doubling the workforce that is somehow impacted by construction projects. These include manufacturing of equipment and building materials, services, and trade-related activities.

The state's building industry considers 125,000 new living units as the minimum standard for a good year. During the boom years of the 1970s and 1980s, new residential permits averaged about 210,000 per year and soared over 300,000 in 1986! More than 160,000 living units were constructed in Southern California alone during peak years. That number dropped well below 60,000 during the early 1990s recession, when California's construction industry took a big hit; Southern California's construction industry was also one of the last in the nation to recover. Only 85,000 new permits were issued for the entire state in 1993. The "only" in that sentence reveals the relative size and importance of California's construction industry compared to any other state.

Non-residential construction averaged $14.8 billion during the 1980s boom, but it was only about $8 billion going out of the recession during the mid-1990s. Heavy construction also played a big role in the building industry. It was especially fortified by earthquake repairs and retrofitting throughout the 1990s, particularly when there was public support from bond measures. Transportation projects have always helped fuel this industry. Jails that sprouted around California during the early and mid-1990s and school facilities later in the decade also strengthened this economic sector. By the late 1990s, the industry was recovering remarkably and growing again

Resorts in Palm Springs are being upstaged by enormous developments farther south in the Coachella Valley. Leisure activities and retirees continue to fuel the construction industry here.

THE CONSTRUCTION INDUSTRY RESPONDS TO NEW DEMOGRAPHICS

The recession forced a restructuring of California's construction industry. Numerous smaller construction firms went out of business, while some larger companies, including L.A.-based Kaufman & Broad Home Corporation, shifted their operations to other western states. Several larger companies remaining in California were able to hold on through the recession only because they had more capital and diversity. As one example, with 850,000 acres, San Francisco-based Catellus Development Corporation became arguably the largest construction-firm landholder in the state. (However, much of this was Mojave Desert land, which Catellus negotiated to sell to environmental groups by the end of the century.) As a result of recession losses, California Building Industry Association memberships dropped by more than half from the late 1980s through the early 1990s. Foreign companies also began moving in to fill the perceived void.

A few surviving firms, especially smaller companies, started a new trend that is changing the state's urban landscapes. Instead of constructing expensive units on the extended suburban fringe, they focused on smaller existing spaces in urban areas. These firms are building less expensive units for less profit. They are attracting first-time buyers and more diverse, lower-income groups within cities as they monitor the movement and success of surrounding employers. This trend is encouraging some of the new Californians to crowd together in more densely-populated urban centers. Here was another economic trend that fit the new California demographics—urban infilling.

---

in response to demands rippling out from a growing population, economy, and real estate market.

The lagging construction industry finally moved forward with the booming California economy into the late 1990s. As building start-ups increased, the Construction Industry Research Board's (CIRB) normally optimistic predictions were at last realized. Due to new jobs and lower unemployment, increased immigration, and lower interest rates, nearly $20 billion of new housing units were anticipated during the final few years of the century. Southern California was especially looking north toward the Silicon Valley, where remarkable economic growth resulted in a housing shortage within an industry that couldn't build fast enough.

San Diego's Construction Industry Rebounds No economy suffered more than San Diego from the early 1990s recession's housing slump. This was partially a result of manufacturing jobs lost to nearby Tijuana and a lull in past population explosions. Interestingly, heavy construction projects led San Diego out of the building recession as the housing industry recovered more slowly. Major projects in 1997 included expansions of former Jack Murphy Stadium, the San Diego Convention Center, and the Hyatt and Marriot downtown hotels. These were followed by other planned projects including the sewage treatment plant at the border, and the expansion of Lindbergh Field airport and I-5.

By 1997, construction jobs were increasing, and apartment and hotel vacancy rates were falling in San Diego. A dramatic increase in housing construction followed. This recovery continued into the next years and accompanied investments in San Diego's infrastructure that propelled it into the twenty-first century.

Aerospace

During the mid-1900s, the state of California, and L.A. County in particular, became the nation's largest aerospace and defense industrial center. Growing airline industries and spacecraft and missile defense contracts helped make giant aerospace corporations (such as McDonnell Douglas and Rockwell) household names. This is one reason California continued to lead the United States in industrial job formation throughout much of the twentieth century. It also helps explain why California was hit so hard by defense cuts and downsizing during the recession. Corporate consolidation and cuts in defense contracts left some California communities (especially in L.A.'s South Bay) staggering into the 1990s.

A Rand Corporation computer analysis of defense contracts between 1987 amd 1991 showed a loss in L.A. County aerospace jobs of 20.3 percent, compared to 10.7 percent for the rest of the country. Nearly 20 percent of California's 100,000 aerospace job losses in that period were at McDonnell Douglas because of competition for defense contracts from other companies. Veering from tradition, only 15.5 percent of competitive, fixed-price defense contracts were awarded to California companies during that period.

Several factors were responsible for California's losses: breakdowns in infrastructure, employees' deteriorating and crowded living and working conditions, and the high cost of doing business in Southern California. It seemed that the very attractions that brought these companies to California decades ago had disappeared. Many claimed that the California problem was really a Los Angeles problem as the industry hit bottom in the early 1990s. The results were very familiar to Californians—

BOEING CONSUMES ROCKWELL AND MCDONNELL DOUGLAS

Changes in the state's aerospace industry became evident again in August, 1996, when Rockwell International Corporation announced plans to sell its space and defense operations to Boeing for $3.2 billion. Here was the company that bought North American Aviation in Southern California in 1967, named itself North American Rockwell, and moved its headquarters to El Segundo. This was the company that was renamed Rockwell International Corporation and was the focus of California's aerospace industry with operations in Seal Beach, Downey, Canoga Park, Anaheim, and Texas. Californians could not believe that the giant that built U.S. space shuttles had decided to bail out and sell to Seattle-based Boeing. Thousands of jobs and billions of dollars were at stake.

Both companies anticipated positive financial windfalls from the transaction. Rockwell (still a $10 billion per year company) now had the cash to expand its non-defense businesses in factory automation systems, aircraft avionics and communications gear, semiconductors, and automotive parts. These were considered to have greater growth potential than the less reliable government space and defense contracts. Rockwell would also have the revenue to acquire telecommunications companies, especially in wireless and multimedia communications, and companies developing electronic and satellite-based guidance systems.

Rockwell could use the extra cash especially to increase its dominance in the semiconductor market which provided 26 percent of the company's "new" annual profits in the mid-1990s. Sales at its Newport Beach-based semiconductor unit were expected to top $1 billion in 1996; this was Rockwell's fastest growing business. This group already was producing about 70 percent of the modem chip sets used in fax machines and personal computers worldwide and had just introduced chips for the cordless telephone and other wireless communications markets.

Remaining Rockwell units (after the sale to Boeing) depended on foreign markets for 43 percent of their sales. It was clear that Rockwell had its sights on some of the new growth sectors in California's economy—advanced technologies, communications, and trade (industries to be reviewed later in this chapter).

Meanwhile, Boeing hoped to smooth out its periodic drops in private jetliner and commercial aircraft business with government space and defense contracts; these would now account for about one-third of its nearly $25 billion annual revenues. However, Boeing had just begun its acquisitions. Within months after the deal with Rockwell, Boeing announced its intentions to acquire mammoth McDonnell Douglas Corporation for more than $13 billion. This would make Boeing Southern California's largest industrial employer, with 42,000 workers (including 20,000 former McDonnell Douglas employees in Long Beach and 5,600 in Huntington Beach).

Boeing would become a $48 billion corporation with a total of 200,000 global employees and the world's largest supplier of combat jets, spacecraft, and jetliners. Anxiety in California about a Seattle-based corporation becoming the dominant aerospace company was cushioned by several factors: Boeing was now the leading commercial aircraft company and the second-largest U.S. defense contractor. It now represented a more balanced company that might restore stability to the California industry.

Boeing also had back orders for commercial aircraft, and it would use the newly acquired (and formerly emptying) McDonnell Douglas defense factories in Long Beach to fill the orders. Employees' futures at the big Douglas Products Division (now Boeing's) plant in Long Beach suddenly depended on new orders for passenger jets. In the short term, there were plenty of winners, but were California's economy and its workers among them?

MERGER MANIA LEAVES CALIFORNIA OUT OF THE AEROSPACE SPOTLIGHT

After corporate giant Raytheon acquired the defense electronics business of renowned Hughes Electronics, impacting thousands more jobs, yet another bombshell hit California's aerospace industry in July, 1997. Lockheed Martin Corporation announced it would acquire Northrop Grumman Corporation for $11.6 billion. Northrop was headquartered in Century City, Los Angeles, and had nearly 47,000 employees, 13,000 in Southern California. Lockheed's headquarters were in Washington state suburbs. If the merger was successful, Lockheed would become the world's greatest supplier to militaries. When the U.S. government enforced antitrust laws to block the merger, both companies refused to break off key operations; in a dramatic turnabout, the proposed merger failed in 1998.

This was what some said would be the end of massive mergers, consolidations, and downsizings in this industry. After all, there weren't many aerospace companies left to merge. Yet, the damage to California aerospace was done; once the headquarters of four giant defense contractors, Southern California was struggling to hold on to its last one.

MAQUILADORAS IMPACT LIFE
AND LANDSCAPES

The billions pumped into border economies had profound impacts on Tijuana and other cities, especially in San Diego and Imperial Counties. Tijuana's population increased by 5 percent per year, a rate double the rest of Mexico, straining the city's infrastructure. Of more than 100,000 Mexicans who migrated from their country's interior to the northern border during twenty months in the mid-1990s, more than 60,000 of them found jobs at Tijuana's maquiladora factories. By 1996, maquiladoras employed more than 750,000; job opportunities were increasing by up to 20 percent per year in some regions through the 1990s. It was compared to the great migrations into America's industrial belt during the years around World War II, and it was the greatest migration trend in Mexico since the 1960s.

Such rapid growth created terrible problems just across the border. Up to 300,000 new immigrants were seeking shelter at one time. Tijuana streets were jammed for the lack of transportation, while dirt roads, crime, and pollution stretched for miles around the city. Many squatters' barrios had no services or infrastructure, such as power, water and sewage disposal. The result was that many recent immigrants made quick money for a few months or years and returned to their homelands in Mexico. Others continued their migrations into the United States. Numerous highly skilled managers and corporate executives located their families and advanced high-tech operations on the U.S. side, boosting San Diego's economy.

Solutions to infrastructure and environmental problems were expected to cost more than $8 billion within ten years. As local governments looked for help, North American Development Bank (NADBank) was set up by NAFTA to finance and solve these problems. As utilities are deregulated, energy shortages are being solved by outside utilities, such as California's big four power companies. Wastewater and purification projects were first planned by NADBank in such places as Brawley, California. The hope is to catch up with revolutionary economic and migration trends and create better living and working environments that will stabilize border populations.

corporate mergers, consolidation, downsizing, and complete restructuring of the aerospace industry.

The succession of mergers that threatened to take defense headquarters out of state could not kill California's aerospace and defense economy. Without these major headquarters, Southern California's aerospace industry still supported hundreds of thousands of aerospace workers, hundreds of aerospace subcontractors, manufacturing and testing facilities, and eleven engineering schools. It had evolved into a weaker economy of smaller firms and subdivisions of larger out-of-state firms. The series of rather complicated mergers reviewed on page 369 produced the new, restructured aerospace and defense industry that would fly California, with considerable turbulence, into the twenty-first century.

These corporations' stories simply reflect the tumultuous nature of the state's broader aerospace industry. It is increasingly difficult to predict the future of these or any other dynamic California industries as the state's economic landscapes evolve at accelerated rates.

Computer Parts

Here is another expanding California manufacturing industry that is dependent on other sectors of the economy. The manufacture and assembly of computers and their parts will be considered in a following section on high-tech industries.

Maquiladoras Reshape Manufacturing Landscapes

One of the most profound developments to impact California manufacturing industries during the late twentieth century was the growth of maquiladoras. These new factories were built just across the border in Mexico. The number of these industries exploded as trade agreements between the United States and Mexico decreased tariffs for goods made in these factories and shipped into the United States. California's wealth of technology had finally blended with an enormous pool of cheap Mexican labor. During the 1990s, the full effects of the North American Free Trade Agreement (NAFTA) were remarkable in California and Mexico, though the trend began long before that. Some manufacturing industries were pulling away from California cities to employ the Mexicans who rushed to work in the new factories along their border.

During the 1990s, Tijuana's unemployment rate dropped below 2 percent. NAFTA and the collapse of the peso had drawn corporations from around the world. Within single years, maquiladora factories added more than 100,000 new jobs to Mexican border towns as payrolls grew by more than 10 percent. Signs announced "Se Necesita Personal" everywhere, especially in such areas as the Mesa de Otay industrial zone of Tijuana. All of this occurred as the rest of Mexico's unemployment rates skyrocketed in the midst of economic disaster. Even U.S.

exports *to* Mexico soared to record billions of dollars per year.

Due in part to these trade agreements, more than $8 billion of investments were directed into Mexico in 1996 alone. As ties between Mexico and California companies and consumer markets grew stronger, other foreign countries, especially from Europe and Asia, jumped into the act. Though tens of thousands of California manufacturing jobs were lost to the maquiladoras, companies from around the world helped Tijuana become one of the great manufacturing centers, including the world's largest TV production center. Such companies include Hitachi, Sanyo, Maxell, and Matsushita. Korean corporations considered purchasing the Port of Ensenada and building a rail to the border factories.

By the late 1990s, South Korean Samsung, U.S.-based Corning Glass, and Asahi Optical of Japan planned one of the largest factories on the California-Mexico border for either Tijuana or Mexicali. It would make glass for computer and TV monitors, lasers, and big-screen TV projection lenses. The U.S.-South Korean-Japanese venture would be a $250-million glass plant with up to 5,000 employees. They join the expanding list of high-technology companies attracted to Mexico by NAFTA and low-cost labor.

From trade and finance, to providing services and infrastructure, you can see how sweeping changes in manufacturing industries might create ripple effects through multiple sectors of the economy. More advanced economies and their landscapes are reviewed next.

Tertiary and More Advanced and Complex Industries

We have reviewed how more advanced industries soared past manufacturing to lead the modern California economy. From high-tech, entertainment, and tourism to retail, trade, and real estate, a diverse economy has emerged. Government, transportation, and other infrastructures and services are required to support this complex economy.

High-Tech Information and Computer Services

Silicon Valley California's Silicon Valley is more successful than its competitors (such as the high-tech corridor along Route 128 in Massachusetts) because it represents a local economy with business and social cultures that promote industrial systems built on regional networks. Silicon Valley firms are more flexible and dynamic as they compete with the changing international marketplace. (Though the late 1990s Asian economic crisis slowed growth considerably, the valley didn't sink into depression as some had warned.) Collective learning between colleges and businesses encourages companies to adjust as they make specialty products for related tech-

nologies. Instead of Silicon Valley's open and hierarchical structures, Massachusetts' Route 128 firms have more rigid and secretive structures. Otherwise, the two may represent similar companies and locations.

Competition, Social Capital, and Geography Transform Modern Silicon Valley What factors have led to Silicon Valley's recent success? UC Berkeley planner Anno Saxenian called it "**Regional Advantage**" in her book of the same name. She argued that firms are independent and creative, but still maintain relationships with customers and suppliers. Entrepreneurs and business leaders may guard some new innovations, but frequently consult with one another to solve problems and create improved hardware and software. Harvard political scientist Bob Putnam refers to the openness and density of relationships between technology experts and business leaders as "**social capital**." As individual leaders reach out and rely on one another, each firm becomes more productive than if it worked alone.

The need for software programmers alone has transformed the Bay Area's economic landscapes; software engineering leads creation of new jobs in high-tech fields. Industry executives maintain strong ties with Stanford University with donations and equipment because it has one of the nation's top computer science schools. Graduates are in high demand. Experts in state-of-the-art data-base programming, computer networking, and multimedia product development can often write their own tickets; bidding wars are most intense in Silicon Valley. One result is that software-related jobs accounted for 90 percent of the 8,900 jobs added in Santa Clara County during 1996.

The Silicon Valley led California out of the recession and into the mid-1990s recovery. Restructured and newly resurging technology companies thrived. Unemployment rates in Santa Clara County dropped well below 4 percent, far below state and national averages. Employees armed with high salaries were buying expensive homes, cars, and other items that helped push the region's booming economy into the late 1990s. The $95 million Tech Museum of Innovation in San Jose celebrates the industries responsible for such trends.

Such success has fueled competition between many California communities for new high-tech and especially biotechnology firms. Cities such as Davis are trying to attract newer firms that are balancing the geographic advantages of the Silicon Valley with its overcrowding problems. Vacaville has successfully created a biotechnology cluster. Midway between the Bay Area and Sacramento, these new industries are finding lower costs and more space away from major cities, but they remain close enough for easy commutes when required.

By 1998, the Asian economic crisis knocked the wind out of high-tech industries with the strongest ties to Asia. However, there is reason for continued optimism. Com-

HISTORY OF THE SILICON VALLEY

How did the Silicon Valley achieve its global leadership status? The answer involves an interconnected chain of events that have had economic and geographic implications for more than a century. This is a lengthy, fascinating story packed with plenty of useful lessons about economic geography and the success of industry. Countless publications have examined Silicon Valley's success stories. One of the better reviews of this place and its industries appeared in the Spring/Summer 1990 edition of *American Heritage of Invention and Technology*. James C. Williams wrote the article, "The Rise of the Silicon Valley." Take a deep breath, and we will plunge into these stories for a better understanding of this region and its economy.

A 25-mile stretch of California farmland became the heart of America's electronic industry (see Map 10.2). The Santa Clara Valley was home to prune, apricot, and cherry orchards, and famous canning and packing industries into the 1960s. Then, a series of events caused it to evolve into the Silicon Valley.

It started when regional electric power companies built hydroelectric plants in the Sierra Nevada using the Pelton waterwheel, which was developed years earlier in San Francisco for the gold mining industry. By the early 1900s, high-tension, long-distance transmission systems had been developed by a new cooperative style of research and development between company engineers and university engineering professors. This technology helped provide electricity to California coastal cities.

STANFORD BECOMES A CATALYST

In the meantime, Stanford University had accepted its first students in 1891; within ten years, its electrical-engineering program became an important partner with the California electric-power industry. Thanks to this university-industry cooperative research and development, Stanford designed the first high-voltage laboratory in the West in 1913 and the nation's first two-million-volt university laboratory in 1926.

Professors and other researchers worked to make Stanford the national research center of electrical engineering. They included electrical engineer visionaries such as Harris Ryan, followed by Frederick E. Terman. As head of Stanford's electrical-engineering department in 1937, Terman brought Stanford graduates William Hewlett and David Packard back together to form an electronics business, which grew quickly during World War II. Stanford's electrical engineering department had grown into a full-fledged research program by then.

After World War II, Stanford's electrical-engineering program was drawing some of the best faculty and students and had established strong connections with private industry. Stanford's Electronics Research Laboratories (ERL) built strong ties to outside electronics firms, military, and commercial interests who would convert new discoveries into practical hardware. Terman was a leader as Stanford University established its Applied Electronic Laboratory and built even closer ties to private industry and the military during the 1950s. High-technology companies, such as Hewlett-Packard, formed strong partnerships with Stanford, benefitted from the research, and donated huge sums of money to the university during the 1950s.

SILICON VALLEY DEVELOPS

By 1960, more than forty high-technology firms occupied the 450-acre Stanford Industrial Park. The Santa Clara Valley had become a center for the electronics and aerospace industries. High-technology firms such as the NASA-Ames Research Center moved into the valley. These firms came from across the country to settle from Palo Alto to San Jose; electrical engineers from all over the world flocked in. The Silicon Valley was established after Fairchild Semiconductor opened in Mountain View and began mass producing integrated circuits and training young engineers and scientists. By the early 1970s, former Fairchild employees had started up to forty-one new semiconductor companies, mostly in the valley.

By the mid-1970s, companies like Intel had developed the first microprocessors that led to the first affordable home computers. The Homebrew Computer Club became the focus group where computer experts and intellectuals in the valley met to share new engineering and technology ideas and discoveries. One of the club members, Hewlett-Packard's Stephen Wozniak, got ideas from club meetings and teamed with Steven Jobs to start Apple Computer in Cupertino in 1976. By 1984, their computer sales soared over $1.5 billion.

The Silicon Valley has recently become even more famous as high-tech firms expand across the valley. Semiconductor and computer hardware and software firms have especially thrived through the 1990s. As the power of the microchip doubled every eighteen months, the number of millionaires in the Silicon Valley doubled at least at the same rate. Individual success stories abound. According to the *Los Angeles Times*, Kim Polese (president, CEO, and chairman of Marimba Inc.) became one of the top twenty-five most influential Americans during the 1990s. After only one year in business, up to 50 million people were using her company's software to surf the Internet.

HISTORY OF THE SILICON VALLEY *continued*

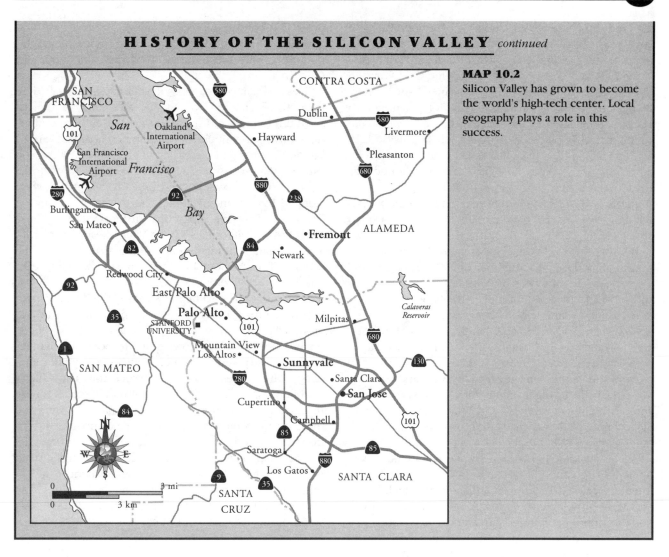

MAP 10.2
Silicon Valley has grown to become the world's high-tech center. Local geography plays a role in this success.

It might look like the Silicon Valley before it filled up, but it's Vacaville, midway between Sacramento and the San Francisco Bay Area. Here, high-tech industries will find cheaper land and plenty of space to build, in contrast to the intensively developed Silicon Valley. It is not far to major cities.

puter, communications, and software companies accounted for more than one quarter of America's economic growth during the 1990s. Industry analysts declared it one of the most exciting eras ever. Biotechnology and other newer high-tech firms continue to prosper within this same environment. Decentralization, flexibility, and innovation are the rules. And it all started around 1900 with that fledgling electronics industry.

High-Tech in Southern California It could be argued that high technology industries were going strong during the 1940s and 1950s in Southern California long before the Silicon Valley. They grew from innovations in missile and aircraft research and development, and in the electronics industry. By the 1950s, high-tech firms in Southern California had strong ties to the defense industry. Consequently, they were clustered in a few Los Angeles Basin (such as southern Santa Monica Bay) and San Diego locations. By the 1970s, high-tech clusters were centered along freeways, including the Newport (55) and San Diego (405) Freeways interchange in southern Orange County and in the Chatsworth/Canoga Park areas.

By the 1980s and 1990s, the end of the Cold War and the explosion of technology in business and society changed the emphasis in Southern California's high-tech industry. Sophisticated aerospace technology was still in high demand at places like NASA's Jet Propulsion Laboratory (JPL) in Pasadena. Just as JPL contracted with local private firms, so did those firms use the laboratory as a resource for new innovations in technology. One example is in developing terrain mapping and global positioning systems to help airplanes navigate around obstacles.

JPL was thrown into the spotlight again with its mission to Mars during the summer of 1997. Scientists and the public were captivated by pictures from its Pathfinder and new information transmitted by its Sojourner as it rolled along to sample Mars' landscapes.

However, Hollywood and the entertainment industry has also developed a healthy appetite for advanced technologies. By the late 1990s, hundreds of new firms had grown to meet the demands for hardware and software for special effects, digital film editing, sound production, and entertainment on the World Wide Web. A multimedia technology industry had also grown to produce computer games, CD-ROMs, and content for the Internet.

According to a 1997 report by the Economic Development Corporation of Los Angeles County and the Los Angeles Regional Technology Alliance, high-tech industries were growing fast in the L.A. area. The region was home to more than 19,000 firms and 330,000 jobs that were related to technology. Some estimates claim that up to 15 percent of all jobs in the region are technology-related. High-tech industries ranging from computer hardware and software, to aerospace, to biotechnology and entertainment thrive for several reasons: the region's creative atmospheres, trade with Asia and its Pacific Rim location, favorable ports, world-class universities, a highly-skilled labor pool, and good weather. That Asian market slump in the late 1990s was one of few events to put a damper on these trends.

Venture capitalists and the Los Angeles Community Development Bank were even investing in low-income empowerment zones that included South-Central Los Angeles in the late 1990s. They anticipated rapid growth of high-tech industries in L.A. into the twenty-first century.

San Gabriel Valley to Orange County Mostly Taiwanese immigrants have created a multibillion-dollar computer industry in Southern California, and it is based in the San Gabriel Valley. Small, specialized computer firms combine efforts to assemble complete computer systems within the region. Thousands of workers assemble com-

puter parts and equipment from Asia to sell here and globally. By the late 1990s, there were more than eight-hundred Taiwanese-American firms in Southern California.

Ties to Asian companies had strengthened Pacific Rim trade, the economy of the San Gabriel Valley, and all of Southern California. Estimated sales at Southern California's Taiwanese-American computer companies were $3 billion per year and increasing up to the late 1990s. You can see why many business people in the San Gabriel Valley, some of whom were already wounded, were stunned by the unexpected Asian market slump in the late 1990s. This area is part of a "**golden triangle**" linking northern California's Silicon Valley design firms with Taiwan manufacturers, then with the assembly and distribution firms in Southern California. (Taiwan is a leading producer of computer parts.)

Southern California mainly supplies the business people to this triangle. These entrepreneurs cluster in and around Walnut and the City of Industry. As in Silicon Valley, the clustering allows quick response to changes in the industry and consumer requests. Many are members of the Chinese Computer Association. The valley's warehouses, loading docks, security systems, Chinese restaurants, shopping, and schools have all attracted these business people. Some of these companies stretch into Orange and Ventura Counties. Mandarin is often the business language, and tea is served at meetings instead of coffee and soda. Primarily Chinese-American neighborhoods are found in Rowland Heights, Walnut, and Diamond Bar. A residential and commercial (especially warehouse) real estate boom has followed.

Irvine The Irvine Spectrum is a sprawling 3,600-acre planned business community where the Santa Ana (I-5) and San Diego (405) freeways meet. Into the late 1990s, it included more than 2,200 companies and 36,000 employees; it was growing faster than its developers, the Irvine Company, had ever imagined. Irvine Spectrum boosters were trying to lure technology companies from around the world as they compared it to the Silicon Valley and other technology centers. However, it had become more of a regional center as it attracted mostly fast-growing entrepreneurs (known as "gazelles") from L.A.'s crowded urban core. Smaller high-tech centers have sprouted for similar reasons northwest of L.A. in Chatsworth, Valencia, and Thousand Oaks.

The Irvine Spectrum initially attracted larger corporate headquarters and manufacturing facilities. Recently, it has gained new tenants both from the growth of high-tech companies and also from firms moving farther away from urban centers to seek more land and less congestion. Several specialized, high-tech firms (such as Wonderware Corporation, an automation software company) start small, but end up leasing larger and larger spaces

ONE MORE HIGH-TECH SUCCESS STORY

It is difficult to overstate the impact of modern technologies and the success of high-tech firms in California from the 1990s into the twenty-first century. Here is one example. In 1987, two Chinese immigrants, David Sun and John Tu, started Kingston Technology Corporation in Fountain Valley with only $4,000 cash. Kingston supplied PC manufacturers and made memory boards to add to older computers. As consumers required increasing amounts of memory for their computers, Kingston thrived. Their profits quickly soared to hundreds of millions of dollars as they marketed their memory components. They became famous for taking good care of their employees and for donating large sums to community causes.

During 1996, nearly 70 percent of the company's market was in the United States and that was expected to quickly grow above $2 billion. During that same year, Kingston Technology Corporation was bought by a Japanese firm called Softbank Corporation for $1.5 billion. The new Japanese owners plan to market Kingston products in Japan and throughout Asia. The result should be even greater long-term profits for this company competing within an industry that seems to have no limits to rapid change, an industry that is transforming California landscapes in revolutionary style.

until they control their own buildings within the business park.

Growth at the Spectrum was so fast into the late 1990s, developers were rushing to keep up with needed infrastructure and services, such as the expansion of the Irvine Entertainment Center. Smaller centers began erupting on more plentiful land farther out on South Orange County's fringe. However, Irvine Spectrum developers expected to use its prestigious reputation as a gathering place for high-tech companies; they look toward filling it with 5,000 companies and 150,000 workers within the first two decades of the twenty-first century.

Other Cities Compete for the High-Tech Pie Some developers and city officials hope that remodeling old industrial spaces of Culver City will make it a center for the new media industry in L.A. They are trying to lure the kind of computer technology and talent responsible for the urban renewal in San Francisco's Multimedia Gulch. Creative individuals once saw now famous Multimedia Gulch as an inexpensive and attractive area to locate their innovative, high-tech companies. Many city leaders consider Culver City to have similar potential. It is also on L.A.'s West Side—close enough to downtown and near the entertainment industry.

Officials hope that new firms will move this city away from the aerospace-based economy and landscape of past years to a modern center of technology. This potential has brought developers like Frederick Samitaur Smith to remake industrial spaces in Culver City. The trouble is getting computer technology, software, and entertainment firms to concentrate in one area of sprawling L.A. Meanwhile, other cities are competing for that high-tech distinction, including other communities on the West

Side, the Pasadena/Glendale/Burbank corridor, and what USC hopes will become the Figueroa Corridor between USC and downtown.

With such centers as Silicon Valley and Multimedia Gulch, the Bay Area certainly has the edge on technology-intensive activities, including development of software and new computer languages. However, development of entertainment-related products and activities are probably destined for Southern California. Thousands of jobs and billions of dollars are at stake while Southern California grows as the entertainment and media capital of the world.

Santa Barbara Coast By the late 1990s, high-tech companies were clustering along the Santa Barbara coast, revitalizing the economies of Santa Barbara, Carpinteria, and Goleta. Previously, the region lost about 7,600 defense and electronics-related jobs since the 1980s, and negative ripple effects were felt well into the 1990s. More recently, some software companies have doubled in size. The number of companies increased from 95 to 134 in the area from 1994 to 1996, and that growth continued into the late 1990s. Communication companies are experiencing similar trends.

The climate, environment, lifestyles, and the talent out of UCSB are contributing factors to this growth. Government officials are encouraged by groups such as the Santa Barbara Region Economic Community Project. They lure high-salary, high-tech industries that are nonpolluting. Consequently, surrounding communities are encouraging software, telecommunications, and medical technology firms to move in. The region's growth will be restricted by its physical geography—a 25-mile coastal strip bounded by the ocean on one side and mountains on the other.

Biotechnology According to the *International Journal of Technology Management*, California was the acknowledged leader in the economic development of high technology through the 1990s and the driving force in the emerging biotechnology industry. Biotechnology is expected to create economic changes similar to the earlier electronics and semiconductor industries. However, there are high stakes and high risks regarding the unpredictable nature of this new industry.

California receives massive funding for research from the National Institute of Health. Northern California, L.A., Orange County and San Diego all compete for funds. Northern California (with the Silicon Valley), UC Berkeley, and Stanford are all famous for their biotech industries. However, San Diego (where the cooperative Connect program merges interests of scientists and businesses known for biotech work) has also become a biotech powerhouse. Groups such as the Southern California Biomedical Council, which represents more than forty biotech, law, and finance companies, are working to increase the industry's competitive edge in their regions.

By 1998, University of California's BioSTAR project identified 391 biotechnology companies in the state. Demonstrating the importance of highly skilled workers and research in this industry, ninety-eight of these companies were founded by UC scientists from the state's nine different campuses. Most of them were at UC San Diego, Berkeley, and San Francisco. Numerous other universities and colleges across the state were also expanding their biotech programs and pursuing joint research with business.

Entertainment

During the mid-1990s, $17 billion per year was generated by the film and TV industry in California, and it was growing toward the twenty-first century. Movie and TV studios and film and production crews require support services and staff. Companies were shooting in more than two-hundred locations each day in the L.A. area alone. In addition to generating revenue, production companies were seen impacting countless California neighborhoods and landscapes destined to be displayed before audiences around the world.

After losing some of this business to other states and countries into the early 1990s, local officials and community groups worked with business leaders to bring this industry back to California. They were successful for several reasons. California, and L.A. in particular, has the advantage of ideal weather and quick access to industry workers and post-production facilities. To encourage film production crews, several communities, including Los Angeles County and city, streamlined their permit processes. City officials also worked with neighborhood groups to mitigate inconveniences caused by film crews.

Los Angeles formed the Entertainment Industry Development Corporation to help film crews expedite their shooting and cut production costs.

CBS Studios claimed that the entertainment industry was responsible for generating more than 11,000 jobs each year in the Los Angeles area into the late 1990s. The industry was buying $9 billion in goods and services each year, from food caterers to building supplies.

Particularly the east side of the San Fernando Valley is reaping economic benefits from entertainment's surge. Burbank's media district plans to increase production at the Walt Disney Co., Warner Bros., and NBC lots. Realtors report that 50 percent of Studio City and one-third of Sherman Oaks home buyers are in the entertainment industry. As this economic boom carries toward the twenty-first century, some neighbors complained about the typical negative side effects of increased traffic, noise, and congestion.

California's entertainment industry has managed to exploit its popularity and the growth of the technology and communications revolution. This has led to growing foreign investments in Hollywood, especially from Asia. South Korea's largest food company, Cheil Jedang, invested $300 million to become the second-largest investor in DreamWorks SKG in 1996. They wined and dined DreamWorks' Jeffrey Katzenberg; he even chatted with South Korea's president at the presidential mansion.

Such efforts are typical of large South Korean conglomerates, known as chaebol. South Koreans staged a mini-invasion of Hollywood in the 1990s as they invested in film, video, and TV partnerships with some of entertainment's biggest companies. They see the creative industries as a good risk, perhaps because many of these modern Korean companies are run by younger, more Western-oriented executives. By 1998, the risks of working in the global marketplace hit California's entertainment industry; shock waves rippled through as Asian markets faltered.

Powerful connections bind California's entertainment and tourist industries together. Disneyland and Universal City are two obvious examples. Hollywood's movie and TV industries keep the world's popular culture spotlight focused on California. Tourists then stream in to visit the attractions and amusement parks. The competition for these entertainment and tourist dollars in California is fierce.

Tourism

Individual Attractions During the summer of 1996, Magic Mountain's engineers raced to perfect their new Superman roller coaster ride so that it would travel at the promised 100 mph. It was not ready before the start of school, but it was up and rolling for the next summer season.

Ghirardelli Square represents just one of the many tourist attractions that make San Francisco California's number one tourist destination city.

While Magic Mountain struggled through its annual race to get its new attractions on line, Disneyland advertised their last summer of Light Parade down Main Street in 1996; it was a profitable strategy. Disneyland typically draws more than 50,000 people per day during summer days. That number grew to more than 80,000 per day during the fall weekends that marked the end of the Electric Light Parade in 1996. For the first time, entrances to the park were closed on some weekend days due to overcrowding. Disneyland broke its own records with well over 14 million visitors in 1995 and 1996. On July 5, 1997, Disneyland celebrated its 400 millionth visitor.

Orange County has grand plans to expand its tourist industry into the twenty-first century, partly because the world's most famous theme park has greater plans that will celebrate the California Dream. A $1.4 billion expansion of Disneyland called Disney's California Adventure adds three themed lands centered on Hollywood, the beach and the state's wilderness areas. Anaheim approved it in early October, 1996. Plans include a Golden California Area with white-water rafting, cave exploration and hang-gliding over the Golden Gate, a palm-lined Boardwalk Area with surfing, a Hollywood Studio District, and other attractions.

Disney's California Adventure is expected to eventually attract 7 million people per year and create 14,500 new jobs. Furthermore, it is expected to generate $35 million per year for Orange County/Anaheim and another $35 million per year for the state of California. Already in a more cramped, diverse urban setting, some Anaheim residents complained that the expansion would create too many crowding problems. Short-term thinkers argued that Disneyland should not get bond rate guarantees from city taxes. Regardless, the project continues to move forward.

Additionally, an expanded Anaheim Convention Center was also planned at a cost of $150 million. A few miles away, Knott's Berry Farm in Buena Park already has a beach-themed tribute to California stereotypes. It is the scale and innovation of Disney's plan that makes it different. It is expected to be a complete vacation resort, and Anaheim will be confirmed as an international tourist destination.

Orange County's Tourism Council was formed in 1996 as an addition to the powerful Orange County Business Council. This mostly volunteer group of business people is encouraging a regional, cooperative approach to tourism to replace local competition. Their intent is to give Orange County a distinct and separate identity from the rest of L.A. Like many tourist destinations, they were considering a memorable logo or tag line to make Orange County more recognized by tourists who may otherwise think of it as Disneyland, or part of L.A.

Competition for tourist dollars is fierce. While Orange County's Tourism Council struggled to raise $1 million of private funds for promotion of their county, Las Vegas was spending $50 million per year on similar promotions.

To the south, the Irvine Entertainment Center opened in November, 1995, and attracted more than four million visitors to its twenty-one-screen theater complex in less than one year. The Irvine Company planned to double the center's size by adding entertainment outlets and retailers. Such enormous entertainment centers and regional malls have popped up across California; they are attracting Californians and tourists from around the world. Almost simultaneously, Ontario, in the Inland Empire to the north, completed a similar mammoth project. Outlet malls such as the Great Mall of the Bay Area, once the largest on the West Coast, with 210 outlet stores, are also attracting tourists. You will also find tourist buses parked outside outlet malls located in unlikely places, such as near Barstow and Banning.

In the hills overlooking the San Fernando Valley, Universal Studios is considered *the* movie park. During the late-1990s, MCA planned a $3 billion expansion of Universal City. New office buildings, hotels, shops, restaurants, and entertainment attractions are to be added to its existing Universal Studios Tour, CityWalk, and amphitheater on its 415 hilly acres. MCA claimed that the 11 million additional square feet of development would pump $1.6 billion into the local economy and add 13,000 jobs.

However, MCA ran into more barriers than Disney in designing its project. The development lies partially within unincorporated county land and partially on L.A. city land. Both entities must cooperate in order for MCA's expansion to go forward. Additionally, neighbors, such as those in the Studio City Residents Association, are concerned about traffic, noise, crime, lighting, and other congestion problems that an enormous development might bring. Developers were forced to scale down the expansion.

Did you know that Venice Beach Boardwalk competed with all of these more formal amusement parks for the number one tourist attraction in the state? Residents there have also complained about the congestion and isolated acts of violence during peak weekends. These are just some examples of attractions, projects, and problems impacting the Los Angeles region's booming entertainment and tourist industries. They are certainly changing California landscapes.

Similar issues about growth in the tourist and entertainment industries apply to other California cities. Spending in San Diego's tourist industry, with its Sea World and internationally famous zoo, approached $4 billion into the late 1990s. Up the coast is Legoland, San Diego County's new 128-acre theme park in Carlsbad. In this competitive market for theme park dollars, Legoland officials hoped to prosper by catering to younger children and their parents in a safe environment.

The Bay Area has Paramount's Great America in Santa Clara and Marine World Africa USA in Vallejo. Just over the hill on Hwy. 17 is the Santa Cruz Beach Boardwalk, one of the few traditional beach amusement parks that has survived through the decades in California. Millions of annual visitors to San Francisco kept it competing with cities like Las Vegas for the number one tourist destination city in the nation. Many of California's smaller urban areas were also cashing in on tourist dollars.

Nature and Impact of Tourism California is still the nation's number one tourist destination, though it is now getting strong competition from places like Las Vegas and Orlando. California attracted 295 million tourist visits and $55.2 billion in travel spending during 1995. Tourism grew nearly 5 percent in 1996 to almost $58 billion in spending, accounting for nearly 670,000 California jobs. More than 80 percent of trips made in the state were by California residents, making Californians most important to the industry. Additionally, the state often attracts up to 11 percent of the U.S. domestic leisure market.

Later in the 1990s, California expanded its advertising campaigns to attract more tourists. Focus was on family tours, adventure, romance, and natural beauty. Besides the previously mentioned expansions, there are new attractions, such as Turtle Bay Park and Museum in the Shasta Cascade region. As the state broke out of the recession, hotel occupancy rates and room rates were rising into the late 1990s.

More than 9 million people from other countries visited California in 1995. Individual external events, such as currency rate changes and natural disasters, have their impacts from year to year. The top ten countries that sent visitors in 1995 were:

Mexico	3,000,000+
Japan	938,000
Canada	827,000
Britain	592,000
Germany	567,000
Australia	264,000
France	256,000
Taiwan	255,000
Korea	236,000
Italy	159,000

Source: California Division of Tourism and *Los Angeles Times*

Millions visit California to attend business and other conventions of all sizes. They have enormous impacts on a range of businesses, from transportation services to hotels and restaurants. This is one reason you could find the southwest's four largest convention centers in California during the 1990s. Here are their sizes in square feet:

Los Angeles Convention Center	867,000
Anaheim Convention Center	602,000
Moscone Center (San Francisco)	442,000
San Diego Convention Center	254,000

The geographic distribution of tourism and travel impacting the state is not surprising. Following are estimates for the top eleven tourist impacted counties in the state (in dollars and jobs) during 1994. Growth rates into the late 1990s were around 5 percent per year.

County	Travel Expenditures	Employment (Jobs)
Los Angeles	$11,850,000,000	122,180
San Francisco	5,950,000,000	46,620
San Diego	4,850,000,000	68,090
Orange	3,550,000,000	48,040
Riverside	2,750,000,000	34,180
Santa Clara	2,130,000,000	26,800
San Bernardino	2,000,000,000	28,850
Alameda	1,800,000,000	19,800
San Mateo	1,660,000,000	30,770
Monterey	1,223,000,000	17,100
Sacramento	1,170,000,000	14,090

ECOTOURISM

The importance of ecotourism and the money it generates in California is often overlooked, especially because these activities do not fit into neat economic categories. Because ecotourism is so difficult to define, it appears in other sections of this book, particularly Chapter 9. When goods and services are provided to tourists seeking experiences with nature, we have ventured far beyond the more basic primary and secondary sectors of the economy. As mentioned in previous sections, some authors have referred to these services as GEMS (gas, food, motels, and related retail). Clearly, these travellers require transportation to get into natural settings, food to eat when they arrive, and a place to stay or even camp out. Clothing, cameras, film, fishing gear, educational materials, and other equipment might be purchased or carried along. A multitude of smaller, rural California economies rely on these tourists and their purchasing power.

However, they are actually visiting to experience the beauty and serenity that only a more natural, "unspoiled" or pristine environment can offer. As they escape to the peace and quiet, these tourists become campers, hikers, sightseers, and leisure seekers. They may fish, hunt, or, more likely, do some bird watching. Regardless, they have become the most basic consumers of what nature has to offer. Take away or destroy the natural environment that attracted them, and the tourists will disappear.

Note that all are heavily populated Southern California or Bay Area counties, except for the last two. Besides serving as extensions of L.A. Basin population centers, Riverside and San Bernardino Counties attract additional visitors with their mountain and desert resorts. Monterey County has Big Sur, Hwy. 101, Monterey, and Carmel resorts. The capitol in Sacramento usually draws very different kinds of visitors—those doing business with the state.

What these statistics do not show is the *relative* importance of tourism in a given county compared to its size and economic strength. Nearly every county on the bottom of the list of fifty-eight counties is in the Sierra Nevada or northern California. Just a few travellers and tourists in one of these counties can make a big difference in their tiny economies, and their landscapes show it. As an example, Modoc County comes in last in tourist dollars. What do you think would happen to this county's little economy if they did not have the $26,440,000 and 370 jobs generated each year by travel and tourism? How would little towns in other regions (such as Truckee, reviewed in the previous chapter) survive without tourism? How would their landscapes change?

The importance of tourism in these smaller rural communities was underscored in the early 1990s in northwestern California. Residents and officials were concerned that a rare, grisly murder and trial in Hawkins Bar (east of Eureka in rural Trinity County) would have high costs. Hawkins Bar is a rustic community of miners, loggers, and retirees along the Trinity River. Record legal costs of several hundred thousand dollars, law enforcement and attorney time, and jail space were taxed, but residents saw the greatest threat from decreased tourism.

Jeff Kohlhagen, owner of a market and bait shop in Big Bar along the Trinity River worried, "Tourism is all we've got up here, and news like this can really hurt. It's not like we're Miami Beach. Things are weak already, so any decline and you're in big trouble." Sheriff Paul Schmidt said, "We're not the Wild West or anything. This was a heinous crime that made people sick. . . . But should people stop going to Disneyland because of the L.A. Riots?" Yet, all of this was reported hundreds of miles away at the other end of the state, in a *Los Angeles Times* article on December 27, 1992.

Other Forms of Tourism, Travel, and Entertainment Cruise ships play important roles in many California port economies. A ban on gambling on cruise ships stopping at California ports was rescinded in 1996, and the cruise lines began returning. Gambling is now allowed between two different California ports. It is estimated that California lost more than $300 million and thousands of jobs between 1993 and 1996 due to the ban. As the cruise-ship industry grew 600 percent worldwide in one decade, California dropped from seventh place in the world in cruise-ship calls to tenth or eleventh.

The cities most affected are San Diego, L.A., San Francisco, and Avalon (on Catalina Island). The new stops probably mean $15 million per year for San Diego alone. The number of cruise line passengers using the Port of L.A. in San Pedro grew by 30 percent in fiscal 1996, to nearly one million. This made the Port of L.A. the busiest cruise port on the West Coast, with most cruise lines destined for Mexico.

California also has a $500 million ski resort business, which includes equipment and services provided for skiers and snowboarders. The California Ski Industry Association is a San Francisco-based trade group representing thirty-nine California resorts. According to them, California is the nation's second-largest skiing state, with 7 million skier visits per year (compared to number one Colorado's 10–11 million annual visitors). Mammoth Mountain is the state's—and one of the world's—largest and most profitable single ski resorts. Its proximity and

Mammoth Mountain is one of the largest single ski resorts in the world. Thousands of visitors from Los Angeles race up Hwy. 395 for a weekend to race down the powdered slopes.

easy access to Southern California via Hwy. 395 and its almost ideal ski conditions help make it successful.

Bear Mountain is 70 miles east of L.A. in the San Bernardino Mountains at 8,000 feet near Big Bear Lake. It has 690 acres, 11 lifts, 35 downhill trails, and a 9-hole golf course. In 1995, it was sold for $18 million and then resold, along with two northern California resorts (Northstar-at-Tahoe and Sierra-at-Tahoe), to ski operator George Gillett, Jr., for $127 million. (If the Tahoe resorts were merged, they would form the largest ski resort in California. Combined, they attract more than one million skiers per year.) The Gilletts made plans to enhance Bear Mountain's summer business, perhaps with summer mountain biking.

Obviously, tourists must eat. Add Californians who travel to eat, and you can see how many restaurants rely on tourism and travel. During the 1990s, Gladstone's restaurant along the Pacific Coast Highway in the Pacific Palisades had the highest sales (gross) of any restaurant in the state (about $13 million in 1996). They were selling 1,000 bowls of clam chowder and 200 pounds of crab each day. After a drop in customers, they increased sales by emphasizing entertainment with their eclectic food selections. Geography has blessed Gladstone's; it would be difficult to find this style of restaurant in California with a more favorable location. About 40 percent of all Gladstone customers are from outside L.A. County. Other restaurants around California such as the Hard Rock Cafe and Planet Hollywood have enjoyed fame and success with similar formulas.

Some prefer to travel California in style. EagleRider Motorcycle Rental in Torrance made nearly $1.5 million per year during the mid-1990s by renting Harley-Davidson motorcycles in California and some other states. Customers especially include European tourists, who want to see America on a Harley, and others who just want to participate in the culture. Most cannot afford the average price of about $20,000 per bike. EagleRider was growing fast and expanding by renting vintage automobiles. Here is more proof that especially in California, it is often difficult to find the line separating the tourist, travel, and entertainment industries.

The list of tourist- and travel-related industries is long, and we can only include some examples. Consider the important connections to retail sales in California, our next topic.

Retail

During 1996, California retail sales were growing faster than the nation for the first time in nine years. These trends carried California into the twenty-first century. Major California retailers include Sears, Kmart, Macy's, Mervyn's, Wal-Mart, Target, and May Department Stores. Major retail chains moving to or expanding in California into the late 1990s included Sears, Bloomingdale's, Mills Corp., Dillard Department Stores, Wal-Mart, Home Depot, Robinson's-May, Macy's, Saks Fifth Avenue, and Emanuel/Emanuel Ungaro. Most of these expanding retail chains faced a common problem of geography; the best sites were already taken by the end of the century.

Nevertheless, the first Bloomingdale's stores in California opened in November with three stores in Southern California and one in the Bay Area. These stores quickly led all Bloomingdale's in the nation in sales. Macy's West, based in San Francisco, moved into Southern California in 1996, and its statewide sales also led the chain's other

Specialty stores like this one in San Francisco will only survive in urban areas with large populations.

CREATIVE CARTOGRAPHY IN RETAIL

California's major retailers are using the power of creative cartography. According to the South Coast Plaza shopping center, South Orange County has 17,000 households with $1.45 billion in discretionary income. Some residents traditionally avoided the South Coast Plaza and Fashion Island shopping centers due to traffic congestion. Then, the $1.5 billion San Joaquin Hills Transportation Corridor opened in November, 1996. The two shopping centers produced different maps showing how the corridor easily spills motorists directly toward *their* centers.

Advertisements for these shopping centers further claim that one-hour traffic jams to get to the malls have been cut to a fifteen minute trip. A South Coast Plaza advertising blitz claims the tollway is a shortcut to South Coast Plaza. In reality, it dumps motorists right between the two centers. It is no surprise that Fashion Island was a co-sponsor for the tollway opening ceremonies and also has its own advertising campaign.

In the midst of these map wars and retailers' rush to grab consumers in South Orange County, Cal State Fullerton released a study showing that the average wages in northern Orange County are only 93.5 percent of southern Orange County's. This helps explain why so many retailers target the south part of the county.

national stores in December. Saks Fifth Avenue planned to at least double its Southern California stores and open three new stores in northern California in the late 1990s. This provides competition with Bloomingdale's for the high-end, upscale market.

Saks also considers Southern California to have significant profit potential. Consequently, Saks planned to expand its giant Southland flagship in Beverly Hills during the late 1990s. It already had stores in Costa Mesa, Palm Springs, and San Diego. Note that each of these locations was picked for their proximity to the high-end markets. There is a lesson in economic geography here. These stores must locate near, or provide easy access to, higher-income groups. Walk around Union Square in San Francisco. Study the individuals visiting each store. Who will you find around Neiman Marcus' rotunda? You will probably notice the connection these stores make with their high-spending target populations.

In this section, we focused on major retailers, though there is much more to California's retail economy. Numerous smaller, specialized retailers have made their marks on every California city. You will find them from Old Town Pasadena to Old Sacramento, from San Diego's Horton Plaza to Santa Monica's Promenade, from Ontario Mills to the most generic suburban-style retail landscapes cloned in places like Redding. Except for isolated, gigantic retail outlets that have erupted in rural California, the largest and most specialized retailers are found within California's great population centers.

Trade

For years, California has been the nation's top exporting state. In 1990, according to *Business America*, the state accounted for 15 percent of all U.S. overseas sales of goods. California exports totaled $58.4 billion in 1990, 70 percent higher than 1987 and 9 percent higher than 1989. The next decade brought remarkable increases in

this trade until the Asian economic crisis hit especially high-tech export industries, such as those in the Silicon Valley.

In the Spring, 1993, edition of *Foreign Affairs*, James D. Goldsborough wrote that California, with its powerful economy and population, requires its own foreign policy. He argued that improved relations with Mexico, the Pacific Rim, and other countries would bring great economic benefits to the state. He also argued that California will benefit most from the controversial North American Free Trade Agreement (NAFTA).

A few months later, California's World Trade Commission, under its new leadership, announced it would play a more active role in international trade and business. The commission was trying to gain more prestige in the business sector. Soon, publications like *Business America* were announcing how U.S. Export Assistance Centers were becoming part of the president's national export strategy. They are designed to give U.S. companies more organized federal support in export promotion, export finance, and technical assistance.

During the mid-1990s, demand for California products increased exports and helped lead California out of recession. Exports rose 15 percent in 1994, 22 percent in 1995, and continued strong toward the twenty-first century. California exports as much to the world as it does to the nation. The state traded more than $18 billion with Japan and $9.5 billion with Canada, its first and second trade partners. (However, Mexico became the top destination for the state's exports during the late 1990s during the Asian economic slump.) The U.S. Commerce Department reported that California maintained its lead as the nation's top exporting state during the 1990s with at least 15 percent of the nation's total foreign sales. Map 10.3 shows the locations of California's ports

Nine of the state's fifteen top export markets are in the Asia-Pacific region. The Silicon Valley pushed ahead of the Los Angeles-Long Beach area with nearly $27 billion

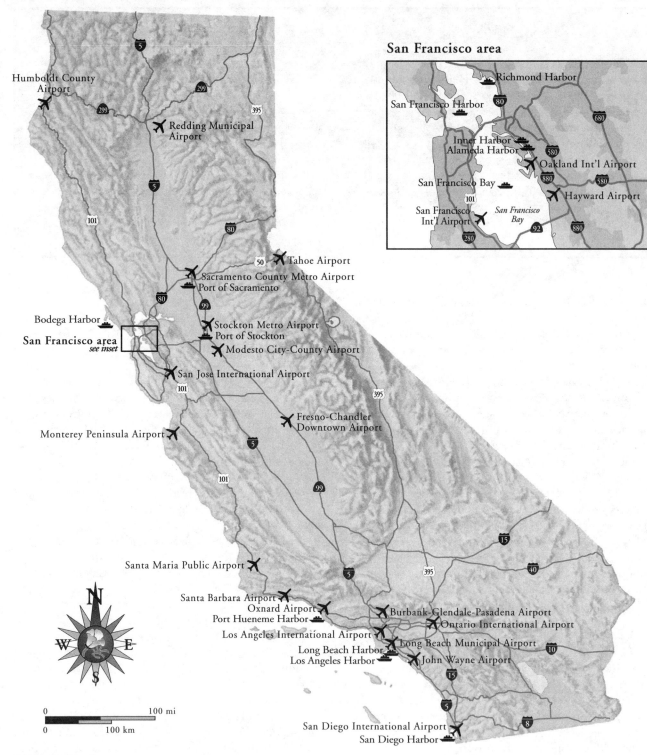

San Francisco area

Humboldt County Airport

Redding Municipal Airport

Tahoe Airport

Sacramento County Metro Airport
Port of Sacramento

Bodega Harbor

San Francisco area
see inset

Stockton Metro Airport
Port of Stockton

Modesto City-County Airport

San Jose International Airport

Fresno-Chandler Downtown Airport

Monterey Peninsula Airport

Santa Maria Public Airport

Santa Barbara Airport
Oxnard Airport
Port Hueneme Harbor
Los Angeles International Airport
Long Beach Harbor
Los Angeles Harbor

Burbank-Glendale-Pasadena Airport
Ontario International Airport

Long Beach Municipal Airport
John Wayne Airport

San Diego International Airport
San Diego Harbor

Richmond Harbor
San Francisco Harbor
Inner Harbor
Alameda Harbor
Oakland Int'l Airport
San Francisco Bay
Hayward Airport
San Francisco Int'l Airport
San Francisco Bay

0   100 mi
0   100 km

N W E S

MAP 10.3
Trade is vital to the California economy. The state's seaports and airports are some of the busiest in the nation.

in exports in 1995, an increase of more than 34 percent. That made San Jose the fastest-growing export area in the United States and very close to the leader. Apple, Intel, and other high-tech firms in that region and their electronic products were given much of the credit. L.A.-Long Beach area exports increased by more than 11 per-

cent to nearly $25 billion. By the late 1990s, the Asian economic slump hit harder in the Silicon Valley, allowing Southern California to gain economic ground relative to the north.

Export jobs include longshoremen at L.A. and Long Beach Ports (the nation's largest), workers in Silicon Valley computer firms and Hollywood studios, and laborers on Central Valley farms.

Trade with Latin America For years, California has worked with several Latin American countries to build stronger ties. Why did the California Chamber of Commerce, along with numerous other business groups, lend its enthusiastic support to the enactment of NAFTA during the early 1990s? As of 1993, California accounted for 16 ercent of America's total shipments of manufactured goods to Mexico, and that was with tariffs existing prior to NAFTA. As NAFTA was enacted, Mexico continued as California's fastest growing market, taking about 10 percent of the state's exported manufactured goods. This is one reason that when Mexico's president toured California in 1999, he was given so much attention.

The growth of maquiladoras (reviewed earlier in this chapter) have helped confirm Mexico as California's Latin American trade star. Communication represents one great example of the connections with Mexico. Telephone traffic between Mexico and the United States is the second highest in the world, just behind the United States and Canada. Mexico's local and long distance telephone market should grow from $6 billion to over $9 billion just into the new century. New competitors are airing TV commercials and laying fiber-optic cables across Mexico to spread modern communication technologies.

Numerous California businesses are looking beyond Mexico to future trade agreements with other Latin American trade partners, such as Chile.

Asia APEC is the eighteen-member Asia-Pacific Economic Cooperation forum. It accounts for half the world's economic output and 46 percent of global merchandise trade. The organization is trying to enhance trade and economic development. However, there are huge gaps between rich and poor countries of the forum, and this causes conflict. According to the *Los Angeles Times*, gross national products per capita for APEC members in 1994 ranged from the top three (Japan at $34,630, United States at $25,860, Singapore at $23,360) to the bottom three (Philippines at $960, Indonesia at $880, China at $530).

Several Asian economies representing more than 3 billion people were advancing rapidly out of poverty. Asia was expected to account for up to one-half the world's economic growth during the final years of the twentieth century. Then, the Asian economies unexpectedly sputtered and staggered in the late 1990s. These downturns sent powerful ripples through California's economy.

About one-third of California's economy is, in some way, tied to trade with Asia. The state's economy is bigger than Indonesia, Singapore, Thailand, the Philippines, Taiwan, and China, all important trading partners. California is especially selling technology, particularly environmental technology, to these countries. Fast-growing

Asian countries are contracting with western companies for water treatment and purification and other environmental technologies they desperately need.

Evidence of this trade industry can be found in the *Asian Environmental Business Journal*, a San-Diego-based newsletter. Developed economies of the United States, Western Europe, and Japan spend about $368 billion per year on waste management and air and water purification; Asia's more populous developing countries spend only $16 billion per year. Consequently, California universities, institutions, and companies are poised to play important roles in cleaning up Asian environments.

Fortunately, California has already established strong links to Latin American and Asian leadership, as many foreign leaders were schooled here. There is a $110 billion per year two-way merchandise trade between Southern California and Asia alone, as overseas companies set up factories here. Even greater total trade occurs in Hollywood films, music, and TV shows, engineering and financial services, and especially education. Academic links to overseas companies and leaders are similar to the links that Stanford and UC Berkeley have to the Silicon Valley.

Thousands of students continue to stream in from Asia, especially to Southern California, for college. Stronger links are evident between major Asian corporations and USC, UCLA, UC Irvine, and other California universities. Universities continue to recruit experts on Asia and Latin America to strengthen these ties. California colleges and universities are selling knowledge for the future economy.

Today's estimates are that up to 25 percent of the world's output of goods and services are produced in Asia. Asia may produce up to 50 percent of goods and services by 2020. Such forecasts became more uncertain after the Asian markets fell in the late 1990s.

A Few Examples of Trade with Japan Usually, a weak yen means cheaper Japanese products will flood into California, causing loss of jobs and a larger trade deficit. A weaker dollar means cheaper U.S. products flow into Japan, boosting California industries, just as in the few years up to 1996. The yen dropped to a low below 90 yen per dollar in 1995. When it began strengthening again into 1996, U.S. economists became worried. Such market fluctuations could mean billions in trade to either country. Then, in 1998, after the Asian market collapsed, Japan dropped to second behind Mexico in accepting exports from California.

One export important to many Californians is beef. Sales of U.S. beef to Japan totalled $2.1 billion in 1995, a 17 percent increase over the previous year. Much of that export is from California. Countless trends and rumors of contamination can drive the fluctuation in this market. This is why the U.S. Meat Export Federation and the California Beef Council work to "educate" Japanese consumers about high quality U.S. beef. Meanwhile, Kirin

Brewery Co. Japan moved its U.S. headquarters to Santa Monica in December, 1996, to be closer to its West Coast customers. Kirin is Japan's largest brewer, but its strongest U.S. market is on the West Coast and in Hawaii. It entered into a partnership with Anheuser-Busch in Van Nuys to use and expand their Van Nuys plant.

China Trade   With the China economy growing at double digits during the mid-1990s, the United States had a trade deficit with that country. However, the United States also exported more than $13 billion of products to China during 1996, and that number was also increasing each year. China mostly consumes airplanes, agricultural commodities, and technology from the United States, while we buy textiles, apparel, and light manufactured goods from China.

China is being called an "800-pound gorilla" by some economic experts. California exchanges goods and services from cotton to technology with China. Average incomes are relatively small in China, but the population is huge; some claim that there are already one million millionaires there. Some experts expect the Chinese economy to become number one in the world by early in the next century, growing ahead of Japan and the United States. They still have a long way to go, particularly since the Asian economic slump of the late 1990s slowed this economic momentum.

By the time the Chinese government took control of Hong Kong on July 1, 1997, shock waves had already rolled through California. California is serving as a place of business, of safe investment, an adopted home, as a refuge for friends and relatives, and as an educational outpost for children of wealthy people from Hong Kong. California has a large stake in developments there. Hong Kong's ties to California have been strengthened as wealthy Hong Kong citizens grow uneasy over the transition of power to China. Secondary headquarters were established here, families moved to second and permanent homes, and billions of dollars in investments were made in California.

Binational living has certainly increased since the 1980s, as reviewed in Chapter 8. U.S. immigration laws have encouraged this by granting eventual citizenship to those who invest more than $1 million in companies with ten employees or more. California's popularity is due to its mild climate, proximity to Asia, and its higher-education system. Hong Kong's wealthy can especially be found in the San Gabriel Valley's Asian-style shopping malls, restaurants, and nightclubs as transpacific connections continue to grow.

Hong Kong bought $3.4 billion worth of California products in 1994 to become California's tenth largest export market. Hong Kong was the third largest trading partner behind Japan and China at the Port of Long Beach. Hong Kong is the world's eighth largest trading economy and has the busiest container port. High in-comes are the rule and unemployment is less than 3.2 percent. It is the capital of Chinese overseas and Pacific Rim business communities. Though many of their investments in California are hidden, more than six-hundred businesses and companies belong to the Hong Kong Association of Southern California.

The ties are obvious. Tung Chee-hwa is a shipping magnate who was chosen to run Hong Kong by the Chinese government. His company, Orient Overseas, was the first Hong Kong company to ship containers to Long Beach in 1969, and it now operates a 101-acre container terminal. Ronnie Chan is a billionaire developer with a master's degree from USC who now heads the Hong Kong-based Hang Lung Group. He made eighteen trips to the United States in 1996 and has a branch office in Costa Mesa. Centaline Realty in Alhambra is a branch of one of Hong Kong's largest real estate firms. It assists Hong Kong investors in California industries, buildings, and hotels.

In 1996, Hong Kong investors and developers bought the Biltmore Hotel and adjoining building in Los Angeles and the Regent Beverly Wilshire Hotel. The Hong Kong-based Park Lane Hotels International owns hotels in San Francisco and Oakland and developed the Pacific Renaissance Plaza in San Francisco's Chinatown. Hong Kong investors also own the Hilton developments in Woodland Hills, Pleasanton, and Whittier.

Korea   Japanese investors were stung by the California real estate market slump during the early 1990s. Despite these uncertainties, according to the *Far Eastern Economic Review*, Korean firms are gradually developing commercial and residential properties as they focus on development, rather than just buying real estate in California.

Sae Hyun Uhm runs his high-risk commercial and residential Los Angeles-based development firm called K. Young. He represents one example of Korean investors in California's real estate market. In 1996, he planned to build the $106 million Palladian project in Glendale (the first speculative commercial project in Southern California in five years) and Water Garden II in Santa Monica. He was first supported by his father in South Korea, but scandal and hard times have hit his business there and also affected Korean business in general within California. When the Asian markets slumped in the late 1990s, Asian investments in California's entertainment industry waned; uncertainties were cast over future developments such as the Palladian project in Glendale. More information about Korean Americans in California can be found in Chapter 8.

Russia's Far East   Other promising areas of trade with Asia include Russia's Far East. After their fur trade evaporated, the Russians sold Fort Ross for $30,000 in 1841.

More recently, political and economic instability kept California industry away from Russia. Today, more than 300,000 Russian-speaking people live in California.

Russia is currently trying to interest California in trade with its Far East region, particularly to exploit Russia's timber and oil resources there. In the past, clever leaders in Washington State beat California to trade deals with Russia while California was overwhelmed by trade potentials in other Asian nations. In 1995, California exported more than $300 million of goods to Russia, a $60 million increase over 1994. That left Russia just thirty-second on California's list of world trade partners. Today it represents only one example of the enormous potential for trade with Asia.

The focus of this section has been the remarkable growth and potential for trade with Pacific Rim countries. Though situation factors may not be as favorable, California has also established strong economic ties with nations beyond the Pacific, such as European countries. This global involvement is expected to continue within one of the world's most powerful and vibrant economies.

Effects of Trade on California Landscapes   The Port of Oakland handled the highest volume of farm produce in California during the 1993–1994 fiscal year (1.15 million metric tons). Fruits, vegetables, and other products went to places like Japan, Hong Kong, France, Germany, and Taiwan. The Port of Long Beach followed Oakland with 1.04 million metric tons, and Los Angeles followed it with 718,594 metric tons of produce.

In 1994, the Port of Oakland and the Southern Pacific and Union Pacific Railroads agreed to develop an intermodal yard that will host all major railroads serving California. This $80 million development was called the Joint Intermodal Terminal (JIT) project and is part of a larger $600 million expansion of the area. Oakland was strengthening its reputation to compete as one of California's classic **break-of-bulk** ports, where goods are transferred from one type of transport to another.

The new Harbor Transportation Center in the Port of Oakland was established due to a growing need for container and chassis staging areas and the need to consolidate freight with the increase in shipments to the West Coast. It is designed to become a multisectoral service provider. The 80-acre harbor has warehouses and truck chassis parking for eight transport companies, Union Pacific Railroad, and the West Oakland Truckers Co-Op. These expansions caught the attention of trade publications such as *American Shipper and Distribution.*

It was in 1995 that the Los Angeles Customs District soared ahead of New York to become the nation's busiest port. The L.A. District includes the ports of L.A. and Long Beach, L.A. Airport, Port Hueneme, and Las Vegas airport. International trade increased another 14 percent to $80.9 billion during the first half of 1996. Expanding economies on the Pacific Rim, especially Japan and China, were cited as reasons, as well as increased exports of electronics (computer chips), cars, and aircraft parts. These trends were threatened by the late 1990s Asian economic crisis.

The Ports of Los Angeles and Long Beach are the top two container ports in the United States. After posting remarkable increases since the 1994–1995 fiscal year, they are also planning to expand for anticipated growth. According to the *Journal of Commerce and Commercial,* intermodal cargo is now being rerouted from the Pacific Northwest to southern ports.

In October of 1996, the Port of Los Angeles experienced the busiest month of its ninety-year history. The number of containers handled through the Port of Long Beach during that year also soared over 3 million for the first time at any port in North America. More than 4 million cargo containers moved through the port in 1998, a 17 percent increase over the previous year and another

Ships, cranes, trains, and trucks keep goods moving in and out of San Diego.

record. Of course, this confirmed Long Beach as the number one container port in the United States. Meanwhile, more than $1 million per day was spent during part of the 1990s to strengthen and expand Los Angeles and Long Beach ports' infrastructure for more growth.

Long Beach has always been a Navy town, but it is changing fast. Due to the early 1990s recession and military closures, Long Beach lost more than 50,000 jobs as its unemployment rate soared up to 8 percent. It was one of the hardest hit by the military shutdowns and layoffs. By the mid-1990s, some proponents of a new container terminal claimed it could create up to 650 jobs and $1 million in annual revenue for the city. Members of the Long Beach City Council created controversy when they decided to level the closing Long Beach Naval Station to make way for the terminal. The station would be replaced with a parking lot for shipping containers for the Port of Long Beach. The Council anticipated more international trade, high-wage jobs, and other economic benefits.

However, when Long Beach residents viewed the 170-acre naval station, many wanted it for other uses. Questions were raised by retirees, taxpayer groups, and architecture and history buffs. These groups launched their own campaign to keep the gym, playgrounds, and open park atmosphere for the community. This conflict between local business interests and some residents got national and international attention when it was revealed that much of the land would be leased to a Chinese shipping company. By 1998, members of the U.S. Congress also tried to block the deal, using it as political ammunition to fuel anti-Chinese sentiment. Long Beach proponents remained determined to build the container terminal, regardless of the company destined to use it.

What are the chances that some politicians from around the country were blocking the expanded Long Beach port to get trade for their districts or states? Could jealousy or fear have played a role as California's mammoth trade economy grew to even more astounding proportions? Was there fear that foreign interests would gain too much influence in our port? These local planning and national trade issues and conflicts are having enormous impacts on the future economy and landscapes of Long Beach and its neighbors. Fluctuations in global markets, including the late 1990s Asian economic problems, are also impacting California harbors.

Real Estate and Related Economic Activities

Trends in real estate and housing markets often reflect broader changes in California's economy and landscapes. They also indicate how and where Californians are willing to spend and invest their money and time. Perhaps this is why a multitude of institutions and publications struggle to keep track of these trends. They include publications such as *Mortgage Banking*, which noted in 1994 that during the recession, housing demand in California was in a state of flux. Job declines, corporate cutbacks, and business out-migration affected all segments of the home-ownership market.

The real estate market cautiously emerged from recession during the late 1990s, after economic restructuring and recovery had settled in across the state. Enormous spatial variations ruled during this recovery.

By 1998, home prices were soaring again in the major metropolitan areas; a real estate boom had returned to California. During a one-year period from 1997–1998, median home values increased at the highest rates in the nation. All of the top five, and six of the top ten, U.S. metropolitan areas with the greatest increases in median home values were in California. Here is the list of the top five:

San Francisco +19.8%

Oakland +17.7%

San Diego +16.3%

Orange County +13%

San Jose +11.9%

Los Angeles/Long Beach came in tenth in the nation with a 6.7 percent one-year jump in home sales prices. These data were compiled and presented to local media by Experian RES, an Anaheim-based real estate research firm. To increase accuracy, they only compared homes that sold at least twice during the period.

According to the California Association of Realtors, median single-family home prices soared over $205,000 in California during 1998. That was more than a 10 percent increase in just one year. The seasonally adjusted rate of home sales also increased to more than 607,000 during one year. This activity represents a lot of money and real estate changing hands; economic ripple effects were felt far beyond real estate and financial offices.

The nation's leader in the real estate frenzy continued to be the San Francisco Bay Area, particularly the Silicon Valley. In 1998, median home prices in San Francisco exceeded $330,000, while they topped $375,000 in Santa Clara.

Silicon Valley Real Estate The Silicon Valley was California's hottest housing market as its high-tech economy boomed into the late 1990s. Buyers were lining up to compete for new housing like they did in Southern California during the 1980s. Software engineers, managers and entrepreneurs were buying "absolute dumps" for more than $250,000. Median home sale prices rose about 5 percent in 1996 to more than $264,000 in the area, and they soared faster into the late 1990s.

In high-scale communities like Atherton, median prices approached $1 million. More and more secretaries, clerks, and lower-income workers were being forced farther away as apartment vacancies dropped below 1 percent. Home builders were having trouble keeping up with demand; Kaufman & Broad Home Corporation sold out a 120-house development within about four months in 1996. Such stories were becoming more commonplace throughout California toward the end of the decade.

Houses in upscale communities such as Atherton, Woodside, and Palo Alto have been purchased as "scrapers" for more than $500,000, only to be then torn down and replaced with much larger and modern homes. More established neighborhoods like the College Terrace section of Palo Alto are also being impacted by this "mansionization." A backlash has developed as the city of Palo Alto near Stanford University imposed a moratorium on residential demolitions after historical homes were leveled. Neighbors were concerned about losing the character of their communities with the destruction of the architecture that defines them. In some areas, such as the Willow Glen neighborhood in old San Jose, buyers have taken out newspaper ads and gone door-to-door searching for sellers.

Almost one-third of the state's employment growth came from Silicon Valley firms in 1996—that is 100,000 jobs in Silicon Valley alone. Real estate-related businesses were thriving, as expected. Some furniture sales were up 40 percent from the previous year, and they included upgraded merchandise for those who could afford it. Interior designers are also expanding their territories. The growing economy created more high-quality jobs, which created more homes, which fueled service industries used by new residents with disposable income. Ripple effects transformed Silicon Valley landscapes at a furious pace.

Southern California Real Estate Within California, more than seven-hundred buyers purchased homes worth more than $1 million during a single three-month period of 1996, according to DataQuick Information Systems. Southern California led the trend, with more than 250 homes in Los Angeles County and more than 60 homes in Orange County sold for over $1 million. The figures are even more impressive nearing the end of the decade. During one quarter in 1998, a record 1,555 homes were sold for more than $1 million in California and 20 percent of the buyers paid cash!

The L.A. area contains 60 percent of the state's homes valued at more than $1 million. Here are three examples from just one quarter of 1996, including one of the most expensive homes in Southern California. Called Pacific Reflections, it is an 11,000-square-foot Laguna Beach mansion with views of the ocean that sold for more than $14 million. Then, an estate in Brentwood sold for more than $18 million, probably with additional property, and a Santa Monica home sold for more than $6 million during that same quarter. Such prices indicate where the wealth in California is as prices continued up into the new century.

Extremes in Southern California's home prices (printed in the *Los Angeles Times* and various real estate publications) may reveal where the money is, where the region's economy is thriving, and where it is not. Remember that Southern California median housing prices were up to $161,000 by 1997 and were rising fast into the late 1990s. Here are the extremes in 1996 median home prices for areas with ten or more home sales. The data provide valuable geography lessons.

> *Los Angeles County:* Median home prices were more than $500,000 in Bel-Air, Beverly Hills, Brentwood, Malibu, Pacific Palisades, Palos Verdes Peninsula, and San Marino. (Note the west side clusters.) Prices near or below $100,000 were in Lake Hughes, Lancaster, and Littlerock (the lowest at $80,000). (Note high desert locations.)
>
> *Orange County:* Median home prices were above $400,000 in Corona del Mar (highest, and only location above $500,000), Newport Beach, and Villa Park (the only inland location—in the hills above Orange—instead of on the South Coast). Prices averaged below $150,000 in Midway City, Santa Ana, and Stanton (the lowest at $113,000).
>
> *Riverside County:* Indian Wells median prices averaged $370,000 and in Rancho Mirage, $200,000; all other locations' prices were lower. Median home prices were below $80,000 in Blythe, Coachella, Desert Hot Springs ($65,000), and Mecca.
>
> *San Bernardino County:* Median home prices above $150,000 were in Alta Loma, Chino (the highest at $175,000), Lake Arrowhead (barely at $155,000), and Upland. None averaged near $200,000. Median prices below $60,000 were in Cedar Glen (next to Lake Arrowhead), Joshua Tree, Morongo Valley, Trona ($48,000), and Twentynine Palms (barely making this lowest list).
>
> *Ventura County:* Above $200,000 were in Somis ($359,000), Thousand Oaks, and Moorpark. Median prices at or below $150,000 were in Santa Paula, Fillmore, and Port Hueneme ($129,000). Note the much narrower range in Ventura County compared to other areas in Southern California.

You Are Where You Live It is obvious that home value statistics can reveal much about the economy and landscape of any California county. Moreover, these statistics help reveal even more about the *people* who choose to live in certain California locations.

You are where you live; this is a rule recognized far beyond the real estate and home services industries. Your address often determines your actions and your purchases, which reveal who you are and how you spend your money. **Consumer segmentation** is a $100 million business that categorizes each lifestyle and applies nicknames to them. Young marrieds look for suburbs with good schools; young singles look for more urban, hip neighborhoods.

Demographic data from the U.S. Census are analyzed. Private and public information about your activity and purchases is compiled. You become part of a "tribe," defined as those who share your ZIP code (usually between 2,500–7,500 households). More specific information may come from census blocks (200–500 households) or the extra 4 digits on your ZIP code (5–12 households). Various researchers put you into a category of similar lifestyles and buying patterns. Different names for the groups depend upon the company doing the research.

From Bedrock America, Movers and Shakers, Upper Crust, Urban Singles, White Picket Fence, Food Family Life, and Stars and Stripes, to Money and Brains, American Dreams, and Kids and Cul de Sacs, where do you fit in? Shotguns and Pickups might refer to people without college degrees who resist continuing education but who view Cadillacs as status symbols. New Ecotopia consists of those who moved to rural areas, taking their urban habits with them.

Numerous businesses from restaurants, retail chains, and grocery stores to banks and alarm companies use this information to locate customers, to stock shelves, to advertise, and to offer services. This "birds of a feather" concept is as much art as science, and it often holds true even as people move in and out of a neighborhood. The most stable neighborhoods have the good schools and job opportunities that increase real estate values and tax structures. You might expect the opposite in the poorest neighborhoods. Geographers revel in the study of such connections.

Government

During the 1990s, the number of government jobs in California broke through the two million mark. What and where were these jobs? Why are they important to California?

The governor of California signed a $63 billion budget for the 1996–1997 fiscal year for California alone. (The state's budget soared much higher into the new century.) It included $28 billion for K–12 education spending, which also increased dramatically into the twenty-first century. UC's, CSU's, and community colleges got $5.2 billion combined, with annual increases on the way.

The Center on Juvenile and Criminal Justice stirred controversy when they reported that in 1980–1981, 9.2 percent of the state's general fund went to higher education and 2.3 percent to corrections. In the 1996–1997 budget, higher education got 8.7 percent and prisons 9.4 percent. Californians debated what seemed to be ominous trends. State prisons got nearly $4 billion. The state's prison population was up to 141,000 and still growing. About $16.6 billion went to welfare and other social programs. Controversies will continue to rage over where and how Californians decide to spend their tax dollars, but one thing is certain; we are talking about enormous amounts of money and jobs.

Though proportions were similar, the California state budget for 1997–1998 was more than $66 billion, increasing to more than $81 billion by the end of the decade. The big differences were that the state was finally taking in more money than anticipated, and much of that surplus was going to education. These figures give you an idea of what the state spends and how it impacts the economy. However, there are many other local and federal government jobs and services.

Compared to all general economic categories, total government jobs in California recently ranked a distant third behind booming services and trade, but they had nudged just ahead of fourth-place manufacturing. Most state and local expenditures and jobs are parts of the infrastructure deemed necessary to hold our economy and society together. These workers provide services directly to Californians and businesses who demand them.

Defense Spending　Huge sums of federal dollars also flow back to California to provide services to Californians. Some of that spending, such as military and research and development, creates jobs in California that contribute to greater national goals. However, changes in defense spending have had substantial impacts in California, especially since World War II. During the 1980s, U.S. defense spending in California doubled, reaching about $60 billion. Nearly two-thirds of that went to the dominant players in Southern California's high-tech industry—defense contractors Rockwell, McDonnell Douglas, Hughes Aerospace, and TRW. During the recession that followed, total defense contracting in California dropped to $51 billion by 1992, causing about 22 percent of California's 550,000–800,000 job losses. According to the Legislative Analyst's Office, the 337,000 aerospace jobs in 1990 dropped nearly 45 percent to 191,000 in 1994.

Evidently, the early 1990s recession hit California hardest after the state became too dependent on defense spending. Especially damaged by cutbacks were local economies in San Diego, Long Beach, L.A.'s South Bay, Monterey Bay, the Bay Area, and inland cities near mil-

TATTOOS AND THE MILITARY ECONOMY

Like any other economic activity, defense spending generates a multiplier effect of indirectly related industries and jobs that ripples through the economy. Some of them are quite obscure. Long Beach, San Diego, and Bay Area economies have been dependent on the Navy for most of this century. Local tattoo studios thrived in these areas. By the late 1990s, Grimm's Tattoo Studio in Long Beach had declined from employing ten full-time artists to just two. Much of the decline was caused by Navy moves out of the area and the closing of the Long Beach Shipyard by 1997.

Tattoos began as Captain James Cook's English Navy sailors got them as souvenirs while mapping the South

Pacific in the eighteenth century. Today, they include hundreds of images, including typical sailor cartoon tattoos, such as Popeye. Lucky's Tattoos in San Diego is run by a former artist from Grimm's; it was estimated in the mid-1990s that about 50 percent of the clients were military, especially from the U.S. Navy Base in San Diego. By the late 1990s, tattoo artists were benefitting from a more general client base, thanks to popular trends. Tattoo shops were springing up throughout California, far removed from military sites. Yet another California industry had been weaned from its reliance on defense spending.

itary bases. Most of these communities searched for more sustainable industries that could replace their military economies. Economic diversity became a battle cry in many of these communities.

Due to the recession, downsizing of the aerospace industry, closure of the Long Beach Naval Station in 1991, and the shipyard in 1997, more than 27,500 Navy jobs disappeared from the Long Beach area during the 1990s. More than 50,000 total jobs left the area. This had a $4 billion per year economic impact on the region. If the Long Beach area were a state, it would have been fifth nationally in jobs lost due to military downsizing. The mayor, city council, and community leaders responded by encouraging the growth of new economic activities centered on trade, tourism, and high technologies.

Other Government Services There are plenty of other categories of government services that impact the state's economy and landscapes. Parks and recreation is an obvious example. Consider the national and state parks that serve as open spaces, retreats, playgrounds, reserves, historical landmarks and educational opportunities for millions of Californians and others from the United States and around the world. Some of the most spectacular park landscapes in the world continue to fuel a tourist industry (previously reviewed) that has grown to more than $55 billion per year. Local parks and recreational activities also play vital roles in creating quality living and working environments within an increasingly crowded state.

Social services designed to stabilize society and provide security and safety nets to struggling residents play vital roles in every developed country in the world. Californians are in constant debate about the extent of these services. In California, 2.7 million people received grants under Aid to Families With Dependent Children in the mid-1990s; this was the state's largest welfare program.

About 1.8 million recipients were children. The six counties representing the greatest percent of California recipients were as follows.

| County | Aid Recipients | |
	Individuals	Percentage of County Population
Los Angeles	881,000	32.8
San Diego	195,000	7.3
San Bernardino	193,000	7.2
Sacramento	145,000	5.4
Fresno	121,000	4.5
Orange	118,000	4.4

Within a few southern L.A. County ZIP codes, clusters of up to 50 percent of local populations were on some form of welfare. Some may be surprised to find clusters of more than 20 percent of the population on welfare in the Antelope Valley and other communities far removed from California's inner cities. (Struggling rural communities were reviewed in the previous chapter.) Counties with the most food stamp recipients in 1996 were:

Los Angeles, 1,030,812

San Bernardino, 218,194

San Diego, 202,673

Sacramento, 166,740

Orange, 145,613

Fresno, 137,439

Riverside, 125,601

Alameda, 120,229

Santa Clara, 94,375

Kern, 90,475

These statistics give you an idea of where the greatest number of people struggle in poverty in California. Of course, they are associated with the state's largest population centers, where the majority of social services must also be clustered. They *do not* usually reflect the large *percentage* of populations struggling in poverty within smaller, distant rural communities. Such statistics became more important during the late 1990s; cuts in welfare and other social programs made larger ripples through the poorest and most vulnerable communities.

Fortunately, California's healthy economy during the end of the 1990s helped keep welfare roles and unemployment far lower than earlier in the decade.

Infrastructures and Connections

Millions of Californians and billions of dollars are involved in efforts to keep California and its economies working efficiently. Can you imagine what would happen to California without education, safety, power, transportation, communication, water, and sewage treatment and other waste disposal? Parts of these infrastructures are private and others are public, but all of the people providing these services are responsible for improving the living and working environments of Californians. Certainly, the state's economy would collapse without them. Standing alone, they also represent a large piece of the state's economic pie.

Several of the private industries and public agencies that make the state's infrastructure have already been examined in this book, such as in Chapter 6 on the state's water supplies. We have room for just a few additional examples here.

Education   During the mid-1900s, California gained a reputation for building one of the best public education systems in the nation. Budget cuts and other problems during the 1980s destroyed that image. Going into the twenty-first century, the number of students enrolled in the state's public K–12 school system soared past 5.7 million. Yet, according to data in a nonpartisan report published by EdSource, Inc., Californians had neglected their public schools. The state spent $1,000 less per student than the national average (ranking forty-first among all other states and last among the ten major industrial states in spending per student). In the same study, the state ranked fiftieth in the number of students per teacher and principal.

Though those budget cuts, the recession, and other problems also took their tolls on higher education

through the 1980s and 1990s, the combination of public and private colleges and universities (though now far more expensive than in past decades) is still matched by no other region on the planet. These schools have traditionally helped produce the skilled labor force so essential to the success of modern, cutting-edge industries in the state.

Most California industries recognize the importance of public education, and some are donating money for school improvements and starting several school-to-work programs across the state. They include groups such as "Workforce Silicon Valley," sponsored by the Santa Clara Manufacturing Group. After all, private industry's links to Stanford, UC Berkeley, and other colleges helped make the Silicon Valley success story. By the late 1990s, most California citizens, officials, and businesses were rediscovering the long-term benefits (and shorter-term costs) of supporting a sound educational system.

Intrastate Transportation   The greater L.A. area has $430 billion gross output of goods and services per year, and about 25 percent of that depends on international trade. Traffic and trade are expected to bring 700,000 jobs to Southern California in the next twenty years. Cargo traffic in Southern California alone is expected to increase from more than 2 million tons to 6 million tons by 2015. Our location on the Pacific Rim and near Mexico is increasing the flow of passengers and goods. This is why the Southern California region has started a total of $4.3 billion worth of airport, port, and rail expansions, the country's largest capital expansion program. Building this infrastructure is just as important to intrastate transportation.

We must efficiently transport products and people within California if we are to thrive economically. The state's shipping industry connects California's coastal cities. The nation's greatest ports are Los Angeles/Long Beach; the Bay Area and San Diego are not far behind. An impressive (and infamous) interstate and state highway system and the state's impressive railways extend these links into an inland web. The network is completed with one of the busiest and more advanced air traffic networks in the world. (The air route between San Francisco and L.A. remains one of the busiest on earth.)

The importance of transportation was underscored in 1997 when state leaders argued over how to distribute highway funds raised from state gas taxes. One of the persistent problems was that these funds were raised from a tax on each gallon of gasoline. After the 1970s energy crises, motorists were buying cars with better gas mileage. As a result of increased fuel efficiency, although the number of cars and the miles they traveled on California highways increased, motorists were actually paying less taxes per mile driven to support the highway

ALAMEDA CORRIDOR

The ports of Los Angeles and Long Beach have invested and risked the most time and money of all the parties who will benefit from the $2.4 billion **Alameda Corridor** project. International trade into the ports is expected to triple within the next twenty-five years. A twenty-mile, high-speed freight route will include three parallel train tracks. The project also includes a widened Alameda Street artery for trucks that will connect the railroad yards near downtown L.A. with the port and its many railroad tracks. Railroad lines would connect right up on the docks.

The cities of L.A., Long Beach, Compton, Lynwood, Vernon, and South Gate must agree on the finances and rules for the Alameda Corridor Transportation Authority. Businesses along the route may lose during short-term construction, but they will win in the long run. About 90 miles of currently zigzagging railroad tracks will be consolidated into the corridor, eliminating congestion caused by up to 200 different street crossings. One of the tracks will be at ground level to service the many industries along the corridor; the other two will be for transport of goods between the downtown train yard and the port. More than 180,000 tons of cargo per year at San Pedro Bay and 180,000 jobs are expected to be generated by 2020.

---

system. By the 1990s, California highways were being used more and maintained less and the deterioration was noticeable, partly because those gas tax revenues dropped during the two previous decades.

State engineers recently claimed $2.5 billion was required to prevent seven California toll bridges from collapsing during an earthquake. Five of the bridges, which needed about 93 percent of the repair expenditures, were in the Bay Area. They included the San Francisco-Oakland Bay, San Mateo-Hayward, Richmond-San Rafael, Benecia-Martinez, and Carquinez Bridges, all serving about 600,000 vehicles per day. The San Francisco-Oakland Bay Bridge (damaged and temporarily closed after the 1989 Loma Prieta quake) would require somewhere between $1.5–1.7 billion in repairs and support. Bay Area residents and leaders were engaged in heated debate over what design they would choose for their beloved, historic Bay Bridge. Work was also needed on Southern California's Vincent Thomas Bridge in San Pedro and San Diego-Coronado Bay Bridge. Bridge tolls do not even begin to cover construction costs.

Leaders debated about how much transportation funding would go to support public transportation systems that could ease traffic on existing highways. Highway improvements, extensions, and connector roads were also needed, especially at truck-crossing points, such as Otay Mesa and Calexico East, on the booming Mexican border. Local leaders lobbied for funding to support transportation projects that would help their communities.

Airports Within every California urban center, leaders are scrambling to meet the demands of increasing air traffic. All of California is recognizing that it is at a crossroads, not just at the edge of the continent. Here is an example of the problem in the L.A. area alone. The following are predictions of passenger growth in the region's airports taken from officials and published in the *Los Angeles Times.*

Airport	Passengers (in millions)	
	1996	2015
LAX	53.9	98
John Wayne	7.2	12
Ontario	6.4	18
Burbank	5.0	12
El Toro	0	12–30
TOTAL	72.5	152–170

Today's 74 million passengers per year in the Southland will double in twenty years. LAX is expected to expand from its current 58 million passengers per year to 98 million passengers and 4 million tons of cargo per year by 2015. San Diego and Orange County already send more than 100 commuter flights per day to LAX. Expansion is a political controversy in each of these cases. Residents near the airports are concerned about noise and traffic, pollution and congestion, and property values. Ontario's expansion is much more popular because it is recognized as overdue by surrounding communities and industries. It serves the Inland Empire region of more than 3 million people, creating about 30,000 new jobs per year.

As this growth continues, officials are spending $300 million to expand Ontario Airport so that increased pas-

San Diego's airport is crowded, small, and dangerously close to the city's office towers. A debate rages over where to locate a new, expanded facility that will better serve San Diego.

sengers and cargo could make it the state's third-largest airport. The Southern California Association of Governments projected 34 million passengers per year by 2020 (up from 7 million in 1975) for Orange County alone. This is assuming a fully operational John Wayne Airport and completion of the new El Toro Airport. Proponents of El Toro Airport claim that no operational restrictions on the airport will make it more popular and successful. The airport site is the 4700-acre El Toro Marine Corps Air Station, which was closed in 1999. In familiar battle cries, residents of especially southern Orange County worry about degradation of their environment and lower property values caused by all the air traffic. Businesses and residents of northern Orange County tend to support the new El Toro Airport for its economic benefits and job creation potential.

Communications   California has the most area codes of any state; there were twenty-six area codes by 2000. Companies are adding lines as customers acquire the newest technologies. Additional phone line requests are skyrocketing as more modems and fax machines are used in California. More than 650,000 new phone lines were installed in 1996 alone, nearly double the previous year. And this was *not* due to new housing starts. The vast majority of those lines were in Southern California coastal cities or the Bay Area. These trends also continued into the twenty-first century.

Modern telecommunication projects are now being established to connect workers in the home to the office. Desktop videoconferencing, telephone-to-PC integration, and other technologies offer remarkable opportunities to change production in the workplace, and to impact economies, transportation, and urban landscapes.

From High-End to Low-Wage and Low-Skill Services

We emphasized how California's economy evolved as advanced trade and services have eclipsed primary and manufacturing industries. In our review of the state's economy, you may notice that various types of services have been considered separately. What is the impact of the service industry on the state's economic landscapes? The answer to that question must include a definition of service industries and their roles in our modern cities.

Nonbasic service industries are generally defined as economic activities that supply urban residents with goods and services that do not have export implications. These activities grow with California cities and are considered vital to the successful operation and internal functioning of California's urban centers. They provide essential retailing, banking, wholesaling, transportation, health, education, government, and office services to a city's residents and workers. Nonbasic services contrast with the basic sectors of a city's economy, which are those export activities that keep capital flowing into the city from other regions.

We hear the stories about people in higher-income services, such as management, high-tech, and finance, living the California Dream. These jobs require more education and skills. Financial and business services are examples. If you do not believe financial and business services are important in California, note these facts: In 1997, the top six savings and loans in the United States were in California. According to the U.S. Treasury, eight out of the ten top savings and loans institutions were based in California. Think of all the advertising, information, and other business services that require education and skills. Millions of Californians are making their

OTHER INFRASTRUCTURE

From water treatment to flood control, from waste disposal to recycling, industries that provide billions of dollars of these vital technologies and services are thriving throughout California. New businesses are sprouting to provide services that may be less traditional.

One example involves perceived threats to water quality that are driving a lucrative bottled water industry, especially within the state's urban areas. California is, by far, the number one consumer of bottled water in the United States. Purchasing from large and small companies, Californians consumed more than 788 million gallons of bottled water in 1995, and the industry was growing rapidly into the twenty-first century. From distilled to spring water, the product comes in many different varieties. The MWD and other water agencies continue to claim their water is of high quality, and it only costs about one-tenth of a cent per gallon compared to $1 per gallon for many bottled products. Regardless, the number of water businesses continues to grow.

Another example is Marplast in Moorpark, which was expected to grow to $1.8 million in sales during the late 1990s (six times the original size) by making powerful toilet plungers from recycled milk jugs. Like many innovative entrepreneurs, Martyn Keats could not get money from a bank, so the California Integrated Waste Management Board loaned him $200,000. His loan was quickly bought with other successful loans by the Community Reinvestment Fund. What a great way to recycle good project money!

Perhaps we've crossed a boundary by including recycled toilet plungers as part of our infrastructure, but how we deal with our solid waste determines our level of development and the quality of our living conditions. Building an infrastructure that encourages recycling will have enormous impacts on our manufacturing industries, and this is the perfect example. Besides, anyone who buys and uses one of these plungers has a clearer view of how various economic sectors are tied together.

---

fortunes, or at least comfortable livings, in these industries.

There are far more people on the low end of the economic scale who provide services for the fewer number of people on the high end. They are the custodians, restaurant workers, parking attendants, day laborers, and temporary employees we see every day. They provide the manual and repetitive labor that keeps our cities working. Of course, many hope to eventually work their way up the economic ladder and get their piece of the California Dream.

California's youth, students, and others with less education, skills, and experience often filled these jobs through the mid-1900s. Increasingly (especially during the mass migrations following the 1960s), employers relied on another traditional labor pool filled with motivated individuals who work for less—recent immigrants. These trends have led to some oversimplified generalizations and stereotypes regarding California's low-wage service labor force, and they are having profound impacts on our society as the gap between haves and have-nots grows. One thing is certain—this growing sector of the state's economy is playing a major role in the economic restructuring that is pushing California into the twenty-first century.

One general economic trend has made it easier to identify groups left behind in this low-wage service sector. This trend, among other economic changes, was highlighted in the March, 1995, issue of *International Journal of Urban and Regional Research*. The shift from

manufacturing to services in Los Angeles was blamed for closure of manufacturing plants in the inner city. African Americans who lost jobs must now compete with Asian (especially Korean) and Latin American immigrants for low-wage service jobs and low-cost housing. These changes have increased competition and tension between a multitude of cultural groups in cities from Sacramento and the Bay Area to the Mexican border. Such trends also helped lead California toward a two-tier society.

Fast-Food Fever It would be difficult to find a more competitive industry than California's fast-food restaurants and services. Since the mid-1900s, California's fast-paced lifestyles and willingness to experiment with food from other regions and cultures was nicely matched with the convenience of drive-through windows and take-out restaurants in the midst of a car culture. The state's exploding fast-food industries have been taking lessons in economic and urban geography ever since. Fierce competition has kept the price of the basic taco and hamburger so low, many of us wonder how profits are made.

Glen Bell opened his first taco shop in Downey in 1962; his Taco Bell chain quickly grew to dominate the Mexican fast-food market. (Mexican food was less popular outside California during the 1960s and 1970s.) Del Taco and Naugles grew during the 1980s to compete. Both were headquartered in Orange County until Del Taco consumed Naugles.

By the mid-1980s, taco shops were mainstream. During the 1990s, Taco Bell controlled about 70 percent of the Mexican-style fast-food market in the United States, with its familiar Mission-style architecture. The corporation keeps profits high by opening new restaurants as novelty wanes at each region's original restaurant. The problem with this approach is that each new restaurant starts with fresh business. Unfortunately for investors, added restaurants not only compete with other fast-food chains, but eventually with restaurants of the same chain that are too close together. The winners are fast-food consumers in this hyper-competitive environment.

Special Delivery Services Specialized delivery companies play important roles in every California city. Bicycle messengers delivering letters and packages can still be spotted in more dense, compact urban settings where interacting businesses are just blocks apart. (As more business transactions were done by fax or on the Internet during the 1990s, some of these delivery service companies' profits were eroded.) Delivery companies will use small vans or trucks for larger items or for more distant runs out to a city's periphery.

By 1996, Pink Dot grocery delivery company already had 45,000 Southern California customers and five warehouses. Their employees will take your grocery list, do your shopping, and deliver the groceries to you. Though most deliveries were on L.A.'s West Side, Pink Dot was expected to open in several more locations, one in Orange County. Its customers, often in two-income families, are too busy with work and other responsibilities to do their own shopping.

By the end of the 1990s, there seemed to be someone ready to offer a specialized service for almost anything a Californian might need. These inexpensive services are having profound impacts on the state's cultures and landscapes.

◆ ECONOMIC DEVELOPMENT AND GROWTH: PLANNING FOR THE FUTURE

California ranks high with developed economies in almost every traditional measurement of **economic development**. GNP per capita and energy consumption per capita are among the highest in the world. Nutrition, health, education, and other public services compare favorably with most other developed economies. Though there are still clear differences, gender gaps are closing as women play more prominent roles in the state's economy.

However, the gap between the wealthy and poor widened considerably during the 1980s and 1990s, and there were particular differences between ethnic groups. This is a situation traditionally more indicative of a less developed country. All of these trends, both positive and negative, contribute to the amount of crime, pollution, and stability in a society. They also reflect the quality of living and working environments and the general measure of happiness of the state's people.

What is the future of California's powerful economy and the landscapes it creates? Here are just a few examples of some issues and trends to follow.

Cooperation and Partnerships

Regional business groups and other organizations have teamed up to tackle much broader industrial and geographic problems in the state. They include Joint Venture Silicon Valley Network in San Jose, the Santa Clara Manufacturing Group, and several other organizations previously reviewed here.

California is in a period of investment mania, which usually leads to high innovation and productivity. This has encouraged individuals and businesses to pool their money to improve local economies. **Venture capitalists** are individuals and private partners who lend money to companies involved in high-risk endeavors. Financial backers hope these companies, usually in high-tech areas, will grow into successful, stock-issuing enterprises. California has the largest share (about one-third) of U.S. entrepreneurial efforts funded by venture capitalists. According to statewide publications such as the *Los Angeles Times*, nearly $2.3 billion was raised in 437 deals between entrepreneurs and venture capitalists in 1995 in California, and nearly three-fourths of that was raised in the Silicon Valley. Investments continued to increase toward the end of the 1990s.

Partnerships in the Bay Area

Many of the nation's largest venture capital firms are along a quarter-mile stretch of Sand Hill Road in Menlo Park, all within walking distance and within sight of Stanford University. One society called the Band of Angels represents sixty dues-paying former and current Silicon Valley entrepreneurs, executives, bankers, and other sources of capital for new companies needing a jump start.

Recent government cooperation and streamlining and cuts in business taxes and fees have often encouraged short-term economic growth. One example of this business friendliness includes the two counties and twenty-five cities, including San Jose, around the Silicon Valley who consolidated and streamlined permitting processes. Counties and cities within regions throughout California are cooperating with one another and with businesses to create common, simplified building and business regulations and code interpretations. All of these factors combined by the mid-1990s so that *Fortune* magazine voted San Francisco and the Bay Area the best urban center for business in the United States and second only to the world's best, Singapore.

Los Angeles' South Bay Partnerships

Traditionally, L.A.'s South Bay is considered to include sixteen cities from L.A. Airport and the 105 Freeway south to Long Beach. The South Bay Economic Development Partnership was formed in 1995 among companies and local governments that will work together to further diversify the economy. (Long Beach really has its own economy, but Torrance is the second-largest economy in the region.) During the recession, employment dropped by 50 percent in the area. More recently, the movie and other entertainment industries have moved to Manhattan Beach and surroundings. High-tech and international trade is diversifying the economy, leading to further recovery. Logistics companies have also become highly automated and high-tech as they are involved in the transfer of containers from the ports of Los Angeles and Long Beach.

By 1996, a total of thirteen cities in this part of southeast L.A. County had banded together to enhance the economic clout of the region. The cities include Compton, Cudahy, Downey, La Habra Heights, Lakewood, La Mirada, Maywood, Paramount, Pico Rivera, Signal Hill, Long Beach, Norwalk, and Huntington Park. Long Beach gets two votes, and the other cities get one. A total of twenty-seven cities have been invited to join.

The area was once the county's industrial powerhouse, but it was still stinging from defense cutbacks and aerospace layoffs into the late 1990s. Instead of competing against each other for government contracts and businesses, companies were working together as a stronger coalition to recover from the recession. City leaders (especially in Long Beach) were pushing ahead to develop vacated naval land and expand the port with developments designed to add thousands of jobs and $1 million per year to city revenues. It was hoped that the new economy and partnerships would continue to bring high-paying jobs in trade, technology, and tourism.

Rising Above Past Defense Cuts and Base Closures

Most California communities who haven't already recovered from the hardships of late 1980s and 1990s defense cuts at least have a plan. Here are a few examples.

Officials in Pico Rivera were cooperating to replace the Northrup Grumman Corporation's aerospace plant when it shuts down by the year 2000. Northrup once employed about 5,000 and was the center of Pico Rivera's economy, which is why officials compared the plant closing to the effects of a large military base closure.

Pico Rivera wants to establish a diverse balance between many types of industries, jobs, and tax revenues for long-term economic stability. This will probably include a mix of industrial and manufacturing uses on the 200-acre site along Washington Boulevard. One proposal included a giant mall. Another was for a $3.2 billion theme park called the Las Americas Cultural Center. It was supported by the Norwalk-based national Hispanic Education Foundation and would include an aquarium and rain forest simulation. These were options discussed within just one community.

Norton Air Force Base officially closed in 1994, taking 10,000 military jobs. It was one of numerous base closures decided on by the 1988 national base closure committee. San Bernardino made Norton's conversion the most ambitious development project in the Inland Empire. A coalition of cities and agencies created the Inland Valley Development Agency to speed the conversion. More than $120 million of public funds were invested to convert the base and build the infrastructure that has attracted over eighty new companies and agencies to the site. They include aerospace, an entertainment center, an accounting firm, and others. By the late 1990s, the community was gradually recovering from the base closure, but too slowly for many locals.

In San Diego, many residents and politicians protested a decision by the Marine Corps to move helicopter squadrons from closing bases at Tustin and El Toro to Miramar Naval Air Station in San Diego. Nearby residents, some in upscale neighborhoods, were concerned that the noise will decrease quality of life and property values. Even some developers sided with the protesters, fearing a decrease in housing values in the San Diego area. They urged that the move be made to March Air Force Base in Riverside, where locals reeling from defense cuts wanted the helicopters.

San Diegans who argued for the helicopter squadrons feared losing more military dollars. Other proponents felt that helicopter noise could be the lesser of two evils. They suspected that if the military is not using Miramar, it may be targeted as the site for San Diego's much needed international airport. That would mean noise twenty-four hours a day, an ironic twist for San Diegans against the military helicopters! However, an airport at Miramar would also help San Diego in its desperate search for an expanded airport facility and it is a superior airport location. These are great examples of the choices facing several California communities as they diversify and convert their once military-dependent economies; they all involve substantial impacts on California landscapes.

Remote Ridgecrest in the high desert was named "the secret city" by the Navy in the 1950s due to top secret military operations in the area. Then, the population increased ten times by the 1990s, partly thanks to the Naval Air Weapons Station at China Lake, employing up to

8,000 people. As China Lake laid off about 2,000 from 1991 to 1996, the Ridgecrest economy staggered. The town was hoping for future help from the SELENE (Space Laser Energy) project that would use laser technology to power satellites.

Many consider Ridgecrest's location perfect for the space laser industry. The town has 260 cloud-free days and minimal atmospheric distortion for laser beam technology. Some locals hope that Ridgecrest will become the space-power beaming center of the world. Hundreds of jobs may be generated by the SELENE project alone. It could lead scientists, electricians, maintenance workers, and entrepreneurs to the area. Local proponents argue that once officials who make the final decisions learn about the geographic advantages, Ridgecrest will get the project.

One of California's most magnificent conversion success stories is at the 500-acre Sacramento Army Depot. It employed less than 2,000 until it closed in 1994. It was quickly converted into a manufacturing site for Hewlett-Packard, supporting more than 5,000 jobs into the late 1990s.

A Rosy Future?

The massive economic **restructuring** outlined in this chapter has changed California forever. As the importance of defense and manufacturing waned, an explosion of service and trade industries has left us with a labor of minds and a low-skilled, low-wage workforce to serve them. Painful social upheavals and restructuring have also left us with a population and labor force that better matches this two-tier economy.

In California today, at least 60 percent of all jobs require community college or university training after high school as compared to 30 percent during the 1970s. The information economy with knowledge-based industries is more competitive, and could enhance the two-tier society. As an example, by the late 1990s, some studies showed those with only street addresses earned one-half the average income of those with e-mail addresses.

According to the Center for Continuing Study of the California Economy in January, 1997, California's population will continue to increase about twice as fast as the national average well into the twenty-first century. Increasing job opportunities and incomes around the state were cited as major reasons. They also warned that the state will suffer from major infrastructure and overcrowding problems if it doesn't devise a plan to deal with this expansion; such problems could slow growth.

California is experiencing job growth from 14.6 million in 1996 to 17.4 million in 2005, a 19.4 percent increase, nearly double the nation's percentage. During 1997, the state's unemployment dropped to 6.5 percent (the lowest in seven years), and it dipped below 6 percent as the decade ended. As jobs were created at the rate of 400,000 per year, California's economy was racing past the rest of the nation. California incomes were projected to rise from $808 billion in 1996 to $1.1 trillion in 2005, a 35.3 percent increase, again much larger than the nation.

The traditional base of the state's economic growth in the past included the three As: aircraft, apparel, and agriculture. The new economic base is well established and includes technology, tourism, entertainment, business services, and foreign trade. California also continues as a leader in manufacturing even after all the defense cuts. Even real estate and construction industries roared back by the late 1990s. Nonetheless, problems continue to emerge where there are no long-term public and private investment strategies. These include plans for infrastructures previously noted, including schools, transportation, communication, and other services.

The Future Silicon Valley

Experts have recently looked to the Silicon Valley to provide a glimpse into California's economic future. By the late 1990s, San Jose was America's most manufacturing-intensive city, with 30 percent of its workers making chips, circuit boards, and communications equipment. The need for prompt shipment of sophisticated electronic products had moved manufacturing back to northern California.

Solectron Corporation of Milpitas in the Silicon Valley manufactures circuit boards and other computer equipment. It encouraged learning by giving seventy-eight hours of training per year to each of its employees and paying for their other college courses. From 1991 to 1996, it grew from 2,000 to 13,000 employees and from $250 million in revenues to $2 billion. Cisco Systems was a three-year-old San Jose firm that led in developing tools for computer networking. Within those three years, it had 700 job openings, all requiring at least a community college education and knowledge of computers.

A 1997 U.S. Bureau of Labor Statistics report put San Jose and the rest of Santa Clara County at the top in average pay for workers of metropolitan areas in the nation. Average salaries in 1995 rose 8.4 percent to $42,409 per year, and they continued soaring into the late 1990s. San Jose edged out New York as the top paying metropolitan area in the nation. An explosion of well-paying, technology-related jobs requiring highly skilled workers was fueling these trends. Other national surveys have confirmed Silicon Valley's lead. The Los Angeles Metropolitan Area ranked nineteenth of 311 metropolitan areas in the nation with average salaries at $32,445 in 1995, while Orange County ranked twenty-eighth at $30,315 per year. California ranked seventh among the fifty states with average pay at $30,716. The state and nearly every California city inched up in the rankings into the twenty-first century.

Optimism Spreads

Throughout the state, smaller firms have been creating jobs faster than the large corporations could downsize. One extreme example is the explosion of new, home-based virtual companies. Employees work from their homes using phones, electronic mail, and internal computer networks.

Optimistic projections for Southern California's economy include growth especially in smaller aerospace and apparel industries, and professional management services, particularly consulting and engineering. Additionally, international trade, motion picture and TV production, retail sales, tourism, wholesale trade, new home construction, and real estate and health services could lead the way.

San Diego's Economic Future

San Diego's economic trends and future may provide another glimpse of the state's future. During the 1980s, San Diego boomed with growing defense industries such as General Dynamics, but this sector had fallen apart by the early 1990s. In response, San Diego in 1996 was just completing its computer-telecommunications networks link between city government, businesses, schools, hospitals, and libraries. This was all part of its $4 million program to realize the promise in San Diego's new logo—City of the Future.

By the late 1990s, San Diego was making an economic comeback based on a knowledge-based economy. This city was banking on competitive growth industries such as telecommunications, biotechnology and medical instruments, software and computer electronics, and tourism to propel it into the future. By 1996, San Diego already had 200 telecommunications firms, more than 350 software companies, and 200 biotech and medical products companies. It added 20,000 jobs per year as its unemployment rate dropped below 5 percent by the end of the century, lower than California and the rest of the nation. Research support comes from UC San Diego, San Diego State, Scripps and Salk research institutes. Clearly, San Diego's economic focus has become research, education, and community.

Though California and Mexico may disagree over how to handle crime, drugs, illegal immigration, and other issues, businesses on both sides of the border are cooperating to create one of the world's greatest manufacturing regions. The San Diego-Tijuana region now has more than 4 million people, the largest of any U.S./Mexico border area. It is often considered by scholars and businesses as one metropolis that happens to have an international border cutting through it. This is a change from past separatist and some more recent government policies.

There is growing awareness that maquiladora industries are fueling economies on both sides of the border. Maquiladoras were growing at about 10 percent per year through the 1990s, mostly due to cash from Asian firms wooed by joint efforts by Mexico and California. By 1996, there were more manufacturing jobs in Tijuana (about 130,000) than in San Diego County. Up to 8,000 of those employees live on the California side and commute to their jobs in Mexico. The advantages to California are the supply and service businesses in San Diego and other parts of the state that service the maquiladoras. More than $800 million of the $5.4 billion of goods and services imported to the maquiladora industry comes from California, and that is expected to keep growing.

Asian and other firms are looking for cheap labor in Mexico and the high-tech products California offers. Company headquarters, engineers, and executives are often located on the California side, while assembly is on the Baja side. Even more demand for California exports from contractors, designers, chip-makers, and raw materials are expected as Baja's plants move toward more high-tech products. This increases growth in California's high-tech and services sectors to replace lost manufacturing jobs. Both sides are currently winning in this mix.

Nearly every economic study projects that these ties between California and the rest of the world, especially Latin American and Asian economies and cultures, will continue to grow. Mexican and Asian economies, politics, and crime problems are increasingly catching the attention of Californians. The Asian economic crisis of the late 1990s sent powerful reminders of the risks of competing in this global marketplace. Such developments will also steer a course toward even more ethnically-diverse economic leadership within the state. That is why we have given these topics considerable attention in this and previous chapters. You will notice these important trends in the new, restructured economy as they increasingly impact California landscapes into the twenty-first century.

Economics and Urban Landscapes

Throughout this book, we have stressed the connections between each topic and chapter. California's modern economic trends often determine the nature of its urban landscapes; it would be difficult to find a better example of such powerful connections. California cities serve as centers for business and commercial activity; tertiary and more advanced activities and service economies rule, and all of these sectors continue to grow fast. It is true that a few primary and a few more secondary economic activities continue to exist around these urban landscapes, particularly specialized manufacturing. However, the number, variety, and complexity of services increases as California cities grow.

Look for formal knowledge-based information, service, and trade activities in the new urban landscapes, including within major retail outlets and professional office spaces. In an increasingly two-tier urban society, you will also find services requiring fewer skills, especially in cities, such as Los Angeles, with large numbers of recent immigrants. These services are more common to less developed countries and include artisans, peddlers, vendors, and other less formal, even underground, economic activities. You will recognize all these activities as they shape California's urban landscapes.

Within California's cities, you will find the towering central office complexes that dominate city centers, or central business districts (CBD). You will often find low-tech artisan, craft-based industries of workmen and craftsmen dominating landscapes surrounding the city center. Dispersed farther out in the periphery (and increasingly important) are the major and minor high-tech industries. Obviously, these various sections of the state's cities are not exclusive; different industries often mingle and thrive together within rich, diverse urban settings.

More recent trends are reshaping California's urban areas. Instead of merely emphasizing CBD office towers filled with business services, the state's cities are increasingly being renewed as some of the most impressive entertainment and cultural centers in the world. They are being reconfirmed as California's crown jewels, the cultural beacons that define our society.

Certainly you can see how an understanding of the economic issues we have reviewed in this chapter helps us understand the urban landscapes we review in the next chapter. Moreover, an understanding of the spatial relationships between various industries, urban activities, and landscapes will help us plan our cities so that they are more efficient and livable.

SOME KEY TERMS AND TOPICS

Alameda Corridor	high tech	restructuring (economic)
break-of-bulk	manufacturing	secondary industries
consumer segmentation	maquiladoras	social capital
economic development (measures)	quaternary industries	sweatshops
entertainment	quinary industries	tertiary activities
golden triangle	regional advantage	venture capitalists

Additional Key Terms and Topics

Asia-Pacific Economic Cooperation (APEC)	Gross National Product (GNP) per capita	ports
commercial economy	history (economic)	recession
corporate profits	immigrant workers	services
creative cartography	industrial revolution	Silicon Valley
distribution of income	information revolution	site
downsizing	knowledge-based economy	situation
economic diversity	labor of minds	specialized delivery
economic growth	low/high–skill/pay jobs	taxes
economic growth indicators	manufacturing clusters	telecommunications
efficiency	modern technologies	tourism
entrepreneurs	North American Free Trade Agreement (NAFTA)	tribes (economic)
foreign trade	Pacific Rim	two-tier economy/society
global market	partnerships	white collar
Gross Domestic Product (GDP)		working environments

Chapter 11

California's Urban Landscapes

A host of dynamic forces continue to create dramatic change in California's cities. These processes are often complicated and interconnected, but it is possible to understand them and even anticipate how they will change our urban landscapes. They involve human population and behavior and economic and political trends. These are just a few examples of the forces or processes—from local to global scales—that are changing our cities. If we are to understand our urban landscapes, we must first identify and appreciate the processes that have shaped and are shaping them. In this chapter, we will examine such processes and then demonstrate how they have historically molded and are currently shaping specific urban landscapes.

Our cities might be considered to be a series of individual, but interdependent, systems. Flowing into and out of each of our cities are diverse people, materials, capital, ideas, and trends—a wealth of matter and energy with spatial dimensions. How does each California city utilize and transform these diverse, concentrated resources? How does each city become more efficient by making stronger internal connections between its various parts? How do our cities exploit their external connections, such as their roles in the global marketplace? How will our cities make necessary adaptations and change to compete into the twenty-first century?

The processes, issues, trends, and questions already introduced here are vitally important to our cities and cannot be dismissed as generalizations. Instead, they must be addressed if we are to understand the diversity, connections, and rapid change that combine to create and transform the state's urban landscapes. We appropriately conclude our geography of California with this systematic survey of the state's urban geography.

San Francisco and Market Street from Twin Peaks.

KEY ISSUES AND CONCEPTS

◆ California cities represent powerful economic and cultural centers, the crown jewels of the state's modern civilization. More than 80 percent of all Californians are concentrated within urban areas.

◆ A host of activities and landscapes helps us distinguish urban from rural settings. They include nucleated, nonagricultural settlements, more specialized services, complex activities, and broad economic influence in surrounding service areas. The state's larger urban areas exhibit central business districts (CBDs) and suburbs. Some even grow together into enormous conurbations, such as in the Los Angeles, San Francisco Bay, and San Diego areas.

◆ Powerful economic, political, cultural, and other forces within and beyond our cities are molding urban activities and landscapes.

◆ California cities continue to grow mostly due to immigration from other countries and some states. Suburbs grow (often with people escaping urban centers) until they also become self-sufficient urban realms; the increasing importance of freeways and the automobile during the last half of the twentieth century fueled these urban extensions.

◆ After World War II, flight to the suburbs stranded the poor in the state's inner cities, creating urban blight. California cities have since

launched efforts to rebuild their economic and cultural centers; these urban face-lifts were slowed by recession, but they were encouraged by gentrification and investments from government and private industry.

◆ The state's major cities must function with diverse economic foundations, both as political, entertainment, and cultural centers, and also as centers for business, government, education, religion, and services. They must maintain and modernize their infrastructures, such as transportation and communication systems.

◆ As the state's cities expand and grow into one another, their structures have become more complex. They often compete for resources and influence at the expense of regional cooperation, planning, and problem solving.

◆ Several models might be used to understand the internal structures of the state's cities, but multiple nuclei are most evident in California.

◆ Factors of site and situation have influenced the location and growth of California cities. These factors continue to change with increasingly advanced technologies and evolving local and global economies.

◆ Common, interconnected issues and problems within the state's cities include homeless, urban sprawl, poorly planned growth and development, transportation, zoning, and other ordinances. Too often, short-term solutions are proposed to remedy these long-term problems.

◆ Government and business are working together to improve the vitality of our cities. Such efforts include Community Redevelopment Agencies (CRAs) and Business Investment Districts (BIDs). Sports arenas and entertainment centers, a return to outdoor or open shopping and entertainment districts, and high-tech urban planning are also playing roles.

◆ California cities continue to grow outward and together to create the state's three enormous conurbations in the Los Angeles, San Francisco Bay, and San Diego/Tijuana areas. Most of today's newest urban areas are growing inland, particularly within southern California's Inland Empire and in the Central Valley, where rapid growth is reproducing issues, problems, and landscapes familiar to urban Californians.

◆ THE GROWTH AND EVOLUTION OF CALIFORNIA'S URBAN AREAS

Defining California Cities

Urban areas are usually defined as nucleated, nonagricultural settlements where more complex economies expand beyond the once dominant primary activities. California's urban areas have many sizes and often subjective labels—from towns to cities to metropolitan areas—depending on one's perspective and experience.

A hamlet grows into a village when it offers specialized services for people clustered in the settlement and those near it. A village may grow to offer even more specialized services. As its population increases, its economic influence reaches farther out to attract business from a larger surrounding service area or hinterland; it becomes a more influential town.

The town may continue to grow, offering more specialization to a much larger hinterland. Eventually, it will form a central business district (CBD) and suburbs connected to it that help define a true city or metropolis. Redding, Sacramento, Fresno, and Bakersfield may be good examples of such cities because they are the main commercial centers for their areas. When various metropolitan areas then grow together, we may recognize an expansive megalopolis or **conurbation**. Cities have grown together in and around the Los Angeles Basin, the San Francisco Bay Area, and the San Diego/Tijuana area, creating three such expansive urban giants in California.

Regardless of the terms used to describe urban areas, they usually represent multifunctional, nucleated settlements with central business districts and both residential and nonresidential land uses. Examples of almost every size of urban settlement abound throughout California, except north of Sacramento, where no city approached a population of 100,000 near the end of the 1900s. Meanwhile, we continue to watch as the drama which transforms rural landscapes to urban centers unfolds again and again across the state.

It often begins with a self-sufficient rural settlement. This small settlement grows until social and residential agricultural and other primary activities and features yield to urban activities and features. Structures are built along main roads in a linear, cross or starlike pattern. As the main street grows, so do roads linked to other nearby settlements. Economies become less self-contained and extend still more connections to these surrounding communities.

California cities grow as migrants flock in. Other world cities have also experienced dramatic growth from migrations. However, in modern California cities, international and interstate migrations continue to be more responsible for swelling urban populations rather than rural to urban movements within the state. Once established in urban California, residents who escape farther out to the edge of urban areas are not only extending the urban fringe, but are creating and expanding new urban areas of their own. Map 11.1 shows the locations of major California cities.

Suburbs Grow into Independent Urban Realms

Once California's central cities are established, their **suburbs** grow. At first, these suburbs are not self-sufficient and may have specialized land uses dependent on the dominant city. Some residential, manufacturing, and commercial activities may not survive without connections to the economy of the larger city. Especially since World War II, use of the ubiquitous automobile has accelerated the growth of California suburbs.

White flight after World War II also played an important role in decentralizing California's cities and expanding its suburbs. During the mid-1900s, many of the state's urban families accumulated more disposable in-

MAP 11.1
California's growing urban areas are the state's economic and cultural centers. Cartographers located these cities based on population and their importance as commercial and local/regional centers.

come; with their cars, they became more mobile. Often, these families were established by individuals who had moved to California after World War II, chasing the growing number of middle-class jobs in aerospace, construction, and other manufacturing industries.

Instead of facing and solving the inevitable problems associated with California's fast-growing cities (such as racial and cultural tensions, poverty, crime, pollution, and congestion), those who were able—predominantly white families—fled the cities. They found larger lots and houses, open spaces and parks, sprawling school facilities and playgrounds, and growing communities with healthy economies. All of this was available at affordable prices in the extensive suburbs distant, at least in perception, from those city problems.

In Southern California

Soon, the suburbs began to take on their own identities as they became more independent. By the 1970s, Southern California suburbs were growing into more distant, self-sufficient, outer (or edge) cities. Many of these suburbs eventually duplicated and even improved the functions of the traditional centers. Eventually, ties became weaker with the central cities of Los Angeles and Long Beach, which were older cities once responsible for suburban growth. Secondary centers on L.A.'s West Side (including Century City) and in the San Fernando Valley grew to become classic examples of this urban sprawl.

During the 1970s, Orange County gradually severed ties with Los Angeles as it developed more independent functional units. Besides the traditional centers of Santa Ana (the Orange County Seat) and Anaheim, new economic and cultural centers erupted within the urban sprawl, especially toward the coast. By the 1980s, Huntington and Newport Beach, Costa Mesa with South Coast Plaza on its border, Irvine, and other southern Orange County cities were earning their own identities.

Farther out on the urban fringe, growing population centers still struggle to define themselves. These include communities in the hills west of the San Fernando Valley to the Ventura-Oxnard Plain, and in Canyon Country where we now recognize Santa Clarita. Communities in western Riverside and San Bernardino Counties (the "Inland Empire") sprouted and thrived. These suburbs even grew beyond the mountains into the high desert's Antelope Valley. Rapid growth in these areas has created great population centers. Nevertheless, they continue to share historical and functional ties, albeit fewer, with their mother city of Los Angeles.

In the Bay Area

In the Bay Area, economic and population growth also shifted away from crowded San Francisco. The City was the financial center and dominant city in the western United States for nearly one-hundred years until the mid-1900s. Then, it was eclipsed by L.A. By the 1980s, San Jose's population suddenly surpassed its mother to the north and became California's third-largest city. The entire South Bay, with its high-tech Silicon Valley, had grown into a world-famous economic powerhouse.

The focus of attention was also moving east, past Oakland and Berkeley, into the inland valley suburbs of the East Bay; places like Walnut Creek, Concord, and even Antioch boomed. More recently, citizens became anxious about the quality of life in Sonoma County's expanding North Bay communities. They include Petaluma, Rohnert Park, and Santa Rosa, communities responding with a host of regulations to slow and control rampant growth and development.

San Diego

San Diego, now California's second-largest city, had many lessons to learn from its sisters to the north. Compact San Francisco with its narrow streets was built before the automobile; it is also confined within its tiny area on the peninsula. Neighboring San Francisco Bay cities and their suburbs accepted great migrations from that crowded peninsula; within its tiny municipal boundaries, "The City" soon became known as the city in search of a suburb. Meanwhile, Los Angeles was known as the suburb in search of a city.

Though San Diegans scoffed at the giant conurbations growing to their north and even formed groups such as "Not Yet L.A.," San Diego's city limits were vast, and the forces of growth were overwhelming. It all just happened a little later there. White flight, wealth moving away from a central core that had hardly developed, and an explosion of populations and economic activities into the surrounding suburbs had the same results as elsewhere— San Diego was decentralized. The populations spread to produce a weaker density gradient where numerous, extensive suburbs to the north, east, and south assumed increasing economic and cultural significance and authority.

Urban Realms/Suburban Lifestyles

On the outskirts of California's three largest urban areas (the L.A., San Francisco Bay and San Diego areas), shopping malls, commercial districts, and business and industrial parks merged into centers now sometimes called **urban realms**. Each urban realm is now a separate and distinct economic, social, and political center within its larger conurbation.

The office towers, service industries, and cultural attractions that have erupted next to what were once typical California suburban malls are examples. They are strewn across San Diego County to the north and east of the city, and they will soon connect San Diego with Tijuana. Within the Los Angeles conurbation, these separate urban realms are scattered across the San Gabriel Valley (especially along I-10), throughout the San Fernando Valley, and in Orange County and the Inland Empire of Southern California. Their clones have sprung up in the Antelope Valley and are spreading north into Canyon Country and west along major transportation routes to the Ventura-Oxnard Plain.

Similar urban realms in the Bay Area now attract economic and cultural attention far to the north, east, and

CAR CULTURES

Regional shopping malls with their stacked parking structures in the suburbs continue to grow into more self-sufficient centers of economic and cultural activity. This car culture has increasingly dominated California's urban landscapes since World War II. Many years ago, commuting by car to work, shop or to recreation and entertainment centers replaced traditional walking and gathering at family and community meeting places. Gradually, a smaller proportion of people gathered in parks and community centers.

Today, you might find suburban residents hidden in their backyards for barbecues and other leisure activities or in front of the TV when they are not commuting to work, school, or the mall. After driving home, cars disappear behind closing electric garage doors. Where are the people who once entered their homes through their front doors? The suburban stereotypes of impersonal, generic lifestyles with no real sense of community are enhanced.

Does this personal independence come with a price tag? There are the horror stories of commuters spending so many hours each day driving from Santa Rosa or the Delta into San Francisco and back. Others may commute from Lancaster (in the Antelope Valley), Moreno Valley (east of Riverside), or south Orange County to their jobs in Los Angeles. Today, those who moved out to San Diego's suburbs are also experiencing gradually increasing commute times as populations grow and traffic becomes more congested. Even subdivided ranches in the western Sierra Nevada foothills are filling with commuters who work in Central Valley cities such as Sacramento.

Many of the people who moved out into these open spaces are now also complaining about those who have followed and brought the crime, congestion, and environmental degradation that everyone tried to escape in the first place. As long as there is such affordable housing, a perception of better living environments, and a car culture, millions will be willing to make that big move to California's new and more distant suburbs.

---

south of San Francisco. Some have even referred to inland East Bay's urban realm as Contra Costapolis, mocking the rapid growth spreading through Contra Costa County.

These newer centers are now expanding with their own suburbs. Families looking for more open space and even cheaper land are now filling the Delta and commuting into Bay Area cities for work. Farther south, they are settling in the southern San Joaquin Valley to commute over the mountains and into the Los Angeles Basin. Now, the future urban realm look-alikes are breeding next to cities in the Central Valley such as in areas surrounding Sacramento and Fresno and other regions of the state once so obviously rural.

Back in the City
Left Behind?

Just as white flight and the movement of wealth out of California's inner cities after World War II and into the 1980s created economic growth in the suburbs, it devastated the urban communities left behind. Near downtown Los Angeles, Long Beach, Oakland, and even in emerging cities like San Diego and San Jose, **inner-city** transitional neighborhoods were stranded and neglected. Many of those with the disposable income and mobility to migrate to the suburbs did, and they took their money with them.

These commuters made their way into the city office towers and industries by weekday, but they took their paychecks home to the suburban malls and shopping and entertainment centers by night and on weekends. Many of those downtowns which once displayed their bustling retail districts, flagship stores, and entertainment and cultural centers became virtual ghost towns at night and on weekends, after the workers had returned home. An enormous tax base that could have expanded and strengthened the infrastructures and increased the efficiencies of California's inner cities had shifted to the suburbs.

The poorest inner-city residents were less mobile and least capable of taking the risk to migrate out. By the 1960s, urban blight glared out at everyone who journeyed through California's inner cities and transition zones. Overt racial segregation and past discrimination was replaced by class segregation, but the results were the same. Urban unrest, racial tension, crime, deteriorating living environments, and a lack of financial resources to deal with these problems often exacerbated inner-city decay through the 1970s and into the 1980s. Similar patterns developed even in some of California's smaller cities, such as Santa Ana, Berkeley, Sacramento, and Fresno.

Matters were made worse when individuals and businesses who tried to invest in the struggling communities ran into another formidable urban foe—**redlining**. Mortgage and insurance companies often refused to issue loans or insurance in deteriorating neighborhoods that were considered high risk. For a brief time, geography fate would help turn the tide for many of these struggling urban neighborhoods that once represented California's traditional economic and cultural centers.

Gentrification Changes the Landscape

During the 1980s, a combination of factors brought hope to California's inner cities. First, as businesses recognized their complementary positions within cities, a number of impressive redevelopment projects were completed in every major urban area. Businesses were encouraged to stay and some moved into and around the renovated CBDs, though sometimes at the expense of low-income families and businesses with smaller profit margins. Perhaps the greatest symbol of this trend was the completion of the tallest building in California, the First Interstate Tower, at more than 70 stories, on Bunker Hill in L.A. These developments helped maintain and sometimes enhance the concentration of jobs, including many high-paying professional positions, in the cities.

From San Francisco Bay to the Los Angeles Basin and San Diego, major retail centers and entertainment and cultural attractions were added to encourage those workers in the financial districts to stay and even relocate into the city. Weary commuters in middle-, upper-middle, and higher-income brackets began returning to some of the struggling neighborhoods. Moving into and renovating old apartments, homes, Victorians, and warehouses, they brought capital back to the cities and slashed their commuting times, but often displaced lower-income residents. These changes were common to many cities in the United States during the 1980s.

Upscale, ambitious professionals who led the charge became known as YUPPIES (young, upwardly-mobile, urban professionals), and "**gentrification**" was coined

to describe the process of renovating these inner-city neighborhoods. They were protected from redlining by their higher salaries, favorable credit reports, and often government-guaranteed loans to encourage redevelopment of blighted inner-city areas.

Where did the lower-income families go? Some moved to nearby neighborhoods where gentrification had not yet arrived. Others were unable to relocate near or far and became part of the burgeoning numbers of homeless so common to California's inner cities during the late 1900s. Still other poor families finally detached themselves from the inner city in a turn of events that surprised even some of the most astute city planners. Some disadvantaged families followed an example set years ago by the more privileged and mobile groups before them; many of these minority and low-income families began moving to safer and more affordable housing in the distant, growing suburbs.

They moved into lower-income suburban neighborhoods in the hills and valleys east of San Diego and the San Francisco Bay Area. In the Los Angeles area, neighborhoods in and around Lancaster, Palmdale, San Bernardino, and Riverside became more culturally and economically diverse. California suburbs were no longer necessarily white or culturally generic. Yet a new trend was making its mark on California's human landscapes, a trend that may have started with gentrification.

Effects of Recession on Urban Landscapes

Unfortunately, the boom of the 1980s died with the recession that stretched into the early 1990s. The once ubiquitous YUPPIES began retreating from many of their aggressive gentrification schemes in city environments; their jobs and salaries were washed away in a flurry of mergers, downsizings, and bankruptcies. Hopes for re-

Some might thank gentrification for transforming a clogged, polluted Venice canal system into this aesthetic urban environment. Property values soared after this successful redevelopment.

vitalizing California's inner cities dwindled with them. The effects of the recession, statewide tax cuts, and evaporating revenues drained nearly every California city's resources to near bankruptcy. Due to these events and poor financial management, the entire County of Orange declared bankruptcy.

Several new and once promising upscale city apartment and condominium complexes failed miserably and were left with more than 50 percent vacancy rates, as were many new office buildings completed just before the recession. Los Angeles was especially hard hit; struggling speculators and developers stopped the planning and construction of new office towers in Los Angeles through the mid-1990s, until the economy had recovered. The recession confined gentrification to more isolated pockets of urban success stories well into the 1990s.

San Francisco stood out as an exception to the general downward trend. After some years of social and economic upheavals exacerbated by the 1989 Loma Prieta earthquake, gentrification not only held on, but accelerated into the 1990s to revitalize The City. A new generation flooded The City, looking for space to live their cosmopolitan lifestyles or establish their innovative businesses. These events caused rents and real estate to skyrocket. San Francisco was experiencing the economic and cultural renaissance through the 1990s that most other California cities could only dream of. It continues to display, almost any time of day, the innovation, cultural attractions, excitement, and economic prosperity that are the envy of almost every city.

Recent Changes and Trends

Rapid and dramatic changes continue to make their marks on California's urban people and landscapes. From financial districts to transition zones, from wealthy gated communities to the most distant suburbs, California's cities have become extremely complex, and some have evolved into unique economic and cultural centers. Once an urban trend is recognized or assumed, one or more California cities seem to break through the assumptions and rules to blaze a new trail.

Within major conurbations, such as the Los Angeles and San Francisco Bay areas, freeways are no longer jammed just going into the city centers in the morning and out to the suburbs during evening rush hours. Instead, transportation corridors are often crowded going in all directions all day. Commuting to jobs across town or from more densely populated communities *to* urban realms and distant suburbs has become commonplace.

Minority families are no longer limited to inner-city neighborhoods, while suburbs are no longer only middle- and upper-middle class white communities. The mix of classes, ethnic, and cultural groups within and surrounding California's cities has become more complex; mobile Californians are increasingly willing to seek new employment opportunities and living environments. Natural, cultural, and political geographic boundaries are playing less important roles in these decisions as we move into the twenty-first century.

Such a mobile, opportunistic, and changing population has created some great new challenges for California cities. How do we plan our urban areas or communities when we are not sure what new trends to expect? Since the planning process is designed to increase the efficiency and success of our cities as we improve living and working environments, how do we encourage and manage the trends that will result in positive growth? Then, how do we instill a sense of community in residents who are so mobile that they show little interest in their neighborhoods? These are questions confronting big and small cities in the state.

If we ignore these challenging questions, we submit ourselves to a future of total urban chaos. If we are to

The incredible cost of rebuilding an at-risk San Francisco-Oakland Bay Bridge is only overshadowed by the tragedy and chaos that could result if it is damaged beyond use by an earthquake. Oakland is seen across the Bay from the San Francisco side.

find answers, we must first understand some of the processes and events that have helped shape California's modern urban landscapes. That has been the purpose of the first section of this chapter. Now, we must also better understand how our cities function within their complex geographic structures. These more specific topics are covered in the next section of this chapter.

◆ STRUCTURES AND FUNCTIONS OF CALIFORNIA'S CITIES

California Cities Lead the Way

Why should we be so concerned about the structure and health of California cities? The answer is because more than 80 percent of all Californians live in cities. That percentage jumps much higher if we include more distant suburbs. These cities are the traditional centers of our economy and culture. California's urban areas contain a wealth of cultural history, and they are the crown jewels of the state's current civilization. They represent a history rich with the struggles, triumphs, and failures so unique to the California experience. They represent who Californians are and what we aspire to be. When California's urban areas thrive, California prospers; when its cities sputter, the entire state stumbles.

Too frequently, futurists, planners, and problem-solvers have tried to use models from cities in other states, and even countries, to understand California's urban centers. Of course, California cities will always share some similarities with urban giants in other regions of the nation or the world; that is one theme of this section. However, scholars often fail when they try to overextend their models to make sweeping assumptions and generalizations about California cities based on examples from other regions of our globe.

It is often more rewarding to consider the differences in the sites, situations, and time periods in which California cities have been built and continue to grow in comparison to other great cities. This may be upsetting to those who want to force California cities into nicely bound models and generalities that worked in other parts of the world. However, here is an opportunity to better understand the uniqueness of each California city and urban community so that we can plan for the future and solve problems.

After all, California has already assumed its role—from manufacturing to high-tech industries, from fashion to entertainment—as one of the world's greatest and most innovative economic and cultural centers. Californians now have an opportunity to show the world how its great cities, which are the geographic foci of these innovations, can be planned to be more efficient as they offer better living and working environments for their residents. As any visitor or resident of a California city

knows, there is certainly room for improvement and enormous potential for future success.

What Makes California Cities Tick?

Before we examine some of the issues and problems confronting individual urban areas in California (in the next section), it is important that we review some of those traditional concepts regarding the structure and function of all California cities. Therefore, this section begins by illustrating how many California cities might share some basic characteristics with cities in other regions.

However, the discussion will evolve to illustrate how California cities contrast with many common models and even with one another. And though each city in California deserves separate consideration, there is room to examine only several of California's unique urban areas. We continue with our goal to gain a better understanding of California's urban landscapes and the people and forces that have shaped and are changing them.

An Economic Base

Each city must have an economic base to support its populations. Usually, when the economic base strengthens and diversifies, the city will grow; when the economic base weakens or stagnates, the city will struggle. In most California urban areas since the 1800s to near the end of the 1900s, with a few exceptions, growing and more diverse economies have attracted larger and more diverse populations. Some California cities have gained notoriety as functional, commercial, and service centers not only for their regions, but for the entire West Coast. This has helped make California the number one state in a host of secondary and tertiary economic activities and beyond, from manufacturing to professional and personal services and from wholesaling to retailing.

There are many examples of how California cities have thrived or struggled as they attempted to build diverse economic bases. Many years ago, factories (mostly light industry) spread across sections of the cities, such as the southern part of San Francisco and in the East Bay, and east of downtown L.A. and into its South Bay. These manufacturing centers were vital to the economic health and growth of the cities. This also encouraged a concentration of wealth, economic activity, and populations in and around California's urban areas.

During the Cold War, billions in defense dollars and thriving aerospace industries further bolstered the economies of many California cities, such as the growing urban realms of the Los Angeles area's South Bay. California's three great conurbations were also aided by their famous harbors. (Los Angeles/Long Beach finally became the number one shipping harbor in the United States in the 1990s.) When the defense money and aerospace industry finally sputtered during the recession of the late 1980s to early 1990s, more futuristic, high-tech information and entertainment industries came to the cities' rescue. These serve as just a few historical examples of how important diversified economies are to every California city.

Centers for Professional and Personal Services   Professional and personal services always follow the people and their capital, and California has been no exception. Financial institutions that moved in with the Gold Rush eventually became rooted in San Francisco along with the legal firms, insurance companies, and other growing corporations servicing the new state. (Bank of America continued as the number one bank in California with its world headquarters in San Francisco until a 1998 merger.) By the mid-1900s, San Francisco gave up its leadership role to faster-growing Los Angeles as the number one financial center of the West. Despite this, The City and its Bay Area continued to thrive and grow throughout most of the century.

Heading toward the late 1900s, it became clear that professional and personal services had eclipsed manufacturing especially in and around the CBDs representing California's three conurbations and in many of its other cities. The delivery companies, temporary employment agencies, restaurants and other food vendors, and companies offering products and services for the office are but a few examples; these professional and personal services are all important parts in the economic engines that drive California's urban economies.

Wholesale and Retail Centers   The San Francisco, Los Angeles, and San Diego areas also became famous as great wholesale and retail centers during the 1900s. The state's cities have helped make California the number one retail state in the United States. These are the cities where greater volume and competition keeps the price of many big-ticket items (such as cars, furniture sets, or entertainment centers) lower. Major retailers locate their **flagship stores**, the crown jewels of their corporations, within these conurbations to exhibit the latest products that will help define their companies.

Where populations with disposable incomes are greatest, **specialty stores** abound. From condom shops to specialty lingerie, from 24-hour car parts stores to 24-hour computer stores, from health food stores for vegans only to companies that will shop for and deliver your groceries, you can choose specialty goods and convenience services in California cities that most smaller towns cannot offer.

Entertainment and Cultural Centers

Entertainment and tourist industries are as important and renowned in California cities as anywhere in the world. They not only serve residents and visitors, but provide

L.A.'s Music Center, with its dancing fountains and world-class productions, brought some people back to its downtown. The nearby Disney Center should add to this cosmopolitan atmosphere.

thousands of jobs and pump billions into the California economy. From "snowbirds" escaping winter snows to "zoners" escaping Arizona's summer heat, San Diego draws the crowds to its coast, its zoo, its entry to Mexico, its Sea World, and other attractions. The Los Angeles area has everything from the beach and its Venice Boardwalk, to the great theme parks (Disneyland, Knotts Berry Farm, Universal Studios, Magic Mountain, etc.), to Hollywood. To the north, San Francisco competes with Las Vegas for the number one tourist destination city in the nation. On any night, each of the state's large cities now offers rich and diverse experiences in the performing arts.

Farther from the centers of its greatest cities, California's urban realms and suburbs have realized the economic and cultural potential of entertainment. The performing arts continue to grow and thrive in Orange County's South Coast Plaza. Theaters, skating rinks, and other forms of entertainment are built into many of the suburban malls. In 1996, two major theater chains completed the largest group of theaters in the nation in Ontario (40 miles east of L.A.)—across the street from one another!

Sports buffs will find that every major national sport has at least one organization playing in northern *and* southern California. Baseball is just one example. There are the San Francisco Giants and Oakland Athletics, the Los Angeles Dodgers, the Anaheim Angels, and the San Diego Padres. Except for a few weekday nights, each date in the summer offers a major league baseball game in both a northern *and* southern California city. Distant from the urban centers, in the suburbs and beyond, are the popular and lucrative small, hometown minor-league baseball teams.

The story is similar for the National Basketball Association and professional football, although football league owners took their losing teams away from the L.A. area in the 1990s when taxpayers refused to pay wealthy owners to stay. The increasing popularity of professional soccer and other sports helped fill this void in L.A. before professional football returned.

Business and Government Administration Centers

California cities have also naturally evolved into business and political administration centers. Along with world corporate headquarters (such as Wells Fargo Bank and Chevron Oil in San Francisco, and Arco Oil in Los Angeles), are the government headquarters to serve the people and their businesses. These are more than just county seats.

Sacramento can thank government services provided by the state capitol for much of its growth. State and other regional government centers are well established in the San Francisco, Los Angeles, and San Diego conurbations, as well as other major California cities; they not only provide services, but employ thousands. The link between businesses and the government services they require helped contribute to the growing office towers in California's central cities during the 1900s.

Centers for Education

Educational functions have probably been more critical to California cities than anywhere else in the world. During the 1900s, its public colleges and universities evolved into the greatest higher educational system the world had ever known. It is not surprising that these educational institutions have helped California stay on the cutting edge with the brain power, innovations, and technologies that keep the state competitive. The most renowned examples include the first, UC Berkeley, simply known as "CAL," and the giant of the south, UCLA.

Though other University of California and California State University campuses have had greater impacts on their smaller, local communities, the entire UC and CSU systems have supplied the educated and trained labor force vital to California cities. Private universities such as Stanford and USC and other smaller colleges also provide their share of trained researchers and professionals to private industries and public agencies in California cities. California's community colleges represent the largest and most extensive community college system in the world. They have also trained and prepared an enormous work force, and they have helped citizens make smoother transitions to higher education.

Religious Centers

Churches, synagogues and other places of religious worship may be dwarfed by the office towers that rise above every city center and urban realm in California, but California cities continue to serve as centers for organized religious worship. For examples in the Catholic tradition, just look up the hill to that giant, concrete, washing-machine-agitator-shaped St. Mary's Cathedral in San Francisco, or consider the visibility of the new cathedral site in downtown Los Angeles.

The great Mormon Temple along Santa Monica Boulevard stands out on any night as a landmark on L.A.'s West Side. Great numbers and diversity make California cities the centers for not only every major religion, but for smaller sects and less popular religions from around the world. Community churches within the urban centers often help form the foundations and weave the social networks that unify neighborhoods. Almost any religion, philosophy, or lifestyle can be found thriving, making its own economic and social impact in a California city.

Military and Defense

Military activity has impacted California economies and cultures since the Spanish first settled here. Navy activity and shipyards have poured billions of dollars and thousands of jobs especially into the economies of California's great port cities in the Bay Area, Long Beach, and San Diego. Also, during the twentieth century, military bases especially boosted the economies of smaller cities, such as Marina (near Fort Ord), Oceanside (near Camp Pendleton), and communities near bases in the Inland Empire and Mojave Desert.

The end of the Cold War and the closing or downsizing of many of these military bases since the 1980s has diminished the traditional role of the military in California's major cities. Now, California cities are looking to those closed bases for new industrial spaces, airports, educational institutions, parks, open space, and other developments to diversify their economies.

City Infrastructures and Services

Finally, transportation, communication, and other services are the crucial links that bind all these urban functions together. Every competitive urban center in the world functions with extensive transportation and communication systems designed to move massive numbers of workers and residents, goods, and services.

Ground Transportation The remarkable public transportation system in San Francisco has successfully linked workers to their jobs and businesses to other businesses for most of the twentieth century. When the suburbs and urban realms grew around The City, much of the region joined together to build Bay Area Rapid Transit (BART), which conveniently linked numerous once-distant Bay Area cities and communities by modern rail.

The contrast to this was Los Angeles, which chose instead to tear down its highly successful and world-renowned urban transportation system centered around its Red Cars. (You will find a brief summary of the troubling events that led to this loss later in this chapter.) Like growing tentacles, the freeways quickly replaced Red

Sacramento is working on public transportation that might keep it from becoming another Los Angeles.

Cars after World War II. At first, especially during the 1950s and 1960s, the freeways provided a quick connection to the city from the suburbs.

Unfortunately, the suburbs grew faster than freeways could be built and growing numbers of individual commuters were already saturating the lanes by the late 1960s and into the 1970s. During the last three decades of the twentieth century, commuting times dramatically increased over the same distances in the L.A. area. By 1990, more than 38 million car trips per day were taken over 30,000 miles of roads and more than 700 miles of freeways in the L.A. region. Less than 5 percent of commuters were using public transportation while the average rush-hour freeway speed dropped below 35 mph.

Consequently, transportation has become one of the most crippling barriers facing the Los Angeles area's economic future. Today, L.A. struggles to build light rail systems to link communities south, east, north, and west of downtown. It struggles both to complete the central Metro Rail that will link these systems and to make the freeways more efficient in the long run. These are more than local political and personal power struggles; the results of these struggles will literally determine whether Los Angeles can survive as an economic and cultural leader into the twenty-first century. Meanwhile, average rush-hour freeway speed dropped to about 17 mph into the twentieth century, and there is no more space for new freeways.

Hopefully, California's newer cities will learn from these examples. To the south, San Diego started its growth, incredibly, by emulating its despised neighbor to the north. Its economy boomed and its population expanded throughout the last half of the twentieth century. For a few years, it was the fastest-growing city in the nation. Those ubiquitous freeway tentacles grew out to the north, east, and south to link the extensive suburbs with the city; the suburbs grew faster than the freeways. The freeways are now crowded and commute times have

increased along several corridors. Sound familiar? San Diegans now complain that their rush hours on I-5 and I-15 must be as bad as L.A.'s.

Recognizing the irony of all of this, more futuristic San Diegans were able to muster enough public support against a well-organized opposition to begin experimenting with their own light rail system. San Diego's own version of red cars quickly became popular and successful during the 1990s (a surprise to opponents) as the city pushed ahead to expand the system. Even smaller, but growing, California cities (such as Sacramento), with their limited revenue, are attempting to expand their own light rail and other public transportation systems, as they look on with horror at what happened to short-sighted Los Angeles.

Air Transportation   It is also difficult to overstate the importance of convenient air transportation to and from every California city. Less than 10 miles apart, busy San Francisco and Oakland International Airports serve populations on opposite sides of the bay. San Jose and smaller airports in the Bay Area have provided more options for passengers jamming the airways of this megalopolis.

In the Los Angeles area, those who find California's greatest airport (LAX) too distant or crowded use Burbank, Long Beach, Ontario International, John Wayne Airport in Orange County, or even smaller local airports. As Ontario Airport expanded with new terminals in the late 1990s and plenty of room, officials considered it one of the best candidates for growth. In contrast, a scheme to make Palmdale International Airport a prime destination and to shuttle passengers from there into the L.A. Basin failed several years ago. (Palmdale was still hoping to catch overflow from the LAX expansion into the 21st century.) By the end of the 1990s, plans were being debated to greatly expand LAX and to build an enormous international airport in Orange County in place of the closing El Toro Marine Corps Air Station.

Though surrounding neighborhoods, especially in southern Orange County, loathe the prospects of more noise, pollution, and congestion, leaders across the region recognize the importance of these airports to local economies.

San Diegans battled for decades about where to relocate their airport; the current airstrip is confined by a growing city and its office towers. As leaders even considered floating a new airport out in the ocean and a joint San Diego/Tijuana airport, San Diego's airport problem has repeatedly erupted as the city's most hotly-debated issue. It is a reminder of how important reliable air transportation will be to future California cities and how difficult it is to find room for new airstrips.

Communications   Like transportation, communication services have always been critical functions provided by every California urban area. The ease and convenience of communication and interaction is what attracted many complementary economic activities to our cities in the first place. Today, modern communication and information technologies are providing private industries and public agencies with new, revolutionary ways to do business.

Modern telecommunications and virtual businesses, especially in the service industries, are changing the landscapes of every California city. Could the results be fewer commuters and vehicle miles? Will this decrease the importance of city centers, urban realms, or any form of urban center? What impact will high-tech communications have on our public transportation systems? These and other questions loom as the high-tech information revolution sweeps through our urban economies and cultures, causing changes that could rival the industrial revolution.

There are numerous other services that prove vital to a city's infrastructure. What would happen to California cities without quality water, pollution control, and waste treatment facilities? They would certainly be unlivable.

Future Functions of California Cities

Today, California cities continue to function as the economic and cultural centers of our society. We have concentrated our political and economic power in our urban centers. They represent our centers of hope and innovation. They also concentrate the social problems related to the economic and cultural upheavals that inevitably result from such rapid change. California's extremes, whether good or bad, are exaggerated in its urban areas. How we deal with these changes and problems is exposed to the world in our cities.

If they are to be successful, our cities must continue to serve as commercial and service centers; they must continue to have concentrations of capital and labor for production. Increasingly, they must be centers of knowledge and international business and trade. They must offer goods and services for consumers, and they must have efficient infrastructures, including transportation and communications systems, water delivery, and treatment facilities.

One of the most recent trends in California urban areas is their reemergence as entertainment and cultural centers. In some California cities, especially Los Angeles, leaders in the late 1990s noticed that office towers were not filling as expected although the early 1990s recession had ended. Efforts to reestablish downtown Los Angeles as the region's cultural and entertainment center were designed to solve this problem and complete the city's recovery. The new sports arena, entertainment, and retail complex was planned to complement adjacent convention center activities and to refocus attention downtown.

Los Angeles and some other California cities were using more successful California cities as role models during the late 1990s. San Francisco has already turned its revitalization into a renaissance of astounding proportions. It has become California's, and perhaps the nation's, most lively and renowned urban playground. San Diego used such attractions as its Horton Plaza, Gaslamp Quarters, and new Convention Center to create an impressive facelift that revitalized its economy. Smaller cities, such as Santa Monica and Pasadena, have also realized incredible economic growth and other benefits due to their focus on culture and entertainment. Other large California cities, especially Long Beach, are committing substantial resources to rebuild their downtowns as the cultural and entertainment centers they were once meant to be.

If California cities are to compete globally and with one another, all of these functions must be connected within an efficient structure. As these city structures evolve, they form more tangible human landscapes that can be measured, scrutinized, and planned. The physical structures of California's urban areas are considered next.

California City Structures
Economic Functions Often Determine Urban Structures

As California's cities grew through the first half of the twentieth century, they often followed patterns similar to their counterparts in the rest of the nation. They established vital connections to surrounding rural landscapes and activities and to other urban areas. Basic economic sectors were first established to export goods and services outside the cities in exchange for the capital that flowed back into the cities. This led to an early accumulation of wealth and concentrated populations in urban areas of the San Francisco Bay Area, the Southern California coastal plains, and growing hubs in the Central Valley.

Subsequently, **nonbasic economic sectors**, which provide services for the growing populations who reside in the cities, gained increasing control over urban economic activities and their landscapes. In California, especially during the last half of the twentieth century, the multitude of legal, financial, and public services required by urban residents has made the growing nonbasic sector even more vital to the success of our cities.

The results are evident in every part of California's urban landscapes, industries, and labor forces from educational institutions to medical centers, from entertainment and retail centers to specialized business and government services; each city must now maintain its own balance. It must not only serve its residents and sustain its internal affairs, but reach out beyond its borders as an established regional, national, and sometimes even a global hub.

California cities have now developed to represent somewhat distorted versions of Walter Christaller's **central place theory**. In a modified view of this theory, California cities have evolved into central places that compete with other cities. The larger cities serve larger markets because they can offer more goods and services at more competitive prices than smaller cities. In this urban hierarchy, the largest cities have become very complex because they control huge urban influence zones; smaller cities are less complicated and dominate smaller areas. Especially in California, as larger central places and their surrounding realms of influence expanded, their suburbs grew more quickly; these suburbs eventually became new central places, claiming their own functional territories separate from the larger urban core they once relied upon.

Modern communication technologies and the new global economy will further complicate all of this. California industries and cities using new transportation and communications technologies to take advantage of their geographic positions, especially in regard to the Pacific Rim, will thrive; those bound by outdated constraints of geography and distance will struggle. Cutting-edge planning and the most efficient operations will be required for each California city to remain healthy and wealthy.

Where California Cities Begin and End

It is already difficult to define the boundaries of some California cities so that they can be planned to operate more efficiently. In many more isolated California towns and smaller cities, the CBD and the town boundaries are easier to delineate. Issues and problems facing these

Yet another reminder that physical barriers seem to be the only controls on urban sprawl in the Inland Empire. Red tile roofs, freeways, and industries continue filling the valley and marching up the slopes.

towns are often well-defined and somewhat easier to manage.

How do we define the centers and edges of California's larger cities? CBDs are often recognized as the central cores of cities, and they are almost always within a city's official political boundaries. However, California's largest urban areas most often extend far beyond one specific city's political boundaries. Should we consider the entire urbanized or built-up area or the greatest extent of urban development as part of the same city? Should we include the extensive, low-density suburbs that have grown beyond the edge of that city as part of the same urban area?

Perhaps a city's **functional region**—the area over which a city's interactive and interdependent functions (as previously discussed) are united—best defines its boundaries. Interconnected economic activities and infrastructure patterns, including transportation systems such as BART in the Bay Area or the L.A. area's freeway system, may provide clues to the extent of this more practical functional region.

Recognition of these urban boundaries is required before solutions to urban problems and planning for more efficient cities can be realized. Issues concerning the economy, crime, homeless, education, growth, land use, pollution, transportation, and other infrastructure problems transcend city and county boundaries. There are many examples of issues so complex that no one community or city can approach in isolation.

Traditionally, we have attempted to use definitions to help us with the dilemmas facing more specific urban areas. We recognize a metropolitan area as a large-scale functional entity that includes numerous different urbanized areas within a whole, integrated economy. In California, we now have huge, multimetropolitan complexes that are two or more continuous, extended major urban areas that have grown together. You will find these megalopoli or conurbations in the San Francisco Bay Area, the Los Angeles Basin, and the San Diego/Tijuana area.

They continue to reach out to absorb smaller surrounding cities. We have long recognized Standard Metropolitan Statistical Areas so that an urban region's census data, problem solving, and planning can be considered within a larger functional unit. Groups of cities and counties also voluntarily gather into government associations so that wise planning decisions are made for the entire region. The Association of Bay Area Governments (ABAG, headquartered in Oakland), the Southern California Association of Governments (SCAG, headquartered in L.A.), and the San Diego Association of Governments are examples. These regional organizations include hundreds of cities and dozens of counties. They play vital roles in establishing leadership in planning and coordination, seeking new forms of financing for infrastructure (such as ports, airports, highways, and public transit), and encouraging international trade.

BREAKING THROUGH BOUNDARIES TO SOLVE REGIONAL PROBLEMS

During most summer afternoons, air pollution drifts from San Francisco into the East Bay and San Jose, and from Los Angeles' West Side into the San Gabriel Valley and Inland Empire. It similarly drifts with the sea breeze from coastal San Diego toward eastern foothill communities. Within each of these regions, polluted runoff flows in the opposite direction from those inland communities to the west, toward and frequently into the ocean. On a much grander scale, the same holds true for summer sea breezes that flow across the Delta from the Golden Gate and split north into the Sacramento Valley and south into the San Joaquin Valley. Surface runoff flows in the opposite direction through the Sacramento and San Joaquin Rivers and into the Delta and Bay.

Resulting pollution sources and problems know no legal boundaries. Unfortunately, in each case, this pollution is decreasing the quality of living and working environments as it flows across numerous county and city boundaries. Most of the larger, growing cities of the Central Valley are not only legally separated, but are clearly separated by expansive farmlands. Even these distant communities must deal with the same pollution in the air and water as it flows through their jurisdictions.

Such complex issues and problems require statewide cooperation on a scale that ranges far beyond any definition of specific urban areas. How can one community build efficient transportation, communication, and other infrastructures and services without planning with adjacent communities? These are planning and infrastructure decisions that clearly impact neighboring communities.

All of this defining and boundary drawing must be considered if we are to avert urban chaos and build the foundations for the futuristic planning and efficient operation of our cities that will assure their success. Meanwhile, our cities continue to represent rather orderly land uses that have resulted in competition for sites between social groups and economic functions. Let's go inside California's cities to examine their complex landscapes and structures in more detail.

Internal Structures of California Cities

Like most cities of the world, each California city has a **CBD (central business district)** where economic activity, highest land values, and the tallest buildings are usually concentrated. Before the car and the urban sprawl that accelerated during the mid-1900s, better defined CBDs were more vital to California cities. Even after this sprawl, it is easy to recognize these financial districts as centers with the most intensely used and highest valued land.

Walk down Montgomery Street where it meets Market Street in San Francisco or up to the First Interstate Tower (the tallest in California) on Bunker Hill in Los Angeles during rush or lunch hours. Their towering skyscrapers dwarf the thousands of people scurrying through the streets; these are still vibrant financial and business centers. Downtown San Diego is easily recognized from San Diego Bay or Horton Plaza as its old and new office towers spring up southwest of Balboa Park and I-5. Oakland and San Jose in the Bay Area, and Long Beach and other cities in the L.A. Basin are often overlooked as parts within their larger conurbations; yet, they have defined

CBDs. They have also accumulated their own rich cultural histories, and independent economic and political power.

CBDs are evident in even smaller cities, especially those once more distant from and less reliant on the larger conurbations. Riverside and San Bernardino, hubs of the Inland Empire, are examples. Even more independent cities in the Central Valley, such as Sacramento, Fresno and Bakersfield, have established CBDs. Look for the greatest concentrations of tall buildings and activities such as transportation; even the most casual observer might notice these CBDs.

Models of **City Structures** Especially within the complex structures of California cities, similarities to other cities and classic models fade away beyond the CBDs, and land value patterns may become very confused.

The concentric zone model certainly does not adequately describe California cities. Ernest Burgess used this model while studying Chicago's urban structure in the 1920s. It paints a series of four rings, each more distant from the CBD. In this model, the inner city neighborhoods or zones of transition are found just beyond the CBD. Here are the high-density, low-income slums and ethnic ghettos with their old, deteriorating structures. California's cities have such struggling neighborhoods and pockets of poverty, which include some areas labelled "skid row." However, there may also be noticeable upscale districts and neighborhoods, often gentrified and perched along waterfronts or on hillsides with views, just as close to the CBDs.

The next ring outward would include independent working people's homes who labor in nearby industries.

These are often second-generation citizens with modest homes on small lots. Within the next ring outward are the middle class and even wealthier, upscale neighborhoods with apartments, condominiums, and single-family homes. Living here are people who can choose higher commuting costs for the privilege of better living environments. The final and most distant ring consists of commuters living in low-density residential suburbs. While viewing the most salient features of California cities, we can find some similarities to the concentric zone model. The expansion of inner rings toward the outside as cities grow is one example. Closer analysis of any California city reveals too many exceptions.

The sector model divides the city into sections resembling pieces of a sliced pie. Homer Hoyt is given credit for this 1930s model. The pieces, which widen out away from the CBD are often organized along certain transportation corridors. The low-rent residential areas of slums and ghettos with the poorest living conditions are surrounded by noisy and polluting transportation and heavy industrial activities. As expected, the upscale, high-rent residential neighborhoods are surrounded by green space, recreational and educational centers, and intermediate-rent residential neighborhoods. The middle class find themselves within a pie slice somewhere between these two extremes. Though many of these sections can be identified in California cities, they are rarely shaped or organized according to the sector model, and they are often not connected to the CBD.

Of the three classic city models, the **multiple nuclei** model usually works best for California cities, especially within the state's modern conurbations. Chauncy Harris and Edward Ullman submitted this model for scrutiny in the 1940s. Though there may be an original and dominant CBD, there are other major nodes of growth or separate nuclei. Each of these additional nuclei serve special functions that take advantage of the local geography. Figure 11.1 shows the three classic city models.

Multiple Urban Nuclei in the Bay Area   Oakland became the center for the East Bay and the second largest city in the Bay Area due to regular ferry service to San Francisco, improved rail transportation, and a dredged port. This secondary nucleus and its smaller neighbors, such as Richmond, Berkeley, and Alameda represented attractive alternatives for industries and commuters crowded out of congested San Francisco into the 1900s. Oakland took advantage of its more than 20 miles of waterfront. Meanwhile, educational activities helped support growing communities around UC Berkeley and Stanford University.

Due to a concentration of skilled, educated entrepreneurs and an abundance of land that San Francisco could not offer, the urban area from Redwood City past Stanford, Palo Alto, and Mountain View and into San Jose became known as the Silicon Valley in the 1970s. By the 1980s, this Santa Clara Valley was famous as the world's center for innovation in the computer industry. This is also one reason why San Jose passed Oakland and San Francisco to become not only another separate nucleus in the Bay Area, but the third-largest city in California. New nuclei continue to erupt from Fremont and Hayward into Contra Costa County's "ContraCostapolis" and into the North Bay.

Multiple Nuclei in Southern California   The multiple nuclei model also works better to explain the internal structures of Southern California cities. Smaller communities were first connected by rail and then freeway to the Los Angeles CBD; many are examples of secondary nuclei today.

After a sleepy beginning marked by conservative transplants from the Midwest (especially Iowa), Long Beach recognized its geographic advantages. By the early 1900s, the port was developed, oil fields were producing, and the Navy had arrived. Among the industries that brought capital and jobs through the middle of the

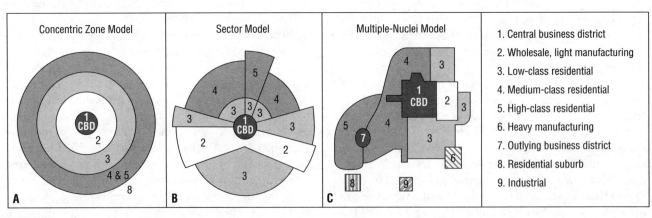

FIGURE 11.1
Though major California cities may exhibit some characteristics of all three classic internal models, multiple nuclei cities are the rule.

century (often fueled by defense spending) was the giant McDonnell Douglas. Long Beach continues as the third largest city in Southern California with its own complex structure of various industries, transportation corridors, upper and lower-income neighborhoods, urban issues and problems. Long Beach and its harbor share boundaries with Los Angeles and its harbor and the many other neighbors that combine to make the Los Angeles conurbation.

On L.A.'s West Side, another interesting financial center eventually erupted, connected by the Wilshire Corridor. The office towers at Century City sprouted in part to serve higher-income professional, entertainment, financial, and other business leaders who tired of the inconvenience caused by the commute to crowded downtown Los Angeles. As office towers sprouted in nearby West Hollywood, Westwood, and throughout west Los Angeles, a new financial center is recognized, complete with the wealth, congestion, and urban problems once concentrated in L.A.'s CBD. Perhaps what distinguishes this financial center is the concentration of higher-income neighborhoods surrounding it, including nearby Beverly Hills and Bel Air.

Extending farther west is Brentwood, Pacific Palisades, and the Santa Monica/Malibu coast. It is no coincidence that the West Side nucleus just reviewed represents the closest major financial center for these upper-income communities. Similar nuclei have erupted in places like the hills of Studio City and in Woodland Hills (Warner Center) along Topanga Boulevard. Numerous other economic and cultural centers have grown in Glendale, Burbank, and Pasadena, and they have erupted around the malls along I-10 in the San Gabriel Valley and where major freeways meet in Orange County.

The San Diego area is a classic example of how urban sprawl has been directed mainly along freeway corridors where multiple nuclei have grown north, east, and south of the city. Some of the freeways follow historical railroad routes where separate towns originally nucleated. Today, connections with Tijuana and other blooming border cities are producing remarkable changes in landscapes within the San Diego/Tijuana conurbation.

Each of California's nuclear centers could be considered urban realms and may be dominated by various industrial, manufacturing, wholesale and retail, or financial center activities. The nature of these industrial and business activities and the jobs they offer often determine whether low-, middle-, or upper-income communities or stereotypical residential suburbs surround them. Or, perhaps the types of surrounding suburbs determine the center activities. Regardless, each of these urban realms also still has at least some important connections to that larger and more dominant parent CBD.

Though the multiple-nuclei model may work better than the concentric zone or sector models in describing the internal structures of California cities, it is still not adequate. In some California cities, overlays of all three models might help explain their structures. Now, we will do better to consider the complex nature and unique character and history of each California city.

◆ SITE, SITUATION AND THE FUTURE OF CALIFORNIA'S URBAN LANDSCAPES

Our brief review of the history, structures, and functions of California cities has brought us back to question how and why our cities evolved to produce the urban landscapes we see today. We now have a better understanding of our modern cities and the processes that are shaping them. The next step, naturally, is to question the future of California's urban landscapes. Which cities will prosper and grow and why? The future of these cities will probably be determined by whether their geographic sites and situations are made more or less desirable by local and global events and trends. Lessons from the past will also be used to more accurately forecast our urban future.

Site

You may recall that site refers to the exact position of a place. In this chapter, we refer to the exact position of geographic features within the city or the geographic position of the city itself.

Historical Site Factors

Most of California's first settlements and then cities were located near abundant natural resources. The Spanish established their missions, presidios, and pueblos where reliable water sources and good farmland were found with large populations of American Indians and defendable space. It is no surprise that many of their settlements had some of the largest concentrations of Native Americans and now have some of the largest concentrations of modern populations. The exact site where the Spanish founded Los Angeles is in dispute, but the general location is known. It was chosen due to its proximity to the Los Angeles River water source. More hostile natural landscapes sometimes provided sites for security and defense, such as the Presidio in San Francisco, which overlooks the Golden Gate, the only passage into the Bay. Even the American military continued to use this as a strategic defense site well into the 1900s.

The Mexican ranchos encouraged populations to disperse across more favorable rangeland, but the discovery of gold in 1848 changed all of that. Within two years, tens of thousands had moved into Mother Lode towns. When gold was found, the towns boomed; where it

When the military handed San Francisco's scenic Presidio over to The City, it provided opportunities and challenges other California cities could only dream of. This is the Presidio Museum, a very small part of this huge chunk of land.

wasn't found or the sources ran out, the people left and the towns died. As these dramas were played out time and again in the western Sierra Nevada foothills, Sacramento and San Francisco grew and prospered.

Sacramento thrived along the main waterway between the Mother Lode and San Francisco; San Francisco, with its protected Bay and Pacific access, often served as the point of entry for Mother Lode activity, and it quickly became the financial center of the West. Both site and situation played roles in the explosive growth of these wild west cities and in the dominant role northern California played in the state's early history.

Favorable Site Factors Change

As the Gold Rush faded, other site factors encouraged cities to grow elsewhere in California. Due to mild weather, long growing seasons and extensive flatlands, Southern California's coastal plains first became famous for outstanding farming opportunities and later attracted large numbers of people and industries to their blossoming cities. Hollywood and the defense industry brought more wealth and attention as boosters took advantage of the mild climate and available land. By the mid-1900s, Los Angeles had eclipsed San Francisco in size and stature, and San Diego would soon follow. With the passage of time, Southern California coastal cities began to benefit more from these favorable site factors.

The time had ended when California cities were limited in location to areas that were defendable and secure or had an abundant natural resource. Left behind in the rush to build California cities were the towns in rural California. Located near timber and mining resources, they were constrained by limitations of these resources and other restrictions that were required to ensure their long-term sustainability. Meanwhile, agricultural service towns grew faster where the land was most productive and agribusiness flourished, such as in the Salinas and Central Valleys.

For towns to grow into influential cities, they had to diversify their economies and decrease their reliance on agriculture. This is exactly what happened in the expanding cities of the Central Valley. Evidence of increasing economic diversity is obvious today in cities like Bakersfield, Fresno, and Modesto. The sites of Stockton and Sacramento have been improved by their deep water channels and access to shipping lanes. Ironically, as these Central Valley cities grow, they are consuming the very fertile land that helped get them started so many decades ago.

By the mid-1900s, more modern site factors were encouraging the growth of California's new urban giants. The San Francisco Bay Area, Los Angeles Basin, and San Diego waterfronts had established large, influential harbors. When nature wasn't cooperative enough, the harbors were improved or built, such as along the Oakland waterfront or at Los Angeles and Long Beach Harbors. These represent **head-of-navigation** sites where shipping lanes, railheads, and truck and air transportation corridors meet. They are important break-of-bulk sites where the mode of transport is interrupted and changed.

Adding to the capital brought by commercial shipping at the ports was the military presence. Due to the great harbors, military influence has been outstanding from the shipyards and Navy activities in the San Francisco Bay Area to Long Beach and especially in San Diego; there, the Navy has had a profound impact on the region's economy and culture. The military also established bases where inland and desert sites offered vast open spaces and abundant land.

Modern Site Factors

A few natural site factors continue to play important roles in California's major urban areas. California's coastal areas are still famous for their mild climates and natural beauty. However, the most desirable sites are filled and the people are being drawn to the abundant inexpensive sites only available in the inland valleys and deserts. These modern settlers experience hotter, smoggier summers in many of the inland valleys, and the much harsher environment of the desert is often balanced by open spaces and solitude. However, it is difficult to imagine what natural site factors will draw people to these population centers once their landscapes are filled with the congestion and urban problems they have tried to escape.

It is clear that we are creating site factors within our built environment that overshadow those of our natural environment as we decide where to settle, live, and work in California. It is no longer important to locate near a water source when your water is channelled to your urban area from a river more than 200 miles away. Instead, we may seek urban communities that have the best drinking water quality or that use recycled water to create beautiful green spaces or scenic lakes.

There is obviously no longer a reason to locate urban areas on sites that can be defended from foreign attack because missiles can travel thousands of miles. Instead, we search for sites with low crime rates or where security is so tight, we can protect ourselves from one another. And the climate at your location may not be as important when you spend most of your time inside, whether it be your apartment or condominium, the office, indoor gym, or urban mall. New building technologies have even allowed us to break away from the flatlands that were so conveniently jammed with urban populations; we now extend the city high into some of the most rugged terrain.

Modern technologies are changing our perceptions of the urban environment and our site considerations. Even as we run out of traditional spaces, we are creating new choices and opportunities. These new developments and innovations are not only changing our perceptions of where urban areas can be located, but they are having impressive impacts on the internal structures and landscapes of all cities in California.

Situation

Situation refers to the location of a place in relation to its surroundings. Like many other world cities, California's urban areas are dependent on the physical and cultural characteristics, the resources, and activities of the surrounding region and beyond. From northern to southern California, from smaller to larger urban landscapes, examples abound and continue to multiply.

Historical Situation Factors

At first, growth of California's cities was slowed by poor accessibility. The Spanish settlers and the Mexicans after them constantly struggled with their remoteness. By 1850, San Francisco and Sacramento had experienced remarkable growth by providing access and services to the distant gold country. However, even during the Gold Rush, frenetic 49ers were either detoured or killed by the desert and mountain barriers they had to cross to get to the gold fields. These same barriers and sheer distance from a westward-expanding America kept many regions of California wild and unpopulated even after the railroads made their connections from the east. This also underscored the importance of the coastal cities with major shipping ports where people and cargo could flow relatively freely in and out of the state.

Situation Factors that Benefit Smaller Cities

Little Crescent City has long been the focus of activity for all of Del Norte County; its harbor is used by commercial fishing industries, while primary products from nearby agriculture and especially timber lands are shipped out from there.

Eureka has been even more successful in exploiting its situation in relation to the timber and agricultural resources that flow into it from rural landscapes and often out on ships. Fishing resources are important to almost all these small northwestern cities. Due to those surrounding resources and Humboldt Bay, Eureka is the largest city and most active port in northwestern California. Ironically, these same communities benefit from the tourists seeking relief and recreation among the surrounding resources that have not been harvested. Where the mix and diversity of economic activity is the richest, the larger towns grow and thrive in the long run.

Along California's central coast, urban centers first exploited surrounding farmlands and other resources. Later, many grew to serve travelers and tourists visiting some of the most scenic coastal landscapes in the world.

Redding has grown to become the largest city in the northern end of the state by exploiting its situation. It has long been an agricultural service town for a large region of inland rural northern California, but it has also profited from surrounding timber production and other primary industries. It serves as a stopping point for travellers between California and Oregon along I-5 and a staging ground for tourists and others seeking recreation in the surrounding mountains and parks.

Dwarfed by Redding, little Red Bluff, like other towns in the region, hosts the same types of activities, but on a much smaller scale—agricultural services, timber, and a turn-off to Lassen Volcanic National Park. To the south,

Downtown Eureka and its Victorian district represent an urban center surrounded by rural landscapes.

urban centers up and down the Central Valley have always depended on the remarkably productive farmland and agribusiness surrounding them.

On the other side of the Sierra Nevada, Bishop has grown to support similar activities, except the tourists, especially from Southern California, are more evident as they race to some of the most popular ski resorts in the world. There are also plenty of fishing and hunting opportunities in the region. Similar situational factors helped to make Owens Valley a convenient source of water for Los Angeles' thirsty masses.

Modern Situation Factors Shape Our Urban Giants

In Southern California, cities grew throughout the 1900s as they successfully sold their convenient situations— surrounded by beautiful beaches, snow-capped and forested mountains, and desert recreational opportunities in wide open spaces, all within a few hours drive.

The Silicon Valley later became famous for its innovation and technology, partly because it was surrounded with cutting-edge educational institutions and some of the most educated and skilled workers in the world. San Jose and surrounding cities blossomed throughout the late twentieth century due to this situation.

On a much grander, global scale, California's situation continues to have a profound impact on its cities. Decades after some Californians tried to sweep aside the state's Spanish and Mexican heritage, our proximity to Latin America has been reemphasized, celebrated, and sometimes exploited, especially in our cities. Today, the futures of California and Latin America are tied by powerful economic and cultural forces. The Latino influence is evident in almost every human landscape in the state.

Just as profound are the changes brought by Asians, their cultures, and their landscapes. California is home to more Asians and more diverse Asian cultures than any place outside Asia. Much of California's economic and cultural future can be found in our Chinatowns, Monterey Parks and Koreatowns, in our Japantowns, Little Tokyos, and Little Saigons. Powerful economic ties with Asia are only strengthened by the high-tech and information revolutions. Our cities, situated across the ocean from the giant Asian markets, will have much to gain as focal points on the Pacific Rim, especially as the new global economy sets sail.

The Future Significance of Site and Situation

Legendary factors of site and situation that helped build California cities are fading fast. The changes are rapid. Impacts of the high-tech/information revolution are forcing us to cast aside traditional assumptions and models. As more workers and industries use new technologies and information systems and as more virtual offices and businesses go on line, will we need cities? Will these developments encourage an even greater dispersal of populations? How will these changes affect our rural landscapes and smaller towns? It is certain that California cities must, and can, continue to evolve and redefine themselves if they are to survive the tumultuous years ahead.

California's Modern and Future Urban Landscapes

We have finally established a general foundation in urban geography. We can use this knowledge to understand issues and solve problems in modern and future California cities. Additionally, we can use this information to better understand the connections, diversity, and change that define our urban landscapes.

One of the most exciting aspects of modern geography is its relevance and applicability to the real world, which is what this next section is all about. We are now ready to pick out a few specific issues and problems that are transforming California's urban landscapes. Here are just a few examples of how we can use some basic geographic concepts to reflect on the past, critique our modern urban landscapes, and plan for a better future.

◆ EXAMPLES OF ISSUES AND PROBLEMS WITHIN CALIFORNIA'S URBAN LANDSCAPES

For decades, California natives and outsiders have tried to understand the nature of the state's cities. Most agree that there are numerous factors setting California cities apart from most others around the nation and the world. It is rare when experts and visitors can identify or agree on the nature of those differences. Certainly, there is healthy debate about how to solve our urban problems as we try to make our cities more livable. Ironically, there may be more agreement on the direction in which California's urban areas are headed.

We begin this review of our modern and future cities with some ideas taken from Professor Thomas Bender at New York University. Though he is an East Coast scholar, Bender's clear and poignant observations on the state of U.S. cities are relevant to California's urban areas. His writings were edited for major California publications such as the *Los Angeles Times*, in 1996. They serve as inspiration for the next few paragraphs, a general critique of California cities.

Earlier in this century, our cities were our economic, cultural, and innovative centers, but suburbanization and decentralization of the population may have hurt our cities and stifled discovery and creativity.

Modern California cities are increasingly becoming landscapes with several tiers, but two of them are particularly noticeable. First, there are the financial districts with their economic transactions and electronic connections more and more controlled by the global market. These are now the profitable production sectors of the city. Nearby are entertainment, cultural, and retail zones that provide spaces to visit and shop. The Balboa Park Complex in San Diego, Costa Mesa Performing Arts Center, Central Library in L.A., and Opera House in San Francisco are examples.

Gritty, lower-income working class neighborhoods represent the second tier. These are the sectors that many middle- and upper-class residents usually choose to ignore. They are often rough, grey, and blighted, but they are sometimes colorful, festive landscapes dominated by powerless minorities, immigrants, and poor. There is little mixing between the high-income cultures' creativity and low-income cultures' innovations. Especially since the mid-1900s, different classes in our cities have been successfully separated by space and financial and cultural barriers.

Some argue that, especially in the suburbs, true innovation, creativity, and culture have been lost in the middle- and higher-income version of "City Lite." Here, consumption drives the atmosphere at safe, generic malls and entertainment centers where everyone knows what to expect. Such critics see an atmosphere that stifles true art and creativity, innovation, and culture. Life in the generic City Lite reveals no passage of time. The City Lite is simply consumed and replaced with no historical connection.

Those critics also argue that the most ambitious urban projects are no longer public, but private developments. They include fun zones, theme parks, and office towers cut off from the average citizen, especially from the poor, and with no easy street access. Even many residential communities have become gated fortresses.

The reality of interdependence, of a common environment, and of common goals may be lost in California's modern cities. Is this because our cities have grown too large, and most people's area of concern is so small? Is it because each city sector and neighborhood has broken away as an independent self-interest group? These concerns, often with a slightly different twist, seem to appear repeatedly in modern studies of California cities.

Common Issues and Problems are Connected

Typical examples supporting the previous arguments were flowing out of USC's Southern California Studies Center and other research institutions throughout the state into the late 1990s. The Center reported that the L.A. region was progressing economically as it exploited its location on the Pacific Rim. However, crime, pollution,

and a splintered government that cannot coordinate planning efforts were slowing progress. The USC study considered five counties and 177 cities as part of Southern California. Those ominous numbers help define the planning problem! They found local governance to be chaotic in this region, where so many different and complicated industries, cultures, and legal jurisdictions shared regional issues and problems.

Authors of the USC study noted the painful economic transition toward high-tech, entertainment, services and trade. They recognized the large recent immigrant population. They also acknowledged that, in the midst of growing wealth, nearly one-fifth of all Southern California residents were still living below the federal poverty level. That gap between the rich and poor was glaring as more teenagers in the area dropped out of school and experienced a higher rate of violent deaths than the national average. These trends are common to many California cities.

It is ironic that USC, in another study, ranked the Los Angeles area second (just behind New York) and San Francisco third in the nation in the number of cultural assets, including theater groups, classical and ethnic radio stations, and library holdings. (Recall from Chapter 8 on cultures that when cultural assets per capita were ranked, San Francisco led the nation.) This confirms a previous notion—extremes that help define California are magnified in its extraordinary cities. How will we deal with these contradictions?

Urban Sprawl in California

In California, the growth of our cities' suburbs into urban realms and the expansion of new suburbs from these urban realms continues. These trends have already received plenty of attention in this and other chapters. It is difficult to miss their enormous impacts on California's landscapes. Just how much attention does this issue deserve? Should it be considered a major problem? In 1995, Bank of America, the state's largest financial institution, and the Greenbelt Alliance issued a report called "Beyond Sprawl." It criticized urban sprawl for causing pollution and deterioration of the quality of life, and it warned about a host of future negative impacts.

For decades, Californians relied on suburban growth not only to escape from their cities, but to provide jobs in construction and related industries. Real estate interests and developers played dominating roles in state economics, politics, and planning throughout the twentieth century. Giant corporations, such as Kaufman and Broad Home Corporation in Los Angeles, grew with astounding success as they erected one housing project after another on the next available tract of vacant land at the urban fringe.

Even during the last decades of the 1900s, it was common in Los Angeles and other California counties that up

HOMELESS

One problem shared by every California city since the 1980s involves the large number of urban homeless. During the mid-1990s, it was estimated that on any one night, L.A. had 42,000 homeless people and San Francisco had 10,000–15,000 street people.

These homeless are more visible on San Francisco streets for several reasons. First, it is a more compact city. Second, hundreds of homeless live in Golden Gate Park (a major tourist attraction) and other tourist sites, including downtown streets. Third, San Francisco has a reputation of being sensitive to homeless issues and even had a well-organized group of militant advocates; social welfare programs such as food, clothing, and low-income housing handouts attracted homeless from across the nation. However, there is a five-year waiting list for the most subsidized rental units for the poorest homeless in The City.

Nearly every California city has struggled with homeless issues. Factors and events similar to San Francisco's have, historically, exacerbated homeless problems in smaller compact cities, such as Berkeley and Santa Monica. Earlier in the 1990s, when Berkeley officials began placing volleyball courts for surrounding residents in People's Park, some homeless staged a near riot. They protested infringement on the territory they had staked out in the park as another example of a policy to get rid of homeless. Years later, the Berkeley City Council voted to prohibit homeless people and their dogs from sleeping on busy avenues. There are countless other examples of conflicts in urban areas across the state.

Local conflicts erupt when residents who want to help the homeless tangle with those who want to get rid of them. The courts have repeatedly entered these controversies. In 1990, the Legal Aid Society in San Diego sued the City Council to stop San Diego police from confiscating the shopping carts and belongings of homeless. This tactic has

been used by several other California cities. A few days later, police were arresting "panhasslers" who blocked paths and used aggressive language. In 1991, a federal court ruling struck down California's century-old antipanhandling law as an infringement of freedom of speech. San Francisco voters responded in November, 1992, approving an ordinance to ban the most obnoxious forms of panhandling, including the touching or blocking of pedestrians.

A few months later, dozens of homeless in a makeshift village hidden among bushes next to the Hollywood Freeway near downtown L.A. were forced to leave. Department of Transportation officials cleared out roadside landscaping that concealed them and replaced it with ground cover in early February, 1993. Caltrans officials found men, women, children, and pets living in plastic-wrapped houses built of scrap lumber, tree branches, and cardboard. Some of the shelters were even partially furnished. Nearby residents complained about their fires, lack of sanitation, and crime they blamed on some of the homeless. Caltrans officials estimated that as many as 1,000 homeless slept each night along the Hollywood Freeway between Hollywood and downtown L.A.

In 1997, Sacramento residents and leaders fought over what to do about the estimated 10,000 homeless in their county. The Sacramento City Council got tough when it sued the privately-funded charity called Loaves and Fishes. Up to 1,000 homeless guests would gather each day for meals, showers, and a school for homeless children. Neighbors and the city complained that, after meals, unkempt homeless would pour through nearby neighborhoods. Yet, Sacramento officials became sensitive about gaining an image as a mean city. A similar conflict erupted in Buena Park, when a church pastor allowed up to thirty homeless people to stay on church property. Neighbors complained and pressured the city to enforce its no-

---

to seven out of the ten top contributors to County Board of Supervisors candidates were developers. By the early 1990s, a Los Angeles Ethics Commission study found that nearly 40 percent of the money supporting lobbyists at L.A. City Hall came from real estate and developer interests. Other major corporations and businesses, most of whom engaged in city business, accounted for another 30 percent of all lobbyist money.

The results are evident from the Bay Area to the Central Valley and south to the Mexican border; for decades, developers and construction companies spread more concrete, asphalt, and housing developments across California landscapes than any other place on earth. Some of these communities provided new living spaces that enhanced the quality of life in a region. Others were ill-

advised and poorly planned, ravaging California landscapes and contributing to the deterioration of living and working environments.

Leaping and Spreading

Threats from impatient developers to push for uncontrolled growth have become reality in many parts of California. When Marin County officials enforced their slow-growth policies, developers leapfrogged to the north of them to Petaluma, Rohnert Park, Santa Rosa, and other Sonoma County communities. As these North Bay suburbs expanded, they sprouted their own malls and urban problems. Today, their commuters jam Hwy. 101 to get to work in the urban centers along San Francisco Bay.

HOMELESS *continued*

camping laws in a controversy that dragged on from 1996 to 1998.

Part of the plan to renovate downtown Long Beach in 1997 was a ban on social service programs there. The city blocked a proposed expansion of the Salvation Army's Beach Haven Lodge, a pre-parole facility for nonviolent offenders being released from state prisons. Nonprofit charities around the state were watching as Long Beach and other California cities from Sacramento and San Jose to San Diego considered zoning laws to restrict homeless, mentally ill, and recovering substance abusers who move into downtown districts looking for social services.

For years, local governments have competed to be tough on homeless and move them on to the next community. The traditional exceptions, such as San Francisco, Berkeley and Santa Monica, initially gained softer reputations that attracted homeless. Clearly, this is a perfect example of a state and national problem that had been thrown on the backs of individual, smaller urban communities. Many smaller cities simply could not afford the cost of supporting thousands of homeless, although a few concerned local governments experimented with their own solutions.

SEARCHING FOR SOLUTIONS

San Diego was one. The city allowed up to five-hundred homeless to sleep on thin mattresses on the floor of San Diego's famous Municipal Gym (called Muni Gym) in Balboa Park. Homeless were allowed in at 5 P.M. when public basketball ended, but they had to be out of the way by 9 A.M. the next day. The experiment began during heavy January rains in 1993. Previously, Muni's three full-sized courts were *the* place for basketball in San Diego County and were used from morning till midnight seven days a week. Hours had to be cut and some leagues cancelled for the experiment.

All of this was a response to a homeless tent city that had been erected illegally in a parking lot at Balboa Park. As usual, police prepared to remove the tents and homeless. City officials acted when the media planned complete coverage.

In Santa Monica, merchants urged visitors to stop giving handouts to panhandlers. They argued that only more aggressive panhandlers were accumulating small change to support their substance abuse. Contacts between visitors and the larger populations of more timid and hidden, truly needy homeless were rare, giving the public a warped perception of the homeless problem. Instead, concerned visitors were encouraged to drop their spare change into strategically-located dolphin receptacles. This money was then channelled to organized programs that help homeless get the training, jobs, and housing that might get them back on their feet.

In San Francisco, a relatively successful, comprehensive program known as the "continuum of care" was a national model by 1996. It first allows the needs of homeless to be assessed in temporary shelters. Then they are moved to transitional housing where psychological counseling, job training, and other assistance are available. Permanent subsidized housing is the next step for each person. Some federal government HUD grants go to cities with such comprehensive programs to support housing and job training.

Homeless people in California's cities have come from around the nation. Finally, a statewide and national problem was being approached with a more sweeping, long-term solution. This is an example of how competition between cities for funds to help the homeless was working better in the long-run than competition to get rid of the homeless.

Each day, thousands drive in bumper-to-bumper traffic through miles of bucolic Marin County landscapes that separate their city jobs from their distant suburban homes.

In 1998, residents of Ventura County overwhelmingly revolted against urban sprawl. They voted to take the power of approving new sudivisions on land zoned for agriculture or open space away from their County Board of Supervisors. Such developments would have to be approved by voters. It was called the Save Open Space and Agricultural Resources (SOAR) campaign. Four cities in the county also voted to restrict growth within their own urban boundaries. Simultaneously, voters in San Luis Obispo County were expressing reservations about uncontrolled growth. Residents from northern California to San Diego County were testing and implementing various measures to control growth in their communities into the final months of the century.

Moreno Valley Moreno Valley is perhaps the best example of urban sprawl that leaped east of Riverside as commuters tested the limits of lengthy commutes into the L.A. area. Known for its vast fields of corn, sugar beets, and alfalfa before the 1980s, Moreno Valley became the fastest-growing city in the United States during part of the 1980s. It advertised itself as a "city poised for the twenty-first century, a city of promise." The peak periods saw more than 1,000 new homes per month purchased on cheap land that was easy to develop; L.A. and Orange County housing prices had skyrocketed out of reach for these families.

SUBURBS IN THE RIVER

Here is a bizarre example of where unbridled development and urban sprawl had taken us by the late 1990s. About 98 percent of the water from the upper San Joaquin River watershed never flows directly past Fresno and into the Central Valley, due to dams and canals for farms. Now, there is controversy about developing the river itself. The problem started when Friant Dam was built in 1942, drying up half of the river. County recorders worked with families on the Fresno and Madera County sides of the river; they unwisely divided land on both sides of the river all the way into the middle of the river bed. The river land was used for pasture and then sold to developers.

Developers wanted to build two golf courses and several hundred homes and condominiums right in the river bottom, claiming flood control projects make it safe. Projected development is *in* the river bottom, not on the bluffs or banks! Sure enough, the river flooded in early January, 1997, before any developments. Opponents say the development threatens a rare riparian habitat, and it ruins the proposed San Joaquin River Parkway. This would have included trails, picnic tables, and other recreation and open space opportunities along the twenty-two miles from Friant Dam to California 99.

In 1992, the Fresno County Board of Supervisors approved the first large-scale river bottom development at Ball Ranch, including 721 dwellings and a golf course called "Scottish Links." Though that project was scaled down, there were proposals on the Madera County side of the river to build other developments, which would include several hundred homes on and near the river bottom. Remember, all of this area flooded in January, 1997.

Though there is plenty of land left for development in Fresno County, the developers want to build on the river. This is the same region where law enforcement officials, including the FBI, had recently launched an investigation called Operation Rezone. Results of the investigation sent at least nine politicians, developers, and lobbyists to jail for land-use corruption. The continuing investigation included some of the parties trying to develop the river. Lawyers representing developers are threatening to sue if they do not get their way. One wrote that if they do not develop, "housing and urban development will therefore be required to leapfrog over this area, thereby disrupting the otherwise orderly expansion of urban facilities."

When the city of Moreno Valley incorporated in December, 1984, the population was only 45,000; it grew to nearly 120,000 in five years, and it was booming financially. By the end of the 1990s, it had grown to define a huge bedroom community with a population of more than 138,000. However, growth and the new developers' fees and construction it brought were required to finance the city. When that growth stopped in the early 1990s, the city was near financial collapse. Without the income from developers' permit-processing fees, the city had to lay off nearly half its staff.

By the mid-1990s, some were calling Moreno Valley the worst-developed city in the state. It had not established a strong manufacturing and retail base, and the

Issues of flood control, fires, and unplanned growth—this could be somewhere near Moreno Valley or any other Southern California suburb that presses against its hills and open spaces, but this scene is in eastern San Diego County.

housing projects were not generating enough property taxes to pay for the services they required. It was a middle-class community with median household incomes of $45,000, and it was an ethnically diverse population of 57 percent white, 23 percent Latino, 13 percent African American, and 6 percent Asian.

The recession, 3,000 jobs lost at nearby March Air Force Base, and the collapse of real estate that devalued properties and dropped property tax revenues by 20 percent made matters worse. The city also gave $23 million of future sales tax back to developers of the regional retail mall to get them to locate there. Otherwise, business and industry just did not follow the people and their houses. The city even cut developer fees to encourage them to build more housing tracts instead of going elsewhere. These were fees that would help build streets, parks, flood control, and other services and infrastructure. By 1996, Moreno Valley officials were trying to get citizens to accept special taxes to keep the city afloat.

By the end of the century, Moreno Valley officials had finally discovered the importance of a diverse economy in a well-planned urban landscape. The future looked brighter as Moreno Valley cruised into the twenty-first century.

Antelope Valley   In the high desert north of Los Angeles, Palmdale experienced similar problems when it grew from 23,000 to 113,000 in ten years. In contrast to Moreno Valley, officials strengthened its economy with new redevelopment and retail projects that brought in money.

Southern Pacific once laid the tracks that would double the price of land in this area. Palmdale was founded in 1886 as Palmenthal by Swiss and German immigrants who thought the Joshua Trees were palm trees. Much later, it became the Antelope Valley's first city. Due to Edwards Air Force Base, World War II, and then defense plants and the Cold War, it became the aerospace capital of the United States. It was once the fastest-growing community in the country.

This story illustrates the extremes that are California. After incorporation in 1962, a plan emerged to locate the next big Southern California international airport there. By 1968, the L.A. Department of Airports had planned a tunnel and monorail to L.A. through the San Gabriel Mountains for passenger transport. Palmdale's isolation eventually killed the plan. By the 1980s, explosive growth made it an extended suburb for commuters to L.A. Buyers would camp out for a chance to purchase an inexpensive house during the boom period.

Then, by the early 1990s, the recession and defense cuts made Palmdale the number one foreclosure city in the country. During the late 1990s, it was rebounding by promoting a more balanced, diversified economy. Like Moreno Valley, its population has also become more cul-turally diverse. Lancaster and other Antelope Valley suburbs were suffering and then recovering from similar events.

Within the Gates

Yet another popular trend has become common, but not exclusive, to California's notorious suburbs—gated communities. By the late 1990s, Canyon Lake, in southern Riverside County, contained about 12,000 residents. That made it the nation's second-largest gated and walled community. Canyon Lake was built in 1968 as a retirement and weekend retreat community, protected by a surrounding wall. Encroaching populations from the west quickly filled it during the 1980s with younger families and wage-earners. They were willing to commute into L.A. and Orange Counties, skipping past less fortunate suburbs filled with the same urban problems people were trying to escape.

Canyon Lake was finally incorporated in 1991 to escape the control of the Riverside County Board of Supervisors and to keep nearby cities from incorporating it. Most city services—police and fire protection, animal control, etc.—are contracted out. The $1,302-per-home Property Owners Association (POA) dues pay for trash, grounds and roads upkeep, and other services. The city has a $2.2 million budget, and the POA has a $7 million budget. There are serious restrictions, including an architectural committee whose members decide on paint color for homes. There are no sidewalks, no street lights, and motorcycles are banned.

Canyon Lake offers residents security, prestige, and strict land-use restrictions in an environment with a golf course, athletic fields, tennis courts, lakefront recreation, water skiing, fishing, an equestrian center, clubhouse, and pool. Most of the residences are middle class, but a few homes are million-dollar mansions. Here, there is a nice architectural mix uncommon to most California suburbs and housing tracts. A private security company patrols the grounds. The Riverside County Sheriff's department records very low crime rates, usually committed by people who live within the gates. For schools, serious shopping, and entertainment, residents must visit nearby Perris and Lake Elsinore. It is one of only six incorporated U.S. cities that are entirely closed; Rolling Hills on the Palos Verdes Peninsula and Hidden Hills near Calabasas are also on the list.

Retiring in Style in the Suburbs

California's retiring populations are searching for similar security within specialized communities. As baby-boomers born between 1946 and 1964 turn fifty, many are rejecting traditional planned retirement communities in favor of "active adult" communities catering to ages over

SUBURBAN MALLS

The extent of this urban sprawl in California is noticeable when examining the number and size of suburban malls. In 1996, the largest malls in California by millions of square feet of retail space were:

Del Amo Fashion Center, Torrance—3.00

South Coast Plaza, Costa Mesa—2.92

Lakewood Center Mall, Lakewood—1.75

Ontario Mills—1.70

North County Fair, Escondido—1.52

Northridge Fashion Center—1.52

Mission Valley Center, San Diego—1.50

Eastridge Shopping Center, San Jose—1.47

Sunvalley Shopping Center, Concord—1.40

Glendale Galleria, Glendale—1.39

This list changes to include a host of additional California malls when other measurements, such as entire acreage or retail sales, are used.

The Ontario Mills mall, opened in 1996, covers 131 acres at the junction of the I-10 and I-15 freeways about forty miles east of L.A. It was actually the largest mall in the nation when its theme park and other attractions were added to the shopping complex. Dining and entertainment cover about one-fourth of the space; entertainment is a big draw. There are two-hundred outlet and specialty stores hoping to draw crowds from Orange County and L.A. developers expect it to attract 15–19 million visitors per year, more than Disneyland.

Multiple-screen movie theaters and now megaplexes with 12 or more screens have become more common and many of them are in suburban malls. At the Ontario Mills mall, the AMC megaplex theaters and Edwards megaplex were dueling across the street from one another in 1996 to open a total of fifty-two screens with all the latest visual and audio technology. Some estimated that each company spent up to $40 million to complete each megaplex. The AMC thirty-theater complex alone, with seats for 5,700 would be the largest so far in the world. The city of Ontario refused to step in as industry experts and residents were wondering how either megaplex in this ego contest will ever be successful. Anticipating the size of Ontario Mills, financiers for additional malls planned nearby either pulled away from or simply abandoned their proposed projects.

Economic geography was working to keep other malls at reasonable and profitable distances from one another. By the late 1990s, population growth and cheap land prices were finally luring retailers into more distant Inland Empire locations to catch up with development. San Bernardino County already had the Montclair Plaza in Montclair, the Inland Center Mall in San Bernardino, and a large mall planned for Redlands. Other malls in the Inland Empire region include the Desert Hills Factory Stores in Cabazon, Riverside County. Way out in the Mojave Desert, The Tanger Factory Outlet Center opened near Barstow's Factory Merchants Mall. By the end of the 1990s, these remote malls were competing with yet another trend as many new retail developers were returning closer to city centers.

fifty-five. Uniformity and enforced activities are out. Instead, builders are preparing California "communes" of safe, warm, healthy atmospheres with hiking and nature trails for a more sophisticated and active crowd. The new communities will cater to diverse people; even some older residents in their 70s might be working. Kaufman and Broad Home Corporation is gearing up for a demand of low-income apartment and condo projects for seniors. (This trend will also impact the state's urban centers.)

The first Leisure World was built in Seal Beach in 1961. Several years later, the Laguna Hills Leisure World was built. It is now California's largest retirement community, with nearly 18,000 residents, an arts and crafts center, equestrian center, golf course, and five swimming pools. A firm was hired to remodel Laguna Hills in the late 1990s because acquiring land for new developments that size would be impossible. A lighter and brighter renovation was planned, including moving the famous giant golden globe away from the freeway, although no one could agree where to move it.

During the early 1990s, Del Webb Corporation built its "crown jewel" Sun City near Palm Springs off I-10. According to the *Los Angeles Times*, this gated community and its companion community in Roseville, just north of Sacramento in northern California, were the best-selling housing developments in California during much of the 1990s. Baby boomers are rejecting the large "old people's" communities in favor of smaller, collegiate retirement developments where residents can get to know each other. Such smaller developments are planned in places like Walnut Creek in the East Bay.

When Will it Ever End?

We end this topic of suburban sprawl mania with more proof that it will continue in California. One of the latest proposals evolved toward the end of the 1990s, when

VIRTUAL HOMES AND BUSINESSES IN CALIFORNIA

Now that we have noted and considered these issues and problems, let's consider a few possible solutions. As we enter the twenty-first century, the effects of new technologies on this urban sprawl are uncertain. We are looking for ways to get people out of their cars so that they can live more efficient and productive lives. Perhaps the next step will be to establish telecommunication projects so that workers can realize the same functionality at home as in the office.

How will improved desktop videoconferencing, telephone-to-PC integration, and other technologies change where we live and how we go to work? How will they change the nature of our cities and suburbs? Will more people be encouraged to abandon our cities or will we rediscover the cultural treasures they have to offer? (Home-based businesses are considered later in this chapter.) Consider how the answers to these questions will shape California's future human landscapes.

Home builders and buyers are already changing the way we buy and live in our homes. By the late 1990s, buyers were developing virtual floor plans for their custom homes. By 1996, corporations such as Centex in the San Joaquin Valley and Presley Homes (a Newport Beach-based company, building its Boardwalk development in Huntington Beach), were decreasing the number of model homes in favor of virtual, custom models that are designed by the buyers. With these technologies, developers don't have to wait to market and sell each of their designed models. This is changing the very nature of suburban landscapes.

What will life be like inside these homes? In 1996, all eighty-seven homes in the Chino Hills development built by West Venture Homes were wired and computer ready. One home, known as CyberHome, already had more than fifty different computers and other electronic devices for work, kitchen chores, entertainment, and other functions. So much for driving to work and hiring low-income houseworkers to do the chores while you're gone! Radical changes are in store for suburban (and urban) life in California.

---

developers planned a giant new community called Newhall Ranch near Magic Mountain in the Santa Clarita Valley. Originally, it was planned to house 70,000 people on about 12,000 acres. Conceptually, the homes, services, schools, business park, golf course, lake and recreation areas were included to allow residents to stay in their community. Developers would carve five distinct modern villages out of the hills down to the Santa Clara River.

Newhall Ranch developers continued negotiations to scale down their project at the request of locals who were concerned about overcrowding and damage to river habitats. The final "scaled-down" version pushed through by L.A. County in 1998 against the protests of neighboring Ventura County and environmentalists included a projected population of 60,000, with a 200-acre business park and golf course, and more than 6,000 acres of dedicated open space on the 12,000 total acres.

As if in a recurring California dream, local publications noted that every L.A. County supervisor received political contributions from the developers, including nearly $70,000 to one politician. Opponents promised to continue their fight, claiming that water supplies were inadequate. The only differences between this and countless similar controversies throughout the state were the size of the development and the concessions required to get the plan passed. Originally, the Newhall Ranch development was the largest master planned community in L.A. County history. Regardless of the final size,

it is designed to extend L.A. suburbs nearly twenty miles farther out when it is completed in 2025.

Transporting People in Our Cities

Now that the realities of urban sprawl have set in, we can look to the Los Angeles area to see the enormity of California's urban transportation problems (see Map 11.2). There are plenty of lessons here. During the early and mid-1900s, Pacific Electric Trolley Red Cars ran through L.A. on as much as 1,000 miles of track. You could ride from the beach to the valley; surrounding communities were connected to downtown by one of the world's greatest urban transportation systems. As the Red Cars were sold and dismantled, freeways and cars replaced them. There are lingering questions about why L.A. surrendered its public transportation system to the consortium of car and tire manufacturers and oil interests that eventually shut it down.

At first, if you had the money, the car brought the independence and freedom that helped define the California Dream. By the 1970s, same-distance freeway commute times were increasing in jammed rush-hour traffic; leaders were scrambling to clean up the choking air pollutants belched out by cars going nowhere.

This was not supposed to happen; Angelenos had become less healthy and less efficient. By the 1990s, rush-hour freeway speeds averaged about 34 mph; they were dropping below 20 mph by the twenty-first century.

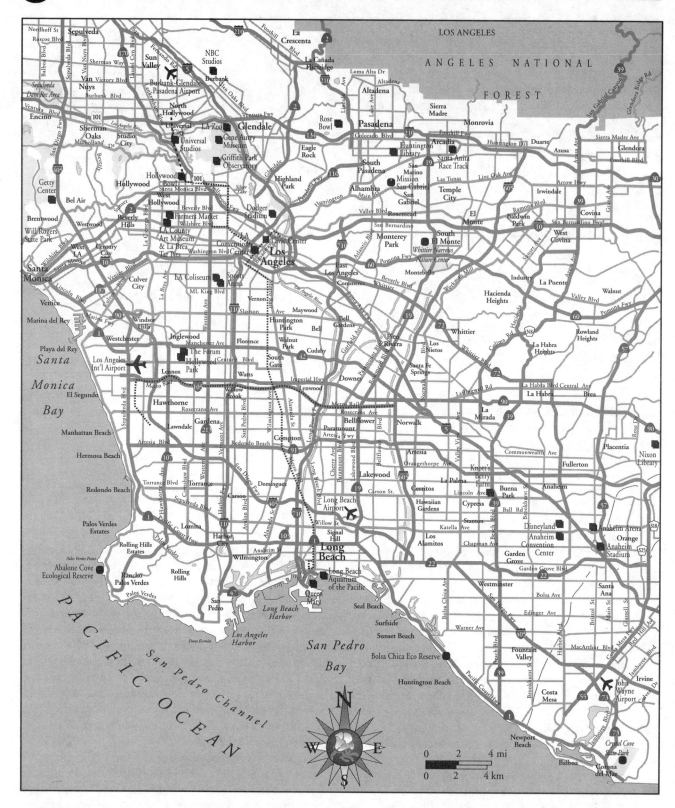

MAP 11.2

L.A. commuters are suffering from increasing traffic congestion on the busiest and most extensive freeway system in the nation.

BETTER FREEWAYS

SOUTHERN CALIFORNIA'S INTELLIGENT FREEWAYS

Let's consider the car solutions first. Caltrans (California Department of Transportation, the state's transportation agency) developed its first Advanced Transportation Management Centers in Los Angeles, Santa Ana, Riverside, and San Diego. They are called information, navigation, and traffic management tools, or "intelligent transportation."

The new technology focuses on quick diagnosis of traffic snarls and rerouting cars around impasses. It includes detectors and cameras that show when traffic slows, traffic engineers who control the cameras to determine what kinds of emergency services must be sent to the scene of an accident, and quick communications between motorists at the scene, the California Highway Patrol, and Caltrans. Messages to motorists are displayed on fixed, overhead changeable electronic message boards and also on mobile message boards ahead of approaching traffic. Caltrans computers use the message boards to relay information about alternate routes. Local city-operated traffic systems can then keep traffic flowing smoothly through side street detours. These efforts and Santa Monica Freeway's "smart corridor" show how many Southern California public agencies are finally working together to solve traffic problems.

Eventually, it is hoped that the traffic and detour information will be transmitted directly into vehicles with GPS systems. Firms throughout the area are embracing smart transportation technologies. Los Angeles, Orange, and San Diego counties already have much of the monitoring equipment installed, so they hold the greatest potential in the state for the success of this technology. Before these traffic management centers were started, drivers lost 40 million hours per year due to traffic delays in Orange County alone. It is estimated that the costs were $15 million per year in lost productivity and income to businesses and individuals. These first efforts were designed to increase speeds by 5 percent and decrease freeway trips by 12 percent.

Especially the Santa Monica Freeway may serve as a model for the future because the cost of building new highways is forcing better management of what already exists. Other innovative Southern California projects include the toll road on the Riverside Freeway (91) through Santa Ana Canyon, elevated carpool lanes on the Harbor Freeway, and automated highway testing in San Diego County.

Orange County took an additional step by taking bites out of their little remaining open space. Final sections of the fifteen-mile San Joaquin Hills Transportation Corridor opened in November, 1996, ahead of schedule. It was expected to shorten driving times between Laguna Niguel and Newport Beach from up to an hour down to 20 min-

utes. Tolls of $.25 to $2 are paid by transponders or in cash. The full road was expected to handle up to 70,000 vehicles per day after one year. This is one of three major toll roads in south Orange County that total seventy miles and were to be completed by 2003. The Eastern Toll Road connected the Inland Empire to coastal Orange County cities in 1998. Some officials and residents worried that these projects would usher in an era when roads will only be accessible to those wealthy enough to pay for them.

Others argued that any traffic relief would be worth the risk. Orange County's traffic problems were highlighted in the 1998 edition of the *Guinness Book of World Records*. The Orange Crush—where the Orange, Garden Grove, and Santa Ana Freeways meet—was named the most complex highway interchange in the world! Its on and off ramps carried 629,000 cars per day with 66 lanes, 34 routes, and 13 bridges.

Still not convinced how serious Southern California's transportation problem is? The California Department of Transportation also plans more than 326 miles of high-occupancy vehicle (HOV) lanes in Los Angeles County by 2025 at a cost of more than $6 billion. Another ninety-nine miles of elevated freeways will total $4.5 billion.

CARS IN THE SAN FRANCISCO BAY AREA

Things haven't been much better in San Francisco Bay Area urban centers and suburbs, where many cities are separated by water and linked by bridges. By 1992, California government agencies were working to increase transportation facilities required by the growing population centers east of San Francisco. Caltrans planned two new commuter lanes on Interstate 80 for $318 million, and the state planned to enlarge a freeway interchange in Walnut Creek for $310 million. Meanwhile, the Contra Costa Transportation Authority planned a $506 million commuter

You have several choices to ride public transportation on Market Street in San Francisco. Your options expand if you use the BART or MUNI tunnels below street level.

BETTER FREEWAYS *continued*

rail extension and $50 million in roadwork. It is clear that state officials were considering very costly solutions that continue to focus on the automobile as they try to solve crippling transportation problems.

The city of San Francisco has a fascinating history—and sometimes hatred—of automobile transportation. Developed before the car and confined on the tip of a peninsula, this is one of the state's few compact cities with narrow streets. During the 1950s, Caltrans proposed an interconnected web of major freeways through The City to connect the peninsula, Bay Bridge, and Golden Gate. This proposal included slicing through several neighborhoods and destroying Golden Gate Park's panhandle.

Citizen group protests against the plans drew up to 10,000 people and the plans died during the 1960s, to Caltrans officials' dismay. The double-decker Embarcadero and Central Freeways survived, spilling vehicles on to surface streets at their abrupt ends. However, no freeway has ever cut through the entire city.

When the Embarcadero Freeway was damaged by the 1989 Loma Prieta earthquake, the city decided not to rebuild it. Caltrans warned of impending traffic gridlock that never happened. The double-decker freeway was finally demolished. This has opened up the Embarcadero to the bay and allowed spectacular improvement of the waterfront; such urban renewal eventually spread all the way into South of Market, a sector of the city just south of Market Street that was formerly an urban decay mecca. On the other side of town, the old Embarcadero Freeway once

spilled tourists and consumers into Chinatown. That puts merchants in Chinatown among the few who miss this concrete eyesore, and they do not hesitate to complain about their losses.

In August, 1996, Caltrans had to shut down San Francisco's double decker Central Freeway for earthquake repairs. They warned that traffic could jam up to 45 miles down the peninsula *and* across the Bay Bridge into the East Bay, adding up to two hours to daily commutes. Surprisingly, after one month, none of that had happened, and there may have even been some easing of traffic congestion. The *San Francisco Chronicle* called it "San Francisco's greatest mystery of 1996." No one was sure where the 80,000 vehicles per day went as rush-hour volumes on the Bay Bridge declined by 10,000 per day. Only some of the usual car commuters were counted as additions to regular public transportation users.

This encouraged many citizens to lobby to get the freeway permanently destroyed. Residents of Hayes Valley, an area of restored Victorians west of Civic Center, were especially enthusiastic about ending commuter traffic spilling off the old Central Freeway that sliced through their neighborhood. Caltrans warned that traffic would gradually increase again. Today, Los Angeles, San Diego, and San Francisco are examples of how "build it and they will come" seems to hold true for freeways and parking garages. Fortunately, it also is true for most forms of alternative and public transportation in California.

Throughout Southern California, 4 percent of all workers used public transportation, 14 percent carpooled, and 77 percent drove alone. Some studies showed average rush-hour speeds dropping below 35 mph in every major California city. Gridlock was showing its ugly face in every city across the state. Room was running out to build more freeways, and taxpayers were revolting against their incredible costs. Consider today's costs of buying land and destroying neighborhoods and businesses to run a new freeway through an urban center. In most urban areas, new freeways have become an unrealistic, if not impossible, option.

Officials and planners are designing solutions they hope will combine to ease these staggering transportation problems into the twenty-first century. They include car-pool lanes, private toll roads, superstreets, rail lines, and an improved bus system, which serves about 85 percent of L.A. County's public transportation users. A study by the Texas Transportation Institute in the late 1990s indicated a dire need for solutions. According to the study, the Los Angeles area ranked number one in the

nation in traffic congestion, the San Francisco area ranked fifth, San Diego ninth, and even San Bernardino-Riverside Counties ranked tenth in the national competition for the most gridlock.

More Cars or Mass Transit?   Even Sacramento and other smaller California cities are being clogged by cars. Is the best solution to build more roads for cars or to build mass transit? As each city responds, there are many lessons to learn from California's past successes and failures. These decisions will have profound effects on the state's urban landscapes, its economies, and the quality of living and working environments.

By the 1990s, dire predictions resulting from research into the state's urban transportation problems were widespread. Publications such as *Work Watch* reported that commuters' average rush-hour speeds on the state's highways had declined to 31 mph. With only traditional transportation improvements, traffic congestion was projected to increase by 360 percent from 1990 to 2010. Average rush-hour speeds on Southern California freeways might drop to 11 mph. Proponents of mass transit claimed that efficient systems could carry as many as seventy times the people as highways, generate only 1 percent of the hydrocarbons, and cost one-tenth as much to build per mile.

Mass Transit in California Cities

The number of bus- and rail-passenger trips had decreased by more than two-thirds from 1950 to 1990. After massive cuts statewide in the 1980s, only 6 percent of Californians used mass transit by 1990. Resulting urban gridlock forced many local and county governments to reevaluate their dilemmas and commit to rail and other mass transit systems.

During the 1990s, Californians showed increasing enthusiasm for railways to improve intercity and other urban mass transit. The state's commuters flocked to existing train routes such as Amtrak's L.A. to San Diego line and Bay Area Rapid Transit (BART). Planners warned that urban Californians will also have to live closer together and closer to work.

Gradually during the 1990s, trolley and intercity passenger trains were returning to the California landscape. In 1990, more than six California cities, including San Francisco, Bakersfield, and L.A., were building new lines or adding to existing ones. New light rail systems were being developed or expanded in San Diego, Sacramento, and Santa Clara County. More Californians were also beginning to use existing systems. BART was handling more than 50 percent of rush-hour traffic into San Francisco from across the bay. With expansion, its ridership was also expected to increase.

The San Diego trolley system ridership increased at an average of more than 12 percent per year from 1983 to 1990 and was more popular than almost anyone predicted. It includes lines from downtown to the Mexican border; the system is planned to be 113 miles long by the twenty-first century. L.A.'s new rail system will be the largest of them all. It is planned to cover about 150 miles and carry more than 500,000 people/day when completed. The success or failure of L.A.'s system will have an impact on plans for future urban rail systems. In the late 1990s, communities were still participating in heated battles to determine who would get the first lines.

Commuter passenger trains are being considered throughout California. Amtrak's San Francisco to San Jose Caltrain was the state's only commuter train in 1990, but that changed with the addition of links from L.A. to its suburbs during the 1990s. Meanwhile, the L.A. to San Diego line was carrying more than 17,000 riders per day.

Proponents of mass transit still face serious obstacles. First, light-rail projects have often been financed by increases in state and local sales taxes. Recent antitax laws requiring a two-thirds majority vote for any tax increase have slowed many public transportation projects. Second, proponents also argue that mass transit is not given a fair chance to compete because the real costs of car travel are subsidized. Consider an example where the cost of fuel may be only $.85 per 8–10 miles. Real costs, including highway maintenance, parking (including space taken from productive urban activities and businesses), street cleaners, and wear and tear on vehicles, are about ten times the fuel costs. This reveals real costs of more than $8 per 8–10 miles! Mass transit proponents argue that once individual drivers must pay the full environmental and economic bill for the costs of urban car trips, they will more readily choose mass transit.

Mass Transit in the Bay Area There are numerous transportation options to or from Market Street in San Francisco. To feel like a tourist, one can take a nostalgic cable car up a steep hill. When this system became obsolete for daily commuters, The City spent a fortune to fix it up and has made many times that fortune by attracting visitors and tourists who want to ride the cable cars. Underscoring differences between the two cities, it was all L.A. could do in the 1990s to recreate the tiny Angel's Flight car up to Bunker Hill—a must stop for L.A. visitors. Yet, Angel's Flight is scarcely an amusing toy model by San Francisco standards.

Commuters in San Francisco can take the electric or gas-powered buses on surface streets, or they can plunge down into MUNI's network of underground street cars, many of which eventually come to the surface in surrounding neighborhoods. There are also buses out of The City, headed to communities to the South, East, and North Bay areas. However, if you travel to a host of communities in the East Bay or toward Daly City, you'll probably want to hop on BART. Map 11.3 shows some major public transportation systems in San Francisco.

BART is an example of short-term, costly investments delivering substantial long-term profits. BART was opened on September 11, 1972, at a cost of $1.6 billion, which was way over budget. It was the first new transit system built in the nation in sixty years, and it was the most highly automated transit system ever built at the time.

The first few years of operational problems and labor disputes were capped with a fire in the Oakland–San Francisco tube in 1979. Opponents found fuel for their ridicule. However, the system's reliability and popularity improved noticeably after these initial setbacks.

Following the Loma Prieta earthquake in October, 1989, the Bay Bridge and other freeways were unusable. However, BART worked just fine and accepted thousands of new commuters. Many stayed with the system. When BART celebrated its twentieth anniversary in 1992, it included 71.5 miles of track and 34 stations. Tracks connect Daly City, Richmond, Concord, and Fremont. Each weekday during the 1990s, 260,000 commuters used it, including nearly half of those travelling

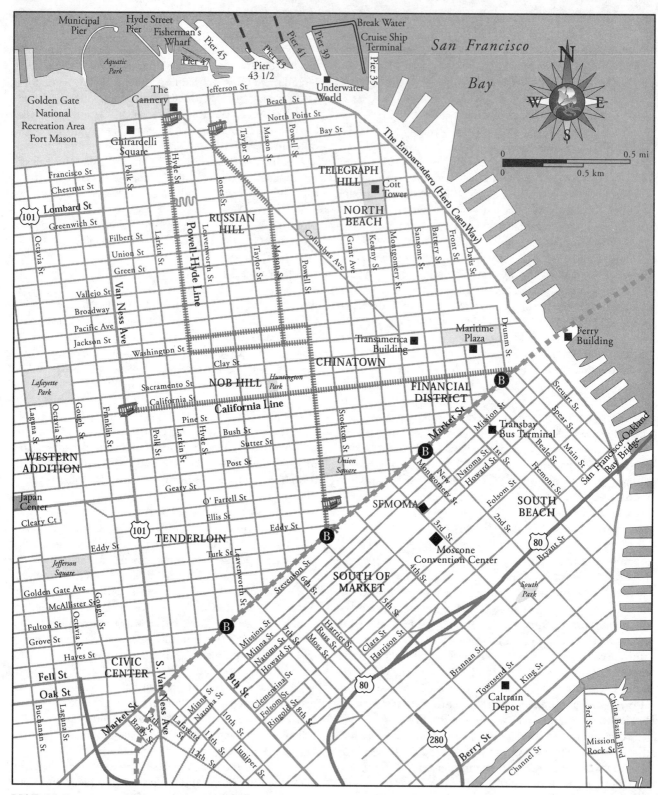

MAP 11.3

Successful public transportation systems are popular among San Francisco Bay residents. Modern BART and nostalgic cable car lines are shown here in downtown. Above and below BART, you will find a variety of opportunities to ride The City's popular MUNI system.

PUBLIC TRANSPORTATION TRANSFORMS
SOUTHERN CALIFORNIA URBAN LANDSCAPES

Transportation planners are now hoping to attract off-hours riders who want to attend special business meetings, shop, and visit museums and theaters either in downtown L.A. or at other stops along the way. The entire Metrolink system is planned to eventually serve seventy stations in L.A., Ventura, San Diego, Orange, Riverside, and San Bernardino Counties. It already includes lines to Long Beach, Santa Clarita, Ventura County, and inland valley locations.

Redevelopment projects are expected to spring up along L.A.'s new transportation corridors, revitalizing local communities and bringing a completely new face to the city. Stations along Metrolink's 404-mile rail network connecting downtown L.A. with those six counties are being planned to include huge parking lots, village greens, and shopping malls. The stations will offer easy commuting connections to local services, housing, and retail centers. Incentives will be offered to businesses and residential developers to locate next to public transport stations and along rail lines instead of along freeways.

Metrolink hopes that at least one complete, liveable community will locate at a station in each of the six counties. Their forty-five stations increased to fifty-seven during the late 1990s alone, as ridership continues ahead of projections. Projects planned by communities near stations include civic centers, day-care centers, theaters and other entertainment attractions, retail centers, and restaurants.

---

between the East Bay and San Francisco. BART had become one of the most successful urban transportation systems in the nation, one that many Bay Area residents claim they could not live without.

A $1 billion repair and modernization job and three new segments were being planned for BART at the end of the twentieth century. One 8.7-mile, $1.2 billion segment was designed to finally connect San Francisco to its airport (ranked as the seventh busiest in the world) by 2001; other extensions will go to the two East Bay communities of Pleasanton and Pittsburg. Bay Area residents were realizing, along with L.A. and other California cities, the costs of past planning mistakes and waiting too long to build convenient transportation systems.

Public Transportation in the Los Angeles Basin Los Angeles has an entirely different public transportation story. Charming Union Station was built in the 1930s over L.A.'s old Chinatown. It quickly became an architectural landmark in the midst of one of the world's most successful urban transportation systems, starring the famous Pacific Electric Trolley System's Red Cars. After the system was dismantled in a chain of events that stir controversy to this day, the stage was set for a transportation nightmare that would strangle L.A. into the twenty-first century.

By the late 1900s, many Angelenos grew to despise the freeways they once loved. Yet, L.A. County's undernourished Metropolitan Transportation Authority (MTA) bus system was carrying only about 350,000 people per day during the 1990s; most of the other 9 million were traveling by car. Residents use ominous terms such as "the traffic monster" to describe rush-hour gridlock. Officials are desperately seeking solutions.

By 1996, the Union Station to Westlake/MacArthur Park subway had been extended another 2.1 miles west along the Wilshire corridor from downtown L.A. to Western, adding three more stops. MTA officials spent $578 million over five years to build the extension, making it the costliest public works project in the western United States. L.A.'s new subway, with a total of eight stops, finally linked Union Station with the bustling Wilshire corridor. With the addition, this "Red Line" now extended nearly 5.5 miles. Its Wilshire and Vermont Stations were the deepest and had the longest escalators of any subway west of the Mississippi.

This entire subway ride takes about thirteen minutes, a fifteen-minute decrease from the traditional bus ride. At $289 million per mile, the L.A. Red Line is one of the most expensive subways in the world. However, it is also the center of the region's sprawling and expanding 404-mile Metrolink train system/rail network that is connecting to it. This includes a connection to the popular L.A.-Long Beach Blue Line.

Original plans were to extend the subway to Hollywood by late 1998, to the San Fernando Valley by 2000, and to the Eastside by 2003. Ironically, some businesses were complaining that construction barriers hurt business in the short term, while other community groups continued competing for the first extensions and rail links to the system. Others argued that the subway was costing too much, draining revenue away from other public transportation options. Most of the conflicts boiled down to the same old dilemmas—inadequate funding and too much competition for too few mass transit projects, all of which were desperately needed.

In the November, 1998, elections, frustrated L.A. taxpayers signed the subway extension death warrant. It ends in North Hollywood. Voters overwhelmingly approved an initiative that prohibited the use of future transportation funds for any subway extensions to new communities in the L.A. area. L.A. was forced to consider other options to solve its transportation nightmares.

Using Zoning and Other Ordinances to Shape California Cities

Here are some examples of ordinances backed by citizens and leaders designed to improve the quality of living and working environments in California cities.

Home-Based Businesses

Many California cities are struggling with what to do about home-based businesses. Advantages of running smaller businesses at home include more time with the family, fewer commuters on the roads, and lower costs of doing business. Due to the high-tech revolution, these businesses are becoming more common. Across California, neighborhood groups are worried about the extent of these businesses and their potential to disrupt community life.

Cities are predictably passing ordinances that allow, but regulate, home-based businesses. Besides assessing certain taxes and fees, regulations may prohibit disruptions in the neighborhood and alterations to buildings. There may be restrictions on the number of client visits, deliveries and pickups, mechanized equipment, visible advertising, light, dust, fumes, noise, hazardous substances, and retail sales. Note the obvious conflict here between individual property rights and residents' rights to determine the nature and quality of their communities.

By the late 1990s, more than three million home-based businesses operated illegally in California. Yet, within L.A. County alone, at least seventy-seven cities had legalized and regulated home-based businesses. Businesses not allowed may include adult entertainment, animal training, automotive repair, ambulance service, funeral homes, garment manufacturing, gun stores, restaurants, retail sales, tow truck services, and various heavy or loud machine services. Opponents of these businesses are afraid of neighborhood nuisances and claim the city can never regulate them properly. Proponents who want to be legal say they cut traffic and smog and allow parents to be with their families. This is a controversy that will probably escalate into the twenty-first century.

Response to Disasters and Natural Hazards

A growing controversy intensified after January, 1997, when a series of storms caused forty-six of California's fifty-eight counties to be declared disaster areas. Here was yet another costly disaster. The $2 billion price tag included 20,000 damaged or destroyed homes. Some state senators declared that it was time for better zoning laws in California that would minimize future damage and cost to taxpayers.

Trains, highways, housing tracts, and office buildings crowd together in once rural Oxnard. Ventura County voters have recently expressed their displeasure with uncontrolled growth.

This was not a controversy about the location of farms, ranches, park lands, and other extensive land uses. Rather, citizens and officials were questioning the practice of building dense, intensively developed housing and industrial projects on lands vulnerable to frequent natural disasters. Critics argued that assisting citizens and businesses in need after an unusual disaster was one thing; repeatedly replacing the homes and businesses of people who persisted in building in harm's way is another. There are many cases when debris from such damaged homes becomes nature's tools to do even more damage to other homes.

There are a host of examples that are costing taxpayers millions in every California urban area. Developments can be found too close to rivers and streams, perched on unstable steep slopes, at the edge of breaking ocean waves, and plopped right in the middle of wild lands that frequently burn.

Lobbyists representing developers and the California Association of Realtors reacted quickly to the mere suggestion of any building restrictions. They stated that they find restrictions on development, rebuilding, and resale "repugnant." These events magnify a clear need for balance between private property interests and the government's ability to act for the general good of public health, safety, welfare, and our pocketbooks.

Examples of Other Urban Zoning and Ordinance Issues

There are a host of other laws that are used by leaders and activists to improve their communities, though not everyone has the same vision of community. One example can be found in a working-class neighborhood in west Santa Ana that has grown from its more rural roots. It took just one neighbor to complain about crowing roosters that had, for decades, cut the silence of the morning air. The City of Santa Ana, due to an ordinance

CEMETERIES IN CALIFORNIA

Besides their obvious historical value, cemeteries play important roles in every California urban landscape. In 1914, San Francisco banned public cemeteries due to the scarcity of land. This is one reason why, just to the south, the city of Colma became known as "home to a thousand live bodies and a million dead ones." With this distinction, it was declared a "necropolis" by some.

Colma actually has about 1,100 residents and fifteen cemeteries, thanks to cemetery-friendly zoning laws. More than 350,000 people are buried in Cypress Lawn Memorial Park alone. However, when the Colma City Council approved a high-volume crematory across the street from the Winston Manor development, and more than three-hundred houses, many citizens protested.

Residents of Winston Manor realized their troubles were compounded because they actually lived on the South San Francisco side of the boundary with Colma. Though South San Francisco urged Colma to relocate the crematory to a more hidden spot, like its other four crematories, there was little they could do within another city's jurisdiction. Residents complained they had moved to the area to be near the peace and quiet offered by surrounding cemeteries, not to breath crematory fumes. However, owners of the crematory and others countered that it would be a state-of-the-art facility, and residents would not even know it was there.

Californians across the state are rediscovering and remodeling their cemeteries. This movement to salvage historic burial grounds includes community clean-up crews, amateur genealogists, and professional preservationists from San Juan Capistrano to Santa Rosa. By the late 1990s, California had fourteen cemeteries on the national Register of Historic Places and had named twenty-eight cemeteries as historic landmarks. They were being recognized as valuable open spaces surrounded by exploding populations and more intensely-used land.

Rose Hills Memorial Park north of Whittier is the largest cemetery in North America. It is famous for its advertisements and more than 7,000 rose bushes. It inters more than 10,000 people per year, mostly locals, and each year it claims to light the tallest Christmas tree overlooking the San Gabriel Valley. It was sold in 1996 for $240 million, the money going to charity.

The antithesis of Rose Hills may be Westwood Memorial Park Cemetery where several wealthy and famous L.A. celebrities and entertainers are buried. Although it is tucked away in an unlikely spot and surrounded by high-rise developments, it remains a tourist stop. Part of Woodlawn Cemetery in Santa Monica is now being transformed to accept up-scale clients for $20,000 per plot instead of the previous highest prices of $7,500. Burial plots are becoming far more expensive within these dense urban landscapes.

As urban cemeteries across California run out of space, many are building huge mausoleums, sometimes several stories high. A traditional cemetery normally holds up to 1,500 graves per acre with ground plaques. A mausoleum can hold from 5,000 to 15,000 crypts per acre. Sunset Mission Mausoleum at Inglewood Park Cemetery is an example. The mausoleum at Resurrection Cemetery in Montebello is another. Until now, mausoleums in the United States were reserved for the wealthy and famous. They have recently become more affordable.

Each modern mausoleum in California must be built under strict earthquake codes and other guidelines, though they are not acceptable to all religions. Orthodox Jews, traditional Muslims, and others usually practice in-ground burial in the dust-to-dust tradition. Buddhist and Hindu cultures use cremation. The profound connections between California's population densities, cultures, economics, and urban landscapes are obvious when we consider where we put our lost loved ones to rest.

---

banning farm animals, was forced to order the roosters' owners to get rid of them. When the owners refused to comply with what they claimed was a ridiculous law that ignored the history of the neighborhood, the media showed up in full force. The city, trying to save face, backed off.

Communities around California are restricting yard sales to keep neighbors from setting up commercial businesses where they might sell new merchandise. Some yard sales are seen as a threat to established businesses that must locate in business districts and pay taxes. Restrictions in L.A. County limit residents to two garage sales each year held from from 7 A.M. to 6 P.M. Artesia and Beverly Hills have even stiffer garage sale restrictions and a $25 permit. Other cities around the state have

smaller fees for permits, but similar restrictions. Though some politicians are sensitive to complaints of commercial activities in residential zones, other inner-city representatives consider such sales as opportunities for low-income residents to make extra cash.

Nearly every major city in California has also struggled with how to regulate and zone for adult book stores and sex shops. During the 1990s, this controversy was played out in Canoga Park with the same issues and intensity typical in numerous other communities. On their old-fashioned shopping street is an adult book store/sex shop that city officials and many residents claim is an attraction for illegal activities, including prostitution, loitering, and lewd conduct. The Canoga Park business (Le Sex Shoppe) on Sherman Way was first ordered to close

LIQUOR STORE DENSITIES

Images of urban blight often include low-income, inner-city neighborhoods flooded with liquor stores. During the 1990s, state law limited Type 20 licenses (for beer and wine only) to one license for every 2,500 people in a community. These were easier to get than Type 21 hard-liquor licenses. The most recent legislative attempts to solve neighborhood problems target the way populations of individual census tracts are counted.

However, there are few patterns and plenty of surprises in liquor licenses per capita across California. Much of the current densities are the result of local histories before state laws were passed. The newest law is also problematic because it counts the entire population, including children, to establish liquor license per person ratios. This could increase liquor licenses in low-income areas with large families. Incredibly, past laws resulted in some parts of South-Central and East L.A. having fewer high-ratio liquor license census tracts than most of L.A. County. In contrast, though industrial/commercial Santa Fe Springs has few residents, many people shop there; consequently, it has one alcohol outlet per 1.5 residents.

It turns out that small cities are more affected by the new law, while the city and county of L.A. are below the liquor-license limit. Napa County, which led the state in the number of new alcohol licenses during much of the 1990s, has surpassed the one license per 2,500 people limit. Consequently, legislation had to be passed to exempt winery tasting rooms. This practice of tacking exemptions onto existing legislation obviously pits antidrunkenness advocates against liquor industry lobbyists. Even oil com-

pany lobbyists stepped in to block efforts to stop gas station mini-markets from selling alcohol. Opponents of liquor sales at gas stations claim it encourages drinking and driving.

Another issue, which is not addressed in the new law, is that liquor licenses in the suburbs are often given to larger supermarkets that sell many kinds of food and other products. In poorer, inner-city neighborhoods, the licenses are usually for smaller liquor stores. Unfortunately, the original law did not allow discrimination based on the type of applicant for a license. Consequently, this also blocks larger supermarkets that sell liquor from locating in neighborhoods that are trying to stop liquor selling. Therefore, the "liquor store on every corner" along South-Central L.A.'s busiest streets continued to be the only option for many residents without major markets nearby.

Further evidence of the complexity of this problem was evident when the state Department of Alcoholic Beverage Control revealed that San Francisco has one of the highest concentrations of liquor stores and establishments per capita. San Francisco has 803 hard-liquor licenses, but should only have 303 under the new state law. Population in The City would have to double before new liquor licenses could be issued. Yet, liquor is not recognized as such a problem there. Many people in this compact city do not have cars, and they cherish their restaurants and corner markets. Consequently, only a limited number of local neighborhood groups, mostly in the Bayview and Mission districts, have tried to limit liquor licenses in San Francisco.

at 10 P.M. rather than 2 A.M. Unsatisfied residents wanted it closed to help create a family neighborhood and shopping district.

The owner of Le Sex Shoppe claimed First Amendment rights. He defended his business as law-abiding and clean and claimed that he is being blamed for all of L.A.'s problems. Nevertheless, surrounding businesses and neighbors continued their efforts to shut it down. Once again, you can see how many of these conflicts involve classic battles between personal property rights and the rights of citizens to determine what kind of community they will live in.

Card clubs have become another source of controversial income for some communities who are concerned about the effects of legalized gambling. In 1996, the Gardena City Council gave major tax breaks to its two card clubs to keep them from going out of business. The city once received 12 percent ($4.5 million) of its general fund from the Normandie Club. It is the largest of the two remaining Gardena card clubs and one of the oldest (more than 50 years old) in Southern California. Gardena

had six card clubs in 1980, but fierce competition between them and from other gaming opportunities in the region drove the other clubs out.

Newer and bigger clubs, such as the Hollywood Park Casino at the racetrack in Inglewood and the Radisson Crystal Park Hotel and Casino in Compton, had more than one-hundred tables each. Each community tries to weigh the negative effects of gambling with the revenue these clubs bring in. Many cities are competing to get these clubs and their revenue so that other fees and overhead are kept down.

Throughout California, male day laborers who wait in groups for contractors to pick them up have been criticized by nearby residents and businesses. Some residents cite problems with drinking, harassing women, trash, and lack of bathroom facilities. Several communities have passed ordinances outlawing solicitation on public streets by day laborers and their employers. To guard worker's rights, a few cities have constructed formal hiring facilities across from home improvement centers and other gathering places.

DRIVE-THROUGH RESTAURANTS

Neighbors throughout California are organizing bans on drive-through restaurants. This is more than just a traffic and noise issue. It continues a trend in California of communities trying to salvage their identities by discouraging chain stores and strip malls. Pedestrian-oriented shopping districts are favored among many residents who are preserving the architecture and personality of their communities. This was the case when the Sierra Madre City Council, like many communities, banned drive-through restaurants in 1996. Much of Sierra Madre's old architecture remains, with only one older drive-through facility for a bank.

Claremont banned new drive-throughs except along the San Bernardino Freeway. West Hollywood was one of the first to ban them after incorporation. Burbank and South Pasadena are experimenting with such bans on new drive-throughs. All of this is seen as a backlash against the corporate sameness invading and disrupting communities across the state.

Critics of the drive-through bans often argue that motorists are already driving along busy travel corridors, and their stopping creates no additional problems. They also argue that the industry and motorists will only take their money to the next city that allows drive-throughs.

In 1996, Malibu responded to claims of day laborer problems, which included laborers gathering on street corners looking for jobs, congregating in front of stores, intimidating customers, and disturbing the peace. A city-sanctioned nonprofit labor exchange was set up in the early 1990s as a solution. However, the city was still troubled by the same problems in 1997. Recent studies in L.A. City and Glendale have shown that 75 percent or more of these workers are legal residents with work papers. Many of them were laid off construction jobs and speak fluent English.

Preservationists and community activists across the state are also fighting to save historical architecture and enhance the unique personalities of their communities. These issues are at the heart of the classic battle between Caltrans (in a recent coalition with Alhambra residents) and preservation officials over the proposed 6.2-mile extension of the Long Beach Freeway (710). It will cut through El Sereno, South Pasadena, and Pasadena, including historic districts and homes in El Sereno and South Pasadena. Since these preservationists and others concerned about the new freeway cutting especially through South Pasadena and other historic neighborhoods have blocked it, traffic spills out on Valley Boulevard in Alhambra.

Enter Alhambra residents. By early October, 1996, Alhambra filed suit with the California Department of Transportation to force them to complete that 6.2-mile Long Beach Freeway extension. They estimate that 100,000 cars congest Alhambra streets each day, pouring out millions of tons of pollutants. Consequently, their streets require $380,000 in annual repairs due to the extra traffic pouring off the dead-end freeway. (Alhambra also complained that the Alameda corridor project would bring even more traffic into their communities and asked for further study before construction on that project begins.)

It has become clear that in our crowded urban environments, each community's zoning, preservation, and development policies create ripple effects felt for years far beyond their legal boundaries. You can often see the results of these policies and laws as you compare and contrast California's urban landscapes.

Short-Term Remedies for Long-Term Urban Problems: Examples

There are lessons to be learned from communities who became so desperate and vulnerable in the early 1990s recession. Some may have bought short-term gains by selling away their hopes for long-term recovery and stability. Construction in California fell in the early 1990s to one-quarter of 1980s levels. Consequently, many cities made it easier for developers to build, ignoring the long-term impacts of unplanned growth. In the 1980s, Modesto's growth was twice the state average, and it was one of the first California cities to impose a fee system to make developers pay the cost of funding the roads, fire stations, parks, and other infrastructure required to support developments.

By 1992, in an attempt to cope with a median income at 85 percent of the state average, unemployment rates at 18 percent and almost zero growth, Modesto leaders cut their fee systems by more than 30 percent. Civic leaders then hoped to impose a half-cent sales tax or get federal transportation funds to make up for some of the cuts in services, such as traffic signal projects. Slow growth advocates' concerns about residents bearing the tax burden were summed up by one citizen who told the *Los Angeles Times*, "We can't subsidize growth. We are getting stiffed. We need more developer fees, not less. Why should it hit our pocketbooks?"

In 1992, Moreno Valley officials were giving tours and lunches, sending out coupons to developers and promising a 15 percent reduction in fees for new businesses that would generate fifty or more jobs and a 5 percent reduction for those who would generate twenty-five jobs within two years. Site inspectors were available around the clock. As a city councilman noted, they were laying out the city's carpets and opening doors. Moreno Valley's cash reserve dropped from $16 million in 1989 to just $2 million in 1993. They were forced to lay off almost half the eighty-person Planning and Building Department staff, but there was concern that more cuts might delay permits and inspections, driving developers away.

The problem was that Moreno Valley had earlier failed to balance its housing growth with job-creating and tax-paying industries. Citizens were suffering not only from their long commutes, but from the lack of infrastructure and services.

Burbank once depended on aerospace and entertainment for a strong economic base. In the midst of the early 1990s recession, city officials sold a city-owned parcel for a $2.3 million loss to a software company after Lockheed Corporation moved out. Burbank also gave up about $1.2 million in property tax revenue to keep IBM subsidiary Cadam, Inc. Officials hoped it would bring 250 jobs to Burbank. They also softened a 1990 law controlling residential development. In an interview with the *Los Angeles Times*, former City Council member Mary Lou Howard said, "Developers should pay their own way and it should not be up to the community members to pay for new development. In the long run, the taxpayers will be picking up the tab. I don't think that's appropriate."

These examples underscore the balance which must be achieved between short-term and long-term approaches in urban planning. Certain policies may bring jobs and income to make leaders and politicians look good in the short-run but will taxpayers and services suffer in the long-term? How do we distinguish between good and bad development and growth? How can communities from Eureka and Redding to San Diego and Indio move toward a more balanced approach when making these planning decisions? These issues are debated in cities across California.

Urban Planning in Modern California

Volumes have been written about California's cities and efforts to make them more efficient and liveable. The state's urban landscapes are considered in every reputable modern treatise on urban geography. The first part of this chapter summarized the evolution of these cities and some of the issues and problems that have developed.

It is now time to look into the future. It would be impossible to address all the myriad planning issues and decisions that are launching California's urban landscapes into the 21st century; we will only have room for a few of them here. Because we have already considered the nature of California suburbs, we will now focus more on planning within city centers.

At least two major trends were transforming California's big cities during the 1990s. First, downtowns in larger cities that were reserved for traditional office ac-

Art, architecture, and open space combine to create a pleasant working environment in downtown Los Angeles.

tivities and business services into the 1980s were being invaded by and planned as entertainment and cultural attractions during the 1990s. From sports arenas to music centers, nearly every major California city was attempting to remake itself in grand fashion. Many of these cities were competing with one another to both recover financial resources that had flowed out into the suburbs for decades and to recover from the budget crises caused by tax cuts and the recession into the early 1990s.

A second major trend involved the evaporation of public funds that once drove **Community Redevelopment Agencies (CRAs)** to boldly rebuild and improve our cities. Budget crises and the real estate slump cut the public funding that once allowed officials to section off blighted areas of cities so that developers could invest and remake them. Today, you will find modern office towers and other developments in every California city that erupted from these earlier CRA efforts.

From CRAs to BIDs

Bunker Hill in downtown L.A. is one of the best examples of CRA developments in the state. The L.A. Community Redevelopment Agency started with the renovation of Bunker Hill in the 1960s. Once the old Victorians on the hill were demolished, sleek, towering steel and glass skyscrapers sprouted in their places. The Los Angeles CRA has since spent more millions on such redevelopment projects as the Central Library, Convention Center, Skid Row, Historic Core, South Park, Little Tokyo, and 7th Street Marketplace garage.

More recently, the L.A. CRA played a role in placing the city's modern cathedral. Location of the new cathedral is on a 5.8-acre property bounded by the Hollywood Freeway, Grand Avenue, Temple Street and Hill Street. The hilly site was picked because of great visibility. It will include a 120-foot-high bell tower, giant crucifix, seating for at least 2,600, and Latino-style courtyards, plazas, and colonnades. L.A.'s CRA bought the property from the county for $10.85 million and immediately sold it to the archdiocese for the same price.

However, due to funding problems, CRAs (though still important) no longer represent such reliable redevelopment tools. This resulted in minimal changes to California's downtown skylines during the first half of the 1990s.

When CRAs are not practical, **Business Investment Districts (BIDs)** have recently emerged in their places. In this new scheme to improve and fortify our crown jewels, local merchants and businesses agree to pay special taxes or fees that will remain in the community to fuel downtown and main street face-lifts and redevelopments. Property owners agree to these self-assessed surcharges to improve a district with beautification and activities that focus more attention on their area. Successful BIDs improve retail sales and increase tax revenues for cities, which then spend money to improve infrastructures. The hope is that these concerted efforts will bring people and their business back to revive the urban core.

Governments and Businesses Combine to Rebuild Urban Centers

BIDs started in the 1960s when local merchants pooled additional funds to finance parking lots. By the 1990s, merchants were using BIDs to create destination shopping districts, especially where city governments were struggling. The BIDs are organized and renewed by property owners who cannot conveniently pack up and leave when a local economy is struggling.

Focus on Southern California Urban Centers Santa Monica's Third Street Promenade's success led to a remodeled Palisades Park and the Santa Monica Pier upgrade. Incoming high-end stores have pushed out community-oriented businesses, which the city is hoping will locate nearby to enhance adjoining streets downtown. Santa Monica continues these improvements that have grown to historical proportions in one of America's most famous and successful small cities.

Santa Monica also was one of the first cities to take a chance with outdoor malls. They proved, along with San Diego's Horton Plaza and Gaslamp Quarter, that open-air shopping and entertainment districts in California could not only be successful, but could outcompete and outclass any generic indoor mall. These experiences show there is a dramatic snowball effect that can revitalize downtowns. Old Pasadena's BID has had similar successes. Old Town earns the city of Pasadena nearly $1.5 million per year in sales tax.

Communities throughout the L.A. area, such as Eagle Rock and Westwood, are planning to draw the overflow crowds from these amazing urban success stories. Now, BIDs are springing up all over California where merchants are creating downtowns with personalities to replace drab, generic suburban-style malls. These old town centers are being redeveloped and promoted as pedestrian-friendly places to shop and live. They are designed to replace "mall fatigue." Retailers are also returning to downtowns with urban entertainment center themes. An excellent modern example of themed retailing is The Block in the city of Orange. There, you will find more than 800,000 square feet of shops, restaurants, theaters, and clubs in a comfortable fantasy land setting completed at the end of the century.

On the smaller scale, Monrovia, Covina, and other cities are reestablishing a sense of place and community, or civic intimacy. This reverses the trends since the 1960s when people and shopping centers shifted out along new freeways and housing projects, devastating main streets across California.

Azusa is now working to revitalize its downtown by narrowing its Azusa Avenue, slowing traffic, and replacing or fixing up the old buildings. The entire project should cost $8–10 million into the twenty-first century. Other cities are also revitalizing their downtowns with beautification and renovation efforts and movie theaters. Proponents of movie theaters cite that they bring in the crowds. Opponents sometimes cite overcrowding, traffic, and unruly young people. Others emphasize the need to get people to live downtown and de-emphasize the "theme park" approach. Similar debates continue in cities throughout California.

Government and private interests and revenue are combining to rebuild our state's urban centers with these new projects. In Southern California alone, more than $700 million was made available in grants and loans from a combination of U.S. HUD economic development grants, loan guarantees, and lending commitments from commercial banks for commercial business loans and technical support. These resources target the area's most impoverished neighborhoods within designated "**empowerment zones**," areas where loans have traditionally been difficult or impossible to get. A total of nearly $1 billion is expected to be made available in the area between 1996 and 2006.

The first loan by this L.A. Community Development Bank was to a 150-employee garment manufacturing firm in South-Central L.A. The clothing manufacturer has been in operation since 1954 and needed the loan to continue. It will expand operations and job opportunities with the loan.

This support is being felt in communities outside L.A. city. Maywood is the most densely populated city in California, with 30,000 residents on only 1.1 square miles. It was using federal loans targeted for local businesses and housing and recreation to build better recreational facilities, especially for kids. It received other federal loans for redeveloping commercial projects.

Partnerships Rebuild Cities Throughout California In 1996, the James Irvine Foundation and Trust for Public Lands created the California Center for Land Recycling to

OXNARD REDEVELOPS

For decades, merchants moved their businesses out of downtown Oxnard. Like other CBDs, you can see struggling retailers and abandoned storefronts as Oxnard competes with indoor malls and retail strip centers. About 450 downtown businesses include pawnshops, discount stores, and one-room eateries. At the center of town is Plaza Park, where homeless gather. Until the 1960s, it was a thriving CBD with upscale clothing stores. Then, the city began a program to promote business outside of downtown, and to lure giant tax-generating businesses along the Ventura Freeway. The Esplanade Mall opened on the outskirts of Oxnard.

Small downtown merchants suffered. After years of panels, committees, and studies, a master plan in 1993 fo-

cused on a 50-square-block area to attract millions of dollars of private investment back to the CBD during the next two decades. During the previous seven years, $25 million in redevelopment money was poured in to improve downtown Oxnard. Ten million dollars of that went to the Heritage Square project, where turn-of-the-century farmhouses have been redesigned to accommodate an assortment of businesses from lawyers to insurance agents and hair stylists. The city hopes this project, opened in 1991, will be the catalyst for future redevelopment into the twenty-first century.

locate "**brownfields**." These are abandoned and sometimes polluted vacant urban properties that can be targeted for commercial use, light industry, housing, parks, open space and wildlife habitat. Private investors will then be found to develop the land.

The Irvine Foundation, based in L.A. and San Francisco, contributed $2 million to start the project. It will locate six to ten redevelopment projects across the state within two years, focusing on lots in places like South-Central L.A. Then, it is hoped that banks and other financial institutions, many of whom are stuck with such properties after defaults, will invest in developing inner-city brownfields.

The emphasis of this latest discussion was on Southern California to illustrate the profound regional connections which must be considered by urban planners. Remember that similar developments are sweeping across the landscapes of cities throughout northern and central California. We will consider a few examples from these urban hot spots later. First, we take a brief look at urban sports arenas and then the future of planning in California.

Sports Arenas and Entertainment Centers

Sports arenas and stadiums are some of the most visible landmarks in any California city. They, and the home-town sports teams that use them help establish a sense of pride and identity; they can serve as public meeting places that help bind a city. Modest, more intimate minor-league baseball stadiums popped up in several smaller California cities through the 1990s. They often become the summer's cultural focal points and meeting places for these communities. In California's larger cities, giant arenas and stadiums have been replaced or remodeled in costly, and often controversial, attempts to re-

make downtown landscapes. There are examples in every California city.

Arenas in the Bay Area During the late 1990s, about $1.1 billion in renovation and construction was planned for sports facilities in the Bay Area. San Franciscans, in 1997, approved a plan to convert 3Com (once known as Candlestick Park) into a giant $525 million stadium-retail mall complex. Proponents cited the advantages of no cost to taxpayers because sales taxes should pay the interest on the bonds, and a boost to the economy of nearby Bayview Hunter's Point. Baseball's San Francisco Giants will soon move to their new, privately financed, more intimate Pacific Bell Park in China Basin, closer to downtown.

Across the Bay, Oakland had lured the National Football League's Raiders back with a $64 million deal to restore the Oakland Coliseum in the 1990s. Oakland suffered $30 million in renovation overrun costs and was spending millions per year in unexpected expenses, all for a transient team that had once, years before, abandoned them for Los Angeles.

Oakland's National Basketball Association's Golden State Warriors were also pushing for the costly renovation of their aging adjacent Oakland Arena. Understandably, these investments were being criticized by activists concerned that the money could go to schools and infrastructure improvements more vital to the city. To the south, San Jose's $162 million arena was already home to the National Hockey League's Sharks.

New Sports Facilities in Southern California Cities In San Diego, Jack Murphy Stadium's facelift was completed under controversy in 1997 to become Qualcomm Stadium amid rumors that Los Angeles might steal the city's football pride. Baseball's Padres and the NFL's

COMMUNITIES SEEK THE RIGHT IMAGE

URBAN SIGNS AND SLOGANS

What is the most visible evidence of the nature of a California city and its residents? Signboards or the lack of them are clues about the constituents within a community or neighborhood; they provide a general idea of city spatialization. Some California communities ban or regulate all billboards to keep their neighborhoods from appearing tacky or too commercial. Others have celebrated their flashy signs. There are plenty of examples, but a drive along Sunset Boulevard in West Hollywood or a stroll along CityWalk certainly reveals something about Southern Californians' mind-set and their perceived fascination with cutting-edge popular culture. You can see evidence of local cultures in smaller signs and graffiti.

Many California cities develop slogans or nicknames to reflect the desires of residents and civic leaders in a community. These efforts are also good for tourism. They may be historical, funny, or wishful thinking.

Bellflower changed its city slogan from "21 Churches and No Jails" to "The Friendly City." By the mid-1950s, it had fifty-one churches, and the city claims to have more churches per capita than any other U.S. city. This is one signal of a culturally and religiously diverse population. Here are some recent, more interesting slogans for various California cities. Do you think they fit?:

Bakersfield: "Nashville of the West"

Baldwin Park: was "City in Motion," but image consultants helped change it to "A New Perspective"

Calipatria (− 184′): "Lowest Down City in the Western Hemisphere"

Claremont: "A Bit of New England With a Sombrero on It"

Laguna Beach: "Riviera of the West Coast"

Los Angeles: "City of Angels"

Oceanside: was "Tan Your Hide in Oceanside," but changed to "Take Pride in Oceanside"

Oxnard: was "Kissed by the Sun, Hugged by the Sea," but now "Upcoast Oxnard, Where Life Takes on New Meaning"

San Pablo: "Little City With the Big Inferior Complex"

Santa Barbara: "Riviera of the Pacific"

Torrance: "Halfway to Everywhere"

Sources: Los Angeles Times, Internet, and local chambers of commerce.

WORKING ON ORANGE COUNTY'S IMAGE

On January 14, 1997, the Orange County Tourism Council launched a plan to organize its competing tourist businesses in a cooperative effort to bring in more tourist dollars. This is the result of the 1994 county-sponsored "tourism summit" attended by local hotel, attraction, and visitor bureau leaders. The idea was to expand the collective efforts and cooperation exemplified by the Anaheim/Orange County Visitor and Convention Bureau.

The county, attempting to show differences from L.A., announced its new slogan—"Orange County, the Perfect California." The logo included a palm tree, ocean wave and the sun. The Orange County Tourism Council also proposed that tourist businesses pool resources to improve services such as transportation and signs for visitors. There was little agreement on how to fund these improvements, though tourism is a $5.5 billion industry in Orange County.

Chargers stayed, keeping a spotlight on inland Mission Valley. San Diego had already invested in their new Convention Center and a host of other urban attractions. A smaller, more intimate baseball stadium was also in the works.

In Orange County, Anaheim finished a $100 million attempt to improve and scale down their Anaheim Angels baseball stadium. Meanwhile, Anaheim's National Hockey League Mighty Ducks were playing in the $120 million Arrowhead Pond. Anaheim sent clear signals it would not willingly yield any more spotlight to southern Orange County cultural centers growing around South Coast Plaza, Costa Mesa, Irvine, and Newport Beach. Simultaneously, the competing Irvine Company advertised their prime location with six movie theater centers, five performance theaters, and 460 area restaurants. All were once part of Irvine Ranch landscapes, including Tustin Ranch and Newport Beach and Coast.

Perhaps the grandest urban plans at the end of the 1990s involved the new arena, known as the Staples Center, in downtown Los Angeles. This $250 million sports arena is anchored adjacent to the struggling Convention Center to revitalize and refocus attention on the entire area. In a blow to Inglewood, it is the new home for the NBA's Lakers (who moved from the aging Forum) and hockey's L.A. Kings. Meanwhile, renovations of L.A.'s Coliseum (near USC) were designed to bring professional football back to L.A. and renew the entire Figueroa Corridor. The remaking of L.A.'s Civic Center with convenient connections to the Music Center, Disney Concert Hall, and other cultural attractions would confirm L.A.'s new direction. Like many California cities, a renewed emphasis on culture and entertainment was considered key to L.A.'s successful urban future.

You can see that nearly every major California city was looking to sports, music, entertainment, and other cultural centers to redefine itself and renew its landscapes. This involves considerable competition between cities and costly investments by local businesses and governments.

Even in Fresno, a familiar controversy developed when proponents of a new city baseball stadium clashed with those who claimed the stadium would cost taxpayers in the long run. Meanwhile, Fresno's minor league team considered moving to other cities where there might be greater support into the twenty-first century. Will these projects settle in to successfully restructure and stabilize California's urban landscapes? Or do they represent new trends that will force every California city to repeatedly rethink and rebuild its downtown with costly improvements?

High-Tech Urban Planning

By the mid-1990s, publications such as *Planning and Computer World* were reporting on new technologies being used by modern urban planners. The California Urban Features Model (CUF) is a computer modeling tool developed by UC Berkeley's Institute of Urban and Regional Development to show planners how proposed policies will affect development. It uses a geographic information system that performs spatial analysis and data integration, much more than simply mapping displays.

Professors and students at UCLA's Graduate School of Architecture and Urban Planning developed the Urban Simulation Environment. It is a new urban planning and simulation system designed to allow planners and citizens to review planned developments in a virtual reality environment. The simulator produces a three-dimensional, photo-realistic image of an area as it would look after planned changes to landscapes are complete. The system was developed by Silicon Graphics Inc. to store sonic and visual data from text, geographic information systems, videotaped aerial and ground footage and other sources. This video format is more user-friendly for citizens than blueprints and charts.

◆ LOOKING FOR INTERESTING TRENDS AND URBAN PLANNING

Starting With the Los Angeles Area

In the movie *Escape From L.A.*, released during the summer of 1996, a giant earthquake separated L.A. from the mainland. The city became a deportation camp for criminals. Here's what the movie's director, John Carpenter, said about today's L.A. in an interview with Steven Smith of the *Los Angeles Times*: "It's the cutting edge of America. We're what America is going to be like. We're multicultural, we try our best to get along the best we can, and we're poised over the edge of the apocalypse."

Channeling Growth into Centers

On July 17, 1996, the L.A. City Council voted nine to four to adopt a long-term plan to absorb 820,000 more people into the city by 2010. The plan anticipated that L.A.'s population will reach 4.3 million, an inevitable increase resulting from birth and immigration rates in certain pockets of the city.

Proponents support more density around the following growth areas at three different levels:

◆ larger, more intensive high-rise developments in regional centers such as downtown, Hollywood, Century City, and Warner Center

◆ mid-size community developments and centers as focal points with three- to eight-story buildings for offices, hotels, and theaters, in places like Los Feliz and Studio City

◆ smaller business districts around transit stops created by the Red Line and Metrolink

The plan includes encouraging pedestrian-friendly communities and centers linked by modern mass transit systems, while protecting residential neighborhoods from overbuilding. Can you visualize such future urban landscapes?

Critics include many neighborhood organizations trying to slow or stop growth who feel that such growth is ruining their communities. They do not want high-density, multi-family condos and apartment buildings in their neighborhoods. Proponents argue that the growth expected by the Southern California Association of Governments (SCAG) will not be stopped, but should be planned for and the centers of growth should be anticipated.

This new 1996 plan is the first revision since 1974. It sets guidelines for land use, development permits, and zoning for the future in L.A. The plan reemphasizes the original "center concepts" that did not work in the past because there were no restrictions on growth in pockets, but there was plenty of growth without planning. Individual neighborhoods as centers of businesses and housing will now be connected by transit lines.

Some critics not only argue against growth concentrated in their neighborhoods, but also argue that there is inadequate planning for an infrastructure (sewers, parks, schools, etc.) that will serve the crowds and congestion. An additional 320,000 people will flood the communities of Boyle Heights, Silver Lake, Echo Park, South-Central L.A., Hollywood, and Wilshire, representing 40 percent of the city's entire growth by 2010. Another 310,000 are expected to crowd the San Fernando Valley to 1.5 million people by 2010. About 75 percent of the growth and new developments are expected on 5 percent of L.A. land, in major centers and along thoroughfares. Century City on the West Side and Warner Center on the west end of the San Fernando Valley are examples of such centers that have met expectations. Many other centers were not successful because of too much scattering and unplanned growth.

Westwood Westwood Village has already experienced the results of growth as a regional center. Westwood village grew slowly after UCLA opened in 1929, but it became a regional entertainment attraction during the 1960s to 1970s. Before the 1980s, Westwood Village was famous for its pedestrian-friendly environment, restaurants, movie theaters, and UCLA campus. By the late 1980s, Westwood became too popular and had problems with unruly crowds of young people, crime, and even riots on some weekend nights. Merchants complained as streets had to be blocked off.

By the 1990s, Century City, Westside Pavilion, Universal City Walk, Santa Monica's Third Street Promenade, and Old Pasadena had stolen the spotlight. Rents remained high in Westwood through the recession, although its flawed image drove many businesses out. Surrounded by UCLA, the sleek skyscrapers and snarled traffic along Wilshire, and the wealth of Brentwood and Bel-Air, Westwood still stands out. Today, Westwood merchants and L.A. City are working together to restore a family-friendly atmosphere.

The effort includes a BID supervised by the Westwood Village Community Alliance, which is planning for better police services, more convenient parking, new landscaping, and expanded theaters. They are trying to create an atmosphere that will draw the older, wealthier crowd back. However, the planned new theaters, businesses, and housing are feared by some who see new traffic and crowd problems. There will be more debate about this redevelopment. Will it attract more problems or the "desired" crowd?

The heart of the controversy involves a proposed $100 million, sixteen-screen movie and retail complex with dozens of shops and restaurants called the Village Center Westwood. Though the plan is to draw back revenue lost to Third Street Promenade and Century City, some neighbors are concerned. They argue that the wrong crowd may return and that the plan is too big to conform to the Westwood Village Specific Plan adopted by the city in 1989. Neighbors are also concerned about the more than 10,000 car trips it will generate per day and the additional 4,700 movie theater seats that will give Westwood more than 10,000 total seats. Merchants want the foot traffic into their shops; neighbors resent the large nighttime crowds.

Playa Vista Who wins the award for the single largest planned development in Los Angeles? During the 1990s, it was Maguire Thomas Partners' Playa Vista Project. Original plans included a residential, office, hotel, retail, and marina community, 28,635 residents, and work places for 20,000 in the open space next to Marina del Rey. By the mid-1990s, DreamWorks SKG had joined the project with plans to build the first major L.A. studio in sixty years. They planned 3.2 million feet of studio and entertainment center facilities. It is to be a model for future building in the area, and it has included an impressive public relations campaign.

However, some community organizations questioned the accuracy of the $4 million environmental impact statement. They cited the development's impact on air quality, traffic, open space, views, and runoff. They also questioned its effects on what is left of the Ballona Wetlands, the largest remaining coastal wetland in L.A. County. Some complained about the poor balance between high-cost housing and low-wage jobs that would cause frequent commuter trips. This is already an area with traffic gridlock during rush hour, critics argued.

Long Beach In recent years, Long Beach has exploited its location between Los Angeles and Orange County, luring industries and employees from both areas. The Port of Long Beach, already the nation's busiest, continues to expand. Defense-related jobs lost during the recession have been replaced within a more diverse economy by retail, trade, tourism, and technology industries. Regional connections and its advantageous situation are being cleverly used to fuel improvements in specific city landscapes. Long Beach is boldly redeveloping its downtown and waterfront. Its new Aquarium of the Pacific, opened in the summer of 1998, is the linchpin of these plans. City officials hope to refocus the spotlight on this vital part of a city that was overlooked for too many years.

A Sense of Community

We began this section on modern urban trends and planning by using the L.A. area as an example of how new growth will be channeled to create public meeting places and other local focal points. It may be surprising to some to find that even L.A. has its smaller neighborhood centers. Locals may identify with these centers, which are more important to them than the larger city. District signs represent efforts by locals to set themselves apart from the larger L.A. and organize distinct neighborhoods, such as Carthay Circle, Rancho Park, and Eagle Rock.

Perhaps the most extreme example of this behavior was exhibited by residents of the San Fernando Valley in the late 1990s, when a powerful group of citizens and business leaders mounted an aggressive drive to secede from L.A. City. As their efforts gathered more steam toward the twenty-first century, they attracted the attention of scholars such as Mark Purcell at UCLA. He recognized this exceptional example of "metropolitan political fragmentation" and the politics of urban growth. He studied the curious coalition that bound traditionally antigrowth homeowner associations in the southern valley with the traditional progrowth business community, including local chambers of commerce, across the valley.

Valley VOTE (Valley Voters Organized Toward Empowerment) members claimed they were not receiving their "fair share" because they were not getting back in services from the city what they paid in taxes. They also argued for more local autonomy in land use decisions. They complained that their demands fell upon deaf ears at L.A. City Hall and into a sea of red tape and bureaucracy. They noted that more than seven major U.S. cities combined could fit within the City of L.A.'s contorted boundaries, but they neglected to emphasize that citizens in each of those smaller cities might have problems similar to theirs.

Opponents to valley secession included L.A.'s traditional growth machine, such as Bunker Hill businesses, city government and the *Los Angeles Times*. Lower-income groups also feared what they saw as another attempt to separate L.A.'s wealthier valley populations from the inner-city poor. (Median incomes and home values in the San Fernando Valley are substantially higher than the rest of L.A.) Even if successful, efforts to make the San Fernando Valley its own city will take many years and millions of dollars. It may be more interesting to watch how such an unlikely valley coalition will manage their new city after splitting from L.A. No doubt, communities within L.A. and other major California cities will be watching closely.

Other cities have incorporated within L.A. County in order to gain control of their local landscapes. Orange County completely broke away from L.A. County in 1889. Palos Verdes Estates incorporated in 1939 to gain control from L.A. County government. Some studies show that this is typical of people and cities around the world. Generally, people become less interested in events more than two to six blocks from their homes. There are plenty of examples beyond L.A. in every California city.

Before this discussion of California's urban future ends, we must look into the future of other California cities. Local developments have created other urban centers, such as at 3rd and Mission in San Francisco and San Diego's Gaslamp Quarter.

San Francisco Bay Area

It could be said that San Francisco was not herself during the 1980s. First there was the slump that started with AIDS, then the 1989 Loma Prieta earthquake, and the

Crunched on steep hills, the steel and concrete towers of downtown San Francisco create an impressive urban landscape from almost every vantage point.

recession that slowed The City into the early 1990s. San Francisco has since emerged with more vitality and confidence than ever and it is getting plenty of attention from media inside and outside of California. Though up to 6,000 homeless and a struggling school system are lingering signs of past struggles, the recession ended earlier in The City than in most of the state. To the south, the Silicon Valley also flourished through the 1990s as confidence quickly returned to the entire area.

Officials of the same corporations who left during the 1980s were returning in the 1990s. They are eager to share San Francisco's compact downtown where so many banks, law firms, port facilities, a stock exchange, government offices, insurance companies, delivery and other services, and cultural attractions are easily accessible. This is where businesses have congregated for convenience to get things done.

The Yerba Buena Gardens redevelopment project is one of the best examples of The City's revitalization. This nineteen-block project is South of Market, centered around 3rd and Mission. It includes a new Museum of Modern Art and the Center for the Arts, a luxury hotel, and new apartments. Anyone familiar with that old, decaying San Francisco landscape known as South of Market could hardly believe what has happened here.

Dozens of cutting-edge software companies have also moved in to this area now known as "multimedia gulch." Thanks to these developments, some are calling San Francisco the multimedia capital of the world. The city-

CAN A CITY BE TOO SUCCESSFUL?

All of this success and attention has created some problems in the Bay Area. What precious few living spaces are available reflect the high cost of housing. This is keeping more than low-income groups from settling. If you want to rent a place in San Francisco, you have to get on a long list of hopeful applicants who are willing to pay exorbitantly high moving-in costs and give up their garages. (Living with a car and without a garage in The City can be a parking nightmare without rival.)

Housing opportunities are not any better in the booming Silicon Valley. Its successful high-tech economy has produced California's hottest housing market. As noted in the last chapter, buyers are lining up to compete for new housing like they did in southern California during the 1980s. With their bounties, software engineers, managers, and entrepreneurs are bidding on overpriced homes. More and more secretaries, clerks, and lower-income workers are being forced farther away as apartment vacancies drop below 1 percent. All of this has caused surges to ripple through real estate, construction, furniture, and interior design firms, as Silicon Valley landscapes are transformed. The pace of change is remarkable in the Bay Area.

Back in The City, there is another toll to pay for this turmoil. Perhaps no other landmark better represents the history, beauty, and endurance of San Francisco than the Golden Gate Bridge, The City's number one tourist attraction. It stretches 6,450 feet across the water. Its 3-foot-thick cables, if unravelled, could stretch around the equator three times.

This great bridge also represents the stresses and troubles people endure when they live life on the edge. The east side of the bridge was opened to pedestrians in 1937; the first suicide was less than 3 months later. No fences or other barriers have been built because wind resistance already causes swaying up to twenty-seven feet, and fences would destroy the view.

Today, because an average of one person a month jumps off the Golden Gate Bridge, thirteen emergency phones on the bridge are directly linked to suicide hotlines. Official suicides off the bridge totalled more than 1,000 by 1995. Some believe the actual number should be at least doubled because many bodies are never found. An average of two people per week are dissuaded from jumping.

---

scape around the cyberspace magazine *Wired* was transformed within three years. Restaurants and business activities have created an almost campus-like environment.

Revitalizing the civic center is the new high-tech library; it has its critics, but is attracting big crowds. (The old library will be an Asian Art Museum.) City Hall has also been remodeled in such grand style that it attracts sightseers. The City's museum of European and classical art—the California Palace of the Legion of Honor— has been expanded and remodeled and has doubled the number of visitors.

Additionally, citizens passed a bond measure in 1995 to build a new 42,000-seat, $265 million baseball stadium in China Basin on the bay. Planners hope to open the compact, more intimate city stadium by the year 2000. In 1997, city leaders encouraged citizens to support the $525 million renovation of 3Com Park, once known as Candlestick Park. This is actually a massive stadium-retail mall complex designed to generate jobs and sales taxes. It is planned as an employment-maker for nearby Bayview Hunter's Point.

After the 1989 quake damaged the Embarcadero Freeway, it was torn down and replaced by an open atmosphere looking across the bay with walkways and restaurants. The multi-million dollar Embarcadero project is almost complete and very successful. At the tip of the peninsula, the 1,480-acre Presidio was once an Army headquarters, but its closing has allowed it to become part of the national park; plans for recreation, open space, education centers, a digital-arts complex, housing, and museums abound.

A Bright Future for The City

San Francisco's culture and atmosphere are attracting young, highly educated and skilled professionals from around the region and the world. Many Silicon Valley professionals are now moving into San Francisco and commuting to the San Jose area so that they can share in the night life and culture of The City.

Since the mid-1990s, the mayor and other city officials have encouraged such organizations as the San Francisco Partnership to attract new businesses and corporations into the city. This atmosphere of working together is paying off. San Francisco's workforce was expanding by more than 10,000 per year during the mid-1990s.

Records are also being set for tourism; more than 16 million people per year are visiting The City. Hotels average at least 75 percent occupancy rates, and the expanded George Moscone Center is booked 15 years into the future. City officials, business leaders, and citizens agree that this is another memorable turning point in the history of San Francisco.

PLANNING FOR GROWTH IN SMALLER CITIES

More than 200 miles northeast and over two major mountain ranges from the central coast is the very different Mammoth Lakes ski resort facing very similar issues. The Shady Rest tract was about 25 acres of forest and grass in the middle of Mammoth Lakes Village, which is also beginning to look more like a city. This green space was used by residents for walking, bicycling, and picnicking. In 1996, the majority of the Town Council accepted an agreement between a Mammoth Lakes developer and the National Forest Service that would allow the developer to swap his more environmentally sensitive private land in the National Forest for this Shady Rest tract. He planned 52 houses and 120 apartments, all badly needed affordable housing units for entry-level families and individuals.

Only seven acres will be left for a park. Members of the Heart of Mammoth preservation group and other slow and no-grow proponents were fighting it, saying it is the last major natural space within the community. The developer and his backers claim Mammoth is already surrounded by open space and does not need it in the middle of town.

By 1999, Mammoth Lakes had a good start on expansions and developments worth one billion dollars. They included expensive townhouses, condominium complexes, and a golf course. Mammoth was growing into one of the great destination resorts on the planet, impacting natural and human landscapes in the surrounding region. South of Mammoth, residents had just settled an argument over the size and extent of a regional retail outlet mall in Bishop. This promised to be just the start of similar battles over the soul of that town.

Regardless of the location, growth and planning issues that pop up repeatedly across the state usually follow the same line. Slow-growth activists who want to preserve the personality and integrity of their communities react against business people and developers who are looking to build the next urban or suburban center. You'll find different characters representing both sides of conflicts in communities from Crescent City, Eureka, Arcata, and Redding to the Mexican border.

On June 14, 1996, The City honored *San Francisco Chronicle* columnist Herb Caen, who later died of cancer. He proclaimed that a San Franciscan who dies and goes to heaven can only conclude, "It's nice, but it isn't San Francisco."

Planning the Future in Other Northern and Central California Cities

Consistent population and economic growth around Monterey Bay was interrupted when Fort Ord ended up on the military's downsizing hit list. Except for this bump in the road, Santa Cruz, Salinas, Monterey, and Carmel and other less well-known communities have been growing into urban centers.

Santa Cruz was once a conservative little beach town, attracting visitors from the Bay Area and Central Valley. By the late 1900s, it had gained a reputation for its progressive politics, alternative lifestyles, and UC campus. Then, the 1989 Loma Prieta earthquake destroyed much of Pacific Avenue and the city's vibrant business section. By the mid-1990s, the city was fully recovered; it still draws those visitors from the Bay, the Central Valley and more distant locations, and its economy continues to diversify.

Monterey is flourishing, primarily due to tourism and the Monterey Bay Aquarium, converted canneries, pier, and other attractions. Just to the south, Carmel residents have been struggling to manage the area's remarkable growth. By 1997, Carmel had formed a beach task force to figure out how to accommodate beach visitors and tourists. One controversy was the placement of portable toilets for summer tourists; residents were concerned about some visitors relieving themselves in public. Other residents complained that the portable toilets were placed too close to their homes.

The love-hate relationship Carmel has with its tourists received more attention in recent years. The town was started as a quiet and quaint artists colony, and some residents want it to stay that way. There are now more than seventy art galleries and 4,500 residents on about one square mile that is Carmel. Into the late 1990s, there was still no mail delivery and no street addresses; residents collect their mail at the post office. No more than 10 percent of most store merchandise can be decorated with the word "Carmel" or other local place names. T-shirt and formula (chain) stores are restricted to discourage tacky, souvenir-seeking tourists.

However, this is a town where 30 percent of the municipal budget comes from sales taxes and another 28 percent comes from hotel taxes. One article in the *Los Angeles Times* estimated the number of annual tourists at 1.5 million. The town is trying to attract older, quiet, more affluent, art-and-antique tourists who stay in bed-and-breakfasts. This is a narrow slice of the California population, but Carmel is just a dense, compact point on the coast within a state with an exploding population and economy. Many residents have fought attempts by former Mayor Clint Eastwood, developers, and other business people who try to bring malls and other generic projects to the town.

Planning the Future in San Diego

San Diego has received much-deserved attention in this book, from its border patrols and maquiladoras, to its tourist and high-tech and other modern industries that have turned it away from reliance on military spending and toward the twenty-first century. California's second-largest city has earned its own book. In this very limited space, we can only begin to review some of the cityscapes and planning issues it and its neighbors will carry into the twenty-first century.

San Diego has as much potential as any West Coast city to become one of the world's leading international urban centers (see Map 11.4). There are the maquiladoras just across the border and the growing industries and communities on the California side. There is enormous foreign investment, especially from Asia, and much of it is related to the maquiladoras. There are relaxing trade barriers fueling these new economies, though some investors became nervous during the late 1990s Asian economic crisis. There is the beautiful setting, including scenic coastlines, San Diego Bay, Mission Bay, and tourist attractions, and there is one of the mildest climates in the world.

San Diego's potential may best be realized while looking across the city from Point Loma on any sunny day. It is not confined on the tip of a peninsula as is San Francisco. It is not yet choking in the grit, gridlock, and smog that help define Los Angeles, although it may stumble in that direction. In addition, it does not suffer through the searing, stagnant summer heat and thick, cold winter fog that settles on and encloses some Central Valley cities. Perhaps this is why San Diego gained a reputation

as one of the nation's fastest-growing cities during the 1980s.

It is true that San Diego is not yet L.A. It and its suburbs still have plenty of room to grow up and out. Will San Diego's future be marred by chaos, planning mistakes, and regrets about what could have been? Or will San Diegans accentuate their setting and plan a cutting-edge urban center where the California Dream can still be realized? Positive answers to these questions might be found in their popular and successful trolley cars, at Horton Plaza and the Convention Center, or the way their high-tech industries connect with local universities. Negative answers might be found in poorly planned suburbs with generic malls and on the expanding concrete tentacles that connect them.

San Diego Grows Up

San Diego once had a respect and image problem. It was once ridiculed as the suburb of L.A., Navy-base-with-a-zoo attached, the branch-office city, and the cultural cul-de-sac. In 1972, the Republican National Convention was moved (just six weeks before it started) from San Diego to Miami. Republicans claimed the city was not ready for such a big event.

Its inferiority complex has since evaporated. In 1996, Republicans held a successful national convention in the new Convention Center. The city spent about $13 million to sponsor the convention, but made up to $30 million from it. Though reporters and cameras brought it into the spotlight and helped change its image during the 1996 Republican Convention, the city regularly hosts larger conventions and events. San Diego has been the sixth largest city in the country for several years, and it has certainly separated itself from L.A.

San Diego is gaining a more cosmopolitan atmosphere and a sense of culture. Its Spanish history and

Ordinances ensuring direct sunlight for each San Diego space have helped keep new office and hotel towers from clustering. Is this good planning? How has it shaped the San Diego skyline as the city grows out?

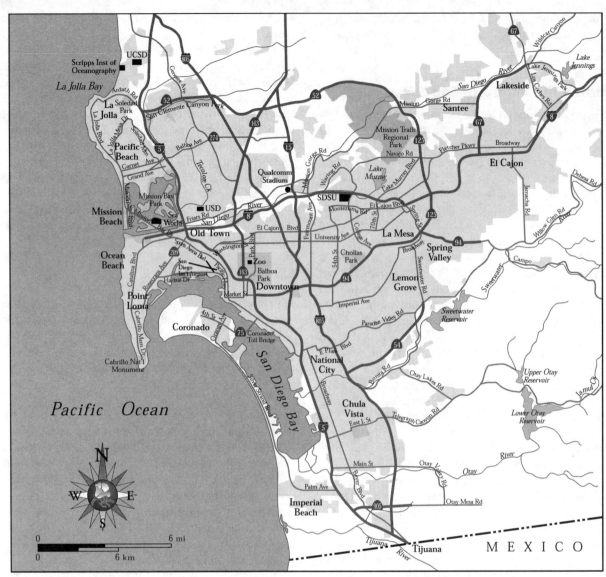

MAP 11.4
San Diego is the state's second-largest city, and it continues to grow.

architecture, its coastal location, its diverse economy and cultures are among a host of factors that are building San Diego's unique identity. As an example, at least five main nightlife centers have developed in the area. The downtown Gaslamp Quarter has restaurants, clubs, and live music. The Garnet Avenue Strip in Pacific Beach is considered the Melrose Avenue of San Diego and there's La Jolla's upscale Prospect Avenue. Across the border, in Tijuana's Avenida Revolución, you can find rowdy parties and Ugly Americans, while Tijuana's Zona Rio is where you will find more high-society Mexican clubs.

We haven't even mentioned the string of vital activities and landscapes along the San Diego River and I-8 in Mission Valley. Travelling east from Ocean Beach and Mission Beach, we pass Sea World and Old Town. We can look up from Hotel Circle developments to Mission Hills, Hillcrest, and University Heights. Farther inland is a renovated Qualcomm Stadium, formerly Jack Murphy Stadium and still home to football's Chargers and baseball's Padres. East on I-8 from there is San Diego State University. If we follow I-8, we encounter La Mesa, El Cajon, and other cities draping their suburbs across the eastern San Diego area's hills and valleys.

And what is to become of the northern San Diego area and county? What role will educational institutions such as Scripps Institution of Oceanography and the University of California play in the future? How will well-known landscapes with familiar names such as La Jolla and Del Mar change? Look at the open spaces, valuable land, and opportunities for development between Encinitas and Oceanside and inland to Vista and Escondido. Finally, what will happen to the one great gap between the Los Angeles and San Diego areas we call Camp Pendleton?

Instead of becoming like L.A., will San Diego finally become another extension of L.A.? Will the valleys and mesas be scraped, paved, and become so urban that we will no longer recognize them? Today, San Diego is thriving with a new, diverse economy (reviewed in the previous chapter). Some would argue that it is the state's last urban giant where the California Dream can still be realized.

Central Valley Cities Emerge

Throughout this book, there have appropriately been numerous and lengthy references to Central Valley cities. (The review of Sacramento on page 31 serves as one example; there are numerous others in Chapter 9 on primary economies and rural landscapes.) Within this valley are the most recent major California cities to erupt on their own, relatively independent of the state's three giant coastal conurbations. However, the crowding and congestion in California's coastal cities has affected some of these Central Valley cities. More people crowded away from the coast are considering Central Valley urban centers as options. This is one reason some of them were the state's fastest-growing urban centers during the final years of the twentieth century (see Map 11.5).

Can this growth continue? What will be the nature of these cities and their newly built landscapes? Answers to these questions will depend on many factors, such as how these urban centers affect and absorb the large proportion of poor working families in the valley. During the late 1990s, more than 20 percent of the populations in Tulare, Fresno, and Merced Counties were on public assistance as unemployment rates ran as high as 16 percent. It is true that many of the poor are in rural areas, but as nearby cities grow to consume more farmland, they will attract these people.

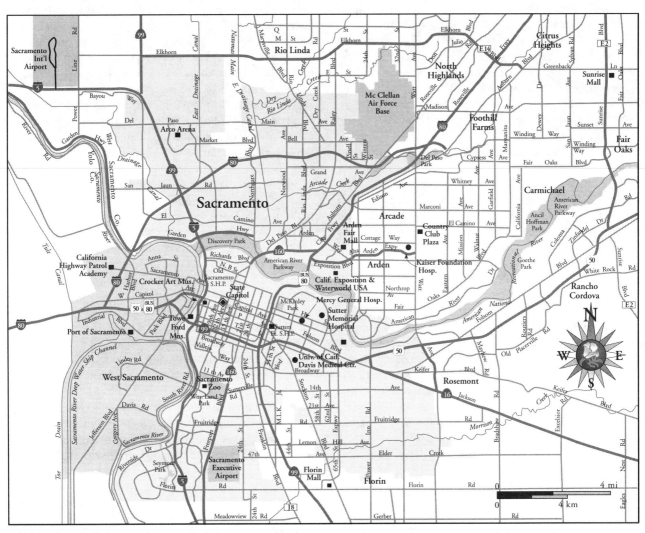

MAP 11.5

Central Valley urban areas, such as Sacramento, continue to grow and spread across fertile farmland.

Downtown Sacramento was built next to its river, a waterway that has been important to the city since the Gold Rush.

As Central Valley cities look for more traditional planning and diverse economies, there are also grand schemes for growth and job creation by such developers as Norman Jarrett. During the late 1990s, he proposed a giant, $4 billion Gold Rush City theme park and entertainment complex near Lathrop, south of Stockton. The development would include hotels and motels, a farmer's market, four theme parks, three golf courses, 8,500 houses, shopping, entertainment, commercial, and educational activities.

Gold Rush City would be linked by San Joaquin River waterways and freeways to Sacramento and the Bay Area. Little Lathrop showed interest while others questioned the wisdom of locating such a development on a muddy flood plain. The biggest problem was finding an investor to build what Jarrett claimed could bring up to $100 million per year to the area and what critics claimed would be a bust.

Repeatedly, we have demonstrated how such developments and issues have created planning controversies in every California city. Now, they are popping up in the Central Valley. We have also witnessed how the Central Valley and its cities have, like their coastal counterparts, become so culturally diverse. There are Fresno's Armenians and Bakersfield's Basque and the enormous diversity of Asian, Latino, and African-American cultures that have put their roots into Central Valley cities. Emerging are trends and issues strikingly familiar to the state's larger coastal cities.

◆ REDISCOVERING DIVERSITY, CONNECTIONS, AND CHANGE

It is only a matter of time when Central Valley cities boast of their own participation in programs such as the Cultural Tourism Initiative, started in 1997. This is a joint venture between San Francisco, Los Angeles, and San Diego to develop sixteen ethnic-themed trip itineraries lasting three to five days in each city's region. State and local officials were hoping to increase tourism options. Visitor bureaus and cultural tourism directors from each of the three cities are working with the state's tourist industry, artists, and museums.

The Cultural Tourism Initiative will advertise in several languages, including English, Spanish, Japanese, and German. Millions should be attracted to these educational journeys. Planned itineraries and options include various ethnic, cultural, and lifestyle themes that are easily visible and experienced throughout California's urban centers. (Many were highlighted in Chapter 8 on California's ethnic groups, cultures, and lifestyles.)

These programs will also offer local residents opportunities to learn more about their own neighbors and to build the cultural bonds and cooperation required for our cities and our state to work more efficiently. Recognizing and celebrating this rich cultural diversity is just one way we will improve the living and working environments for individuals and families throughout California. Perhaps such positive, futuristic thinking and planning will push California into a magnificent twenty-first century.

How many residents and visitors will recognize the powerful connections between California's diverse natural and human landscapes? Who will appreciate how natural environments and resources, human populations, migrations, cultures, economies, and rural and urban people interact? How many will use these lessons to manage inevitable change for the better and to build communities and landscapes that are more livable?

How these complex questions are answered and how problems are resolved will not only determine the nature of California's future landscapes; it will also determine how, and whether, California leads the world into the twenty-first century.

SOME KEY TERMS AND TOPICS

brownfields	empowerment zones	nonbasic economic sectors
Business Investment Districts (BIDs)	flagship store	redlining
central business district (CBD)	functional region	specialty store
central place theory	gentrification	suburbs
city structures	head-of-navigation sites	urban realm
Community Redevelopment Agencies (CRAs)	inner city/transition zone	white flight
conurbation	multiple nuclei	

Additional Key Terms and Topics

break-of-bulk sites	immigrant populations	site
car culture	infrastructure	situation
cemeteries	light industry	specialized land uses
center concepts	main street	specialized services
city functions	manufacturing centers	Standard Metropolitan Statistical Area
"City Lite"	megalopolis	suburban lifestyles
city models	metropolitan areas	tax base
commuters	minority groups	tiers in the city
corporate headquarters	modern/future issues	transition zone
cosmopolitan	neighborhood centers	urban blight
cultural centers	neighborhoods	urban boundaries
decentralization	political centers	urban fringe
density gradient	poverty	urban housing
economic base	public transportation	urban planning
edge cities	redevelopment projects	urban sprawl
entertainment centers	regional government associations	urban systems
financial districts	religious centers	urban transportation
gated communities	retail districts	virtual homes/businesses
hinterland/service area	retirement communities	young, upwardly-mobile, urban professionals (YUPPIES)
historical architecture	segregation	zoning
home-based businesses	self-sufficient settlements	
homeless	service centers	

References and Further Readings

CHAPTER 1 AND GENERAL SOURCES FOR CALIFORNIA GEOGRAPHY

Human Geography Texts

Countless human geography texts can be used to clarify general concepts and definitions used especially in Chapter 1 and the last half of this book. Only a few are listed below.

de Blij, Harm J. 1996. *Human Geography: Culture, Society, and Space.* New York: John Wiley & Sons, Inc.

de Blij, Harm J., and Peter O. Muller. 1994. *Geography: Realms, Regions, and Concepts.* New York: John Wiley and Sons, Inc.

Fellmann, Jerome, Arthur Getis, and Judith Getis. 1997. *Human Geography: Landscapes of Human Activity.* Dubuque, IA: Wm. C. Brown.

Hartshorn, Truman A., and John W. Alexander. 1988. *Economic Geography.* New Jersey: Prentice Hall.

Rubenstein, James M. 1994. *An Introduction to Human Geography.* New York: Macmillan.

Professional Geography Organizations and Their Publications

These geography publications occasionally contain articles that provide information specific to California. Information from these publications and organizations has been accessed for this book. They will serve the reader looking for more specific articles in geography.

Annals of the Association of American Geographers (AAG). 1710 Sixth St. NW, Washington, D.C. 20009-3198. *The Professional Geographer* is the forum and journal of the AAG.

Association of Pacific Coast Geographers. Dept. of Geography, California State University, Sacramento, CA 95819-6003. *Pacifica* is the journal of the Association of Pacific Coast Geographers.

National Council for Geographic Education (NCGE). Indiana University of Pennsylvania, 16A Leonard Hall, Indiana, PA 15705. *Pathways in Geography* is the journal of the NCGE.

National Geographic, National Geographic Society. 1145 17th St. NW, Washington, D.C. 20036-4688.

California-Specific Books

Allen, James P., and Eugene Turner. 1997. *The Ethnic Quilt: Population Diversity in Southern California.* Cal State University Northridge Center for Geographical Studies.

Altman, Linda Jacobs. 1997. *California.* New York: Benchmark Books.

Bright, William, and Erwin G. Gudde. 1998. *California Place Names: The Origin and Etymology of Current Geographical Names.* Berkeley: UC Press.

California Road and Recreation Guide. 1998. New York: Benchmark Maps.

Clark, Thurston. 1996. *California Fault: Searching for the Spirit of State Along the San Andreas.* New York: Ballatine Books.

DeLorme Mapping Co. 1990. *Atlas and Gazetteer of Northern California and Southern California.* Freeport, Maine. Two Sets.

Donley, Michael W., Stuart Allan, Patricia Caro, and Clyde P. Patton. 1979. *Atlas of California.* Culver City, CA: Pacific Book Center. (Out of print)

Durrenberger, Robert W. 1976. *California: Patterns on the Land.* Palo Alto, CA: Mayfield Publishing Co.

Fay, James S., and Stephanie W. Fay. 1995. *California Almanac.* Santa Barbara, CA: Pacific Data Resources, frequently updated.

Fraccia, Charles. 1997. *The Golden Dream.* Graphic Arts Center Publishing.

Fradkin, Philip L. 1995. *The Seven States of California.* New York: Henry Holt and Company.

Fremont, John Charles. 1995. *Geographical Memoir upon Upper California.* Fairfield, WA: Ye Galleon Press.

Gudde, Erwin G. 1959. *1000 California Place Names.* Berkeley, CA: UC Press.

Hardwick, Susan Wiley, and Donald G. Holtgrieve. 1996. *Valley for Dreams: Life and Landscape in the Sacramento Valley.* Lanham, MD: Rowman and Littlefield.

Hart, James D. 1987. *A Companion to California.* Berkeley, CA: UC Press.

Hartman, David N. 1972. *California and Man.* Santa Ana, CA: Pierce Publishers, 3rd ed.

Highway 99: A Literary Journal Through California's Great Central Valley. Edited by Stan Yogi. Berkeley, CA: Heyday Books, 1996.

Holden, William M. 1988. *Sacramento: Excursions into its History and Natural World.* Fair Oaks, CA: Two Rivers Publishing.

Hornbeck, David, and David L. Fuller. 1983. *California Patterns: A Geographical and Historical Atlas.* Mountain View, CA: Mayfield.

Jaeger, Edmund D. 1965. *The California Deserts.* Palo Alto, CA: Stanford University Press, 4th ed.

Johnston, Verna R. 1998. *Sierra Nevada.* Berkeley, CA: UC Press.

Karinen, Arthur E., David W. Lantis, Gary L. Peters, and Rodney Steiner. 1995. *California.* Dubuque, IA: Kendall/Hunt.

King, David C. 1978. *Windows on California.* Boston: Houghton-Mifflin.

Lantis, David W. 1989. *California, The Pacific Connection.* Chico, CA: Creek Press.

Libero, Chiara, and Susanna Perazolli. 1997. *California, Places and History.* New York: Stewart, Tabori, and Chang.

Miller, Crane. 1983. *California: The Geography of Diversity.* Mountain View, CA: Mayfield.

Oxford, June. 1983. *The Capitol that Couldn't Stay Put.* Fairfield, CA: James Stevenson Publisher.

Pelta, Kathy. 1994. *California (Hello USA).* Minneapolis, MN: Lerner Publications.

Pitt, Leonard, and Dale Pitt. 1997. *Los Angeles A to Z.* Berkeley, CA: UC Press.

Robinson, W.W. 1979. *Land in California.* Berkeley: UC Press.

Schad, Jerry. 1998. *California Deserts.* Helen and Billings, Montana: Falcon Press.

Walters, Dan. 1992. *The New California: Facing the 21st Century.* Sacramento: California Journal Press.

Wuerthner, George. 1993. *California's Sierra Nevada.* Helena, MT: American and World Geographic.

Periodicals and Other Sources with Information Specific to California

AAA (Automobile Club of California/California State Automobile Association) Maps. Offices throughout the state, including San Francisco and Los Angeles. 1-800-222-4357

California Coast and Ocean. 1330 Broadway, 11th Floor, Oakland, CA 94612.

California Country (a periodical). 1601 Exposition Blvd., Sacramento, CA 94705.

California County Fact Book. County Supervisors Association of California. 1100 K St., Suite 101, Sacramento, CA 95814.

The California Geographer, California Geographical Society.

California Geographic Alliance (North). Department of Geography and Planning. California State University, Chico CA 95929-0425.

The California Handbook (a periodical). California Institute of Public Affairs. P.O. Box 10, Claremont, CA 91711.

California In Print (a state government research periodical). 815 North La Brea Ave., Suite 197, Inglewood, CA 90301.

California Journal: Independent Analysis of Politics and Government. A StateNet Publications journal. 2101 K St., Sacramento, CA 95816.

California Magazine. P.O. Box 2585, Boulder, CO 80322.

California Schools. (Education issues in California.) 3100 Beacon Blvd., Sacramento, CA 95691-3473.

California State Library and State Librarian of California, Room 220. California State Information and Reference Center, Room 301. Library and Courts Building I, 914 Capital Mall, Sacramento, CA 95814.

California State University, Northridge. Department of Geography. California Geographical Survey, Dr. William Bowen, Professor of Geography. 18111 Nordoff St., Northridge, CA 91330.

California Weekly Explorer. Law and Company. 579 S. State College Boulevard, Fullerton, CA 92631.

Magellan Geographix. 6464 Hollister Ave., Santa Barbara, CA 93117.

Northern California Monthly. 7660 Morningside Dr., Loomis, CA 95650.

Outdoor California. California Department of Fish and Game. Resources Building, 146 Ninth St., Sacramento, CA 95814.

Pacific Discovery. Academy of Sciences periodical. Golden Gate Park, San Francisco, CA 94118-4501.

San Diego Society of Natural History. San Diego Natural History Museum Library. P.O. Box 1390, San Diego, CA 92112.

Sunset Magazine. 80 Willow Rd., Menlo Park, CA 94025-3691.

Thomas Brothers Maps, including *California Road Atlas and Travel Guide.* 17731 Cowan, Irvine, CA 92714.

University of California Press, 2120 Berkeley Way, Berkeley, CA 94702.

Williams, Larry and Jerry Williams. *California Atlas.* California Geographic Alliance—North. Department of Geography, California State University, Chico, 1997.

Major Newspapers

Played critical roles as sources of information for this book, particularly the *Los Angeles Times.* These papers provided updates to current events in California that will eventually appear in other publications, but would have been too late for this one. Thank you, California newspapers, but special thanks to:

Los Angeles Times. P.O. Box 60164, Los Angeles, CA 90060-0164.

The New York Times. 229 West 43rd St., New York, NY 10036.

Sacramento Bee. P.O. Box 15779, Sacramento, CA 95852.

San Jose Mercury News. 750 Ridder Park Drive, San Jose, CA 95190.

CHAPTERS 2 AND 3   SOURCES FOR THE GEOLOGY OF CALIFORNIA

Books

There is a growing list of books and parts of books that address the geology of California. The following books were repeatedly consulted in the two chapters on geology. They are listed in order of importance to the author. They also offer a wide range of approaches to anyone studying California's geology. Each reader may rank them differently, depending on individual interests and expertise.

Norris, R. M., and R. W. Webb. 1990. *Geology of California.* New York: John Wiley & Sons, 2nd ed.

This is a thorough and exhaustive work. It is mostly a region-by-region assemblage of studies up through the 1980s. There is something here for everybody, but be careful: nongeologists could be overwhelmed!

Harden, Deborah R. 1998. *California Geology.* Upper Saddle River, New Jersey: Prentice Hall.

A slightly different, but needed, perspective, this is a more recent attempt at California geology contained within one publication. Well-organized, easy reading.

The Geotectonic Development of California. Edited by W. G. Ernst. Englewood Cliffs, New Jersey: Prentice-Hall Inc., 1981.

More specifically focused on California's tectonic history, this also gathers many studies together. It is far more technical and discipline-specific than Norris and Webb.

Hill, Mary. 1984. *California Landscape: Origin and Evolution.* Berkeley, CA: UC Press.

This is a more light-hearted approach designed to catch most everyone's attention. It is a good beginner's guide.

This should be in a separate category:

McPhee, John. *Assembling California.* New York: Farrar, Straus and Giroux, 1993.

Written by a great author for the average reader.

Other Publications and Organizations

Following are a number of other publications/organizations relevant to these two chapters on geology; those marked with an asterisk could be helpful to anyone looking for very specific maps or geologic studies in California, others offer more general surveys.

California Division of Mines and Geology, California Dept. of Natural Resources.
    801 K St., MS 14-33, Sacramento, CA 95814-3532.
    185 Berry Street, Suite 210, San Francisco, CA 94107-1728.
    107 S. Broadway, Room 1065, Los Angeles, CA 90012-4402.

California Geology Magazine. California Department of Conservation, Division of Mines and Geology. Refer to addresses for Division of Mines and Geology.

Clark, Thurston. *California Fault: Searching for the Spirit of State Along the San Andreas.* Ballantine Books, 1996.

*Cooke, Ronald U. 1984. *Geomorphological Hazards in Los Angeles: A Study of Slope and Sediment Problems in a Metropolitan County.* Boston: Allen and Unwin.

*Ellen, Stephen D., and Carl M. Wentworth. 1995. *Hillside Materials and Slopes of the San Francisco Bay Region, California.* Denver, CO: U.S. Geological Survey.

Fradkin, Philip. 1998. *Magnitude 8: Earthquakes and Life Along the San Andreas Fault.* New York: Henry Holt and Co.

Guyton, Bill. 1998. *Glaciers of California.* Berkeley, CA: UC Press.

Harbaugh, John W. 1974. *Geology Field Guide to Northern California.* Dubuque, Iowa: W. C. Brown.

Hill, Mary. 1975. *Geology of the Sierra Nevada.* Berkeley, CA: UC Press.

Hodgson, Michael E., and Risa Palm. 1992. *After a California Earthquake: Attitude and Behavior Change.* Chicago: University of Chicago Press.

Hunt, Charles B. 1975. *Death Valley: Geology, Ecology, Archaeology.* Berkeley, CA: UC Press.

*Kelsey, H. M., D. C. Marron, and K. M. Nolan. 1995. *Geomorphic Processes and Aquatic Habitat in the Redwood Creek Basin, Northwestern California.* Menlo Park, CA: U.S. Geological Survey.

*Kruckeberg, Arthur R. 1985. *California Serpentines: Flora, Vegetation, Geology, Soils, and Management Problems.* Berkeley: UC Press.

Minch, John, and Thomas Leslie. 1991. *The Baja Highway: A Geology and Biology Field Guide for the Baja Traveler.* San Juan Capistrano, CA: John Minch and Associates.

National Geographic. National Geographic Society. 1145 17th St. NW, Washington, D.C. 20036-4688.

Nature. Macmillan Journals Ltd. London, England.

Science News. Science Service. Washington, D.C.

Sharp, Robert P. 1978. *Field Guide to Southern California* and *Field Guide to Coastal Southern California.* Dubuque, Iowa: Kendall/Hunt Geology Field Guide Series.

United States Geological Survey. Menlo Park and 600 J St., Sacramento, CA 95819-6129.

CHAPTER 4

General introductory and more advanced books on weather and climate can be found in bookstores and libraries across California. The Internet is your best bet for up-to-date weather information for California or around the globe. The following list of books and other publications includes only five sources of information that specifically address California's weather and climate. There really are no others!

California-Specific Weather Resources

Baily, Harry P. 1966. *Weather of Southern California.* Berkeley: UC Press.

Felton, Ernest L. 1965. *California's Many Climates.* Palo Alto, CA: Pacific Books.

Knox, Joseph B., and Ann Foley Scheuring. 1991. *Global Climate Change and California.* Berkeley: UC Press, 1991.

National Weather Service Offices: Eureka, San Francisco, Sacramento, Hanford/San Joaquin Valley, Oxnard/Los Angeles, San Diego. Weather radio broadcasts and links on the Internet.

Newspapers throughout the state. The *Los Angeles Times* has the best weather page.

National Publications

Bulletin of the American Meteorological Society. 45 Beacon St., Boston, MA 02108-3693.

Weatherwise Magazine. 1319 18th St., NW, Washington, DC 20036-1802.

Organizations

American Meteorological Society. (Refer to the Bulletin for address.) Local Chapters.

California Weather Symposiums. Sierra College Natural History Museum. 5000 Rocklin Road, Rocklin, CA 95677.

CHAPTER 5

Since the 1700s, scientists have studied and debated about the nature of California's living organisms. Whether the studies were organized according to biomes, vegetation belts, or C. Hart Merriam's Life Zones, they added to our understanding of California's diverse and fascinating plants and animals. In 1959, Phillip Munz and David Keck published a landmark study of California life forms. They organized California's plants into communities, a system that changed the way we look at the distribution of plants and animals in the state.

Books

There have been some stellar studies since, most of them following Munz's and Keck's lead or modifying their work. The following is a list of books that were used throughout this chapter. These selections represent a broad range of approaches to this subject; each will appeal to very different readers with very different interests and backgrounds.

Barbour, Michael G., and Jack Major. 1998. *Terrestrial Vegetation of California.* California Native Plant Society Special Publication No. 9, Expanded Edition.

This is one of the most thorough and exhaustive studies of California plants ever! It is written for those who have previous experience studying this subject, and it is *not* for those who only want a general introduction.

Ornduff, Robert. 1974. *Introduction to California Plant Life.* Berkeley, CA: University of California Press.

The antithesis of the first reference, this one is for the beginner who wants a more general introduction to California plants.

Holland, V. L., and Keil, David J. 1989. *California Vegetation.* San Luis Obispo, CA: California Polytechnic University.

This is a successful attempt to bridge the gap between the two extremes listed above.

Schoenherr, Allan A. 1992. *A Natural History of California.* Berkeley, CA: University of California Press.

This is a bold attempt to examine the different elements of California's natural history. It is thorough, but it breaks into a region-to-region study of California's plants and animals.

Bakker, Elna. 1984. *An Island Called California: An Ecological Introduction to its Natural Communities.* Berkeley, CA: University of California Press, 2nd ed.

This is a classic and delightful trip through California's natural communities to visit its plants and animals. A must for anyone interested in California's living creatures!

Additional References and Further Readings

Alden, Peter, and Fred Heath. 1998. *National Audubon Society Field Guide to California.* New York: Alfred A. Knopf.

Barbour, Michael, Bruce Pavlik, Frank Drysdale, and Susan Lindstrom. 1993. *California's Changing Landscapes: Diversity and Conservation of California Vegetation.* Sacramento: California Native Plant Society.

Berg, Peter. 1978. *Reinhabiting a Separate Country: A Bioregional Anthology of Northern California.* San Francisco: Planet Drum Foundation.

Bulletin of the California Insect Survey. UC Press, 2120 Berkeley Way, Berkeley, CA 94720.

California Native Plant Society. 1722 J Street, Suite 17, Sacramento, CA 95814. (Thirty local chapters statewide).

Dawson, E. Yale. 1966. *Cacti of California.* Berkeley, CA: UC Press.

Dunning, Joan. 1998. *From the Redwood Forest.* Vermont: Chelsea Green Publishing Co.

Fremontia. California Native Plant Society quarterly publication. 1722 J Street, Suite 17, Sacramento, CA 95814.

Frenkel, Robert E. 1970. *Ruderal Vegetation Along Some California Roadsides.* Berkeley: UC Press.

Jameson, Jr., E.W. and Hans J. Peeters. 1983. *California Mammals.* Berkeley: UC Press.

Johnston, Verna R. 1994. *California Forests and Woodlands: A Natural History.* Berkeley: UC Press.

Herpetology (reptiles and amphibians). Southwestern Herpetologists Society. P.O. Box 7469, Van Nuys, CA 91409.

Herpeton (from the same group as above, but more technical).

Hickman, James C. 1993. *The Jepson Manual: Higher Plants of California*. Berkeley: UC Press.

Keator, Glen. 1998. *The Life of an Oak: An Intimate Portrait*. Berkeley, CA: Heyday Press.

Knute, Adrienne. 1992. *Plants of the East Mojave*. Cima, CA: Wide Horizons Press.

Kruckeberg, Arthur R. 1985. *California Serpentines: Flora, Vegetation, Geology, Soils, and Management Problems*. Berkeley: UC Press.

Mason, Herbert. 1957. *Flora of the Marshes of California*. Berkeley: UC Press.

Matthews, Mary Ann. 1997. *An Illustrated Field Key to the Vascular Plants of Monterey County*. Sacramento: California Native Plant Society.

Minch, John, and Thomas Leslie. 1991. *The Baja Highway: A Geology and Biology Field Guide for the Baja Traveler*. San Juan Capistrano, CA: John Minch and Associates.

Minnich, Richard A. 1988. *The Biogeography of Fire in the San Bernardino Mountains of California*. Berkeley: UC Press.

Sharsmith, Helen K. 1982. *Flora of the Mount Hamilton Range of California*. Sacramento: California Native Plant Society.

Shuford, W. Dave, and Irene Timossi. 1994. *Plant Communities of Marin County*. Sacramento: California Native Plant Society.

Small, Arnold. 1994. *California Birds: Their Status and Distribution*. Vista, CA: IBIS Publishing.

Smith, James P. 1981. *Keys to the Families and Genera of Vascular Plants in Northwest California*. Eureka, CA: Mad River Press.

Western Birds (formerly *California Birds*). Western Field Ornithologists. 3924 Murrietta Ave., Sherman Oaks, CA 91423.

Whitney, Stephen. 1979. *A Sierra Club Naturalist's Guide to the Sierra Nevada*. San Francisco: Sierra Club Books.

Wiggins, Ira. 1980. *Flora of Baja California*. Palo Alto, CA: Stanford University Press.

CHAPTER 6

Like other chapters in this book, countless sources have been used and are available regarding this topic. Many pieces of information have been gathered from the general sources listed after the first chapter of this book. Here are the most important California water-specific sources used in this chapter.

The California Water Atlas. Edited by William L. Kahrl. Sacramento: Governor's Office of Planning and Research, 1979.

Gottlieb, Robert. 1988. *A Life of its Own: The Politics and Power of Water*. San Diego: Harcourt Brace Jovanovich.

Hundley, Jr., Norris. 1992. *The Great Thirst: Californians and Water, 1770s–1990s*. Berkeley: UC Press.

Kelsey, H. M., D. C. Marron, and K. M. Nolan. 1995. *Geomorphic Processes and Aquatic Habitat in the Redwood Creek Basin, Northwestern California*. Denver, CO: U.S. Geological Survey.

Mount, Jeffrey F. 1995. *California Rivers and Streams*. Berkeley, CA: UC Press.

Nadeau, Remi A. 1974. *The Water Seekers*. Santa Barbara, CA: Peregrine Smith.

Reisner, Marc. 1986. *Cadillac Desert: The American Desert and Its Disappearing Water*. New York: Viking.

Water Agencies (with their own publications)

California Department of Water Resources. 1416 Ninth Street, Sacramento, CA 95814 (P.O. Box 219000, Sacramento, CA 95821-9000).

California Highwater. California Department of Water Resources, P.O. Box 388, Sacramento, CA 95802.

California State Water Resources Control Board. P.O. Box 2815, Sacramento, CA 95814.

California Water Clearinghouse. Association of California Water Agencies. 910 K St., Suite 250, Sacramento, CA 95814.

Coachella Valley Water District. P.O. Box 1058, Coachella, CA 92236.

East Bay Municipal Utilities District (MUD). 375 11th St., Oakland, CA 94607-4240.

Imperial Irrigation District. 333 E. Barioni Blvd., Imperial, CA 92251.

Los Angeles Department of Water and Power. Public Affairs Division. P.O. Box 111, Room 1509, Los Angeles, CA 90051.

Metropolitan Water District of Southern California. P.O. Box 54153, Los Angeles, CA 90054-0153.

Monterey County Water Resources Agency. 893 Blanco Circle, Salinas, CA 93901.

APPENDIX B

California Coast and Ocean. California State Coastal Conservancy. 1330 Broadway, Ste. 1100, Oakland, CA 94612-2540.

California Coastal Commission. 45 Fremont Street, San Francisco, CA 94105. *Coastal Access Guide*—check for the latest update of this and other publications.

Dawson, E. Yale. 1966. *Seashore Plants of Southern California*. Berkeley: UC Press.

Lynn, Ronald J., and James J. Simpson. 1987. The California Current System: The Seasonal Variability of its Physical Characteristics. *Journal of Geophysical Research* 92 (November 15): 12,947–66.

Morris, Robert H., Donald P. Abbott, Eugene C. Haderlie. 1980. *Intertidal Invertebrates of California*. Stanford, CA: Stanford University Press.

Ricketts, Edward F., and Jack Calvin. 1968. *Between Pacific Tides*. Stanford, CA: Stanford University Press.

Scripps Institution of Oceanography. University of California at San Diego, La Jolla, CA.

Scheffer, Victor B. 1976. *A Natural History of Marine Mammals*. New York: Scribner.

California Current: A Collection of Readings for Geography 158. Edited by David Siegel. UC Santa Barbara, 1997. Readings included: Bascom, Willard. "Waves and Beaches." 1980. Carlucci, Epply. "Plankton Dynamics of Southern California Bight." 1986. DeSantis, Marie. "California Currents." 1985.

Lights Manual: Intertidal Invertebrates of the Central California Coast. Edited by Ralph I. Smith and James T. Carlton. Berkeley: UC Press, 1975.

UC Press Series of California Natural History Guides. They are too numerous to list here, but can be very helpful. Example: Hinton, Sam. 1987. *Seashore Life of Southern California.* Berkeley: UC Press.

CHAPTER 7

Human History of California

California's historical events and references to historical publications are referenced throughout this book. Here are some interesting publications, organizations, and agencies focusing on California history:

California Historical Courier (publication of the California Historical Society), San Francisco, CA.

California Historical Society in San Francisco. 2090 Jackson St., 94109 or 678 Mission St., 94105.

The California Missions. Edited by Sunset editors. Menlo Park, CA: Sunset Books, 1979.

California Office of Historic Preservation. Sacramento: California State Parks, 1996.

Chang, Anita L. 1992. *The Historical Geography of the Humboldt Wagon Road.* Chico, CA: Association for Northern California Records and Research.

Dana, Richard Henry. 1937. *Two Years Before the Mast: and Twenty-Four Years After.* New York: Collier.

Delgado, James P. 1996. *To California by Sea: A Maritime History of the California Gold Rush.* Columbia, South Carolina: University of South Carolina Press.

Heizer, Robert F., and Albert B. Elsasser. 1980. *The Natural World of the California Indians.* Berkeley: UC Press.

Hinton, Leanne. 1994. *Flutes of Fire: Essays on California Indian Languages.* Berkeley: Heyday Books.

Holden, William M. 1988. *Sacramento: Excursions into its History and Natural World.* Fair Oaks, CA: Two Rivers Publishing.

Hornbeck, David, and David L. Fuller. 1983. *California Patterns: A Geographical and Historical Atlas.* Mountain View, CA: Mayfield.

Howard, Thomas Frederick. 1998. *Sierra Crossing: First Roads to California.* Berkeley: UC Press.

Hunt, Rockwell Dennis, and William Sheffield Ament. 1929. *Oxcart to Airplane* (of the Series California). San Francisco, Los Angeles: Powell Publishing.

Lake, A.I., and Arlene C. Rourke. 1990. *Gold Fever: Wild West in American History.* Rourke Book Company.

Lapp, Rudolph M. 1997. *Blacks in Gold Rush California.* New Haven: Yale University Press.

Libero, Chiara, and Susanna Perazolli. 1997. *California, Places and History.* New York: Stewart, Tabori, and Chang.

Marinacci, Barbara, and Rudy Marinacci. 1980. *California's Spanish Place-Names.* Houston, Texas: Gulf Publishing Co., 2nd ed.

Nava, Julian, and Bob Barger. 1976. *California: Five Centuries of Cultural Contrasts.* New York: Macmillan Publishing Co.

News From Native California. Heyday Books, P.O. Box 9145, Berkeley, CA 94709.

Osio, Antonio Maria. 1996. *The History of Alta California: A Memoir of Mexican California.* Madison, Wisconsin: The University of Wisconsin Press.

Oxford, June. 1983. *The Capitol that Couldn't Stay Put.* Fairfield, CA: James Stevenson Publisher.

Pittman, Ruth. 1995. *Roadside History of California.* Missoula, MT: Mountain Press.

Rolle, Andrew. 1998. *California, A History.* Arlington Heights, IL: Harlan Davidson, 5th ed.

Rohrbough, Malcolm J. 1997. *Days of Gold: The California Gold Rush and the American Nation.* Berkeley, CA: UC Press.

Rush, Philip S. 1953. *Historical Sketches of the Californias: Spanish and Mexican Periods.* San Diego, CA: Southern California Rancher/Neyenesch Printers.

Starr, Kevin. State librarian in the 1990s, historian, USC professor, and author of numerous books on the history of California.

Tales of California. Edited by Frank Oppel. Secaucus, NJ: Castle Books, 1989.

They Came Singing: Songs from California's History. Edited by Karen W. Arlen, Margaret Batt, Mary Ann Benson, and Nancie N. Kester. Oakland, CA: Calicanto Associates, 1995.

The Way We Lived: California Indian Reminiscences, Stories and Songs. Edited by Malcolm Margolin. Berkeley: Heyday Books, 1981.

Population

Many of the specific sources used for Chapter 7 provide up-to-date records of population trends and their ramifications in California. Some are traditional, general publications, others publish periodically, and still others can be found on the Internet. A few examples follow.

Allen, James P., and Eugene Turner. 1997. *The Ethnic Quilt: Population Diversity in Southern California.* Cal State University Northridge Center for Geographical Studies.

Allen, James P., and Eugene Turner. 1991. *An Atlas of Population Patterns in Metropolitan Los Angeles and Orange Counties.* California State University Northridge, Department of Geography.

Allied Van Lines. 221 S. Beverly Dr., Beverly Hills, CA 90212-3807 or 11231 San Fernando Rd., San Fernando, CA 91340-3409.

American Association of Retired People (AARP), with chapters throughout the state, including Sacramento, Los Angeles, Lakewood, and Riverside. 1-800-424-3410.

American Demographics. P.O. Box 68, Ithaca, NY 14851.

California Department of Finance. Population Research Unit. 915 L Street, Sacramento, CA 95814.

California Research Bureau. Library and Courts Building II, 900 N Street, Room 300, Sacramento, CA 95914.

California State Library and State Librarian of California, Room 220. California State Information and Reference Center, Room 301. Library and Courts Building I, 914 Capitol Mall, Room 220, Sacramento, CA 95814.

California State University, Northridge. Department of Geography. California Geographical Survey, Dr. William Bowen, Professor of Geography. A variety of socioeconomic maps. 18111 Nordoff St., Northridge, CA 91330.

Center for Continuing Study of the California Economy. 610 University Ave., Palo Alto, CA 94301.

Central American Refugee Center. 1245 Alabama St., San Francisco, CA 94110.

Population—a research journal. Princeton University Office of Population Research. 21 Prospect Ave., Princeton, NJ 08544.

Public Policy Institute of California. 500 Washington St., Suite 800, San Francisco, CA 94111.

San Jose Mercury News. 750 Ridder Park Drive, San Jose, CA 95190.

U.S. Census Bureau. Bureau of the Census, Los Angeles Regional Office, 15350 Sherman Way, Suite 300, Van Nuys, CA 91406.

U.S. Immigration and Naturalization Service (INS). Offices in major California cities.

USC School of Urban and Regional Planning. 3535 South Figueroa, Los Angeles, CA 90089.

CHAPTER 8

There exists an exhaustive list of publications and organizations with volumes of information about California's ethnic groups, cultures, and lifestyles. Some of the sources that were used in Chapter 8 are listed below.

African American Genealogical Society of Northern California. P.O. Box 27485, Oakland, CA 94602-0985.

Allen, James P., and Eugene Turner. 1997. *The Ethnic Quilt: Population Diversity in Southern California.* Cal State University Northridge Center for Geographical Studies.

Allen, James P., and Eugene Turner. 1991. *An Atlas of Population Patterns in Metropolitan Los Angeles and Orange Counties.* California State University Northridge, Department of Geography.

Anti-Defamation League. 720 Market St. #800, San Francisco, CA 94102-2501 and 7851 Mission Center Ct. #320, San Diego, CA 92108-1328.

Armenian Society of Los Angeles and in numerous communities throughout the state. 721 South Glendale Ave., Glendale, CA 91205.

Asian American Economic Development Enterprises, Inc. 320 West Newmark Ave., Monterey Park, CA 91754.

Asian Pacific American Legal Center of Southern California. 1010 South Flower St., Suite 302, Los Angeles, CA 90015.

Asian Pacific Policy and Planning Council.-L.A. 300 W. Caesar Chavez Ave. Suite #A, Los Angeles, CA 90012. Bowers Museum. 2002 N. Main St., Santa Ana, CA 92706.

Burns, Ric. The American Experience. PBS documentary, "The Donner Party." 1992. Steeplechase Films Production: WGBH Boston Presentation.

California African American Museum. 600 State Drive, Exposition Park, Los Angeles, CA 90037.

California Department of Parks and Recreation. "The Spirit of Allensworth" (Video). Col. Allensworth State Historic Park, State Route 1, Box 148, Earlimart, CA 93219.

California Parks and Recreation Society, 7971 Freeport Blvd., Sacramento, CA 95832-9701.

Caminos Magazine (for the Latino community; published in English). P.O. Box 54307, Los Angeles, CA 90054.

Chinese American Voters Education Committee—San Francisco. 415-397-8133.

Chinese Historical Society of Southern California. P.O. Box 862647, Los Angeles, CA 90086-2647.

Council on Islamic Education. 9300 Gardenia Street #B-3, Fountain Valley, CA 92708 (P.O. Box 20186, Fountain Valley, CA 92728.)

Dharma Publishing. 2910 San Pablo Avenue, Berkeley, CA 94702.

Ethnic Los Angeles. Edited by Roger Waldinger and Mehdi Bozongmehr. New York: Russell Sage Foundation, 1996.

Filipinas, monthly periodical. 655 Sutter Street #333, San Francisco, CA 94102.

Godfrey, Brian J. 1988. *Neighborhoods in Transition: The Making of San Francisco's Ethnic and Nonconformist Communities.* Berkeley: UC Press.

Guerin-Gonzales, Camille. 1994. *Mexican Workers and American Dreams: Immigration, Repatriation, and California Farm Labor, 1990–1939.* New Jersey: Rutgers University Press.

Hermandad Mexicana Nacional. 804 South Anaheim Blvd., Suite #B, Anaheim, CA 92805.

Heer, David M., and Pini Herman. 1990. *A Human Mosaic: An Atlas of Ethnicity in Los Angeles County, 1980–1986.* Panorama City, CA: Western Economic Research.

Hispanic American Family. 10654 Woodbridge Street, North Hollywood, CA 91602-2717.

Hispanic Times Magazine, published in Spanish and English. Hispanic Times Enterprises. Van Nuys, CA.

Homeless Prenatal Care. 995 Market St., Suite #310, San Francisco, CA 94103.

Houston, Jeanne Wakatsuki, and James D. Houston. 1973. *Farewell to Manzanar.* New York: Bantam Books.

Institute for Women's Policy Research. 1400 20th Street, NW, Suite 104, Washington, D.C. 20036.

International Migration Review. 209 Flagg Place, Staten Island, NY 10304.

Islamic Center of Southern California. 434 S. Vermont Ave., Los Angeles, CA 90020.

Islamic Council of California. 3420 West Jefferson Blvd., Los Angeles, CA 90018.

Islamic Society of Orange County. 9752 13th St., Garden Grove, CA 92844.

J. Paul Getty Museum. 1200 Getty Center Drive, Los Angeles, CA 90049.

Japanese Americans Citizens League. 1765 Sutter St., San Francisco, CA 94115.

Korean American Chamber of Commerce. 3440 Wilshire Blvd., Suite #520, Los Angeles, CA 90010.

Korean American Coalition. 3421 West 8th St., 2nd Floor, Los Angeles, CA 90005.

Korean American Times, published in Korean and English. Los Angeles, CA.

Korean Community Service. 650 N. Berendo St., Los Angeles, CA 90004.

Lao Family Community Agency. 4903 East King's Canyon Road, Fresno, CA 93727.

Lapp, Rudolph M. 1997. *Blacks in Gold Rush California*. New Haven: Yale University Press.

La Prensa San Diego (Latino community periodical in San Diego published in Spanish and English). 1950 5th Ave., San Diego, CA 92101.

Los Angeles Multicultural Collaborative. 1010 South Flower St., Suite #304, Los Angeles, CA 90015.

Lowrider Magazine—Pomona.

Marinacci, Barbara and Rudy Marinacci. 1980. *California's Spanish Place-Names*. Houston, Texas: Gulf Publishing Co., 2nd ed.

Mitchell, Don. 1996. *The Lie of the Land: Migrant Workers and the California Landscape*. Minneapolis: University of Minnesota Press.

Museum of Tolerance. 9786 West Pico Blvd., Los Angeles, CA 90035.

The Nation. P.O. Box 1953, Marion, OH 43306-1953.

NAACP, 1100 Wayne Avenue, Suite 830, Silver Spring, MD 20910. Local chapters throughout California.

National Association of Women Business Owners. Los Angeles Chapter: 1804 W. Burbank Blvd., Burbank, CA 91506.

National Underwriter. 505 Gest Street, Cincinnati, OH 45203.

Native American Cultural Center. 13252 Garden Grove Blvd., Garden Grove, CA 92641.

New Life (Korean community in California, published primarily in Korean). Hollywood, CA: Korean Community Service.

News From Native California. Heyday Books, P.O. Box 9145, Berkeley, CA 94709.

Pakistan Link. Pakistan Link Publications, Inglewood, CA.

Saito, Leland. 1998. *Race and Politics*. Urbana and Chicago, Illinois: University of Illinois Press.

Sanderlock, Leonie. 1998. *Making the Invisible Visible: A Multicultural Planning History*. Berkeley: UC Press.

Social Science Research Quarterly. Institute for Social Science Research, Los Angeles, CA.

Templeton, John. 1991. *Our Roots Run Deep: The Black Experience in California*. San Jose, CA: Electron Access, Inc.

Transpacific. (Asian-American focus.) P.O. Box 4260, Malibu, CA 90264-4260.

UC Berkeley Department of Ethnic Studies, 506 Barrows Hall, Berkeley, CA 94720-2570. Leanne Hinton, Linguistics Professor, UC Berkeley.

UC Davis. (Theresa L. Dillinger.) 1 Shields Ave., Davis, CA 95616.

UCLA School of Public Policy and Social Research (Paul Ong). 405 Hilgard Ave., Los Angeles, CA 90095.

USC's Southern California Studies Center. Los Angeles, CA.

Women in Business. P.O. Box 265, Palos Verdes, CA 90274.

Wyatt, David. 1998. *Five Fires: Race, Catastrophe, and the Shaping of California*. Reading, MA: Addison-Wesley Publishing.

CHAPTER 9

Here are a few publications and organizations with more recent information regarding California's primary industries and rural landscapes. Some have offices throughout California and produce publications throughout the year. Others might be found on the Internet and still others are local activist groups:

Bradshaw, Ted K., and Brian Muller. 1998. Impacts of Rapid Urban Growth on Farmland Conversion: Application of New Regional Land Use Policy Models and Geographical Information Systems. *Rural Sociology* 63 (March).

Bulletin of the California Insect Survey. UC Press, 2120 Berkeley Way, Berkeley, CA 94720.

California Crop and Livestock Reporting Service. P.O. Box 1258, Sacramento, CA 95806.

California Department of Fish and Game. Resources Building, 146 Ninth St., Sacramento, CA 95814.

California Department of Food and Agriculture Publications: (California Agricultural Statistics Service: Annual Bulletin. 1220 N Street, Room 243, Sacramento, CA 94814).
Crop Weather Report
County Agricultural Commissioners' Report Data
Dairy Industry Statistics
Dairy Information Bulletin
Dot Maps showing fifty major commodities
Field Crop Review
Fruit and Nut Review
Grape Crush Report
Grape Acreage
Livestock Review
Poultry Report
Summary of County Agricultural Commissioners' Reports
Vegetable Review
Walnuts, Raisins and Prunes (Price Report)

California Department of Forestry. P.O. Box 944246. Sacramento, CA 94244-2460.

California Farm Bureau Federation. 2300 River Plaza Drive, Sacramento, CA 95833.

California Farmer. 2300 Clayton Road #1360, Concord, CA 94520.

California Forestry Association. 300 Capitol Mall, Suite #350, Sacramento, CA 95814.

California Grocer. P.O. Box 2671, Sacramento, CA 95812-2671.

California Grower. P.O. Box 370, Carpinteria, CA 93014.

California Plant Pathology. University of California Agriculture Extension Service, 147 Hilgard Hall, Berkeley, CA 94720.

California Rural Legal Assistance (CRLA). 631 Howard Street, Suite 300, San Francisco, CA 94105.

California State Mining and Geology Board. 801 K Street, MS 24-05, Sacramento, CA 95814.

The California Tomato Grower. P.O. Box 7398, Stockton, CA 95207.

Cazin, Lorraine Jolian. 1998. *Yosemite.* Mankato, MN: Crestwood House.

Hardwick, Susan Wiley, and Donald G. Holtgrieve. 1996. *Valley for Dreams: Life and Landscape in the Sacramento Valley.* Rowman and Littlefield.

Hunt, Charles B. 1975. *Death Valley: Geology, Ecology, Archaeology.* Berkeley, CA: UC Press.

International California Mining Journal. P.O. Box 2260, Aptos, CA 95001-2260.

Jaeger, Edmund C. 1965. *The California Deserts.* Palo Alto, CA: Stanford University Press, 4th ed.

McCormick, Maxine. 1988. *Sequoia and Kings Canyon.* Mankato, MN: Crestwood House.

Mitchell, Don. 1996. *The Lie of the Land: Migrant Workers and the California Landscape.* University of Minnesota Press.

The Northern California Review of Business and Economics. California State University Center of Business and Economic Research, Chico, CA 95929.

Outdoor California. California Department of Fish and Game. Resources Building, 146 Ninth St., Sacramento, CA 95814.

Pacific Fisherman. 23182 Alcalda #K, Laguna Hills, CA 92653.

Sierra Club of California. 85 Second St., 2nd Floor, San Francisco, CA 94105-3441.

Society of American Foresters. 5400 Grosvenor Lane, Bethesda, Maryland, 20814.

Trinity Bioregion Group (AEGIS). 202 Wurster Hall, UC Berkeley, CA 94720.

United Farm Workers Union (UFW). Offices in San Francisco, San Jose, Oakland, Los Angeles, and other locations. Farm Worker Movement Recruitment. P.O. Box 62, Keene, CA 93531.

U.S. Bureau of Land Management Public Land Statistics. Office of Public Affairs, 1849 C Street, Room 406-LS, Washington, DC 20240.

U.S. Bureau of Mines. Washington, DC 20241.

U.S. Department of Agriculture (USDA). Natural Resources Conservation Service. Hanford Soil Survey Office. 680 Campus Dr., Suite E, Hanford, CA 93230.

U.S. Department of Agriculture (USDA). Rural Utilities Service. 14th and Independence Ave., South Building, Washington, DC 20250.

U.S. Department of the Interior. 1849 C Street NW, Washington, DC 20240.

U.S. Forest Service. P.O. Box 96090, Washington, DC 20090-6090.

University of California Division of Agriculture and Natural Resources. California Agriculture. UC Davis. 1 Shields Ave., Davis, CA 95616.

UC-Sustainable Agriculture Research and Education Program. UC Davis. 1 Shields Ave., Davis, CA 95616.

Western Agricultural Publishing Company. 4974 East Clinton Way, Suite 123, Fresno, CA 93727.

Western Growers Association. 17620 Fitch St., Irvine, CA 92614.

Western Grower and Shipper. P.O. Box 2130, Newport Beach, CA 92658-8949.

Wine Institute. 425 Market St., Suite 1000, San Francisco, CA 94105.

Yogi, Stan, ed. *Highway 99: A Literary Journey Through California's Great Central Valley.* Berkeley, CA: Heyday Books, 1996.

CHAPTER 10

Here are a few sources and organizations with more recent information regarding California's modern, advanced industries. Some have offices throughout California and produce publications throughout the year. Others might be found on the Internet and still others are local activist groups:

Nearly every California city and/or economic region has at least one publication dedicated to the business community. They are usually, but not always known as "journals." Check the local phone book listings for city government or for the Chamber of Commerce.

Association of Bay Area Governments (ABAG). Joseph P. Bort MetroCenter, 101 8th St., Oakland, CA 94607. (P.O. Box 2050, Oakland, CA 94604-2050.)

Business America. U.S. Department of Commerce. Washington, DC 20230.

California Builder and Engineer. (Heavy construction industry.) 4110 Transport Street, Palo Alto, CA 94303-4915.

California Computer News. (Micro-computing applied to business, government, and education.) 9719 Lincoln Valley Drive #500, Sacramento, CA 95827.

California Department of Finance. Population Research Unit. 915 L Street, Sacramento, CA 95814.

California Legislative Analyst's Office.

California Manufacturer. 980 9th St., #2200, Sacramento, CA 95814-2742.

California Ski Industry Association. 74 New Montgomery, Suite #750, San Francisco, CA 94105.

California Trade and Commerce Agency. Office of Economic Research. 801 K Street, Suite 1700, Sacramento, CA 95841.

California World Trade Commission. 917 7th St., Sacramento, CA 95814.

Center for Continuing Study of the California Economy. 610 University Ave., Palo Alto, CA 94301.

Computerworld. International Data Group, Farmington, Mass.

DataQuick Information Services. 4640 Admiralty Way, Suite #231, Marina Del Rey, CA 90292.

Economic Development Corporation of Los Angeles County. 515 South Flower St., 32nd Floor, Los Angeles, CA 90071.

The Economist. (A weekly news magazine.) 111 West 57th St., New York, NY 10019.

The Engineer of California. (News/jobs.) 626 North Garfield Ave., Alhambra, CA 91801-1448.

Entertainment Industry Development Corporation. 7083 Hollywood Blvd., Suite #500, Hollywood, CA 90028.

Far Eastern Economic Review. Citicorp Centre 25th Floor, 18 Whitfield Road, Causeway Bay, Hong Kong.

Foreign Affairs. Council on Foreign Relations. New York, NY.

Hispanic Business. 360 South Hope Street #300-C, Santa Barbara, CA 93105-4017.

Hispanic Reporter. (Business and trade.) 3121 West Temple Street, Los Angeles, CA 90026.

Institutional Investor. Institutional Investor, Inc., Rye, New York.

International Journal of Technology Management. Interscience Enterprises. Geneva, Switz.

International Journal of Urban and Regional Research/Planning. Urban Studies, University of Glasgow, Glasgow G12 8RT, Scotland.

Journal of Commerce and Commercial. (Published daily, except weekends.) New York, NY.

Los Angeles Regional Technology Alliance. 746 W. Adams Blvd., Los Angeles, CA 90089-7727.

Money Magazine. The Money Publishing Co., N.Y.

Mortgage Banking. 1125 15th Street NW, Washington, DC 20005

National League of Cities. 1301 Pennsylvania Ave. NW, Washington, DC 20004-1763.

The Northern California Review of Business and Economics. California State University Center of Business and Economic Research, Chico, CA 95929.

Pacific Shipper. 562 Mission St., #601, San Francisco, CA 94105-2916.

Public Policy Institute of California. 500 Washington St., Suite 800, San Francisco, CA 94111.

Santa Barbara Region Economic Community Project. 12 East Carrillo Street, Santa Barbara, CA 93101.

Southern California Association of Governments (SCAG). 818 West Seventh St., 12th Floor, Los Angeles, CA 90017-3435.

Southern California Biomedical Council. 515 S. Flower St., 32nd Floor, Los Angeles, CA 90071.

Stoll, Steven. 1998. *The Fruits of Natural Advantage: Making the Industrial Countryside of Los Angeles.* Berkeley and Los Angeles, UC Press.

Tech Museum of Innovation. 201 South Market St., San Jose, CA 94113.

U.S. Bureau of Labor Statistics. P.O. Box 193766, San Francisco, CA 94119-3766.

UCLA Anderson Forecast. 110 Westwood Plaza, Gold Hall B302, Los Angeles, CA 90095.

U.S. Commerce Department. Washington, DC 20230.

U.S. Department of Labor. Office of Public Affairs. 200 Constitution Ave. NW, Washington, DC 20210.

Wall Street Journal. Published by Dow Jones. New York, NY.

CHAPTER 11

Many sources used in this chapter could prove useful to researchers looking for more specific information on urban geography. Additionally, there are visitor's guides available in major bookstores in every California city.

American Demographics. P.O. Box 68, Ithaca, NY 14851.

American Society of Landscape Architects. 4401 Connecticut Ave. NW, 5th Floor, Washington DC.

Amtrak. Contact local Amtrak stations for train schedules.

Association of Bay Area Governments (ABAG). Joseph P. Bort MetroCenter, 101 8th St., Oakland, CA 94607. (P.O. Box 2050, Oakland, CA 94604-2050).

Automotive News. Crain Automotive Group. Detroit, Mich.

Business Improvement Districts (BIDs) in each major city.

California Center for Land Recycling. 116 New Montgomery St., Suite 300, San Francisco, CA 94105.

California Department of Transportation (Caltrans). Headquarters: 1120 N Street (P.O. Box 942873), Sacramento, CA 95814. District offices (12) in most major California cities.

California Public Utilities Commission. 505 Van Ness Ave., San Francisco, CA 94102.

Chambers of Commerce and other local business associations.

Church groups may provide sources of information about specific cultural groups in each California city.

City and county planning and building departments.

City councils.

Community Redevelopment Agencies (CRAs), such as L.A. Community Redevelopment Agency.

Davis, Mike. 1992. *City of Quartz: Excavating the Future in Los Angeles.* New York: Random House Vintage Books.

Davis, Mike. 1998. *Ecology of Fear: Los Angeles and the Imagination of Disaster.* New York: Metropolitan Books.

Fulton, William. 1997. *The Reluctant Metropolis.* Point Arena, CA: Solano Press.

Garreau, Joel. 1991. *Edge City: Life on the New Frontier.* New York: Doubleday.

Gleeson, Brendan J. 1989. *Homelessness and the Politics of Turf: The Case of Venice, California.* University of Southern California, Los Angeles, Department of Geography.

Godfrey, Brian J. 1988. *Neighborhoods in Transition: The Making of San Francisco's Ethnic and Nonconformist Communities.* Berkeley: UC Press.

Herman, Robert D. 1996. *Downtown Los Angeles: A Walking Guide.* Claremont, CA: City Vista Press.

James Irvine Foundation Trust for Public Lands. The Irvine Foundation. 777 So. Figueroa, Suite #740, Los Angeles, CA 90017.

Koegel, Paul. 1988. *Understanding Homelessness: An Ethnographic Approach.* University of Southern California, Los Angeles, Department of Geography.

Libraries in cities and colleges throughout California. The new and remodeled Los Angeles City and San Francisco Libraries are exceptional examples.

Local historical and preservation societies, conservancies, and environmental groups, such as Friends of the L.A. River.

Los Angeles Magazine. 1888 Century Park East 920, Los Angeles, CA 90067.

Los Angeles Micro-Geographer. City of Los Angeles. Community Development Department, Community Analysis and Planning Division, Los Angeles, CA 90012.

Museums are playing active roles in every major California city. The J. Paul Getty Museum is one of the most recent examples in Los Angeles.

Nation's Cities Weekly. Published by The League, Washington, DC.

Neighborhood, community, and homeowners organizations and associations, such as Blythe Street Prevention Project and Mothers of East L.A.

Parr, Barry. 1996. *San Francisco and the Bay Area.* Oakland, CA: Compass American Guides of Fodor's Travel.

Pitt, Leonard and Dale Pitt. 1997. *Los Angeles A to Z.* Berkeley, CA: UC Press.

Planning. San Francisco City Planning Commission. San Francisco, CA.

Sacramento Magazine. P.O. Box 2424, Sacramento, CA 95812-2424.

San Diego Association of Governments (SANDAG). 401 B Street, Suite 800, San Diego, CA 92101.

San Diego Magazine. 4206 West Point Loma Blvd., San Diego, CA 92138.

San Fernando Valley Partnership. 1019 Second St., San Fernando, CA 91340.

San Francisco Bay Guardian. 2700 19th St., San Francisco, CA 94110.

San Francisco Magazine. San Francisco Publications and Communications, Inc. 45 Belden Place, San Francisco, CA 94104.

San Francisco Partnership. 465 California St., Suite 950, San Francisco, CA 94104.

Southern California Association of Governments (SCAG). 818 West Seventh St., 12th Floor, Los Angeles, CA 90017-3435.

Transportation authorities in each major California city, such as L.A.'s MTA, Southern Cal Regional Rail Authority, Alameda Corridor Transportation Authority, Contra Costa Transportation Authority, San Francisco's MUNI, and BART (Bay Area Rapid Transit) P.O. Box 12688, Oakland, CA 94606-2688.

U.S. Department of Housing and Urban Development (HUD). 451 7th Street SW, Washington, DC 20410.

Universities. Numerous universities are researching California cities and helping to plan and solve problems. Just a few examples include: (addresses on other lists.)

UC Berkeley Institute of Urban and Regional Development. www.ucb.edu

UCLA Department of Geography and the former Graduate School of Architecture and Urban Planning. www.ucla.edu

USC's Southern California Studies Center and School of Urban and Regional Planning. www.usc.edu

California State University Northridge Department of Geography's California Atlas and other resources. www.csun.edu

Urban Affairs Quarterly. Sage Publications. Beverly Hills, CA.

Visitor and Convention Bureaus, Tourism Councils.

Wired—a San Francisco cyberspace magazine. http://www.wired.com/wired

Wolch, Jennifer R. 1991. *Skid Row USA.* University of Southern California, Los Angeles.

Index